B. TRAVEN

B. TRAVEN

The Life Behind the Legends

KARL S. GUTHKE

Translated by Robert C. Sprung

LAWRENCE HILL BOOKS

Library of Congress Cataloging-in-Publication Data

Guthke, Karl Siegfried, 1933–
[B. Traven. English]
B. Traven : the life behind the legends / Karl S. Guthke :
p. cm.
Translation of: B. Traven.
Includes bibliographical references and index.
ISBN 1-55652-132-4 : $24.95 —ISBN 1-55652-131-6 (pbk.) :
$14.95
1. Traven, B.—Biography. 2. Authors, German—20th
century—Biography. I. Title.
PT3919. T7Z6813 1991
813′.52—dc20
[B] 90-26277
CIP

First published by Büchergilde Gutenberg, Frankfurt am Main,

Translated from the German by Robert C. Sprung

Printed in the United States of America
First edition

This edition has been made possible through the
financial help of Inter Nationes.

Cover: Drawing of B. Traven by Antonieta Figueroa.
Reproduced with the artist's permission.

Published by Lawrence Hill Books, Brooklyn, New York
An imprint of Chicago Review Press, Incorporated
814 North Franklin Street
Chicago, Illinois 60610

5 4 3 2 1

Para Chelena

CONTENTS

The biography of a creative man is completely unimportant.

—B. Traven

Life is worth more than any book one can write.

—Hal Croves

Ese lugar común de que "lo más interesante de su obra, es su propia vida," a nadie se le puede aplicar más justamente, que a B. Traven.

—Luis Spota

PREFACE

That "B. Traven" is the greatest literary mystery of the century is a commonplace circulating for some time around the world, in tabloids as well as in scholarly handbooks. The name B. Traven is a pseudonym; it appeared on the title page of more than a dozen books, primarily novels, first published from 1926 to 1960, with more than thirty million readers worldwide by now. Readers—some highbrow, some less exacting, some politically engaged, some with more literary interests—were drawn to books like *The Death Ship*, *The Treasure of the Sierra Madre*, and *The Cotton-Pickers* not least by the aura of mystery that even today envelops their author. Who was the man behind this unique phenomenon?

The man who called himself B. Traven, the man who claimed to be an American exile in Mexico but wrote his books in German, always placed great importance on keeping the author and his work separate in the minds of his readers. The work, not the writer, was important. He tried to focus the public's attention on his books while himself remaining hidden in the wings.

His *works* have secured a permanent place in literary history—German, American, and Mexican. Their readers may vicariously enjoy exotic experiences beyond their usual sphere of existence, but at the same time they cannot mistake the voice of the philosophical anarchist appealing to social awareness and offering alternatives to Western patterns of life and thought. The chronicle of the impact of Traven's work is a complex success story that is not without its curiosities. Overnight sensations, then blacklisted by the Nazis and rediscovered after the Second World War, some of Traven's books have today entered the ranks of school texts, not only in English translation but also as textbooks helping English-speaking students learn German or Spanish. In Germany, they are used to instill in students a sense of social responsibility. One school reader containing a chapter on Traven is simply entitled *Vorbilder für Deutsche* (*Models for Germans to Live By*). Traven's novels and stories are the subject of university lectures and seminars on both sides of the Atlantic, and they have been the focus of international and interdisciplinary conferences. The film version of one novel, John Huston's *The Treasure of the Sierra Madre* starring Humphrey Bogart, has become a classic. Radio plays and television and stage versions of Traven's fiction have appeared with regularity for decades, primarily in Europe. Traven books were printed in deluxe editions, as pocketbooks and garishly illustrated versions reminiscent of comic books, and eventually in a handsome edition of collected works (to say nothing of the numerous translations into some three dozen languages).

The *author*, however, remained hidden in shadow. Even to his death in 1969 he was "the man in hiding," to quote the title of a recent work on Traven. One could make him out in the darkness, to be sure: a presence shrouded in mystery, the eternal revolutionary without a party, the nameless one with a high profile who was seen as a sort of forerunner by Brecht and later by the beat generation, even, in the 1970s, as a countercultural "hero of the 'alternative lifestyle.' " But the image was by no means clear. And when reporters, publishers, literary sleuths, and other amateur detectives tried to sharpen the image, Traven withdrew. He was always on the run. Stories about Traven thus became the domain of the illustrated magazines and tabloids, which were ever ready to serve up new "revelations" or "decipherings" of the pseudonym of the enigmatic man in the spotlight. As these "solutions" contradicted one another, the speculations proliferated. The distinguished-looking Hal Croves, who in 1959 traveled as Traven's representative to Germany for the premiere of the movie version of *The Death Ship* accompanied by an elegant woman—was he the author of the world-famous novels? But didn't this man allegedly place a phone call from Berlin to Traven in Mexico City? Was Traven the son of a Norwegian fisherman or of an American farmer from the Midwest or of a German theater impresario? Was he the German-Polish locksmith's apprentice Otto Feige from Schwiebus near Posen? Or a bastard son of Kaiser Wilhelm II? He supposedly bore a striking resemblance to both.

B. Traven became a phantom. "The only date known for certain in the life of the mysterious author B. Traven," we read in 1982 in the German magazine *Stern*, in a commemorative article on the (putative) one-hundredth anniversary of Traven's birth, "is the date of his death."

An attempt is made in this book to determine what can be found out and what can be pieced together about the life of the "man nobody knows" (the title of a collection of his stories). Although Traven's life excites interest ultimately because of his novels and stories, here the works themselves are treated more peripherally. The focus is on the man who wrote them, the aspect Traven himself considered "unimportant" while admitting it was not without interest. "My life story," he wrote as early as 1926, "would not disappoint." When his editor Ernst Preczang encouraged him in the mid-1920s to write a "biographical novel," since he had "doubtless experienced much," Traven answered from his hideaway on the Mexican Gulf Coast with a resounding no, without failing to add: "Doubtless experienced much? Twenty volumes in the Brockhaus encyclopedia format are too little to publish even part of it."

Whether Traven's life was his most adventurous novel, as he intimates, may remain an open question; in any case, not all of his life can be reconstructed. Yet the surviving evidence allows us to sketch a more or less detailed picture: a picture of the course of Traven's life, his environment, his personal relationships, his circles of acquaintances, his "experiences"—an image of the life that gave birth to the work and that was in turn molded by it. For the greater the fame of the German exile in Mexico became, the more the public's attention was drawn to "B. Traven," the more urgently the public wished to know the real identity of this man who was so in love with his own anonymity—and the more Traven felt urged to flee from fame. This flight included cultivating the image of a "man of mystery" through mythmaking and using multiple pseudonyms, the inventive lie, the bluff, and the double bluff. Thus the gringo's life as B. Traven—or, more accurately, as the man who didn't want to be B. Traven—was a creative achievement in itself, a work of art born of the spirit of the Mexican present and the trauma of the European past. *Quel homme*!

What *sort* of man? The following chapters are also meant to give an impression of the personality of the man who lived and fashioned this life. As for Traven's origin, the hypotheses to date are all undocumented and implausible. Whether my own conclusions are an exception is not for me to judge.

Though this book is not able to disclose every facet of this extraordinary life—a limitation due in some measure to Traven's lifelong desire to cover his tracks—it may be considered the first Traven biography, being the first to make exhaustive use of the Traven estate and the archives of his German publisher, Büchergilde Gutenberg, as well as less central sources previously unknown or unused. Rolf Recknagel's *B. Traven* is subtitled "Contributions to a Biography" rather than a biography proper—rightly so, though his pioneering study remains valuable, especially for its bibliographical sections. Its most recent edition, the third (1982), bears no substantial changes from the first edition of 1966. The book thus originated without the benefit of the documentary material in Traven's house, and even the 1982 version makes only fleeting reference to the Traven estate. Recknagel also takes little or no note of the other document collections and archives that I explored in my preparation of the present volume. As a result, his work throws particularly insufficient light on Traven's Mexican period. It is disproportionately influenced by the effort, which was of interest in the 1960s, to prove that Ret Marut, the German revolutionary sentenced to death in 1919, and B. Traven were indeed one and the same. Recknagel's attempt at biography is further handicapped by the author's presentation of Traven's life "predominantly through his literary works." Frederik Hetmann's *Der Mann, der sich verbarg* (*The Man in Hiding*) (1983) contributes little more factual information about Traven's life than Recknagel's study; Will Wyatt's *The Secret of the Sierra Madre: The Man Who Was B. Traven* (1980) details the BBC producer's search—to my mind unsuccessful—for Traven's identity.

Thanks, above all, to Traven's widow, Señora Rosa Elena Luján, *B. Traven: The Life Behind the Legends* is more substantial and better documented than other studies. She made accessible the holdings of the Traven estate (in Mexico City and Cuernavaca), with a generosity and hospitality for which I cannot sufficiently express my gratitude.

I offer my thanks to the following publishing houses, archives, and institutes for copies of letters or other documents and for permission to use them: Büchergilde Gutenberg, Frankfurt; Fritz-Hüser-Institut für deutsche und ausländische Arbeiterliteratur, Dortmund; Stadtarchiv Schwerin; Akademie der Künste, Berlin; Arbetarrörelsens Arkiv, Stockholm; Hill & Wang, Inc., New York; Alfred A. Knopf, Inc., New York; the Library of Congress; Pattee Library, The Pennsylvania State University; Houghton Library, Harvard University; Marut archives (then in private hands, now at the University of California, Riverside); the National Archives. Thanks are due to Max Schmid for providing copies of letters in his collection, to Gerd Heidemann for most generously showing me his Traven collection and granting permission to use copies of some of his texts. For discussions and correspondence about Traven I thank Ferdinand Anton, Michael L. Baumann, Gabriel Figueroa, Gerd Heidemann, Lawrence Hill, Philip Jenkins, William W. Johnson, Herbert Arthur Klein, Peter Lübbe, Helmut Müssener, Jan Papiór, Helmut Pfanner, Fritz J. Raddatz, Rolf Recknagel, Armin Richter, Max Schmid, Ernst Schürer, Ray Spencer, H. D. Tschörtner, Christopher von Warnstedt, Bernhard Werner, Will Wyatt, and above all Rosa Elena Luján. Edgar Pässler provided invaluable assistance through his intimate knowledge of the subject. Finally, I recall with great gratitude the months spent in 1984 as a fellow of the Humanities Research Centre at the Australian National University in Canberra. A substantial part of this book was written there.

Postscript 1991

I thank Barbara Flanagan for her careful copyediting of the English translation, Shirley Cloyes, director of Lawrence Hill Books, for her thoughtful editorial suggestions, and, finally, Robert C. Sprung for the good humor and resourcefulness with which he went about the daunting task of recasting my German into eminently readable English; reviewing his translation, I have learned a lot about writing.

The German edition of this book appeared in hardcover in 1987 and in paperback in 1990. To bring the English edition up to date, I have made some minor changes, corrections, and additions.

1

A DEATH AND A DEATH SENTENCE

Mexico and Munich, 1969 and 1919

"Shrouded in Mystery"

It is well past midnight—late even by Latin American standards—when the phone rings at Calle Río Mississippi 61 in Mexico City. The call wakens Rosa Elena Luján, B. Traven's widow. She listens in disbelief as the caller identifies himself as Luis Echeverría, the president of Mexico, calling from Vienna where he is on a state visit. After apologizing for overlooking the transatlantic time difference, Echeverría explains that in his first talks with Austrian Chancellor Bruno Kreisky the two discovered that they shared an admiration for the novels of B. Traven. Since they were unable to resolve a number of questions about Traven's books, Echeverría had offered to get answers in the most direct manner possible. Señora Luján answers his questions and further promises to send the chancellor two of the most recent Traven volumes. Later that morning a courier from the Palacio Nacional appears at the iron gate of her home to collect the books.

Bruno Kreisky's thank-you note of March 8, 1974, was anything but routine. In it the statesman reveals his interest in the author and asks for a reference to a reliable biography of this man who is "shrouded in mystery" (whose works, incidentally, had been translated by his colleague the Danish Prime Minister H. C. Hansen and who reportedly was Albert Einstein's favorite author). Kreisky explains that his generation saw B. Traven as "the great activist poet of our youth." Traven's books, which Kreisky says he had read while in prison, evoke "special memories."

"Shrouded in mystery": Kreisky was not exaggerating. The man who hid behind the pseudonym B. Traven spent decades of his life literally as a fugitive into anonymity. But his cover-up incited the world press to attempt to solve his mystery. As a result, he became, in the words of the daily *Die Welt*, "probably the most mysterious figure in contemporary letters."

Ashes in the Jungle

A few days before the *Welt* notice, on March 26, 1969, Traven had died an old man at his home on Calle Mississippi, a short walk from the imposing Independence Monument in the center of Mexico City. Even at the very end of his life, he had not allowed the public more than a glimpse behind his veil of secrecy. The news of his death gained national and international attention. One of the first condolence telegrams sent to the Mexican family of this German exile came from the president's palace, signed by head of state Gustavo Díaz Ordaz: "Few writers have penetrated so deeply into the Mexican soul and have written about our land and people with such breadth of understanding as B. Traven. His books, translated into all major languages, have spread the name of Mexico throughout the world. Mexico will always remember him as a brilliant writer and a great friend."

Reporters, photographers, and television crews swarmed through the three floors of the writer's elegant home. The next day, the country's leading daily, *Excelsior*, reported Traven's death in a lengthy front-page tribute. Extensive pictorial essays on his life, death, and *misterio* appeared in the periodicals *Mañana*, *Siempre*, and *Impacto*. They told of a man who had emigrated from central Europe and had gained fame in Mexico; who had come ashore in 1924 at or near Tampico as a casual laborer with just the clothes on his back; who wrote his novels in German while stubbornly denying that he was German, maintaining that he was born in America and that English was his native tongue. His novels were available in three dozen languages, with many million copies in print—25 million in 1969, according to the story in *Die Welt* (32 million in

1982, according to *Stern* magazine). No wonder the report from Mexico was heard around the world.

Traven's body was cremated on March 27, in a ceremony attended by prominent figures from Mexico's art circles. Traven had stipulated that his ashes be scattered over the Río Jataté in the Chiapas jungle. The southernmost state of the country, Chiapas had served as the backdrop for his novels that depicted the exploitation of Indians in the mahogany *monterías*—the notorious logging camps populating the area at the beginning of the century. His wish was honored. Tuxtla Gutiérrez, the capital of Chiapas, was the scene for a day of remembrance, sponsored by the governor and the mayor, on April 17. Traven's widow and her two daughters landed at the airport at noon. Amid great ceremony, they handed over the wooden urn containing Traven's ashes. The governor presided over the official tribute at the Palacio Municipal. An exhibition of Traven's books opened late that afternoon at the newly founded University of Chiapas, and that evening saw the first of nine literary readings by well-known Mexican authors—their way of paying homage to the "gringo" who had introduced Mexico to world literature.

Tuxtla Gutiérrez in Chiapas: for Traven, this was not just another way station in his many travels through Mexico and the rest of the world. To him, it was the very cradle of civilization. He liked to think that the human species originated in the New World, specifically in southern Mexico and Chiapas. In his 1928 travel book *Land des Frühlings* (*Land of Springtime*),* in which he stated his theory of the origin of the human race, Traven had this to say about Tuxtla Gutiérrez:

> The Governor's Palace in Tuxtla Gutiérrez makes you think about the problems that are today stirring up all of humanity—problems of races, peoples, and economic systems. Every day something happens in this Governor's Palace that heralds a new era in the history of mankind. Nowhere else on this continent—not in Mexico City or any other Mexican capital—can you witness what is really happening in Mexico so clearly, so simply, so naturally, with such elementary clarity, as in Tuxtla Gutiérrez and this Governor's Palace. No other state in Mexico has as high a percentage of pure-blooded Indians, no state exhibits

*Traven/Marut's books, stories, and other writings that have not been translated into English are nonetheless referred to in the text with English titles. The Bibliography includes existing English translations of Traven/Marut's works.

such a remarkable amalgam of people as Chiapas. Highly sophisticated Mexicans and Europeans alongside great masses of the most primitive Indians such as the Lacandones—and between them lies every level of civilization imaginable. A hundred thousand or more Indians here speak their own traditional language. Living by age-old manners and customs, they are adapting to contemporary European civilization bit by bit, but they are doing so very slowly and reluctantly. Every place has reached another, higher level of civilization than the one which lies further back. Pure, ancient Indian communism next to ultramodern capitalism in its most ruthless manifestation. New-fangled farming methods employing the latest tractors and other machinery alongside agricultural tools and implements made of hardwood and stone such as had been common long before the Toltecs had arrived with their highly developed civilization. . . .

And all these elements seek and find common ground in the Governor's Palace at Tuxtla Gutiérrez. In the Governor's waiting room we find an American mine owner, a millionaire many times over, who wants to have concessions confirmed or has some other request. Next to him sits the explorer who has come to ask the Governor for a letter of safe-conduct. Beside him, the coffee planter ready to dispute his taxes. In their midst sit chieftains and emissaries from a dozen Indian tribes who cannot communicate with each other since each speaks a different language; each wears different clothing. . . .

There is no better place to see how greatly the affairs of men have been transformed in the last ten years. The Governor rises and greets everyone who enters his chambers—be it the multimillionaire mine owner or the representative of a distant Indian tribe—with precisely the same gesture of politeness. He may have more time and patience for the Indian than for the mine owner, since the Indian has difficulty expressing himself even with the aid of an interpreter. The battles raging today throughout the whole world between capital and labor, between races and nations—those battles are all fought and concluded here in this one room. Virtually nowhere else do all the problems of all people alive today appear in one place and in such concentrated form as here. . . . They appear here in their natural, naked, primeval form. . . . And if you are convinced, when one gets right down to it, that all men come from the same mold, that they all react in the same way to the same impulses, that the basic nature of all problems can be reduced to very simple formulas—then you can study the very essence of all questions right here. . . . One can pursue so many questions here so successfully, it is as if one actually stood at the cradle of civilization—or at least in civilization's nursery.

To return in death to Tuxtla Gutiérrez, to the source and the heart of life—Traven would have liked the symbolism.

On the morning after the ceremonies in the capital city, a handful of the mourners left the airport at Tuxtla Gutiérrez in three-seater planes manned by bush pilots. They headed for the remote Indian village of Ocosingo, which lies in a small valley of the Sierra Madre through which the Río Jatatė flows. Ox-cart paths were the only other route to the village. Traven had come here often since the mid-1920s. Equipped with camera, typewriter, books, notebooks, and, curiously, a gramophone, he and his Indian guide would undertake solitary jungle expeditions looking for authentic material for the novels set in Chiapas. The Tzeltal Indians who lived there, members of a Mayan tribe like the neighboring Lacandones, were Traven's friends, his "brothers," his "soul mates," as he called them. They gave him bows and arrows and entrusted him with ceramic cult objects. Now, on April 18, 1969, residents of Ocosingo, in particular Traven's guide, Vitorino Trinidad, shared their vivid memories from the 1920s and 1930s of the man who then called himself Señor Torsvan. They recalled him asking tirelessly about every aspect of Indian life and then working the material into his novels (news of B. Traven's novels had reached even this remote spot). His books were theirs, too, in a sense.

It was fitting that the tribute paid to Traven's ashes in Ocosingo was more in touch with local custom than the one in the capital city, where black Sunday suits and white shirts had dominated. True, the Ocosingo town council had offered a series of formal speeches in a special meeting, attended by Traven's widow, her daughters, some friends, and journalists. But the real flavor of the event was Indian, particularly that afternoon as the funeral procession wound through the village: fireworks and Mexican music played on marimbas, hand drums, and flutes, with schoolchildren lining the streets throwing flowers. The procession headed for the most humble of the straw-covered mud huts at the edge of the village—"*el jacal más humilde del pueblo*" in the words of the local paper—where the wake was held. That night hundreds of Indians walked by the urn resting on a table in the hut and said farewell in the dim light of four candles. The air was thick with the smell of tamales chiapanecos—pork, cornmeal, and plums wrapped in banana leaves.

Early the next morning a single-engine Cessna took off for the nearby *finca* San José El Real, where Traven had often been a guest of the Bulnes family. A cameraman from the TV crew emptied the ashes over the Chiapas jungle. Seated beside him was Traven's friend the sculptor Federico Canessi. With hurricane winds forecast, the mourners returned from Ocosingo to Tuxtla Gutiérrez. On their departure the mayor of Ocosingo announced solemnly that his town would henceforth bear the name Ocosingo de Traven.

This last act—the scattering of his ashes over the jungle of Central America—would have been to Traven's liking not only late in his life. He had pondered the circumstances of his death a full two generations earlier, when he had been an actor, journalist, and revolutionary living under the name Ret Marut, a fact that had been established for some time, though he authorized his wife only on his last day to divulge it after his death. In the anarchistic journal *Der Ziegelbrenner* (*The Brickburner*), which Marut published from 1917 to 1921, first in Munich and from late 1919 with the imprint Vienna, he once wrote of his desire to die a nameless death, to vanish into nothingness—a wish that was finally fulfilled in the jungle of Chiapas. "As soon as I feel the hour of death approaching, I will crawl like an animal into the heart of the bush where no one can follow me," he wrote in 1918. "There, with great devotion and reverence, I will wait for infinite wisdom. I will then die without a sound, crossing over amid stillness and silence to the great unity from which I first came. And I will be thankful to the gods if they allow hungry vultures and outcast dogs to eat their fill on my corpse, so that not even a single white bone remains." Four decades later, in 1958, at the end of the final version of the novella "The Night Visitor," the author returned to this particular notion of death, in words closely parallel to his remarks in *The Brickburner*.

Life on the Run

Traven's conception of death, ironically, comes close to characterizing his life. His longing to vanish, in death, without a trace and to return to the elements from which he came echoes his lifelong hunger for anonymity, for disappearing without a name, or with a fictitious name, so that his true identity would be lost forever. The life of a pseudonym is the life of a dead man, of one who does not exist. In Mexico, B. Traven presented himself not only as the engineer and innkeeper Torsvan, but also as his own literary agent Hal Croves. And back in his *Brickburner* days, in 1918, the man who called himself Marut wrote: "*I am nothing but the result of my time*, yearning to vanish namelessly into the great oneness, just as today . . . I must scream out my thoughts *with no identity at all.*" The way Traven wished to live was thus barely distinguishable from the way he wished to die. He would have viewed an anonymous death as the crowning achievement of his anonymous life.

The life of the best-selling Mexican author B. Traven actually stood in the shadow of death, for Marut's "death" was the basis of Traven's "life." The death of Marut, however, was not just the metaphorical metamorphosis into a new identity that Traven had in mind when he wrote in his Tampico diary on July 26, 1924, "The Bavarian of Munich is dead." The truth was that he narrowly escaped physical death fifty years before his actual death in Mexico City.

That had been during the collapse of the Bavarian Republic of the Workers', Soldiers', and Farmers' Councils, which had established itself during the chaotic days after the First World War. Marut was one of the intellectual leaders of the Räterepublik (Republic of Councils), although the offices he held in the spring of 1919 were relatively low-profile. He served on the Propaganda Commission of the Provisional Revolutionary Central Council as one of the censors of the local newspapers. He was also chairman of the Preparatory Commission for the Creation of a Revolutionary Tribunal. When government troops under General von Epp moved into Munich on the first of May to root out revolutionaries, a group of White Guards recognized Marut on the street and arrested him. He was brought into the ministry of war, where a summary court of dubious authority questioned him and brought a charge of high treason, which would have been routinely punished by the death sentence and immediate execution. But since Marut was not prepared to confess, he was whisked away to the former royal residence, speeding along streets lined with the blue-and-white and black-white-and-red banners of the triumphant royalists. There a court-martial dispensed summarily with labor leaders, revolutionary soldiers, Spartacists, and Red Guards. In a matter of minutes, a Free Corps lieutenant made life and death decisions between puffs on a cigarette; if any question of guilt remained, the suspect was brought to the courtyard where a firing squad did away with him on the spot. Under the circumstances, Marut expected a death sentence, but shortly before his turn to appear before the lieutenant, a scuffle broke out in the waiting room between the prisoners and guards. Marut used the opportunity to escape. "Two soldiers apparently felt a spark of humanity within them for a brief moment, as they saw how the most precious thing that a man possesses, his life, was being mistreated. They were not uninvolved in his escape. Thanks are due to them for saving the life of a fellow human being," Marut wrote in his *Brickburner* report in December of that year (writing of himself, as he often did, in the third person).

It was Traven's life that was saved on that day. Marut, wanted for high treason by the Munich public prosecutors, disappeared without a trace in the underground. He spent the next several years on the run in various European countries, resurfacing in the summer of 1924 on the Gulf Coast of Mexico in the state of Tamaulipas, calling himself B. Traven or B. T. Torsvan or Traven Torsvan. A series of novels started appearing as early as mid-1925 under the pseudonym B. Traven. They featured Mexican cotton pickers, vagabonds, gold prospectors, and Indians. Their most memorable figure was an American sailor named Gales who lacks a passport and travels on a "death ship." These novels catapulted the obscure revolutionary to world fame in his new persona.

A death sentence in Munich and a death in Mexico—the half century that lay between harbored the life of an author whose name became synonymous with "mystery." His name enjoyed the limelight, while the man behind it hid in the wings. Until his death, he publicly denied any connection with Marut—whose existence in Germany can be documented from 1907, first as an unknown actor and from 1912 as a journalist and short-story writer. And as soon as the writer B. Traven became known worldwide, the man who lived in Mexico as Traven Torsvan and later also as Hal Croves flatly denied being the best-selling author. His was an obsessive flight into anonymity, a determined rejection of modern conceptions of individuality and originality, of the person and the self, reminiscent of Rimbaud in Abyssinia or T. E. Lawrence in the Royal Air Force.

As a result, fascination with the author threatened to overshadow interest in his works. The biographical riddle became irresistible: legends, rumors, hypotheses enveloped him—all the more as Traven himself occasionally helped promote the mystery and encouraged the proliferation of hearsay. This may have been psychological calculation designed to promote sales of his books, or he may have felt that the legends offered him protection. Still, the farther one reaches back in the twilit regions of B. Traven's past, the dimmer it gets; his beginnings are veiled in darkness. We can easily imagine why he adopted a new name in his chosen land and tried to pass himself off as hailing from America. He clearly did not want to be identified as Marut, the German anarchist and traitor wanted by the authorities. From the 1930s on, he may have feared the fiery tempers of the southern Mexican landowners whose exploitation of the Indios he lambasted in his Mahogany Novels. Furthermore, it is conceivable that a writer with Traven's sense of independence simply wanted to avoid the inconvenience of personal publicity. Or the anarchistic conviction that the individual is insignificant may have lain at the bottom of his never-ending game of hide-and-seek.

Yet the question Who was Ret Marut? remains unanswered even today. For Ret Marut, like B. Traven to follow, is believed to be an assumed identity. Why did he camouflage himself with this pseudonym, or why did he feel compelled to do so? Were the reasons criminal or political? Psychological or even psychopathic? This question, more than all other Traven mysteries, has engendered a host of fanciful speculations and contradictory scholarly theses. We are often told that even on his deathbed Marut/Traven did not reveal his true background: Was he a son of Emperor Wilhelm II or Emperor Frederick III, or of another Hohenzollern, or of a nobleman of similar stature? Was he the son of a Norwegian fisherman or of a midwestern American farmer? Was he a former theology student from Cincinnati or a German-Polish locksmith's apprentice from Schwiebus near Posen? Perhaps the more fitting question is Did he himself know who his father was? Did he really have a secret of this kind to guard and take with him to the grave? Or did he, as a child born out of wedlock, elevate his own lack of an identity into a philosophy of anonymity and a rejection of the cult of personalities? Or was all the mysterious to-do nothing but a public relations trick on a grand scale?

To pursue these questions is not inappropriate, even if one is primarily interested in Traven's *works*. Traven's and Marut's opinion, repeated often, that only the printed word, not the author, is important is an extreme philosophical position. Consciously or unconsciously, the strategy of negating the role of the author is a challenge to uncover the reasons for the smoke screen. Traven's assertion did in fact backfire, particularly because the theme of who one is and how one proves it permeates his works. It was surely a complicated, unusual, and adventurous life that enabled this mystery man—who was no average man even in his low-profile period in Munich—to write novels that were to fascinate millions of readers and hold them spellbound even today. And as the novels took on lives of their own, the author's life took new twists. His world fame inspired literary critics-turned-amateur detectives to direct their searchlights on the psyche and the past of the man who seemed to have more than philosophical reasons for keeping things in the dark.

What kind of man is constantly on the run from his own fame, trying to remain anonymous and avoid all publicity yet nonetheless doing everything in his power to promote his fame? Traven displayed such conflicting behavior even in his early days in Mexico when, as a German revolutionary trying to pass himself off as an American or a Scandinavian, he wrote novels in the mosquito-infested bush. It is not difficult to see that this was a man who relished a good mystery. But while there may be a certain amount of truth to the proposition that one can learn important information about the inner man from the "facts" that he fabricates about himself, where in Traven's case does one draw the line between truth and fiction? And what can one conclude from this line, assuming that one could draw it with some degree of certainty?

Paul Theroux called Traven's life and work "the greatest literary mystery of this century." Here was someone who had apparently realized the fantasy of millions: He had traded his identity for a new one that he himself had chosen with total freedom. He had enacted the adventure of vanishing into thin air and being reborn, phoenixlike, as someone else—literally a self-made man. And he accomplished this in a world where regulations infiltrate even the most private corners of every citizen's life. A fairy tale for modern times seemed to have become reality in the life of the unknown man known round the world—a life that provided untold numbers of readers with vicarious wish fulfillment. "Lucky he who can be someone else!"

But what sort of life was it really? Can we ever hope to untangle the twisted skein of legends and rumors to get at the truth? When, where, and how did it begin? What insights can we gain from the pre-Traven period, when the mystery man was Ret Marut, who played a role, albeit a rather obscure one, on the German literary and political scene? And how did his life subsequently take shape, both externally and internally, under the assorted aliases in Mexico, after dramatic personal experiences and historical events made someone else out of him entirely, namely that representative of world literature who became well known and at the same time unknown as the novelist B. Traven? "Only he who has lived life has the right to depict life," we read in the *BT-Mitteilungen* (*BT News*), a newsletter authorized by that great portrayer of life in the New World.

Was Traven's a life at all—or was it rather a legend, a rumor of a life?

2

ARMCHAIR ADVENTURES

Hide-and-Seek and Guessing Games, 1925 to the Present

Nameless in Tampico

Traven began playing his game of obfuscation even before he gained worldwide renown. Early on, he expressed a philosophy based on the insignificance of the individual, reviving Marut's thoughts along these lines. *Das Totenschiff* (*The Death Ship*), published in April 1926 by Büchergilde Gutenberg, loomed large in the literary world and beyond, selling 120,000 copies in German alone in the first ten years. Traven saw to it, however, that any questions about the author were headed off even before the book's release. In the essay "Mein Roman *Das Totenschiff*" ("My Novel *The Death Ship*") in the March 1926 issue of the publishing house's magazine, *Die Büchergilde*, he refused to divulge any information about himself:

> Anyone who applies for a job as a night watchman or a lamplighter has to write a résumé and submit it within a certain period. From a worker who creates spiritual values, one should never demand a résumé. It would be impolite. One tempts him to lie. Especially when he believes, for whatever reasons, that people would be disappointed by his true life story. This is not the case with me, however. My life story would not disappoint. But my life story is my own business and I would like to keep it to myself. Not because I am an egoist. But rather because of my desire to be my own judge in my own case. I would like to

> make it totally clear. The biography of a creative man is completely unimportant. If the man cannot be recognized in his works, then either the man is worth nothing or his works are worth nothing. For that reason, the creative man should have no other biography than his own works. In his works, he exposes his personality and his life to criticism.

A month later, *The Death Ship* inaugurated the success that would only increase with the publication of *Der Wobbly*, later called *Die Baumwollpflücker* (*The Cotton-Pickers*), in 1926, *Der Schatz der Sierra Madre* (*The Treasure of the Sierra Madre*) in 1927, *Der Busch* (*The Bush*) in 1928, *Die Brücke im Dschungel* (*The Bridge in the Jungle*) in 1929, and the later books. *Die Büchergilde* did not fail to allude to the exotic wilderness from which these novels reached the German reader—sent from tropical Tampico with just a post office box as a return address. Similarly, on June 21, 1925, the Social Democratic newspaper *Vorwärts*, which published the first part of *Der Wobbly* in serial form as *Die Baumwollpflücker* that summer, introduced its new novelist as an adventurer: an oil driller and worker on a cocoa plantation in Central America, a brush clearer and orange picker, a mule driver and "trader among the wild Indian tribes of the Sierra Madre, where the natives still hunt with bow, arrow, and club" and where one must travel thirty-five miles to the nearest store for paper and ink. The public, at first merely curious, grew impatient.

When pressed for more details about himself or when asked to provide a photograph, this foreigner writing in German left *Vorwärts* as much in the dark as *Die Büchergilde*. Editors at Büchergilde Gutenberg tried to appease their readers in March 1927:

> It is clear that works such as Traven's can derive only from an extraordinarily rich life experience. Traven has tried his hand at many jobs: he was a farmhand, a sailor, a baker, a cotton picker, a gold miner, to name but a few. He has worked in the oil fields of Mexico and has driven herds across wide stretches of land. We have received many requests for more information about him. But Traven will send us neither a picture nor a biography, since he considers these unnecessary.

The February 1928 issue of *Die Büchergilde* struck a similar chord: "We are asked again and again to provide information about the author's background. But we can say nothing at all about B.

Traven the man, since he simply refuses to speak about himself. We would not provide such information in any event, since we share Traven's view that in each work of literature both the poet and the man reveal themselves." From *Die Büchergilde* in 1931: "Next to nothing is known about B. Traven, and Büchergilde Gutenberg, in accordance with the author's wishes, will not divulge the sliver of truth that is known about him to the rumormongers of the bourgeois press." Traven had so instructed his publisher, most forcefully in a letter to Büchergilde staff member Johannes Schönherr:

> "Who is this man? Think of the mystery that surrounds him!" Ask questions like that and the person becomes more important than his work. But I desire that the person be totally unimportant. If the person cannot be found in the work, then it helps nobody to provide his date of birth, his age, and his shoe size. And if you can find the person in the works, then you don't need to know more about him. Anything else that you hear about him is more or less the same as old wives' tales. I have no mystique. I simply don't consider myself and my personality important enough that someone else should be concerned about them. You can certainly exert your influence so that people don't discuss whether or not I provide information about my private life. I don't see why this should be the case—I am not applying for a job as a mailman or president of a country.

That philosophy did not keep Traven from publishing in *Die Büchergilde* two more or less autobiographical essays as early as February 1928—essays that could only fan the flames of interest in the mystery man's personality. The first, entitled "Der Bungalow" ("The Bungalow"), was illustrated with photographs taken by Traven of the Mexican jungle and Indian life. In it he described a hut on the edge of the jungle, next to an Indian chief's or priest's funeral pyramid overgrown with tropical vegetation. One of the stories in the collection *The Bush* (to be published in 1928) was set here and written here as well, he said in the essay—and the same held true of other Traven stories, the reader could well assume. "An ideal poet's retreat?" Traven asked, satirizing the German cliché of the poetic life of romantic isolation. He reveled in portraying the adverse circumstances of his "poet's" existence in the backcountry of Tampico: mosquitoes by the score, giant lizards and snakes in his hut, jaguars and "lions," scorpions, finger-long spiders, tarantulas as large as a hand, and "whole armies of large ants running through the house"; total absence of human company, no electricity, no furniture, little water, and so on. As early as 1925, when he had described, in correspondence with Büchergilde editor Ernst Preczang, the many hardships he encountered while writing *The Cotton-Pickers* in the tropics, he had not failed to mention the hammock that he made for himself or his lack of writing paper. It is apparent from these remarks that Traven was seeking to awaken understanding of, sympathy for, and even curiosity about the European thrown into such an inhospitable lot.

At the same time as he rejected the importance of biography, he promulgated all sorts of information that would spark interest in him and make his life appear as anything but "completely unimportant." This apparently contradictory behavior might seem to be merely a clever business maneuver, but that interpretation misses the complex personality and difficult situation of this author. To be sure, Traven did have a healthy sense for business and advertising, demonstrated in his correspondence with his publisher. He could certainly understand that by insisting on anonymity, "attention is drawn to precisely that which I would like to keep out of the limelight," namely to himself rather than his works. But that irked him, he told Johannes Schönherr, although the publicity helped sales of his books.

More important than the commercial aspect of this amalgam of obfuscation and revelation was a psychological paradox that must have weighed heavily on Traven. Imagine his day-to-day life: in the 1920s, the threadbare, untrained casual laborer Torsvan working on haciendas and oil fields on the Gulf Coast while his nom de plume was becoming a byword in Europe; in the 1930s and 1940s, the inconspicuous innkeeper Torsvan in Acapulco cashing Traven's royalty checks; in the 1950s and 1960s, the nondescript gringo Hal Croves walking incognito through the streets of Mexico City to the palm-shaded newsstand and the main post office and observing the giant advertisements for *El barco de los muertos* (*The Death Ship*) on the roof of a publishing house "on the most elegant street in Mexico" and the billboards touting the film based on his *Rebellion of the Hanged*, to which moviegoers flocked week after week. "There are dead men," he wrote as Ret Marut in 1918, "who are more alive than the living." Did he not see himself as one of these living dead? Wasn't his life a form of death—but a death that was determined to play a role in life—more effective than the life of the living, "who are dead from their first day in school, even though they will tell you, 'we are alive, since we have the power!' " The desire to be both dead *and* alive—who can read the mind of the man in the prime of life in Tamaulipas or of the old man in Mexico City who, with a false identity card in his pocket, opened his nameless post office box to discover that sales of his books numbered in the millions? They were his books, but then again not "his" books.

The "Bungalow" essay was followed in the same issue of *Die Büchergilde* by "Mitteilung" ("Notice"), dated October 18, 1927, in the form of a letter signed "B. Traven." In it, *Die Büchergilde* insisted in 1931, Traven "revealed more about himself than he would ever do again." What Traven said in his "Notice" (and repeated in his own *BT News* in 1951) may have looked like a publicity stunt, yet it was more than that. It was provoked by an unauthorized addendum with which the magazine *Das Buch für Alle* had introduced Traven's story "Ein Hundegeschäft" ("Indian Trading") in 1927. The addendum insinuated that the author of the story—presented as a German—depicted the roguish behavior of Ascension, the Indian protagonist, as "characteristic of the Indian mentality." Traven's "effusive rebuttal" (his own words) in the "Notice," like so many of his comments, comes across as the release of a pent-up need to communicate. He identified completely with the Indians. Offering no explanation, he simply maintained that the Mexican proletarian was his "brother," closer to him than a blood brother. He was thus particularly offended by the magazine's affront to the Indians, especially its implicit disparagement of their struggle for liberation, which the gringo writer now adopted as his own literary cause:

> I know the courage, the dedication, the sacrifice—unknown and inconceivable in Europe—with which the proletarian Indian in Mexico fights for his liberation to reach the light of day. It is a struggle for liberation the likes of which has never before been seen in the history of mankind, not even in the history of the struggling proletariat. To date I have not succeeded in making a single chapter of this struggle for liberation accessible to the European working class in objective, historical form or in a work of art. For all the writer's or poet's tools as I have possessed them to date fail me when faced with the enormity and variety of the cultural, societal, and economic side effects and logical

> consequences of this Indian-proletarian struggle for liberation. But be this as it may, and no matter how much and how painfully I am compelled from within and without to feel the full impact of this violent event in world history, this colossal cultural event, so that I might capture it in words and sentences and vivid images—against my will and without my prior intention the impression was given that I had authorized a sentence containing an affront to the Mexican Indians and thus an affront to the Mexican proletariat. This hurts me more than a bodily wound ever could.

This somewhat self-pitying portrayal of a white man identifying with the jungle, its torments, and its people piqued interest rather than satisfying it. Even more remarkable was Traven's heated attack in his "Notice" on the other falsehood that *Das Buch für Alle* had promulgated—Traven's nationality: "I am not to be counted among the Germans, since I have no right to be counted among them." He noted that he possessed this right "neither by birth nor by extraction"—and thus invalidated the distinctions that others were to make between his citizenship and his nationality. If he was not a German, as he stated, then what was he? "Whoever is acquainted with just one of my books knows that I have never concealed my nationality," he continued. Was he an American like Gales, the narrator of a good deal of the early prose? This identity was not expressly ruled out, but Traven did attempt to cover his trail. His "true countrymen," he immediately added, were those with whom he was connected "not by chance through the place of my birth, but those I belong to with my consciousness and on the basis of my philosophy. They do not live within the boundaries of a single nation, regardless of how wide one draws the boundaries." Traven thus blurred the concept of nationality, recasting his argument in terms of supporters of the same cause or members of the same class—without expressly identifying the cause or class: In spite of his half-revelations, Traven was still holding tight to his anonymity, even though it threatened to become only an illusion.

One would expect such a philosophy of namelessness from the former Ret Marut, the perennial anarchist. But Traven's philosophical justification at the same time has all the earmarks of a diversionary maneuver. He pushed his German background from center stage. Yet in doing so he, perhaps unintentionally, suggested a different nationality, rather than no nationality: American. This suggestion was reinforced in a letter that Traven sent in the late 1920s to Büchergilde Gutenberg in which, between the lines, he identified himself as an American. (The letter was meant for private consumption only, and Traven was very upset when the journalist Manfred Georg published it, without Traven's authorization, in *Die Weltbühne* in 1929.) "Workers," he wrote in the letter,

> should not respect any figures of authority, neither kings nor generals, nor presidents, nor artists, nor transatlantic fliers. Everyone has the duty to serve mankind according to the best of his powers and abilities, to make life easier for others, to bring them joy and direct their thoughts to great goals. I fulfill my duty to mankind, as I have always done, as a worker, as a sailor, as an explorer, as a private tutor on remote farms, and now as a writer. I don't feel like a person who wants to stand in the limelight. I consider myself a worker within the community of men, nameless and fameless as every worker who contributes his share to propelling mankind one step further along. I feel like a single grain of the sand which makes up the earth. My works are important, my personality is unimportant, just as unimportant as the personality of the cobbler is unimportant who sees it as his duty to make good, well-fitting shoes for his fellow man.
>
> We—I speak here of the Americans—have been so plagued and hounded by the press that it is really a tragedy for anyone who is hit by it. Our great authors live like hermits in order to escape the shameless press. Upton Sinclair is the most enviable of all: through his works he has succeeded in being totally ignored by the press. Sinclair Lewis often spends time in Germany under a different name. Our greatest dramatist is always traveling around the world in order to avoid the public eye. He has found a double, whom he has hired and who has to make appearances at every conceivable location around the world in order to confuse the reporters and hence the public regarding the true whereabouts of that dramatist. Lindbergh—really a fine young man—slips away to Mexico every few weeks to avoid reporters who want to know what he has had for breakfast, how many hours he slept the night before, and what films he enjoys most. His life in the United States is more wretched than that of a prisoner. He cannot go to the theater, attend a concert, or see a film, since he is hounded to death wherever he goes. Now his young fiancée is the object of public scrutiny: the whole world wants to know her brand of underwear and whether she's been in love before and with whom.

> I hope that people finally understand what I'm getting at: I do not wish to give up my life as an ordinary man, as one who lives an unassuming, simple existence among men. And I wish to do my share so that authority figures and authority worship vanish, so that every man strengthens his own awareness that he is just as important and indispensable for mankind as everyone else, regardless of what he does, and regardless of what he has done.

The message about his nationality that is implied here was openly stated in a letter Traven sent at about the same time to Charlot Strasser, an adult education lecturer in Zurich who had devoted the final chapter of his 1929 book *Vier neue amerikanische Dichter* (*Four New American Writers*) to the "German-Mexican B. Traven." "B. Traven is an American, he was born in the United States; both his parents were Americans and were born in the States," Traven is quoted as saying in the letter to Strasser. (Along with this letter, Strasser also reprinted Traven's letter published by Manfred Georg regarding the right to anonymity, with the addition "The typesetter who sets my book is just as important to cultural life as I am, and for that reason one should be no more concerned about my personality, about my private personality, than about the personality of the typesetter.")

Inventing a Past: The Log Cabin in the Midwest

The German best-sellers were thus written by an American—one who supposedly either wrote them himself in German or, after composing them first in English, entrusted them to a translator (as Traven sometimes chose to maintain). This scenario could help explain a curious aspect of Traven's use of language. On the one hand, the author (or translator) "doesn't know proper German," as a bewildered Kurt Tucholsky noted in *Die Weltbühne*; specifically, he peppers his prose with anglicisms or "awful Americanisms." Yet the author's (or translator's) command of German extends from proletarian jargon and provincial dialect to the heights of literary allusion and esoteric academic reference, to say nothing of his extensive knowledge of German geography and culture.

But couldn't the author and translator be one and the same? This is in fact the version that Traven promulgated in the 1920s: He wrote at least some of his works originally in English, he noted, but he was also responsible for their German versions. (A partial English manuscript of *The Death Ship* in Traven's estate confirms this often doubted story for at least one of the novels.) Traven pursued this line of reasoning in the self-portrait he sent to Strasser (speaking of himself in the third person, as he often did):

> His mother tongue is English. Although he writes a great deal in German, he nonetheless writes half, if not more, first in English, since he finds it easier to record difficult chains of reasoning and intricate dialogues first in English to clarify them to himself in words and sentences. *The Death Ship*, *The Bridge in the Jungle*, the bulk of *Land of Springtime*, the first book of *The Cotton-Pickers*, as well as the majority of the novellas in *The Bush*, most notably "The Night Visitor," were originally written in English. The difficulty, not to say the impossibility, of finding a publisher for his books in the States gave him the idea of rewriting his books in German and offering them in Germany.

Once Strasser bruited about these autobiographical revelations of the anonymity fanatic in 1930, it became impossible for Traven to keep up the "man without a country" story. The author of *The Death Ship*—a novel about an American sailor without identity papers, suspect as autobiographical—had no choice but sooner or later to flesh out the American past he claimed to a complete, or at least sufficiently detailed, fictitious biography that ended with his settling in Mexico. In so doing, he did not need to look further than his own statements that his life could be found in his own novels; and, indeed, from this time on, the biographical details he divulged often recalled the youth of Gales, the narrator of some of Traven's early prose. Charles H. Miller, with Traven's assistance, published such a biography in 1966 in his introduction to Traven's *The Night Visitor and Other Stories*. But what could Traven have hoped to accomplish by publicly claiming to be an American?

Since the 1930s one reason for Traven to emphasize the American scenario may have been that his game of autobiographical hide-and-seek had meanwhile tipped off the press hounds that he was "probably wanted by several German prosecuting attorneys for robbery or the like," according to a 1931 *Büchergilde* essay, "Traven und sein amerikanischer Verleger" ("Traven and His American Publisher"). The following year *Die Büchergilde* felt compelled to hint more broadly: "Numerous newspapers now think they have discovered why B. Traven lives so mysteriously and hidden. An Austrian newspaper reports that he is probably wanted by prosecuting attorneys and the police of several countries. A newspaper in Prague reports that he was probably involved in several political murders in Germany and Austria and for that reason is now forever on the run." B. Traven surely read that, either in his threatened idyll on the Pacific coast near the still undeveloped Acapulco or in the highlands in the politically explosive capital city. When he himself spoke of such rumors, however, he did so in a tone of amusement.

But, then, what about the English manuscript draft of *The Death Ship*, which contains a seemingly unconnected digression that might be suspected to reveal a part of Traven's own past with which he had not yet come to terms? The segment follows the description of the dingy deckhands' quarters on the *Yorikke*, where the sailors, without names or passports, waste away their lives, the by-products of the touted European civilization that lowers "real men into the average."

> Our democratic age does not like exceptions, nor outsiders from the general rule. Therefore we are so terrible poor of great men. Great men always have some secret as to their personality, always have something to hide as to their past. Not necessary that this secret has to be a murder or a holdup. Nevertheless, it is his secret that gives a great man that shade of mystery which is essential for his power over the average.

Whoever so matter-of-factly connects a mystery with a capital offense *and* in the same breath rejects the mere thought may, according to Freud's rule of denial, actually have committed some wrongdoing or believe that he has something of the sort on his conscience—or he may not. Determined psychologists might point out that in *The Death Ship* Traven states that every skipper automatically thought "cutthroat" at the sight of a deathship sailor. They might also become alerted by Traven's occasional insistence that he wanted to be his "own judge" in his "own case." Notwithstanding Traven's preoccupation with anonymity and his denunciation of the cult of authority, which also arises in *The Death Ship* in impersonal philosophical garb, have we not perhaps hit on a sore spot? The answer must be that we do not know.

It was, in any event, a matter of life and death for the former Ret Marut, as soon as he found refuge in Mexico, to treat as preposterous any ties back to Germany. (Even in his final days in Mexico, Traven publicly denied his identity with Ret Marut, as well as any German background.) And once strict anonymity was no longer tenable after the "Notice" of 1928, after Georg's article of 1929, and after Strasser's publication of 1930, it made sense for Traven to give center stage to his presumed American origin, youth, and citizenship. In the privacy of the Prussian and Bavarian bureaucracy, he had already claimed American birth as Ret Marut. (At one point, perhaps in 1914 at the start of the war, the originally stated English nationality, registered by the actor with the Düsseldorf police in August 1912, was changed by an official stroke of the pen to American, which does not exactly lend it credibility; and in Munich, Marut was officially registered as an American during the war.) After 1930 Traven thus returned to this story.

In the long run, the public, its curiosity growing as quickly as the author's fame, could not be satisfied with the single scrap of information that Traven was an American. That was no more satisfying than the clichés that only the work was important and not the author or that Traven's biography and personality could be found in his works. No photograph, no address except for an ever-changing post office box, no parents, no date or place of birth. That was not enough. In an era of increasingly widespread communication and public visibility, it was only understandable that readers wanted more.

But not until the mid-1930s did Traven venture out of his shell—and into the realm of fiction. On February 6, 1936, he recommended that his Swedish publisher, Axel Holmström, use the biographical statement that had appeared on January 26 of that year in the (New York) *Daily Worker* on the occasion of its serialization of *The Death Ship*. This statement, by journalist Edwin Seaver (possibly relying on information from Traven himself), was retold as follows by *Die Büchergilde* in its June 1936 issue: "*The Death Ship* is, without question, at least partially the story of his own life. At the age of seven, he was a bootblack, newspaper boy, and milkman's helper. Before the age of twelve, he had already gone to sea. And he apparently formed the basis of his education during his time as a sailor." Traven says nearly the same about Gales's youth in *The Death Ship*.

Johannes Schönherr of Büchergilde Gutenberg furnished further biographical details using "material from correspondence hitherto unpublished." In 1947 he gave a lecture on the life of the mystery man, about which *Leipziger Volkszeitung* had the following to say:

> Traven, the author of *The Death Ship*, is according to his own account not a German, but a North American born in the midwestern United States. His parents were likewise born in the United States. Traven's ancestors come from Scotland and Norway, not from Germany, which Traven visited only once, shortly before 1914. He is able to document his presence in Mexico since 1911; he had first set foot in that country back when he was a cabin boy at the age of ten. His background is virtually the same as Jack London's: he too grew up in the proletarian sections of the large American cities and was on his own at the age of seven and never went to school. Those acquainted with his works know that he was a baker, sailor, cotton picker, laborer, and waiter before he became a writer. In 1911, he left a Dutch freighter where he had been badly treated and settled in the state of Sinaloa. He found it impossible to publish his inflammatory books in the United States in his native tongue, which gave him the idea of offering them in Germany. "I am, after all, not the only well-known author who writes in more than one language," remarks Traven.

The newspaper report concluded: "Now all the legends and rumors about Traven . . . are finally laid to rest." One can well imagine Traven's delight. Nothing could have been more important to Traven Torsvan than Schönherr's assertion that the author had been in Mexico before 1924—at the time when, as Ret Marut, he was actually an actor in various German provincial towns and the *Brickburner* revolutionary in Munich. Similarly, his Mexican alien registration card of 1930 recorded that he, an American born in Chicago on March 5, 1890, entered the country at Ciudad Juárez in 1914.

As time went on, Traven fitted out this non-European, pre–World War I biography with all sorts of realistic details that do not always agree. Shortly after the Second World War, he wrote to the American correspondent William W. Johnson that until age thirty-five he had not spent more than twenty-six days in school and that as a twelve-year-old he deserted a Dutch freighter in Mexico, where he worked as an apprentice to an electrician. And Charles Miller's biographical introduction to *The Night Visitor and Other Stories*, composed apparently under Traven's watchful eye in Mexico and published during the author's lifetime, added that Traven liked to regale his friends with stories of how at an early age he would skip school and earn money as a messenger, a shoeshine boy, and a newspaper boy. In polyglot Chicago, so the story went, he would pick up the languages of the immigrants. He "probably" had little knowledge of family life and parental love under these circumstances, Miller asserted. Around 1900, Traven signed on aboard a tramp steamer as a cabin boy; until about 1920, he traveled with the merchant marines of many countries and got to know the world. In Mazatlán, the harbor on the west coast of Mexico, Miller reported, Traven's presence was officially registered in 1913. He made numerous trips to Mexico from various parts of the world until he finally settled in the state of Tamaulipas on the Gulf Coast "about 1920."

Traven himself published extensive biographical information for the first time in 1952 in the *BT News*. Details from the essay "Who Is B. Traven?" then echoed through many newspapers and magazines around the world. This "official biography" included the following information:

> B. Traven was born around the turn of the century in the midwestern United States, in the same region that brought forth a number of other well-known authors, including Buzzell, Hecht, Sandburg, Masters, Lindsay, Anderson, and Dreiser. On several occasions, first in 1928, Traven wrote in German magazines that he had no German ancestry on either side. . . .
>
> Traven's mother tongue is English, and he writes his books in English. His works were published in fifteen other languages before they appeared in the United States. This is due largely to the political conditions in the United States between 1919 and 1929. His books were first printed in Germany since B. Traven found a good translator; further, at the time his books appeared in Germany, Germany was the freest country on earth, as far as art, literature, and scholarship are concerned.
>
> Both of B. Traven's parents, although of northern Scandinavian descent, were born in the United States; and on both sides B. Traven comes from a long line of sailors. Since the age of seven, Traven has lived on his own and has had to make his own living. He has never gone to school. His school is life, harsh and unrelenting life itself. He first came to Mexico at the age of ten, when he got to know the harbors of the Pacific coast as a cabin boy on a Dutch tramp steamer. There he became the world-renowned novelist. He has lived in Mexico for forty

> years, with shorter or longer interruptions for journeys to other countries and continents.
>
> His books, which are always based on what he himself has seen and experienced, provide the reader with insight into the jobs he has held. He has been a sailor, a cotton picker, a casual laborer, a petroleum driller, a baker, a cattle drover, a gold prospector, a farmer, a private tutor on remote farms, an explorer, a medicine man, a midwife, and a lawyer in Indian villages. B. Traven has undertaken year-long expeditions through unexplored regions of Mexico, and has lived among the Indians as one of their own.

In *Canasta de cuentos mexicanos* (*Basket of Mexican Stories*), Spanish translations of selected stories edited by Rosa Elena Luján and published in 1956, a few additional details were sketched in, which the *BT News* passed on to the German press in 1957 in these words:

> B. Traven, of Norwegian descent, was born around the turn of the century in a simple log cabin on a farm in the midwestern United States. When he was only seven years old he found himself forced to earn his own living. At ten, he sailed as a "kitchen boy" aboard a freighter, which threatened to come apart at the seams any day. . . .
>
> A perpetual rover, he spends many months in Switzerland (in Geneva and in Davos) only to return to his farm in Chiapas (Mexico). He says that Chiapas "is the most beautiful and enchanting corner of the world. Were it not for what one calls 'Casiquismo' [political "bossism"] in Mexico, Chiapas would be paradise, the most beautiful country in the world, where one could live and die contented."

The final sentences bring to the fore the most compelling component of this biography: the yearning for exotic, primeval, far-off lands, which recalls *The Brickburner*. "The only thing that one knows for sure is that B. Traven, like so many other restless spirits, withdrew from white civilization," according to the *BT News* in 1953. In the next breath the article recalled Rimbaud's mysterious disappearance as an ivory and slave trader on the "Gold Coast" [*sic*], Gauguin in the South Seas, and Lafcadio Hearn in Japan. "Traven belongs to this band of adventurous, freedom-loving men with strangely flashing eyes. . . . For several years he lived among the Lacandones, a dying race of Indians, in the inaccessible reaches of the jungles."

What is one to make of the "official biography"? Some of the details relating to Mexico are false (Traven's farm in Chiapas to which he claimed to return from the equally fictitious journeys to Switzerland); others correspond roughly to the truth (his occupations). But what about his alleged childhood in America?

However much one would grant that Traven himself may have been convinced of his birth in America, the more or less detailed American biography that leads up to his arrival in Mexico before the First World War is the story of an escape artist. This biography is not convincing, not only because of the inconsistencies between the various versions but also because Traven's novels appeared without exception first in idiomatic, albeit not flawless, German, with English versions being published by Knopf only in the 1930s. And the English of Knopf's rather free translations was somewhat Teutonic, even in the stylistic revision by the publisher's editor Bernard Smith. (Years later, Smith attested to the presence of Germanisms in the texts furnished by Traven.)

The story of an American background has never been documented, although the attempt was made on several occasions. A number of people who had the chance to converse with the Mexican recluse, whether he presented himself as Torsvan or as Hal Croves, noted the strong German accent in his English. Further, the English that occurs on rare occasions in Traven's German novels not only is in some cases unidiomatic but also has a downright comical Teutonic flavor (as in "Smile, work, and give the poor"). The same holds true for Traven's English draft of *The Death Ship* and other English texts by Traven. Also, the knowledge of things American demonstrated in the novels and stories is hardly so profound that it unequivocally shows that the author grew up in the American tradition. Whoever believes that this is merely a matter of opinion need only consider the following case, which speaks volumes.

A nine-page typescript in German, with handwritten corrections by Traven, entitled "Die Lebensgeschichte eines erfolgreichen Mannes" ("The Life of a Successful Man"), "von [by] B. Traven," lies among the author's papers. It originated in the early Tampico days (before ca. 1930), as shown by the return address typed on the first page. The life in question is that of the American newspaper tycoon Frank Andrew Munsey, who, as stated in the first sentence, died on December 22, 1925, shortly after which Traven may have written this essay. On the penultimate page he describes a newspaper as the "Organ der 'Bostoner Tee Partei,'" ("organ of the Boston Tea Party"), "which had played such an important role in the American Revolution." No American, no one who grew up in America, even if only until the age of ten, as Traven maintained, would speak of the "Bostoner Tee Partei." While any American child knows that the Boston Tea Party refers to a group of Bostonians jettisoning a cargo of tea from a British East India Company ship into Boston Harbor—a revolutionary act humorously referred to as a "party"—Traven, not knowing any better, falsely translated it with the German word *Partei*, which can only mean "political party." If this "Life of a Successful Man"—was it translated, in part, from the English?—had been published in the 1920s, as Traven apparently had hoped, it would have taken a none-too-perceptive observer to explode Traven's story that he spent ten years growing up in America.

Legends, Exposés, Rumors

Traven's insistence on an American background, meant to satisfy the public's curiosity, only fanned the flames of legend and rumor. The more people investigated, the less they found. Even those who knew Mexico well were unable to ferret out Traven. The Swiss archeologist Gertrud Düby, who had lived in Chiapas for years, wrote in the East Berlin *Sonntag* in 1948:

> Many of Traven's books are set in the Mexican state of Chiapas. He describes remote regions where strangers rarely set foot and where every foreigner remains etched on the inhabitants' memories, even if he has spent but one night on the secluded farms. Usually only the natives stop over here; sometimes traders bring their wares on donkeys; hardwood cutters and chicle tappers stop on their way, and explorers rest here. I myself have combed every corner of the state and could not discover who Traven is. He must have spent the night at the same places as I, he must have studied the native customs in the same Indian villages as I, and yet no one there can say who Traven is. Under which name, with which mission could he have journeyed through those villages? As a trader, woodsman, mule driver, or explorer? Or is he perhaps one of the lone farmers?

The rumor mill was quiet only during the Nazi era. Traven was persona non grata in Germany. Nonetheless he distanced himself from any and all German writers in exile. He did not meet face to face with any of the antifascist German writers who had fled to Mexico, although they basically shared his political sentiments and admired his works (during the war they apparently helped stage a production of *The Rebellion of the Hanged*). After the war, it was believed for years—as the *BT News* kept reminding its readers—that a reward of three thousand dollars (five thousand according to some versions), allegedly offered by *Life* magazine, awaited the unmasker of the mystery man. The story was exposed in 1957 as an advertising ploy of Traven's Mexican publisher Rafael Arles Ramírez. The filming and release of *The Treasure of the Sierra Madre* added to the pandemonium in 1947–1948, with Traven himself, the press reported, assisting in the production in the guise of his own agent Hal Croves at a salary of one hundred dollars per week. According to Traven's letter of introduction presented by Croves to director John Huston, Croves knew Traven's works better than Traven himself did. Naturally people suspected his real identity. Croves responded by writing a letter to the editor of *Time* magazine, asserting that had Traven been hired, he would have commanded a thousand dollars a week. Oddly enough, though, Croves shared some of Traven's quirks: He did not allow himself to be photographed, and he bristled when addressed as Bruno. He repeated the imposture in 1959 at the Ufa production of *Das Totenschiff* in Berlin; disguised again as Croves, he went so far as to feign making a phone call to Traven in Mexico to clear up a technical detail. He reportedly employed the same subterfuge in 1962 at the filming of *La rosa blanca* (*The White Rose*) in Mexico City. Strange incidents added to the aura of mystery. In the 1940s Traven scheduled a rendezvous on the beach of Acapulco with the actress Lupita Tovar, wife of Hollywood agent Paul Kohner, but he failed to show up at the appointed hour—or rather, a man walking along the beach failed to identify himself as Traven. Bernard Smith, Traven's editor at Knopf, had a similar experience during his visit to Mexico City in 1936. Traven arranged for a young woman to show Smith and his wife the sights of the city following a detailed daily itinerary. Meanwhile, Traven himself was nowhere to be seen, though the Smiths had the lingering suspicion that their every step was being watched. Similarly, journalist William Johnson reported that when he visited the home of Traven's translator, Esperanza López Mateos, in Mexico City about 1946, part of the living room was separated by a heavy curtain. Although he could see or hear nothing from behind the curtain, he felt in talking with López Mateos that "someone" had stood behind the curtain the entire time.

In 1948, the Mexican journalist Luis Spota came dangerously near the truth of Traven's identity in an intrusive interview with the innkeeper Torsvan in Acapulco, garnering international attention. In the late 1950s, Wolfgang Cordan sparked a spirited debate in the German press with his essay "Ben Traven: Ende der Legenden" ("Ben Traven: An End to the Legends"). His piece loosed an avalanche of readers' letters, rebuttals, and new theories, each more fantastic than the last but including some realistic ones as well. Cordan answered them rather lamely in the magazine *Die Kultur*. From 1951 to 1960, the *BT News* did its part to ensure that talk of B. Traven never ceased (its efforts included agitated attacks on Cordan's piece). Its ostensible goal, however, was "to combat the never-ending stream of overblown false reports about the author's identity."

In the next decade, *Stern* reporter Gerd Heidemann enticed Traven fans with extensive photo essays that had a ripple effect in the rest of the popular press as well as on radio and television. His thesis was that Traven was a son of the last German kaiser. An interview with Mexican journalist Luis Suárez, which appeared on October 19, 1966, in the widely read magazine *Siempre*, caused repercussions in the international press as well. Public attention was revived in 1969 when Traven died and again from late 1978 on, when the BBC, at lavish expense, promulgated Will Wyatt's discovery that Marut/Traven was the German-Polish locksmith's apprentice Otto Feige from Schwiebus near Posen. The putative centennial of Traven's birth, 1982, stirred up the hornets' nest yet again, with its many retrospectives, such as that in *Stern*. Senior Travenologist Rolf Recknagel's biography enjoyed a well-timed third edition that year; *Der Mann, der sich verbarg* (*The Man in Hiding*) by Frederik Hetmann, a popular entry with little new substantive information, joined the ranks in 1983. The multivolume edition of Traven's collected works published by Büchergilde Gutenberg and Diogenes Verlag also helped keep Traven in the public eye from 1977 on. As in earlier decades, talk continued to revolve more around the author's personality than his works: Who was B. Traven?

A typology rather than a history of the answers that have been offered to the puzzle of Traven's identity may provide some insight into the needs that were filled and continue to be filled by this curious phenomenon of twentieth-century literary life.

The *BT News* in 1957 bemusedly reviewed the potpourri of unconfirmed hypotheses regarding Traven's identity, maintaining that this sort of hullabaloo was in itself uninteresting to the serious Traven devotee:

> None of the investigations to date which attempt to clear up the question of Traven's background has been executed with scholarly precision. They are based on legends, sensational exposés, and vague conjectures, without exception lack an airtight, logical, documented line of argumentation, and for that reason are unconvincing. If one compares the results of these professional literary detectives with one another (a source of amusement itself), one is faced with an impossible hodge-podge of mutually exclusive theses and becomes entangled in a web of contradictions, so that the entire question begins to lose its interest in the eyes of any reasonable person.

Traven kept a close eye on the contents of the *BT News* and had surely given his imprimatur to this dismissive remark. Nonetheless, he himself contributed to the canon of Traven identities, for example in a letter to Alfred Knopf in 1933. Perhaps he felt safer the more tangled the skein of legends became.

In the letter to William Johnson of about 1946, Traven was at it again. He said that some people in the United States had taken him for an American black man or for a woman; that German newspapers billed him as a Hohenzollern prince who had emigrated to Mexico; but that he was also purported to be a shipping magnate from the West Coast of America who had written books critical of the social structure to soothe a troubled conscience. Reporters, Traven continued, had simultaneously spotted him on a ship in the North Sea and on a train in Brazil "nibbling at pumpkin kernels."

More such nameless characters lurk in the obscure recesses of Traven scholarship; the fugitive Austrian archduke, the convict from Devil's Island, and the Stalinist spy are among the more fanciful. Gertrud Düby reported from Chiapas that Traven was rumored to be a leper in Mexico who was seen only with a bandaged face or a German ranchero who lived somewhere in the jungle of Chiapas, several days' journey from the nearest village, in a "house full of books." Düby, to be sure, had not seen either of the two characters in the flesh. The Norwegian journalist Edvard Welle-Strand thought he had met Traven—as a nameless intellectual—in the 1920s on a coal steamer in the North Atlantic bound for Spitzbergen. The *BT News* revived the story in 1959: "In answer to our questions, B. Traven explained that he would neither confirm nor deny this encounter and that everyone could think what he wished."

Such were the nameless characters that emerged from the exotic romanticism of the literary sleuths. Other hunches, particularly from Mexico, were more concrete, naming identifiable candidates. Some reporters wasted no time in pointing a finger at Gertrud Düby's husband, the Danish Lacandones archeologist Frans Blom, who had lived many years in Chiapas (a story Gertrud Düby herself related with a chuckle in her *Sonntag* article). But Blom was by no means the only candidate in Chiapas. When Gerd Heidemann was rummaging about there in the 1960s, he found that it was nothing special in that state to be identified as Traven. The exiled Germans of the Heine Club in Mexico City apparently made a sort of parlor game out of identifying one or another of the émigrés in Mexico as Traven. The writer Ludwig Renn, for example, saw Traven in the German plantation owner Lothar Schlamme in Chiapas, and many shared his view. Others were equally off the mark in their nomination of the teacher José Weber in San Cristóbal.

Setting his sights a bit higher, Traven himself informed William Johnson in his letter that Mexican president Plutarco Elías Calles was suspected as the enigmatic best-selling author. Adolfo López Mateos, one of his successors, turned out to be a stronger candidate, beginning as early as his tenure as state secretary in the 1950s. It certainly ranks as one of the curiosities of modern political life that a head of state, on an official visit abroad, was asked at a press conference whether he was Traven, as happened to López Mateos in Buenos Aires in 1960. Charles Miller, relying on information from Traven himself, recounts this story in his introduction to *The Night Visitor and Other Stories*. The rival version that López Mateos's sister Esperanza was the phantom novelist was one of the earliest and longest-lived of the rumors. This hypothesis at least had a certain logic, since Esperanza López Mateos was Traven's Spanish translator and assistant and the joint holder of his copyright from about 1941 until her death in 1951; further, she was listed as coeditor of the *BT News*. Journalist Antonio Rodríguez was one of the chief peddlers of this story, starting in 1946 with a series of articles in the Mexican magazine *Mañana*. Traven retorted that Señorita López

Mateos could write much better books, as time would tell. Rodríguez himself related this rejoinder in an extensive report in *Siempre* in 1964. In 1946 Rodríguez had not had a shred of evidence, relying instead on his vivid imagination. In 1964, however, with much fanfare he published a quotation from a book by Esperanza López Mateos that had apparently been printed privately in 1943, entitled *La carta y el recuerdo* (*The Letter and the Memento*). Rodríguez took the quotation to prove that López Mateos was a great Mexican writer and as such "could have" written at least Traven's *El puente en la selva* (*The Bridge in the Jungle*). Not exactly a coup worthy of an Inspector Maigret. On the occasion of the Mexican presidential election in 1959, the *BT News* returned to both López Mateos legends in an extensive report, quoting exhaustively from the Mexican press and referring also to *Life* magazine: How strange that after Esperanza's death nothing more had appeared by Traven; how remarkable that the recently elected president had stated that he "truly wished that . . . he could really be B. Traven, since Traven writes such extraordinarily good books."

During the filming of *The Rebellion of the Hanged* in Mexico three years after Esperanza's death, the daily *Esto* related that a number of the crew thought they had uncovered the "real" Traven in the American assistant director John Bright, who reportedly adopted the posture during the filming that he was authorized to make decisions in accordance with the author's wishes. The *BT News* did not fail to play up this canard (*Esto* itself had labeled the rumor as false), adding that of course there was nothing to the story: Traven had not been in Mexico for quite some time.

If such disparate individuals could pass for the inscrutable Traven, it made a certain amount of sense to pin responsibility for the novels on a collective instead of an individual, particularly since this approach would satisfy the claims of both Europe and America. An anonymous article in the magazine *Sie*, entitled "Traven hat nie gelebt!" ("Traven Never Existed!"), did just that, asserting that there had never been a *single* Traven and it was thus no accident that the search for him had gone in circles. The writer's argument was that anyone who, like Traven, hides from the public eye must have committed a felony that is not subject to a statute of limitations and for which every country, including Mexico, recognizes extradition treaties—namely murder. "But this is impossible. Never would a man with such a serious crime on his conscience make himself the focus of the attention and interest of a worldwide public," the writer reasoned. Hence there was not a single Traven, but the name must harbor several persons. "And now all of a sudden the pieces finally fit together," the writer concluded. "The novels—examined by stylistic experts—at times appeared to have been translated from English into German and at others looked like German originals. When one searched for the writer in Mexico, he was suddenly in South America, the United States, or Switzerland. The novels and stories depict the most disparate settings with the same intimate knowledge of detail. All of which is hard to imagine in the case of a single author." To be specific, the writer claimed "with certainty" that the collective consisted of five people: three Germans, an American, and a German-Canadian. At the time of the report, 1949, they were working together in Honduras, apparently in Tegucigalpa. For support, the writer referred to an unnamed authority who had not yet completed his investigation but who nonetheless could supply the names of the members of the authorial team. The non-Germans' names were not revealing; the American was "said to be" a certain McClean (no first name); the Canadian was "reportedly" called "Thiel or Theel," with no further identification. With the Germans, the anonymous researcher had more luck:

> The names of the three Germans are Bretting, Holthusen (an engineer), and Wollank. Bretting is from Hannover and left for Central America because of a dueling incident in which he had been involved at the University of Göttingen after the First World War. He does not do the writing but is the initiator and creator of the seminal ideas of *The Death Ship*. Holthusen, a few years younger, served in 1910 in a Hamburg infantry regiment but was demoted because of insubordination and was sentenced to prison. He too fled to Central America—to Mexico. Holthusen is very wealthy, they say.
>
> The oldest is Wollank. Little is known about him—save that he was the one who published *The Brickburner* along with Ret Marut. Marut himself originally belonged to this group but died in 1934 in Tegucigalpa, Honduras, where he was living under an assumed Spanish name.

Evidence? This strange article, which its unnamed author surely penned with all seriousness, concluded: "We have not the slightest doubt that Traven fans will raise plenty of questions and probably protests as well, demanding more detailed information. Today we are not yet able to furnish this information. The man who has set for himself the task of solving the Traven case is still in the midst of his project." But a follow-up report on this dubious "work in progress"—one that could have written *finis* to the case with the same self-assurance as the original piece—never materialized. The road remained clear for the next industrious sleuth who might come along.

Just how many sleuths did come along can be illustrated by a few highly prosaic (and never before published) examples in Traven's estate. They demonstrate how contemporaries of every description identified themselves or their relatives (and thus their extended selves) with the man whose name represented wish fulfillment and unrealized possibilities. Letters from people otherwise unknown started pouring in to Mexico City at the time of Heidemann's *Stern* reports in the 1960s and shortly after Traven's death, all of them maintaining or suspecting that the renowned incognito was a long-lost relative. For example, a seventy-seven-year-old pensioner from the Breisgau wrote that Traven was a cousin he had not seen since 1913: "Our fathers were brothers." One woman asked whether Traven might be her father's brother, who came from Danzig (where Marut had worked as an actor) and went to sea, never to be seen again. "I greet you as the brother of your departed husband," wrote a man from Berlin in 1969 to Señora Luján. On June 21, 1968, a singularly original message was sent to Traven from Yugoslavia: "You are the son of Count Blagay of Castle Bostani and Margareta Travnik from the village of Veliko Mlacevo." A letter to Traven from Dortmund dated October 9, 1968, ranks as one of the most bizarre, yet revealing examples of imaginative identification with the man who perfected the art of phoenix-like personal metamorphosis. Omitting the salutation, the letter wasted no time in getting to the point: "I am B. Traven." The recipient was instructed to send an agent to "inform me about everything."

Things looked a trifle more promising for the likewise unknown Slovenian shepherd Franz Traven, who was in the running as early as 1959 amid the publicity surrounding the Ufa filming of *Das Totenschiff*. The *Frankfurter Allgemeine Zeitung*, like other German newspapers at the time, reported that in the tiny village of Utik in Slovenia, the elderly Martin and Ivana Traven had identified a photograph of Hal Croves as that of their brother Franz. Born in 1883, Franz had left for America in 1910 after completing his military service, returned shortly before the First World War, and then, as a soldier on the Russian front, disappeared one day after confiding to comrades that he wished to go back to America. A photo unearthed by the family supposedly reminded them of Hal Croves; the siblings put most stock in their brother's short fingers, similar to Croves's. The last issue of the *BT News* quoted the article at length and subjected it to scrutiny: It finally freed the author of the novels of the despised Christian name Bruno, but beyond that it was just as absurd as the fact "that people today identify Hal Croves with B. Traven."

This last statement gives a glimpse into the precarious psychological plight of the aging Traven, who was known to many as Hal Croves. However understandable the proliferation of legends in an age in which enigmas and mysteries are increasingly scarce and however understandable even Traven's own support for this spawning of legends, the humor with which he denied such reports seems strained. We hear the laughter of someone who was trying to save his skin, perhaps his very life. Similarly, in the *BT News* in 1957, under a title more befitting a humor magazine—"Who'll Laugh Along?"—the writer (Traven himself no doubt) cast aside the Marut-Traven equation and in the same breath rejected as equally absurd the claim of a Hamburg woman that Traven was her betrothed who had fled the altar and disappeared across the sea, as well as a Frankfurt woman's assertion that Traven was her lost fiancé who in happier days had written her letters, the wording of which she had discovered in *The Death Ship*. Laughing, the former Marut was actually quaking in his boots.

Completely unknown candidates have their allure since a refutation of their claims (or the claims made on their behalf) must rest on the same shaky foundation as their candidacy: No one knows under which name Ret Marut was born. It is a different matter with the well-known names from literary history who have been identified from time to time with Traven. In his letter to William Johnson, in which Traven revealed his enjoyment at the mythmaking surrounding himself by naming several nameless candidates, he also mentioned Jack London. It is common knowledge that London committed suicide in California in 1916. But just as there is no lack of theories that Christopher Marlowe was only apparently stabbed to death in a Deptford inn in 1593 and lived on as the originator of Shakespeare's dramas, so too—as early as the 1920s—did the scuttlebutt make the rounds that Jack London's suicide was faked; he lived on as—who else?—B. Traven. Superficially, this is not wholly implausible, since Traven's literary temperament is closer to London's than to most other writers'. But what of the original editions in German? Traven himself offered a curious answer in his letter to Johnson, without of course vouching for the reliability of this or any other thesis: "London merely pretended to have committed suicide so as to 'get away from it all,' especially from his complicated love affairs and marriage problems, whereas in fact and secretly he went to Mexico, changed his name and to avoid being recognized had his further books and stories published in German first and translated into English from the German with intention to destroy his original style." Traven had written to Charlot Strasser around 1929 that his life "bore far greater similarity in every respect" to that of Jack London than one could conclude even from the novels themselves—surely the words of a man who enjoyed a good smoke screen.

The tale of a well-known writer's fantastic disappearance and rebirth in a new identity borders on literature—the art of the possible and of the imaginary become real. The line of thought seems to be that the author is a man of a thousand possibilities who can make anything a reality and therefore can himself perhaps also be what he chooses to be. Jack London was not the only one to stir the fantasy of the Traven sleuths. Another was newspaperman and storyteller Ambrose Bierce. Tired of the American dream, in 1913—a year after his *Collected Works* were published—he is said to have slipped across the Mexican border never to be heard from again, save under the pseudonym B. Traven, whose novels, however, show few signs of the macabre fantasy of Bitter Bierce. When and by whom this rumor originated is unclear. Conventional wisdom has it that in 1914, when Bierce was already over seventy, his colorful life ended under mysterious circumstances at the siege of Ojinaga. By the time of the spectacular success of *The Death Ship*, he would have been in his mid-eighties, and when *Aslan Norval*, Traven's last novel, was published, he would have been about one hundred twenty, with still a full decade to go. Once again, a good mystery proves more enticing than the banal truth.

Gerd Heidemann in *Postlagernd Tampico* (*General Delivery, Tampico*), related a story that illustrates the absurd lengths to which some Traven detectives would go. A scholar approached Heidemann several weeks after Traven's death claiming to have solved the Traven riddle (by the very methods of stylistic comparison that years previously had revealed the identity of Marut and Traven so clearly that Traven was terrified by such scholarly competence): None other than Nabokov had hidden behind the pseudonym, the scholar asserted. Equally absurd was the candidacy of Herbert Baldus, the German South America expert who was endorsed by Büchergilde Gutenberg after it had been taken over by the Nazis in 1933. The short-lived effort probably received no attention and certainly was commercially motivated, since the real Traven naturally would have nothing to do with the Nazified Büchergilde from the beginning.

A more romantic and adventure-packed contribution, from Czechoslovakia, recalls the Jack London story. In a 1964 article entitled "Traven Unmasked" in the magazine *Kulturní tvorba*, Ivan Růžička asserted that the creator of the novels that had gained world fame under Traven's name "could be none other than Arthur Breisky, a very promising writer of the Czech decadence":

> Breisky, a great admirer of Baudelaire, Verlaine, Nietzsche, Wilde, and Hamsun, tried to affect an aristocratic manner, although he was only a minor customs official; *blagueur* and dandy, he became notorious because of his temporarily anarchist leanings. He considered himself a *poète maudit*. At the age of twenty-five, he suddenly and surprisingly left his Bohemian homeland in order to escape the constraining conditions of the Czech Parnassus, which he had just climbed with his first publication, a collection of fictional portraits of famous personalities. Early in 1910, Breisky showed up in the United States, but even in the New World fate did not favor his plans: Although talented and fluent in several languages, Breisky could land a job only as an elevator operator in a German hospital in New York, where he was found on the morning of July 10, 1910, with his skull crushed beyond recognition. Naturally, this led many of his friends to believe that the deceased was not really Breisky, but that this had been just one of the many disappearing acts Breisky engineered in order to create a new identity for himself. This theory was further reinforced by the autopsy results, which showed signs of a Jewish ritual which was improbable in Breisky's case.
>
> In short, Ivan Růžička revived the theory that Breisky continued his life under a new name, and he connected it in an ingenious manner with the mystery of B. Traven. He tried to

> prove, in fact, that the pseudonym B. Traven was only an anagram derived from shuffling the letters NEV ART B = NEW ART Breisky. The theory naturally fell out of favor when new discoveries were made about Marut's similarities to Traven.

An adventurous identity switch never fails to beguile. Gabriel Figueroa, the noted Mexican cameraman, told journalist Judy Stone that his friend Traven must have had as many as twenty passports. Metaphorically that is certainly correct, and it is not entirely off the mark in real terms. For it seems that since his first years in Mexico, when he lived in the Tamaulipas jungle in such penury that he could not even pay the customs fee for his forwarded clothing, Traven preserved official papers of other people (presumably brought from Munich) with which he might have been able to identify himself in an emergency. He held on to them until his death, surrounded by the Old World elegance of the Zona Rosa of Mexico City. Among these documents were the army reserve I.D. of an ironworker named Laurentius Brennig, born in 1882 in Weilbach in Bavaria, and the identification card of his friend Anton Räderscheidt from Cologne. Ret Marut's estate contains a similar item: the Prussian lieutenant's commission of a certain Karl Kreitz, dated 1894. And Marut left Germany after the Munich debácle with the passport of Götz Ohly, a friend from the *Brickburner* years, according to Ohly's own testimony.

Obituaries, Usurpers of Fame, and the "Other Man"

Anyone as obsessed with his own anonymity or pseudonymity as Traven faces three risks. First, he may be declared dead, even if it is only a feint meant to elicit a rebuttal. Second, others may circulate works under his name hoping to capitalize on his fame and force him to publicly identify himself. Third, one could maintain that the author shunned the public eye since he himself was reaping what someone else had sown—far from creating the novels that gained fame (and royalties) under his name, he might at best be their translator or editor, a parasite who based his novels on the experiences of someone else. The man who called himself Traven was spared none of these three scenarios, with the ensuing ballyhoo in the press making the mystery man even more mysterious.

Reports of Traven's demise were sprinkled through the press during his lifetime. Such accounts, like the one in the article on the Traven collective, appeared logical at least on the surface. Had not Traven, in an interview with Mexican journalist Luis Spota in 1948, brought up this theory himself? Had not the last of his rapidly produced chain of Mexican novels, *General from the Jungle*, appeared in 1940, followed after a long hiatus by the novel *Aslan Norval* in 1960, which was in many ways atypical and in any event not "Mexican," its authenticity questioned both before and after its publication? Thus Marut/Traven, who had narrowly escaped a death sentence and come to Mexico, where he had lived for decades, was forced to "prove" that he was indeed alive—long before *Aslan Norval*, in fact. The *BT News* amply documents this irony: The "Bavarian of Munich," who had expressly recorded his own death in his diary, must now, in the face of the rumors of his demise, desperately fight for the recognition of his existence as Traven. Luckily for him, the various accounts of his death were so inconsistent as to discredit one another. Also, they were oddly balanced by the reports, likewise picked up by the *BT News*, that Traven was in an insane asylum and "therefore cannot be found or revealed." Further adding to the confusion was the story in the Mexican press that Traven stood ready to get married and thus "the veil masking the author's true personality will finally be lifted. . . . This will doubtless be recorded as a major event in the literary life of the entire world." An early rumor of Traven's death even beat the Spota interview to the punch: German émigrés who had fled to Mexico to escape the Nazis were said to have published "some of [Traven's] books" during the war in Spanish pirated editions. Their "shameless" pretext was that "Traven died long ago in Puebla and his books could therefore be reprinted without permission or royalty payments," according to the *BT News* report of the incident. "To prove that he was still alive," the *BT News* continued, Traven responded by publishing *Una canasta de cuentos mexicanos* (*A Basket of Mexican Stories*) in 1946. Subsequent issues of the *BT News* denied the story that Traven's life had ended in the fall of 1950 in a suburb of Zurich and dismissed the rumor that he had died in 1948 in Angelopolis as Jacob Torice. In 1957 the *BT News* was still passing along stories of Traven's death, denying his rumored suicide in Puebla. Later, the newsletter recalled that the Mexican daily *El Nacional* reported the death of Esperanza López Mateos with the headline "Murió B.

Traven" ("B. Traven Is Dead"). Other issues of the *BT News* discussed in general terms the alleged death of the author who for so many years had apparently not published anything, for which one could "easily" cite "a hundred reasons." The truth is that some new pieces—above all *Macario* (1950)—had appeared in print between *General from the Jungle* and *Aslan Norval.*

Traven's efforts to prove his own existence also took the form of reactions against "literary pirates" who attempted to take advantage of the Traven name and thus created further unwanted publicity. This latter chain of events came to pass in spite of Traven's responses to the "obituaries"—after all, the *BT News*, where Traven's rebuttals were published, did not enjoy a particularly wide audience. Thus in the early 1950s publishers and magazine editors received book manuscripts falsely billed as Traven's works that the author himself, so the stories went, had not brought to market for some fanciful reason—if the manuscript peddler did not bill himself as Traven outright.

The *BT News* repeatedly took up arms against such piracy. In the December 1953 issue, for example, an article entitled "In the Shadow of Traven's Fame" ridiculed the plottings of a certain Herbert Reckefuss, who in the previous year had allegedly tried to hawk his works to publishers in Bern in the guise of "the so long-lost B. Traven." Starting in 1954, the *BT News* also often mentioned the case of Heinz W. Schilling from Bochum, who, like Reckefuss, was otherwise unknown. Schilling supposedly undertook to sell no fewer than six new Traven novels to various German publishers and editors, after he had, in 1953, peddled an adventure story entitled *Catceria* as Traven's. The public prosecutor of Bochum began an inquiry that had to be suspended for procedural reasons but that nonetheless entered into the record the astounding story of two alleged Traven typescripts that had reportedly been uncovered in 1943 in the air-raid shelter of Schilling's family home, which was destroyed in the bombing. The manuscripts had so suffered from fire and water damage that they had to be recopied and even partly reconstructed before being offered to publishers some ten years later. The man with the six new Traven novels was not Schilling, however, as the *BT News* corrected itself later, but yet another member of the "Society of False Travens," namely a certain Kurt Adler from Berlin-Tempelhof, against whom legal proceedings were also inaugurated (in 1956, in Berlin). Adler maintained in court that he had published under the name of Traven from 1925 to 1933 but allowed the pseudonym to be entered on his identification papers only in 1953—and claimed to have received word of the existence of another Traven only as a result of the proceedings in Berlin.

Similar was the case of the Berlin sea captain who called himself Jack Bilbo but whose real name was Hugo Baruch. Though he did not attempt to sell Traven manuscripts, he did claim to be B. Traven. While held in an English internment camp during World War II, he announced himself one day as the famed author of *The Death Ship* and other Traven books. When his fellow prisoner Emil Rameau related the news in *Die Westküste*, the supplement to the émigré newspaper *Aufbau*, Traven wrote to the publisher on September 12, 1944, dismissing the announcement but at the same time attempting to lend credence to his "official biography" (as a seaman, a ship's stoker, and, since 1914, a Mexican resident). The letter was printed in 1948 in the American magazine *Tomorrow* in an article about Traven by William Reid McAlpine, which Traven shortly thereafter described, in a letter to Wolfgang Paulsen, as the only one that was authoritative.

Other such usurpers of fame have included a certain Fedor Gonzala in Zurich, a would-be Traven from Sweden, and the Mexican film director Chano Urueta, who during the filming of *The Treasure of the Sierra Madre* told the Union of Mexican Authors and Composers that the novel was his literary property and that he had chosen the pseudonym Traven for "personal reasons." (His claim was dismissed as "loco.")

Plagiarists are a related species of literary pirates. They too created quite a stir about Traven, particularly in the Nazi period, when a German copyist was safe from any protest or threat of prosecution since Traven, as an avowed antifascist, was powerless in his land of origin. One of these cases is interesting in that it combines plagiarism and the "other man" hypothesis. An alleged German sea captain named Tex Harding had published in 1936 in the *Münchner Illustrierte Presse* a "true story" called "Kesselbum," in which he had copied pages on end from *The Death Ship*. *Die Büchergilde* pointed out in 1936 that this was not simply a matter of individual sentences being lifted but that the plagiarism extended even to the term coined by Traven that Harding found irresistible as a title. When a reader alerted the writer to certain parallels with *The Death Ship*, Harding wrote, as *Die Büchergilde* reported: "The beginning of the 'Kesselbum' has something in common with the book you mention only insofar as that other author composed the above-named passages on the basis of my own experiences."

This is probably the earliest formulation of the hypothesis, at times even presented as fact, that Traven had written up, translated, or reworked the experiences of an "other man." The hypothesis has taken various forms and has featured quite a cast of "other men" whose experiences purportedly lay at the heart of the novels or who supposedly served as the authors of the original manuscripts (which Traven then reputedly translated or reworked). A clear distinction exists, of course, between such "other men" and those who tried to pass themselves off as Traven, as Reckefuss, Bilbo, and others had done.

The breed of "other men" may have been on Traven's mind when, in old age, he noted on the back side of a calendar page from May 1967, probably with thoughts of death not far away: "Anonymity its threats. Possibilities of danger."

Paradoxically, the threat arose because the "other men" or "original authors" could be neither confirmed nor refuted so long as Traven remained hidden and his typescripts and manuscripts were not examined. His game of hide-and-seek included having the typescripts of his published texts returned to him from the publisher, thus securing the possible evidence in the hands of the man who had no interest in stepping into the limelight. Indeed, he was so circumspect that even in his earliest days in Mexico he very rarely signed by hand his typed letters to his publisher or even furnished them with a handwritten *T*. As a rule they were simply signed with a typewritten "B. Traven." The *BT News* spoke of this risky practice in a discussion of the "highwaymen" ever on the prowl, citing a letter Traven sent to the publisher Kiepenheuer and Witsch on the occasion of the Schilling incident:

> If I do not personally sign this letter—a custom I follow in all my letters—the reason is concern for my security. As matters have developed, the danger exists that Heinz Schilling from Bochum would perhaps forge my signature, which until now is unknown to him, in an effort to clear himself. One who has already spent years peddling fraudulent manuscripts and false claims certainly no longer has any scruples about a forgery as simple as that of a signature.

From the start, the idea was not entirely implausible that an "other man" had had the experiences that lay behind the novels and had, in addition, perhaps written the original versions or at least some of them. After all, how could a German about whose presence in Mexico nothing was known (apparently a real novice) arrive at such a thorough knowledge of Mexico—a country that in those days was more exotic, romantic, and remote than it is today, in the age of mass tourism? And as word went around after the Second World War that Traven and Marut were one and the same, Traven's background proved that he was indeed such a novice. How could someone compose in so few years so many novels that apparently were based on real-life experience if he did not rely on the experience of others? And did not the German of these books often sound as if it had been translated from English? No less a stylist than Kurt Tucholsky, justifiably bewildered at the "awful Americanisms" in the Traven novels, hit upon this idea in 1930. Did the author perhaps rework someone's experiences or even go so far as to translate the texts of an "other man" who wrote English?

In principle it would be only natural that a European émigré who depicts the Mexican environment—depicts it furthermore somewhat didactically or in the manner of a cicerone, which is Traven's hallmark—*also* relies on experiences and reports of others, natives or gringos with long-standing Mexican experience. Traven himself never denied that he had such sources of information; in *The Land of Springtime*, in describing a sojourn in the backcountry of Chiapas, he notes:

> Since not much work can get done on a hacienda during such a strong rain, and all outside work is wisely put off until the rain stops, I had plenty of time to speak with the people. And there is much, very much, that I would never have heard or learned had I not been rained in there. These people, who have lived here for generations and stand in the most intimate relationship with the land and its inhabitants, particularly with its native population—they see, hear, and understand everything in a completely different way from those who live predominantly in the state's cities. Much of the information I received here about the life of the Indians was told to me in a completely different way than in the cities. And by weighing the reports of these hacienda people against those of the city folk, one comes a step nearer to the truth.

Traven's Indian guide Amador Paniagua also doubtless furnished him with further details about life in the logging camps, which he depicted in the novels of the 1930s.

Such borrowings are a matter of course, but they do not justify the assumption that Traven was nothing but a ghost writer, translator, or editor of the works of an "other man." To the objection that the author's knowledge of the country and its customs was too thorough for the recently arrived Traven to have possessed, one must ask on which criteria this authenticity argument is based. Neither Mexicans nor those who have lived in Mexico have put forward this contention; rather, it has been asserted by literary critics who lived far from the scene and certainly did not themselves know Mexico through many years of experience. Does not their impression that Traven, even in his early days, depicted Mexico "authentically" simply attest that Traven is a compelling storyteller, a writer who knew his trade?

Finally, it should be food for thought that it was Traven himself who originated the hypothesis of an "other man" (more than a decade after the letter from Tex Harding, which referred only to *The Death Ship*, a novel with no Mexican backdrop), in the 1948 interview into which the Mexican journalist Luis Spota inveigled him. Traven, driven into a corner, used every means at his disposal to throw the obtrusive newspaperman onto the wrong trail since he had come close enough to the secret Traven was guarding. The first full-fledged proponent of the "other man" hypothesis may well have been inspired by such hints in Traven's own remarks—this was the Swiss writer Max Schmid, who argued the case in a series of articles in the Zurich *Tages-Anzeiger* in 1963–1964. Schmid's articles form the basis for all the later hypotheses of the existence of an unidentified, ghostly "other man" in Traven's life and work. In the final analysis, then, such speculations, whether or not their authors acknowledge or even know it, go back to Traven himself, who had no lack of inspiration when it came to disguising the authorship of the Traven novels. (One version that made the rounds in the popular press would have been a particular source of amusement for Traven. According to the West Berlin *Tagesspiegel*, Traven, as Hal Croves, was the "other man" behind at least *The Death Ship*—he then supposedly related his experiences to Adolfo López Mateos, who recorded them in Spanish with the help of his sister.)

The speculations concerning that éminence grise, the "other man" whose experiences or writings Traven reputedly exploited, create two categories of candidates: those known—or at least identifiable—and those whose identity remains unknown.

The first character is easier to dispose of, not least because the various claims contradict one another. Symptomatic of the entire complex is the claim put forward in the British radical publication *News from Neasden* in the spring of 1981. Whether it is to be taken at face value or as a joke is relatively unimportant, because the thought pattern behind it had become a popular notion—its intended readers were assumed to be well acquainted with it. The magazine's editors reported that they had received a series of letters from Australia on the basis of which they were now publishing the claim of an "other man" behind the Traven novels, a man who at that time was almost ninety years old. His name was not given, although the publishers appeared to be acting as his legal agents, since the claimant directed that his share of the royalties from the Traven novels be transferred to them. How did Marut, with his feet barely planted on Mexican soil, come upon his stories? The man from Australia provided the answer: He himself related them in 1924 to the German ex-revolutionary and journalist in a bar in Tampico, using his own experiences in Mexico as a basis; the two then "worked together": "I just let him have my stories and he rewrote them a little." Marut/Traven allegedly promised the Australian half the royalties for the Mexican novels. (*The Death Ship* and *Aslan Norval*, the Australian said, were Traven's own works.) Once the money began cascading in after the film versions, Traven, the story went on, had bandits kidnap his partner and take him into the jungle, where he lived for twenty years until he was able to escape. And now he wanted his share of the royalties.

Whether fictitious or not, there was nothing new about this sort of claim. It was in the bars of Mexico City, not Tampico, that Captain Jack Bilbo allegedly told his story of a death ship sunk off the coast of Mexico, from which an attentive German journalist then fashioned *The Death Ship*. The latter may have expressed his gratitude by using the initial *B*. At least this is what Bilbo wrote to Rolf Recknagel in 1967. This "other man" story does not hold water, if only for one simple reason. This is the same Bilbo who, in an English internment camp during World War II, had tried to pass himself off as Traven rather than as the "other man." He again maintained that he was Traven after the war, in the south of France, where he lived as an innkeeper and amateur painter.

No landlubber, Captain Bilbo left the Mexico novels to Traven. An "other man" of a very different stripe, however, laid claim to them: a German-born attorney, Ewald Hess, who lived in Chiapas. He hoped to gain recognition for providing pivotal assistance in the creation of the Mahogany Novels of the 1930s, or at least of some of them. Hess's version seems to have been first published in June 1957 by Wolfgang Cordan, who reported that in San Cristóbal Las Casas, Hess had "always referred to himself as coauthor of *Der Karren* [*The Carreta*] and *Regierung* [*Government*]. The truth is that Traven had spent many hours each day with Hess. The most likely scenario is that Hess had prepared the material which Traven then refashioned in his unmistakable style. . . . The relationship was severed. Hess spoke bitterly of Traven. And when asked for samples of their cooperative efforts, he responded three years ago that he had burned everything in a fit of rage." Hess's estate consequently contained nothing of the sort, the report continued. In October 1958, Cordan added: "Much could be said about the Hess-Traven collaboration. But since the death of this witness in 1957 gave welcome occasion for denials and insinuations, our report must follow the living witnesses." The denials to which Cordan was referring were apparently two issues of the *BT News* that flatly rebuffed the notion that Traven had ever "come in contact" with an attorney named Hess or with the Bulnes family in Chiapas—whom Traven most certainly knew, as proved beyond question by correspondence found in his estate. And of course Traven, posing as the German-speaking "Norwegian" Torsvan, knew Hess as well. One of the "living witnesses" whose testimony Cordan curiously failed to relate, namely Hess's son, told the reporter Gerd Heidemann that Torsvan had made notes on his father's reports and that Hess had actually dictated several of his "stories" to his daughter, who typed them for Traven. But Hess was embittered in the end, Heidemann related, since Traven had in a manner of speaking embezzled "his material" by writing the books that Hess had wanted to write himself, publishing them "under his own name." It may be true that Hess, through his stories about the Mexican revolutionary period, contributed some details to the Mahogany Novels; but this is a far cry from proving that he qualifies as a coauthor or an "other man" behind the books.

We can pass a similar judgment on the candidacies of those who did not themselves claim to have furnished Traven with their experiences but whose involvement has been maintained by others. Gerd Heidemann, who did not put much stock in Hess's candidacy, believed that the experiences at the heart of *The Death Ship* (and perhaps of other Traven novels as well) derived from the stories told by a customs official and adventurer from Mecklenburg named August Bibeljé: The *B.* in B. Traven thus might pay subtle homage to him. Not surprisingly, it was Bibeljé's widow who had put Heidemann on this trail. She, like the women previously mentioned, had discovered all sorts of details from the life of her husband in the Traven novels. Heidemann discovered that August Bibeljé had been a volunteer soldier in the Spanish Civil War. This man had presented himself to his comrade Ernst Fallen de Droog as the "Brickburner" at the time and confided to him that Traven was "not a person, B. Traven is a joint enterprise," as Fallen de Droog reported in September 1967. Since this "Brickburner" had been killed in battle on New Year's Eve 1937—Fallen de Droog had buried him himself—one must wonder how the later novels and other writings of Traven came about.

Not as Bilbo or as Bibeljé did Ursula Bourba of Cologne interpret the *B.* in B. Traven. For her, it was a tribute to her husband, who died in 1942, the Russian-born, stateless ship's engineer Wladislav Bourba. She too recognized the experiences of her husband in *The Death Ship*, and when the Cologne Arts Association sponsored an exhibition in 1978 composed largely of graphics by the Cologne painter Franz Wilhelm Seiwert that came from Traven's estate, she recalled that her husband had brought several of precisely these works across the sea to safety during World War II. Further, she recalled hints from her husband that convinced her that *he* was the actual author, while the mystery man in Mexico, whom Bourba had assisted in *Brickburner* days, had merely appropriated his works. The report of Hartmut Wilmes, which I am following here, is not quite clear about the extent of Traven's role. Wilmes speaks of Traven as the "agent and at best coauthor" of Bourba. Bourba, like Marut, had reportedly fled to Mexico after the collapse of the Republic of Councils in Bavaria. In one way or another, according to this theory, which Wilmes considers "convincing," Bourba emerges as an "other man" who to a certain extent also apparently put his own experiences on paper.

These "other men," despite the lack of documentary proof, are at least identified by name and a biography that could conceivably be fleshed out. The waters are murkier with the second version of the "other man" hypothesis, which does not even honor its candidate with a name—not to mention documentable biographical facts—but nonetheless emphatically posits his existence. This version relies on the anglicisms or Americanisms in the Traven novels (which suggest a translation from the English of an "other man" and thus exclude the German-speaking "other men") and on the opinion that Marut had spent too little time in Mexico to have written at least the early Traven novels, which brimmed with supposedly profound knowledge of the country and its customs.

This version of the "other man" hypothesis received its first full-fledged treatment in 1963–1964 and enjoyed a revival around 1980 through the incontrovertible evidence of Will Wyatt that Marut had first arrived in Mexico in the summer of 1924, not 1923, as had been assumed until then. This gave Marut even less time to have composed on his own the novels that began appearing in Germany in mid-1925. Thus several reviewers of Wyatt's book (but not Wyatt himself) returned to the hypothesis of an English-speaking—more specifically, American—coauthor or even sole creator of first versions, which, of course, nobody has ever seen. Traven supposedly went so far as to "steal" the texts from this nameless figure, according to some "Traven nuts," in the words of the London *Times*. These ideas never got beyond the stage of mere conjecture, as Wolfgang Bittner noted in 1982: "The question remains open whether one and the same person wrote all the books published under the name B. Traven. . . . Perhaps linguists can shed more light on this chapter." *Stern* magazine asserted that "anyone who traded his own identity so cavalierly with that of any other certainly had an easy time of adopting the other's experiences as well."

But even before Wyatt revealed the date of Marut's arrival in Mexico, *Das B. Traven-Buch* (*The B. Traven Book*) in 1976 assured its readers that there was nothing unsettling in the notion "that several narrators, writers, and translators had taken part in the production of the Traven books." The only open question was the "role played by other participants."

Just as speculative as such occasional assertions are the more extensive studies on this theme. The first is the series of articles on the "other man" by Max Schmid in 1963–1964. Schmid's argument was reprinted essentially unchanged in 1976 in *The B. Traven Book*, where it won an incomparably broader readership that could also put greater stock in the argument because of references to the hypothesis elsewhere in this volume.

Schmid's argument was simple. He presented a chain of events as factual without offering the scantiest concrete evidence. "Only one thing is certain," wrote Schmid: "Ret Marut gave the B. Traven works their literary form, but the experiences depicted in *The Death Ship*, *The Cotton-Pickers*, *The Bridge in the Jungle*, *The Treasure of the Sierra Madre*, and many of the *Bush* stories derive largely not from his own range of experiences, but rather are based on the manuscripts of another man who had settled in Mexico a full decade before him." The latter thus had at his disposal a richer store of experience, as the supposedly realistic and authentic depiction of Mexican life would require. This "other man"—his name, according to Schmid, was "presumably" Bendrich Torsvan—was essentially identical with the fictitious American Gales, who narrates some of the early novels and stories. He was thus the American trade unionist and labor agitator, the sailor and cotton picker, gold prospector, drover, baker's assistant, and so on who appears in the early works, and he had already written his autobiographical manuscripts in English before he met Marut shortly after Marut's arrival in Mexico. The German journalist then translated the manuscripts into German on the spot (hence the anglicisms, one might point out), at most adding his anarchistic philosophy, and published the German texts under the pseudonym B. Traven. Further, Marut "apparently" traded his identification papers with those of Torsvan (if that was, in fact, his name) so that he could live thereafter under the new identity in his chosen land. He also adopted the biography of his partner, and thus that of Gales to a certain extent, while the true Bendrich Torsvan (who incidentally was Marut's cousin according to this version) disappeared in the jungle of Tamaulipas never to be seen again—as Gales does at the end of "The Night Visitor." Of this Torsvan (of whom not a shred of documentary evidence exists) Schmid then constructed a rather detailed biographical portrait. He simply patched together motifs from the early novels and stories into a coherent biography, which was largely identical with the life story of Gales: birth on a ranch in Wisconsin, youth in Chicago, cabin boy, sailor, oil driller, drover, farmer in Mexico. This essentially corresponded to the "official biography" that Traven circulated as his own. Schmid granted, however, that Marut himself—now living under the name Torsvan—authored the later novels, notably the Mahogany Series but also *The White Rose* (1929). (The first-person narrator Gales had correspondingly bowed out of those novels.)

The "other man" theme was taken up by Michael L. Baumann in *B. Traven: An Introduction* in 1976. Baumann retained the basic framework of Schmid's scenario, but he did not presume to be privy to the biographical details of the "other man" and original author, which Schmid believed he could deduce from the fictional texts. Baumann's version of the "other man" story was propounded not only in his book of 1976 but also in the *Dictionary of Literary Biography*. Yet, while Schmid claimed that he possessed "conclusive evidence of the existence of such an 'other man' " but failed to provide any proof (beyond the simple equation "fiction equals biography"), Baumann spoke not of biographical fact but rather of a hypothesis and conceded that there was no documentary evidence for the existence of the "other man."

Reason itself contests the existence of an "other man." Why couldn't a seasoned journalist like Marut assimilate within a year authentic, though not exactly profound, knowledge of his surroundings and use the persuasive power and fantasy of a professional writer to depict his *own* "experiences" (recorded to a certain extent in the diaries that are preserved in the Traven estate)? To calculate the span of time that would have been necessary for accumulating and then for recording his experiences implies an odd view of literature. As for the anglicisms on which Baumann, unlike Schmid, relies heavily, if those in the early novels and stories of the man who had written immaculate German under the name Marut are to be taken as traces of translation, one must ask: Could they not in some cases be translations from their author's *own* English? Traven often maintained, in fact, that he had first composed some of his early works in English. There is no reason to doubt this in light of his English original manuscript of parts of *The Death Ship*, which is preserved in the estate. Further, if anglicisms in the early novels are taken as telltale signs of translation, how does one then explain the same anglicisms in the later Mahogany Novels, which neither Schmid nor Baumann (in 1976) attempted to pin on an "other man"? And how can one explain the anglicisms in the travel book *Land of Springtime*, clearly Traven's own, to say nothing of the anglicisms in letters and occasional essays? They are easily explained (as are those found in Traven's prose works, which he did not translate from his own English originals): Marut/Traven, who wished to pass as an American, created his own English-speaking atmosphere in Mexico, using English whenever possible and almost entirely avoiding German except in his writing. Experience shows that anglicisms quickly insinuate themselves under such circumstances, even when one is not trying to burn one's bridges, as Traven was. Early on, his first diary (beginning in 1924), written in English like all the others, recorded his contacts with British or American oil companies and Americans in the Tampico area; and even at home on the Calle Mississippi in his final years, Traven spoke English among his Mexican family. He wrote letters in English even to Spanish-speaking friends such as Gabriel Figueroa and Esperanza López Mateos. Torsvan's and Croves's everyday language was English.

In short, undocumented as it is, the "other man" hypothesis is untenable.

Burden of the Past

Casting a look backward, we are confronted with an overgrown thicket of venturesome hypotheses and conflicting claims of identity, of manifold identifications by Travenologists and ingenious mystifications by the master of the bluff and the double bluff himself. Over the decades Traven developed ever more sophisticated means of pulling the wool over the public's eyes; but we should not overlook the psychological background of this maneuver, which renders the biographer a chronicler of emotional anguish. B. Traven, like Rimbaud or T. E. Lawrence, has become synonymous with mystery, adventure, and the allure of total self-obliteration and self-transformation, of metaphorical reincarnation and a radical new beginning. As such, he has come to represent the wish fulfillment of millions; he has attained the status of a romantic cult figure, and he certainly knew how to play his role with bravura when necessary.

But this fantastic feat of sovereignty over one's destiny, this fairy tale for modern times, should not let us overlook the deep shadows encroaching on this life—the twisted skein of legends and hypotheses, the rumors and attacks, the death reports and usurpations of identity. Traven would seldom have *enjoyed* his sensational role-playing. One detects an undertone of fear in his calendar notation in old age on the dangers of anonymity. Many of his comments in conversation and correspondence as early as the 1920s bear the Cain's mark of a man alone who has condemned himself to isolation and yet does not feel emotionally at home with the idea: Ever on the run into anonymity, into self-denial, he nonetheless wishes to have an effect and somehow see his work acknowledged. His books—like those of any author—are meant first and foremost as an act of communication. Yet he denies himself the response to his initiatives as he flees into pseudonymity. The occasional traces of delusions of grandeur in his letters as far back as the 1920s are best taken as a compensatory release.

Why was this man—up to his death—always on the run from himself? The oft-cited right to privacy, by itself, is as unsatisfying an answer as the philosophy of anonymity, which stresses the importance of the work rather than its author. Let us recall the considerations touched on in Chapter 1.

One explanation is that Traven did not wish to be recognized as the revolutionary who was wanted after the collapse of the Bavarian Republic of Councils. There is certainly something to that. But this explanation could apply only to the first period in Mexico and not the later years, when he realistically no longer had any reason to fear charges of high treason (according to his own testimony in *The Brickburner*, in fact, the death sentence was never formally pronounced); and even an act of vengeance from right-wing circles in Mexico was hardly conceivable during the later years. Further, Traven had certainly lied to the Mexican authorities, according to everything that we now know about him, when he covered up the trail leading back to Germany (he presented himself as an American who had entered the country in 1914). But even if the authorities had wished to make life difficult for him, a successful, world-famous author who circulated among the country's artistic trendsetters, as Traven did in the later decades of his life, could count on the goodwill of those in power. Even the conceivable fear of reprisals from the big landowners in Chiapas, whom he had depicted in the *montería* novels as brutal exploiters of the Indios, could not suffice as the sole motivation for anonymity during the later years.

Why then the lifelong smoke screen, the lifelong bluff? This much has emerged as fact from the long and not always pleasant quest for B.T.. his identity with Ret Marut. True, the "Marut equals

Traven" equation has been halfheartedly questioned from time to time, as late as the 1980s. Even *The B. Traven Book* bristles at "the thesis gaining credence that Ret Marut . . . is B. Traven." Yet none of these second thoughts rests on documentary evidence or the rules of logic; they fail to convince. Recknagel's research—preceded by similar suppositions and claims by Erich Mühsam, Oskar Maria Graf, Leopold Spitzegger, and others—has confirmed the identity of the two beyond a shadow of a doubt, as have manuscript materials in Traven's house, such as the diary note of July 26, 1924 ("The Bavarian of Munich is dead"), and the letters Irene Mermet, Marut's friend from his German period, wrote to Traven when he was in Mexico in the 1920s. This is decidedly not "a question of faith or a matter for Interpol," as Lothar Creutz wrote in *Die Weltbühne* in 1967.

Traven/Torsvan *was* Ret Marut. The secret that the man who gained fame in Mexico was guarding may, in the final analysis, have been the secret of Ret Marut, whose existence is first documented in 1907 as an actor and director at the Essen municipal theater. The name Ret Marut is generally believed to be an alias. The man it cloaked apparently was fleeing from his own past. But from what sort of past? Who was on the run?

Götz Ohly, Marut's friend from *Brickburner* days, who died in 1958 and who had harbored the fugitive Marut in Berlin on his odyssey through the underground, stated tersely in 1949 that Marut/Traven "has very weighty reasons for remaining hidden; he already had such reasons when he was in Munich." Such reasons had nothing to do with his role in the Bavarian Republic of Councils, Ohly implied. He suggested that he knew Marut's real identity, or at least the time and place of his birth. We can no longer ascertain whether this was merely a ploy to get attention. Ohly did not specify the name, nor did he hint at what sort of "very weighty reasons" Marut had for vanishing into pseudonymity—were they criminal, psychological, political, or familial (illegitimacy)? And were they the reasons that, even in the 1960s, traumatized the man whose success was already well established? When an entourage from *Stern* magazine impinged on the publicity-shy old man in 1963 and perhaps came dangerously close to uncovering his secret, anxiety attacks in the form of hysterical blindness plagued him for days, according to his widow, Rosa Elena Luján. One night during that time, Traven burned papers from his past, she recalls.

For decades, the sleuths have pored over the mystery of B. Traven. They have usually assumed that Traven himself knew his own identity. It is clear that he knew how to pose a sphinx-like riddle; whether he possessed the answer remains an open question, however. In *The Death Ship*, the American sailor Gales, often cited as Traven's double, remarks that he needs no papers—he knows who he is. Did that hold true for Traven as well, or did he perhaps see himself forced into the role of a Kaspar Hauser of modern literature?

3

TRAILBLAZING IN NO-MAN'S-LAND

The Search for the Beginnings, 1882–1907

Intellectual Games

B. Traven was Ret Marut—but who was Ret Marut? The equation, although no longer doubted, at most relates one mask to another, or several others (Torsvan, Croves, and so on). But who hid behind those masks, playing roles with gusto or in agony? The search for the man who was "probably the most mysterious figure in contemporary letters" begins and ends with the question "Who was Ret Marut?" Literary sleuths keen on solving "the greatest literary mystery of this century" must today focus their energies on that question.

The beginnings of this perplexing life are shrouded in darkness. None of the venturesome searchers who have trekked into the nebulous pre-Marut (pre-1907) period has returned with any hard evidence. The most fruitless attempts have come from speculators taking their cue from the author's noms de guerre. These attempts have proved to be mere intellectual vagaries, wholly undocumented, and usually unimaginative as well. What does one gain by learning that the name Traven is in fact a family name in Yugoslavia? What use is the assertion, even if it were true, made by none other than Captain Bilbo in a letter to Traven biographer Rolf Recknagel, that *Traven* means "the traveler" in nautical jargon? Equally pointless are the speculations that *Traven* alludes to the German word *trauen* ("trust") or *B. Traven* to *betrauen* ("entrust"). For others the trail leads to the river Trave and, more specifically, the city of Lubeck on the Trave, sometimes rumored to be Traven's birthplace or his mother's hometown. Gerd Heidemann reported that Traven's widow herself made the Traven/Trave connection, although this is no doubt based on a misunderstanding. Señora Luján assured me that it was Heidemann who first brought into her house the picture of the river Trave that Judy Stone reported as hanging in Traven's study after his death.

Equally questionable are the attempts to decipher the name Marut. Marut has been documented as a family name in Poland—a dead end in this maze, as is the discovery that Marut is an anagram for *Traum* ("dream"), which then might lead some to see a connection with *Traven*. One rumor has it that one of the novellas sent by Traven to *Vorwarts* editor Karl Döscher bore the author's name Traum, which Döscher then changed to Traven. Others surmise that Marut borrowed the name Traven from a certain Ada Traven, an actress in his days at the Düsseldorf Schauspielhaus, although that was not her real name either. Ada Traven, the story continues, was none other than Marut's friend and colleague on *The Brickburner*, the actress and publisher more widely known by the name Irene Mermet. But no Ada Traven is documented in the personnel records of the Schauspielhaus or the Düsseldorf municipal theater for the period in question. The game is not over yet, however: *Marut* forms an anagram not only for *Traum/Traven* but also for *Armut* ("poverty"). Those looking for "evidence" may note—again, to no avail—that the early story "Brief nach Berlin" ("A Letter to Berlin") is signed "Artum" by its fictitious narrator, while the satire "Honesty" appeared in the Düsseldorf *General-Anzeiger* in 1913 under the name Ret Murat.

Others are quick to point out that in the Rigveda the Maruts were a type of storm god whose origins were apparently known only to themselves. A little free association recalls the storm motif, echoed in the name of the *Death Ship* protagonist Gales and in Torsvan too (Thor, god of thunder), as well as in Traven's plans to found a publishing company with his collaborator Esperanza López Mateos under the name Tempestad. The "storm" also recalls Marut's idiom in his Munich magazine *The Brickburner*, evidenced in such outbursts as "The storm draws near! Day is dawning!" Could Marut's real name have been Sturm? One might apply the same sort of creative guesswork to any of Traven's pseudonyms, including Georg Steinheb (hitherto unknown), which appears on the title page of *Das Vermächtnis des Inders* (*The Indian's Legacy*), an unpublished novel found in Marut's estate. But, of course, all such speculations lead nowhere.

The name Maurhut helped inaugurate another wild goose chase. Traven published his first book, *An das Fräulein von S . . .* (*To the Honorable Miss S . . .*), in 1916 under the name Richard Maurhut. Could not Marut be an alias derived from Maurhut, and might not Maurhut, though widely assumed to be a pseudonym, be our man's real name? A few have supported this hypothesis, among them Leopold Spitzegger in the Viennese magazine *Plan* in 1946 and Manfred George in *The New Republic.* The Maurhut hypothesis circulated, though unconfirmed, as early as 1918, among the Munich police authorities. The Marut estate includes a letter to Marut dated July 24, 1918, from his "Brickburner journeyman" Götz Ohly (who addressed him with the formal "Sie"): The recipient, Ohly noted, was more to him than merely Ret Marut; he would prefer to call him Richard Maurhut, but then Marut would surely get angry. Is this just an allusion to Marut's authorship of the 1916 novel *To the Honorable Miss S . . .* or to his true name as well? The letter gives no clear answer. Nor does *The Brickburner.* In response to a reader's letter in 1918 that unmasked him as Maurhut, whose novel was praised lavishly in the journal, the editor noted with a shrug, "And what if that were the case?" He would be proud to be Maurhut, though at the same time he distinguished between himself, Ret Marut, and Maurhut as if they were three separate entities. Of course, even if Marut's true name had been Maurhut, this, too, simply replaces one enigma with another.

Speculations based on the names thus serve only to draw us deeper and deeper into the labyrinth.

Traven himself, of course, concealed his roots or put out a false scent, even before 1919, although he presumably did so more systematically thereafter. We might thus put a bit more faith in some of the statements from the Munich period than in those made later in Mexico. Unraveling the mystery, however, is further complicated by the fact that Traven's knowledge about his background was probably limited. The issue of a valid identity—provided by official documentation—that pervades his novels and conversations raises the suspicion that Traven was an illegitimate child. His widow said that he never had a birth certificate and that Traven told her his birth had been recorded only in a family Bible. It is certainly not by chance that the *BT News* in 1957 included the following in its reports of Mexican *curiosa*:

> In Mexico there are no illegitimate children. But there are unmarried couples here who have children. The names of the father and mother are recorded on the child's birth certificate. But this document says nothing of whether the father and mother were legally married. In Mexico an "hijo natural" (a child born out of wedlock) has the same rights, including the right of inheritance, as any child born of legally married parents.

One born out of wedlock who knows only part of his past—his mother, but not his father—may feel justified in creating his own past, in inventing a background and a name, a family and a family history. "I can choose my own country; I can choose my own parents," Traven reportedly quipped. His prodigious talent for spinning yarns extended to his *consciously* obscuring his own biography, sometimes losing track of the factual basis of his tales. Traven's widow said that she could relate only Traven's stories about his early youth, since she could not draw the boundary between the biographical truth and the writer's fantasy. The life stories told by the *Death Ship* sailors are presented as fiction, not fact. Was it any different when Traven talked about his own life? Did he have a story in mind that he might want to write? His widow had occasion to ask herself such questions. Raskin, in *My Search for B. Traven*, quotes from a conversation with Rosa Elena Luján: "I don't think he could have told the truth, even if he wanted to. . . . It was so tangled in his mind that even he didn't know the truth anymore." An illegitimate child might very well develop diversionary strategies—a person who from an early age suffers from the dilemma of not knowing his own father, who fears questioning, and who, like the narrator of *The Death Ship*, arrives at the conclusion that the only protection against people and their questions is lying. Such a person may adopt, as an expression of sublime freedom or of painful self-consciousness, not merely one name and one nationality, not merely one date of birth, one place of birth, and one family history, but several. He may confuse them easily, as Traven/Torsvan did in the interview with Luis Spota, or even sometimes forget them, temporarily changing identities unconsciously or playfully. (Señora Luján relates that Traven once forgot the name under which he had checked into a Mexican hotel, making it difficult for him to reclaim the room key.) In his years in Mexico, his widow has noted, he would easily change his stories, claiming that his father had been an American farmer or a Norwegian fisherman or an impresario, only to cloud the issue again with mysterious references to noble ancestry. Are such ploys sheer fantasy, a thirst for recognition, or theatrics to offset traumatic beginnings? Possibly all of these.

Official identification papers, whether passports or birth certificates, became objects of loathing to Traven. The revolutionaries in the Mahogany Novels destroy official papers, thus validating or confirming their own existence. Mexico was for Traven the place where one was not asked for identification, "where it is considered tactless, in fact insulting, to question someone about his name, his occupation, his origin and plans"—so he states on the first page of his first Mexican novel, *The Cotton-Pickers*. Anyone can present a birth certificate, the innkeeper Torsvan told Spota in Acapulco in the 1948 interview—but how, he continued, does one know that the holder of such papers was the person thus documented? Better to have no personal identification papers at all, it seems. Not surprisingly, Ret Marut used to state his place of birth as San Francisco, where all official documents had gone up in flames during the earthquake of 1906.

In providing information that no one could confirm, he may well have fabricated *all* of the details concerning his past—or again perhaps not all. The registration form filled out in Munich on July 6, 1914, and bearing Marut's signature records that "Ret Marut" was born on February 25, 1882, in San Francisco, the son of William and Helene Marut née Ottarrent (father's occupation: "impresario in San Francisco"); the Munich register of occupations filled out on July 11, 1917, gives Marut's nationality as "North American." But his many attempts to procure American papers failed without exception. The Munich registration form, under the heading "Proof of Identity," records as a later addition: "Identification paper from the Düsseldorf police dated 4 October 1915, according to which he had submitted passport and other papers for the purpose of naturalization" and "according to Marut's personal statement of 27 January 1918 the application was denied"—doubtless because his U.S. nationality could not be proved. Also, no records confirm the existence of a William Marut at a San Francisco theater—the closest name discovered is a Heinrich Maret, who was active there in the 1880s.

The grounds for suspicion grow more numerous: The man born out of wedlock creates his identity as he wishes, fashioning a fictional existence, transporting himself, in a manner of speaking, into the realm of "literature." It is revealing to recall a story that Traven, in his Marut days, told his fiancée Elfriede Zielke (from whom he separated in 1914). He had been born on a ship, he said, and his birth had been registered in San Francisco. Recknagel refers in this connection to a quotation from Herman Bang's novel *Denied a Country*, cited by Marut in *The Brickburner* in 1919: "The man without a country is free, and I was born on the ocean which connects all worlds. . . . I *have* a homeland, Sir, and it is *myself*. There I am both king and subject. . . . I am my own homeland, where I myself am ruler." A copy of the German translation of the novel, a 1918 edition, is preserved in Traven's estate.

A "German" from America

In spite of these difficulties, what can we deduce, if not document, about Traven's early years? One important point was touched on in Chapter 2: that Traven had an essentially German background, having grown up with German as his principal language. The use of German in the early Marut stories and *Brickburner* articles reinforces this premise—the German there is free of anglicisms. Conversely, Traven spoke English with a German accent and never wrote it without Germanisms. Disputing the claim that German was his mother tongue, however, Traven said he grew up speaking English—which does more to confirm the German background than call it into question. His godchild Gabriel Figueroa, Jr., vividly recalls Traven teaching him German children's songs.

Traven (and Marut) himself may have sincerely believed his emphatic contention that he was born in the United States. He may simply have remembered remarks made by his mother. In 1978 Rosa Elena Luján reportedly said that the "only thing" B. Traven heard from his mother was that he had been born in the United States. She made similar remarks to Wyatt and to me as well. Traven was apparently convinced of this story, and there is in fact no reason for dismissing it out of hand. As long as the contrary is not proved, the story of an American birth cannot be rejected. This point, of course, has relevance only for the question of original citizenship, not necessarily for that of native language. For Traven may indeed have been born in America, being taken to Germany while still a child (as his widow has in fact stated, recalling Traven's own remarks). The reference in *The Brickburner* to "the Germany of my most sublime childhood dreams" may allude to birth in a foreign country and moreover to German ancestry or even German-speaking parents. Traven may have been born in America of parents who came from Germany or were of German ancestry, even though a 1912 registration card filed by Marut in Düsseldorf originally indicated that his nationality was British (which may signal that one of his parents held British citizenship or perhaps dual citizenship). Traven's widow and one of her daughters told me on several occasions that Traven spoke *British* English (both in vocabulary and accent), which practically rules out an extended early period in America. At the same time, the use of British English does not necessarily imply that he spent his early years in Britain or had a British or an Irish mother—a character that surfaces from time to time in the Traven mythology—but more likely points to his learning English in a German-speaking country. For this British coloration cannot be isolated from Traven's German accent when he spoke English (well documented) or from his highly Germanic written English. Most plausibly, Traven studied English in Germany, with German as his mother tongue or "best language," learning it in relatively early youth, even if he had actually spent his first years in an English-speaking country.

Traven himself may have been unwittingly admitting to such a scenario when he wrote on October 21, 1929, to Manfred Georg, thanking the critic for a favorable article and stressing anew that he had been born in America of American-born parents. This, then, Traven implied, would make German, of which Georg maintained Traven had total mastery, his *second language*. Georg's own style, Traven noted, proved to him, "once again, that one can fully express one's thoughts, making them unambiguously clear for the reader, only when one is in the happy position of expressing oneself in one's native language. A language which is not one's mother tongue, even if one adopts it at a very early age, even if one applies one's greatest efforts to master it, always leaves one in the lurch when one wishes to take the most beautiful and the best that one has in one's heart, to express it in words and make it understandable to others." Traven was not speaking the truth, of course, when he assured Georg that he had already been in Latin America for more than fourteen years, and the remarks on his imperfect command of German follow from the American persona of the "official biography." But does not a glimmer of truth shine through in his incidental remark on the early-adopted "language which is not one's mother tongue"—namely that Marut, born in America, came to Germany while still a child and learned his German (primarily) from that point on?

When Marut filled out his "Application for Registration—Native Citizen" at the U.S. consulate in London in March 1924, he completed the statement "I last left the United States on . . . " with the response "1892." If that is true, and if Marut was actually born in 1882, as he often maintained, he would have left the United States at the age of nine or ten (although he would not necessarily have spent the entire nine or ten years in America). If, however, 1890 is the correct year of birth, as Traven maintained repeatedly in later years, he would have been considerably younger when he left the United States. In any case, German may thus have actually *become* his "best language." He may have spoken it like a native German—and yet have come from America. But did he really speak German like a native?

The story that Ret Marut spoke German "with a slight accent," originating with Marut's companion Elfriede Zielke and related by her daughter, is confirmed nowhere else and is by no means conclusive in itself. The daughter could not speak from personal experience, since her contact with Marut, even by mail, was cut off when she was about six. Further, is the reference to a foreign, specifically English, accent or merely to a trace of dialect? A former secretary at the Düsseldorf theater, Maria Ludwig-Morian, who knew Ret Marut during his acting days in Düsseldorf ("1913–1914," she said), described him in a letter of condolence dated April 20, 1969, to Señora Luján: "He was a quiet, withdrawn man, and occasionally I accompanied him and his large Airedale on short walks. He was always very reserved, but often spoke with me about his literary projects. When the war broke out in August, 1914, Ret Marut disappeared without a trace. . . . He was not an American, but a German, surely from the eastern part of Germany."

We cannot state with certainty where in the socioeconomic landscape the man who called himself Marut had his roots. As an illegitimate child, which he probably was, he may well have had roots in two very different social strata. The proletarian themes and sympathies of *The Brickburner* and of many Traven novels do not necessarily confirm that the author himself was a proletarian. Many critics, overwhelmed by these themes, do not question that Traven himself was a proletarian. Kurt Tucholsky declared so in 1930 in *Die Weltbuhne*, and as late as 1968 the knowledgeable Charles H. Miller included a chapter called "B. Traven, Pure Proletarian Writer" in David Madden's *Proletarian Writers of the Thirties*. Such attempts to pin down the author's social background, however, have yet to enjoy the benefit of any evidence.

Traven's own remarks, as so often, are conflicting. On the one hand, he declared his allegiance to the proletariat, as he may have done even in the *Brickburner* passage cited in Chapter 2, in which, denying German ancestry, he proclaimed that his "true countrymen" were those who did not live within the boundaries of a single nation and among whom he counted himself by virtue of his "consciousness" and his "world view." But does his profession of closeness to the proletariat describe his actual background or even one side of his background? In his letter to his Büchergilde editor Ernst Preczang of October 26, 1929, Traven cited his "long experience as a working proletarian, not as a salon proletarian or a literary proletarian, but as a proletarian who stood in the ranks because his economic situation compelled him to do so." This does not unequivocally refer to his roots; Traven may have had in mind the situation into which he was forced by adverse circumstances in Mexico and perhaps earlier in Germany. In a letter to Charlot Strasser he maintained that Jack London and he were "both real proletarians, both grown up in proletarian conditions, in the tumult and crowds of the proletarian quarters of large American industrial cities." But this is a mere rehashing of the "official biography," with its fictional account of early years in Chicago. Traven must have been pleased to see Strasser publish this letter in his book *Arbeiterdichtung* (*Workers' Literature*).

On the other hand, Traven distanced himself from the proletariat. On October 11, 1925—*The Cotton-Pickers* (called *Der Wobbly*) had just been completed—he wrote to Preczang that he would "feel deeply unhappy" if he were classified as a "poet of the working class." He would respond to such identification by immediately writing a novel "waving the capitalist banner." He told his editor:

"I do not see workers, nor do I have the workers in mind. I always see just people. It is only a matter of chance that these people who appear in my writings are mostly workers. First, it is workers with whom I have lived the most, and second I have found, seen, experienced, and personally felt that the worker, the proletarian, is the most interesting and most multifaceted man, a thousand times more interesting than your recently deceased Stinnes, than our Rockefeller or Morgan or Sinclair or Coolidge, or Gloria Swanson or Tom Mix or Mary Pickford or Henny Porten [a German actress], to return to your country."

As early as January 1919, Ret Marut noted in *The Brickburner* that he felt "better" under the dictatorship of the proletariat "than I have felt under any government in my entire life. . . . For where the proletariat has governing power in its hands, capitalism heads for certain destruction. And destruction of capitalism means there can never be another war! . . . My personal freedom is secured!" But he then distanced himself immediately from the proletariat as a class with the proviso "although I am not a worker and do not belong to the proletariat." But who threatened to take away the freedom vouchsafed by a proletarian government? His "greatest opponents" were "the bourgeois," he said in the same *Brickburner* article. Was Marut perhaps not a proletarian by birth, but rather a bourgeois or wealthy capitalist disillusioned with his "native" class? This is not necessarily made more plausible by the considerable financial means at *The Brickburner*'s disposal, to which Marut admitted on occasion, or by his remark in his theater days that he did not have to depend on his salary. For these private funds need not have been his own or those of his immediate family. This scenario would, however, accord well with Gabriel Figueroa's recent revelation that Traven told Esperanza López Mateos (who called Traven Mauricio) that he was the son of Emil Rathenau, the powerful industrial entrepreneur and founder of the AEG and father of Walther Rathenau, the German foreign secretary during the Weimar Republic. Intriguing as this revelation is, it is, however, not supported by documentary evidence.

Traven's level of education, a more promising clue, seems to point more strongly to a nonproletarian or bourgeois youth. A reference in *The Brickburner* to his "Quarta [third-year] classmates" implies his having attended a Gymnasium, where he might have learned English. But we cannot be sure, nor can we tell whether his knowledge of other languages (how extensive was it?) is attributable to higher education—more accessible to the child of the bourgeois than that of the proletarian—or was acquired in a later period, independently. The same question mark must hang over all the traces of his literary, historical, and scientific knowledge, since these traces surface for the first time—as quotations and allusions—in the works of Marut and Traven, when the author was long past school age. That Traven played the piano and violin, as his widow reports, may (but need not) point to more socially elevated beginnings. The same can be said of his refined manners, which Lawrence Hill referred to in *The New York Times Book Review*. Finally, one must not forget that the educated man's sympathy with the proletariat may point not to a definite social stratum but rather to the outsider status of the intellectual or to a (partial) descent from the free-floating "fifth estate" of artists, bohemians, and the like.

Another aspect of Marut's background surfaces on occasion in *The Brickburner*, particularly in connection with a dispute with the anti-Semite Dietrich Eckart. Eckart thought Marut was a Jew, while Marut countered by maintaining his "unadulterated Germanic heritage" without wishing to be "proud" of it: "Our family history can be traced back several centuries; to the best of our knowledge and belief, no drop of Jewish blood runs through our family." Traven made a similar remark on May 23, 1933 in a letter to Büchergilde Gutenberg in Zurich.

A Child Without a Family, a Vagabond on the High Seas

Traven's widow has recalled that Traven said remarkably little about his early years even among his family. He never seems to have mentioned his first name, to say nothing of his actual family name. Was that intentional or only by chance, or was it because Traven himself did not know? In his final years, he was called "Skipper" at home, while friends called him "Hal." His collaborator Esperanza López Mateos, in her letters to him in the 1940s, addressed him as "Viking." María de la Luz Martínez, with whom he managed the orchard and restaurant El Parque Cachú in Acapulco in the 1930s and 1940s, apparently addressed him as "Mister." It was not until he reached Mexico that he adopted Traven as his first name (and Torsvan as his last). If the *B.* in B. Traven stood for his true first name, he never revealed what that name might be, except that he dismissed Ben, Benno, Bernard, and above all "that immortal Bruno." Does the *B.* perhaps subtly recall the model for the character Stanislav in *The Death Ship*, who was named Berthold in the (handwritten) English first draft and who, according to Rosa Elena Luján, saved Traven's life? We do not know.

Traven's childhood, according to his very occasional remarks in later years, apparently did not include siblings, father, aunts, uncles, cousins, grandparents—or even a steady circle of associates. He apparently never mentioned any such figures: They seem never to have existed. He did mention a few episodes, in spite of all his reserve—or was it poor memory or perhaps a lack of events and people worth remembering? One of his recollections was that as a small boy, he followed a funeral procession, only to be found later at the cemetery; another recollection of his childhood was that he was taken to a spa. Yet the only other person that figures in such recollections is his mother—a lonely childhood, reminiscent of several Marut stories. While he almost certainly grew up without a father, Traven must have spent his first years with his mother. He expressed little love for her and rebelled against her strictness (or so Señora Luján seems to remember). A strange light thus falls on the paean to maternal love that stands as a dedication to the novel *The Bridge in the Jungle*: "To mothers everywhere! Mothers of every people, every country, every language, every race, every color, every creature under the sun!"

What is known of Traven's mother, or what can we surmise? She seems to have played a role only in Traven's reminiscences of his *earliest* youth, according to Señora Luján's recollection. By the time he reached his teens, she apparently was no longer a factor. Marut allegedly told Elfriede Zielke that his mother committed suicide when he was twelve. Traven's widow never heard that story from Traven; it may have been Marut's way of evading questions about his past. When Marut applied for an American passport in 1917 at the U.S. consulate in Munich, he stated that his mother had died "during his infancy." It is not implausible that Traven grew up without his mother from a relatively early age, although not necessarily from the age of seven—as Gales, the narrator of *The Death Ship*, does and as the "official biography" has it—at which age he claimed that he was on his own, working as a bootblack, newspaper boy, dishwasher, and the like. Such a scenario might also explain the dominance of the mother figure in the Marut stories. Mother and son apparently did not have a fixed home in the early years. Señora Luján heard Traven say he traveled much as a child with his mother. These trips may have had some connection with his mother's occupation: According to Traven's comments to his wife, his mother was an actress or singer who went on tour, perhaps also in the United States (a scenario that might account for his claim of a childhood spent in America). Less certain is the assertion made by the actor Ret Marut to Elfriede Zielke that in childhood he traveled all over the world as a member of a ballet troupe.

As to his mother's nationality, Traven never told his wife, to the best of her recollection, that his mother was German. Some assume that her native language was English and that she hailed from England or Ireland. Elfriede Zielke was among those who believed this version. A Scandinavian background surfaces from time to time. Traven himself wrote on May 25, 1946, to Axel Holmström, his Swedish publisher: "Our family came from Norway, but I myself have never seen it." It is well known that in Mexico he often presented himself as a Scandinavian or an American of Scandinavian extraction.

The sea almost certainly was a part of Traven's early history. The "official biography" relates that Traven, starting at quite an early age, went to sea for a number of years. Marut often claimed extensive experience as a sailor, and Traven stressed his seafaring to Señora Luján. In connection with his "Application for Registration" in London in 1924, he told the American consulate that he ran away from home at the age of ten, signed aboard a ship bound for Australia in 1892 as a cabin boy, and remained at sea until 1900. In his letter to Manfred Georg in October 1929, Traven noted that for economic reasons he occasionally returned to his "old occupation . . . namely that of sailor, and within that profession a simple sailor, stoker, coal drag, machinist, oiler, greaser, cleaner." In the 1930s, responding to Anton Zischka's "plagiarism" from *The White Rose*, Traven emphasized that he himself had traveled as a stoker and machinist's assistant on those oil tankers that Zischka knew only from hearsay. In 1951 the *BT News* claimed that "B. Traven's depiction of the boiler room is so true to life because he worked, shoveled coal, and stoked in such boiler rooms, was scalded and scorched in a room like that." He spoke of his seafaring days with a certain casualness when he wrote to Axel Holmström on April 26, 1939: Even when he was a sailor things did not go as badly as they were going now. There is no reason to doubt such assertions: Traven must have been at sea for an extended period in his youth. (The Marut estate includes a notebook with drawings of nautical signals and, on loose pages, sailors' knots accompanied by explanatory notes. The notebook may date from the period before 1907.)

What then did Traven see of the world in his seafaring days?

At home on the Calle Mississippi and earlier in the apartment on Calle Durango, the "skipper" spoke of experiences in China, India, and Australia (when he filled out the "Application for Registration" in 1924 he stated that he had been in Australia). The Marut estate includes a carbon copy of a letter of May 14, 1914, in which Marut assures an unnamed publisher that he spent five weeks in Indochina, specifically Saigon, fifteen years earlier. While vacationing with his wife on the west coast of Mexico, Traven told her that Mazatlán had been one of his ports-of-call as a sailor. Charles Miller's biographical introduction to *The Night Visitor and Other Stories*—based on materials provided by Traven—states that Traven had been there in 1913—when Marut is documented in Germany! This may heighten suspicions that in references to his own background, Traven easily blurred the boundaries between truth and fiction, fact and mythmaking. The line is particularly blurry for references he made while in Mexico, when he took every opportunity to burn all bridges leading back to Marut.

Somewhat more stock might therefore be put in the résumé recorded in London in 1924 under the name Marut. For the years 1892–1900, beginning with the date that the child allegedly born in San Francisco ran away from home at the age of ten, he named the following stations in his travels: Sydney, India, Singapore, Rotterdam, India, Rotterdam once again, Hamburg, Rio, San Francisco, Rio, New York, Rotterdam. (He stated that he subsequently worked as an actor in Vienna and Germany, with some of the locations named—Danzig and Düsseldorf—actually corresponding to those at which Ret Marut appeared onstage.) This background sketch (handwritten by someone other than Marut) begins as follows:

> Applicant is the son of William Marut and Helene Marut (nee Otorrent [*sic*]) and was born he says in San Francisco, Cal. on —. He ran away from home when he was ten years of age, having signed on as a Kitchen boy on a ship bound for Australia

> (1892–summer). After 5 or 6 weeks he left there, Sydney, and proceeded to India. Then to Singapore and from there to Rotterdam finally (1895). From there on another ship to India and after 18 mos cruise returned to Rotterdam (1897). Then to Germany and on another boat from Hamburg proceeded to Rio and from there to Frisco and return to Rio (1899). From Rio to N.Y. and having changed there proceeded to Rotterdam (1900). Stayed in Rotterdam waiting for another boat (1901). Then to Germany remaining short & from there to Vienna where he took up the study of languages.

Remarks in *The Brickburner* correspond to these geographical reference points. Marut recalled that he was not unfamiliar with the "vocabulary of the docks of Rio"; he likewise claimed to have visited Asia. In 1917 the *Brickburner* editor made the general statement that he "lived abroad," and from the context one can conclude that he meant England and America. In 1919 he remarked that he "was familiar with practically all countries of the world and had lived for many, many years in many non-German-speaking lands." From *The Death Ship* one could, if one assumed that the novel were autobiographical down to the individual details, conceivably flesh out the picture with all sorts of information. But here one proceeds at one's own risk.

A Skeleton in the Closet?

As if the waters were not murky enough already—thanks in part to Traven's own mystifications—Marut also may have been compelled to adopt an alias for some reason we do not know. It has been speculated from time to time that he must have had a skeleton in the closet. That an actor adopts a stage name is nothing unusual. It is unusual, however, that no one has ever succeeded in peering through Ret Marut's mask to uncover his real identity. Ret Marut—an exotic-sounding pseudonym fit for an actor—appeared from 1907 to 1915 primarily in less prominent German theaters. He himself did his best to cover up the past, as he would do later in Munich as a journalist and revolutionary. The shadows enveloped him literally as well: He insisted on speaking at *Brickburner* events in Munich with only a reading light on.

Traven sleuths have speculated from the beginning that something serious underlay Marut/Traven's persistent game of biographical hide-and-seek. We recall that in his handwritten English draft of *The Death Ship* Traven wrote that what lends great men their "mystery" and thus their power over the average man is always a "secret," something in their personality or past that they had to conceal. Not that this was necessarily a murder or robbery, he added. Armed with Freud's essay on denial (that which is denied even before a question is asked points to the truth), one is tempted to read between the lines of Traven's striking discussion and conclude that something criminal might indeed be lurking in his past: "The weaklings," the *Death Ship* passage continues, "have always good police records and fine passports. And it is the weaklings and the cowards that make the criminals of the big cities. A strong heart knows how to struggle and he likes to struggle for his life." We do not have to assume that *The Death Ship*, or even the first draft of it, recounts literally the autobiography of the man who wrote it, but the passage was later cut by the author, with nothing even remotely similar retained in the published version. The strange connection between "mystery" and "murder" surfaced on the other side of the Atlantic a full forty years later. In a letter of October 28, 1964, Traven assured the American writer and editor Sanora Babb, with whom he corresponded extensively about getting his short stories published, that there was nothing wrong with a "mystery"—"as long as mystery does not stand for murder."

It would be hasty to conclude that the old prospector Howard in *The Treasure of the Sierra Madre* has let the cat out of the bag with his piece of worldly wisdom: "It's not what we do that burdens us. It's always the memories [of actions, one presumes] that gnaw at our soul." The voice of experience? Ulrich Schnapauff thought so in his commemorative article on Traven in *Die Welt*. "Another reason for the heavily guarded incognito cannot be ruled out," Schnapauff wrote. "Perhaps Marut/Traven/Torsvan/Croves was guilty of a crime in his youth. Two years ago an anonymous caller told *Die Welt* that Traven came from Eastern Europe and had committed murder while traveling in America."

Another neat solution, but undocumentable—and yet strangely irresistible. Traven, master of both autobiographical cover-up and autobiographical striptease, wrote in *Die Troza*, one of his Mahogany Novels: "When you have a name that keeps coming up in police reports, court rulings, and prisoner lists, you are well advised, if only for the sake of self-preservation, to drop it and look for another one that is less well known and worn. Life is more comfortable from then on, until one is again in the position of having to shed one's skin. A new, usable name is always much safer, if one can produce a brother or sister, or best of all a father [!]." Is the author sharing secrets—secrets akin to those of the *Death Ship* sailors, each of whom has something on his record and none of whom gives his real name?

In Marut's early story "Der fremde Soldat" ("The Unknown Soldier") why the curious fascination with a soldier dying in a field hospital who is described in the final scene as follows: "And no one knows who he is, what he is, where he comes from"? In *The Brickburner*, Marut quoted from Herman Bang's *Denied a Country*. He related the passage on the birth of the protagonist on the high seas and cited the subsequent curious statement: Homelands cripple people; one should climb to the mountaintops, then one would no longer see states and boundaries, "and there will be no more codes of law, crime is no crime, disgrace is no disgrace, shame is no shame, there will be no more penal codes and no [legal] paragraphs." *The Death Ship* contains a similar fantasy: "Where my homeland is, you ask? There, where I am and where . . . no one wants to know who I am, no one wants to know what I'm doing, no one wants to know where I've come from—there is my homeland, there is my fatherland." For Traven Mexico was that land. In the Mexican novels we repeatedly hear of insurgents burning official documents: "Once they are all burned, no one will know who he is any longer, what his name is, and who his father was [!]." Similarly: "Only then, when no registers or a single document can be found on the earth, will we be truly and forever free." In his *Büchergilde* essay "My Novel *The Death Ship*," Traven said he considered personal freedom to be at its height before the First World War. Then one could travel to Philadelphia and Borneo, to Brussels and New Zealand, "without a passport, without a visa, without a birth certificate, without a certificate of good conduct issued by the police, without a divorce decree, without a marriage license." In all these instances, do we not sense a dark cloud in the background?

And why, in response to the public's attempts to approach him, did he insist on serving as his own "judge?" Answering a reader who took offense at the books touted in *The Brickburner*, Marut unleashed the following in 1918: "What I do is law because *I* do it: concerning my actions *I* am the judge, not anyone else on the earth."

He then continued, disproportionately irritated, with an invective against readers who sent letters to "try to sniff out holes in my clothing in order to get at me." In his *Death Ship* essay he lodged the protest—so common in his later years—that his "life story" was his "own business" and he wished to keep it to himself: "Not because I am an egoist but rather because of my desire to be my own judge in my own case." For Marut had a harsh verdict for the public justice system. "Every man," he said in *The Brickburner* in 1920, can "become a murderer under certain circumstances, even the most peace-loving man." In such a case, the murderer himself had "many just excuses which can be understood and grasped upon considering the roots in the human soul and human drives." The "judge," he contended, has as little feeling for such explanations as the hangman or the prosecutor; official justice becomes a parody or open perversion of the law, to the extent that the law has anything to do with justice. Marut struck a similar chord in his essay "Indizien" ("Circumstantial Evidence") in the magazine *März* in 1916, inveighing against the legal practice of treating such evidence as proof (this is his sole nonliterary work outside of *The Brickburner*):

> Our system of justice continues to adhere to the medieval view that the suspect is to be viewed a priori and without further consideration as guilty. The judge has but one goal, namely to prove the guilt of the suspect. Neither prosecutor nor judge seriously entertains the possibility that the suspect may in fact be innocent. One actually senses very often that the prosecutor would feel very awkward if the accused were proved innocent. That is of course perfectly understandable, since then the prosecutor's entire argumentation, so carefully constructed, would collapse and his logic would suffer a defeat. The guilty man alone has the incredibly difficult task of proving his innocence against the prosecutor's accusation, which is assisted by every official means available. But it is much more difficult to prove innocence than guilt. Even the most harmless man often cannot supply an alibi. And since proving innocence is much more difficult than proving guilt, the accused should—if the judicial process should not make even greater allowances in his favor—be seen and treated as absolutely innocent until he is proved guilty. The miscarriages of justice would certainly be fewer.

A similar message surfaces in *The Death Ship*: One who cannot prove his innocence is guilty.

Now, quoting Traven in this manner is somewhat misleading: In the proper context, the effect of such passages is diluted as the author wished (or did he?). No incontestable conclusion can be drawn from the accumulation of such quotations. Yet we recall the "very weighty reasons" that Marut had, as early as his Munich period, for "living in obscurity," according to Götz Ohly. One such reason may have been his radical leftist politics in 1905 and 1907, directly preceding his rebirth as Ret Marut the actor at the Essen theater. *The Brickburner* stated that in those years he told the "Social-Democratic" workers and "Social-Democratic voters" that the victory of the Social Democrats would unleash "robbers and murderers" on society, or at least on its revolutionary element. Perhaps Marut became involved in a brawl at an election meeting and from then on—rightly or wrongly—believed he was guilty of some wrongdoing. The story of the Alsatian worker Paul told by Stanislav in *The Death Ship* comes to mind ("I don't know his real name. . . . He said his name was Paul"). This Paul, shoved across the border from France to Germany, had "gotten into revolutionary affairs" and was arrested and "exiled for Bolshevist activities, of which he knew nothing":

> He was given two days to make himself scarce, or else got six months in the workhouse. When he got out of the workhouse, he got two more days, and if he was still around, then the workhouse or jail or an internment camp awaited him. They don't have workhouses nowadays, or don't call them that anymore, he told me. But they have similar facilities instead. Those fellows always come up with a new trick, when they get rid of an old one for some reason or other. What do they know of a man's motivation? In their view there are only criminals and noncriminals. Whoever cannot prove that he is definitely not a criminal, is one.

Then there is, in *The Death Ship*, Kurt from Memel, who came from a politically volatile border region, as did Stanislav and Paul. Another example of the human jetsam of the post–World War I era, he neglected to declare his national option. He spent some time in Australia and got into some sort of "mischief" there: "A story of strike breakers with strike breakers getting beaten up, and one of these curs fell down and couldn't get up anymore. Kurt couldn't go to the consul to get in the clear, because when it's got something to do with a strike or stories that smell of communism, the consuls all team up, even if a few months prior they were ready to spit on each other. The consul would have certainly tipped off the police about him, and Kurt would have had to do twenty years. . . . Kurt managed to reach England without papers."

Perhaps we are on the trail of those "very weighty reasons" that compelled the mystery man to put on the Marut mask. Was it conflict with ruling powers, authority, the establishment? Was it an actual crime, or one that was involuntary or imagined, or was it a mere suspicion against him? Such thoughts come naturally when one recalls Traven's remark "The creative man should have no other biography than his own works. In his works, he exposes his personality and his life to criticism." Traven's refusal to have his books published in the United States in the 1930s (or his insistence that, if they were published, it would be done without publicity) to some also seemed to imply "that he does not want his books to appear in America because he is wanted by the American police," rather than the German authorities. Traven himself, in an amused tone, referred to such speculations in a letter to his first American publisher, Alfred Knopf. On balance, these speculations add as little to our knowledge as the guessing games involving pseudonyms, class background, and native country. All these paths are enveloped in fog. If the fog lifted suddenly, we might find that the long-awaited answer proved to be quite banal. An unlikely eventuality, however, when one thinks of the hysterical blindness that afflicted Traven when *Stern* magazine was intent on pursuing his secret in 1963. Señora Luján told of the night he burned papers from his past in the fireplace at his Calle Durango home. Were they papers only from his Marut past or also those from *Marut's* past? Questions and more questions.

The Metamorphoses of Ret Marut

Paradoxically, we have an easier time dealing with the *answers* to the decades-old questions about Traven's background—even the answers that have lately made headlines and purport to shut the books on the case once and for all: Ret Marut was none other than Charles Trefny, the Freiburg theology student from St. Louis and Cincinnati; Ret Marut was the illegitimate son of Kaiser Wilhelm II; Ret Marut was the German-Polish locksmith's apprentice Otto Feige from

Schwiebus near Posen. None of these arguments holds water, in my view. But perhaps we can replace them for the time being with a new hypothesis that at least has the advantage of opening up fewer questions than it answers. One may, however, find more compelling the not implausible assumption that no answer can be given at all, since Traven himself did not know it.

The identification with Charles Trefny takes its cue from a 1919 issue of *The Brickburner*. In a protest against the clergy's praying for the nation's military victory, Marut wrote that he was not really qualified to talk about such theological matters: "I gave up my study of theology prematurely (had to give it up, actually, since I was 'dismissed' because of two 'improper' questions I asked during a lecture, and was 'most strictly' forbidden—the reprimand was in Latin—to attend any other activities of that faculty)." In his dissertation entitled "Das Revolutionserlebnis im Werk von B. Traven" ("The Revolutionary Experience in the Works of B. Traven"), Peter Lübbe notes that from 1898 to 1912, only *one* American was among the theology students dismissed from universities in German-speaking countries—a certain Charles Trefny. The academic records of Freiburg list Trefny as born in St. Louis in 1880 and graduated from "St. Xavier College" in Cincinnati. He was expelled from the University of Freiburg in the Breisgau in 1903 "because of offenses against morality," as the university records state. A Freiburg newspaper revealed that this entailed "improper conduct" with children, to whom Trefny presented himself as a physician administering vaccinations. On the strength of this evidence, Lübbe considered it "certain" that Trefny and Marut were one and the same. Recknagel followed suit in an essay of 1976, although in the 1982 revision of his biography of Traven he considered the matter conjectural but still included Trefny's expulsion in his list of important dates in the life of Marut/Traven and in the biography proper as well. But the Trefny-Marut connection does not even merit consideration as a hypothesis. In 1983 I learned, as had Recknagel, that no Charles Trefny could be found either in the records of Saint Xavier High School in Cincinnati or in the archives of Xavier University there for the period in question. Was "Trefny" an alias, too? Recknagel and Lübbe note that, like Trefny, Gales, Traven's double in several of the novels and stories, had a penchant for "doctoring"—hardly relevant. And is Marut's remark in *The Brickburner* about his theology studies, which lies at the heart of this whole argument, to be taken at face value? Or is it not simply a playful fiction, the ironic undertones of which are effective in their context? Needless to add, the offense cited in *The Brickburner* is not the same as Trefny's. If Marut and Trefny were the same, would Marut not have grown to early adulthood in America? A very doubtful proposition. Finally, Trefny is listed in the enrollment register at Freiburg (reproduced in Recknagel's book) as a son of "Karl Wilh. T." from St. Louis—apparently nothing in his background to account for Traven's theme of illegitimacy. Or did Trefny, too, invent his father?

The press has widely publicized speculation that Ret Marut's father was Kaiser Wilhelm II or another of the Hohenzollerns. It is difficult to pin down the origin of this version, which was quite popular in the 1960s through Gerd Heidemann's sensational report in *Stern* magazine. A certain resemblance may have played a role. Recknagel claimed that the "legend of the 'Hohenzollern Prince' " had already made the rounds as early as 1917–1918 in the Department of Censorship of the Bavarian Ministry of War, according to a 1962 statement of Rudolf Pfannkuchen, an alleged "*Brickburner* journeyman", who in turn was quoting Marut's friend Götz Ohly. This is hearsay, thirdhand information. Ferdinand Anton, the archeologist who accompanied Heidemann on his visit to Traven in 1966, maintained that around 1920 rumors of Marut's descent from the kaiser circulated among Marut's friends in Cologne. The assertion is undocumented. The journalist William Reid McAlpine noted, in an article that Traven touted as authoritative, that in the early 1930s German newspapers said Traven was a Hohenzollern prince who had emigrated to Mexico. Again, no evidence to that effect exists.

One might not miss the mark in supposing that Traven himself was the first to leak the Hohenzollern story, not necessarily because he took it seriously. More likely, playful as he tended to be and illegitimate as he presumably was, he would have shaken off troublesome questions with this story. To a man with the political leanings of *The Brickburner*, the last German kaiser surely loomed large. Traven may have gradually created an imperial fictional background for himself, which would have accorded well with his penchant for psychologically therapeutic teasing and mystification. One recalls the German worker named Wil'm from the English version of *The Death Ship*—no relation to Kaiser Wilhelm, we are told—or the comment that "only stranded princes and dukes" got the 8–12 watch on the *Yorikke*. Recknagel, in a wild leap of logic, concluded from this that, "as a 'stranded prince' he [Ret Marut] found his way into the realm of the death ship sailors on the *Yorikke*." Traven, writing to Esperanza López Mateos, did in fact claim to have come from a great family, saying that their hereditary characteristics had a curious history—but this reference is clearly tongue in cheek. Similar hints may likewise have been meant playfully, particularly those dropped in conversation. When the journalist Judy Stone visited Traven at his home in Mexico City in May 1966, Traven's first words to this perfect stranger were, "Forget the man! What does it matter if he is the son of a Hohenzollern prince or anyone else?" He may have made a similar ambiguous comment to Heidemann, giving rise to a misunderstanding, possibly because of the language barrier. Señora Luján has denied the reports that she told Heidemann or Judy Stone that her husband was a son of the kaiser or of another Hohenzollern (through a relationship with an actress or singer of Norwegian or perhaps American extraction), and she published a rebuttal to Heidemann in *Siempre*. She assured me as well that she had never presented such notions as fact, nor have I any reason to doubt her testimony. Señora Luján told Heidemann that during a trip to Germany in 1959 to see the premiere of the film *Das Totenschiff*, Traven went out of his way to show her the monument in the Grunewald erected to Wilhelm I, grandfather of Wilhelm II and father of Frederick III. Heidemann related that while standing in front of the monument Traven remarked: "I am descended from him." This detail was conspicuously absent from the story I heard from Rosa Elena Luján. Heidemann also quoted Señora Luján as stating that while Traven was alive, a portrait of the kaiser hung in his study—which she was likewise unable to confirm when I spoke with her about this. Traven did, however, own a photograph of the kaiser, as Señora Luján noted in her introduction to *The Kidnapped Saint and Other Stories*.

The only scholar who has taken seriously the relation to Wilhelm II, who indeed has claimed it as fact, is Rolf Recknagel, a significant contributor to Traven research. More specifically, he made this claim in 1976 in the catalogue to the exhibition at the Berlin Akademie der Künste entitled *Literaten an der Wand* (*Writers Up Against the Wall*). He did not revive the claim in the 1982 edition of his book *B. Traven*, nor however did he deny it there, and that edition still includes the suggestive passage regarding the "stranded prince." It is nonetheless interesting to inspect Recknagel's argumentation of 1976, which purportedly solved "the final riddle in the case of Marut-Traven." Recknagel took his cue from a gossip column on Berlin society in the Paris *Nouvelle Revue* of October 15, 1883. The column reported that the twenty-four-year-old prince, later Wilhelm II, "likes to amuse himself"; but the crown that the princess could expect would reconcile her to "her husband's little infidelities." From that bit of gossip Recknagel concluded that Traven was the son of Wilhelm II and a mistress:

> This mistress was probably the Irish actress Helene Mareth from Pennsylvania. She spent a number of years touring with a company through North America and turned up about 1880 at the court in Potsdam. Her illegitimate son was reportedly born in early 1882. Cared for by a governess, he spent his childhood in Schloss Cronthal (in the Taunus mountains), in Brandenburg and Hannover. The father of Crown Prince Wilhelm, King Frederick III (1831–1888), knew this child, named Alfred Wilhelm, through his wife Victoria, born Princess Royal of Great Britain and Ireland. The animosity between Crown Prince Wilhelm and his parents grew unabated. Frederick III reigned a mere 99 days after the death of his father, Wilhelm I (died March 9, 1888). On June 14, as Frederick III lay dying in the New Palace near Potsdam, the military sealed off the castle. Guards stood at every door at the "express order of His Majesty, Crown Prince Wilhelm." A search was on for the diary of Frederick III and his wife Victoria's letters. To no avail: weeks earlier the diary and letters had been deposited at the Royal Archives in London. Only the will was found, which Wilhelm II chose to ignore. A countess, the chief lady in waiting, and the Kaiser's wife were taken to Cronthal.
>
> Helene Mareth had meanwhile returned to North America with her son (programs of various German theaters there, such as one in Cincinnati, list her as "Maret" and "Mareth"). The son Alfred W. Mareth received training particularly in ballet. When the company made a guest appearance in Germany shortly after the turn of the century, Alfred W. Mareth went off on his own, to take up the study of theology in 1902 at Freiburg under the alias "Charles Trefny." He was expelled in 1903 for "immoral acts" and imprisoned for a year. We lose track of him for the subsequent years. . . .

> In 1908 we again pick up his trail as an actor and director going by the name Ret Marut.

The catalogue provided no evidence for the details about Helene Mareth's background and history, nor about the identity of her son and Trefny. Wyatt, painstakingly retracing this path with various expert testimony, could locate neither an illegitimate son of the crown prince nor an actress named Helene Mareth in Europe or America. I myself have not uncovered a trace of Helene Mareth in the history of the German theater in North America, not even in the well-researched history of the German theater of Cincinnati, where, according to Recknagel, she appeared onstage. The result of this investigation, however useful, was predictable. The notion of Wilhelm II's paternity bears all the earmarks of fiction, of a playful fantasy—the anarchist as the bastard of the establishment.

Also, a more generic version of this legend has circulated, further arousing suspicion: It was not necessarily Wilhelm but "a Hohenzollern" of some sort who fathered the man of mystery. The story could be proved only if the imperial family acknowledged this illegitimate son; the less one could expect such an acknowledgment, the more the rumor could flourish. Thus in the late 1960s a totally new version of the noble descent "of one of the most important writers of our century" surfaced in the press: Rather than an illegitimate son, Traven would have been an illegitimate half-brother of Wilhelm II, a son of Frederick III. The sole "argument" put forward to date for this thesis is the "uncanny" resemblance between alleged father and son. In the meantime, purveyors of this theory have tried to console Travenologists with the announcement that "the B. Traven archivists have already found several references that give weight to this thesis." So we hear from Marc Kuhn in 1967 in the *Stuttgarter Zeitung* and in the Zurich newspaper *Volksrecht*. But no supporting evidence has yet come to light. Until then, this thesis does not merit further discussion; talk of it has quieted down in recent years, as it has about Traven's noble birth in general.

The theory currently in vogue, which holds the final answer for most critics, ironically points toward the very opposite end of the social spectrum, the proletariat—namely Will Wyatt's sensational solution to the riddle of Traven, presented in his BBC-TV program in 1978 and then in his book *The Secret of the Sierra Madre* in 1980.

The breakthrough for Wyatt's discovery of Marut's "true" identity was made possible by the U.S. government's 1966 Freedom of Information Act. Wyatt approached the State Department with a request to examine the file of Marut/Traven, who had always claimed to be an American citizen. (Jonah Raskin, who put him on this trail, had made the same request a short time earlier.) The file revealed that in the winter of 1923–1924, Marut attempted to obtain American papers through the consular division of the American embassy in London, which then turned for instructions to Washington. Boylston A. Beal of the American embassy in London wrote on January 22, 1924, to Norman Armour, assistant to an undersecretary at the State Department, in this regard: The alleged American Ret Marut, who claimed to have been born in San Francisco in 1882 and who had connections with "communist circles" in London, was in Brixton Prison for failing to register as an alien. He had "confessed," the letter went on, that his true name was Herman Otto Albert Max Feige and that he was born in 1882 in Schwiebus, Germany; his mother was a "mill hand" and his father a "potter." He had come to England in the summer of 1923 en route to Canada and was then sent back from Canada to England because his papers were not in order. Investigations by the German police in Berlin and Schwiebus had not turned up anything. Nonetheless the prisoner, demonstrating good knowledge of the area, seemed "well acquainted with that town [Schwiebus] which makes it apparent that he has had some connection there." Wyatt uncovered a photo of Marut in the American Marut file, which Beal had enclosed and in which Beal claimed to note a similarity with "a well-known German" (Kaiser Wilhelm II?). Wyatt found other photos (which in no way recall Wilhelm II) in the British Home Office. Other documents at the Home Office, discussed by both Raskin and Wyatt, revealed that while in England Marut used the aliases Adolf Rudolf Feige, Albert Otto Wienecke, Barker, and Arnolds.

The conclusion of the story, as told by the London documents, was that Marut was released from prison on February 15, 1924, and left England that same year, perhaps in April. By summer he was already in Mexico. But was it Otto Feige who then set foot on Mexican soil?

That is a given for Wyatt. His tantalizing search for Traven led him to the registry of births in the town of Schwiebus, now the Polish Swiebodzin. The registry confirmed that a Hermann Albert

Otto Macksymilian was in fact born there on February 23, 1882—two days before the birth date on Marut's Düsseldorf registration card (a date Marut stated on other occasions as well)—as the illegitimate child of the factory worker Hormina Wienecke. The father, who claimed the child as his own three months after it was born and married the mother at that time, was Adolf Rudolf Feige, who worked as a potter in a brick factory, a Ziegelbrennerei (Marut would later publish *Der Ziegelbrenner*).The register of births also revealed that Otto Feige had a brother thirteen years his junior, whom Wyatt then interviewed in Wallensen, in Lower Saxony. The brother (and a sister born in 1893) confirmed the existence of their brother Otto born in 1882 but knew little about him, save this: He spent the first six years of his life in Schwiebus with his maternal grandparents; he was a good student who could not study theology as he wished, but rather learned the locksmith's trade in Schwiebus. He served as a soldier in Bückeburg from 1902 to 1904, the siblings continued, after which he lived with his parents in Wallensen, where he caused quite a stir as a political agitator and left his family in about 1904–1905. The only word from him came in the form of a letter "after the First World War," in which he informed his family that the British authorities were about to expel him from England. Both brother and sister recognized photographs of Marut (taken in London in 1923) and Traven (taken in Mexico from 1924 on) as those of their lost brother. They themselves were able to come up with a photograph from about 1902 of their brother Otto.

Was this incontrovertible proof of the "Feige equals Marut/Traven" equation? "The full life of this extraordinary man now stands revealed," Wyatt claimed. The documentary validity of photographs, however, must remain a matter of opinion. More than twenty years lie between the final photograph of Otto Feige and the London photos of Marut (an earlier photo of Marut, from 1912, is very indistinct). How the siblings, in 1978, could claim to recognize him as their brother in those photographs must raise some eyebrows. They had seen him last when they were nine and eleven years old—more than seventy years in the past. Of course, as Wyatt himself granted, they *expected* that the photos Wyatt presented to them would be those of their brother. The siblings knew nothing of the Marut-Feige connection that Wyatt claimed, nor that "their brother" had been an actor or a journalist.

At most Wyatt proved Otto Feige from Schwiebus was in London in 1923–1924, and this only if one makes rather generous assumptions regarding the letter from England to the Feige family: that the letter was sent not at just any time "after the First World War" (the siblings were not more specific), but specifically in the winter of 1923–1924 (as Wyatt assumes), and that it was the Otto Feige who disappeared in 1904–1905 who sent this letter to his family as the first sign of life after a silence of twenty years. Was it he and not Ret Marut? We may recall a trick pulled by the former Marut in 1948, when he was living in Acapulco as Señor Torsvan. Incensed at a report by Luis Spota in the Mexican magazine *Mañana* saying that Torsvan was Traven, Torsvan typed a letter in the name of Traven and had someone, perhaps his agent, send it from London to the Mexican magazine. The letter, quickly revealed to have come from Mexico, stated that the writer, Traven, lived in London and was not identical with Torsvan. Might not the master mystificateur Marut/Traven have attempted a similar trick in 1923–1924 in the name of Otto Feige?

Strictly speaking, then, Wyatt discovered that Ret Marut *presented himself* in 1924 as Otto Feige. Whether that was his true identity is another matter entirely. Wyatt believed so, and his reviewers have widely embraced the Marut-Feige connection. But let us play the devil's advocate.

Wyatt found among the U.S. State Department documents a further application by Marut for American papers. In March 1924, barely out of prison, Marut again petitioned the American embassy. He again presented himself as an American named Ret Marut born in San Francisco in 1882 (a handwritten curriculum vitae, not in Marut's hand, was presumably dictated). Details from this background profile: "kitchen boy" and sailor from age ten; in Germany and Austria since 1901 to study languages; actor since 1907; in Danzig in 1912; in Düsseldorf, 1912–1915; in Munich, 1915–1919; an odyssey through western Europe to Canada and back to England; arrest in London in November 1923; release from prison on February 15, 1924. The details concerning the period beginning in 1907 thus correspond to well-known facts about Marut, even if Marut understandably failed to mention his editorship of *The Brickburner*. But as to the pre-1907 period: Why did he not now disclose himself as Otto Feige, if that was in fact his true identity? His ultimate goal was to gain passage to the United States. He had just been released from prison as the German Otto Feige. After the many abortive attempts to pass himself off as an American, would he not have been in a better position to achieve his goal by admitting to the name and nationality to which he had already "confessed" to the British authorities? The petition was denied, in any event. Embassy official Boylston Beal had the final word on the subject in 1926: Although the embassy assumed that Marut was Otto Feige, "his identity has never been absolutely established." Perhaps, then, Marut simply tried to *pass himself off* in London as Otto Feige from Schwiebus in an attempt to conceal his true identity.

Why should Marut have told the truth at all in his "confession"? Wyatt believes that Marut made a deal with the English police: He would tell the truth, and in exchange the London police would set him free rather than deport him to Germany, where Marut, wanted for high treason, rightly had to fear for his life. (If that were the deal, the police reneged on their part of the bargain: Marut's "confession" that he was the German Otto Feige was passed along to the American embassy, which then denied his passport petition, in which he claimed American birth.) Wyatt himself admitted that this deal is no more than a guess. The speculation is indeed not conclusive. First, at that time economic considerations commonly dictated that alien prisoners of that sort be set free and monitored until their departure from England, a fact Wyatt himself found out. Further, what should Marut have expected to gain from confessing the truth about his past, if this truth compelled him to adopt the pseudonym Ret Marut in the first place? According to Ohly, Marut had "very weighty reasons" for concealing his past even while in Munich. Why should he have delivered up *those* secrets to the police?

Is it not more likely that Otto Feige was a borrowed name, the name of another, actual person? Wyatt's answer: Marut was able to provide the occupations of Otto Feige's parents; he used the maiden name of Otto Feige's mother, with two of Feige's Christian names; he also used the full name of Otto Feige's father, including both Christian names, as an alias. All this proves to Wyatt that these must have been Marut's own parents and not those of an acquaintance or relative. How else could he have come by such detailed information and remembered it so long? But is this such an inconceivable feat for Marut—particularly when one considers that Schwiebus had only eight to nine thousand inhabitants at the turn of the century? This is precisely the sort of trickery we have come to expect from Marut/Traven, a man forever on the run. Is it not natural that the master of deception would have stored away biographical details about a safe double, one to whom he possibly further bore some resemblance (a relative perhaps), so that he could adopt that person's identity under duress? This scenario may indeed have ended with the letter to Otto Feige's parents in Wallensen typed (one would think) in the guise of a son from whom they had not heard in two decades—precisely in the hope that the Feige family would assure the police investigators that they did have a son named Otto in London. Further strengthening the case that Marut used the Otto Feige "confession" as a false alibi is that Marut's statements did not correspond *exactly* with those at the Schwiebus registry office. Marut supplied Feige's Christian names, but in a different sequence from that in the register of births, and the birth date that Marut "always" gave differs by two days from Otto Feige's actual birth date.

This is not to say that Wyatt's discovery leads nowhere. Its principal value is in revealing the path to Schwiebus. Boylston Beal, the American embassy official in London, stressed in his letter to his superior in Washington that the alleged Otto Feige, then in custody under the name Marut, must be "well acquainted" with Schwiebus. In light of Marut's detailed knowledge of Otto Feige, perhaps Marut too grew up in Schwiebus. Marut is not documented there as an actor, even though the Berliner "Neue Bühne," to which he belonged in 1910–1911, made guest appearances at that time in the province of Posen. It may be that Otto Feige was a lost relative or schoolmate or other boyhood acquaintance of Marut's. Marut would then have been in a position to know all of Feige's Christian names, those of the father and the maiden name of the mother, who likewise came from Schwiebus (in his earliest years Otto Feige grew up at the home of his mother's parents in Schwiebus, who were named Wienecke). (It is less likely, but not impossible, that Marut gained such detailed knowledge in Wallensen or that he first met Feige sometime around 1905, when both were active politically on the anti-establishment side.)

A final consideration: Schwiebus lies on the periphery of the German-Polish border region (the center of which was Posen) that became Polish territory after the First World War—a mere fourteen miles within postwar Germany at that time. Marut/Traven was well acquainted with its ethnic and political problems; they were of interest to *The Brickburner*. Is it merely a coincidence that the second main figure in *The Death Ship* is a sailor named Stanislav born in Posen, who as a victim of shifting boundaries and nationalities becomes a man without a country or passport, a nonperson, as Marut himself was in London in 1924? This Stanislav left his homeland as a teenager under a borrowed name and would sooner kill himself than return to Germany. He read Cooper's *Leatherstocking Tales* in his youth—as Ret Marut had done, or so Marut said in *The Brickburner*, in a passage that in the very next breath addresses the issue of German-Polish nationality.

All this suggests not that Marut was Otto Feige but that he was familiar with his world, his environment, most likely from an early age. So Wyatt's research, instead of proving the identity of Marut and Feige, does however reinforce the view that Marut was a German or grew up in Germany, specifically East Germany, as a Düsseldorf associate of the immediate prewar years asserted. And this does indeed represent an advance in our understanding of the Traven mystery, since it strengthens the supposition that German was Traven's mother tongue or "best language."

Other considerations argue against Wyatt's "solution." True, at the time his book was published (1980), the press widely hailed it as containing the answer to the riddle. Even the *Sozialgeschichte der deutschen Literatur von 1918 bis zur Gegenwart* (*Social History of German Literature from 1918 to the Present*) (1981) presented the Feige thesis as fact. The few who expressed doubt did not provide reasons for their position, except Raskin. The others included Nicolas Walter in a letter to the editor in the *Times Literary Supplement* in 1982 and in his review in the *Spectator* in 1980, Michael Baumann in 1981 in the *Dictionary of Literary Biography*, and Wolfgang Bittner in the *Neue Zürcher Zeitung* in 1982. The doubts seem to have multiplied in the meantime. The latest Traven book, Frederik Hetmann's *Der Mann, der sich verbarg* (*The Man in Hiding*) does present Traven and Feige as one and the same but concedes that "the connection between Otto Feige and Ret Marut . . . cannot be considered as proved beyond a shadow of a doubt." The basis for Hetmann's reservation is that in 1924 the German police, while (he assumes) investigating in Wallensen or Bückeburg, where Otto Feige had done his military service, were unable to turn up the appropriate entries in the list of residents. But what if Marut had said nothing at all of Wallensen or Bückeburg to the London police? Hetmann also reports that the Travenologist Theo Pinkus considered Wyatt's research "unconvincing" but failed to provide an explanation. H. D. Tschörtner pointed out in 1982 in the East Berlin magazine *Sonntag* that Traven's "educational level and early knowledge of English" did not fit the proletarian Feige and that Feige had been "at other places in the world than Ret Marut at certain points in time." Recknagel, the pioneer of Traven research, played up the latter explanation for rebutting Wyatt, an explanation based, however, on a misunderstanding requiring a brief digression.

In the index to the 1982 edition of his B. Traven biography, Recknagel states flatly that Feige was "mistakenly viewed by BBC TV as the original B. Traven." The explanation of this statement constitutes the sole reference to Feige in Recknagel's book. It simply claims that Feige "spent some time in the US during the [First World] War," when Ret Marut is documented on the other side of the Atlantic. Recknagel provided more details in his rebuttal of Wyatt in December 1982: "But how can Otto Wienecke alias Feige, who lived from 1914 to the end of 1918 in Minidoka County, Idaho, be identical with the 'Brickburner' Ret Marut, who lived in Germany between 1917 and 1921?" This clearly illustrates another case of mistaken identity, namely Recknagel's confusion of Otto Feige with a certain Herman Feig in Idaho (Wyatt, incidentally, had learned previously of this Herman Feig from the U.S. State Department file and mentioned him briefly in his book). To get to the heart of the matter I secured copies of the relevant State Department documents through the U.S. Justice Department and the National Archives. A summary of the facts follows.

Norman Armour in the State Department wrote to William J. Burns, director of the FBI, on February 7 and again on March 1, 1924, requesting any available information on Ret Marut alias Herman(n) Otto Albert Maximilian Feige, who had been arrested in London. He enclosed a photograph. Burns ordered a number of regional offices to investigate the matter. Word came from Portland, Oregon, on March 12, 1924: A file was found, not on the Feige being sought but rather on a Herman Feig (spelled Feige on rare occasions in the ensuing correspondence; but this is clearly a slip of the pen, since the original letter from Portland refers *repeatedly* to the person in question as Feig and makes a clear distinction between Feige and Feig). This Herman Feig was reportedly living in

Minidoka County, Idaho, in August 1918. The Portland report mentioned a letter dated August 26, 1918, sent from the district attorney in Rupert, Minidoka County, Idaho, to the district attorney in Boise concerning the farm hand Herman Feig. Feig was arrested on August 22, 1918 under suspicion of espionage, having allegedly remarked, while loading hay, that the kaiser would rule the world, a fact of which he was proud, and that the war was not yet over. The letter from the Rupert district attorney, retyped in toto in the report from Portland, described the interrogation. Feig stated that he had been in the United States for seventeen years, was born in Germany, and was not naturalized. In response to the Portland report, an agent from the FBI regional office in Pocatello, Idaho, which had jurisdiction in the matter, turned to the sheriff in Rupert, asking whether this Herman Feig might be the Otto Feige London inquired about. Sheriff W. B. Cole answered on April 4, 1924: One of the former witnesses against Feig stated that the photo (of Marut) was not that of the accused.

Recknagel's argument that Ret Marut could not have been Otto Feige of Schwiebus—Wyatt's contention—because Otto Feige was in Idaho during the First World War collapses like a house of cards. This is not the way to refute Wyatt. The witness's failure to identify Marut's photograph as that of the man accused in 1918 at best confirms that the accused was not Ret Marut, who in any case is documented in Munich in 1918. It does not prove that the Herman Feig in Idaho was, as Recknagel assumes, identical with (Hermann) Otto Feige from Schwiebus. Herman Feig was in America from about 1900–1901 (while this admittedly comes from his own testimony, we have no reason to doubt it), when Otto Feige is documented in Germany. Recknagel allows himself to be tricked by the similarity of the names, and his "proof" that Marut was not Feige is illusory.

That the names are similar is not really as unusual as one might think—even if they were identical. The U.S. Immigration and Naturalization Service furnished me with information about an immigrant named Herman Feige, who had no connection with either the Herman Feig in Idaho or the (Hermann) Otto Feige from Schwiebus. Born on December 20, 1882 in Dammer near Kraschnitz in Silesia, this Herman Feige came to America on December 28, 1906, lived in 1911 in Hardin County, Texas, and was naturalized on October 4, 1916 in Douglas County, Nevada. I received this information in response to my question of whether Herman(n) Otto A. M. Feige's entry into the country had been registered—so this information also seems to confirm that Otto Feige from Schwiebus never came to the United States, at least not officially. Señora Luján has a copy of a letter that strengthens this argument: The U.S. Department of Labor informed Norman Armour on February 12, 1924 that it could find no proof of residence in the United States for Herman Otto Albert Maximilian Feige. To verify this information, I turned in 1983 to FBI headquarters and various regional offices asking whether Herman(n) Otto Albert Maximilian Feige could be documented in the United States in the period from about 1904 until 1924. No trace could be found of him in the records in Washington, D.C. (Central Records System); Salt Lake City; Butte, Montana (which has jurisdiction over Idaho); Portland, Oregon; San Francisco; Los Angeles; Sacramento; or Chicago.

In sum: Recknagel's "proof" that Marut and Feige were not the same unravels, since Feig and Feige were not the same person.

We can entertain other thoughts in questioning the contention that Marut was Feige. First come the psychological considerations.

A fixation on problems of identity, illegitimacy, official documentation, and proof of one's existence—a fixation bordering on a compulsion—clearly runs through the works of Marut/Traven. This fixation points toward illegitimate birth and the lack of papers, toward the lack of a homeland, a home, a father, a family. Such was not the case with Otto Feige from Schwiebus. True, he was an illegitimate child. But the father acknowledged his son three months after his birth and at that time officially married the mother. Otto Feige did not even necessarily know of his illegitimacy. And even if he had learned of it, there would be no basis for the trauma that weighed so heavily on Traven. True, Otto Feige spent his earliest years with his grandparents; but both parents lived in immediate proximity, and he lived with them after the age of six or seven, along with his brothers and sisters. Otto Feige knew who his father was and knew him personally; his mother and father were near him until his late teens, until about 1900, when the family moved to Wallensen, while Otto remained in Schwiebus. His birth, like his parents' marriage, was officially registered and could have been confirmed at any time in the very town where he spent his youth and adolescence.

We may understandably not know "everything" or even much about the youth and early manhood of an inconspicuous figure like Otto Feige. But Wyatt's discoveries about his youth do not explain Traven's preoccupation with illegitimacy and ignorance of one's father. In contrast to B. Traven, Otto Feige did not need to create a fictional father, whether romantically high-born or humble. Further, he was at home in the place where he lived for two decades from birth. Traven/Marut, on the other hand, to all appearances never had such a feeling of home. Would not someone who grew up like Otto Feige, over the course of many years of marriage, have made just one reference, whether intentionally or not, to brothers and sisters, father, childhood friends, relatives, and hometown—instead of only to his mother? There can be no doubt: The identification of B. Traven with Otto Feige is not proved.

Those not impressed by the logic of psychology might consider the following, not as a trump card but as the closing argument, which, viewed along with the other evidence, makes Otto Feige's candidacy as the real Ret Marut even less likely.

We read of Marut's prehistory as a sailor in a letter he wrote on May 14, 1914, a carbon copy of which is in the Marut estate. Marut sent the letter from Düsseldorf to an unnamed publisher, to whom he had sent the (still extant) typescript of his novel set in Indochina entitled *Die Fackel des Fürsten* (*The Torch of the Prince*). The publisher had apparently questioned whether the novel was based on the author's own experiences. Marut, who also mentioned two of his published stories in this letter, assured him that he spent five weeks in Saigon some fifteen years earlier. The sojourn in Saigon would thus have been about 1899–1900. There is all the less reason to doubt Marut's truthfulness since at the same time he provided a detailed list of his sources for the novel; that inspires confidence. And why should Marut have lied about visiting Indochina? If he had wanted to lie, he could have claimed a more intimate acquaintance with places and customs. Furthermore, the tone of this letter sounds anything but desperate. With an air of self-assurance and detachment, the author even advised the publisher to reject the novel if he doubted whether the piece was suitable for his publishing program. In no way did Marut attempt to ingratiate himself, nor was he particularly forward; we have no reason to suspect that he was bluffing.

We have come full circle: While Marut was in the Far East around 1900 (compatible with the information put on record in 1924 in London), we can place Otto Feige in Germany, thanks to Wyatt's research. Otto Feige thus could not have been Ret Marut/B. Traven.

The Trail to Traventhal and Marutendorf

If not Otto Feige, who *was* Ret Marut? We do not know. Perhaps Traven himself did not know.

But before falling back on that conclusion, we should consider yet another potential clue that seems more promising than the other evidence submitted thus far.

On April 10, 1935, B. Traven wrote a highly unusual letter, with only a typed signature as was his custom, bearing the elusive return address "c/o Alfred A. Knopf, 730 Fifth Ave., New York City." The addressee was a "Dear Sir" in the U.S. Library of Congress:

> Enclosed, please, find an Opera Program
>
> Czar und Zimmermann
> Opera by Lortzing
>
> which I want to present to the Library of Congress as a gift.
>
> Five years hence this program will be one hundred years old. It is the only of its kind in existence and it has, for its rarity, most likely no price.
>
> Warmbrunn, meaning Hot Springs, where that opera performance took place was, so I understand, in those times a watering-place frequented exclusively by the high nobility of Prussia including the Prince of Prussia Wilhelm who was later to become Wilhelm I, the first emperor of the German Empire created 1871. As you will note the company performing here is a Royal Prussian Privileged Company one of its members belonging to the Prussian nobility herself.
>
> Warmbrunn is found in the mountainous western section of Silesia and according to the informations [*sic*] I have is still a summer resort of some importance.
>
> The date is August 8, 1840. While the actors are already called Herr, formerly Monsieur, the actresses are still called Madame or Demoiselle and it was not, to my knowledge, until thirty or forty years later that the actresses were called Frau or Fraeulein. In this case the only exception is the actress belonging to the nobility who is called Frau [von Sternwaldt].

The abbreviation Sgr., as found for the prices of the tickets, stands for Silber-Groschen, a money worth 12½ Pfennig in silver of which eight made a silver mark and twenty-four a silver thaler.

In the case that you would have no use for this program because of not fitting in any needs of the Library of Congress' may I ask you to return it.

B. Traven
c/o Alfred A. Knopf
730 Fifth Ave.
New York City

Very truly yours,

B. Traven.

The Library of Congress still has that letter and the playbill.

Let us take a moment to survey the situation. Ret Marut, having narrowly escaped his adversaries in Germany, found refuge in Mexico under a new name. His was the unpredictable life of the adventurer, vagabond, and outsider—from his disappearance underground in 1919, to his reappearance in the New World in 1924, through the early 1930s when he lived in Acapulco. And throughout these years—so one may conclude from the letter to the Library of Congress—he preserved that playbill from 1840, carrying it with him in the jungle and the oil camps, on the cotton farms and his expeditions in Chiapas. Why? And why did he have this playbill in the first place, having probably brought it with him from Germany? How did he know that it was the only existing copy, as he stated in the letter? Or was he just going to make sure that the Library would keep it? And why the specific reference to Frau von Sternwaldt? Does it not appear as if he wished somehow to protect her memory from the passage of time and the forgetfulness of historiography? And how did Traven know that "von Sternwaldt" belonged to *Prussian* nobility? Why, in the same breath, the reference to the Hohenzollerns, particularly Wilhelm I? Traven curiously insisted on pointing out to his wife a monument to this kaiser on their trip to Berlin in 1959. Have we finally discovered the root of his jeu d'esprit about his liaison with the Hohenzollerns?

According to R. Blum's *Allgemeines Theater-Lexikon* (*General Theater Lexicon*), the Faller theater company listed on the playbill did in fact give preseason performances in Warmbrunn, a spa in the district of Liegnitz in the Riesengebirge region of Silesia, then under Prussian administration. But why would Traven, almost a century later, have gone out of his way to keep posterity from forgetting this? The Frau von Sternwaldt of 1840, whom he singled out, could not have been his mother, but was she perhaps his grandmother or great-grandmother or other relative? We do not know. Traven, in a conversation with Señora Luján about the playbill, intimated that he was in some way related to this Frau von Sternwaldt. He himself may not have had or been able to recall more detailed information, or it may be that he only believed he was related to her in some way. Raskin quotes Señora Luján as saying, "I believe" Traven's mother was named "von Sternwaldt." The matter remains unresolved. Señora Luján does not in fact know the name of Traven's mother.

Judging from her role in *Zar und Zimmermann* listed on the playbill, von Sternwaldt cannot have been a major actress. She appears in none of the biographical reference works on the history of the theater. More curiously, German handbooks of nobility do not mention the name von Sternwaldt. O. G. Flüggen's *Biographisches Bühnen-Lexikon der deutschen Theater vom Beginn der deutschen Schauspielkunst bis zur Gegenwart* (*Biographical Directory of the German Stage from the Beginnings of German Theater to the Present*) lists an actor named Ludwig von Sternwaldt, identified in brackets as "v[on] Warnstädt." This, unlike Sternwaldt, is in fact an authentic aristocratic name, and a Prussian one at that, at least in the form Warnstedt—and the family name Sternwaldt, undocumented in my research, turns out to be an anagram for L. Warnstedt! (The Gotha peerage, while including the Warnstedts, acknowledges neither the family name Warnstädt nor Sternwaldt.) The biographical information in the directory on Ludwig von Sternwaldt is meager: He was born in 1804 in Braunschweig, died in 1880 in Heidelberg (not Traven's father, clearly, but perhaps his grandfather or great-grandfather?), and was an actor in Stralsund, Lübeck, Danzig, Hannover, Vienna, Innsbruck, and Leipzig. In L. Wolff's *Almanach für Freunde der Schauspielkunst* (*Almanac for Friends of the Theater*) and in its continuation, edited by Ernst Gettke, we can in fact find an actor named "v[on] Sternwaldt" or "L. v[on] Sternwaldt" for the years from 1840 at the latest (the first year in which an index was included in the almanac) to 1879. He is also occasionally listed as a director. Gettke's *Almanach* of 1881 records his death: "Ludwig von Sternwaldt, *recte* v[on] Warnstädt." The preference for the pseudonym may be attributable to his illegimate birth, noted in the birth register of Braunschweig for October

11, 1804 (mother: Clara Francisca Spanuth); the Braunschweig Confirmation Register for 1819 names Hauptmann (Captain) Carl von Warnstedt as the father.

For the period from 1838 at the latest to 1882, both Wolff's *Almanach* and Gettke's *Almanach* also list a Frau von Sternwaldt as an actress. Her obituary in Gettke's *Almanach* identifies her as Josephine Stephanie, née Dorsch, widow of Ludwig von Sternwaldt, born on December 25, 1812 in Karlsruhe, died on Feburary 15, 1883 in Heidelberg. Ludwig and Josephine von Sternwaldt only rarely acted in the same place together. They shared the stage in 1840–1841 in Frankfurt on the Oder as members of a traveling theater company directed by Emilie Faller (the same troupe as that on the Warmbrunn playbill). One can closely follow the career of Frau von Sternwaldt with the help of the yearly chronologies of Wolff and Gettke. She seems to have moved around quite a bit, particularly in the provinces: Glogau, Liegnitz, Stade, Bremen, Freiburg, Bamberg, Hannover. She seldom remained longer than a year in the same place.

In 1855, the path takes an interesting twist: In this year for the first time a Fräulein von Sternwaldt appears as an actress (cast as "second and third lover") in Frankfurt on the Oder, where in the same year Frau von Sternwaldt acted as well (as "chaperones and first matrons"). For the year 1856 neither is mentioned, but for 1857 both Frau and Fräulein von Sternwaldt are listed as actresses in Bamberg, and both again for the following year in Augsburg. Ludwig von Sternwaldt had an engagement in Hannover during those years. Thereafter, Fräulein von Sternwaldt is no longer listed in the registers, but in 1871 (and only in this year), in addition to Herr and Frau von Sternwaldt, another actor named Sternwald appears (spelled in this manner, without "von" or Christian names), cast as "hero and lover." After the death of Ludwig and Josephine von Sternwaldt, a "Frau E.v. Sternwaldt" is listed for the 1886–1887 season, working as a prompter at the Deutsches Theater in Newark, New Jersey, as well as an actor named E. von Sternwaldt at the same theater (playing roles of elevated social rank). This is the only instance where the name E.v. Sternwaldt (Frau or Herr) surfaces in Gettke's yearbooks, although the Newark theater company is occasionally listed in later years in the continuation of the *Almanach* (the *New Theater Almanac*) as well. (It is absent in the volumes for the 1880s before 1886.) One explanation may be that the almanacs do not include every German-speaking stage every year, particularly not those in foreign countries. It may thus be that these Sternwaldts were engaged years before the 1886–1887 season, whether in Newark or elsewhere in America. They may conceivably have given a number of guest performances and returned to Germany in 1887 or shortly thereafter. Was Traven their (or Frau von Sternwaldt's)—legitimate?—son, born in America, who then from 1907 at the latest used the stage name Ret Marut? Traven told Señora Luján that his parents had takenly him "soon" after his birth from America to Germany. Was this in 1892, to be specific, the year Marut claimed to have left America? After 1887, when we lose track of Herr and Frau E. von Sternwaldt, the *New Theater Almanac* mentions the name Sternwaldt only once more, in 1907: A prompter named Emilie Sternwaldt (no "von") worked at the Pabst Theater in Milwaukee, Wisconsin, and at the Powers Theater in Chicago. Did the mother return to America as soon as her son had begun his acting career as Ret Marut?

The facts gleaned from the theater almanacs allow no firm conclusions, not least because there may well be gaps in their reporting. But consider the following constellation: Traven's claim to birth and early youth in the United States, although German was his "best language"; the claim that his mother was connected with the stage; the claim that his father had been an impresario in San Francisco; the interest in the name von Sternwaldt; an actor and a female prompter, both of this name, working at a German-speaking theater in America in the decade of Traven's birth. Perhaps it is the right track, even if it becomes lost in the undergrowth like so many others.

But the mist shrouding Traven's beginnings seems to lift a bit in places. The family von Warnstedt had a Danish-Swedish branch, which would correspond to Traven's oft-claimed Scandinavian heritage. The family is old nobility (*Uradel*)—did Marut have them in mind when he stressed that his family could be traced back over "several centuries" and in his allusions to noble ancestry? In the nineteenth century, the von Warnstedt family, to whom the "American" Traven thought he was related, even had an American connection: Two brothers, born in 1819 and 1825, "emigrated to America and were never heard of again." But why would someone who at least *believed* he was somehow related to the von Warnstedt (Sternwaldt) family pick the pseudonyms Traven and Marut? In the nineteenth century, the German branch of the family lived principally in Schleswig-Holstein (its male line died out in the early twentieth century). The pseudonym Traven may point to Schleswig-Holstein, where the name Traven is documented (in Lübeck, for example), even if only in the seventeenth century (in Lübeck at any rate). More enticing is the fact that an uncle and aunt of the siblings lost in America, namely Jürgen von Warnstedt and Charlotte von Warnstedt (married name: von Adeler), lived on what was then Danish territory, approximately nineteen miles west of Lübeck—in a place called Traventhal. Moreover, Marut (Maruthe, Marute) is indigenous to this region; it is the name of an old noble family that died out in the fourteenth century; the name of the village of Marutendorf, seven miles west of Kiel, is thought to be derived from it. A strange configuration: Sternwaldt/Warnstedt-Traven-Marut. Is it unthinkable that the mystery man who had perhaps grown up in or near Schwiebus (under whatever name) surmised something of this configuration, held it as part of dim childhood memories, or thought he actually knew about it—based on what he had heard from his mother in early childhood?

As a rule, inquiry into Traven's background assumes that Traven himself knew more about it, specifically about his father, than he let on—to the authorities, strangers, friends, and even his wife. If this were the case, why did nothing involuntarily slip out over the decades? Isn't the converse more plausible: that Traven himself did not know who he was, who his father was, or did not know precisely, beyond a shadow of a doubt? (This is not irreconcilable, of course, with the speculation connecting him to the actress von Sternwaldt.) True, his double Gales remarks in Traven's American version of *The Death Ship* that he doesn't need any papers, since he knows who he is. But the precise meaning of this is unclear from the context, and it is also unclear if Gales intends to tell the truth at all. Gales, apparently born illegitimate, does not know the name of his father (according to his own testimony and to all appearances). In the American version of *The Death Ship*, he says he does not know whether his family name was that of his mother or whether his father had "added" his name. In 1977 Raskin wrote in the magazine *Liberation* that after six months of research at Traven's house after the author's death, he felt that Traven himself did not have conclusive knowledge about his parents' identities. In that case, Traven would have had nothing to hide, aside perhaps from the assumed illegitimate birth; he only pretended that he did; and that would, as already intimated, help explain his apparent knack for fabricating stories about his background. This "solution" is attractive, not least because it severely restricts the scope of the guessing game. But is it not just as speculative as its converse, namely that Traven knew something and was hiding it?

This question cannot be answered with certainty. But two pieces of possible evidence merit consideration. The first is a letter from Traven dated October 21, 1935, to Lewis Gannet of the New York *Herald Tribune* (no signature, only a typewritten "B. Traven" at the bottom), in answer to two of Gannet's letters. In the first, Gannet had asked Traven to review books for the newspaper; Traven declined the offer. In the second letter, Gannet had apparently asked: "Who in hell are you?" Traven's answer: "I wish I could tell you that. Fact is I myself don't know it. If I knew it perhaps I could write books no more." Words of truth? We do not know. Traven apparently trusted Gannet. Novelists, he said earlier in his letter, should not review novels as a matter of principle, noting that this remark was not to be printed, as it was only "a friendly and confidential talk." Directly following this remark came the answer to Gannet's second letter. One wonders why this time Traven did not offer up his usual story about his early years in the Midwest, and so on, or simply say, as he did so often, that his life story was his own business.

The second piece of possible evidence: Traven's estate includes a Gotha peerage in French. It seems to have gotten little use and on the endpaper bears the notation "50 c" in pencil, which may indicate a purchase in an antiquarian bookshop in Mexico. Slipped in this Gotha is a publisher's notice in German, with an overview of the entire series of the German Gotha peerage, along with an alphabetical listing of the aristocratic names it includes. Someone—Traven probably, who else?—has underscored several of these names with pencil, not at random, but those that have some similarity, some reminiscence to the names that he himself used (Traven, Marut, Maurhut, Ziegelbrenner): Raven, Murat, Mayr, Mor-Merkl, MacCafry of Kean More, Maurer von Kronegg, Ziegler; but also Krohn, Menaden, and Lichtenberg; Great Britain and Ireland are also marked among the ruling houses. The significance? Have we eavesdropped on Traven *à la recherche de l'origine perdue*? Have we caught a glimpse over his shoulder as he attempts to recall his past using a list of aristocratic names, to remember a name that he had perhaps heard as a child? Did he thus not know his true name, at least his father's, or then again perhaps not his mother's either?

That would explain a lot, above all why all paths taken to reach Traven's youth have led nowhere.

4

RET MARUT

Actor and Writer, Revolutionary and Fugitive, 1907–1924

A Bit Player

The identity of the man who hid behind the pseudonym Ret Marut remains a mystery; perhaps it was a mystery even to himself. Maybe, like his double Gales in *The Death Ship*, he did not even know whether his birth had been officially registered or, if it had been, whether it had been done under his father's or mother's name. He was equally in the dark, one may suspect, about where he was born: Surely he did not believe the claim that he was born in San Francisco, which he often made before his rebirth as B. Traven in Mexico. In any event, all evidence for this story would have been conveniently destroyed in the great San Francisco earthquake.

We can first document Ret Marut's existence when he was already in his mid-twenties (assuming that his oft-claimed year of birth 1882 is correct). But this first bit of hard evidence about the man who a few decades later would captivate millions reveals the most lackluster beginnings imaginable. Marut first comes to light in the 1908 edition of *Neuer Theater-Almanach* (*New Theater Almanac*), a publication of the Association of the German Theatrical Profession. Ret Marut is listed as a "director and actor" at the Essen Municipal Theater for the 1907–1908 season (September–April) as well as member number 8228 of the association. His engagement seems to have started rather late in 1907, since the almanac does not list

Marut in the personnel register of the Essen Municipal Theater, but only in the general name index, apparently as a later addition. Whether this was Marut's first position at a theater is unclear. If he had been employed earlier at a German-speaking theater, it must have been under a different name—a not improbable scenario—since the volumes for the previous years list no Marut. In the résumé that Marut put on record when applying for American papers at the U.S. consulate in London in 1924, he stated that he had worked from sometime after 1901 until 1907 as an actor at a theater in Vienna, under the name Langer. The *New Theater Almanac* indeed lists an actor, director, and "baritone for opera and operetta" named Vincenz Langer, documented from 1904 in Wiener Neustadt and Baden, near Vienna. But since he is listed in those locations until the 1909–1910 season, by which time Marut was documented at other theaters, one might assume that in his London résumé the political fugitive Marut adopted the name of a different, real person (as I suggest he did in claiming to be Otto Feige). The most one might conclude about Marut's actual background from the Langer story would be that he had worked as an actor in or near Vienna before moving to Essen. But as long as the only indication for this is Marut's own testimony, Ret Marut's official year of "birth" must remain 1907.

One can follow his stage career on a yearly basis beginning in 1907 in the *New Theater Almanac*. In 1908 Marut was a director and an actor playing "youthful heroes and lovers" in the towns of Suhl and Ohrdruf in Thuringia, in 1909 an actor at the Municipal Theater of Crimmitschau (Chemnitz district). Was it carelessness or daring playfulness that caused B. Traven to mention Crimmitschau out of the blue in *The Bridge in the Jungle*, just as he casually referred to Suhl in *The Death Ship*, again for no apparent reason? These provincial theaters must have held little appeal for Marut. For already in 1909 he surfaced in Berlin, in the proletarian northern section of the city (Veteranenstrasse 7), "to pursue his studies," as the *New Theater Almanac* notes—in other words, with no regular position at a theater. But for the 1910–1911 season Marut is listed as a member (actor and director) of the Berliner "Neue Bühne" ("New Stage") ensemble, a traveling theater troupe offering guest appearances that season in the provinces of East and West Prussia and Posen. On this tour, from early October 1910 until mid-August 1911, Marut appeared onstage only in small towns, usually in hotels:

in West Prussia (October 1910), for instance in Lobau; in East Prussia (late October until April) in places such as Goldap, Pillkallen, Lasdehnen, Stallupönen, Mohrungen, Preussisch-Stargardt (where he met the photographer and writer Kurt Hielscher, who subsequently gave him a photo portrait that is preserved in the Marut estate); and in the province of Posen (May–August) in Wronke, Zirke, Grabitz, Pinne, and Neustadt near Pinne, among other places. (His appearances are recorded in a notebook preserved in the Marut estate.) This engagement did not continue either but was apparently a stepping-stone to positions at more important theaters. One can easily imagine that while traveling with the Berliner "Neue Bühne" Marut was able to arrange his next engagement.

The 1911–1912 season found Marut, according to the directories of the *New Theater Almanac*, at the Danzig Municipal Theater as an actor and "manager and treasurer" of the local artists' club. In the summer of 1912, he managed to make the leap to a truly important theater with an engagement (albeit a modest one) at the Düsseldorf Schauspielhaus, which at the time enjoyed a considerable reputation throughout Germany owing to the efforts of its directors, Louise Dumont and her husband Gustav Lindemann. Photocopies of the correspondence between Marut and the Lindemanns in the Traven estate reveal that Marut had taken the initiative to join the company in the winter of 1911–1912. When he formally applied for a position, he dropped an offhand remark that has elicited a good deal of puzzlement: His "personal conditions" allowed him "to view what is called a good wage as a matter of secondary importance," he wrote. The Danzig theater, he continued, spent too much of its energies on opera, operetta, and farce, keeping him from pursuing his interest in developing as a serious actor. His appearance "as a solo dancer in a full-length ballet" must not have proved particularly fulfilling either. So Marut traveled to Düsseldorf in late May 1912 to introduce himself in person, and he was engaged there beginning with the 1912–1913 season. In the official Düsseldorf registration form dated August 8, 1912, Marut claimed to be an English subject, born in San Francisco on February 25, 1882; the claim to English nationality was later changed (perhaps at the outbreak of the war) to American.

The engagement at the Düsseldorf Schauspielhaus did bring an end to Marut's tramping about the provinces but apparently did not give him the stature as a serious actor that he had hoped for. He appeared in Düsseldorf for only three seasons. After Louise Dumont informed him as early as June 30, 1915, that his contract could not be renewed in light of the "seriousness of the situation" (referring no doubt to the war), he in turn wrote to the management on August 25 requesting that his contract be terminated: "I am about to enter into very extensive commitments which require my absolute objectivity and complete lack of partisanship in regard to the Schauspielhaus. For that reason I request that at the end of the month you relieve me of my contract." Lindemann acceded on August 31, and on November 10 Marut informed the Düsseldorf registry that he was moving to Frankfurt am Main, a fact recorded on the Düsseldorf registration form. Actually, however, he went to Munich, arriving on November 11, 1915. (The Munich Alien Registration Office noted "here since 11 November 1915" on the back of a letter in which Marut, registered as an American, requested permission to make a short journey on May 21, 1917.) His Munich registration form gives his address as Herzogstrasse 83 as of November 13, 1915, and Clemensstrasse 84 as of November 30, 1915. Marut was no stranger in Munich: In July 1914 he had made an appearance at the Munich Künstler-Theater in guest performances with the Düsseldorf Schauspielhaus. His registration form was thus first filled in on July 6, 1914. It gave his intended length of stay as two to three months, although the financial records of the Schauspielhaus indicate that the guest tour was finished by the end of July.

Marut's stage career presents little worth noting. The evidence—from playbills, theater reviews, letters from and to the Düsseldorf theater and Marut's notebook in which he listed his roles with the Berliner "Neue Bühne"—shows that he usually appeared in minor roles, primarily in the light entertainments then in vogue. He apparently had larger roles only in productions of the provincial theaters and also (in addition to the places previously mentioned) in the town of Idar-Oberstein, where he appeared on a guest tour in Sudermann's *Die Ehre* (*Honor*) as Graf Trast, in Ferdinand Bonn's *Der Hund von Baskerville* (*The Hound of the Baskervilles*), *Othello*, and in the title role of *Kean, Englands grösster Schauspieler* (*Kean, England's Greatest Actor*) (based on Dumas?). Newspaper clippings preserved in the Marut estate referring to these performances do not include any dates.

A few kind words about the actor surface here and there in reviews. Essentially nothing is known about Marut's accomplishments as a director. But more evidence exists for his offstage activities in the spring and summer of 1914 at the Düsseldorf theater. He served as an editorial assistant for the theater's publication, *Masken* (*Masks*) and also was secretary of the Hochschule für Bühnenkunst (Theater Academy), founded in 1914, which was associated with the Düsseldorf Schauspielhaus. Letters from Marut to Hans Franck, publisher of *Masks* and director of the Theater Academy, are preserved in the municipal archives of Schwerin. They discuss planning the first prospectus for the academy's curriculum, particularly efforts to enlist instructors from all over Germany, as well as the academy's expectations of its students. Marut, on behalf of Franck, asked leading personalities in the cultural sphere to participate in the activities of the academy: Hugo von Hofmannsthal, Thomas Mann, George Bernard Shaw, Wilhelm Bölsche, Julius Hart, Maximilian Harden, Martin Buber, Gerhart Hauptmann, Georg Simmel, Richard Dehmel, Anatole France, Marie von Ebner-Eschenbach, Albert Bassermann, Rudolf Rittner, and Max Reinhardt, among others.

The most significant aspect of Marut's theater career—which was to last eight years—was the opportunity to come in contact with modern and classical literature. Serious drama had a place, albeit limited, in the programs of the theaters where he worked, particularly in Düsseldorf, however much the popular lowbrow offerings set the tone. We can hardly make any definitive statements about Marut's educational background; all the more interesting are the sparse signs of his knowledge of literature that come from the documents of these years. Marut wrote on January 17, 1912, to Louise Dumont from Danzig that he was involved in productions of Kleist's *Prinz von Homburg*, *Hamlet* (Marut played the second grave digger), and *King Lear*. The Danzig director, Heinrich Römer, he noted in the same letter, was staging "modern dramas—Ibsen, Hauptmann, Wilde, Wedekind, etc." In Danzig Marut appeared in one of them, Ibsen's *The Vikings at Helgeland*. *A Doll's House* was performed in Crimmitschau, where Sudermann's *Honor* and *Heimat* (*Homeland*) took to the stage as well. In Düsseldorf he participated in productions of *Alcestis* and *The Merchant of Venice*; he appeared as a servant in Lessing's *Minna von Barnhelm* and as a troll in *Peer Gynt*; and he was involved in a production of Schiller's *Don Carlos*. On tour with the Berliner "Neue Bühne" he appeared, for example, in Max Halbe's *Der Strom* (*The River*), Hauptmann's *Der Biberpelz*

(*The Beaver Coat*) and *Die versunkene Glocke* (*The Sunken Bell*), Schiller's *William Tell*, and Hebbel's *Maria Magdalena*. Marut's writings from these years make occasional reference to such dramatists as Schiller, Wilde, and Hauptmann; in *The Brickburner*, which first appeared in 1917, he also mentions dramatists from time to time (Shakespeare, Strindberg, Ibsen, Kleist, Karl Schönherr, Wedekind). In a 1912 Düsseldorf production of J. M. Barrie's *Peter Pan*, Marut appeared in the role of an Indian—an ironic footnote in light of his future involvement with the Indians of Mexico in the guise of B. Traven. A photograph of Marut in this role, in spite of a thick layer of makeup, fleshes out the description provided of the actor by Hennes Frisch, stage manager of the Düsseldorf theater: "Ret Marut had a small build, was slight, very thin, but tough. His body had the tautness of a jockey's. His eyes were a watery blue, his gaze was always intense, his nose pointed, strong, well defined—a tracking dog's nose."

Little is known of the private life of the actor Ret Marut. The facts and dates of it, which Recknagel has brought together in painstaking detail, are sparse indeed. Marut became acquainted with the actress Elfriede Zielke in Crimmitschau and appeared onstage with her in several plays from January to April 1909. While Marut lived in North Berlin at Veteranenstrasse 7, the *New Theater Almanac* also gives a Berlin address for Elfriede Zielke, incidentally just up the street at number 47. Next, Zielke, like Marut, was engaged at the Berliner "Neue Bühne." Her daughter Irene was born on March 20, 1912; in later years Traven was to dispute that the child was his. Beginning with Marut's engagement in Danzig, however, the two appear to have moved apart. "In August 1913," Recknagel reports, they "spent a two-week vacation in Tangermünde, where Elfriede Zielke had a theater engagement at the time. Ret Marut eagerly sketched the old buildings in the town. In late 1914 they broke off their relationship. A certain Herr Garding, a devoted admirer of Elfriede's, had come between them. On Garding's being drafted, his mother prevailed on Elfriede Zielke to promise to marry him, 'since he would otherwise take his own life during the war.' Elfriede Zielke gave her word and wrote to Ret Marut in Düsseldorf informing him of her decision. The crushing news motivated Marut to write the novella *To the Honorable Miss S . . .* (letters of a soldier fallen in action), in which the first-person narrator assumes the role of the unfortunate lover and goes off to his death on the front." In addition, Recknagel notes that "Ret Marut frequently wrote to his daughter Irene from Munich until 1918. . . . His new-year's greeting from 31 December 1917 is still preserved."

In his last year in Düsseldorf Marut met the woman who was to play a role in his life for more than a decade. A register of the students at the Theater Academy includes an entry for "Irene Alda (Irene Mermet)" from Cologne, who entered the school on January 1, 1915, defying her parents' wishes, and withdrew on November 24 of the same year. Irene (Mermet was the name of her adoptive father, Alda her maiden name) arrived in Munich's Schwabing section shortly after Marut's move there; on November 24, 1915 she had already officially registered. She apparently assisted Marut with the production of his radical magazine *The Brickburner*, which began appearing in September 1917, and, operating out of her apartment at nearby Herzogstrasse 45, she also ran the small, quasi-private J. Mermet Press. It was there that Marut, under the name Richard Maurhut, published *To the Honorable Miss S . . .* , apparently the press's sole publication. (The Introduction is signed "J. Mermet Verlag München 23"; it is not included in the Büchergilde edition of Marut/Traven's collected works and may have been written by Irene Mermet.) Irene Mermet's life would remain intertwined with Traven's until his early years in Mexico.

From Actor to Author

After his departure from the Düsseldorf Schauspielhaus, Ret Marut never again appeared onstage. Regardless of what he had in mind in his letter of resignation concerning the "very extensive commitments" that required his objectivity and lack of partisanship toward the Düsseldorf theater, he certainly could not have failed to realize that he was not destined to become one of Germany's bright lights on the stage. As he left Düsseldorf, he was not readying himself for a career in academia: He did call himself a "stud. phil." in his letter of May 21, 1917, requesting permission for a short journey from Munich, and he was identified as a "student of philosophy" in the Munich Occupational Register—but neither is proof of formal academic study in Munich. The Munich University Archives do not document Marut's official registration there.

Nor can it be proved that when Marut left Düsseldorf in 1915 he had any intention of plunging into political journalism, specifically in an anarchist-pacifist direction, the genre in which he was to win a certain degree of fame in the history of German journalism and activist expressionism as the author and editor of *The Brickburner.* After all, it was quite a while until the first issue of *The Brickburner* appeared (September 1917). It is more reasonable to assume that Marut, in leaving Düsseldorf (a move that, it seems, was at least in part prompted by the theater itself), planned to concentrate on his creative writing. But although he had already published his first stories in his Düsseldorf period, he could scarcely have expected to support himself by writing. Honoraria from newspapers and magazines, like his actor's wages in Düsseldorf, must have been a "matter of secondary importance," regardless of whether he really had the personal wealth he hinted at in his letter of introduction to Louise Dumont and on occasion in *The Brickburner.*

In any case, Marut devoted an increasing amount of his attention to literary pursuits even while he was still involved with the Düsseldorf theater. A substantial number of stories and sketches appeared in print beginning in 1912, primarily in the Düsseldorf papers (the *General-Anzeiger* and the *Düsseldorfer Zeitung*), and continuing, during the Munich period, until 1919, when Marut was forced to disappear underground. But the printed materials constitute only a modest selection of his literary output. Marut's estate contains typescripts of two novels: *Der Mann Site und die grünglitzernde Frau: Die Geschichte eines Lebens, das nach einem Ziele strebte* (*The Man Named Site and the Green-Glittering Woman: The Story of a Life with a Purpose*), a theater novel "by Richard Maurhut," and two drafts of *Das Vermächtnis des Inders* (*The Indian's Legacy*), "a novel by Georg Steinheb." The latter is an anticolonial book set in Indochina; other papers in the Marut estate refer to it as *Die Fackel des Fürsten* (*The Torch of the Prince*, the title used throughout this book) or *Die annamitische Fürstin* (*The Annamite Princess*), "a novel by Ret Marut," as the title page of the other draft reads. Marut's estate also includes manuscripts of dramatic and lyrical compositions, among them a copybook of poems, entitled *Lieder eines Menschen* (*Songs of a Human Being*), as well as typescripts of dozens of stories from this period, a number of them with handwritten corrections. Some were published at the time, but it remains to be shown whether others ever appeared in print—the collected works published by Büchergilde Gutenberg include just one such previously unknown text from the estate, the novella *Die Geschichte vom unbegrabenen Leichnam* (*The Story of the Unburied Corpse*). Marut, ever enterprising and industrious, offered some of the apparently unprinted stories to newspaper editors and book publishers. Four rejection slips from *Vorwärts*, dated 1916–1917, lie among the papers in the Marut estate, and on December 10, 1918, the satirical magazine *Simplicissimus* (which was later to accept a story by B. Traven) printed the following barb under the heading "Marginalia":

> A certain Ret Marut publishes a rag in Munich which in practically every issue smears *Simplicissimus* rudely and ineptly to boot. This charming gentleman has been trying year in and year out, and even during the war, to contribute to *Simplicissimus* by sending in dozens of sketches and novellettes; but his submissions were always declined by our editorial board as inadequate.

Marut was equally unsuccessful with the seven "Pieces" he sent on July 15, 1915, to Gustav Lindemann, apparently for the Düsseldorf theater publication *Masks*, adding, "if necessary, I can send more."

"More" there surely was. The Marut estate includes tables of contents for two prose collections that never materialized: *Der goldene Berg* (*The Golden Mountain*), "Novellas by Ret Marut," and *Die Himmelfahrt* (*The Ascension*), "Satires, Grotesques, Paradoxes, and Anecdotes by Ret Marut." Both are stamped, undoubtedly by a publisher, as received on July 8, 1913; each item intended for the collections is identified parenthetically in the table of contents as existing either in manuscript form or as previously published in newspapers. These lists include a number of Marut stories known before the lists were found in the 1980s but also a few short stories and satirical pieces that have been located since then in German daily newspapers (*Vorwärts*, *Berliner Tagblatt*, *Bremer Bürger-Zeitung*, and *Frankfurter Zeitung*) with the help of Marut's (unfortunately undated) parenthetical references. It is conceivable that even more material of this sort could be ferreted out in the German press from the period up to 1919. In any event, it is certain that Marut's creative output in the years 1912–1919 was more extensive than the Marut volume of Traven's collected works would indicate.

Although this chapter of Marut/Traven's literary production may be incomplete, two points may nonetheless be made.

First, Marut played a very minor role in the literary life of his day. The widely scattered publication of his pieces weakened their effect—they appeared in the Social Democratic *Vorwärts* as well as in bourgeois regional papers, in the political weekly *März* as well as in popular periodicals for the entire family such as *Westermanns Monatshefte* and *Reclams Universum*, while one prose piece was published in the almost unknown magazine *Licht und Schatten*. A few other literary works appeared in Marut's *Brickburner*, which did not have a particularly large audience. The slim volume *Der blaugetupfte Sperling* (*The Blue-Speckled Sparrow*) (1919) was the only collection to reach the bookshops, accompanied by the non-committal message "Published by The Brickburner" rather than a clear reference to Marut's authorship. Few copies were printed, we may assume, and the only book Marut published with "his" name (Richard Maurhut) on the title page, the novella *To the Honorable Miss S . . .* (1916), could scarcely have found a substantial readership as a title in Irene Mermet's virtually private publishing house. This publication history leads to the conclusion that the writer, though he succeeded in publishing a fair number of his smaller pieces, did not make a coherent or more than a superficial impression on the general public. Even if Marut sleuths, combing through the daily newspapers, were to unearth pieces as yet unknown, their findings would not be likely to change this assessment.

Second, in terms of its literary or artistic merit, Marut's prose rarely rises above the level of the popular literature of the time. Here and there we find thematic points of contact with the later works of B. Traven, which may not be without interest, but the dominant impression gained from a thorough survey is that the "two" authors were qualitatively quite different. Victor M. Mai, editor of the literary section of the *Düsseldorfer General-Anzeiger* in Marut's day, did indeed hit the mark when he wrote in 1950 concerning the Marut/Traven identity: "Marut must have undergone major emotional shocks to reach the level of Traven's accomplishments."

The biographer might find Marut's prose to be fertile ground for studying Traven's psychological development from both a chronological and a thematic perspective. A chronological study is not feasible, however, since the absolute and relative order of the stories is largely uncertain: Date of publication and time of writing may not always lie near each other, as is demonstrably the case with a number of the stories in *The Blue-Speckled Sparrow.* A fact unknown until now, for example, is that the satirical piece "Malkunst" ("The Art of Painting") from this volume first appeared as "Roter Mohn" ("Red Poppy") on December 11, 1913, in *Vorwärts*, which further published the book's title story on November 10, 1913, as "Die grüngesprenkelte Eule" ("The Green-Spotted Owl"). Several other stories that appeared in *The Blue-Speckled Sparrow*—"Der Schauspieler und der König" ("The Actor and the King"), "Betrüger" ("Deceivers"), "Der Herr Kommerzienrat" ("The Business Executive," identical with "Titel" ["Titles"]), and "Die Geschichte vom schlangenklugen Dichter" ("A Writer of Serpentine Shrewdness")—are included in the tables of contents that Marut compiled in 1913 for his planned but unpublished collections. One can only hazard a guess at the dates of other pieces in *The Blue-Speckled Sparrow* until any first printings, if they exist, or other pertinent information comes to light.

If we group Marut's prose by theme rather than date, a few dominant concerns emerge that can be linked with the author's biography—certainly with the external events and perhaps with psychological developments as well. These main thematic groupings are also represented in the unprinted texts. In some cases more than in others we feel justified in taking Traven at his word when he remarked, referring to himself, that the author "can be recognized in his works" and that he could write only about that which he had experienced himself.

What can be gathered from the main themes of Marut's literary output—*To the Honorable Miss S . . .* , the short stories, the caustic vignettes and satirical anecdotes, the bizarre and humorous commentaries on everyday life?

The war stories constitute the largest, relatively self-contained group, although thematic overlaps occasionally occur between the groups (according to Recknagel, Marut "performed behind the front [Metz, Strasbourg]" while touring with the Düsseldorf Schauspielhaus). Other clusters of stories, dating in part to before August 1914 (based on the dates of the first printings), include the following subjects: theater and literature; art and business; the human side of daily life in the provinces and the big city (Berlin); the critical demasking of bourgeois society, particularly of its upper classes and business interests; criticism of politics in the authoritarian state; and the relationship between a son and his domineering mother, with the father figure conspicuously absent.

The latter theme, sounded in "Der Idiot" ("The Idiot") (1912), Marut's first story to appear in print, is surely the most tantalizing for the biographer. One is tempted to read thinly veiled autobiography into the striking image of a strong mother, wavering between a ruthless, egocentric exploiter and a concerned, loving parent, with the son's accusatory self-emancipation struggling against his sentimental attachment. The conflict of mother and son is delineated with particular harshness in this story. Thoughts of financial gain and social advancement destroy a fundamental human relationship. The bourgeoise Bernhardine Leisetritt, owner of a coal business, fails in her attempt to cheat her enterprising and good-natured son out of his inheritance by claiming that he is feeble-minded. She hoped to use the money to facilitate her own social climbing, but her plot backfires and the son, who has just reached legal age, severs all familial ties.

The mother figure appears as an emotional, rather than material, exploiter in the story "Deceivers" (1919). The mother comes between her son and his playmates, his chosen career, marriage, his political associations, and his grand humanitarian ambitions, demanding his "eternal gratitude for giving life to her child." When the son finally buries her after "sixty years of renunciation and doing without," he is struck by a heart attack within the hour. "In his pocket he carried a vial of prussic acid, in case events had taken a different turn." The narrator crassly draws the moral: This vampirelike mother "deceived" her son, she "cheated life itself out of the best it has to offer."

Typical of Marut's characterization is the son's ambivalence toward the domineering mother. Even his first printed story not only ends with the son's emphatically cold, insultingly abrupt departure from his parents'—or rather his mother's—house (only in the final passage is it also referred to as the "father's house," but this is a German idiom and, in any case, the father does not appear at all in the story); it also ends with a moment of deep emotion, bordering on the sentimental. The final paragraph of "The Idiot" runs:

> He stood for a moment in the hallway. Tears welled up in his eyes. It was still his mother, his sister. This was still his home. He wanted to go back to the door and ask for forgiveness. But he clenched his teeth. He went down the stairs, into the stable,

> where he petted the horses and shook the horsemen's and the workers' hands. He slowly looked around the courtyard once again. And then he left his father's house.

Such ambivalence comes as no surprise. Only the writer with depth of feeling is capable of sarcasm that is more than a hollow gesture. But the same writer stands in danger of going to the other extreme at times, as in those prose pieces in which the narrator gives in to the temptation to indulge in his own emotions. This is the case in the story "Kleines Kerlchen!" ("Little Fellow!") (1914), the main characters of which tellingly appear not as mother and son but as Mama and Bubi. The father comes into play only by his exclusion: "Papa was a pilot. He crashed and died instantaneously." This background information may explain the mother's intensity of feeling for her son and her attempts to monopolize his affections. "Bubi must always love Mama and always stay with Mama. Mama doesn't have anyone else in the world besides Bubi," the mother says with pathological possessiveness to her child, who is not even of school age. The depiction of the intimacy between the two does not avoid the sentimental, and the story climaxes in the maudlin sacrifice of the child for the mother: Bubi, looking out the upstairs window, sees his mother walking up the street, about to be hit by an oncoming car; hallucinating that he can fly, he leaps out of the window to save his mother—"her brave little darling" in whose fantasy and longing (so one may interpret the death leap) the image of the father is alive after all.

The mother figure makes her presence felt even in the war stories. In one of the highly charged vignettes called "Geschichten vom Bahnhof" ("Stories of the Railway Station") (1916), an "old woman" says farewell to her son who is returning to the front. In another, a young child is unaware that he is seeing his father, who is likewise returning to war after a leave, "perhaps for the last time in this life" and is left behind sitting alone with his mother on the railway platform. The pacifist story "Mutter Beleke" ("Mother Beleke") (1915) presents a lighter treatment of the mother-son relationship. The mother advises her son, "Don't be in no hurry, Herbert dear, them Russkies bite!" When this admonition, which becomes a familiar quotation in the son's military outfit, is repeated by a "cheerful voice" in the field, it raises such peals of laughter among the son's fellow soldiers that they tumble headlong into the battle and take the Russian village for which they were fighting, an achievement the captain could not have accomplished otherwise. "The solicitude of a loving mother" triumphs pointedly even in questions of military strategy.

Whether he deals in sentimentality, sarcasm, or humor, Marut lays it on thick (as Traven was to do). Marut's treatment is heavy-handed and bordering on the banal in sketches of petit bourgeois life in the big city such as "Das teure Souper" ("The Expensive Supper") (1913), a bizarre story of a man who fails to pay his bill in a restaurant; the scurrilous piece "Ehrlichkeit" ("Honesty") (1913), and "Vom Anschluss" ("Connection") (1913), a fanciful vignette about the human contact that some lonely hearts find while they wait in the post office for a telephone connection to come through. The frame of the more ambitious novella *Die Klosterfrau* (*The Story of a Nun*), which Marut published in 1918 in *Westermanns Monatshefte*, also ridicules the banality of daily life, though its ghost theme borders on the fantastic.

The bourgeois world under the kaiser is subjected to a crass polemical treatment in a number of the small prose pieces that we might call vignettes of social criticism. The shrill tone of *The Brickburner* is occasionally anticipated in these works. Marut, even in this early prose, cynically exposes the criminal machinations of big business—American in "Geschäft ist Geschäft" ("Business Is Business") (1912). The satirist George Grosz could not have made a more venomous attack on the duplicitous sexual morality of the German middle class than Marut does in "Brief nach Berlin" ("Letter to Berlin") (1912). Likewise, Marut sends up the supposedly cultivated upper class with its unbounded thirst for titles and medals in "Titles" or "The Business Executive" (1919/1912 in Bremer Bürger Zeitung) and "The Blue-Speckled Sparrow" or "The Green-Spotted Owl" (1919/1913). He further lays bare the exploitation and psychological mistreatment of industrial and farm laborers by those in power who lack even the most rudimentary sense of humanity, as the sudden rebellion of the suppressed makes brutally clear to them, in "Die Maschine" ("The Machine") (1916) and "Das Seidentuch" ("The Silk Scarf") (1917).

Social criticism turns to the grotesque in "The Story of the Unburied Corpse" (undated), first published after Traven's death. This is a story of an unknown man, found dead, whom both the ecclesiastical and civil bureaucracies refuse to bury. Finally, after 137 pounds of documents have been filed in the case, the military, ironically, furnishes a proper burial for the man who has meanwhile become nothing but "a pile of crumbled, filthy gray bones." This story lambasts society under the kaiser for its thoughtless "official" inhumanity as well as the mode of government that makes such inhumanity the norm. It is only natural that Marut's social criticism in the stories extends to the political sphere, to the heads of state who are ultimately responsible for the ills of society. "The Actor and the King," dubbed a "political grotesque," foreshadows the collapse of the dynastic-autocratic government in depicting the disintegration of a friendship that had existed in spite of class differences: "You smiled," the actor says. "Rather smugly. But if these people should ever cease to play their parts as unpaid extras, . . . then you, my friend, will also cease to be a real king!" In 1918 *The Brickburner* ran a similar piece on the warmongering of outwardly civilized governments—"Höflichkeit der Könige" ("The Politeness of Kings").

The sphere that Marut knew best in his pre-Munich period—the world of the theater—is naturally a particularly fruitful subject for the critical gaze of the writer who seems to compose his words as if arming for battle. Some of his stories dealing with the theater appeared in the Düsseldorf period in the final years of his stage career. But the biographer may view all of them as Marut's way of getting even with the career in which he failed to gain recognition. Marut looks behind the scene and uncovers the pitiful existence of a small-time director, the unreality of the "life" that the "art" onstage tries to depict. With the cynicism of the knowing realist, he reveals the banality of "creating," of pretty appearances. In the world of the theater, success results only when art goes by the wayside, as he shows in "Theaterdirektor Rassmann" ("Theater Director Rassmann") (1913); "Individualität" ("Individuality") (1913); "Regie" ("Direction") (1914); and "Kunst und Leben" ("Art and Life") (1919). Marut does not seem to have shed many tears over his departure from the stage.

A bitter Marut also speaks in his stories of literature and, once, of the visual arts, in observations that are formulated tritely at best. The bourgeois dabbler focuses not on the work itself but on its title and, moreover, on the artist's reputation in "The Art of Painting" (1919, published in 1913 as "Red Poppy"). Marut/Traven's obsession with anonymity springs to mind. The would-be poet Bogumil Scheibenkleber wins commercial success when he hits upon the thought of writing a short novel that contains only one word per page in "A Writer of Serpentine Shrewdness." In "Mein Besuch bei dem Dichter Pguwlkschrj Rnfajbzxlquy" ("My Visit to the Writer Pguwlkschrj Rnfajbzxlquy"), a journalist trying to track down the secret of a famous poet's success discovers him in a mental hospital. Both stories appeared in 1919 in *The Blue-Speckled Sparrow*. Even if *both* should have been written in one form or another at an earlier date, they sound like Marut's embittered farewell to his belletristic pursuits, which had not brought him much further in winning the public's esteem than had his association with the stage. Marut, no longer a young man—he was already in his late thirties when the collection of stories came out—must have had to admit to himself with some sarcasm that his attempts to get a foothold in the cultural life of the Empire, though they may not have been a total failure, at least held no hope for significant public recognition.

Such an overall judgment should make exception for some of the war stories that appeared beginning in 1915. Although they, too, failed to win much acknowledgment, as they were printed in widely scattered and obscure publications, the First World War seems to have given the strongest impulse to the author's creativity during his Marut period, as evidenced also in the virulent pacifism of *The Brickburner*. Many of the war stories—they are considerably more numerous than the prose pieces on other themes—reveal more human substance and a more authentic personal engagement for a serious cause than the other literary works of the pre-Traven period. It is the military, in a humanitarian gesture, that brings to a proper close *The Story of the Unburied Corpse*, which has dragged on for years. Why the military? When the Catholic priest objects to a Protestant being buried in the Catholic cemetery, the captain responsible for the burial order, also a Catholic, tells the priest: "Now let me tell you one thing, as long as there is a war, my comrade is closer to me than a Catholic."

This humanity, which comes alive under cannon fire, is typical of the war stories. With a conspicuous absence of heroic overtones, Marut stresses the bonds uniting all humanity in the face of authorized mass murder. But the stories would not be Marut's, the Brickburner's, work if there were not at least the overtone of accusation against the senseless brutality that celebrates its orgies in the war. Marut thus emphasizes, in a style at times bordering on kitsch, the tender, fleeting moments of human companionship before the backdrop of rampant barbarity—just as B. Traven was later to do in his novels. One of the best examples is "Der fremde Soldat" ("The Unknown Soldier") (1915), a love story about a soldier dying in the field hospital, for whom the nurse, a stranger to him, makes his last moments the crowning experience of his life. The text ends with a typical Marut/Traven motif: "And no one knows who he is or what he is, where he comes from or what regiment he belonged to, whether he was a private soldier or an officer, a worker or an intellectual or an artist. Just another who'll be posted missing, or maybe someone somewhere will be waiting half a century for him to come home again." That the soldier and the nurse are strangers does not prevent them from relating to each other; on the contrary, it makes it possible. Similarly, "Nebel" ("In the Fog") (1916) presents strangers from opposing sides of the war who accidentally meet on a night patrol in no-man's-land and somehow "understand" each other. The French and the German soldiers greet each other without a word, in the semidarkness of the front:

> But in the fathomless depths of their eyes there rested a brief question which men never fail to understand. They slowly lowered their hands. And turned to go.
>
> For the briefest instant there leapt upon them then a second of eternity that stripped them of their uniforms and, unthinkingly, obedient to the one greater will, they reached out simultaneously to take the other's hand, they shook hands in the manner of friends who must part for eternity; they released the other's hand just as quickly and returned by the way that they had come.
>
> What else was either of them to have done, once he had recognized that standing before him was a man?
>
> For they were both stricken by blindness and did not see the enemy.

Only an intermezzo in the shrill cacophony of genocide? The brutality of war, which makes men into marionettes of institutionalized insanity, is often more powerful than the elementary brotherhood we find in "In the Fog." In "Zwei Väter" ("Two Fathers") (1916) Marut strikes up a bitter countermelody. Here the German infantryman, in hand-to-hand combat in the French trenches, impulsively spares the life of his opponent when, a knife clenched in his fist, he thinks of his children and those of his opponent. The spared opponent extends his hand to his savior. But at this moment a French soldier fires at the German. The bullet "split his heart. But that was not enough for it. It sprang from the heart of the one father and shattered the head of the other. It knew no pity with fathers and did its hard duty." Other stories, such as "Liebe des Vaterlandes" ("Love of the Fatherland") (1916) and "Was in Frankreich alles geschehen kann" ("The Kind of Thing That Can Happen in France") (1919), accentuate the senselessness of war between the civilized nations, exposing military fame (on both sides, incidentally) to grotesque ridicule and bitter hatred. The veneer of heroism fails to cover up the war's claim on the lives of sons, fathers, and husbands. A wounded man who had barely escaped with his life is reduced to a cripple; he commits suicide in the army hospital, having just been "healed" by the chief doctor ("Wohingegen" ["On the Other Hand"] [1919]; "Das Mitleid" ["Pity"] [1916]). "Ungedienter Landsturm im Feuer" ("Last of the Reserves in the Fray") (1915) sends up flag-waving patriotism in this battle description:

> I would never have thought that the cannon thunder could get louder, that there should be room in the air for another sound. But it got even louder. And then we saw grenades landing a hundred meters before us, exploding with a frightful roar and tearing up the stony earth, lifting it high as a house into the air in thick clods. Then it became all the same to me, life or death, freedom or slavery, I didn't think of my homeland or the kaiser. For all I cared everything could go to pieces and me with it. What was all that to me! And how stupid and ridiculous it was, that I had brought along soap and toothpaste and stationery in my pack! What good was it! What good that I had learned to write, what good that I had gone to school and taken my examinations! Why did my parents worry themselves about me so much! Everything is stupid and useless. I just wanted to be dead.

To the Honorable Miss S . . . (1916), Marut's most extensive and ambitious prose work and his only novella to appear in book form, exposes the unheroic longing for death of the seemingly patriotic hero. Excerpts from the diary of this officer who died in battle reveal that his death in an assault, praised as an act of heroism by his commanding officer, was in fact a suicide. The depictions of the physical and psychological atrocities of war, worthy of a Goya, again reveal the rage of one who is powerless to act. Yet the horrors of war in this story, astonishingly, act not as motivation for the suicide but as a reinforcing backdrop for the general sense of world-weariness of the nameless soldier—who is Travenesquely taciturn about his background and private life. The real basis of his ennui is disappointment in love—his misinterpretation of an ambiguous but innocuous situation—which has propelled the young man into despair and isolation from which he extricates himself by running into the thick of the fray, appearing heroic to the outside world:

> What care I for life and fatherland? What is war to me? What is this plangent arousal of an entire nation to one mighty purpose of the will? For I stand alone, alone in all the world! As alone and unaided as only a man can be, when suddenly he wakes up to discover as if in a moment of illumination that no one on this earth, not one other single human being, not even the mother who gave him birth, is kindred to him in the ultimate stage of being, that all love and loyalty are nothing but the most unalloyed egoism.
>
> It may be that I committed an unpardonable blunder in preferring discretion to a declaration of my own great love for her. Certainly I cannot demand that she ought to have sensed it. But when for month after month neither she nor I entertained the least thought that did not belong to the both of us, there could be no other admissible conclusion. So, all those to whom I might tell it would say, yours is no more than a pedestrian and tedious love story. And they would find my story, and me not a whit the less, entirely laughable. Just that. And I would concede that they are utterly right to do so. What more could a man do to prove conclusively that he is ridiculous and his story indistinguishable from a thousand others? All of that I freely admit, and a great deal more besides, whatever is desired and demanded of me. Nevertheless, there is none but I who knows that she, and she alone, means life or death to me.

As Marut sees it, the crowned heads conduct war like a family squabble while their increasingly restless subjects bear the brunt of the effort. He attacks the war's senseless destruction by ironically demasking the ideal of military heroism. The inability of the "fatherland," at a time of national euphoria, to offer a meaningful life to the emotionally scarred officer may represent Marut's sharpest condemnation of European politics at the close of its imperialistic phase. Yet it is unmistakable that here, in Marut's most significant published work, a narrator speaks who has insight into those depths of the soul that the politician cannot and the pacifist may not wish to see. The elegiacal *Weltschmerz*, the *mal* of the preceding century, can still be heard here, in striking counterpoint to the shriller tones of social and political criticism. We will find the same in the works of B. Traven.

The Brickburner: Political Agitation

The contrast between a philosophical melancholy focused solely on the individual and moral indignation over the absurdities and brutalities of the war throws a strangely ambiguous light on the pacifist and socially critical journalism to which Marut applied himself in his radical magazine *The Brickburner*, the first issue of which appeared in September 1917. Our knowledge of his *Weltschmerz* might make his political activism seem more like an escape act, a counterpart to the nameless officer's act of "heroism" in *To the Honorable Miss S . . .*—daring on the surface, defeatist in reality. Understandably, the officer's existential crisis caused by a disappointment in love and his resulting death wish have been read as autobiography. And *The Brickburner* itself, for all its political activism, also gives expression to the drive to flee from civilization, if not into nothingness at least to the farthest corners of the world, to the "bushmen." Yet it would be simplistic to reduce the critical and revolutionary impetus of the magazine to the author's supposed *Weltschmerz*. The magazine's sense of political activism is too strong and pointed to allow such an interpretation (and Marut sustained his activism for four years, until the end of 1921). Further, Marut's intensive journalistic activity on behalf of peace and reform of prewar society led him to concrete political engagement. He was to take an active role in the Bavarian revolution of the spring of 1919—a philosophical commitment to which he essentially remained true to the end of his life.

As we pick up the biographical thread leading from Düsseldorf to Munich in late autumn 1915, it comes as no surprise that Ret Marut the journalist and writer, revolutionary and political fugitive is hardly better documented than Ret Marut the actor. *The Brickburner* remains the primary piece of documentary evidence even for factual details of Marut's life in the Munich years. Marut's literary writings during the period preceding the publication's first issue exhibit a fair amount of social criticism and political polemics and provide a glimpse of the author's concerns, but they are of no use for reconstructing details of his factual biography. The same is true of his sole nonliterary piece of journalism published before the first incendiary issue of *The Brickburner*—the essay "Indizien" ("Circumstantial Evidence"), which appeared in May 1916 in the magazine *März*, where Marut also published literary works at this time.

"Responsible for publication, editing, and content: Ret Marut, Munich"—this or a similar message appears in the editorial note at the end of each *Brickburner*, from its inauguration until Marut's disappearance after the collapse of the Bavarian revolution. According to this notice—and there is no reason to doubt it—Marut's magazine was basically a one-man operation, even if anonymous collaborators contributed an article from time to time. Götz Ohly was one such occasional collaborator. It is often assumed that Irene Mermet was involved, particularly before a secretary was hired in the summer of 1918, but her role cannot be defined with any accuracy. She may have limited her activities to assisting with editing, marketing, and the like. The distinction made in *The Brickburner* beginning in the summer of 1918 between the publisher ("the Brickburner") and editor ("Ret Marut")—if it amounts to something more than a flimsy fiction—would most likely point to Irene Mermet's participation of some sort. Perhaps her functions were best described with the designation "publisher." In regard to the authorship of the texts themselves, not a single piece has yet been ascribed to her.

The first issue, brick-shaped and brick red like all subsequent issues, bore the date September 1, 1917, while the war, which had provided so much thematic material for Marut's stories, was already drawing to a close. Before this backdrop, the name of the new magazine reflected the publisher's desire "to furnish with his publication building blocks for a better postwar Germany and for a better world in general." "I never wanted to work for the fall of Germany, but rather for the building of a new Germany from the one choking on its own falsehood," Marut wrote in January 1919. And the first essay of the first issue adopted the building metaphor in reference to the postwar era: "Don't Rebuild the Old—Build the New." This introductory slogan was, however, more upbeat than the general tone of the forty issues that came out in a decidedly irregular tempo. To construct a more humane social order, Marut wrote, one first had to do away with the old. Criticism set the tone—

criticism "of the way things are and of loathsome contemporaries," as the covers sometimes read. The magazine included criticism, polemics, and zestful forays not only against the political and social order but also against harmless parties such as publishers who might intend to send review copies, theater and cinema owners who might think of offering complimentary tickets, and even potential advertisers. A warning on the cover of the first issue was meant to scare off all such potential suitors before they might find their way to the magazine's humble headquarters on the fourth floor of Clemensstrasse 84. The cover of the fourth issue, in July 1918, set new standards for editorial insolence: "People should not attempt to pay a visit, there is never anyone here. We have no telephone," it read. Marut's independence, safeguarded against any conceivable interloper by this alienation tactic, came before all else. He was "of the opinion that a pencil I have bought is in principle worth more to me than a typewriter received as a gift." The articles themselves often adopted a similarly arrogant tone.

Karl Kraus was the only other notable German-language journalist of this century to keep his potential public at arm's length. *The Brickburner* does have something in common with Kraus's *Die Fackel* (*The Torch*), particularly its barbed criticism of newspapers and their deceptive use of language (not coincidentally, Marut occasionally mentioned Kraus in his magazine). *Die Fackel* was rightly seen by critics as a sort of model for *The Brickburner*; Franz Pfemfert, a contemporary of Marut's who published the expressionist journal *Die Aktion*, said as much early on. What is characteristic, however, about Marut's aggressive, expressionist tone is that his pathos-laden pronouncements, meant to herald and awaken ("I scream. I want to be nothing but: word!"), at times appear to be nothing more than a hymn to the individual self (exemplified by the egocentric conclusion "I would like nothing other than to become a true human being"). This attitude is also reminiscent of the Brickburner's pinings to emigrate to exotic climes.

Between the lines one can detect a similar conflict in Marut's style. His is the voice of the outsider who wishes to raise a cry for concerted action to overturn the status quo and reform society but who, through his expressionist outcries, also wishes as an individual to rid himself of the troubles of contemporary life altogether. The result is a curious amalgam of constructive engagement and cynical, egocentric bitterness—regardless of whether Marut's form of expression is a commentary or theater review, a diatribe or a bon mot, a political lead story or a critique of the day's events (or of their coverage in newspapers).

The output of this multifaceted man even included a quasi-scientific—and yet egocentric—essay entitled "Die Zerstörung unseres Weltsystems durch die Markurve" ("The Destruction of Our World Order by the Markurve"). ("Markurve" is a fanciful neologism, apparently formed from Marut + Kurve—"the Marut Curve.") Marut wrote this essay after the collapse of the Bavarian revolution (May 1919), when he was on the run from the authorities; in a postscript it is touted as an improvement on Einstein's theory of relativity. The piece is a theoretical treatise aimed at brushing aside all current mathematics, including mathematical cosmology, viewing its axioms as baseless and every bit as arbitrary as those of theology. There are no straight lines, Marut wrote, only a curve—to be precise a "Markurve," which he likened to a "very twisted spiral" in perpetual motion throughout the universe. Geometric points do not exist, nor do circles, spheres, angles, hyperbolas, and so on. In such a world, in which everything is in perpetual change, nothing can be calculated according to the laws of conventional physics. "By understanding the Markurve," we put aside "all conceptions and definitions which we have had until now about our world order as a whole as well as about its individual parts." Once we acknowledge the Markurve as the governing principle of the world, we can no longer believe in a center of the universe. Rather, every body—the sun, the moon, the earth, and above all the ego—becomes the midpoint. The "scientific" treatise ends in mystical egomania: "I stand in the center-point of the universe," unique, undying, indestructible, unending. "I created this world for myself, when I comprehended it. The world belongs to me, because I comprehend it." Even in a scientific piece Marut exhibits egocentric aggression.

Who would have read a magazine like this, a magazine that was, true to its word, "no magazine or newspaper in the conventional sense" but a publication "far removed" from any political party that set itself the task of safeguarding "the true understanding of culture as Goethe defined it"? In a letter of February 10, 1918, to the press attaché of the Bavarian Ministry of War, Marut stressed this aspect of his publication, calling his intended audience "the intellectuals": "We do not have a single subscriber from the working or lower-middle class; all our subscribers come from the ranks of professors, teachers, students, doctors, officers, artists, writers, independent scholars and industrialists."

How did the readers take Marut's editorial stance? Reaction to *The Brickburner* in the daily press and other contemporary publications was minimal. Letters to the editor arrived at Clemensstrasse from time to time, and Marut reprinted and answered them as if they were life buoys in a sea of disregard. The size of the readership, which certainly fluctuated significantly during the publication's short life span (1917–1921), can no longer be determined, but it cannot have been very significant. The magazine's occasional references to circulation size cannot be taken at face value. *The Brickburner*, according to figures Marut published, did have a worldwide circulation, in a manner of speaking (including a single subscriber in Mexico), but the circulation was most likely limited primarily to Munich and even there did not make a particularly lasting impression. Traven biographer Armin Richter estimates that the average number of copies printed was "relatively small," roughly a thousand. Difficulties with censorship and the underground status of the magazine after the war may have stood in the way of a wider distribution. In light of these problems Marut's journal surely ran at a loss and was no doubt kept afloat and financed in the first place through private funds, which Marut on several occasions in *The Brickburner* claimed to have at his disposal.

The Brickburner's failure to adhere to a regular publication schedule was no doubt due less to an unstable flow of income than to political constraints, though the cover at times included the claim that Marut published the magazine only when he had something to say. Some of the forty issues came out individually and some as double (or multiple) issues, with the number of pages varying unpredictably. Eight *Brickburner* issues (five publication dates) appeared during the war years, nine (three publication dates) during the Bavarian revolution until Marut's disappearance underground in May 1919, and the remaining twenty-three (five dates of publication) during the first phase of the Weimar Republic (early December 1919 to the end of December 1921).

This political backdrop furnished a good deal of the specific and concrete topics of the journal. Yet for all the talk of the real world and political reality, the general theme running through the issues is the more abstract proclamation of the true "human being" whom Marut saw emerging from the world catastrophe. This person may from time to time be defined extremely individualistically, without any "limiting" connection with class, party, nation, or church. Still, the word *Mensch* in *The Brickburner* does not on the whole have a purely solipsistic, egocentric connotation. The more dominant impression is that philanthropic ideas and traditional human rights ideas molded Marut's ideal of the human being as a member of an (admittedly vaguely defined) *community* of human beings. When Marut said that there was "no more precious commodity than the life of a human being," he had not only his own in mind but that of others as well. He envisioned a collective of individuals, of "selves," who have heightened their self-awareness. (Not surprisingly, from the point of view of this philosophy, Marut did not personally isolate himself from the postwar political situation but became actively involved in the Bavarian Revolution.) A typewritten flyer, *Der Selbe* (*The Self*), apparently authored by Marut, demonstrates the extent to which the individual and the community of "selves" are dependent on each other. *Der Selbe* ("published by the Brickburner for the community of selves, Issue 1, 1 May 1919") states: "In my refusal to cooperate I am the strongest of all earth dwellers." Yet, "My life is secure, as long as I value as sacred the life of all my fellow men." Egoism and altruism cannot exist without each other. In *The Brickburner* of January 30, 1919, in the appeal entitled "Die Welt-Revolution beginnt" ("The World Revolution Is Under Way"), Marut said, in what only seems to be a paradox:

> *I can belong to no party*, since I see my personal freedom limited in belonging to any party, since being bound to a party line keeps me from developing into what I view as the highest and most noble goal on earth: *to be a human being*! I wish nothing other than to be a human being, nothing but a human being. And since the "human being" is the greatest thing to me, I am indifferent to everything else which does not lead to this goal and will remain so.
>
> But this indifference ceases for me from the moment when danger threatens my path. And *only for my own sake* do I raise my voice. It is *my* concern, not yours. Your concern is of no importance to me today and will always continue to be of no importance. *The most noble, pure and true love of mankind is the love of oneself. I* want to be free! *I* hope to be happy! *I* want to appreciate all the beauties of this world! *I* want to be joyful! But my freedom is secured *only* when all other people around me are free. I can only be happy when all other people

> around me are happy. I can only be joyful when all the people I see and meet look at the world with joy-filled eyes. And *only* then can I eat my fill with pure enjoyment when I have the secure knowledge that other people, too, can eat their fill as I do. And for that reason it is a question of *my own contentment*, only of *my own self*, when I rebel against every danger which threatens my freedom and my happiness. . . .
>
> We want to be human beings and brothers!

Some critics associate Marut's anarchistic individualism with Max Stirner's philosophy, which enjoyed a renaissance of sorts after the turn of the century (Stirner's main work, *Der Einzige und sein Eigentum* [*The Individual and His Property*] had appeared in 1845). Some proponents stress that Marut/Traven broadened Stirner's extreme, isolationist individualism to include the idea of a community. Wolfgang Essbach has, however, corrected the view of Stirner that underlies this interpretation: Stirner did not in fact subscribe to an individualism that excluded every kind of *union* of self-aware individualists. Marut/Traven, Essbach notes, is thus more in conformity with Stirner than is usually assumed. But since we lack concrete evidence that Marut immersed himself in Stirner's philosophy—evidence such as extensive specific parallels between their works—this connection is not of particular interest to the biographer. In any case, anarchistic, individualistic ideas of all sorts were in the air toward the end of the kaiser's reign. Also, Marut/Traven was such an individual thinker that the question of specific influence becomes somewhat academic.

For Marut, the individual stood in opposition not to other human beings, against whom one would have to assert one's individuality, but rather to the state. A fundamental conviction that he hoped to "protect from perishing" with his magazine was, next to absolute truthfulness, "the idea that the human being is worth more than the state": "The most important thing is not the state, it is the individual human being." Marut's notion of anarchism emerged, however vaguely, from this opposition of the human being to the state and to every form of control by governmental or quasi-governmental authority. It is this anarchistic temperament that gave *The Brickburner* its shape and that would determine the physiognomy of Traven decades later.

While Marut's anarchistic philosophy generally aimed at freeing the self from all governmental or authoritarian control, it took on a particular sense of immediacy in the period of political upheaval at the end of the war and soon thereafter. His anarchistic program in *The Brickburner* thus combined philosophical generalities with commentaries on day-to-day political events. The manifesto entitled "Gegensatz" ("Contrast"), appearing in December 1921, shows a preponderance of the more abstract philosophical considerations. In the theoretical confrontation between the self and the government or state, the sovereign self triumphs in its philosophical invincibility; its power lies in the denial of itself in the face of the state:

> And if I do not recognize the government?!
>
> I need only to wish it, and it no longer exists. A government without the governed. Where is the government? I have none, since I do not respect it, since I do not recognize it.
>
> . . .
>
> Does a single one of your leaders have a goal other than to rule over you or to rule others with you?
>
> Let everyone be a leader!
>
> Let everyone be his own leader!
>
> . . .
>
> The government can murder. It can, if it wants to—and it will do it at the appointed hour—murder 100,000 people. It has power like that. But it does not have the power to compel me to work for it.
>
> . . .
>
> The government with all its monstrous means of power is a wisp of air, if I wish it. And if I wish it, that can also mean: if I do not wish it. In my not-wishing I am stronger than all the powers that wish!
>
> . . .
>
> I support myself on my wishing. And in my not-wishing I am the strongest and most powerful of all earth-dwellers.
>
> . . .
>
> Think! Reflect on yourselves, not on your programs! Let each one become a Self!
>
> . . .
>
> I want to live according to my own laws. I want to be my own king, whose sole subject I am at the same time. No government above me and none governed beside me.
>
> Do the same! Say: I wish it! Say: I do not wish it!
>
> I do not need you. Neither to lead nor to be led.
>
> . . .

Those who produce children remain in slavery. Slaves produce—children. Every child that you produce is a loop in your chain of servitude. Buy yourself a sofa for your living room and produce a child; both are the same, both lead to the same goal.

If you can stuff all your earthly possessions into a bag which reaches up to your hips, and if you can carry this bag on your shoulders, then the cannons will rust and the walls of the oppressor's castles will fall down at the sound of a shepherd's pipe.

. . .

I will not wait for the masses; for I am the masses.

I will not wait for the revolution; for I am the revolution.

Before there is a revolution, there must be a revolutionary!

Before there can be masses, there must be the individual!

Before there can be unity, there must be the unit, the Self!

The word must exist before there can be a fighting song and rallying cry.

Democracy is majority, majority is domination. The majority is the garment under which the nonperson hides the dagger. Majority is the brain cell of those who are unable to think. Majority is the scepter of the deceivers and scoundrels.

. . .

Be yourself, and you will always be at one with yourself!

. . .

Trust only in your own power!

. . .

I am invincible, when I do not wish what another wishes!

You are invincible when you do not do what another wishes!

All of you will be invincible when instead of the masses it is the one person, the individual, who becomes greater and stronger than the most powerful sovereign. The power of the most powerful sovereign collapses at the not-wishing of the weakest slave.

Shall we abolish private ownership of the means of production? No, you foolish chatterers!

Abolish private ownership of your very trousers!

Knowledge is power? No!

Action is power!

Knowledges makes one free? No!

Action makes one free!

This sort of extreme individualism could not ally itself with a particular party program and even in taking concrete political action could not dedicate itself to goals that might be identified with a party. Marut maintained that the Communist party at the time was already being overtaken by a potential successor further to the left and that he himself stood "so far to the left that my breath does not even touch that successor." The revolution in Germany and Bavaria, viewed from this extreme vantage point of the outsider, did not promise the realization of a party program, but rather no more and no less than the liberation of the individual, of one's own, highly personal self.

While Marut's language was in danger of dissipating into vague utopian musings in such instances, he did become more concrete when attacking what he saw as impeding the golden age of anarchistic individualism: war and its causes, that is, the capitalist state and the institutions supporting it, particularly the press and the church. Marut's commentary "Arme Mutter" ("Poor Mother"), more than any newspaper report, reveals the brutality of war that affects all aspects of life and that Marut brings up time and again, even after 1918:

> In a Munich paper of 27 July 1917 there is an obituary marked with the iron cross:
>
> Deeply shaken we report the sad news that my beloved son, our unforgettable brother, Herr . . . Vice Sergeant of the Reserves and fighter pilot, etc., awarded the . . . etc. fell on the morning of . . . in an air battle, after he had just *dispatched* his first enemy aircraft.
>
> The notice is signed by his mother.
>
> Poor mother! Losing a son has made you poor. But that you, as a woman and mother, are sending him off into eternity with this brutal "dispatched"—that has made you abjectly poor. You have become a thousand times poorer, poor mother, than the mother of the "dispatched" who is also weeping a mother's hot tears over her child.

The European nations' thirst for profit, according to Marut, was responsible for the First World War. This generally Marxist view is interesting for two reasons. It anticipates Traven's attribution of the Second World War to the capitalist states' desire to accumulate wealth. And it focuses on the politics of colonialism, which fill the pages of Marut's unpublished novel of Indochina, *The Torch of the Prince* (ca. 1914), and which would occupy the anti-imperialist Traven, whose criticism of "civilization" led him to support the struggle of the Mexican Indians. The First World War, with its "murders" and "tears," Marut wrote, was being fought over who would sell printed cotton fabric to the natives in Africa, Germany or England, and over who would sell razors to the Indians on the Amazon, Remscheidt or Sheffield. Capitalism alone was the culprit. To combat it, Marut insisted, one must stand up "in the name of humanity!" In his radical pacifism Marut even cited Goethe—a questionable sponsor of a call to revolutionary action. But such a call was what Marut's political agitation led up to. Paradoxically, his revolutionary voice was most audible *after* the war, when he protested against a new state being formed—perhaps by the Social Democrats turned bourgeois—which, like its predecessor, in the name of peace and order would once again threaten the freedom of the individual. Instead, the new society should make a more meaningful life possible, Marut asserted, a "livelier, a richer, a stronger life," in which work formed the centerpiece.

The church and the press impeded such a development, and Marut relentlessly condemned them as the mainstays of the war and the status quo. They marched in lockstep to the nationalistic slogans and—here Marut's tone was most strident—as organs of state repression they must be fully uprooted, along with the economic structures and industry in their current form.

The revolution, which had broken out in November 1918 in various parts of the Reich, promised new, freer, less authoritarian forms of these and other institutions and hence of society in general. Marut the anarchist, as both political activist and journalist, welcomed the end of the state—not only of the state as he knew it until then but also of the state absolutely; at the same time he hailed the liberation of the individual. This tone dominates *The Brickburner* dated December 3, 1919. "The state convulses in its death throes. . . . But under the scabs and the tears I can already see the salvation of the individual. Be individual human beings, be only human beings!" Marut wrote. "Of the three—state, government, and I—I am the strongest. Take note of that!" The threatening tone in this provocative aphorism was clearly aimed at the reign of terror that quelled the revolution in Bavaria. Marut himself fell victim to the reactionary backlash. He squared his accounts against the opponents of the revolution most notably in *The Brickburner* of March 20, 1920.

The magazine itself was naturally severely affected by the revolutionary events in Munich. After the suppression of the revolution and Marut's disappearance underground on May 1, 1919, *The Brickburner* appeared "in illegal form," as stated on the cover of the December 3, 1919, issue: "Copies of the publication will be sent to subscribers from any of a number of cities both here and abroad; the postmark never reveals the actual place of publication." Place names listed in the masthead ("Neustadt," "Vienna-Alsergrund") are considered red herrings. Berlin and, in the final stages, Cologne (1921) have been plausibly conjectured as places of publication. But not a clue exists regarding the individual collaborators involved in the operation of the "itinerant press." Marut himself had been on the run since early May 1919, with a warrant out for his arrest. Meanwhile, his opponents were in power throughout Germany.

Revolution in Bavaria

On November 7, 1918, a republic was proclaimed in Munich, as elsewhere in Germany in the final days of the war. The Wittelsbach king was deposed; the royal family fled under cover of night. Kurt Eisner, the Berlin writer and a leader of Germany's Independent Social Democrats, was named prime minister. He based his government on the Workers', Soldiers', and Farmers' Councils that had formed in Bavaria. "The highest authority," announced the red poster signed by Eisner and displayed throughout Bavaria, "is the [central] council of workers, soldiers, and farmers elected by the people, which is instituted provisionally until a permanent representative body is established. The council has legislative power." Eisner experienced an immediate setback when his party received only 2.5 percent of the vote in the Bavarian state elections of January 12, 1919. En route to the state assembly on February 21, where he was to bow to public opinion and announce his resignation, Eisner was assassinated. The delegates dispersed without having taken any action; no new government was formed, and unrest broke out immediately. It was not until March 18 that the state assembly reconvened; it elected the coalition government of the Social Democrat Johannes Hoffmann, who had served as minister of culture in the Eisner cabinet.

Throughout these turbulent months, the local councils and their supervisory authority, the Central Council, heatedly debated whether to proclaim a Republic of Councils to oust the Hoffmann government. The political journalist Erich Mühsam, leftist politicians Gustav Landauer, Max Levien, and Eugen Leviné, and expressionist writer Ernst Toller participated in these debates, as did Ret Marut, one can assume. Their efforts did not bear fruit until April 7, when a Republic of Councils was proclaimed in Bavaria. The Hoffmann government fled to Bamberg. The Provisional Revolutionary Central Council of the Workers', Soldiers', and Farmers' Councils assumed authority, chaired first by Ernst Niekisch and then by Ernst Toller. "People's delegates" took charge of the government departments. But scarcely had the Republic of Councils enacted its first measures—appointment of revolutionary tribunals, creation of the Red Army, socialization of the press, confiscation of arms, reform of higher education, rationing of living space, occupation and regulation of the banks—when units of the Republican Security Troops, supported by the Hoffmann government in Bamberg, staged a putsch on April 13 against the Republic of Councils.

Members of the Central Council were arrested. The result, however, was not a restoration of the status quo but the formation of a second Republic of Councils, in which the Communists, absent from the first Republic, took the helm. Leviné chaired a fifteen-member action committee that called a general strike as a first step in establishing the supremacy of the proletariat. Some members of the earlier, anarchistic Republic of Councils accepted the new government and even offered their cooperation. Meanwhile the Hoffmann government, with support from Berlin, staged an attack. For days the Red Army clashed in and around Munich with White Guard forces loyal to Hoffmann, supported by Free Corps units (former members of the kaiser's army). On May 1 the second Republic of Councils collapsed. The Hoffmann government returned to Munich. Leaders of the revolution and thousands of their supporters stood trial; death sentences were pronounced as late as September 1919.

Marut's role in these political developments can be reconstructed only approximately, even in light of recent archival research and examination of pertinent newspapers. Some information can be gleaned from *The Brickburner* itself. Marut naturally saw the proclamation of the Republic in Bavaria as a milestone on the path toward the fulfillment of the goals that his magazine pursued. Referring specifically to combating the press, he wrote in the January 15, 1919, issue: "Since the day the revolution broke out, I stand in this battle no longer so hopelessly alone as I did before November

7." Demonstrating his fidelity to his cause, he printed in the magazine's first postwar issue (January 15, 1919) all the texts that the censors had struck during the war.

The next issue, dated January 30, 1919, includes the speech "The World Revolution Is Under Way," which had circulated as a flyer throughout Germany since mid-December 1918. It has not been documented that Marut actually delivered this text as a speech. But he did speak at the two *Brickburner*-sponsored lecture evenings in Munich that took place in this period. The first, on December 14, 1918, caused considerable commotion, duly noted in the press; *The Brickburner* itself reported on the event as well. This meeting included a reading of the essays suppressed by the military censors—ostensibly read by someone other than Marut, since "I had more important things to do in North Germany"—a bluff worthy of a Traven-to-be. According to a report in the *Münchner Neueste Nachrichten*, reprinted in *The Brickburner*'s report on the event, the auditorium at the Steinicke art gallery in Munich's Schwabing section was darkened, "and even the speaker stood in the dark; it was only on his manuscript that a dim light fell." The audience protested, but the speaker continued reading, until a "storm of indignation" rose in response to his remark that during the war it had taken more courage to publish a magazine than to lie in the trenches. Singing "Deutschland, Deutschland über alles," the audience left the auditorium. *The Brickburner* described the ensuing tumult with a certain glee: "They pounded their chairs on the floor, they sang and made noise." Marut justified the darkness with an artistic parallel: Just as in a concert it is the music and not the musician that is important, so too in a lecture what matters is the word and not the speaker—a concrete variant of his anarchistic anonymity complex or his effort to do away with the principle of authority. How this accords with the constant emphasis on the cherished "I" is not exactly clear. But it seems to tie in well with Marut's description of the reaction to the second *Brickburner* evening, which took place on December 28: It "went by without incident." That is how he wanted it, he said; whoever expected another free-for-all was *supposed* to be disappointed.

At the first *Brickburner* evening and in the speech "The World Revolution Is Under Way," Marut had again unleashed his scorn of the press, which in his view bowed to authority and was controlled by business interests, holding the public in intellectual servitude.

Continuing the campaign that he had inaugurated in the last phase of the kaiser's reign, he focused his political pronouncements during the post-dynastic Bavarian governments primarily on the socialization of the press (which had been a main point of republican reform from the establishment of the Eisner government to the collapse of the second Republic of Councils). Marut first chose *The Brickburner* as his forum. "I demand the freedom of the press!" he announced on the cover of the issue dated January 30, 1919, when he apparently did not yet have any role in the executive branch of the Republic. In that issue he demanded specifically that the daily newspapers do away with advertising, through which the power groups controlling the economy manipulated freedom of expression and the free flow of information. The cover of the next issue, of March 10, 1919, followed suit with "Meine Forderung" ("My Demand"), which also circulated as a flyer. To make a clean sweep of "journalism which operates in the service of capitalism," it had become necessary, he said, to socialize the press, which meant to expropriate it and turn it over to the "revolutionary proletariat" as a legitimate weapon in its struggle for freedom. When the republican experiment failed in Bavaria as it had elsewhere in Germany, the Brickburner sang a jeremiad to the failure of his favorite cause; the piece, printed on the back cover of the December 3, 1919, issue is simply titled "Menschen!" but translates the expressionistic "O Mensch" pathos into concrete, timely terms:

Human Beings!

> The ennoblement of humankind, the creation of true culture, begins with the elimination and the utter annihilation of the press. In this every application of violence, every act of sabotage and destruction is justified, provided no drop of human blood is shed. Man's cultural needs dictate that he destroy bedbugs, newspapers, and similar vermin, violently if necessary. This need has long been acknowledged and is being demonstrated again and again today. Protests, resolutions, programs for socialization and similar purely intellectual weapons are as fruitless in combating the press as they are in combating lice and bedbugs. Every revolution which does not accomplish this act (removal of the press) at the very outset fails to achieve its goal.

In the meantime, however, Marut had gained access to a forum less "private" than *The Brickburner* for propagating his thoughts on the socialization of the press. And with that forum he must have made a greater impact, if only because by that time he could speak as a member of the post-dynastic government.

The Brickburner itself gives only general and surely incomplete information about Marut's activities during the Bavarian Revolution. In the issue dated December 3, 1919, under the cynical heading "In the Freest State in the World," Marut described the events of May 1, 1919: his arrest, interrogation, and the death sentence averted in the last minute. His alleged high treason, he wrote there, consisted of his membership in the "Preparatory Commission for Forming a Revolutionary Tribunal" and the "Propaganda Committee" of the Republic of Councils. These memberships are confirmed by the minutes of the Central Council meeting of April 8, 1919, by the arrest warrant from the Munich public prosecutor's office, and by the "most-wanted list" (for "high treason") of the *Bayerisches Polizeiblatt* (*Bavarian Police Record*) of June 23, 1919. Further, in the Central Committee meeting on April 17, 1919, Marut was appointed to a commission that was to apply itself to "extremely intensive education in the barracks." The importance Marut ascribed to these positions is clear from his own description in *The Brickburner* (speaking of himself in the third person):

> I will anticipate my later work and state now: to this hour there has not been anywhere on earth a court in which all judgments were delivered with such a deep, humane understanding of every human act as was the case with this Revolutionary Tribunal, which was labeled a court of terror by the Bavarian government and the press-pimps. That this "court of terror" had such a high regard for the office of judges is owed not least to M, who—and I am giving this information to the public prosecutor's office, since it was unaware of it until now—was unanimously elected chairman and spokesman by the Preparatory Commission. The Provisional Revolutionary Central Committee of the Republic of Councils of Bavaria sent M unanimously to this commission. In the meetings of workers' councils, which exercised the highest authority in the Bavarian Republic of Councils, M was unanimously—to be specific, on the recommendation of a printer who worked for a bourgeois newspaper—elected as a member of the Propaganda Committee. M states even today and will always say that this election by revolutionary workers' councils represented for him the highest honor and highest recognition of his work which he had received

> from the November masquerade to the present. In all his activities—he held no offices—which the revolutionary workers had entrusted to him, he supported those ideas which can be read in *The Brickburner*.

Armin Richter's research at the Bavarian State Archives and his examination of Munich daily newspapers allow us to fill in the details of Marut's account. While Eisner was still alive, Marut apparently had no official government functions. On February 24, 1919, during the interregnum following Eisner's assassination, Marut was appointed to the Press Department of the Central Council, where he served as censor of the *München-Augsburger Abendzeitung*, until censorship of bourgeois papers was lifted on March 15. He also published articles in this paper himself, most notably, on March 5, 1919, a polemic justifying the Central Council's control of the press—an ironic role for the man who previously could not do enough to stir up anger over the kaiser's censorship. During this period Marut did his part to support socialization of the press not only through his flyer "My Demand" but also with publicly posted political manifestos and an open letter to Prime Minister Hoffmann. Further, as speaker of the Press Department, he appeared at meetings where socialization of the press was debated. When the Hoffmann government established the Commission for the Socialization of the Press on March 30, 1919, to coordinate all efforts of this nature, Marut was immediately named a member by virtue of his position in the Press Department. With the establishment of the first Republic of Councils on April 7 and the reintroduction of censorship for the bourgeois papers, his position in the Press Department was further solidified: On the same day he was named head of the department and thus chief censor for all bourgeois newspapers in Bavaria. Marut must have viewed this as the height of his activist career. "To work toward the realization of the Council system and the Republic of Councils must be the task of today's revolutionary," he wrote in late 1919 in *The Brickburner*.

The Commission for the Socialization of the Press survived under the Republic of Councils; on the Republic's second day, the commission debated, among a number of press socialization projects, Ret Marut's plan for expropriating the press and turning it over to government control. The public could see his "Sozialisierungsplan für die Presse" ("Plan for the Socialization of the Press") in the *Münchner Neueste Nachrichten* of April 10, 1919, where Marut also published a long piece called "Presse-Freiheit oder Befreiung der Presse" ("Freedom of the Press, or Liberation of the Press"). An article that appeared in *Bayerischer Kurier* (May 3–4, 1919) sheds some light on his additional activities as head of the Press Department of the Central Council: Marut had demanded that an anticlerical essay of his be printed in the Catholic newspaper *Neues Münchner Tagblatt*, but he met with no success. Also not published was a piece (which survives in typescript) on the socialization of the press (entitled, like its published counterpart, "Freedom of the Press, or Liberation of the Press") which the author had hoped to see in the Munich dailies in early March 1919.

Such setbacks may indicate that the position of Marut and his circle was by no means as secure as one might conclude from the self-assured proclamations printed in the press and posted on the kiosks. In any event, the revolutionary who in the spring of 1919 must have thought that his moment had come enjoyed the limelight only briefly. On May 1 it was all over.

Marut described his own involvement in the events of that day in his ironic-polemical article in *The Brickburner* entitled "In the Freest State in the World," published more than half a year after the fiasco of the revolution, when his friends and comrades-in-arms were being imprisoned with the officially sanctioned brutality of the "royal Wittelsbach Social Democrats" and "legally murdered" after a short trial. Marut condemned this brutality more than once in *The Brickburner*, not least in that report of his own arrest and escape. He dedicated the issue of March 20, 1920, to the "memory of Dr. Lewiné [*sic*] who was officially murdered, the memory of Gustav Landauer who was quasi-officially murdered—the former was known to me as a revolutionary of unimpeachable integrity and touching selflessness; the latter became my close friend when I worked with him during the painful and difficult birth of the new era and new morality. . . . Their names are indelibly engraved in the hearts of the revolutionary proletariat." Marut himself, "wanted by the Bavarian government for high treason," escaped their fate, while in East Prussia, for example, which was controlled by the Social Democrats, "a friend of the Brickburner got two years in prison for reprinting as a special edition the first essay of issue 16–17 of *The Brickburner* with the editor's permission and circulating it in several hundred copies." Marut's survival was a matter of chance and, one might say, of the strategy of the born outsider. For he could well imagine what punishment fit his "crime"—his activities in the Republic of Councils, which had become notorious through the official police search for him: fifteen years in jail or execution, as he noted in December 1919, "if one could prove dishonorable motives, which the hanging judges of Bavaria would do without batting an eye, as even the most stubborn reactionary could see from the trials."

According to Marut's own description in *The Brickburner*, the final day of the Republic of Councils, May 1, 1919, passed as follows:

> As M sat in the Maria Theresia café on Augustenstrasse, hoping to meet some of those who had been at the meeting, the trucks of the White Guards had already begun to rush through the streets to free Munich from the red terror. The White Guards wasted no time with high-blown speeches, but recklessly fired their machine guns at the throngs in their Sunday suits filling the streets. Moments later seven innocent citizens were rolling in their own blood on the Augustenstrasse; two of them died in the middle of the street. A few steps in front of the café lay a well-dressed man severely wounded. While the machine-gun fire of the White Guards raged on, M, along with a few people ready to be of assistance, carried the unconscious victim into the café. Only after long examination, a doctor who happened to be in the café was able to locate the wound; the aorta of the left thigh was very seriously injured. An emergency bandage was applied, and an ambulance which was picking up the wounded and dead from the street took the wounded man from the café. The café was closed and M left. He had run no more than a few hundred yards—the streets were still under the fire of the White Guards—when a truck sped to the scene, filled with some sixty infantry rifles and muskets; on it were at least ten shop assistants and students with white armbands and handkerchiefs tied about their arms. The moment they spotted M and recognized him, they ordered the truck to stop. Five men with rifles slung around their shoulders, with a revolver in each hand and four to six hand grenades on their belts, fell upon M, pointing their pistols at him and screaming: "Hands up!" M asked what the gentlemen wanted from him. They said he was a member of the Central Committee, the most dangerous agitator of the Republic of Councils, annihilator of the middle class and destroyer of the press; they therefore had to take him along and if he did not admit that he bore the main responsibility

for the bloodbath which was now going on, they would have to do away with him on the spot. Each of the bloodthirsty buffoons searched M for weapons. The editor of *The Brickburner* was searched for weapons! One can also look for truffles on bare brick, of course, if one has nothing better to do. They found an ordinary house key on his person, which, to the amazement of the imbeciles, could not be used as a rifle. As M now asked where these noble liberators and restorers of order had their warrant for his arrest, the other fellows, who had remained in the truck, pointed their pistols at M as well. Now M requested that the brave liberators allow him to go to his house first, to put his most pressing matters in order before his arrest and possible death. They searched him once again for weapons and machine guns and threw him violently onto the pile of rifles in the truck. In the meantime a number of pedestrians had gathered to watch the incident. The White Guards threw their weight around and began to vilify M loudly, saying that he was principally responsible for the blood which had been and was yet to be shed and that he now was going to get his due. This baiting had no impact on the crowd at all; one of those present simply cried out: "That's M." "So that's M?" the bystanders retorted. Since the public's declaration of neutrality kept them from standing him up on the spot before a firing squad in the proper way, the truck raced away—M faced ten pistols and rifles aimed at him—amid the shouts of the noble saviors and liberators of the middle class. Wherever they passed people on the street, the stout-hearted soldiers roared: "We've really got one now, the most dangerous of all!" Although the good liberators were liberators and as such had at least a vague idea of pride and freedom, they nonetheless needed to get official approval. For as they passed by an upper-class home, they saw a man standing at one of the upper windows. In spite of M being so dangerous and the possibility that M might escape, they ordered the truck to stop, sat up straight in the truck, whoever could stand at attention stood stiffly erect, and then they pulled off their caps and roared deafeningly: "Long live the general! Hurrah, Hurrah, Hurrah!" They seemed to have forgotten their necessary subordination in the midst of the joy and comfort of being slaves again for just a minute and being allowed to offer an ovation to an oppressor; for after the stiffly executed hurrah they shouted up to him: "General, now we've got one, the most dangerous of all." The general, whose calm presence in his apartment provided sufficient evidence of the Bolshevist terror, sent down his benevolent greeting. Highly satisfied, as if each of them had been promoted to the rank of a Prussian corporal, the valiant fighters for Munich's freedom sped off with their valuable booty.

They stopped in front of the Ministry of War. Under heavy cover M was unloaded, again searched for weapons, and then led through a 100-meter lane of weapon-laden war profiteers, coddled sons of the bourgeoisie, elegant pimps and members of the hodgepodge which calls itself the middle class and respectable officialdom, all of whom now wanted to be part of a revolution, now that there was no danger, now that the infamous army troops had already encamped in front of the Residence and had already begun to occupy the official buildings. M was put into one of the back rooms of the Ministry of War. Some legal secretary or the like was charged with watching the room. "Do you have weapons, too?" the guard was asked by the heroes. "Here, have a look!" he responded and produced a Browning from each of his pants pockets, showed one to the prisoner, showed him that it was loaded, holding it right under his nose, while he cocked the gun. "I only wish he would try to escape," said the man, while the captors looked at M as if he were a fatted calf whom they could scarcely wait to slaughter.

Now the interrogation began. First the gentlemen argued among themselves who could best conduct the interrogation. And once the interrogation was under way, each would interrupt the other: "Oh, you really can't interrogate, let me have a go." And so it went for quite a while, until finally they had all interrogated M pell-mell. The interrogation consisted of their accusing M of approximately twenty serious crimes, high treason, inciting soldiers against officers, offending the socialist authorities governing by virtue of their majority, using violence against the legitimate Hoffmann government, and many other crimes for which, according to the desire of the Social Democrat Hoffmann, the death penalty was immediately to be administered. M stated that he had nothing to say here and that he could not recognize these gentlemen as judges after they had simply dragged him by force from the street, a harmless pedestrian. As they saw that they could extract nothing from M, one of the gentlemen suddenly cried out: "Confess of your own accord, or we'll summon the witnesses, and then beware, that will be the end of the matter." Sure enough, witnesses arrived who reported everything as desired. These witnesses, who were always available, particularly if they could witness how a worker was stood up against a garden fence and shot, also played an important role in the trials of the infamous courts of Bavaria, which will one day be recognized as a more fitting symbol for the bestiality, brutality, hypocrisy and degradation of the German middle class and the deceit of German Social Democracy than the War and the denunciation of the November Revolution [1918]. Defense witnesses, whom M named and whom he requested to call, were as little recognized here as by the courts of terror.

After the gentlemen had failed to achieve anything, they left to set out on new adventures. M was left under the strict watch of the man with the Browning. The toughs came back a half hour later. As M, in spite of their repeated attempts, still had nothing to say, they stated they would still make him confess. M was now—two heavily armed men at his sides and two behind him—again dragged through the rows of onlookers outside and brought to the Residence. The picture had now fully changed on the street. Blue-and-white banners flew from the windows. On the public buildings, where the Socialist banners had flown, long since betrayed and soiled by the Social Democrats, black-white-and-red flags now waved. Although the thugs of Mr. Hoffmann, whose feeding trough was beginning to be refilled, called to the rows of bystanders at the Ministry of War and in the Residence that they were bringing a Spartacist prisoner, M was not beaten or derided by any of the heavies. In other parts of the city things were getting much more bestial by this time. At the Residence, M was handed over to a trooper of the infamous army, while the captors and witnesses asked for permission to stay with M so that he would not escape and so that they could be on hand when M was called before the court-martial. A half hour later the order was given that M be brought to the police presidium, where a court-martial was in session. When M was to be taken away, he and his handlers were not allowed out of the ground-floor door, since in the meantime the countercommand had been received that he was to be brought before the court-martial in the Residence immediately. M was again taken back, this time into the anteroom of a great hall where the court-martial was in session. The court-martial in the land of his own compatriots consisted of a dashing lieutenant. This lieutenant dealt with each case in some three minutes: He decided, on the basis of the eyewitness accounts of informers, whether the prisoner was to be shot by firing squad on the spot or whether he was to be set free. If any doubt remained, the prisoner was shot, since it was safer that way. There was not enough time to call defense witnesses or even to call people who could confirm that the prisoner was not a Spartacist or even a leader. The room in which M now found himself was increasingly filled with arrested workers, Red Guards, sailors, girls and boys. M saw among other defendants a sixteen-year-old boy accused of having attacked a trooper of the infamous army and of having spread Spartacist propaganda. From the great hall where the lieutenant decided about the life and death of the prisoners between puffs on a cigarette, workers and sailors with deathly pale faces were continually escorted out. Their eyes, sad and horrified, announced the death sentence to all those gathered. Whether the lieutenant, who was sitting in judgment here over the Spartacists and the supporters of the Republic of Councils who had been informed on, had been appointed by the Hoffmann government or whether he had assumed it of his own will can probably no longer be determined at this point. Thus passed an hour of tormented waiting. M asked his guard whether he might write a note to his friends so that they might know where he was. That was denied. At that point the man who was in line to be turned over to the lieutenant just before M was called up and ushered in. The mercenaries grabbed the man too roughly and a commotion ensued as he resisted—Marut took the chance to escape. Two soldiers apparently felt a spark of humanity for a brief moment, as they saw how the most precious thing that a man possesses, his life, was being mistreated. They were not uninvolved in his escape. Thanks are due them for saving the life of a fellow human being.

The "Traitor" Goes Underground

"Since that hour in which Marut succeeded in escaping, he has been on the run," the account in *The Brickburner* continued. On the run—where and how? We cannot reconstruct the whole story in fine detail. Marut's disappearance was, in all likelihood, not quite as dramatic as *The Brickburner* portrayed it. In any event, Marut had enough time to leave a letter behind for his secretary, Marta Haecker, typed single-spaced and covering an entire page, in which he prescribed precisely how she was to keep the editorial office in operation: She was not to leave checkbooks lying open; she should buy ink, glue, and so on "if the need arises"; if something was confiscated in a search, she must demand a receipt; doors or cabinets that might be broken should be repaired immediately; "always lock the door behind you—don't just slam it shut, lock it"; working hours and breaks for the secretary and an additional assistant were set; Fräulein Haecker might use the table at the window, but when leaving she should draw the curtain; she was to follow precise directions when mail arrived; and, finally, she was to destroy "this letter." For its part, *The Brickburner* reported on the early days on the run:

> M, as long as he still possessed even the least bit of freedom over his actions, immediately after his liberation carried the concept of the Republic of Councils and the idea of the Council system into the Bavarian countryside. In some sixty cities, villages, and towns in Bavaria he spoke to middle-class people, farmers, and workers. He chose a path other than the one currently in favor, a path that brings more success; he used the sole form of agitation which can bear valuable fruit, a form which is ancient and which Christ also applied: speaking from man to man, speaking to the smallest gatherings of people. His audience seldom consisted of more than twelve people. But no middle-class person, no worker, no farmer went away from these intimate conversations without recognizing democracy for the great lie that it is. These conversations were completely informal and everyone who attended could ask as much as he wished about what had been said. It was not at all the intention of the speaker that every listener should go from the spot as an enthusiastic advocate of the Republic of Councils. People who become enthusiastic so easily, who are so quickly convinced, are but rarely the salt with which one seasons. Often M traveled three days in a row to the same place to fulfill his task. He was never turned in by a member of the middle class or a farmer, although those who heard him could scarcely have had any doubts that it was M.

The *Brickburner* press, as Marut put it in "In the Freest State in the World," was meanwhile "as good as wiped out by the henchmen of the Noske-Hoffmann-Epp-Möhl democratic dictatorship." What was left of it was "put into five rooms far away from each other." On the cover of the January 6, 1920, issue Marut further asserted that the Social Democratic government withheld his food stamps and that "in spite of his protest, which was submitted immediately to the Munich housing authority," he was "robbed" of his apartment and the *Brickburner* offices. This protest would hardly have been lodged by Marut personally; after May 1 he would have done anything to avoid his pursuers' traps; the former superintendent of the apartment house at Clemensstrasse 84, where Marut lived and worked, recalled that at the time the building was watched for weeks by the police. Nonetheless Marut may have remained in Munich (or Bavaria) until as late as January 1920. For on the cover of the January 6 issue "the publisher" stated that Marut ("M") and "I" would leave Munich and Bavaria "probably" very shortly. But perhaps that was only a bluff aimed at the Bavarian police. Concerning what happened in the publishing offices, Marta Haecker wrote on June 14, 1967, to Traven: "I . . . continued to operate the *Brickburner* press for some time after your escape, until I had to give up your apartment, the contents of which I was later able to forward to you through an intermediary."

Exactly how that scenario played itself out is unclear. In fact, the *Brickburner* press does seem to have continued its existence in Munich for a period after May 1, 1919. This we may conclude from the lead article, "Die neue Freiheit" ("The New Freedom"), in *The Brickburner* of December 3, 1919, which stated that a partial manuscript for that issue fell into the hands of the police of the Social Democratic Hoffmann regime as a result of the activities of an informer, a one-time publisher of Catholic prayer books, and was confiscated for "stirring up class hatred." The woman at whose house the manuscript was found—although, *The Brickburner* notes, she had no idea of its contents and further "had no political interests," dedicating herself entirely to her "belletristic work and her scientific studies"—was arrested and spent two weeks in custody. Items seized in a search of the woman's apartment included an issue of *The Brickburner*, twelve issues of the *München-Augsburger Abendzeitung*, but also items not necessarily connected with Marut: other Munich newspapers, a book of mathematical formulas, shorthand manuals, and two book manuscripts in English.

Marut's way stations after fleeing from Bavaria and the individual details of his escape route cannot today be determined with any precision. Vienna, Berlin, and Cologne are commonly cited, but it is not possible to reconstruct with certainty just where he was, and when, between 1919–1920 and 1923.

Beginning with the December 3, 1919, issue of *The Brickburner*, the masthead lists Vienna as the place of printing—which may suggest that Marut spent time there; but since the Viennese printing firm given in the masthead could not be verified by an earlier researcher, this may be another red herring, as suspect as Marut's claim that he stayed in Bavaria until the winter of 1919–1920. The Austro-Hungarian currency preserved in the Traven estate, an undated Vienna trolley ticket, as well as a membership card issued in the name W. Schneider for the Vienna "Soup Kitchen 53" do not in themselves prove conclusively that Marut stayed in Vienna after the Munich debacle. Yet it was probably the case. Traven, late in his life, told the Austrian journalist Lampl that he slept under the stars in Vienna as a young man; there is no reason to doubt this assertion. But that is all the information we have—in particular we do not know whether the stay in Vienna was before or after the revolution in Bavaria. The same is true of the reminiscence of Gabriel Figueroa, Jr., Traven's godson, that Traven told him of a steamship voyage on the Danube, complete with many topographical details.

The references to a stay in Berlin are more compelling, although dates and significant details are lacking here as well. Götz Ohly, who worked as Marut's occasional *Brickburner* collaborator in Munich, wrote in 1948 in a letter published in *Die Welt*: "[Marut] fled to Cologne, traveling for weeks on foot, and from there he went to Berlin. . . . He told me and my wife everything that had happened. In the end, he asked me to get him a good passport. Without hesitation I gave him my own, sensing that I would not see my friend for many years to come." The passport was "stolen in Belgium" from Marut, Ohly added on February 25, 1949, in the *Münchener Stadtanzeiger*. Gerd Heidemann related a further detail about Marut's life on the run: Erich Wollenberg, Marut's comrade-in-arms from Munich days, who similarly fled to Berlin about 1920, told Heidemann that Marut and Irene Mermet found shelter in a Berlin attic; Mermet, the story went, took old scraps of cloth and made dolls, which she and Marut sold in the evenings on the Kurfürstendamm (this story is also included in Rosa Elena Luján's "Remembering Traven"). A less colorful but perhaps more significant detail is that while in Berlin Marut may have met the anarchist Rudolf Rocker. Rocker lived in Berlin in the early 1920s and had particularly good connections with Spanish and Latin American anarchist circles; at the International Congress of National Syndicalist Organizations held in Berlin (December 25, 1922–January 3, 1923) he represented the Mexican Confederación General de Trabajadores; it is not inconceivable that it was Rocker who cleared the way for Marut's passage to Mexico.

Marut and Irene Mermet most likely spent the last period of their underground existence, or perhaps most of it, in continental Europe, in or near Cologne. Yet some items in the Traven estate point to a certain period of wandering, possibly before the stay in Cologne. Enticing potential clues are the travel and hiking guides in Traven's library (from 1914–1921). These volumes cover the Mosel and Saar areas, including a part of Luxembourg, the Eifel region and the Belgian Ardennes, the Rhön area, Rothenburg on the Tauber, the Spessart, the Hunsrück, and the mid-Rhineland region. Other documents in the Traven estate point to other regions: a 50-pfennig voucher from the town of Rüstringen in northern Germany, which according to the imprint could be redeemed two years "after the end of the war"; an undated ticket for the Amsterdam Gemeente tram; a Danish 1-krone bill (printed in 1921); a 50-pfennig voucher dated 1921 from the Oldenburg Chamber of Commerce; a voucher (75-pfennig, "valid until 31 July 1921") from Neustadt/Holstein (perhaps the Neustadt that appears in the masthead of *The Brickburner* from December 3, 1919, on: "emergency representative Arthur Terlehn in Neustadt"); a voucher of the town of Limburg printed on November 1, 1918; and, finally, Luxembourg currency printed in 1918.

Such documents, which Traven did not collect or preserve systematically but which were found after his death among his papers and other possessions, "prove" nothing specific but have a certain power of suggestion. The same is true of a curious passage in the *BT News* in 1951. Under the heading "Is Traven a German?" (naturally answered in the negative), the author noted, with a certain strained delight in the absurd, that the biographers hot on his trail unmasked Traven as an actor from Düsseldorf, yet also as the "revolutionary writer from Munich," and further as a "comrade-in-arms in the uprising in central Germany under Hoelzl [*sic*]" (a reference to Max Hoelz). To date no biographer has turned up anything on the third identification. But if one believes that Traven sometimes felt the urge to reveal the truth as a method of camouflage, on the theory that nothing is as incredible as the truth, and since he followed this strategy here in his references to Düsseldorf and Munich, perhaps he has tipped his hand in referring to Hoelz. According to

Wilhelm Kosch's *Biographisches Staatshandbuch*, Max Hoelz allied himself with the Communists after the First World War and organized "during the Kapp putsch of 1920 the uprising in the Vogtland which led to excesses, . . . fled to Czechoslovakia [where Traven had fled as well, according to his widow], and, having returned from there in 1921, led a new revolt in the industrial region of Saxony." While on the run he, too, was in Vienna and Berlin in the early 1920s, before he was sentenced to life in prison. Was Ret Marut one of his "comrades-in-arms"? A further suggestive detail: Marut's friend the painter Franz Wilhelm Seiwert, with whom he had contact before and during his flight, painted a portrait of Max Hoelz in 1921.

Finally, many of the items in the Traven estate point to Cologne—documents that, like those previously mentioned, have survived over the decades by chance: vouchers from the city of Cologne (printed 1918, 1920, and 1921); the book *Köln am Rhein: Ein Wegweiser und Andenken* (*Cologne on the Rhine: A Guide and Memento*) by Georg Hölscher (1919); tickets for the Cologne racetrack; two train tickets from Cologne to Nideggen dated February 25, 1920; a ticket for the Deutsches Theater in Cologne; a ticket for a Cologne movie theater dated May 22, 1922; and a general delivery card issued in Cologne on November 7, 1921.

About the period in Cologne we are somewhat better informed than about the other way stations in Marut's odyssey.

Why Cologne? The area west of the Rhine near Cologne, then occupied by the British, was a logical sanctuary for political refugees from the former Reich, it has been argued: It was foreign territory, in a manner of speaking, and its inhabitants were not particularly well disposed to the Reich. More specifically, Marut and Irene Mermet (who was from Cologne) could count on a circle of friends and like-minded people there. The magnet of this circle, which was primarily composed of artists, was the painter and graphic artist Franz Wilhelm Seiwert (1894–1933). Seiwert, influenced by the expressionists and cubists, was a native of Cologne and lived there his entire life. He was highly regarded during his lifetime, particularly directly after the war. Later he was forgotten for decades, only to be rediscovered in the late 1960s as an artist of international standing. Tristan Rémy, Piet Mondrian, and László Moholy-Nagy were among his admirers. Sympathetic with the proletariat and a political revolutionary, he essentially shared Marut's leanings. He found himself in his element when he joined a circle of intellectuals formed around the writers Carl Oskar Jatho and his wife Käthe in the winter of 1916–1917. Here he took part in discussions of world literature and leftist political philosophy from Kropotkin to Marx, from Tolstoy to Nietzsche. The artists and writers of this circle—including Otto Freundlich, Bekya and Genya Gusik, Peter Abelen, and Franz Nitsche—met around 1920 mostly in the Jathos' country house in the Eifel region's Kall Valley, some thirty miles outside of Cologne. In the tumultuous postwar period, they formed an intellectual oasis, calling themselves the Kalltal Community. They reached a wider audience by publishing a book series from 1919 to 1920 called Publications of the Kalltal Community. Seiwert's graphics were prominently represented in this series, as were writings by the Jathos. The group's guiding principles included pacifism and abolition of the existing power structures, in particular anarchistic opposition to the state. Seiwert himself was politically involved in a manner similar to Marut's shortly after the war (as writings from Seiwert's estate demonstrate). He embraced the goals of the Anti-National Socialist Party, to which the Berlin circle of pacifists associated with Pfemfert's *Die Aktion* was also close. Seiwert had connections to Pfemfert's magazine, having published some of his early work there. Some of Seiwert's texts from around 1919, unpublished at the time, use a language startlingly reminiscent of Marut's: Seiwert speaks of "world revolution," the search for the "human being," and also, referring to Marx, of the "revolutionary dictatorship of the proletariat" that would follow upon the destruction of the existing political power structures. Gustav Landauer, who made a lasting impression on Marut, strongly influenced Seiwert's thought as well. In addition to the Jathos' circle, Seiwert was closely associated with the Cologne Progressives, also called the New-Cologne School of Painting: Anton Räderscheidt, Angelika and Heinrich Hoerle, Marta Hegemann, Wilhelm Fick, and others.

Ret Marut and Irene Mermet (traveling under the name of Scholl) found refuge around 1920 among these groups of Seiwert's acquaintances, although the specifics can no longer be determined. One can assume, as previously mentioned, that the final *Brickburner* issues were printed in Cologne or its vicinity. We cannot dismiss out of hand the conjecture that Seiwert and his acquaintances helped distribute *The Brickburner* once it went underground. (As late as May 1932, remaining copies of *The Brickburner* were offered to "friends of Traven [!]" in the magazine *a bis z*, "Organ of the Group of Progressive Artists" in Cologne, a publication in which Seiwert and Heinrich Hoerle played prominent roles.)

Seiwert's collaboration on *The Brickburner* is not a matter of conjecture, however. His "Sieben Antlitze der Zeit" ("Seven Faces of the Time") appeared in the publication's final issue in December 1921. This series of drawings mercilessly ridicules the militarism and capitalism of the "reactionaries." But Seiwert and Marut had established contact much earlier, at the latest in the spring of 1919. They may have been introduced by Irene Mermet, although it is not known when she first met Seiwert. Their association may also have been brought about through the magazine *Die Aktion*, which considered *The Brickburner* as an ideological kindred spirit. Further evidence of the Seiwert-Marut connection is that Seiwert's portfolio of woodcuts and accompanying text called *Rufe* (*Cries*), after Seiwert unsuccessfully attempted to have the work printed in 1919, was published in 1920 and copyrighted by the "Brickburner Press in Germany" with Neustadt given as the place of publication (there are, of course, many places called Neustadt in Germany). The texts, in spite of a conspicuous affinity with Marut's *Brickburner* tone, were not written by Marut but by Seiwert, as indicated at the end of the portfolio. A "Picture Book of Six Woodcuts by F. W. Seiwert with Verses by Friends," entitled *Welt zum Staunen* (*World of Marvel*), had been published in 1919 by the Kalltal Press. It is unlikely that Marut had anything to do with the text of this volume either—unassuming light verse, tender and childlike—although at least one scholar maintains that Marut wrote it.

Other sources besides journalistic endeavors document the intensive contact between Seiwert and Marut. Numerous works by Seiwert were in the Traven estate (most of which Traven's widow donated to the Ludwig Museum in Cologne in 1978). It is unclear, however, whether Marut/Traven had brought along all these works (more than fifty, according to K. H. Bodensiek) on his voyage to Mexico. Irene Mermet may have forwarded or brought a good number of the items to Traven; unlike Traven, she remained in contact with Seiwert even when she lived in North America, and she wrote to Traven about her communication with Seiwert. In any event, we have testimony of a more personal nature for the friendship between Marut and Seiwert: Seiwert's portraits of Ret Marut preserved in the Traven estate—one ink sketch, the other an oil—as well as Seiwert's handwritten homage to Ret Marut from about 1919:

> And there is Ret Marut, who sees how everything fits together from his own vantage point. Who smashes the old world and lets the new one be born: I am the focal point of the world. Everything that exists flows through Me. Everything exits, is forced out, through Me. I am connected and in touch with the nearest and farthest. Near and far are nothing, I am everything. Birth and death do not exist, only eternal change. Worlds collide into one another, beget themselves in order to disappear once more, to beget themselves again. Everything is unique, and everything is eternal. Worlds and stars and people and plants, everything that exists, dances about each other and into one another in an ever-changing rhythm. We are already receiving word of lands beyond the earth which call on us to realize ourselves, to communicate a message. Everything fixed softens and dissolves, everything flows out in order to find itself, and everything lives under the sign and form of fertility. Today is "the midday of the evolution of mankind," for in us mankind has seen its midday, for we are mankind.
>
> Hail to you, part of myself, traitor Marut!

Finally, a number of *Brickburner* pieces other than the series of drawings in the final issue have been attributed to Seiwert. The Seiwert expert Uli Bohnen, in his biography of the artist, has at least raised suspicions that the manifesto entitled "Gegensatz" ("Contrast") and several other political articles were written in whole or in part by Seiwert. Bohnen further nominates Seiwert as the likely author of two prose pieces written in a poetic vein, which stand out as somewhat incongruous in Marut's publication: "Totengesänge des Hyotamore von Kyrena" ("Death Hymns of Hyotamore of Cyrene") and the legend "Khundar." Seiwert, Bohnen says, is only "possibly" the author of the "Death Hymns," while the legend is "so fundamentally related to Seiwert's early writings both in terms of style and theme that at times whole passages from it could be inserted without much of a problem into the texts of *Rufe* (*Cries*), *Gott-Mensch* (*God-Man*), or *Der Kreuzweg zum Menschen* (*The Way of the Cross to Man*). Or the reverse: passages from them could be incorporated into the 'Khundar' legend without a significant breach arising." A somewhat convincing scenario, but proof is absent.

The Cologne circle, according to an interview Heidemann conducted with two of Marut's acquaintances from this period, arranged Marut's escape from Germany. "Marut was taken by the Anarchistic Association to Rotterdam via Aachen, with money from Onkelchen ["little uncle"], a rich manufacturer who supported our movement." In principle there is no reason to doubt this escape route from Germany in 1923, although I cannot confirm it; nor can I confirm the segment of it that Recknagel claims—from Trier to Luxembourg on July 11, 1923, for which Recknagel cites as proof three train tickets in the Traven estate. The three tickets purchased in Trier that I found in the estate do not bear the date Recknagel alleges, nor are they valid for a trip to Luxembourg: The stations printed on them are exclusively German towns in the Mosel Valley. A train ticket for the journey from Brussels to Antwerp in the estate, the date of which I was unable to make out, may document a later, perhaps the final, stage in Marut's meanderings through continental Europe. In the summer of 1923, in any event, Marut had left the European mainland—not, as is sometimes maintained, with Götz Ohly's passport (which he had lost in Belgium), nor did he use the "passport" of his Cologne friend Anton Räderscheidt—another theory occasionally passed off as fact. (The documents in the Traven estate cited by proponents of this latter view are Räderscheidt's identification card, expired in the spring of 1919, and a "pass" issued to Räderscheidt by the British occupation forces for a single journey from Cologne to Düsseldorf and back in 1919.) If the fugitive had any papers at all upon leaving the country, they probably bore the name Ret Marut. For this was the name he still used in the period that was immediately to follow; indeed, he was soon to attempt to prove his identity with Marut's Munich I.D. card.

A Winter in London

The little we know about the period between Marut's departure from continental Europe in the summer of 1923 and his arrival in Mexico in the summer of 1924 is derived from the Marut file of the British Home Office and the Marut file of the American State Department, both of which were first used by Will Wyatt in his book *The Secret of the Sierra Madre* (1980). These files reveal that from August 1923 to the second half of April 1924, and perhaps a bit longer, Marut was in London, that he had gotten into trouble with the alien registration regulations as a self-declared American failing to register, and that eventually he applied for American papers at the consular section of the American embassy in London. Specifically, this information comes from the London police and court records and the correspondence between the U.S. embassy in London and the U.S. State Department concerning Marut's claim to be an American citizen. These documents throw some light on a previously unknown year in the life of the great adventurer and mystery man at the point when he was about to emerge as B. Traven.

The path to England, curiously enough, was via Canada. The résumé (not in Marut's own hand) made in March 1924 when Marut applied for American papers in London claims that he—the son of William Marut and Helene Marut, née Otorrent [*sic*], born in San Francisco—left Germany in April 1919 and went to Austria as an actor and language teacher, where he "rem[ained] until 1922"; he then spent time in Switzerland, Holland, and Copenhagen; "thence" he traveled to Canada "about July"; he was "rejected and returned to England" by the Canadian authorities.

Marut would not have been a total stranger in England. He may have visited England during his seafaring days; but in any case he had already passed through it on his way to Canada. "He landed in this country last summer," wrote the American diplomat Boylston A. Beal on January 22, 1924, from London to Norman Armour in the U.S. State Department, "and was allowed to pass through as transmigrant on his way to Canada, but he was sent back from there as his papers were not in order." He was back in London on August 19, 1923—or so Marut claimed in March 1924 to the U.S. consulate in London on the "Application for Registration—Native Citizen."

In the meantime, documents show, he was arrested on November 30, 1923, in London for violating the alien registration regulations and was held for questioning. The police took note of his activities, according to Beal's letter, because he moved in "communist circles." There is apparently no mention of that, however, in the court records. The Thames police court, on December 17, decided to deport Marut for "failing to register." But the judge first sent him to Brixton Prison. On February 15, 1924, under instructions from the Home Office, Marut was released but not deported. According to Wyatt, this was not due to intercession by someone influential or to the efforts of the Washington law office of McElroy and Reid, which tried to confirm Marut's claim of American citizenship during his imprisonment (they may have been hired by Irene Mermet, although her name does not appear in any of the documents). Instead, Wyatt attributes Marut's release to the English government's need to cut prison costs. In any event, Marut may not have welcomed his newfound freedom in every respect: The first (English) version of *The Death Ship* was written, at least in part, during his stay in prison, his widow told me, where the nascent Traven felt rather well taken care of.

Questioning by the London police in the winter of 1923–1924 elicited Marut's "confession," which was later to cause such a commotion: that he was in reality Otto Feige from Schwiebus. (The reasons for doubting his testimony are discussed in Chapter 3.) The Feige story is also called into question by the records that Wyatt uncovered. There we read that the mysterious figure came to trial as the American "mechanic" Ret Marut, while the prison records identify him as a Lithuanian "bookseller." It seems that during his stay in London Marut, under pressure to find asylum, donned new personae with more than his usual share of liberality. The file at the British Home Office includes no fewer than five other identities of the supposed Otto Feige: Besides Ret (and Rex) Marut, they are Albert Otto Max Wienecke (Wienecke was the maiden name of Otto Feige's mother), Adolf Rudolf Feige (Otto Feige's father), Barker, and Arnolds. In talking with the American consular officials in London, however, he presented himself simply as Ret Marut.

After his release from prison, Marut lived in the East End of London, a port area where anarchists and radicals often met. He may also have been arrested in this area. Incidentally, the magazine *Freedom*, "A Journal of Anarchist Communism," was published in the East End. It is tempting to imagine Marut leafing through its pages and noting the frequent announcements for meetings of the Anarchist Discussion Circle. Might he not have read with interest in the August 1923 issue the articles "The Tyranny of Passports" and "Mexican Workers' Fight for Freedom" or the essay "Revolutionary Mexico" in the December issue of that year? In these articles, Mexico appears not only as the land of the future but also as the promised land of the born revolutionary, anticapitalist and anarchist, at what was viewed as a pivotal time in world history:

"With unassisted effort," [a journalist is quoted], "there has developed a new consciousness of self-reliance. With the non-interference of high-power 'development' there is emerging a different sense of values, a realisation of the inherent and always neglected possibilities of Mexico itself. . . . For the moment, and for the first time in a generation, the foreign overlords were voiceless by their own consent. Land, a new freedom and dignity for labour, an intellectual renaissance, a new appreciation of things inherently Mexican, an opportunity for Mexico to find itself spiritually, these seem to be the factors emerging out of chaos."

. . .

It has been, and still is, a frightful struggle. The outside world, as a whole, knows nothing of it. The revolutionary world, habitually exhausted by never-ending contests on its home battle-grounds, has but the dimmest conception of how important is the rôle Mexico has been compelled to play. Hardly yet is it conscious that a powerful shout of revolt, first uttered in Mexico by a fearless few, has aroused all Central and South America from slavish torpor.

. . .

The Mexican of to-day is a fighter for his rights; and barely a generation ago he was looked on in the United States as a crushed spirit, with all the fight knocked out of him. Life has sprung up again, invincible.

In some form or other—State Socialism, Trade Unionism, Anarchist-Syndicalism, or Anarchist-Communism—it [discontent] is battling untiringly to cross the border-line of theory and become accomplished fact. . . .

These Anarchist comrades are deported from the United States, which brands them as criminal disturbers of the public peace. They cross the international bridge at El Paso, Texas, and the entire population of Ciudad Juarez turns out to greet them. The town is a blaze of red, and for ten days they are kept busy addressing crowded meetings. Invitations pour in from other cities, and they traverse six large States, making the capitals their headquarters and working thence through the rural districts, for Mexico is still mainly a land of agriculturists. At every railway station large bodies of workers meet them, each union or syndicate carrying its standard and red flags. They march to the public square, and the meeting begins. . . .

Mexico City, the national capital, gives them a great ovation. The streets are thronged by sympathisers, two big parades are

> held, red flags are everywhere in evidence, and the crowd, having stormed the cathedral, rings out welcome to Labour from the belfry. They make excursions into the surrounding country, and when they visit an industrial area the workers habitually desert the factories to attend the meetings.

It is conceivable that among the *Freedom* readers, or even among the Anarchist Discussion Circle, Marut met Sylvia Pankhurst, the pacifist who then lived in the East End (she was the daughter of Emmeline Pankhurst, the women's suffrage activist). The final document in the Marut file of the U.S. State Department, a memorandum dated December 13, 1926, enclosed in a letter of December 15 from Boylston Beal in London to Alexander Kirk at the State Department, reports that Marut was "shielded" in London by two English women: Sylvia Pankhurst and Nora Smythe.

The precise length of Marut's stay in England after his release from prison cannot be determined. In early March 1924 he applied, under the name Ret Marut, for registration as an American citizen at the U.S. consulate general in London. He had scanty supporting evidence: an I.D. card issued by the Munich chief of police dated January 18, 1918, identifying him as a U.S. citizen. The U.S. State Department file also contains a rejected application for an American passport, which Marut had made in Munich in 1917 and which reveals that he had twice before tried unsuccessfully to obtain American papers (1914 in Barmen [perhaps Bremen] and 1916 or 1915 in Cologne). The file also contains notification to Marut in 1915 from the Department of Public Health in San Francisco that his birth in San Francisco could not be confirmed since all birth records were destroyed in the earthquake of 1906. Yet when applying for papers in 1917 Marut had told the American vice consul in Munich that his birth certificate and "other papers" had been lost in a fire in 1910 in Pillkallen (East Prussia). His application for an American passport was declined in 1924, as it had been in 1917.

The rationale of the vice consul in Munich whom Marut had failed to convince in 1917 may speak as well for his counterparts in London, who had to deal with the same case seven years later: "Applicant's memory seems to fail him badly and his manner of replying to pointed questions is reluctant and not convincing." He spoke English "with a remarkable foreign accent, considering his claim to have resided in the United States up to his twenty-second year." In 1924 Marut's attempt to pass himself off as an American apparently was not taken as seriously as it had been in 1917, or perhaps the case was considered resolved by the 1917 decision. Discrepancies in the dates Marut presented may have cast his case in a doubtful light: In 1924 he asserted that he last left the United States in 1892, while in 1917 he gave his U.S. departure as 1901 or 1904 (these two years are recorded in the statement given under oath and the passport application, respectively—perhaps one of the dates is a typist's error). A physical description of Marut can be found in a letter, dated January 25, 1924, from H. Dorsey Newson of the American embassy in Berlin to Boylston Beal: "Height 1.65–1.68 meters, slim, smooth-shaven, healthy appearance, good teeth, dark hair with a large bald spot, slim hands with well-manicured nails, fast gait and well dressed."

Beal's memorandum of December 13, 1926, reveals that Marut, in attempting to prove his American citizenship in London, relied on outside help as well. The memorandum states that Charles Thomas Hallinan, the left-leaning American journalist and former secretary of the American Union Against Militarism, who then resided in London, was in contact with "a mysterious German named Ret Marut" in November 1923. The Labor Bureau in New York had allegedly supplied Marut with a letter of introduction to Hallinan, thinking that he might assist him in gaining passage to the United States. The New York organization, according to Beal, also supplied Hallinan with thirty-four pounds to help Marut; "this was duly handed over." But apparently Hallinan was in no position to assist Marut, either in November 1923 or later, after February 15, 1924, when Marut was a free man again.

In mid-April 1924 Marut was apparently still in London. According to the records of the Norwegian Mustering Authority in London, on April 17 he signed aboard the Norwegian ship *Hegre* as a coal trimmer; two days later, Wyatt determined, the *Hegre* left London for Tenerife. But Marut was not on board: On the Norwegian muster roll of "engaged seamen" Ret Marut's name (domicile: California) has been crossed out. The police seem not to have known that: They relayed word to the American embassy that the undesired alien had left their shores. The embassy forwarded the information to the State Department, which, via a letter by Arthur Bliss Lane dated May 12, 1924, got word to FBI Director J. Edgar Hoover: "This man is reported to have sailed from London on April

18th, on the Norwegian Steamship HEGRI, as a fireman. This ship was bound for Morocco." At this point the authorities broke off their search.

One is tempted to think that Marut himself orchestrated the whole chain of events, which Boylston Beal still did not doubt in his memorandum of December 1926. Was he up to his old tricks when signing on aboard the *Hegre*? When and how he finally left England, whether on a death ship like the *Yorikke* in Traven's novel, whether as a sailor or coal trimmer, what name he traveled under, his intended destination, and where he stopped along the way—all these questions are to date unanswered and are perhaps forever unanswerable.

The one clear fact is that Marut set foot on the coast of the Gulf of Mexico in the summer of 1924. Or was he found there on the beach—shipwrecked, a survivor of a sinking death ship? Recknagel quotes from a letter Traven wrote to Ernst Preczang, his editor at Büchergilde Gutenberg, dated November 18, 1929, which describes "the whole story of my being found on the beach—it was literally on the seacoast." Is that the truth—or is this the voice of the mythmaker identifying with Odysseus, whom Nausicaa, daughter of the Phaeacian king, found shipwrecked on the shores of Scheria?

5

IN A FAR-OFF LAND

The Literary Conquest of Mexico, 1924–1930

The Bungalow in the Bush

The last literary piece to appear in *The Brickburner* was the legend "Khundar" (1920). Khundar, a mythical savior, exhorts his companions at the conclusion of the first part: " 'Up, then, let us go into the wilderness where we will find truth, wisdom, redemption, and life.' " The narrator continues: "And having thus spoken, he went away to a far-off land the very same evening." Whether the fugitive Khundar ever reaches his goal is unclear; the second part of the legend was never written. But the fugitive who penned the story (or who at least published it) arrived in the summer of 1924 in the far-off land of Mexico, which was to be his homeland of choice for the next forty-five years. Aside from brief excursions to Europe and North America, he did not leave it. It is uncertain where he first landed in Mexico, though it was probably one of the harbors on the Gulf Coast, since shortly after his arrival he surfaced in the oil town of Tampico in the state of Tamaulipas on the Gulf of Mexico. The "gringo" from central Europe had more than half of his life ahead of him; he had turned forty-two a few months earlier, if the year of birth claimed by Marut is correct, or thirty-four if one puts any trust in Traven's later, less credible claim.

Mexico—so we read on the first page of his first novel set in Mexico, *The Cotton-Pickers*—was for Traven the land "where it is considered tactless, in fact insulting, to question someone about his name, his occupation, his origin and plans." Nonetheless, though not surprisingly, he chose to adopt a new identity—signaling a radical break with the past—as he embarked on the second half of his life, which would bring him fame. "The Bavarian of Munich is dead," he wrote (in English) in his notebook on July 26, 1924, shortly after his arrival in Mexico. Marut was dead. Throughout the following decades, with almost fanatical devotion, he tried to cover up all trails leading back to the "Brickburner"; as an old man he was still overcome with panic when journalistic sleuths scented his secret. From the 1920s to the 1960s, he regularly presented himself to strangers as an American of Scandinavian extraction, though he spoke English with a thick German accent, or, more rarely, as a Norwegian or Swede (he was blond-haired and blue-eyed, if small in stature). Only hours before his death did he authorize the posthumous announcement that Traven and Marut had been one and the same.

Strictly speaking, he embarked on his new life in Mexico with not one but two new names. For a time, it seems, he went by Traven Torsvan (or B. Torsvan or B. T. Torsvan) as well as B. Traven, both in his private life and as an author. Traveling as the photographer Torsvan, he took part in an archeological exploration to Chiapas in 1926—the Palacios expedition (discussed later)—but he also wrote under this name on occasion: His estate contains a carbon copy of a typescript in English by "B. T. Torsvan" of a newspaper article on the upcoming Palacios expedition, the first page of the typescript (in English) of an essay entitled "The Jungle Dwellers on the Western Banks of the Usumacinta by T. Torsvan," and a letter to "Torsvan" from *National Geographic* dated September 18, 1928, confirming receipt of the essay. On the other hand, the British oil company El Aguila addressed a letter to "B. Traven" on August 4, 1925—as a prospective employee, not as an author. By 1926, after his first two novels had appeared, he used Traven only as a nom de plume. Judging from dated cancellation marks on envelopes in the estate, Irene Mermet at first (April 1925) wrote to "B. Traven" ("c/o Southern Hotel, Tampico"), though later (February 1928, for instance) she addressed her correspondence to "B. Torsvan" ("c/o Hotel Imperial, Tapachula, Chiapas"). In the summer of 1927 the erstwhile Brickburner enrolled at the Mexican National University as Traven Torsvan, and an inoculation certificate issued to "B. Traven Torsvan" and dated February 6, 1926, lies among Traven's papers. Still, in spite of this distinction between the literary Traven and the private Torsvan from 1926 on, he sent the article on the jungle dwellers to the United States in 1928 under the name Torsvan. A possible explanation is that the journalist, writing in English, did not wish to be identified with the novelist B. Traven, who wrote in German; he seems never to have offered German texts for publication under the name Torsvan. As for the much discussed initial *B.*, which Torsvan and Traven have in common, the written documents that remain from the early days in Mexico shed no light on the subject. Traven's estate contains a receipt for a safe in the Banco de México in Mexico City issued to "Berrick Traven Torsvan" on January 5, 1930; but, according to his widow, Traven invented this Christian name since the bank would not permit a mere initial.

To complement his new names (he added a third, Hal Croves, in the 1940s) the immigrant fashioned a new biography, ultimately settling on the following milestones, all of which proved as unverifiable as Marut's claimed birth in San Francisco in 1882. Traven Torsvan (the name which also appeared on his calling card) or B. Traven was born in Chicago on March 5, 1890, the son of Burton and Dorothy Torsvan, née Croves. He entered Mexico from the United States via Ciudad Juárez in 1914 (thus precluding his identity with Marut) and remained in Mexico from that time. This information was recorded on an alien registration card issued in 1930; the parents' names, absent on this card, appear on an identification paper from 1942 and on the death certificate. (The fanciful adumbrations of this biography were discussed in Chapter 2.)

Whether the stranger who arrived in Mexico in 1924 had papers in the name of either of his two new personae is unknown; he probably had no papers at all. In any event, the two new names mark a beginning that was radically new even for the well-traveled and worldly-wise Marut. Yet the former German revolutionary and author of literary works sketching everyday life could still recognize familiar themes in his exotic new surroundings; he may even have realized early on that he could pursue his political and literary interests without significantly deviating from his original course.

Let us imagine his new milieu. Tampico lies a few miles inland from the Gulf of Mexico in the tropical marshlands. Oil pipelines converged here from fields scattered throughout the bush in the state of Tamaulipas, making Tampico one of the world's major oil-exporting harbors since the turn of the century. English and American oil companies controlling the fields had long played a controversial role in Mexican politics. No wonder that leftist labor organizations, socialists, Communists, and anarchists gathered in Tampico to combat the oil "imperialism" of foreign business interests. The social and political tensions of the modern industrial world, familiar to the gringo since his Munich days, came to the fore in this far-off port founded some four hundred years earlier by Franciscan monks on the ruins of an Aztec settlement. But only a few miles westward, the luxuriant rain forest was the undisputed ruler, overgrowing Mayan pyramids, impinging on Indian villages, penetrable only with a machete.

We can reconstruct no more than bits and pieces of the former Brickburner's first weeks, months, and years in Mexico. Aside from letters to Büchergilde Gutenberg, his publisher in Germany, and a few letters addressed to him, a small blue notebook preserved in the estate, eight pages of which Traven used as a diary, sheds the most light on this period. Some of the entries, dated in each case, may have been copied from the original notes at a later point (such scraps of paper still exist from his journey to Chiapas in 1928). In any case, Traven changed the dates of the first five daily entries from late June 1924 to mid-July and then continued with the subsequent entries which required no such changes; further, the author's handwriting seems relatively uniform. The handwriting is clearly Traven's, and the period in question is also clear—July 11 to November 27, 1924, and June 15, 1925, to January 26, 1926—although he did not make daily entries, and from 1925 on he did little more than record the weather, invariably "rain." The diary is written in English, though not without errors and eccentric spelling. Traven has thrown off his German past, but the occasional German word unmasks the pretender who is not quite at home in English. We encounter Stabheuschrecke (walking stick, cricket or insect), Rinden (bark) spider, and Eidec[hse] (lizard). Incidentally, this diary does not begin on the first page of the notebook—several blank pages precede it. Traven may have planned to add entries later for the preceding days or weeks, particularly as the first entries do not appear to depict his very first days in the new country. In any event, it remains interesting that Traven kept such a diary at all (he took similar, carefully dated notes on a more or less daily basis on his expeditions in the years to come). The diary and notes provide a glimpse of the author trying to get a foothold as a professional writer having scarcely arrived in a strange new land. For this little blue notebook, like those that came later, contains material for his novels, including seeds of *The Cotton-Pickers*, his first novel set in Mexico. It also refers to two of Traven's earliest Mexican stories by their German titles.

The scene of the action in the diary is Tampico and environs. Traven makes no mention of any political activity, at least not openly. Scraping together enough to get by seems to have been his chief concern. In July 1924 he rented a cabin from Alex Smith (*S.* in the diary), an American living in Tampico. It was a dilapidated structure on stilts near the small town of Columbus, some "thirty-five miles" from Tampico or, more significantly, from the "nearest store where I could buy paper, ink, or pencils"—so he wrote to Ernst Preczang, the editor at Büchergilde Gutenberg, which would soon publish the first Traven novels. This small cabin would serve as Traven's pied-à-terre for the next six or seven years. Here he penned his first stories and novels, literally in the shadow of a Mayan pyramid that had long before been reclaimed by the forest and that provided the inspiration for the fantastic story "The Night Visitor." Traven stated that the *genius loci* pervaded each of his early Mexican works, stressing that they were based on firsthand knowledge, not on the poor substitute of bookish research. In 1928 he wrote in "Der Bungalow" ("The Bungalow") in *Die Büchergilde*, his publisher's house publication:

> But if one wishes to get to know the bush and the jungle, its life and its song, its loving and its killing, one must not stay in the Regis Hotel in Mexico City; one simply has to go into the jungle, one must live with it, one must love it, one must become married to it. There is no other way. The bush and the jungle tell me their tales only when I bury myself in them, live in them and with them all by myself, unite myself with them unto death and destruction, exclude all other companionship and leave completely behind me and forget the rest of the world beyond the bush, which I love as a friend.

His "bungalow" and the surrounding bush left an unmistakable imprint on his novella "The Night Visitor"—though Traven left it to "literary sleuths, that class of people who merit their own special hell," to "confirm line by line, thought by thought, the extent to which this bungalow may have influenced the novella and its character." When he himself described his working conditions in his 1928 essay, he succeeded in arousing the reader's interest in his personal life, even though he generally refused to divulge any personal information:

> The mosquito plague during certain hours of the day was so frightful that I had to wrap up my hands and head in towels to withstand the attacks of hundreds of thousands of swarming mosquitoes. When the mosquitoes come in such swarms, they sting through clothing, which offers but little protection. My legs and forearms were red from the many successful bites. And every single bite causes an itch which seems unbearable. Going outside does no good, since these pests swarm even thicker outside. You can only hope that the next day brings relief, and relief actually comes when a good solid breeze arises. But as soon as the breeze dies down, these demons are all back in action. These swarms lasted for three full weeks at that time [during the writing of "The Night Visitor"], since the air was hot and humid from the heavy rain showers and was only very rarely disturbed by strong breezes.
>
> But the mosquitoes were not my only house guests. The trees . . . are populated by large black lizards, of the size and thickness of a strong man's arm. These giant lizards come from time to time as guests into the house. Other frequent guests included the snakes, which crept into corners inside the house. One afternoon I encountered two rattlesnakes a hundred feet from the house. One was beaten to death by an Indian, the other one got away. The bite of a rattlesnake is always fatal if medical treatment is not administered immediately. Snakes from three to four meters long and of the thickness of a strong leg live a bit farther from the bungalow.
>
> Jaguars and lions came right up to the house from time to time. The house literally teemed with large scorpions and finger-length red spiders. I would find scores of hand-size tarantulas under stones behind the house. Often enough, in the evening right before sunset whole armies of large ants advanced through the house.
>
> The house stands completely isolated in that area of the bush. I had a fifty-minute ride on horseback to my next-door neighbor. For weeks I often saw no human face; I lived there completely by myself. The nights are long; it is pitch-black night at seven o'clock, even in mid-summer. There is no electric light, even the water for drinking, cooking, and washing is in short supply.

And since frequent washing is not merely a relief here, but a necessity, I had to wash at noon and in the evening with the same water I washed with that morning.

A poet's retreat.

Romanticizing his lack of the comforts of civilization, he even called his dwelling an "Indian hut" in his letter to Preczang of August 5, 1925. His life appeared less exotic, however, in his letter of July 6, 1931, to Smith & Co. in Tampico giving notice, after he had apparently not been living in the bungalow for some time. This business letter (written in English to a Mr. Newell) provides a soberly realistic glimpse of Traven's first years in Mexico:

> There is no rent left to be paid since during the six years I occupied the house I had so much to pay for the upkeep of same that if we check up our accounts properly you would have to pay me quite a little money.
>
> You know that during this long term you did not even furnish a single nail for the upkeep of the shack.
>
> The fence I had to fix seven times because cows and burros and hurricans [*sic*] did sufficient damage to it.
>
> I closed in the whole porch which made the house of higher value than it was when I moved in six years ago.
>
> Five times I had it screened all over to keep the mosquitos out and to make the house fit to live in.
>
> I planted six lemon trees which have taken on so well that soon it will be a real pleasure to see the garden.
>
> The W.C. as we proudly may call it was shaken down by hurricans four times and I had to build it up over an[d] over again.
>
> Two times I had to have the roof tarred so as to keep it in good shape.
>
> One time I had the roof asphalted.
>
> In March this year I had the roof or to be exact three fourths of it roofed anew and again I had it asphalted. It will keep well now for at least three years without any repairs.
>
> And now thinking it over it occurs to me that you charged me for this little shack a rent which even considering everything was excessively high since the house has no water and no electric light.

At times life does not appear to have been so bad there. Traven wrote to Preczang in Berlin on December 2, 1926 that when he thought of the deep snow in Chicago, New York, and Washington, he was glad to be able "to work with the doors open"; with temperatures in the eighties in the shade, the tropics offered him "an ever-blue sky, flowers everywhere and birdsong, and the bush so dear to me sings through my open door all night long." Traven's letters to his German publisher frequently contained such snapshots of the early years in the jungle.

The little blue diary, which is the most immediate source of information about Traven's early life in Mexico, begins with his arrival at the home of the Smith family in Tampico, with the date revised from June 27 to July 11: "Arrived 7^{30}. Mr. S. was allright. The rest of the family seemed not or at least indifferent. When looking after my baggage found Ax missing. In the forenoon with Mr. B. a look after the other land. Told me about his plans. Seems to be good ones. B. said he was expecting my coming. Dinner with S. family. About 3^{30} start for my aim. Nice place. Wants hard work. Nigro in hut. Staying with three cottonpickers. Two Mex.[,] one nigro. Night horrible. No sleep, too many mosquitos. Tent [mosquito net] arrived. Too hot."

The "nice place" that requires a lot of work is the bungalow that Traven rented from Smith. Traven seems to have come there with a certain goal, apparently to support himself by farming a piece of overgrown land. Mr. B.'s identity remains a mystery, no less than the "plans" they discussed. Traven, according to the diary, still met occasionally with B. and Smith over the following weeks; but it is not clear whether common political interests had brought them together or whether Traven, whom, we learn, B. had been expecting, had been in contact with them while still in Europe. Perhaps B. (as in B. Traven?) was *The Brickburner*'s sole Mexican subscriber.

The next day, after the first of those sleepless tropical nights recorded in the diary: "Start work. Clearing a way through gras." On July 13: "Start clearing bush. Move for the night to open hut. Mosquitos." Traven burned off a piece of land apparently intended as a field, and the house required work as well. "Wood for hut," he noted in one instance, and later "no roof"—with no time to spare, since a month later, in early September and with increasing frequency, he recorded "heavy rain," tropical thunderstorms that made the roads impassable. He wrote often of the exotic animals he encountered in his new environment, even in his own hut; he carefully listed them: rattlesnakes, a red and a green snake, variously colored spiders, lizards, beetles, ants "with big tongs" (they made an assault on the rice in the hut and the chewing gum stored under the mosquito netting), scorpions (he already called them by the Spanish name), tarantulas. He occasionally provided an exact head count of the creatures. The future author of jungle stories seems to be training his eye to observe the details of his environment that he would later re-create so skillfully.

He recorded trips to Tampico on occasion. The horse Bala that he soon acquired would have been used for trips in the nearer vicinity. At first it caused a lot of trouble, breaking out of its enclosure; but later, Traven noted, it "follows like dog." Occasionally the diarist took ill. On July 27, 1924, he noted: "Bird-hunter is murdered for his rifle, so his compagnion [*sic*]. Get the missed hatchet."

He earned his living as a day laborer. A cotton plantation and an oil camp were nearby. The first diary entry mentioned cotton pickers squatting in Smith's bungalow. Soon Traven was earning a few pesos as a cotton picker himself—certainly the explanation for the entry of August 18, 1924, which simply states, "Cottonp." The words "Inviting f. dinner. House," appearing a few days later, may refer to Traven visiting the neighboring hacienda owner as his double Gales would do in *The Cotton-Pickers*, where the owner is an American. (Gales seems to lurk around every corner in these diary pages.)

The journal also records Traven's work in the oil fields—another setting familiar from the early prose. On July 19: "Oil camp. Dinner. . . . Borrough [Borrow] goods. Seems without delight. . . . Black sugar. Ax." A few days later, on August 24, B. secured another job for the newcomer—"help drilling"—as a Mr. G. had made a mistake on the job and had been fired. The following day Traven worked in the "pump station," re-created in *The Bridge in the Jungle*. "Work till 5[h] p.m. Bring back Timekeeper, tells there is no job, pays one day wages. Supper. Night in camp." On the way back from work that day, Traven met some Frenchmen and talked with them. On another occasion some geologists gave him a lift in their car. Apparently, Traven was not quite as isolated in this early period as the exotic and romantic description in *Die Büchergilde* would lead one to believe. Rather, he openly and eagerly took in the surroundings and the events soon to be depicted in his novels. He mentioned a "cattle drive"—featured in *The Cotton-Pickers*—in September 1924. Other details that recall the novels: the neighboring hacienda, the unpassable paths, a "mule," the ubiquitous beast of burden in the novels, and Indian dances in the moonlight (one of Traven's early stories was called "Nachttänze der Indianer" ["Indian Dance in the Jungle"]). Above all, Traven became familiar with the oil camps, if only through one-day stints; the El Aguila oil company refused him a regular job (in the letter previously mentioned) and he had to get by with day labor.

Beyond these spare details, we do not know Traven's precise occupations during the first months and years. He could not have been choosy, and he was certainly versatile. Yet at the same time he chose to pursue his writing, which required a substantial amount of free time; the mosquito-ridden evening hours by the oil lamp could scarcely account entirely for the prolific literary production of this period. As for other activities, one is naturally tempted to read *The Cotton-Pickers* and other early works autobiographically point by point and envision Traven leading a life identical to that of the vagabond Gales—as if Traven, seasoned writer that he was, had no imagination at all.

The gringo occasionally presented himself as an engineer in these years—another potential clue to reconstructing his life. The Traven estate includes an envelope from 1930 addressed to "Ingeniero Torsvan," as well as *Kurze Anleitung zum Gebrauch des Normal- und Kubus-Rechenstabes* (*Short Instructions for the Use of the Slide Rule and Cubature Calculator*)—one can imagine the former journalist acquiring some elementary scientific knowledge that allowed him to pass himself off as an engineer in the jungle. (He is also identified as an engineer on his alien registration card of 1930.) The *BT News* in 1952 listed Traven's "occupations" more liberally, referring no doubt to those of the earliest period in Mexico, before the *Death Ship* royalties provided some economic stability:

> His books, which are always based on what he himself has seen and experienced, provide the reader with insight into the jobs he has held. He has been a sailor, a cotton picker, a day laborer, a petroleum driller, a baker, a drover, a gold digger, a farmer, a private tutor on remote farms, an explorer, a medicine man, a midwife, and a lawyer in Indian villages. B. Traven has undertaken year-long expeditions through unexplored regions of Mexico and has lived among the Indians as one of their own.

Similar is the remark introducing the serialization of *The Cotton-Pickers* on June 21, 1925, in the Social Democratic newspaper *Vorwärts*: "He has worked as an oil man, farm worker, cocoa worker, factory worker, tomato and orange-picker, brush clearer, drover, hunter, and trader among the wild Indian tribes in the Sierra Madre, where the 'savages' still hunt with bows, arrows, and clubs."

There is no reason to doubt these details—which appeared in similar form in the March 1927 *Büchergilde* and in the letter of Traven's that Manfred Georg published in 1929 in *Die Weltbühne*—and to suspect that Traven simply adopted Gales's biography. The converse makes more sense: that many of the author's activities left their trace in the novels and stories. Thus, when Traven sent Preczang the story "Die Medizin" ("Effective Medicine")—the first-person narrative of a white man who "rented a small farm" in an Indian village, "on which I planted cotton"—on January 24, 1926, he noted that he wished to see the sketch published in *Die Büchergilde* "because it is 'biography.' " If he were to encounter financial hardship, he would try his hand "planting cotton again," he wrote to Preczang on March 29, 1926. Traven's widow has said that Traven also worked as a photographer, though this was probably not before his expeditions to Chiapas (from 1926 on), when he made a few pesos taking portrait photos of affluent landowners and their families on their remote haciendas.

Before the success of the first novels, he must have barely been able to get by. Income from various jobs, noted occasionally in the diary, was slight. A draft letter among Traven's papers dated December 12, 1924, from Columbus, apparently to the customs office in Nuevo Laredo (on the Texas/Tamaulipas border) reveals the extent of his financial hardship: Three packages addressed to "B. Traven" in Columbus had arrived at the post office in González (near Columbus), and the customs office at Nuevo Laredo demanded 127.50 pesos to claim them. The packages contained "clothes, suits, socks etc.," clothing that he had owned for years, he said. But, he continued, he did not have the money for the customs duty and therefore requested that the packages be returned to the sender. (A curious fact about this handwritten draft of a letter—and a draft was indeed necessary, since his Spanish was still somewhat awkward at this point—is that Traven erased his signature as well as the names of the countries in which the items of clothing in question had been manufactured. The former Marut thus eradicated a clue leading back to Europe. Yet why did he keep the draft for forty-five years nonetheless?)

The sender of those packages was presumably Irene Mermet, either directly or indirectly; she was probably the only one from the former German circle of acquaintances to know of the identity of Ret Marut and B. Traven (as we gather from a letter she sent him dated May 5, 1927). Further, it appears that she actually came to Mexico with Marut/Traven in the summer of 1924. In any event, she was in Tamaulipas by that time. The second entry in the diary, dated July 12 (originally June 28) mentions her: "Looking for I. Not at home." That the "I." refers to Irene Mermet emerges unquestionably from later instances in the diary. The comment that she was not at home may imply that she, like Traven apparently, had been in Mexico for some time, although it is not quite clear where she resided: According to the context in the diary, she must have lived in the immediate vicinity of Traven's bungalow near Columbus—perhaps on the neighboring hacienda. The next day, after Traven had begun his work on his overgrown parcel of land, he wrote (the entire entry for July 13): "See I. Indifferent, but seems a little pleased. Start clearing bush. Move for the night to open hut. Mosquitos. In the afternoon B. came. Coffee. Talk. Showed off." On July 15 Traven noted, however, that he took a letter addressed to Irene ("for I") to the train station, and two weeks later, on July 31, he collected letters and money from the Tampico post office sent by Mermet ("I."): "Canadian money. British consul refuses. At least 18 ps." (By 1925 at the latest Traven rented Box 1208 at the Tampico post office, to which, for example, the letter from the El Aguila oil company is addressed.) Later diary entries again mention receipt of money ("L. with 10$. Great Joy!" and "letter I. 25"). The mysterious "I.c." of November 24, 1925, proves to be a record of Irene's visit to him ("Irene comes"), as is clear from a telegram informing him of her arrival and bearing the handwritten date "11-16-1925."

Irene traveled to the United States in mid-July 1924, apparently to New York City. In the 1960s, an American named George McCrossen recalled that his wife, working in 1924 in a New York theater under the name Dora Malet, brought Irene Mermet home one day. She stayed with them in Greenwich Village for a few days and then traveled as a private tutor with a family to St. Jovite in Quebec for the summer. From there she wrote to Malet and McCrossen on July 30, 1924, that she was delaying until October her plans to return to New York and stay with them. But nothing ever came of those plans, McCrossen reported. Irene Mermet added in the same letter that her friend, whom she had hoped could also find a room at the McCrossens', was unable to travel to New York that winter; he had come down with malaria in the South Seas! (It seems Irene Mermet was as adept at covering up a trail as Traven himself was.) She said further that, although she had no concrete plans yet, she hoped to get a farm in Mexico and take leave of civilization. Nothing came of this plan either, at least not at first. For Irene Mermet wrote on March 28, 1925, to McCrossen, again in a world-weary tone, that she planned to go shortly to Mexico or "maybe Argentine" to flee civilization. But the spring of 1925 did not find her in Mexico—her presence is undocumented, in any event—but instead she arrived there in November of that year, by way of Washington, D.C., from where she wrote to Dora Malet on October 18, 1924, and to George McCrossen on March 28, 1925. According to Recknagel, she worked there as a secretary at the archeology department of a university. She was a student there as well; from July 1926 to June 1928 she was enrolled as a "special student" at George Washington University, the Registrar's Office informed me.

Traven's diary, aside from the "I.c." entry on November 24, 1925, says nothing about a reunion with Mermet on her return to Mexico. The subsequent entries record only the constant rains. It was apparently the first, but apparently not the last, visit Irene Mermet made after the summer of 1924. Among Traven's papers Wyatt found an inoculation certificate dated February 6, 1926, issued to "I. Traven," which he plausibly deciphered as "Irene Mermet." Her letter to Traven of May 5, 1927 reveals that he had sent her $70 for traveling expenses; but whether she then made a trip to Mexico remains unclear, since she said only that she would visit him once her examinations were over. But whether she did so or not, her letters until early 1928 (largely in English) reveal that the two had grown apart. Their interests were too different, however much Irene Mermet was taken by Traven's literary work. In the letter of May 5, 1927, for example, she talked very understandingly and supportively of *The Treasure of the Sierra Madre*, which Traven had sent her. (Incidentally, Irene Mermet, as R. E. Luján remembers from Traven's remarks, typed Traven's manuscripts at first, and she later sent him a typewriter.)

A divergence of interests: Traven immersed himself in the adventure of the primitive and he fell in love with the jungle. Irene Mermet, meanwhile, wished to educate herself, to study higher civilizations; she tried to find herself through intellectual pursuits, reading Nietzsche, Schopenhauer, and Ibsen, and immersed herself in Washington's cultural life, as she told Traven in a letter dated January 23 [1928] (she sometimes included newspaper clippings and book excerpts with her letters). She had missed this sort of cultural stimulation in Tampico, she wrote; she had had nothing to do there. She apparently did not usually accompany Traven on his expeditions scouting for material for his books, whether near his bungalow or farther afield. ("Next week I'll go traveling," he wrote to Preczang on February 9, 1926, for example.) His primary concern was apparently to get a foothold as a writer in the New World, continuing an obsession with writing that was evident in his Munich days. Even in the 1950s and 1960s Traven would occasionally plunge himself into workaholic frenzies, his widow has reported. It became clear that Traven and Irene Mermet would go their separate ways. In 1928 she married the American jurist John Hanna, who became a professor at Columbia University in 1931. After her death in 1956, no one of her former German group knew with equal certainty that B. Traven, long since a literary figure of world standing, was identical with Ret Marut.

Irene Mermet faithfully avoided restoring contact between Traven and his former circle of acquaintances in Germany and thus preserved his secret. She continued to correspond with Seiwert in her early period in America. Along with her letter to Traven of May 5, 1927, she included a letter from Seiwert to herself. She made a clear effort to distance herself from their former friends, who, she noted, still spoke in the same jargon. How wise Traven had been to keep his distance from them, she said. She also mentioned Erich Mühsam's notice "Where Is the Brickburner?" which appeared that year in his journal *Fanal*:

> Doesn't any reader of *Fanal* know where the Brickburner is? Ret Marut, kindred spirit, friend, comrade-in-arms, human being, come forward, do something, give us a sign that you're alive, that you have remained the Brickburner, and haven't become a big-wig, that your brain is not ossified, your arm not lame, your finger not stiff. The Bavarians didn't get you in 1919; they had you by the collar and you escaped their clutches right on the street. Otherwise you would be lying with Landauer and all the others whose spirits were alive—where I would be as well,

> if they hadn't taken me two weeks earlier and carted me away from the midst of the carnage. Now they can no longer get at you. The amnesty passed last year must be applied to you. Now is the time to state for the record how the Bavarian Commune came into being and what it accomplished. The reports to date are clouded by partisanship; they have been stupid and hateful, unfair or self-righteous. I am also too much a partisan, too closely bound on a personal level with the events, too deeply enmeshed in the conflicts about guilt and merit to serve as historian of this revolution with even some degree of objectivity. You were the only one who was actively involved in what happened and who could still perceive, from your vantage point, the evil that occurred and the good that was intended, what was done right and what should have been done better. Gustav Landauer's papers, his letters, his speeches, his activities in his final days will shortly be exposed to public scrutiny. You worked at his side, helping him and encouraging him, when he was the People's Commissioner for Information and Propaganda. We need you. Who knows the Brickburner? Which of the readers of *Fanal* knows where Ret Marut can be found, where he can be reached? If you know where he is, send him this issue. Many ask for him, many wait for him. He is called.

Irene Mermet added in her letter to Traven that she naturally revealed nothing. Seiwert had never asked her, she said, but he suspected some connection.

Politics and Art

While Irene Mermet became politically more conservative—as we can interpret her distancing herself from the early circle of friends—Traven the revolutionary seems to have found in Mexico a politically congenial milieu. The contrast in their attitudes is clearly illustrated in Irene Mermet's letter to Traven of May 5, 1927: The Americans were not imperialists, she contended, as Traven apparently thought. This statement must be read in the historical context of events unfolding in Mexico. At that time Plutarco Elías Calles was the Mexican president; Mexico's domestic and foreign policy hinged largely on conflicts with English and American oil companies and thus indirectly with the U.S. government. Since late 1926 the United States had intervened militarily in the Nicaraguan civil war on the side of the president, Adolfo Díaz, while the Mexican government (which feared a similar intervention) supported Juan Sacasa, who claimed to be the legitimate president. Calles firmly supported labor and intended to implement reforms and was to that extent dangerous to the American oil "imperialists" of which Traven must surely have spoken in a letter to Irene Mermet. His comments to her would likely have been akin to those in his letter to Preczang, his editor, of January 20, 1927:

> Our much-beloved USA, where there's always so much talk about liberating the oppressed smaller nations, is currently stirring up a lot of trouble here on this continent, and whenever the USA makes trouble, the Mexican bandits go on a rampage, pretending to be revolutionaries. The church is now on the side of the gangs of arsonists and bandits, and would at this very moment sign a pact with the devil if that would give them hope of ousting the present government. Conditions today in the USA are as they probably were in Germany before the War. It is the government and a clique of big businessmen who are out to steal, kill, and set fires, and not the people as a whole.

He had a similar message for Preczang on March 5 of that year, writing again from Tampico: "Mexico is already, and will become increasingly so in the coming two decades, the economic and hence political focal point of capitalist and imperialist world politics, but at the same time it is, curiously, also the focal point of anticapitalist and anti-imperialist world politics."

According to his widow and his friend Federico Marín, Traven at that time moved among leftist groups in Tampico and got to know the political activist Augusto Sandino. That sounds convincing, since the Nicaraguan Sandino worked as a mechanic with the Huasteca Petroleum Company in Tampico from 1923 on, before returning to Nicaragua in late 1926 to assist the Sacasa faction with his guerrilla troops. Traven, his widow recalls, said that he collected funds for him.

Sandino had connections with Mexican labor organizations in Tampico, which in the 1920s was a center of the Industrial Workers of the World, an anarchist-syndicalist labor union, the members of which were called Wobblies. (*The Cotton-Pickers* was entitled *Der Wobbly* [*The Wobbly*] in the first book edition in 1926. The IWW is defined there in a footnote as "a very radical labor organization"—the footnote is included in Traven's typescript as well). The first-person narrator of the novel and of other early novels and stories is Gales, a Wobbly from the United States. The presence of such a figure in Mexico is historically entirely plausible. The IWW labor union did originate in North America; but with the U.S. entry into the war in 1917 and the October Revolution in Russia, radical organizations came under pressure in North America and many Wobblies migrated to Mexico, where they allied themselves with Mexican labor groups. In 1921 Tampico already had a local IWW chapter, while in Mexico City the American Wobbly Linn A. E. Gale published *Gale's International Monthly for Revolutionary Communism* from 1919 to 1921. It was hardly a coincidence, one would like to think, that the narrator of *The Wobbly* was called Gales. If Traven indeed honored Linn Gale, who had left Mexico City in 1921, in this fashion, he certainly did not intend to create the impression that the Wobblies were a phenomenon of the past. For even in the mid-1920s they still played a considerable role in Mexico, organizing strikes, agitations, and campaigns. Traven's descriptions of Wobbly activities in his early works derive from exact observation and personal knowledge, rendering the novels an important sourcebook on Mexican social history. It is inconceivable that Traven had *no* connections with the American Wobblies in Tampico and elsewhere in Tamaulipas; perhaps he made his first contacts through the Mr. B. mentioned in the diary, although evidence is lacking. Traven's early works amply demonstrate that he would have had a strong interest in the activities of the Mexican Wobblies. A versatile day laborer like Traven must have met with Wobblies easily and as a matter of course. He read their newspapers: On May 7, 1927, he sent Preczang "two newspapers from May 1, that of the Mexican Communists and that of the Socialists in Tampico, as well as two 'Solidaridad' leaflets of the Spanish-speaking Wobblies."

Whether the German gringo in Tampico had ever read a copy of Linn Gale's magazine cannot be determined; his library does not seem to contain an issue of it. It is more probable, indeed practically certain—and Traven's widow confirms this—that the newcomer read another radical magazine: *El Machete*, the journal, founded in March 1924, of the Sindicato de Obreros Técnicos, Pintores y Escultores, which eventually developed into the official organ of the Mexican Communist party. Its founders included Diego Rivera and David Alfaro Siqueiros, soon to gain international fame for their paintings and murals. In his later years in Mexico City, Traven was friendly with both of them, but they had first met in the 1920s, according to R. E. Luján's recollection. In the early 1920s the two artists, already friends, had returned to Mexico from study in France and had joined the Communist party. With their magazine they sought to implement their political ideas in the favorable climate of the reform-oriented Obregón government and that of Calles after him; Siqueiros was also a labor organizer. Traven, while not a Communist, stood on the side of the Indian population, who represented for him the have-nots in the world of large landowners and the oil industrialists. His engagement is stated clearly in the novels, starting with *The White Rose*, if not earlier. It was natural for him to think that the role played by the Indian was in many respects analogous to that of the proletarian in Central Europe. The *BT News* as late as 1951 still defined the Indian as the "brother of the European proletarian." In other words, the sociopolitical situation in Mexico in the mid- and late 1920s seemed grist for the Brickburner's mill. He could follow his political goals here as well as in Europe; he could remain true to himself. It was thus only natural for Traven to ally himself with radical groups in his early days in Tampico, as R. E. Luján and Marín note, though no such activity is documented.

Mexico City was the nerve center of all Mexican revolutionary activity at the time. Traven soon began to spend time there, in the spring of 1926 at the latest; on March 29, 1926, he sent Preczang a letter with his "new" Mexico City address. But aside from his P.O. Box 1480, he had no fixed residence in the capital. He lived in the Hotel Pánuco on the Calle Ayuntamiento in the center of the city, a modest establishment, rather run-down today. He always stayed in the same room, according to R. E. Luján, which the management kept for him. Sometimes he gave his address as Isabel la católica 17, which was in fact, as his widow indicated to me, the home of Professor Alberto Williams, whom Traven occasionally gave as a reference (as on his alien registration card in 1930). (Recknagel maintains in his chronology of Traven's life that Isabel la católica 17 was then the address of the "Indian teacher" María de la Luz Martínez, who from the 1930s managed the finca and restaurant El Parque Cachú in Acapulco.)

During his stays in Mexico City Traven, no longer dependent on day labor and able to concentrate fully on his writing after the resounding success of *The Death Ship*, circulated among the artists and politicians who gathered around Rivera and Siqueiros, as R. E.

Luján has noted. Their circle included the painter Xavier Guerrero, who studied with Rivera and who also collaborated on *El Machete*, as well as Rivera's brother-in-law Federico Marín, who was Traven's doctor in the 1950s and 1960s and was also his neighbor during the years on the Calle Mississippi. Also on hand were the American political journalist Carleton Beals and Frances Toor, publisher of the American magazine *Mexican Folkways*. The renowned photographer Edward Weston from Carmel, California, who is said to have taught Traven photography informally, also spent time with the Rivera circle, along with his companion the Italian photographer Tina Modotti. In the late 1920s, after Weston had already returned to the United States, Modotti became notorious as a Communist and was deported in 1930.

Some of the group lived in an apartment house on the Calle Sarco, R. E. Luján relates, where they used to meet. Revolutionary politics stood high on the agenda for all of them—Nicaragua and the invasion of the U.S. Marine Corps ("la bellísima" Tina Modotti was a particularly active supporter of the Sandinistas); the social reforms of the Calles government and its relationship with Mexican labor as well as with foreign oil interests; land reform; and church versus state politics (Calles ordered state oversight of the clergy in 1926, which the church answered with the Cristero uprising that left its mark on *The Treasure of the Sierra Madre* and which Traven alluded to in his letter of January 20, 1927, to Preczang). The group was at the political vanguard, and Traven, who in the early days of the Weimar Republic had seen intellectuals and artists fail in their attempts to take part in political life, must have felt at home in this circle, precisely because he had never tied himself to a particular party program. He probably commuted frequently between Tampico and Mexico City, spending an increasing amount of time in the capital. His editors at the Büchergilde often wrote to him there beginning in the spring of 1926, and Traven answered from there; and when he was in Tampico, he left some of his "things" back in Mexico City. For his writing, the remote bungalow in the jungle, with its mosquitoes and rattlesnakes, seemed the more fitting surroundings, though in his correspondence with Büchergilde Gutenberg he tended to depict the Spartan and tormented poet's existence according to the old cliché: the author as sufferer, society's self-proclaimed child of sorrow. "The tropical climate agrees with me better than that of the capital city. It is also too noisy for me here," he wrote to Preczang on August 8, 1926, from Mexico City. "As I pen these lines, Mexico City is roaring and buzzing as it welcomes Lindbergh, who has just come here from Washington with his famous airplane 'Spirit of Saint Louis,' " he wrote in a letter to Johannes Schönherr dated December 14, 1927.

Otherwise Traven does not give much of an impression of Mexico City in his letters of the mid-1920s; nor does the capital city play a role in his novels. The following portrait of the capital in the 1920s comes from Mildred Constantine's biography of Tina Modotti:

> There was furious activity in the city in that year [1923]. The streets were full of tram-cars and *camiones* rushing about; vendors of *pulque*, sweets, fruits and foods, toys and lacquerware were offering their wares. And music—*mariachi* bands on the streets singing for themselves and for the revolution amid the flower vendors offering their almost overpowering fragrances for *centavos*. The acrid smoke of cooking fires mingled with pungent spices. The *Zócalo* (Plaza) was dominated by the Mexican Cathedral, that imposing mixture of architectural styles ranging from that of the Spanish *conquistadores* to the baroque. Across a broad open expanse was the National Palace and other public buildings. The *Zócalo* was also the scene of other kinds of activity. Within the buildings, artists were at work in overalls just like the masons who were working with them (at the same wage scale). Mexicans were arriving in groups to petition for their rights, to ask for schools, or water for the pueblos, or simply to observe and enjoy their capital and their heritage.
>
> This activity extended to areas outside the city. Teachers were carrying books from door to door; art became so popular that open-air art schools for children were founded; painters were telling the story of Mexico and archaeologists and anthropologists were digging the great ruined pyramids and temples to discover the past so that the Indian and the *mestizo* could take their proper place as the foundation for the modern society.

In Mexico City the fugitive from the Weimar Republic quickly seized the opportunity to expand his knowledge of the country through academic study. In 1927, 1928, and 1929, Traven Torsvan enrolled in six-week summer courses at the Universidad Nacional de México. The grade sheets for the courses are preserved in his estate, revealing that his main interest lay in the Spanish language and Mexican cultural history. In the first year, he enrolled in ten hours of Spanish-language classes per week, along with Spanish conversation, writing exercises, and a practical course in phonetics. Going beyond this grounding, he enrolled that same summer in Latin American Literature, The Mexican Revolution, Mexican Archeology, and Mexican Folklore. In 1928 he added Mexican Literature, Geography of Mexico, Aztec Literature, Mexican History, Mexico's Political and Social Problems, and Historical Survey of Mexican Art, which was continued in 1929 (the only course in which he enrolled in the summer of 1929). Traven was not a particularly good student. But he did receive an A in the course on Mexico's political and social problems and in that on Mexican folklore—hardly surprising to those familiar with his Mexican novels. He received his lowest grades (D) in Mexican (Spanish-Mexican, most likely) art history and Mexican literature but also in a highly incongruous course in business correspondence and methods. His interests clearly lay elsewhere. In general, Traven's choice of the other courses reveals him (or so one feels in retrospect) preparing for his future literary production, attempting to acquire the knowledge that would lend his novels authenticity apart from personal experience. Señora Luján has photographs of Traven the student, then in his mid-forties, an elegantly dressed gringo sporting a bow tie.

In his Spanish-language course in the summer of 1927 he met the Danish sisters Helga and Bodil Christensen. They were to introduce him a decade later to Rosa Elena Luján, with whom he would spend the last years of his life. "Torsvan had so much trouble pronouncing the *o* in Spanish," Bodil recalled in the 1970s. "Helga drilled him over and over again hour after hour, until finally he could pronounce it correctly. He would come to our apartment on Calle López and we'd go out to eat, always to the cheapest restaurants. There was a place in Tacubaya you could get enchiladas for a peso and a Chinese place that served a *comida corrida*, a three-course meal, for one peso fifty centavos. Torsvan always knew the cheapest restaurants with the best food. We used to call him 'The Funny Man.' "

Expeditions to Chiapas

It was probably through his contacts in Mexico City that Traven was offered a unique chance to expand his knowledge of the country and pursue the ethnological and archeological studies that were to occupy him for the rest of his life. Traveling as Traven Torsvan, he took part in a scientific expedition that from May to August 1926 explored Chiapas, in the southwestern corner of the country. The expedition was sponsored by the Mexican government and led by the archeologist Enrique Juan Palacios. Traven accompanied the group as a photographer (adding credence to the *BT News*'s assertion that Weston helped him join the expedition). He is listed as a Norwegian photographer ("*fotógrafo noruego*") in Palacios's official report, published in Mexico City in 1928 as *En los confines de la selva lacandona: Exploraciones en el estado de Chiapas.* The idea for this research expedition, which was meant to help formulate a strategy against the locust plague that had been raging for years in the south, originated with the Mexican Ministry of Agriculture. Torsvan's identification card, which entitled him to take part in Palacios's Comisión Científica Exploradora, was issued on May 1, 1926, in Veracruz by the Junta Nacional Directora de la Campaña contra la Langosta. Since Chiapas also had a rich, but little-known, archeological and ethnological heritage, other government offices gradually joined in the planning, changing the character of the expedition. The thirty-member team that was finally assembled included agriculture experts and archeologists, geographers and naturalists, and even a sociologist (Frank Tannenbaum of Columbia University) and a biologist (A. E. Dampf, whom the *BT News* decades later derided for his claim that he was a Traven expert). Traven himself discussed the expedition's goals in an essay, "An Important Mexican Scientific Expedition to Unknown Parts of the American Continent," which he apparently sent to American newspapers; in his typescript he gives himself the byline "Our special Correspondent B. T. Torsvan."

Expedition photographs in Traven's estate show Traven not as the elegant man-about-town of the identification card, but rather as the seasoned explorer, with open shirt, breeches, laced boots, and pith helmet. In one photo Torsvan is seen writing in his small notebook—a glimpse of the author on the job, for he no doubt did not join the expedition simply to gain knowledge of the country that he was making his home, but to collect material for future books. On October 11, 1925, he had already asked Preczang whether Büchergilde Gutenberg was interested in a travel book about Mexico, and his *Land of Springtime* (1928), with its many photos, is the most visible result of the "Norwegian" photographer's explorations in Chiapas. Similarly, his later jungle and revolution novels set in the logging camps, the six-volume Mahogany series (from *The Carreta* of 1931 to *General from the Jungle* of 1940) may also be said to derive ultimately from that 1926 journey.

Traven's expedition diary, a lined octavo-sized notebook, survives. It begins, in typically detailed fashion, with his departure by train from Veracruz, on the Caribbean, on May 21, 1926, and his arrival on the Pacific coast the following day (revealing that he began the expedition along with the team of scientists). After an excursion to Tonalá to examine the pre-Columbian ruins, the expedition progressed inland from Jalisco (in Chiapas), through the Sierra Madre del Sur—a landscape populated by ox carts, which the diarist saw "crawling" by the hundreds along the difficult paths. "At night they camp and they start again at 2 a.m.," he wrote, foreshadowing *The Carreta*. But toward the end of June after only a third of the planned expedition was completed, Traven left the group in Cristóbal Las Casas and continued on his own, accompanied by his Indian guide Vitorino Trinidad (recast as Felipe in *Land of Springtime*). After a stay of several weeks in the region populated by the Chamulas, who at that time had little contact with civilization, the trip ended where it began, in Jalisco on the gulf of Tehuántepec. From there—with an authorization dated August 4 from the Junta Nacional Directora de la Campaña contra la Langosta—Traven returned to Mexico City, arriving on August 6.

Traven found treasure on the Chiapas expedition that no bandit could ever take from him. He must have seen his future as a writer clearly before him, and he systematically made use of his gold mine. He returned on several occasions to Chiapas after the 1926 expedition, exploring the jungles in the deep south of Mexico for months at a time, on horseback or mule. He was accompanied by Indian guides, one of whom was Amador Paniagua, whom Heidemann was able to interview in Chiapas in 1963.

Traven was back in Chiapas in 1927, only a year after the Palacios expedition, if Vitorino Trinidad and José Tarano remembered correctly in their conversations with Heidemann in 1963. The Chiapas trip from January to June 1928, just after *Land of Springtime* appeared, is better documented: a "2,000-mile ride from the Pacific coast to the Atlantic. . . . We will pass through unknown and unexplored territory for most of the journey. Whether and how I'll make it, I do not know," Traven wrote to Johannes Schönherr on November 24, 1927. One day before his departure, on January 5, 1928, Traven related to Schönherr an odd detail: From Tapachula on the Guatemalan border, where he was planning to begin his expedition, he would visit the Mayan tribe of the Lacandones—the staff of the National Museum had told him two days earlier that the tribe did not exist at all. He hoped to find "guides and drovers who do not fear to go there with me." Subsequently, he planned to be in Yucatán about mid-February with his "circus," where "Dr. Morley of Harvard University" was directing the excavations at Chitzen-Itza "and at whose camp I have already ordered a good welcome dinner."

From the middle of December 1929 until late March 1930 Traven was again in the south. (A hunting license issued on December 14, 1929, is among his papers in Mexico City.) He caught the travel bug again at year's end. On December 15, 1930, Büchergilde editor Erich Knauf wrote to the Swedish publisher Axel Holmström that Traven had cabled that he had again "started a rather long journey." Amador Paniagua remembered this expedition as well. In the evenings, he recalled in his interview with Heidemann, Torsvan regularly wrote up his "experiences" on a small typewriter. Then again, on July 1, 1931, Traven informed his Czech translator Serena Koenig in Prague: "This week I am again going on a long trip and cannot receive any correspondence, at least not before November." Amador Paniagua told Heidemann that it was a four-month stay in 1931 that actually did not begin until October; the "Señor ingeniero" went to the Lacandones, bringing them articles of clothing. Traven took many photographs, viewed Mayan ruins, and listened to Paniagua tell of his experiences in the forced-labor camps, the mahogany *monterías*, where he had spent seven years (1918–1925). As they parted, the gringo pressed two hundred pesos into his hand so that he could get married.

As Traven continued to compose the Mahogany series, he would probably have returned occasionally to Chiapas to get a fresh taste of the locale. "These trips are necessary," he stated in his letter to Büchergilde Gutenberg that Manfred Georg published in *Die Weltbühne* in 1929,

> in order to study the country and to collect the material which I offer to readers in the form of novels, stories, travel books, essays, and pictures. I can't make it flow out of my pencil; others can do that perhaps, but I can't. I have to know the people I talk about. They must have been my friends or my traveling

> companions, or my opponents, or my neighbors, or my fellow citizens, if I wish to depict them. I have to have seen the things, landscapes, and people before I can call them to life in my works. For that reason I have to travel to the far-off ranchos and to unknown, mysterious lakes and rivers. I have to have felt fear bordering on insanity myself, in order to be able to depict horror; I have to have suffered all sadness and all heartache myself, before I can allow the figures to suffer it which are to be brought to life. And for that reason I have to travel.

Curious documents among Traven's papers flesh out the picture. On January 16 and 17, 1928, Señor Don T. Torsvan bought three horses in Tapachula (Chiapas), one for 120 pesos, two for 65 pesos each. The Mexican magazine *Siempre* published the list of items Traven planned to take on one of his Chiapas expeditions: metal boxes, waterproof sacks, a hammock, mosquito nets (one with a curtain), a laundry bag, two sheets, slippers, towels, a wash bowl, soap for bathing and laundry, a razor, shaving soap and brush, toothbrush and toothpaste, a comb, various brushes for hair, clothing, shoes, oil for the boots, socks, shirts, "sufficient underwear," and a raincoat. But he also brought along clothing for "banquets, receptions, etc.," a sewing kit (specifying needles, yarn, buttons), notebooks, pencils, a fountain pen, ink and even an eraser, a flashlight, a revolver "for self-defense," a rifle, a feed bag for the horses and mules, stationery, toilet paper, a medicine chest, a hatchet, rope. It seems Traven was armed against any and all eventualities; it is curious to see the amount and diversity of "civilization" this European required in the jungle. The explorer with the pith helmet did not travel *exactly* like Indians, whom he called his brothers. But of course he counted on more civilized contacts. On the 1928 journey "Mr Traven Torsvan" brought along a letter of introduction from Luis Castillo Ledón, director of the National Museum, which he kept till the end of his life; and on the otherwise Spartan expedition of 1926 he paid a visit to the governor of Chiapas.

Traven's archeological interests on these expeditions were probably secondary. True, a certain E. Yarela in San Cristóbal wrote to Sergio Mijares in Pico de Oro (Chiapas) on December 26, 1929, stating that the purpose of B. Torsvan's research expedition was a study of the ruins at Tinieblas and vicinity. But Traven most likely saw the pre-Columbian artifacts primarily as a key to understanding the Indians of his own time. His archeological projects were not insignificant, to be sure. The estate contains a typed note, probably from the Croves period (1940s or 1950s), stating that in 1931 he photographed Bonampak, the Mayan site in Chiapas that has since become famous. "What is more I found the tumb of Cuauhtemoc [the last Aztec chief], the autentic [*sic*] one. But I followed T.'s [Traven's] advice and let that great warrior rest in peace where he fell." His widow has indicated that the Indians showed him the burial site of their national hero—which remained unknown to the outside world—as a proof of their trust in him, which they also expressed by presenting him with the ceramic ritual objects that Traven faithfully preserved.

In addition to his interests in their archeology, daily life, and social customs, Traven was intent on learning about the oppressed condition of the Indians in Chiapas on his travels. (The prerevolutionary history of the white man's exploitation of the Indios in the logging camps, which Traven depicted in the Mahogany Novels of the 1930s, must still have been fresh in the memory of many, not only Amador Paniagua.) To the extent possible for a European, Traven lived the life of the Indians in Chiapas. Or so he stated himself in 1951 in the *BT News*:

> This writer has, with a few short interruptions, spent more than two years in that region alone, unaccompanied by any other man of his race. There he lived, danced, sang, and went on hiking trips with Indians, mule drivers, carreteros; he cured sick Indian men and women, helped pregnant Indian women bring their little Indian babies safely into the world, arranged Indian marriages, and, at night, with or without moonlight, sat under the trees with young Indian women—and sometimes did not just sit. He lacked even the faintest bits of civilization, save those he could bring along in his few packs, in the form of toothpaste and razor blades. . . . Traven did all of this for no other reason than to gather material for his documents; for he does not write fairy tales for adults to help them fall asleep more easily. Rather, he writes documents, that is all; documents which he puts in the form of novels to make them more readable.

But it was not only among the Indios in the jungle of Chiapas that Traven felt at home. In the small town of Ocosingo he occasionally lived at the home of Amador Paniagua's aunt Ernestina Gonzales, who at the time owned a small restaurant. In 1963 she told Gerd Heidemann that the stranger arrived with seven horses;

she recalled that he had developed his film late into the night and that he also brought along a record player, "in order to see if the Lacandones liked music." He donated money, she said, "so that a house could be built to preserve the Mayan stones."

Traven became friendly with whites in Chiapas as well. He liked to stop over at the finca El Chac in the *montéria* region in the heart of Chiapas. Its owner, Ricardo Albórez, told Heidemann in 1963 that he still recalled his friend Torsvan from the 1920s and 1930s. But Traven's most notable friendship was with the Bulnes family, who lived on the San José El Real finca in the same area of Chiapas. He met them in 1928 at the latest (not 1930 as Recknagel claims; the Bulnes family told Heidemann they first met in 1927). Traven was their house guest and became particularly friendly with the *pater familias*, Enrique Bulnes, as can be seen from Bulnes's letters in the Traven estate. Bulnes wrote a neighborly letter on October 5, 1928, for example ("*muy señor mio y amigo*"), assuring Traven that his horses would naturally receive the best care on the finca until his return and offering the family's regards and so on. On December 22, 1929, Enrique Bulnes again wrote cordially to "Sr. B. T. Torsvan" in San Cristóbal ("*Mi estimado amigo*"), promising to care for Traven's "*caballo grande*" and sending Christmas greetings from the family. Traven had sent Bulnes the magazine *Hacienda*. On January 21, 1930, Bulnes thanked Traven for a book and medicine, reported that Traven's horse had been shod, and sent him fresh bread "*para su camino*" to Capulín (Chiapas).

It is useful to relate the day-to-day details of Traven's friendly relationship with the Bulnes family because they were in the mahogany business, the brutality of which Traven subjected to scathing criticism in his Mahogany series. From their El Real finca he left for days on his expeditions in search of authentic material for these novels. To be sure, Traven set the action of the novels immediately before the outbreak of the Mexican Revolution in 1910. But as he stated later, conditions remained more or less unchanged in the 1920s. It therefore comes as no surprise that, according to Señora Luján and the *BT News*, many of the large landowners from the area felt attacked when the novels became known in Mexico and expressed their anger at the writer who repaid their hospitality with such poor thanks. But Traven's relationship with the Bulnes family was never broken off, his widow said. (The claim of an otherwise unknown Fred Gaudat [Traven? Josef Wieder?] in the *BT News* in

1957 that Traven did not know the Bulnes family and never visited El Real does not correspond with the facts.)

The notes Traven made on his journey of 1928, in English on small slips of paper long since yellowed, give a vivid glimpse into his life at this time. Several of them merely catalogue the many photographs he took in Chiapas as far south as the Guatemalan border. Others preserve Traven's experiences in the curious English of the native speaker of German and record geographical facts in an attempt at scientific exactitude. Entries for the week of January 24 to February 1 looked like this (punctuation has been added to make the text more readable):

24. At night with Marcelo in his house, 1^{00h} start for the vulcan. Tacana at 10^{h}, still 400 m to go. Peak in clouds. Stay in Papál. Marcelo leaves, height 2800 m, stay, eat and sleep with Indians.

25. Leave Papál at 7^{h}, arrive crater 9^{15}, height 3170

peak at 10h 3200

crater usually lake, now dry. On peak many carved sticks from Guatemaltecan Frontier mark, phot. crater 8^{25}. . . . leave Papál 1^{45} through jungle after having lost the way. Marcelo house 4^{45}. . . . Earthquake 5^{26}. . . .

26. Taken photos. Coffee plantation on cuadro—45 trees, produces one quintal. . . .

28. Arrive Chicharras 5^{45}. . . . Spend the night in house for Indian laborers, flea pest. Terrible storm all night. Macho and horse break from pasture and are hunted for half the night and all the next morning. When found very late.

29. Leave Chicharras 11^{45}. . . .

30. . . . Macho makes trouble when passing the bridge. Boys refuse to go on, send message after me which is brought by Indian. . . . Have to return to Chanjúl on account of message. Arrive 4^{30}. Boy in helpless state. Camp.

31. Leave Chanjúl 8^{30}

11^{45} 2040 [m. above sea level]

12^{20} 2165

1^{15} 2385

Am far ahead with the horses. Boys only with mule. Boys send word mule doesn't march. Return and find mule down on its fours. . . . With some patience got the mule on its feet again while boy says it is impossible. Passes by an Indio with two mules. Make up with him to change the load of his mule which is very little with the load of my mule until Motozintla. Cost me $7.50 [pesos].

Pinaorte 1^{30} 2400

2^{15} 2520. 2^{30} 2590
Zarragossa 3^{h} 2620
Niquivil 4^{30} 2650–2630.
See the frontier marks, two columns, pict[ures]. Tiendas [Indian stores], robbers.

II.1. [February 1]
Leave Niquivil 7^{h}
Morelia 10^{30} 2260
Valley beautiful. Road high and narrow along the mountain side, deep down below the river bed, stony.
Magueys of all kind.
Bridge 12^{h} 800
Two houses
Rio Blanco, lonely ranch
12^{30} 880. Girls in the door, well dressed, lousing
Junta 2^{h} 800
Meet whol[e] tribe in the road, are migrating. Near a creek a well to do family with horses resting. Beautiful houses, pict[ures].
Tapatzala 4 800
Soon the valley opens with a view of rare beauty
La Nueva 5^{30} 800
Finca cafee in bad condition. Told 400 head of cattle and much sugar cane, things which pay better than coffee. Fine pastures. Jungles with indications of tigers and lions. Always water of finest sort. Peaceful pictures of homegoing cattle. Gets dark.
Arrive Cushú 6^{45} 730. Camp in the plaza with good pasture for the horses and mules. Had and have to doctor the horse. Dogs and pigs eat up all the soap.

Those familiar with Traven's novels are reminded here at nearly every turn of "fictitious" situations and episodes that, in light of these unpublished personal accounts, turn out to be anything but invented in their entirety (or taken over from an "other man's" texts and experiences). The entries confirm, if confirmation were necessary, that Traven based his Mexican novels on what he himself had experienced.

The sketches of the Chiapas expedition of 1929–1930 are even more extensive. I examined the typed version (with corrections in Traven's hand), which most likely was copied from the original handwritten notes. Here are a few excerpts revealing the raw material of experiences and events that would resurface fully developed in the Mahogany series.

1929
December
. . .

29. L[eave] 7:25. Heavy rain. Difficulty passing swollen river close by the ranch. Pico de cerro 2:30. Cruz 1:45. A[rrive] Ocosingo 5:20. El Chorro, two leagues, ruins and one big round stone. San Jerónimo poor. No coffee, no tea. Tea of lemon leaves. Huistanecos followed man whose family was killed. Ambush. Horse returned home alone with saddle. Body never found. Ch[amula] tribe elects pres. each year, and each year from another of the four barrios of which the nation is composed. 1929.I.1. [January 1, 1929] pres. was told by gov. not to resign, stayed in office, town was besieged and surrounded I.1. by nation, at 10:00 pres. and his whole family killed. When after phone call soldiers arrived not one Indian was to be seen. Killers never found.

31. Photos. Chicken of doña E[rnestina Gonzales] are not fed, lay eggs straight somewhere in the garden or in the yard. Men and women extremely dirty. Seem never to wash themselves. Floor covered with pine needles. Also church. Half of the roof of church is missing. . . .

In Comitán and some other places ants are eaten, and sold in great quantities in sacks in the market.

In Capulín the Indians while eating all kinds of snakes, also rattlers, worms, they do not eat turtles nor their eggs. . . .

1930
January
. . .

7. L[eave] 11.30. Rio close to town Rio La Virgen. Crossing rio Chantichác. Difficult crossing, river swollen. Mules to be unloaded. Packs carried by the boy who wades the river. Boy who was to go to his wedding drowned, the boy who was to marry the same girl before was drowned in the river Usumacinta when leaving the monte. A[rrive] Chijilté 5:00.

8. . . . Crossing the river Santa Cruz after nightfall on canoes. A[rrive] El Real 7:10 p.m. In Oco. Indian children with high bellies. . . .

9. Photos.

10. Official dirty and poor, sent to Bacha to enrich himself, selling brandy and jailing the drunken men.

Indians in El Real and in El Rosario clean and intelligent. No brandy sold to them. Fiesta with victrola, all dancing, no brandy, although jolly and gay. Fincas with intelligent Indians more prosperous than others, because the boys are more useful. All floors covered with pine-needles. How by the outrageous way the revolucionary troops acted on his finca the high ambitions of don José de Arcos was killed. Chack . . . Rain god. Camisán near Tenosique supposed to be the burying place of Cuauhtemoc. Ruins near finca El Puente—Comitán called Tenam.

11. . . . Dancing: the boy throws his kerchief into the lap of the girl he wants to dance with. If the girl accepts the kerchief she wishes to dance with the boy, while dancing she holds the kerchief in her hand. She returns the kerchief when the dance ends or when she wishes to cease dancing.

12. Photos of José and Manuel, houses, girls, tambors. 3:00 p.m. 20 deg. shade.

. . .

February 1930

. . .

24. . . . Fell into the creek 9.45. Lost all the sugar and greatest part of provisions wet.

Packed up again 10.30. . . .

25. L[eave] La Culebra 7.45.

Lagunita 12.30. Monkeys, Mono Gritón, by the hundreds in the trees. A[rrive] El Pelhaj 2.00. Trail very mountainous, parts almost vertical. Rocky. Rolling and slipping stones. Picture of camp El Pelhaj. Track of Royal Tiger half the path to El Pelhaj, and right all the time following the caravane of don Marino who is one day ahead.

26. L[eave] El Pelhaj 7.00.

Misty and foggy and wet.

Plants with roots in the air. Big trees carry and feed hundreds of all kinds of plants.

A[rrive] Santo Domingo 2.00.

Camp pitched on the opposite bank of the river. Passing of the mules through the river. It takes 1½ hour. The horse is the most difficult one to get across.

Wild hogs in the trail by the dozens.

Spider's webs horizontal.

Night heavy rain. Flood inside the tent. All wet.

27. L[eave] Santo Domingo 6.45.

No breakfast, no tea, because wood is so wet that no fire can be made. . . .

28. . . . Lake [Santa Clara]. Hardly accessible on account of swampy foreground. Surrounded by virgin forests and jungles. Spoiled by the oxen from the monterias, sent here to feed and for vacation after hard work in the monterias.

Night passes with horrors caused by tecks and millions of mosquitoes. All around dirt from the cattle which accounts for all other kind of vermin on the ground and in the tent. Underbrush left over from former milpas full with miriads of pesterous insects.

Water coming from a natural well beneath an ants' hill very clear. There are several of these wells springing out of the muddy ground.

March 1930

L[eave] Lake Santa Clara 6.20. Sting of some insect in the lips. Lip swells like a thick plum.

Road all mud. Mules are sinking in deep. Riding most of the way out of the question. Fifty times mounting and dismounting.

11.55 Anaité, that is the abandoned monteria Anaité, at the river bank.

. . .

5. . . .

The ruins partly one, partly two halls each, rectangular, like a floor, with niches. Two huge stones with hieroglyphs, very clear cut and very well preserved. Some walls of the halls are covered with ornamented plaster or mortar. Fourteen buildings, but likely some more farther in the jungle. All is covered with a dense jungle.

One building, with door and above a niche, has on the ceiling of the door looking down a stone, serving as the ceiling, in which is cut an historic act.

Three kings making a treaty, the contents of which is written in hieroglyphs on stone tablets.

Yiactchilan. Close by the monteria Santo Domingo which is on the G[uatemala] bank.

L[eave] 3.00.

A[rrive] Anaité 4.45.

. . .

6. Anaité. In the road to Tiniebla[s], near the arroyo Bascán, ruins. Many buildings with sculptures and earthenware. Still visited by the Carribes who have their idols, santitos, in these temples. Buildings have many doors. Incensors of the Carribes. In the road Tenosique to Piedras Negras ruins close to Piedras Negras. These are buildings.

Picts. of doña Victoria Alameya, don Francisco Villanueva Tenosique. Sr. Ulises de la Cruz rec[ommended?] don F. Villanueva Tenosique.

The Usumacinta is not known yet in its full length. Nobody has ever seen all parts of it. This the reason why there is so much mystery about it.

In Guatemala there are living only two Carribe families who have emigrated from Mexico.

. . .

8. L[eave] Anaité 7.45.

9.00 road lost. Cemetry.

1.30 Chicosapote. Bodega y monteria de Juan Noriega y Manuel Villanueva. Giant lizards. Mosquitoes. Tigers. Lizards called Iguana.

. . .

11. L[eave] Ojo de Agua] 7.00. 7.40 Cerro Pedrigal. 7.55 Peak of mountain. 8.05 cerro. 8.30 top.

To the right from the depths of the jungle a cry like the voice of a woman in distress or like mortally wounded. Search does not reveal anything.

In the road many mounds, small ones, might be tombs of a people who wandered this trail centuries ago.

Here the whole jungle is of the same kind one usually may find in regions where there used to be cultivated land. There are certain plants which grow only in places which times ago have been cultivated and which now have been conquered again by the wilderness. Mostly these plants are weeds which are not found in the jungle as a rule, these plants can be seen all over Central-America on abandoned farms. To find them in the jungle is proof that there must have been, perhaps centuries ago, cultivated land. Even certain insects which as a rule are not found in the jungle may be encountered here, insects which belong to regions that were cultivated and that have been turned into jungle again.

Certain regular forms of an artificial kind and shape still visible under the mounds of decaying leaves and branches and trunks indicate as well that all what is now jungle and wilderness has been once populated by men.

Since all caravans have to keep on the trail and since even the men of the caravans when hunting keep as near the trail as possible lest to lose the trail and so their way back to civilisation[;] this jungle has never been penetrated to its very limits. Therefore in the depths of this jungle there are certainly to be found immense proofs of a former civilisation and even more pyramids and temples. But to think of meeting perhaps still populated cities which have never been heard of is out of the question. The only people who still live in this jungle are the Caribes, and these people are few families.

Here frogs have all kinds of size and color. There are frogs that are larger than two big hands, and there are frogs colored green, red, yellow, blue, white. Certain frogs bark like dogs. There are snails that shrill piercingly.

. . .

Nuevo Paraje 3.00. Creek with running water disappears at night. A few yards farther up water can be had.

At Anaité everyone says Buenas Noches to each other, particularly to his parents and to the guests, when the candles are lighted.

. . .

13. . . .

Now, a full week in advance, are beginning the church services in honor of San José. Every night the wife of the mayordomo assembles the women and some men in the chapel where she and the girls of the house sing and pray while the Indian women who do not understand a single word try to follow. Since there are no bells to call for the service some Indians beat drums and play pipes and flutes.

. . .

19. The fiesta in full swing. The capitanes have to feed the whole pueblo. Dances.

. . .

22. L[eave] El Capulín 7.45. Meet the horse. Santa Isabel 10.15. Before arriving at El Real pyramides.

At El Real most of the Indians wear mustaches and beards, rare among the Indians of that region. The flower of the Ceba is like silken hair, colored creamy. Yaxchilán or Yachilum means Very fertile earth. Ocosingo— Great Place.

Fieldwork was not everything. Several of the books that after Traven's death remained in the "bridge" (as he called his study in his Calle Mississippi home) show that he continued to occupy himself with Indian languages, archeology, and the art and history of Chiapas. These books include a worm-eaten copy of Vicente Pineda's *Historia de las sublevaciones indígenas habidas en el estado de Chiapas*, which incorporates a *Diccionario* and a *Gramática de la lengua Tzel-tal que habla la generalidad de los habitantes de los pueblos que quedan al Oriente y al Noreste del Estado* (Chiapas, 1888), Manuel Romero de Terroros y Vinent's *Las artes industriales en la Nueva España* (Mexico City, 1928), Cyrus Thomas's *Indian Languages of Mexico and Central America and Their Geographical Distribution* (Washington, 1911), and Carlos Basauri's *Tojolabales, Tzeltales y Mayas: Breves apuntes sobre antropología, etnográfica y linguística* (Mexico City, 1931).

The Birth of "B. Traven"

Traven's studies and expeditions were ultimately meant to further his literary pursuits. Considering that he tried, almost obsessively, to pass himself off as an American, denying any connection with Germany, it may come as a surprise that he composed his literary works in German. Less surprising was his attempt in his early days in Mexico to establish himself as a journalist and writer of fiction in English: an astonishingly courageous decision for a middle-aged German with no money or connections with the English-speaking publishing world. Traven himself (as discussed in the section "Obituaries, Usurpers of Fame, and the 'Other Man' " in Chapter 2) often claimed that in his early post-German period he wrote in English for the American market, but with little success. "Before I sold a book to Germany, I have peddled my stories around all magazines and editors that exist, or existed, in this country [the United States] and all I sold in five years of constantly firing at them was five bucks, believe it or not," he wrote of this phase of his life in 1935 to the American journalist Herbert Arthur Klein.

Many have doubted these remarks, which are nonetheless confirmed not only by the original English version of *The Death Ship* (noted in the *BT News* as well) but also by bits of evidence in Traven's library, correspondence, and literary papers. There I stumbled upon a German-English, English-German dictionary (by Thieme and Preusser, Gotha and Hamburg, 1859), into which was inserted an advertising leaflet from Tampico, dated October 3, 1926 (also, as chance would have it, a yellowed paper with a typed message that speaks volumes about Traven's free spirit and the spontaneity to which his Mexican family has attested so often: "Never mind an easy life, never mind a life of struggle, do as your heart wants you to do, don't let your brain interfere, at the very end of all things, be they ever so great, ever so small, it is the heart alone which counts"). Traven's library also contains all sorts of trade publications offering help for the budding English author: Frank Farrington's *Writing for the Trade Press* (Ridgewood, N.J., 1917), the anonymous brochure *The Way into Print* (Franklin, Ohio, no date), as well as single copies of the magazines *Author and Journalist* (1927), *The Writer's Monthly* (December 1924), and *The Writer's Bulletin* (November 1927). From these years Traven also kept a few typescripts of articles with which he apparently had attempted to gain an entrée into the American market, including an essay "Women in the Conquest of Mexico" ("Copyright 1925, by B. Traven"), which was never published as far as I can tell. We have already spoken of his illustrated 1928 report on the jungle dwellers on the western bank of the Usumacinta submitted to *National Geographic*, which also apparently never made it into print. ("All the photographs have been taken personally by T. Torsvan from February 1928 until June 1928," according to a note accompanying the typescript.) On November

1, 1926, the editor of *National Geographic* had already returned an article, "The Tzotzil Indians and Their Neighbors," to Mr. Traven Torsvan in Tampico, along with the 101 photographs he had submitted, with the remark "It cannot be adapted to the present needs of The National Geographic Magazine." Traven even tried his luck with *Popular Mechanics*: In a letter dated November 23, 1926, to Traven Torsvan, P.O. Box 972, Tampico, the editor said he would accept for publication one of his photographs and "your interesting story on The Rosary Mill in Chiapas"; the story never appeared, it seems, although the editor enclosed a check for five dollars.

In the mid-1920s, Traven made several more submissions to American magazines, as can be seen from the notebook discussed in the next paragraph. But although one or another of his pieces may in fact have appeared in some American publication at that time (the *Readers' Guide to Periodical Literature* lists nothing under the name Torsvan or Traven), the cases cited here may be considered symptomatic: Traven was not successful as a writer of English in his early years in Mexico.

But from the first, he made overtures to German publishers as well. His earliest diary (1924–1926) records on October 7, 1925: "Mss. Wohlf. Ehre"—a reference no doubt to the short stories "Die Wohlfahrtseinrichtung" ("The Charitable Institution") and "Familienehre" ("Family Honor") published in the collection *Der Busch* (*The Bush*) in 1928. The first page of a typescript, hand-corrected and identified as an "original manuscript," of "Die Wohlfahrtseinrichtung[.] Von B. Traven" lies among Traven's papers. He must have written it at a very early date, since the return address—"B. Traven/ Columbus/Tamaulipas/Mexico"—does not include the Tampico P.O. Box 1208, his first regular address used in transatlantic correspondence. (It appears, for example, on the first and, it seems, only surviving typescript page of his story "Das Feuerfest der Azteken" ["The Fire Festival of the Aztecs"], also in the estate, which apparently never appeared in print.) Traven's papers also include a small notebook from the mid-1920s in which he painstakingly kept track of the German and English texts (novels, stories, articles—all told forty-four titles, some known, others unknown) that he had offered to publishers, newspapers, and magazines on dates precisely recorded. Here we read that *Die Baumwollpflücker* (*The Cotton-Pickers*) was sent to the Kiepenheuer Press in Potsdam on January 18, 1925. The next day he sent the same work to the German Social

Democratic newspaper *Vorwärts*—which *The Brickburner* had excoriated in 1919 as an organ of deceitful demagogues—where it was indeed serialized that summer. In the meantime, he continued to peddle copies of the typescript to several other German newspapers, including one in New York, until April 27, 1925. On March 27, *Vorwärts* editor John Schikowski wrote that he would gladly accept the novel—it was the "first part" of the text that appeared in 1926 in book form as *Der Wobbly*—"and we are offering you an honorarium of 500 Marks for it." He also promised, should Traven have no objections, to offer the manuscript for possible book publication to "our old party press" J.H.W. Dietz.

By that time, Traven was no longer an unknown quantity to *Vorwärts*: He had published the first "Traven" piece there on February 28, 1925, the story "Wie Götter entstehen," which later was reworked and published as "Die Geburt eines Gottes" ("A New God Was Born"). And after serializing *Die Baumwollpflücker* (June 21 to July 16), *Vorwärts* published "Die Gründung des Aztekenreiches" ("The Founding of the Aztec Empire") on August 7, 1925, and "Die Geschichte einer Bombe" ("The Story of a Bomb") on October 24 and 25, 1925. The editors naturally had no idea that their new contributor had long before made his debut in *Vorwärts* as Ret Marut and in that guise had also almost routinely received rejection letters for his short prose pieces. Yet the emerging Traven did not rely solely on *Vorwärts*. The magazine *Jugend*, the estate shows, sent 20 marks to him in Columbus on August 3, 1925, for "Die Dynamitpatrone" ("Dynamite"), which was printed in November, while *Simplicissimus* informed him on October 3, 1925 (writing to P.O. Box 1208 in Tampico) that the (unidentified) "sketch" he had submitted was not suitable for their publication but that in accordance with his request they had passed it along to the newspaper *Die Welt am Montag*. In the meantime, Traven's "The Story of a Bomb" had already made it into the pages of *Simplicissimus* (August 17, 1925).

It was not easy for an author with an unknown name to enter the literary world of the Weimar Republic. What Traven managed to have published was only the tip of the iceberg, however. The *BT News* stated that from 1920 to 1925 (attempting with the earlier date to promote the fiction that Traven had been in Central America and far away from Europe long before 1925) "editors of German newspapers and magazines would now and again receive short stories written in German which were set in Mexico. Their author was someone called B. Traven. The stories were doubtless translations either from American or Spanish.* Very few of those works were published; the majority were returned to the author as unusable. The story that Traven wrote his narratives in pencil on brown paper is a product of some reporter's fantasy. He typed all his works." Büchergilde editor Johannes Schönherr recalled in 1962 that the manuscripts Traven submitted were yellowed and gnawed at by insects.

Most of the stories from this period may well have been rejected. Several did appear in German magazines after the banner year 1925: *Die Büchergilde* included in March 1926 the Indian story "Die Medizin" ("Effective Medicine"); *Westermanns Monatshefte* introduced Traven to its readers that same year with a story that was to become one of his most famous, "Im tropischen Busch" (translated into English as "The Night Visitor"); and "the illustrated family magazine" *Das Buch für Alle* published three other stories based on Traven's experiences in Mexico in 1926, 1927, and 1928: "Nachttänze der Indianer" ("Indian Dance in the Jungle"), "Der Eselskauf" ("Burro Trading"), and "Ein Hundegeschäft" ("Indian Trading") (the estate contains a publisher's agreement for "Nachttänze," dated 1925, providing for an honorarium of 75 marks). Considerably more short pieces were written about Mexico in the bungalow in Tamaulipas. Traven would have intended some of them for publication in German magazines. But once he cemented his relationship with Büchergilde Gutenberg, he probably intended some for a collection of stories. In any event, in 1928 the Büchergilde published twelve Indian stories set in Mexico under the title *Der Busch*, and a second, expanded edition of twenty stories came out under the same title two years later. Most were unpublished until then.

They are all short pieces written simply and unassumingly: sketches, reports of daily life as seen through the eyes of a newcomer to Mexico who eagerly records everything that strikes him as unusual in this "far-off land." The sense of wonder of a European far from home, a civilized man among the natives, infuses practically all of

*Traven again shows his prowess as a master of the bluff, for only he could have been responsible for this statement; the estate includes the carbon copy of a Traven typescript that contains this passage as part of a background story on the filming of *Das Totenschiff*. To be fair, there is reason to believe that some stories existed in English originally, most notably "The Night Visitor," with its play on *hog* and *dog*. Still, it is easy to see how speculation about an "other man" could take a statement like this as its cue.

these texts with freshness and immediacy, however inconsequential their subject matter. For the most part they are not so much stories as colorful snapshots, often anecdotal, telling of happenings in the hinterland, in the tropical bush. Most interesting for the biographer is that Traven, in an extended diary so to speak, reveals much about his own life in his new surroundings (though of course not everything was "experienced" exactly in the manner described). At the heart of almost all these pieces stand the experiences of a white man (sometimes he is called Gales, and often he is the narrator) confronting the natives. One can recognize a thinly veiled Traven as the "Banditendoktor" in the story of the same name ("Midnight Call"), who with the simple items in his medicine chest saves the life of an Indian *muchacho* who had been shot in an ambush and then makes a narrow escape from the soldiers looking for the culprits. Is he not also present as the English-language tutor among the natives and as the cotton planter, as the guest at the nocturnal Indian fiestas, and as the hermit in his hut in the jungle who bargains with the locals for a mule or a dog, bewildered by the strange mentality of his neighbors?

Particularly pointed is the difference in attitude between the Indian and the white man in the sketch "Der Grossindustrielle" ("Assembly Line"): The business savvy of the entrepreneur, who sees in Indian folk art merely a chance to make a dollar, is contrasted with the Mexican's delight in his handiwork, into which he weaves the song of the birds, the beauty of the flowers, and "the unsung songs which he heard in his soul," without thinking much about pesos and centavos. But a glaring spotlight is also thrown on the brutal passion of the Indians and on their naiveté (as in "Die Geschichte einer Bombe" ["The Story of a Bomb"] and "Die Wohlfahrtseinrichtung" ["The Charitable Institution"]). The observer of foreign customs and mores inclines toward the grotesque in "Familienehre" ("Family Honor"), in which the natives can scarcely contain their delight at watching a corpse bloat up so that a European tailcoat, originally much too big, now actually fits him and makes him a "lovely corpse," rendering his funeral a success.

Occasionally the narrator lays bare the natives' realistic attitudes toward Catholic doctrine: A thief seeks to secure the protection of a saint; a saint who fails to help find a lost watch is defaced ("Spiessgesellen" ["Accomplices"]; "Der ausgewanderte Antonio" ["The Kidnapped Saint"]). But Traven also allows the Indians their own—

albeit equally naive—superiority in questions of religion, as in "Indianerbekehrung" ("Conversion of Some Indians"), in which he contrasts the "magnificent, radiant sun god" with the cruel Christian god who lets his son be killed and damns the unbelievers. The confrontation between the interlopers and the natives takes an eerie turn in the most ambitious of these early works, "The Night Visitor," which hauntingly depicts the world that was Traven's in his early period in Mexico. Gales stops over in the primitive bungalow of a strange, self-absorbed American doctor who has chosen to retreat into the Mexican wilderness. A Pakunese chieftain who has rested for centuries in the nearby funeral pyramid, long since overgrown, appears to Gales in a vision—the aura of the pre-Columbian era, translated into mythical, unreal terms, lends the world of the impoverished Indios and uprooted gringos a magical power.

Aside from the short historical sketch "The Founding of the Aztec Empire" and "Götter der alten Mexikaner" ("Gods of the Old Mexicans"), both of which appeared in *Vorwärts*, Traven's first printed German prose was fictional. He attempted journalistic essays more than once, but probably without much originality and in any case without much success. In a letter to Johannes Schönherr of November 24, 1927, he claimed to have also published in *Das Buch für Alle* "some small humorous pieces which I translated from American magazines." (They must have appeared anonymously and for that reason cannot be located with any degree of accuracy among the many humorous pieces in that publication's regular columns.) Perhaps the essay on the founding of the Aztec empire was also more or less a translation, as is probably the case with "Lebensgeschichte eines erfolgreichen Mannes" ("The Life Story of a Successful Man"), a biographical sketch of the American newspaper magnate Frank Andrew Munsey, who died on December 22, 1925, and who was no doubt recalled in many articles at the time. Other unprinted articles may have been similar reworkings.

From *The Death Ship* to *The White Rose*

The stories and other short prose pieces were, with the possible exception of "The Night Visitor," secondary pursuits, journalistic *Kleinarbeit* ("piecework"), as Traven liked to call it in his correspondence with the Büchergilde: "sketches" that he undertook primarily to make some fast cash at a time when he was living from hand to mouth and work was not easy to come by. The most substantial result of his first six years in Mexico—the years, before he settled in Acapulco, when he spent much of his time at the bungalow in Tamaulipas, to which he continued to return from his trips—are the novels: the five novels that, in contrast to the six of the Mahogany series written in Acapulco, do not form an interrelated whole. The five, all published originally in German, are *Das Totenschiff* (1926; *The Death Ship)* and the novels set in Mexico: *Der Wobbly* (1926; published in 1928 as *Die Baumwollpflücker* [*The Cotton-Pickers*], also the title of the first part of the novel serialized in *Vorwärts* in 1925), *Der Schatz der Sierra Madre* (1927; *The Treasure of the Sierra Madre*), *Die Brücke im Dschungel* (1929; *The Bridge in the Jungle*; serialized in *Vorwärts* in 1927), and *Die weisse Rose* (1929; *The White Rose*).

These books established Traven's reputation and even today represent the centerpieces of his fame. The Mahogany series of the 1930s, depicting the exploitation of the Indios in the logging camps of southern Mexico, which erupted in the revolution of 1910, never enjoyed the same popularity, and Traven's attempted comeback twenty years later with *Aslan Norval* actually turned out to be more of setback. But *The Death Ship*, the first of the novels published by the author with the strange new name, enjoyed immediate and lasting popularity, among both members and nonmembers of the Büchergilde Gutenberg book club, which published it. And the Traven titles that followed in rapid succession, culminating with *The White Rose*, were embraced by readers with unusual vigor in those turbulent final years of the Weimar Republic. These books appealed passionately to the individual to assume responsibility for his actions amid the prevailing *Republikmüdigkeit* (Weimar ennui) and hedonistic apathy of the seemingly Golden Twenties. It would be an exaggeration to say that they acted as a purifying and invigorating "storm" through the literary landscape of the late 1920s, as *The Brickburner* had attempted at the close of the Empire and as Traven intended with his projected publishing program in the 1940s, which he hoped to name Tempestad. It would be an exaggeration, but an exaggeration in the right direction.

The merits of these novels do not lie primarily in their literary or artistic value narrowly defined. Kurt Tucholsky realized this when the novels first appeared, though he was also one of the first to recognize the magnitude of Traven's talent. Traven apparently took to heart the maxim of Gerhart Hauptmann—whom he admired, to judge from the Marut story "Liebe des Vaterlandes" ("Love of the Fatherland") (1916)—that "polishing is rarely artistic." From the 1920s to the present day critics have let it be known that this *Wunderkind* of German literature who came from nowhere was no great stylist. He lays it on thick as a narrator, critics note, as when in *The White Rose* he points pedantically to the wagon wheel rotting away in the courtyard as a symbol of the Indians' loyalty to the land. Traven, others stress, had little sense for the aesthetic composition of his epic subject matter; he jarringly interrupts the flow of the narrative with cicerone passages; he handles language carelessly, some claim, to the point of being sloppy—an effect others may view as deliberately unconventional, informal, and antibourgeois; his satire on American-European civilization is unnecessarily trenchant and almost grotesque, just as his adoration of the ancient, natural and unspoiled world of the Central American natives verges on escapism or simplistic romanticizing. Those hoping to find psychological sophistication in the characterizations in these novels would also best look elsewhere.

To acknowledge such criticism does not force us to classify Traven's works as exotic adventure stories or light reading and to attribute their popularity to more or less juvenile instincts beneath the dignity of the "educated." If we did so, we would ignore the basic impetus of this "philosophical revolutionary," which makes us place Traven closer to Thoreau and Whitman than to Jack London (as R. E. Luján puts it in an unpublished text). This basic impetus has given Traven's works a place in the canon of German literature since they first appeared, acting as a refreshing breeze on those inside and outside the cultural elite. Ironically, it was Traven's critics from the clique of the Nazi newspaper *Völkischer Beobachter* who scented the philosophical and revolutionary power of the novels. They branded them the products of a "destructive mind," "devoid of feeling," and lacking any sense of the "positive" or "constructive." Traven rebutted their remarks in an "open letter" to Büchergilde Gutenberg in 1933, just after it had been taken over by the Nazis (the cited characterizations of him by the Nazis are quoted from his letter). In that letter he stated his own critique of society in no uncertain terms and stressed its "constructive" nature (as *he* defined it).

But the "*revolucionario filosófico*," the eternal rebel who denounced every use of force against the individual, was at the same time not naively optimistic. On the contrary: However energetic his revolutionary/anarchistic fanfare for those deprived of their rights in modern society, for those oppressed by totalitarian regimes, all of Traven's novels through the Mahogany series also sound a tone of deep melancholy, not only about the enduringly powerful structure of class society but also about the nature of man, which in spite of all the bright spots, all the moments of fulfillment, remains imperfect—weak, common, and banal. The world is bad, and man is not always good, as Traven's expressionist generation wanted to believe. We cannot attain the object of our desires—or only rarely and momentarily. Thus Traven's novels often enough transmit an air of hopelessness that, though never directly stated, subtly undermines the view of a rosy future and a reformed society. Seeing how the world really operates threatens to frustrate the will. Not surprisingly, heated discussions took place in East Germany in the 1950s about whether Traven—who clearly stood on the side of the oppressed and whose personal record was impeccably antifascist—could be cited as an ideological role model in the rebuilding of the new society. The leftists in the post-Nazi era, like the rightists in the Nazi era, thus missed more or less the same: the "constructive" element, regardless of whether one chooses to call it the "healthy feeling of the people" or proletarian class consciousness. Such reactions correspond not only to Marut/Traven's habit of distancing himself from both the left and the right, without pleading for a middle ground, but also to the nature of the novels themselves.

Traven's first novel, *The Death Ship*, begun in London in an English version in 1923–1924, is still oriented toward European conditions. An autobiographical reading—appropriate in principle—reveals this story of a man without a country as the link between Marut's departure from Europe and Traven's arrival overseas. In it the anarchist settles his account with post–World War I capitalist society, in which those deprived of power and rights by the industrial state are systematically exploited and tyrannized. Specifically, the first-person narrator of this "story of an American sailor" emphasizes that aspect of the tyranny of the state over the individual that affected Marut/Traven personally more than all others: A human being qualifies as a person, a citizen, a valid member of society only when he has the proper papers, which the government bureaucracy alone may issue and deny. In such acts of recognition or denial of legitimacy the state "reveals" its "omnipotence." "It used to be that the princes were the tyrants, today the state is the tyrant." It rules through identification papers. Bureaucracy is "fate." When paper becomes more important than people, people without papers have "no right to live," Traven wrote in 1926 in a discussion of his novel in *Die Büchergilde*. The main characters in the novel, he continued, are precisely such jettisoned members of society—the "involuntary victims of a shameful system," namely "modern capitalism," the living dead, the prime examples of those whom civilization has left without rights or power.

The sailor Gales's fate is sealed—he is dead while alive—from the moment he misses the departure of his ship one day in Antwerp after a night of carousing. He had left his sailor's card on board, which had identified him as an American. His official identity gone, no consul will issue him a passport based on his word alone. Gales enters upon an odyssey through the countries of Western Europe, which one after the other usher him out across their borders under cover of night. His wanderings end in Cadiz, where he signs on aboard the death ship *Yorikke*, a dilapidated freighter that bears contraband and is soon to be sunk on the high seas in an insurance fraud (a motif familiar from Ibsen's *Pillars of Society* no less than from today's news about insurance scandals; in the *BT News* Traven continued to stress the timeliness of the subject matter, and in the 1920s fraud of this sort indeed seems not to have been uncommon). Sooner or later, the crew will go down with the ship; only the officers, coconspirators with the shipping company, are allowed life preservers and lifeboats. But in a sense the crew has long been dead while the *Yorikke* is still afloat—they all lack papers and thus an identity. "They were dead men. Extinguished. Without a country. Without papers. Without a homeland."

As such they are the losers, the exploited. They represent the lowest level of society, the foundation of the capitalism so often attacked in the novel, and the narrator never tires of depicting the agonies of these oppressed and cheated men who are just barely staying alive under inhuman conditions. Traven deromanticizes the traditional view of the sailor by taking as his perspective the sailors' quarters, not the bridge, as Traven claimed Joseph Conrad had done. The death ship itself is an emblem of the industrial state, in which the sailors, deckhands, and coal drags—thrown together from every corner of Europe—represent the proletariat, which keeps this state in running order. An accusation writ in fire.

But the narrator does not merely criticize bureaucratic tyranny and the plight of the proletarian. More fundamentally he is interested in the existential question of the value of the individual born free and equal, whom the all-powerful state declares nameless, a nonperson, or even nonexistent because he lacks identification papers. Apart from all social criticism, Traven strikes a dominant theme that will run through much of his works: The rage of the man without identification over his officially declared nonexistence is transformed into the passionate embrace of this very namelessness as an expression of his true freedom and happiness. Paradoxically, the outcast proclaims his superiority over the authority of the state when he stakes his claim as the outsider—with conviction and with pride.

The American consul in Paris tells Gales that in the eyes of the law he may never have been born, let alone have a right to citizenship and a homeland. Yet Gales finally feels at home among the nameless crew on the death ship, which lends those "without a country and never born" not only a sense of belonging but also an identity. On the *Yorikke* none of the crew gives his true name, none tells his true life story, and neither does Gales. "And so I gave up my good name," he reports almost defiantly. "I didn't have a name any longer." But through this very self-denial he finds himself, creates himself in a manner of speaking: not as the fictional character he has presented to his fellow crew members but as the individual capable of this creative act of the will who has thereby become master of his fate. "I *have* a homeland . . . and it is *myself*," Ret Marut had quoted from Herman Bang's novel *Denied a Country*, foreshadowing Traven's emphatic acceptance of anonymity as the gesture of one who is uncertain of his own "true" name but who is nonetheless convinced of his own worth.

"He who enters here," reads the inscription, reminiscent of Dante, above the crew's quarters on the *Yorikke*, "his name and existence are extinguished. . . . He never existed, not even in thought." This netherworld paradoxically becomes the homeland of the sailor without a country. "Where is my homeland? There, where . . . no one wants to know who I am, no one wants to know what I'm doing, no one wants to know where I've come from—that is my homeland, that is my fatherland." Gales finds a friend in his comrade Stanislav

Koslowski from Posen, who, like an Alsatian and an East Prussian among the crew, lost his citizenship after the war during the bureaucratic shuffle of national boundaries. Stanislav eases Gales's way into the world of the death ship. Eventually Gales gains a certain satisfaction from carrying out his tasks; he learns to love the *Yorikke*, this no-man's-land with a crew of the living dead.

Yet the novel ends with the destruction of even this funereal realm. It is not the *Yorikke* that sinks, to be sure, but another death ship, the *Empress of Madagascar*, to which Stanislav and Gales were shanghaied. The *Empress* appears to be a fully seaworthy, far more respectable vessel than the unsightly and run-down *Yorikke*. The erstwhile revolutionary in the kaiser's Germany cannot deny himself the wordplay: The *Empress* sinks off the West African coast—a broad hint that the nominally dynastic European social and political order was ripe for its demise in the capitalist age, as *The Brickburner* had told its readers years earlier.

Gales survives, however—we do not learn how. In his essay on *The Death Ship*, Traven teasingly denied an explanation, admitting only that one who narrates "must be alive." What survives the collapse of the old European order is, in any event, the anarchistic sense of the individual who has found himself in his defiance.

Gales can thus continue to tell his stories. Aside from the stories in the *Bush* collection, he narrates *The Wobbly*, a tale of vagabonds set in the Mexican hinterland (the locale for all of Traven's subsequent works with the exception of *Aslan Norval*). Compared with *The Death Ship*, this novel seems looser, also less dominated by social criticism. It consists of a number of colorful episodes, Gales's adventures and experiences, with little tying them together aside from his role as narrator—in part no doubt a resourceful reworking of Marut/Traven's day-to-day experiences. The story describes how the indomitable gringo from Chicago blazes a trail in his new environment: as a cotton picker and oil driller, as a day laborer and untrained baker, and finally as a cattle driver crossing hundreds of miles with a large herd. The vignettes, taken together, conjure up a vivid picture of a land and people in a part of the world that was little known at the time. It is a world of Aztec duels and dangers lurking in the bush, of cowboy romanticism Mexican style and of U.S. industrial imperialism, of bandits, plantation owners, Indians, unemployed vagabonds of all races, and of the painted señoritas in the small towns. It is a land of nameless faces in which the nameless can feel at home like the crew of the *Yorikke.* In the midst of all this vivid detail, Traven can only touch upon sociopolitical issues. Still, he depicts a land whose government stands firmly on the side of labor, a land where unions, the syndicates, have a role to play, where "capitalism" and "the proletariat" are topics of the day. The suspicion lingers throughout the novel that Gales is a labor agitator, a Wobbly, a member of the American Industrial Workers of the World. A more unlikely politician would be difficult to imagine: Gales makes light of everything in his boyish manner, traipsing through life in happy-go-lucky style. Yet wherever he appears, strikes erupt and workers demand higher wages and improved working conditions. His philosophy sounds oddly like that of some of the German leftist movements in the 1920s—just as, strangely enough, this American is well versed in things German.

Gales also narrates *The Bridge in the Jungle*, which is more properly a novella than a novel since it revolves around a single episode, an extraordinary event that generates a theme that this novel shares with *The Treasure of the Sierra Madre*, *The White Rose*, and, in a sense, the Mahogany series as well. For *The Bridge*, like the story "Der Grossindustrielle" ("Assembly Line"), contrasts European-American civilization, with its principles of maximizing profit and industrial power, and communal self-sufficiency and fulfillment of the simple needs of life as embodied in the Indians. The critique of capitalism that Traven had brought from Europe (the proletariat versus the owners of the means of production) is translated into equally revolutionary colonial terms: the confrontation of the "colored peoples" and the "white race." This confrontation, too, is familiar from the Marut period: The unpublished novel *The Torch of the Prince* sides with the "primitives" against the evils of "civilization."

The Bridge in the Jungle is set amid the foreign-owned oil fields in the southern part of Tamaulipas, which had become home to Marut/Traven. The gringos—Gales himself, who comes there to hunt alligators, and Sleigh, who lives nearby with his Indian wife in a grass hut—play a secondary role, for this is a story of the Indians. Still, the presence of Western civilization in the thick of the jungle sets off the novel's course of events with its stark symbolism. The "plot" is spare: An Indian *muchacho* drowns in the Tamesi River and is buried within hours in a ceremony attended by the whole village. This death allows the narrator to depict psychological and physical details with a realism never before demonstrated in Traven's adventure stories and fictional social criticism. The elemental pain of the mother at the side of the decomposing body of her child, dressed in a sailor suit from "Manchester, Chemnitz, or New Jersey," is described with gripping exactness. The narrator is similarly realistic in depicting the villagers at the funeral: The native culture has already become so Americanized that, drunk on tequila, the Indians sing the latest American songs at the child's grave.

This detail has further significance: Western civilization, ravaging the natives' idyllic natural state, has ultimately caused the tragedy—and remains lurking in the background as a permanent threat. For the Indian boy, accustomed to walking barefoot, had drowned in the familiar river because he had been proudly wearing for the first time a pair of boots from Texas. The boots had made him stumble, and he hit his head on a plank of the Tamesi bridge, which never would have been there in the first place but for the gringos speculating on oil deposits nearby. Two social orders clash fatefully, with modern industrial society wreaking havoc on the descendants of a great and ancient culture. "The curse of civilization and the reason nonwhite peoples are finally beginning to rouse themselves, is that people are forcing upon the whole rest of the world the views of European and American court stenographers, police sergeants, and drapers as if it were the word of God, which all men must believe or else be wiped out." In *Land of Springtime* Traven had written what may be seen as a commentary on the fateful boots as a symbol of unwanted American civilization: "If the people who live in this great land do not wear shoes, one simply has to force them to wear some, whether or not they want to. And if the people cannot make these shoes for themselves, they must be forced on them, with or without the help of armored ships."

Both cultures lose in the process. The tone of melancholy recalls Marut's novella *To the Honorable Miss S . . .*, with its world-weariness and sense of hopelessness, and it also anticipates the 1958 conclusion of "The Night Visitor," in which Gales disappears into the wilderness never to be seen again, while the bush "[sings] its eternal song" in the tropical night. As the human tragedy is concluded in *The Bridge*, "the jungle sings its eternal song, without a care about what is going on around it. In comparison, men count for nothing." However clear-sighted and engaged Traven's revolutionary philosophy, our image of him would lack depth if he did not also reveal this melancholy side.

The Treasure of the Sierra Madre is far less given to such melancholy moods. It is dominated instead—the impression of the moviegoer applies to the book as well—by the thrill of adventure, gold fever, and the exotic romanticism of the encounter with far-off climes. As in *The Wobbly*, the main characters are a group of down-and-outs: three Americans in Mexico who, having tried all sorts of odd jobs in the oil district, have nothing more to lose and now hope to hit the mother lode as gold prospectors. After months of backbreaking work, they amass a small fortune that they succeed in protecting against both bandits and their own emotions, which explode ever more frequently. But they lose everything when they come down from the mountains with their overburdened mules to the town of Durango, hoping to convert their gold dust into pesos. Their greed erupts into treachery and attempted murder, and what the three fail to do to themselves is perpetrated by Mexican highwaymen, who then, unawares, let the gold dust be blown away by the wind. This story of how gold robs men of their humanity ends almost like a parable: with an idyllic Indian scene, in which the oldest of the prospectors, the worldly-wise Howard, has finally found his peace as a "doctor" in an Indian village. Howard had told his fellow prospectors early on that men were "all equal when gold is involved. All equally villainous, that is." This does not apparently hold true of the Indians, as long as they live according to their traditional communal ways. Unlike the bandits, the "dregs of the cities," the Indians never "fight over gold" because they know that the earth, and not gold, "brings happiness." Traven's contrast of the two cultures and his critique of civilization, formulated so tersely, comes across as simplistic, as it does in *The Bridge in the Jungle* and *The White Rose*. But in *The Bridge in the Jungle* and *The Treasure of the Sierra Madre* at least, Traven's critique is not the sole criterion for success or failure, since their narrative substance engages the reader's attention in its own right.

In *The White Rose*, however, Traven all too crassly points up and thereby trivializes the conflict between American big business and Indian self-sufficiency, delivering an elaborate sermon on the tragedy of "real" human beings confronted by a perverted society. The Indians and Americans vie for possession of the hacienda La Rosa Blanca in the tropical state of Veracruz on the Gulf of Mexico. The hacienda belongs to an old Indian clan that has lived on the site for generations, adhering to its ancient communal lifestyle. An American oil company tries to buy the land from the Indians—in vain, for in their eyes money cannot compare in value to farmland, their "homeland." Yet the business interests finally gain the upper hand by resorting to gangster tactics: bribery and deceit, murder and abuse of the Indians' good nature—in effect a forcible expropriation. Oil rigs shoot up where sugar cane and lemon trees had flourished. "People worked here. They produced here. They made billions here." The novel ends with the overt statement "What do we care about the human being? Only oil is important." Traven does make a forced attempt to interpret the expulsion of the Yanyez family in positive terms as well, as a chance for them to broaden their horizons. But apart from this, *The White Rose* does not stray from its simplistic scheme, making it one of Traven's weaker novels.

In 1961 Traven wrote an interesting essay on the genesis of his novelistic oeuvre. (In a letter dated December 5, 1961, to the Rowohlt press, he suggested that the essay be used as an afterword to the new edition of *The Cotton-Pickers*, but the essay never appeared.) The essay bears the signature "R.E.L." Traven depicts his literary start in Tamaulipas as follows:

> *The Death Ship* was not Traven's first novel published in German; the first Traven novel published in Germany was *The Cotton-Pickers*, which appeared in print fourteen months before *The Death Ship*, after some ten short stories by Traven had already appeared in German magazines and newspapers, all without exception set in Mexico, including "Der Eselskauf" ["Burro Trading"], "Ein Hundegeschäft" ["Indian Trading"], "Tanz im Dschungel" ["Indian Dance in the Jungle"], "Geschichte einer Bombe" ["The Story of a Bomb"], "Nachtbesuch im Busch" ["The Night Visitor"], "Dinamit-Patrone" ["Dynamite"], "Der Wachtposten" ["The Guard"], and others. *The Death Ship* was not even Traven's second novel, nor the third, but rather the fourth. And if one includes another work, also set in Mexico, which was lost, *The Death Ship* was the author's fifth novel. The second novel was *The Bridge in the Jungle*, which appeared in book form three years after *The Death Ship* and had been printed three years earlier in a workers' newspaper in Leipzig.
>
> Traven's third novel was *The Treasure of the Sierra Madre*, which editors at *Das Buch für Alle* in Stuttgart had in manuscript

> form seven months before *The Death Ship* appeared. *Buch für Alle* rejected this novel, claiming it would not appeal to women. But this novel later enjoyed forty-one separate printings and was published in eighteen languages; it sold 1,250,000 copies in the United States, where it was also filmed. Because *The Death Ship* was the first Traven novel to appear in book form and to draw attention to the author, the strangest stories were fabricated about Traven and his life. Yet the truth is that Traven found himself one day without a cent in a port in Tabasco, signed aboard a United Fruit Company freighter, loaded with bananas, which brought him to New Orleans where the story of *The Death Ship* began.

The intervening years may have blurred Traven's memory here or there. Yet his claim, later repeated in the same essay, that he had written another novel, now lost, in his early years in Mexico still piques our curiosity—all the more as we know of Traven's enormous productive drive at that time. His claim seems incredible, yet the estate does contain a typescript without a title (indicating that it was not merely a short story, which would have the title on its first page), beginning with the chapter heading I and the section heading 1, as do other Traven novels; only seven pages survive, and the text ends in mid-sentence at the end of page 7, in section 4. Apparently this is the beginning of the fair copy of a large-scale novel. It is set in Mexico: The protagonist is an American named Burleigh, who had to leave his home state of Oklahoma for mysterious reasons; his family history is presented as a flashback beginning in section 3. At the top right of the first page, Traven recorded in his own hand a date *after* that of *The Death Ship* but still from the Tampico period: "IX.9.28. [September 9, 1928] 4^{h} p.m."

Like the stories, the novels were written in the jungle thirty-five miles northwest of the oil port of Tampico, to which Traven rode or drove from time to time to buy paper and ink (before he got a Remington typewriter). The opening of "The Night Visitor" captures the scene memorably:

> Impenetrable jungle covers the broad plains along the Panuco and Tamesi rivers. Just two railway lines cross this ninety-thousand-square-kilometer stretch of the Tierra Caliente. The settlements which do exist have nestled themselves timidly near the few train stations. Europeans live here only very sparsely and virtually lost to each other. The tiring monotony of the

> jungle is interrupted by a few long ranges of hills covered with tropical bush as impassable as the jungle, and in its depths, which are always enveloped in twilight, all the mysteries and horrors of the world seem to lie in wait. At a few favorable spots where there is water one finds small Indian villages scattered among the hills, settlements which were there before the first white man ever arrived. They lie far from the railway. Mule carts bring what goods they need, mainly salt, tobacco, cheap cotton shirts, work pants, muslin dresses, pointed straw hats for the men and black cotton scarves for the women. In trade they offer chickens, eggs, young donkeys, goats, parrots, and wild turkeys.

Traven more than once delighted in recalling the torments of writing in this milieu. He wrote to the editors of *Westermanns Monatshefte* on July 21, 1925:

> It would make for another interesting story to inform your readers of the hardships one must endure to write a manuscript in the jungle, particularly when the writer does not enjoy the expensive amenities which rich American universities or rich German patrons would supply. Lest I be held for a liar, I cannot tell even you just how much one can skimp when putting a tropical outfit together if one has no means, but more than enough of an adventurous spirit.

And to his editor Preczang on August 5, 1925:

> The novella "Im tropischen Busch" ["The Night Visitor"] was also written in the jungle, and originally in English. In your little magazine you write about the intellectual torments a writer must undergo in order to bring his work into the world. To these intellectual torments, which are unbearable, are added, at least in my case, physical torments which I might one day describe in your magazine. Torments caused by the tropical climate and the tropical environment. Working in this climate, in the simmering fields, does not bother me all that much. But writing in such countries, when one cannot stay in a modern hotel, but must live in shanties or huts, that is truly a living hell. Not only the brain, but also the hands and legs and cheeks, bleeding from the bites of mosquitoes and other demons, rebel against the writer and against his ability to control his thoughts and their images.

Earlier in this letter he discussed *The Cotton-Pickers*:

I wrote the novel in an Indian hut in the jungle, where I had neither table nor chair, and I had to make my own bed out of string tied together in the form of a hammock the likes of which has never before been seen. The nearest store where I could buy paper, ink, or pencils, was thirty-five miles away. At the time I had nothing much else to do, and had some paper. It wasn't much, and I had to write on both sides with a pencil, and when the paper was used up, the novel had to come to a close as well, although it really was just getting started. As I never could have submitted the manuscript to anyone in its illegible state, and as no one would have read it had I done so, I gave it to an Indian, who rode to the station and sent it to America to be typed.

Transatlantic Dialogues

Against this backdrop, it seems miraculous that the vanished Marut found a publisher at all, let alone the uniquely congenial Büchergilde Gutenberg in Berlin. Without much deliberation, the firm adopted the still unknown writer in 1925, offering financial and psychological support. The Büchergilde not only "made" Traven—Traven also made the Büchergilde. For the Büchergilde was to gain its greatest visibility in the literary world as the publisher of the invisible B. Traven. *Vorwärts*, which had serialized *The Cotton-Pickers* in the summer of 1925, brought the two together. On August 6, 1925, the editor-in-chief John Schikowski wrote to Traven, recommending the publisher without whom Traven would scarcely have been able to survive in Mexico, to say nothing of gaining fame on the literary scene:

> I finally have a chance to send you the novel as it appeared in our publication and thank you for the three contributions, one of which ("The Founding of the Aztec Empire") is to appear tomorrow. I did not wish to publish something else of yours while the novel ran in our literary section. But now this "obstacle" is out of the way, and I look forward to any manuscript you may send, particularly fictional pieces. I do not know if our comrade Ernst Preczang has already gotten in touch with you. He wished to publish *The Cotton-Pickers* in a book edition for the "Büchergilde." The "Büchergilde" is a press founded by the German Association of Book Printers, which markets its publications to a well-organized membership (some 15,000 mem-

> bers, I think), so that a relatively large audience is always guaranteed.

It must have seemed like chance to Traven, but *Vorwärts'* role as liaison between him and the Büchergilde had a certain logic. *Vorwärts* called itself the "central organ of the German Social Democratic Party" (as Traven himself could see from the letterhead he received), while Büchergilde Gutenberg vocally promoted the interests of German workers in Social Democratic trade unions during the Weimar Republic. Yet Traven would have had no definite image of the Büchergilde, since the Educational Society of German Book Printers (Bildungsverband der deutschen Buchdrucker) had first established the publishing house and book club only in August 1924, when the fugitive Marut had just landed in Mexico.

The first letter from Büchergilde editor Ernst Preczang, which Traven received even before Schikowski's notice, must have hit the day laborer in the jungle like a bolt from the blue. What was the Büchergilde? Delegates of the Educational Society of German Printers had founded Büchergilde Gutenberg at the meeting of their regional representatives at the Leipzig Volkshaus on August 29, 1924. The Educational Society was an independent organization, though closely allied with the Association of German Printers, about a quarter of whose members in 1924 (some 15,000) belonged to the Educational Society. The printer Bruno Dressler, chairman of the Educational Society, served as the first managing director of Büchergilde Gutenberg. In its early years, its members were predominantly printers. But as its membership broadened, it gradually lost the image of a publisher devoted exclusively to unionized workers.

That would have been impossible had the Büchergilde's program not been equally flexible. Traven, their star author, was himself no Social Democrat, but more of a philosophical anarchist who shunned any party affiliation. And while the Büchergilde embraced "working-class" interests, their prospectuses were designed to provide the reader with precisely what the bourgeois book clubs were offering their members at the time: books with significant content, artistically designed and crafted, and at a relatively low price made possible by the large and quasi-guaranteed readership. The significant content was by no means class-struggle propaganda dressed up in literary garb, but rather—if one must label it—the German cultural heritage of the age of Goethe. This is confirmed by a look at the

August issue of *Die Büchergilde* in 1925, which states that life can be "worth living" only by contact with the "more beautiful world of ideas and enriching culture." The April 1936 issue, the jubilee issue celebrating "Ten Years of Traven," similarly notes that the Büchergilde was "dedicated to the ideals of a working class which strives for a more noble conception of humanity. It wished to serve truth, freedom, justice, and brotherly solidarity, without subjecting itself to a fixed party program." But the Büchergilde did not go so far in its concept of *Bildung* as to give center stage to the more abstract notions of timeless truth and humanity, which had been the lodestones of the bourgeois idea of education in the nineteenth century. Instead, the announcement of *The Treasure of the Sierra Madre* in *Die Büchergilde* of March 1927, in the opinion of Büchergilde historian Bernadette Scholl, reveals many of the criteria by which the editors selected manuscripts:

> The new novel displays the strong points of this narrator which have been so widely recognized: authenticity, spiritual depth, a philosophical conception of the world, vivid characterization, proletarian solidarity, gripping depiction, and, not to be overlooked, the humor which surfaces in places, rising above the misery of the human condition. . . . The reprinted episode "The Ambush" is incidentally not fictitious, but actually happened in Mexico, as the author disclosed in a letter to the editors. Thus Traven's works do not merely provide entertainment but are also, in one respect or another, documents of a land, a people, a class. And it is precisely this which raises them far above the light reading found in such abundance in the book market.

The allusions to the book's proletarian appeal were echoed in announcements of other books and general statements of purpose. But though it published mostly (though not exclusively) leftist authors, the Büchergilde also refused to toe a leftist party line in its choice of writers, at least in the period before 1933, which Bernadette Scholl has researched. As a result, some found fault with the Büchergilde's supposedly halfhearted embrace of the proletarian cause; the Social Democratic critics, whose assistance the Büchergilde had every reason to expect, did not feel totally at ease with its first great book success, *The Death Ship*, because of the novel's anarchism.

On the other hand, Büchergilde books and Traven's novels in particular got favorable reviews not only from the workers' press and leftist literary publications but also from some "bourgeois" newspapers. After all, what was the common denominator between such Büchergilde offerings as Dostoyevsky, Jack London, Georges Duhamel, Goethe, Schiller, Upton Sinclair, Anderson Nexö, Mark Twain (to say nothing of the travel books that were one of the press's specialties)? One can scarcely lump them under the rubric "proletarian literature" or "workers' literature"—in spite of the leftward slant of many of the authors. Such a label would not apply even to Traven's works themselves. For although Traven himself occasionally admitted to a proletarian perspective in his writings, as in his comments on *Land of Springtime* in his letter accompanying the manuscript, he justifiably took umbrage at being simplistically labeled an author of the proletariat or working class, in spite of his sympathy with their plight. If he were so branded, he wrote to Preczang on October 11, 1925, he would "feel deeply unhappy and . . . on the spot write a novel waving the capitalist banner." He said he saw "only human beings"; that these were mostly workers was purely "a matter of chance," since he had mostly lived among workers and had found, "that the worker, the proletarian, is the most interesting and most multifaceted man, a thousand times more interesting than your recently deceased Stinnes, than our Rockefeller or Morgan or Sinclair or Coolidge, or Gloria Swanson or Tom Mix or Mary Pickford or Henny Porten [a German actress], to return to your country."

Most Büchergilde members—and thus the buyers and readers of its books—nonetheless came from the working class, at least in its early period (though Büchergilde titles were also available in retail stores through the affiliated Buchmeister Press). By the end of 1924 the organization had 10,000 members, and by 1927 the number had grown to 40,000; the ranks swelled to over 75,000 in 1930 and to 85,000 in early 1933. The Büchergilde maintained contact with its members and fostered a spirit of community by publishing its magazine, *Die Büchergilde*, and by sponsoring lectures (some on Mexican themes) and promotional contests. The Büchergilde—which was headquartered in Berlin—further fostered a sense of unity among its membership through its branch offices (numbering twenty-seven in 1931) in a number of the large German cities as well as in Austria, Switzerland, and Czechoslovakia.

This extensive network of members (and potential purchasers) could offer its authors—particularly its star authors—"guaranteed sales." Such a relationship afforded essentially the same benefits as a contract with a strictly commercial publisher in Germany in the 1920s. But Büchergilde Gutenberg forced its authors to choose one or the other: The commercial publishers and booksellers naturally had no sympathy for book clubs, which cut out the middle man. Preczang wrote to Traven on this subject on December 11, 1925: "The fight of the publishers and particularly the booksellers against the book clubs has, after heated protests from writers' organizations, officially been called off, though it naturally goes on unofficially. The book dealers fear, with good reason, that a new economic form of book production and consumption is in the making, and they see their sacred profits threatened. . . . Threats of a boycott have to date accomplished only the opposite of what was desired."

Whether or not he weighed the risk involved, Traven immediately accepted Preczang's offer of an alliance. And an alliance it did become, for soon Traven was energetically and ingeniously contributing to all aspects of the production of his own books as well as to the management of Büchergilde Gutenberg generally. Editorial policy, recruitment of new members, program planning, advertising, contents of *Die Büchergilde*, book design, lectures and other events, exhibits of ethnological objects and photographs to inform members about Central America—on all these subjects the would-be entrepreneur offered his thoughts and suggestions to help the Büchergilde "to get on its legs and secure a place where it can then use its legs." His seemingly unstoppable flow of correspondence brims with advice on how the Büchergilde should run its affairs. Some of his recommendations must have raised eyebrows at headquarters. Traven, whose *Death Ship* had established itself as a bestseller by the late 1920s, further made life difficult for his publisher by emphatically refusing to divulge the secret of his identity, his Marut past. He kept both publisher and public in the dark. He would allow no photo, hardly a single accurate biographical detail, no hint of any connection with Germany to be coaxed out of him. Instead, he offered philosophical explanations of his right to anonymity and condemned the cult of personality that valued an author more than the typesetter of his works.

Preczang's introductory letter to Traven was the first step in the whirlwind progression propelling both author and publisher into the limelight. On July 13, 1925, the Büchergilde editor wrote to B. Traven in Columbus in the hinterlands of Tampico—in what must have appeared as a shot in the dark from the Berlin perspective:

> Dear Mister Traven!
>
> I read with great pleasure your novel *The Cotton-Pickers* published in *Vorwärts*. The unique "milieu," the fresh and natural depiction and not least your sense of humor awakened in me the desire to introduce you to our members, who extend through all of Germany and the neighboring German-speaking areas. For that reason I ask: Could we perhaps gain the rights for the German book edition of your novel? Do you have other works completed or in progress, which you might allow us to publish exclusively? As comrade Schikowski from *Vorwärts* informed me, *The Cotton-Pickers* is short and would presumably not fill out our usual book length of 12 to 15 sheets. Provided that you are in fact inclined to offer us the novel, two possibilities are open for our publishing it: (1) publication as a compulsory Büchergilde selection with the addition of a second fairly long story or several smaller stories; (2) publication without additions, by a press which is currently being formed and which is supported by the Educational Society of German Printers. In either case you may be certain of a faultless design of your book. I enclose two issues of our magazine, *Die Büchergilde*, as well as our regulations, to inform you of our objectives. Our association is young and is growing steadily, currently with some 15,000 members. Its leaders work in the spirit of modern social awareness and wish to broaden our readers' horizons beyond the boundary posts erected by nations and philistines. As far as I am concerned, in your novel I sense a kindred spirit and would therefore gladly welcome you as a collaborator. In order to be as complete as possible, I add that travel books, diaries, etc. would also interest us. You have doubtless experienced much and presumably also have photographs available—what about publishing an *illustrated* biographical novel? I would also be happy to publish shorter sketches in our magazine or in *Das Schiff* [*The Ship*], the publication of the Educational Society. In regard to royalties, you would certainly be in no worse a position with us than with any of the private, commercial presses. The Guild, for example, sells its compulsory selections for 1.50 marks and pays the author 15% of this, but guarantees from the outset a certain level of sales, which currently amounts to at least 15,000 copies.

> The above statements, along with the enclosed printed matter, should suffice for the time being. I will gladly answer any further questions you may have. Hoping that you are willing to assist in bringing a bit of fresh air and enjoyment of life into German literature,
>
> Most sincerely yours,
> Ernst Preczang

Traven took up the offer without much deliberation, setting the stage for practically exclusive cooperation. On September 15, 1925, Preczang expressed his hope "for a long-lasting connection" and stated on March 31, 1927, that he "aimed to get *all* your works in our press"—indeed, he said he was even considering an edition of Traven's "collected works." Meanwhile, Traven confessed to Preczang on March 20, 1927: "I think I instinctively fell on the right haystack, when I fell in with you; for only heretics understand heretics, only heretics can spread heresies and only heretics dare to offer support and assistance when heresies are perpetrated."

He had little right to talk of instinct—save in the sense of a drowning man grabbing for a life preserver thrown to him unexpectedly—at least not of an instinctively correct *choice* of a publisher. If anyone had made a conscious choice, it was the publisher and not Traven, and it was not even clear whether the Büchergilde, in its early days, would indeed be able to serve as a dependable life preserver; this much emerges from Traven's early correspondence with the Büchergilde. (He communicated first with the editor Preczang, but after mid-1927 several letters were addressed to Johannes Schönherr. Preczang is the recipient of the letters excerpted in this chapter, unless otherwise noted.)

The letters to Preczang and Schönherr (such as the passages on the torments of working in the mosquito-infested tropics) furnish a lively, colorful picture of Traven's life, writing and publishing in his early period in Mexico after the shaky first year of establishing himself in the exotic "far-off land." They thus afford a behind-the-scenes view of the rise of the Traven phenomenon. The correspondence reveals, in concrete detail, the author in the decisive phase of his literary career—the period that "made" him. We can gain the most penetrating glimpse into this stage of Traven's development by following his correspondence with the Büchergilde from the summer of 1925, when Preczang's introductory letter arrived after some three weeks in transit, until 1927, when the novels establishing

Traven's image and literary fame had appeared on the market in unusually rapid succession: *The Death Ship* and *The Wobbly* (the expanded book version of *The Cotton-Pickers*) in 1926 and *The Treasure of the Sierra Madre* in 1927.

Traven wrote often, and frequently at length, without first waiting for a response from Berlin to his previous dispatch; in his linguistic and cultural isolation, correspondence seems to have taken the place of conversation with like-minded individuals. He rarely received telegrams, and written answers reached him at best forty days after his dispatch of a letter or manuscript. His patience was put to the test in such long-distance communication with an unknown publisher who seemed to promise him the world—particularly when he was waiting for a decision on a manuscript. His very existence hung on word from Berlin. Living as he did from hand to mouth, he wondered if he could count on an advance or would have to try his luck once again as a day laborer in the oil camps near Tampico where unemployment grew from year to year or whether he would have to expose himself to the seasonality of farm work. The gringo spoke often of his sorry state, until the first literary successes let him stand his own ground in his exotic new land.

The Cotton-Pickers occupies a central position in the earliest correspondence with the Buchergilde—Preczang had mentioned the novel in his first letter, dated July 13, 1925. Traven wasted no time in replying. His three-page response from Tampico (typed, as always) of August 5 came abruptly to the point: "The brevity of my novel *The Cotton-Pickers* is due not to the nature of the book, but to circumstances which only rarely determine the length, character, and title of a literary work." There followed the somewhat romantically exaggerated description, quoted earlier, of the novel's development from a manuscript handwritten in the primitive "Indian hut" without furniture through the typing in North America. In the meantime, he noted, he had acquired a typewriter through the financial support of a "friend in America" (then he struck out the words "in America"); but his lack of funds compelled him to look for work once again; "and when I am working, nothing comes of the writing, for working here is quite different from what it is in Europe." Nonetheless, in this letter he plunged into plans and suggestions for his next publications—typical of the entire correspondence. He overflowed with projects and debated their pros and cons in exhaustive detail, beginning with his first letter: "The novel can be expanded to the length which it deserves." Traven had reservations only because of *Vorwärts* readers who, when they saw the novel appearing in book form expanded by a "second part," might see themselves "cheated out of half the novel." He therefore suggested first offering the continuation to *Vorwärts* for serializing as an independent work with its own title. Incidentally, he noted—bringing up the matter for the sake of fairness—that he had already offered the first part to "several German workers' papers" for reprinting; but such printings never hurt the sales of a book, he instructed the Büchergilde. He seemed to overlook that such knowledge of the German book market might expose his background (in other letters he demonstrated detailed knowledge of the techniques and terminology of the German printing trade, even though he did not wish to appear as a German or to reveal familiarity with matters German).

Without missing a breath, as it were, Traven had a second proposition ready in his first letter (as was to be the case in letters to come)—a more practical alternative that would bring him notice and income sooner. He would send the detective story "Der Farmarbeiter" ("The Farm Worker"), which he suggested appending to the existing first part of *The Cotton-Pickers* as printed in *Vorwärts*. Since he was referring to a text that to all appearances is lost, Traven's commentary is of interest:

> This story would easily fit in with the novel, since the protagonist is a farm worker as in the novel. A prominent episode in that novel is the scene where the worker is whipped by the policeman. You will find a similar whipping in "The Farm Worker," only in a more civilized form, illustrating that the laborer in the promised land of the United States is no better off than in Mexico—to the contrary, he is much worse off. That sort of corruption in the police and justice system are not found in Mexico, at least not against workers.

He then appended yet a third suggestion—the unexpectedly discovered author could barely restrain himself. He proposed a collection of stories to be entitled *The Bridge in the Jungle*. It could contain three stories: the title novella, "Indian Dance in the Jungle," and "The Night Visitor"—"all tragicomic, humorous, and tear-raising at the same time" and forming a "strict unity." All three were as yet unpublished. He had, however, offered "Indian Dance in the Jungle" to the magazine *Das Buch für Alle* (where the piece would appear in 1926), while "The Night Visitor" had been accepted by

Westermanns Monatshefte (and would be published there in 1926). The latter novella, he added, was written "originally in English." This was no mere ruse to make himself more interesting; the story bears the telltale signs of an original English composition, as it features a misunderstanding about *dog* and *hog* that is meaningful only in English but that renders the German somewhat clumsy. Had Traven translated this story from the English of an "other man" (and even "stolen" the text), he would naturally have been loath to draw attention to the underlying English version. Rather, the open reference to the English original confirms that in his early period in Mexico Traven intended to survive not only as a German-language author.

Even his first letter bears the traces of Traven's soon-to-be-popularized shroud of secrecy: "No line from this letter may be published. The letter is purely personal," he cautioned Preczang. He correspondingly dismissed the suggestion that he write a "biographical" novel. "Travel books, diaries about my travels and trips with photographs," on the other hand, which Preczang had likewise suggested, would indeed interest him. "Doubtless experienced much? Twenty volumes in the Brockhaus encyclopedia format are too little to publish even part of it," he noted with his typical flair for exaggeration.

Traven's first letter would be incomplete and atypical if it did not bring up the topic of royalties and advances. In this regard he asked Preczang to consider prices in Mexico, "that here 1 (ONE) kilo of potatoes costs .85 Goldmarks, a bottle of beer (ONE QUARTER liter) 1.15 GM, and so forth. Oranges grow thicker here than plums in Germany, without care and without fertilizer, and one (ONE) orange costs .45 GM and even when it is already rotting still costs .35 GM. A liter of drinking water, if one purchases it in large quantities, 12 pfennig and if one purchases it in small quantities, a glass, a fifth of a liter costs 12 pfennig. Yesser! (Yes, sir)" (the latter exclamations written in English).

The letter gives the impression of a man in a hurry, intent on striking a deal with Büchergilde Gutenberg under any halfway acceptable conditions—to forge as permanent a relationship as possible. He must have seen his whole future hanging on this contact. His second letter only three days later, on August 8, 1925, confirms this impression. In reviewing his manuscripts he found a second detective story, "Der Täter wird gesucht" ("Manhunt")—he would send a copy of this as well—which together with "The Farm Worker" could be appended to *The Cotton-Pickers.* (Unless this story is part of the later, second half of the novel, it is likewise lost.) With or without these supplements, Traven hoped to see his first novel appear by Christmas, he said, and suggested code words for telegrams to expedite communication. He also wasted no time in transferring to Büchergilde Gutenberg "the exclusive rights for the German book edition" as well as the rights for all other manuscripts that he was sending and that were mentioned in his two letters. "I will read the proofs if enough time remains." He wanted to know whether Büchergilde titles also appeared "in the regular book trade"; but he stressed that he would "not make any decision subject to" the answer to that question; one way or another preparations for publication of *The Cotton-Pickers* could be made. But at this point it was not even certain that Büchergilde Gutenberg might hold him to his first suggestion, that he properly conclude the novel by the addition of a second part. His main concern was that the novel appear "without too long a delay." Traven was well ahead of the game: He was sending the detective stories, he said, "only to give you a broad notion of the areas I work in, and so that you may perhaps give me indications as to what your members would like to read but cannot get." (Like a few of the other early letters from Mexico, this one concludes not only with a typed "B. Traven," as would later be the rule, but also with a handwritten "T."; only very rarely were the early letters to Preczang or Schönherr signed "Traven" or "B. Traven," and none of Traven's letters to them were handwritten.)

On the same day, August 8, 1925, the budding Büchergilde author wrote a second letter to Preczang, marked by the same impetuous and enterprising tone. He was now sending the stories, but not "Indian Dance," which suddenly did "not seem appropriate" for publication with the title novella "The Bridge in the Jungle," but which might be suitable for the magazine *Die Büchergilde.* He considered adding a few photographs to *The Bridge in the Jungle*— the "title has more significance than merely referring to the setting of the action" and the story was "not fictitious"—provided he could locate a camera. He concluded with a renewed plea for timely action and active promotion of his works:

> I would like to request that you decide as soon as allowed by the Guild's standard procedures.

> Should the pieces, or any one of them, not be what you are looking for in promoting the aims which your association pursues as defined by you or your members, please be totally frank about that. I cannot write according to a formula. I must say what I feel and must express what chokes me up, even if no one accepts it and no one prints it.
>
> If you cannot use the material, I would ask you to keep your ears open for someone who might be interested, a publisher or editor. My knowledge of German magazines and what editors and publishers need is too scant.

Two days later, on August 10, Traven sent yet another letter to the Büchergilde—the fourth within a span of six days: The unexpected life preserver thrown from Berlin seems to have worked wonders. The excitement of these decisive days is evident in this letter. "Tomorrow or the day after" he would send "Manhunt" (he had apparently been busy typing it). Traven could not resist explicating his own text, preventing any possible misinterpretation of its true significance—a habit he would continue in his later letters. Oddly enough, his comments on his detective stories could apply just as well to almost everything he published under the name Traven. He stressed the verisimilitude of his art, which led to enlightenment and the revelation of society's true character:

> Fictional detective stories can be great works of art, yet these stories are not fiction but bare factual reports. I will only publish them in book form if the entire book contains such matter-of-fact reports. As I see it, the pieces are good material for workers' papers if printed intermittently, but not good material for books which someone wishes to treasure as dear friends. Of course, your readers may well have totally different ideas on the subject and see a whole new world opening up before their eyes in these stories, which are prose photographs of the promised land of America. And it is possible that in this roundabout way a sober description of the land and people of a foreign state, a bare report, can be transformed into good reading in the mind of the reader. Only you and the Guild members can judge that. In many respects these two stories, but "The Farm Worker" in particular, have a certain similarity with *The Cotton-Pickers*, since both works depict actual conditions.
>
> In any event I would prefer it if *Vorwärts* or another workers' paper published these detective stories in its literary section; for why shouldn't a worker read detective stories as well, if they

either have artistic merit or reveal the reality of the social order and demystify it?

A spotlight fell momentarily on Traven's personal circumstances:

> I am still looking for work. Since the big American oil companies fire dozens of white men every day, a considerable mass of unemployed workers has developed here in the meantime, so the prospects can't be called promising. I therefore have to work at short literary pieces which sell more easily than larger works, and to date I haven't put away a single peso for the funds which are to take me to new territories.

The expedition to other areas of Mexico and Central America—contemplated partly, no doubt, at Preczang's encouragement (as in his first letter)—materialized the following year in the form of the Palacios expedition to Chiapas (discussed earlier in this chapter).

Before Traven received Preczang's answer or before he could even have expected an answer (to judge from his own precise statements on the time taken by transatlantic correspondence), he wrote yet another long letter from Tampico to Berlin on September 10, 1925. Again, his sense of urgency is understandable, since he was evidently struggling for his very existence. He broke out of his isolation (imposed not only by his own choice) with a vengeance, sensing no doubt the torments of his phantomlike existence (the Traven incognito was already a year old). His lack of communication, bottled up all too long, surfaced toward the end of this letter in his self-important tone (soon to be typical of his letters)—though his boasting, too, remained an ineffectual gesture, since Traven again noted that his letters were "solely private, and of no interest to the public."

Traven asked in this letter whether the Büchergilde might be interested in publishing *The Death Ship*—before his "first" novel, *The Cotton- Pickers*, had even been formally accepted. *Vorwärts* editor John Schikowski had mentioned it in his letter of August 6, 1925. He had sent copies of *The Cotton-Pickers* serialization and had asked: "How do things stand with the second novel which you were planning six months ago? If the price is manageable for us, I would gladly acquire it for our literary section; *The Cotton-Pickers* has met with great acclaim, as we expected." In response, Traven wrote to Preczang: "This novel [*The Death Ship*] is now completed and I can send it off in a few days." He would send Preczang the manuscript, which he asked him to forward to Schikowski (who was on vacation at the time), hoping in the same breath that the Büchergilde would be interested in publishing the "very extensive" text in book form. The tireless businessman—a role his material circumstances forced him to adopt—was full of practical ideas: The new novel should appear as a double volume or in two volumes, "to fetch the price of 3.00 Goldmarks." He reserves the right to publish the book in *Vorwärts* "and in other workers' papers." Should a newspaper reprint it (and if Preczang was interested in signing a contract), the copyright of Büchergilde Gutenberg would be noted in each installment; "you could hardly ask for a better advertisement for the Büchergilde. I think that this will generate many inquiries and you will get many new members in the process." Traven would be entitled to any royalties for these reprints, however, and in the book itself—should it come to that—Traven would be listed as the copyright holder. (Copyright issues were to interest Traven throughout his life.) This was followed by detailed suggestions and alternatives on how the Büchergilde could coordinate the timing of the book and the serializations in *Vorwärts*; Traven stressed the urgency of this matter as well. He would send Schikowski materials for an announcement; assuming that an agreement was reached with the Büchergilde, such an announcement in *Vorwärts* should "expressly" state "that the novel will be published by Büchergilde Gutenberg with a tastefully appointed cover. You may discuss with Dr. Sch. how you wish to formulate this notice." He might write a special announcement for Büchergilde Gutenberg, "but I am not making any promises." In addition, he noted: "I would like it very much if you could soon send me the honorarium or an advance, assuming, naturally, that you acquire the novel in the first place." Traven, surely bluffing a little, seemed to have no doubts in that regard; the mere letter of inquiry from Berlin of July 13 must have boosted his sense of self-worth dramatically. Given the Büchergilde's commitment to "modern social awareness," he felt he had come to the right place, although, as he admitted in the letter of August 8, he had first sent "The Farm Worker" to the eminently bourgeois and capitalist Ullstein press. (Ullstein was to publish an excerpt from *The Cotton-Pickers* as "Das Aztekenduell" ["The Aztec Duel"] in 1929 in *Das Grosse Abenteuerbuch* [*Big Adventure Book*]—the same Ullstein that *The Brickburner*, curiously, had years earlier blasted as an enemy of the people.)The sense of his own importance rings through loud and clear:

I would like to say quite openly: I know, and I know best, what this novel represents and how much it is worth. The simple, elementary fact that I am handing over the novel to you first of all and that I am offering you the first opportunity to acquire it, may allow you to judge how much I value your organization and how much I would like to demonstrate that I am disposed to help it get on its legs and secure a place where it can then use its legs. . . .

In this novel you will come across many sorts of boundary posts erected by nations and philistines which are set to tottering. I hope that people who also claim to be working in the spirit of modern social awareness do not come by and prop up the border posts of the nations and philistines, fearing that many other things could start tottering along with them.

To return to another sentence of your letter, I answer: "Certainly, I am ready to help you bring a bit of fresh air into German literature, a positive feeling about life, and—the primal scream of a new race.[”]

In retrospect, in 1959 in the *BT News*, Traven expressed his euphoria of 1925 in even stronger language—the completion of *The Death Ship* must have indeed represented a milestone in his life. It is a novel that "will set the world's horizons ablaze," he claimed to have written to Preczang in 1925. A text simply titled "Birth Notice!" dated September 2, 1925, gives a more immediate glimpse into the nature of the novel. He presumably sent it first to Schikowski; for Traven, as he informed Preczang on September 10, had sent Schikowski a letter about *The Death Ship*, which Schikowski might give to the Büchergilde editor to read "if he so desires." The text, the richest document on the genesis of the eminently successful *Death Ship* and its significance in the author's "inner" biography, is published here for the first time:

Birth Notice!

IX.2.25

With the usual agonies of conception and labor pains, which were particularly severe in this case, a new novel has opened its eyes on the world—actually just on its birthplace for the time being.

A heavy lad, by weight and character. Weighs two and a half times more than the *Bridge* and more than three times as much as *The Pickers* [die Pickers].

And I created this giant work in precisely twenty days, to the very hour. I wanted to find out what I could accomplish when I set my mind to it. It flowed without a hitch directly into the typewriter. It's ready to be sent off now.

The conception tormented me for several months—tormented me so much that I almost went crazy, since I did not know into what form I should cast it.

I hope that you understand what is meant by Sunny New Orleans and Lovely Louisiana. Then you'll be able to understand what's going on. The death ship is a ship which bears only dead men, people who were left outside when the walls were erected, men without passports, without homelands, thrown to the four winds, damned men, men without names, men who were never born.

It is a tale of the sea. I only know the one book of Joseph Conrad that you sent me. In light of that book I am judging six other books by Conrad. And I feel confident enough to say that with my novel I have so outdone six of Conrad's books that Conrad will be seen as a teller of old wives' tales. It was my intention to dedicate the book to him with the words: In memoriam of J.C. the great writer of fairy tales. He always writes only about the captains and similar fine fellows and if he tells of the crew, they appear as characters or chorus members of an opera.

But here, for once, the crew itself does the talking. And it does not merely speak, it roars. And I'll tell you this much: lightning appears on the horizon and one can hear the first sounds of the trumpets signaling the final settling of accounts between servants and masters. For the time being they are only tuning up for the big concert.

In any event it thunders and hails, so that the pieces are already flying about the ears of those who are still sitting at the feeding troughs. *The Pickers* is no more than a puppet show compared with this dance of the galley slaves rattling their chains. And the consuls will also surely catch a few tones of the blaring fanfare. They will have a few sleepless nights.

Now we'll see who undertakes to publish it. In any event I'll fire it off as soon as I have enough for the postage.

People won't lie back comfortably in the US on their soft cushions and tell themselves: This has nothing to do with us! I have spoiled their fun at the very beginning, since the work is subtitled "The Story of an American Sailor." Now they cannot argue self-servingly: But we're not like those people. And their flag, my goodness! They'll have something to wash now.

> It was supposed to be a love story. You can tell from the opening song. But I can never do with my characters what I wish. As soon as I have breathed life into them, they become independent and go their own way. I can do nothing about it. I can only follow them then and report what they did and said. Nonetheless it is the great unspoken love story of the man who can't get back to his girl.

An interesting aspect of this document of literary *joie de vivre* is first of all the chronology: Traven claimed on September 2 to have penned *The Death Ship* in twenty days. It was thus not Schikowski's inquiry about his next work, at best promising the fleeting fame of a newspaper reprint, that goaded him to start work on the novel that represented his big break, for he could have received the *Vorwärts* letter of August 6 at the earliest during the final week of August. Rather, the reason Traven went to work on the book must have been the unexpected query from the Büchergilde, reaching him in early August, whether he would be interested in a long-term cooperation as a book author. The twenty-day period of composition need not be suspect, since the text, or at least large sections of it, was "originally written in American," as Traven maintained in 1959 in the *BT News* and elsewhere. The novel thus already existed in one form or another. Some critics have more or less politely doubted this contention, but when the English original of part of the novel, in Marut/Traven's own hand, came to light in the estate, the doubters were put on the defensive. The work progressed so quickly because it was only a matter of "rewriting" ("*Umschreiben*"), as Traven put it in his letter to Preczang of November 18, 1929. Not surprisingly, the style bears all the traces of a hasty job—but clearly this is *not* because the gringo in his Indian hut was translating the manuscript of a never-identified original author into German, as the "other man" hypothesis posits with adventurous logic but not a shred of evidence.

The creative frenzy induced by the Büchergilde was in any event a euphoria in a vacuum. For only on September 14 did Traven receive a short note in reply to his first letter. The Büchergilde's response, dated August 28, 1925, could scarcely have met his boundless expectations. Preczang merely confirmed receipt of Traven's manuscripts and said he hoped he could communicate his enthusiasm for *The Cotton-Pickers* to his colleagues who shared in the decision making so that the Büchergilde could in fact publish the work.

Though couched in the most deferential terms ("to tell you the truth, it would be most agreeable to me if . . ."), even this potential offer was contingent on the author's expanding the novel to "standard book length" rather than padding the volume with independent texts. In regard to the other prose works, Preczang said he would read "The Bridge in the Jungle" at the earliest opportunity—this was the only text that was "available," strictly speaking (he apparently had not yet received "Manhunt"). The overall tone of the letter is thus one of interest coupled with restraint, with a bit of diplomatic maneuvering thrown in: "If you would be a bit patient, you will, I believe, soon become a well-known and popular writer at least among the German working class. . . . It is fully in the interest of our organization, the Guild, to attempt to secure the cooperation of worthwhile authors."

Traven answered on the very day that he received this letter, September 14, with a two-page single-spaced letter written in his "bungalow" in the jungle. ("We are in the thick of the rainy season, all the roads are impassable and the prospects of finding work have dwindled to practically nothing. I thus have the opportunity to catch up with a lot of writing and to prepare a number of pieces which otherwise would have had to lie untouched.") He visibly exerted himself to qualify as one of the new organization's "worthwhile authors." Industrious and with a good business sense, but also with inventiveness, the man without a name sought to promote B. Traven. Who would criticize this behavior in the newcomer to Mexico, the intellectual who performed backbreaking farm labor in the blinding sun at the side of illiterate day laborers to eke out a miserable existence? In his dire financial situation he was in no position, as he noted retrospectively in a letter of November 18, 1929, "to compose a book on speculation, only to have to go peddle it."

Now, on September 14, 1925, he pulled out all the stops as his own impresario. "The Night Visitor" had been sold to *Westermanns Monatshefte*, he wrote, with the deal closed by payment of an honorarium; but as of the second half of 1926 that would present no obstacle for its "publication in book form," that is, in a volume of stories. Naturally he also welcomed the Büchergilde's intention to introduce the works meant first of all for an audience of union members "after a certain time to the general book market," where the publishers as a rule were not ready to assume the commercial risk of "very modern literature with social or revolutionary overtones." It seems that the hot-headed revolutionary and the cool-headed businessman cooperated in writing this letter:

> I am convinced that by expanding into the general book market you will gain the means to exert a decisive influence on all of literature. If publishers can sell huge editions of some of their books—which are not always good books—why shouldn't you be able to do the same? And how could you do it more easily than with books recognized as good books by a select and well-read membership? With every book offered by a commercial publisher, there is always the suspicion: Does he want to serve literature, or only his bank account? In the case of an organization such as yours, no one will pose such a question.

Again his tone was one of overenthusiastic self-confidence. For in his remarks on the "decisive influence on all of literature" Traven was surely thinking first and foremost of his own books and their indisputable social and revolutionary "overtones." This eagerness was not merely dictated by a purpose but must also be understood with a view to his being cut off from meaningful communication. He even displayed such enthusiasm for the manuscript that the Büchergilde, he thought, "has little interest at the present time" in publishing in book form, the novella "The Bridge in the Jungle." (Preczang would write on September 15, 1925, that this work had "gone into too much detail toward the end.") Traven claimed on September 14 that he knew of no prose composition that was even faintly as authentic as "The Bridge"—prose that

> depicts as well as this piece the intimate details—and as I may confess—the realities of life in the Central American jungle. And I would contend that in all of German literature no modern work depicts in such minute detail the development of anxiety in a non-European, a nonwhite mother as does this novella. Note that the action of the entire novella takes place at a single place (at the bridge) and the entire novella transpires within twenty-one hours. In spite of the brisk tempo, not a single finger movement is left out and the jungle breathes and sings without pause like a musical accompaniment. Nor do I believe that the "search with the board and the light" has until today ever appeared in European literature or has perhaps ever before been reported by any traveler.

In the midst of this self-generated enthusiasm, Traven did not neglect to bring up practical business matters. Eager as always, he asked Preczang to forward "The Bridge in the Jungle" to *Vorwärts* (where the story was indeed to be serialized, though not until May 14 to June 27, 1927, while the book, with its expanded text, appeared in 1929). He further requested that Preczang pass on to *Vorwärts* "The Farm Worker," which Ullstein had rejected in the meantime. If Preczang did that, as one can assume, nothing came of it. Referring to the difficulties of being an author in a "far-off land," Traven then asked that Preczang assist him in a more general way with business matters:

> Sending my manuscripts back and forth costs not only a lot of postage but also a lot of time, which is worse. My writings are actually always on the ship or on the train, instead of being read by editors. I send off many works to places that surely have no use for them at all, since I have no idea what the newspaper in question is like. If I had a place over there from which the writings could be sent and to which they could be returned, I would be in a better position. I would gladly give up a percentage of my royalties for such business assistance. Would you be able to look around, Mr. Preczang, for such a central office familiar with the needs of newspapers and magazines?

This glimpse into Traven's life in Mexico afforded by the initial correspondence between him and the Büchergilde reveals themes that would arise time and again in the letters of the following years.

In this correspondence Traven often spoke of financial issues (at times he even lacked the pesos for shipping his manuscripts). He brought up his debts, advances, honoraria and installments, reprints and prepublication in newspapers (which Traven the businessman pressed for), the payments for them, and copyright issues. He wrote of his calling again and again at Mexican banks to pick up the funds transferred to him—Traven thought the banks were swindling him with their high commissions and exchange tactics and were getting rich on him by delaying payment. An American bank in Tampico went bankrupt, he wrote to Preczang, causing him to lose his "last few bucks." "Here the state is not so concerned about the citizens as in Europe, here everyone must look out for himself if he does not wish to be run over." All the more so since the prices were so exorbitant and the exchange rates so unfavorable: "A few days ago I bought a nail brush which you can buy in Germany for 25 pfennig, if I am correctly informed. I paid 2.00 pesos for one here, or approximately 4.30 Marks." (He reported extensively on room rates in Tampico on November 19, 1925.) He therefore not infrequently welcomed his royalties "with ardent enthusiasm." The arrival of the "January installment," Traven wrote to Schönherr with more concrete enthusiasm on January 5, 1928, "allows me to buy a second mule, so that the first one doesn't buck if it has too much to carry."

Disruptions in communication were another frequent topic in the correspondence. Telephone calls were never mentioned. Telegrams were exchanged on occasion, though not often. Sending mail by ship took a long time (storms on the Atlantic disturbed the timetable of German literary life), and bandits might blow up the mail train (as he mentioned to Schönherr on October 16, 1927). In addition, letters and packages were returned or were lost because Traven was sometimes away for months at a time from Mexico City or Tampico, his mailing addresses.

The situation was laden with irony, since Traven did not *want* to be reached. In Mexico he continued the game of hide-and-seek begun on that fateful May 1, 1919, when Marut disappeared. Traven refused to send a photo of himself:

> That's right, Mr. Preczang, take care not to ask him for a photo. If my works are unable to conjure up my image with perfect clarity in the mind of the reader, a photograph certainly will not be able to do it. And if you push me too much, I'll go right to a fortune teller on the street—who for 10 centavos lets the infatuated criadas (servant girls) have a picture of their future lover. I'd buy one of those pictures and give it to the press as my own. I'd do it without batting an eye. You have been warned.

"The readers certainly have enough taste," he added, "to deal with my works and not with me." His address was therefore not to be given out. "One is in an enviable position if one cannot be reached—or reached only with difficulty—by people sending letters or packages." A successful author by now, Traven said he would not get personally involved in publicity schemes: "I have no intention of coming to Germany any time soon," he wrote to the Büchergilde on August 21, 1927,

> and when I come, if I ever come, I want to do so as an entirely ordinary private citizen, who travels incognito through the pretty German countryside without being haunted by his dreams—by the fears which grip him when he has to stand on the podium, to talk to a curious mob and be stared at like a caged monkey,

> from whom people expect a few tricks for everybody's amusement. It is certainly conceivable—perhaps yes, perhaps never—that I will walk by the house at Dreibundstrasse 5 [Büchergilde headquarters] and not go in. Yes, sir [written in English]. That's not a quirk. It's simply because I don't want to be a church spire, neither a tiny one, nor a thick gilded one.

He was bitter when the Büchergilde "handed over" one of his letters, which he considered private, to Manfred Georg, who published it in his *Weltbühne* essay in 1929. "After this experience, I will write only sober business letters, cold and concise, in a matter-of-fact style, like a cotton merchant," he scolded Preczang. Consider what that would have meant for Traven: shutting off the only release valve that had made his isolation a little more bearable.

While he himself wished to withdraw from the limelight, he put all the more emphasis on heightening the visibility of the Büchergilde and its book offerings, and especially on promoting the sales of his own books. He was full of advertising ideas. He suggested sending picture postcards, for example, but without an explanatory text, mentioning only Traven's book on Mexico, *Land of Springtime*. "If the reader wants to learn more about the picture, he can buy the book." In the same letter to Preczang, dated March 27, 1927, he continued:

> You can scarcely do enough in the area of propaganda and advertising. The Büchergilde has to have 250,000 members, and it can get these members. Just think of what you could achieve then. And I would like to suggest another propaganda idea in connection with these pictures. . . .
>
> Ten thousand readers for *The Death Ship* is nothing, I want to have 250,000 readers for the book. And I say openly to you that I will not be satisfied with the Büchergilde until it has come up with those 250,000 readers. If not by honorable means, then with machine guns.

Traven suggested in all seriousness that copies of *The Death Ship* be sent to Reichstag members and that the book be made required reading for consular officials. As a result, Germany might become the first country to abolish passport requirements, he wrote on December 2, 1926. (It was not Germany that could first make this claim, but Mexico. Full of satisfaction, Traven informed Preczang on March 27, 1927, that his homeland of choice had the "first

Neuer Theater-Almanach, 1908

Marton, Grete, Ch. Leipzig III.
— Hans, Sch. Hamburg II.
Martoni, Erhard, Sch. Aarau.
Marut, Ret, Reg. u. Sch. (8228). Essen
Marwitz, Lina, Sch. Harburg.
Marx, Anna, Ch. Bern I.
— Elijah, Sch. Bremerhaven

Neuer Theater-Almanach, 1911

— Nikolaus, Ch. Hamburg II.
Martony, Erhard, Reg. u. Sch. (12771). Bochum II.
Marut, Ret., Reg. u. Sch. (14205). Berlin LXII.
Marwilsky Alfred, Sch. Leipzig V.

Neuer Theater-Almanach, 1910

Marton, Hans, Sch. 15654. Berlin XLIX.
— Nikolaus, Ch. Hamburg II.
Martoni, Erhard, Reg., Sch. u. Sekr. 12771). Bochum I.
Marut, Ret., Sch. Studienhalber Berlin N, Veteranenstr. 7.
Marwitz, Lina, Sch. (10998). Primasens.
Marx, Elise, F Sch. Hildesheim.

Adress Register Dusseldorf, 1913

Maruhn, Hermann, Ofenarbeiter, Bruchstraße 44II
Marut, Ret, Schausp.., Mitgl. des Schauspielhauses, Herzogstr. 72
Marwitz, Rudolf, Kaufmann, Bunsenstraße 17U
Marx, Adam, o G. Kirchfeldstr 68aI

Neuer Theater-Almanach, 1909

Suhl in Thüringen.
Vorsaison: Ohrdruf.

(S. u. O., Städte in Thüringen mit ca. 7000 bis 12000 Einw. Die Th. fassen ca. 800 Pers.– Spielzeit: Ganzjährig.)

Eigentümer. In S.: Oscar Kelber; in O.: Bierbrauerei Alt.
Direktion. Oscar Hansen u. Albert Eng-Straube. Ersterer führt zugleich die Oberregie, letzterer die Regie d. P. u. Optte.
Geschäftsführer. Dir. Walter Straube.
Regie usw. Ret Marut, Reg. d. Sch. u. L. Ernst Wiepert, Kpllm. Karl Schmidtlein, Kass. Marie Wagnerfeld, Souffl.

Darstellende Mitglieder.

Herren: Albert Eng (Dir.), I Ges.- u. Charkom. Oscar Hansen (Dir.), I. Held. u. Charr. Ret Marut (Reg.), I. jug. Held. u. Liebh. Werner Olbers, jug. Kom. u. Charg. Karl Petersmann, hum. u. ernste Vät. Walter Straube (Geschäftsf.), I. Liebh. u. Bonv. u. Charr. Max Turnau, I. Charg.
Damen: Riccarda Brock, Soubr. u. munt. Liebh. Grete Hansen (Dir.),

Neuer Theater-Almanach, 1912

Darstellende Mitglieder.

Schauspiel. Herren: Paul Barnay (s. Reg.). Carl Conété, Holzmarkt 27/28. Wolfgang Fritsch, Craueng. 22. Bruno Galleiske (s. Reg.). Adalbert Kriwat (s. Reg.). Ret Marut, Damm 2. Otto Normann (s. Reg.). Max Preißler, Heil. Geistg. 31. Carl Präß, Craueng. 11. Heinrich Römer

Neuer Theater-Almanach, 1913

Darstellende Mitglieder.

Herren: Artur Blask, Hofgartenstr. 9c. Willi Buschhoff, Oberkas... Jaeg-Allee 1. Eugen Dumont (s. Reg.). Arthur Ehrens, Herderstr. 59. ... Peter Esser, Poststr. 22. Franz Everth, Berger Allee 1. Bernh. Goetz... Obercassel, Columbusstr. 86. Paul Günther, Graf-Adolf-Str. 70. ... Henckels (s. Reg.). Julius Herrmann, Obercassel, Balsenstr. 14. Fritz H... (s. Reg.). Paul Kaufmann, Aachener Str. 27. Eugen Keller, Deichstr. Theodor Kigler (s. Insp.). Ret Marut, Friedrichstr. 49. Fritz Rei... Obercassel, Columbusstr. 20.

August 10th, 1948.

Lady:

Enclosed find your letter which I herewith return to you. Had it not been for E.Preczang's explaining letter I would not have understood what in fact you were talking about. It is obvious that your letter was sent to the wrong address. If I understand the whole thing correctly your letter should have been mailed to Film Director Walter Ruttman.

By your letter which you wrote E.P. you state that you were born 1912, evidently somewhere in Germany. At that time I was serving in the U.S. Pacific Merchant Marine and certainly too young to have offsprings. I have never been in Germany in spite of the fact that I was invited many times to go there and lecture. But lecture I could not for my knowledge of German is really insignificant. I write my books and letters exclusively either in English or in Spanish from which they are translated into the languages for which they are meant.

The Fred Maruth story which you mention is not new. It was printed in several German newspapers in 1929, invented by a certain Oskar Maria Graf, a German writer who, apparently is not very punctilious as to what he writes and for whom as long as he sells his ware. He and another journalist of similar quality, by the name of Erwin Kisch, repeated that story so often that, finally, my European agent thought it expedient to stop that tale for good when it, a few months ago, reappeared in a Stuttgart paper. O.M.Graf was compelled to write the editor of said paper a letter by which he publicly admitted that he had invented the story as a sort of possible hypothesis but that he must confess that he could not produce any evidence for what he had told. The Stuttgart paper published that confession of Graf's, admitting at the same time that it felt sorry to have published an article without any truth in it.

I think, lady, that's about all you wanted to know.

Very truly yours

B.Traven.

Traven's letter to Irene Zielke.

Der Ziegelbrenner

Bezugspreis: Zehn aufeinanderfolgende Hefte, Zusendung unter Streifband stets sofort nach Erscheinen: 4,50 M. **Die Abonnenten** erhalten die Hefte in der Regel etwa zehn bis vierzehn Tage **vor** dem allgemeinen öffentlichen Verkauf. Der Herausgeber übernimmt keine Verpflichtung, innerhalb eines bestimmten Zeitraumes eine bestimmte Anzahl (oder eine Mindestzahl) von Heften zu „liefern". Infolgedessen kann der Verlag „Bezugsrechte auf Zeit" nicht annehmen.

Wir bitten, Abonnements nur unmittelbar beim Verlag zu bestellen. Einzel-Hefte jedoch sowie andere Bücher, die der Verlag herausgibt, sind in jeder guten Buchhandlung vorrätig.

Preis des einzelnen Heftes je nach Umfang und Herstellungskosten: 0,40 M. bis 2,00 M.

Kostenlos werden **keine** Hefte abgegeben und sind auch keine abgegeben worden. Werbehefte oder Prospekte gibt es bei uns nicht und gab es auch nicht. Bestellungen werden erst dann ausgeführt, wenn der Betrag eingezahlt ist oder wenn die Sendung unter Nachnahme verlangt wird.

Die drei ersten Hefte sind nicht mehr zu haben. Soweit es uns gelingt, Hefte aus dem Buchhandel oder von Privaten zurück zu erwerben, geben wir sie gern wieder ab, jedoch **nur an Abonnenten.** Jedes dieser Hefte kostet 0,70 M. Heft 1 und Heft 3 werden nur in ganz seltenen Ausnahmefällen noch zu erhalten sein.

Abonnements, bei denen die Nachlieferung der ersten drei Hefte zur Bedingung gemacht wird, bleiben unerledigt.

Das nächste Heft befindet sich im Druck; es wird in wenigen Tagen an die Abonnenten verschickt. Inhalt: Die Rede des Ziegelbrenner und deren merkwürdige Folgen.

Geschäftsstelle des Verlags:
München 23.

Besuche wolle man unterlassen, es ist nie Jemand anzutreffen. Fernsprecher haben wir nicht.

Wir bitten, alle Zahlungen nur auf unser **Postscheck-Konto: 8350 Amt München,** zu überweisen!

3276 29/13, 216

Der
Ziegelbrenner

Zensur

Alle Aufsätze, Besprechungen und Komödien, die während des Krieges dem Ziegelbrenner von der Zensur gestrichen wurden

Preis dieses Heftes
3.60 Mark

Verlag: „Der Ziegelbrenner", München 23

Der Ziegelbrenner, January 15, 1919, front and back cover.

Ret Marut, color portrait (tempera) by F.W. Seiwert, Traven estate.

IN THE METROPOLITAN POLICE DISTRICT.

Register of the Court of Summary Jurisdiction sitting at *Thames* Police Court.

27199—Wt. P. 277—40 Bks.—6/22.—W. & S. Ltd. (12)

The *1st* day of *December* 192*3*

Number.	Name of Informant or Complainant.	Name of Defendant. Age, if known.		Nature of Offence or of Matter of Complaint.	Date of Offence.	Time when Charged.	Time when Bailed.	Doctor's Fee, (if any).	Plea.	Minute of Adjudication.	Time allowed for Payments and Instalments.
7	M. Ryman 386 H	Peter O'Reilly (Labourer)	31	Drunk & disorderly	30·11·23	10·55 pm.		10/6	G	~~40/-~~ or 21 days	n.f.a.
8	W. Paradine 177 H	Jack Deley (Dealer)	30	Drunk & disorderly	30·11·23	8·50 pm.	3am 1·12·23	10/6	G	B.O. £5 6 mos	
9	W. Beadle 117 H	Edward Stevens (Labourer)	32	Drunk & disorderly	30·11·23	8·20 pm.			G	~~40/-~~ or 21 days	7 days
10	A. Hayward 314 H	Archibald Moore (Labourer)	39	Drunk & disorderly	30·11·23	10·35 pm.	7·30 am 1·12·23		G	~~10/-~~ or 7 days	7 days
11	E. Smith 984 K	Frithjof Aberg (Fireman)	28	Drunk & disorderly	30·11·23	10·30 pm.		10/6	G	~~10/-~~ or 7 days	n.f.a.
12	H. Porter 342 H	Hugh Dow (Seaman)	27	Drunk & indecent	30·11·23	10·15 pm.			G	~~10/-~~ or 7 days	
13	F. Bickers C.I.D. C.O.	Ret Marut (Mechanic)	41	Being an alien, viz: American Citizen, did fail to register with the Registration Officer of the district in which he resided.	30·11·23	1·5 pm.			G (Consult)	rem^d 10 Dec	

W. [illegible]
Magistrate Adjudicating.

The *17th* day of *December* 192*3*

Name of Informant or Complainant.	Name of Defendant. Age, if known.	Age	Nature of Offence or of Matter of Complaint.	Date of Offence.	Time when Charged.	Time when Bailed.	Doctor's Fee, (if any).	Plea.
Remands. F. Bickers C.I.D. C.O.	Ret Marut. (Mechanic)	41	Being an alien, viz: American citizen, did fail to register with the Registration Officer of the district in which he resided. (1 from 10 12/23)	30·11·23	1·5 pm			

From the London police file on Ret Marut.

London police photos of Ret Marut.

NOTE.—One copy only of this form should be sent to the Department.

APPLICATION FOR REGISTRATION—NATIVE CITIZEN.

Consular No.

Department No.

I, Ret Marut hereby apply to the Consulate ... of the United States ... for registration as an American citizen.

I was born at San Francisco Cal. Feb. 25, 1882

My father Wm. Marut was born on 1855(?) at San Francisco, Cal.

... immigrated to the United States on or about ... resided ... years uninterruptedly, in the United States, from ... to ... was naturalized as a citizen of the United States before the ... Court of ... on ... as shown by the Certificate of Naturalization exhibited herewith, and now residing at ...

I last left the United States on Aug 19, 1923 ... residing at London England where I am now residing for the purpose of ...

I have resided outside the United States at the following places for the following periods:

Australia and Europe from 1892 to date

I desire to remain a citizen of the United States and intend to return thereto permanently to reside and perform the duties of citizenship within ... years, or when no intention

I am not the bearer of passport No. ...

I have always held myself out as an American citizen and have never been refused registration or a passport as such, and have not taken an oath of allegiance to, or been naturalized as a citizen or subject of, any foreign State.

I am married to ... who was born at ... and is now residing at ...

I have the following minor children by this marriage:

Name	Place of birth	Date of birth	Present residence

OATH OF ALLEGIANCE.

Further, I do solemnly swear that I will support and defend the Constitution of the United States against all enemies, foreign and domestic; that I will bear true faith and allegiance to the same; and that I take this obligation freely, without any mental reservation or purpose of evasion: So help me God.

R. Marut

Subscribed and sworn to before me this ... day of ... 19...

Consul ... of the United States at ...

The applicant's personal description is as follows:

Age, ... height, 5 feet, 7 inches; color of eyes, blue; color of hair, dark brown-grey

complexion, fair; distinguishing features or marks, —

Marut's application for American papers, London, March 1924.

AMERICAN CONSULATE GENERAL,

London: England.
January 11, 1924.

SUBJECT: Deportation Case - Ret Marut

THE HONORABLE

THE SECRETARY OF STATE,

WASHINGTON.

SIR:

I have the honor to report that I have received information from the Home Office to the effect that one Ret Marut was convicted at the Thames Police Court on December 17th of an offence against the Aliens' Order and was recommended for deportation. This man claims to be an American citizen and holds a document issued by the German police at Munich wherein it is stated that he was born at San Francisco on February 35, 1882.

I may mention that a day or two before receiving this information from the Home Office, I also received a letter from McElroy & Reid, Westory Building, Washington.D.C., stating that they had been retained to establish the citizenship of Mr.Ret Marut. In their letter to me they remark"-We have in our possession a large number of documents indicating that Marut was registered in Germany over a large number of years as an American and feel quite confident that reference to letters and papers in our possession will enableus to locate a number of persons who have personal knowledge of his birth here."

2

I shall be glad to be instructed by the Department as soon as possible whether or not an emergency certificate of registration may be issued to this man in order that he may be deported to the United States, although his ordinary place of residence for some considerable time has been in Germany.

I have the honor to be, Sir,

Your obedient servant,

ROBERT P.SKINNER.
American Consul General.

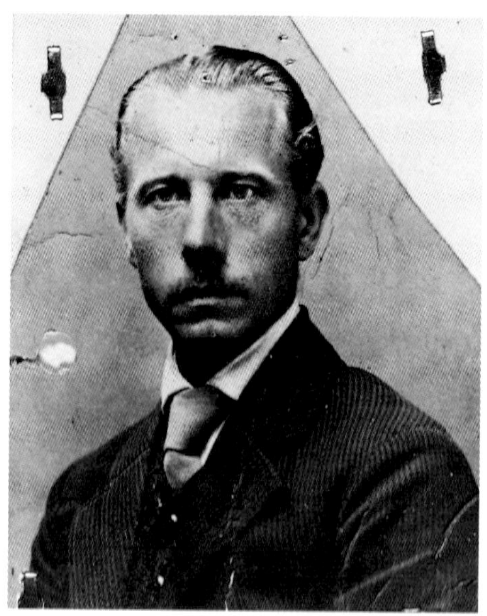

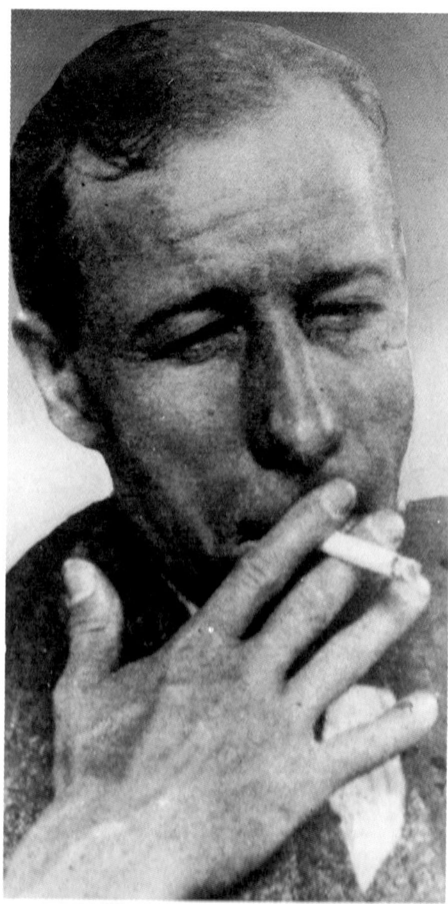

Ret Marut photos, Traven estate.

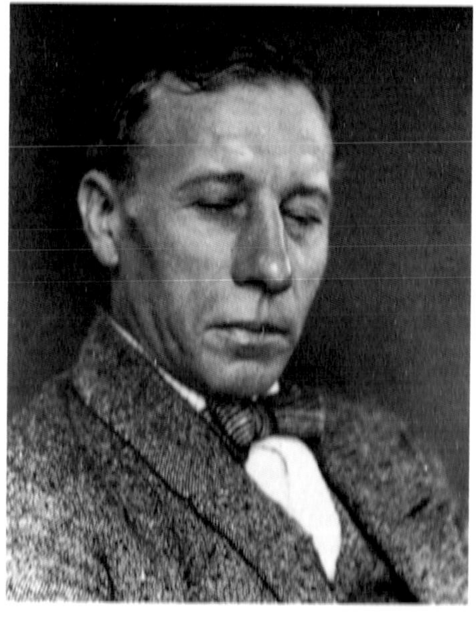

261 Aar og dag. (Date.)	Skibets (Ship's) Navn og beskaffenhet. (Name and description.)	Hjemsted. (Port of registry.)	Fører. (Master.)	Den paamønstredes (Engaged Seaman's) Stilling. (Capacity.)	Navn. (Name.)	Hjemsted. (Domicile.)	Fodselsaar og-dag. (Year and date of Birth.)	262 Anmerkninger (bl. a. ang. hyrens størrelse (Remarks i.e. concerning amount of wages stipulated)
17/4-24	S/S Hegre	Bergen	Haagensen	Matros	Kristian Jörgensen	Kristiansand S	2/1-87	kr. 171,00 pr. md. 3 [illegible]
"	"	"	"	Letmatros	Frederick George Offord	[illegible] London	9/5-1900	kr. 95,00 pr. md. 3 [illegible]
"	"	"	"	Messegut	Terence Barton	Wicklow	22/9-06	kr. 48,00 [illegible]
				~~Kullemper~~	~~Robt Mas[illegible]~~	~~Californ[illegible]~~		
	S/S Vaa[illegible]	Kristiania	[illegible]	Matros	Rolf Skjelin[illegible]	[illegible]	[illegible]	kr. 171 [illegible]
23/4-24	S/S "Sigdal"	Drammen	Mortensen	Letmatros	Anthony John	Hull	7/12-01	kr. 95,00 [illegible]
"		"	"	Salongut	Maurice Clarke	Edinburg	5/2-05	kr. 48,00 [illegible]
				[illegible]	Charles Nash	[illegible]	kr. 48	[illegible]
24-4-24				[illegible]	Arvid Tiren	Trondhjem 23-3-[illegible]	kr. 176,00	[illegible]
25-4-24	S/S [illegible]	Stavanger	Bukkeland	[illegible]	Nigge [illegible] Bidstrup	[illegible] 30-3-[illegible]	[illegible] 176	[illegible]
29-4-	S/S [illegible]	Bergen	Moe	[illegible]	Gideon Gottfred [illegible]	[illegible] 7-9-00	[illegible] 195	[illegible]
30-4-24				Matros	Hans Kristian Kvale	[illegible]	[illegible] 171	[illegible]
30-4-24	S/S [illegible]	Bergen	Olsen	[illegible]	[illegible] Olsen	[illegible]	[illegible]	[illegible]
				Fyrbøter	Emil Skree	[illegible] 30-[illegible]	£12	[illegible]
7-5-	S/S [illegible]	Bergen		Matros	[illegible] Ottesen	[illegible] 2-11-[illegible]	kr. 171	[illegible]
				[illegible]	John Johansen	[illegible] 22-7-98	171	
				Fyrbøter	[illegible] Kristen	[illegible] 8-9-[illegible]	176	
				[illegible]	[illegible]	[illegible]	150	

Den paamønstredes (Engaged Seaman's)

Stilling. (Capacity.)	Navn. (Name.)	Hjemsted. (Domicile.)	Fodselsaar og-dag. (Year and date of Birth.)	(bl. i.e. co[illegible]
Matros	Kristian Jörgensen	Kristiansand S	2/1-87	kr
Letmatros	Frederick George Offord	[illegible] London	9/5-1900	kr
Messegut	Terence Barton	Wicklow	22/9-06	kr
~~Kullemper~~	~~Robt Mas[illegible]~~	~~Califor[illegible]~~		

Muster roll of the Norwegian Mustering Authorities, London 1924 (the lower portion is an enlargement of a part of the upper).

VI/~~27~~ 11. Arrived 7^{30}. Mr. S. was alright. The
rest of the family seemed not or at
least indifferent. When looking after my
baggage found the missing. In the forenoon
with Mr. B. a look after the other land.
Told me about his plans. Seems to be good
ones. B. said he was expecting my coming.
Dinner with S family. About 3^{30} start for my
[illegible]. Nice place. Wants hard work. Negro
in hut. Staying with three cottonpickers. Two
Mex one negro. Night horrible. No sleep, too
many mosquitos. Tent around. Too hot.
12. Looking for J. Not at home. Start work. Cleaning
a way through grass.
13. See J. Indifferent, but seems a little
pleased. Start clearing brush. Move for the
night to open hut. Mosquitos. In the afternoon
B came. Coffee. Talk. Showed off.
14. Burned the inner place. Prairie fire beautiful.
21. rattlesnake caught by three Mex

Diary, 1924 (Tamaulipas, Mexico).

UNIVERSIDAD NACIONAL DE MEXICO

ESCUELA DE VERANO

CERTIFICADO DE ESTUDIOS AÑO DE 1928

EL ESTUDIANTE TRAVEN TORSVAN HA HECHO LOS ESTUDIOS ABAJO ESPECIFICADOS EN LAS CONDICIONES QUE SE INDICAN, Y HA MERECIDO LA CALIFICACION QUE EN CADA CASO SE MENCIONA.

NUMERO DEL CURSO	CURSOS	CREDITO EN UNIDADES	NUMERO DE HORAS POR SEMANA	NUMERO DE SEMANAS	ASISTENCIA A LAS CLASES	PORCENTAJE	CERTIFICADO DE ASISTENCIA	CERTIFICADO DE EXAMEN	CALIFICACION
235	Literatura Mexicana	2	5	6	30	100%	SI	SI	"D"
241	Geografía de México	1	2	6	12	100%	SI	SI	"B"
257	Aztec Literature	1	3	6	18	100%	SI	SI	"B"
161	Correspondencia y Métodos Comerciales	2	5	6	30	100%	SI	SI	"D"
243	Historia de México	1	3	6	18	100%	SI	SI	"B"
202	Gramática Avanzada	1	3	6	18	100%	SI	SI	"B"
246	Los Problemas Políticos y Sociales de México	2	5	6	30	100%	SI	SI	"A"
252	Ojeada Histórica sobre el Arte Mexicano	1	2	6	12	100%	SI	SI	"D"

NOTAS:
A.—EXCELENTE.
B.—BIEN.
C.—REGULAR.
D.—PASE.
F.—REPROBADO.
I.—TRABAJO INCOMPLETO.
W.—ABANDONO DEL CURSO.

MEXICO, D. F., A 17 DE agosto DE 1928.

EL DIRECTOR.

SOLAMENTE SE CONCEDE EXAMEN A LOS ALUMNOS QUE HAYAN ASISTIDO AL 80 POR CIENTO DE LAS CLASES DADAS.

Certificate of Traven's attendance at summer school, 1928.

B. Traven making expedition notes.

Members of the Palacios Expedition.
Traven is second from right.

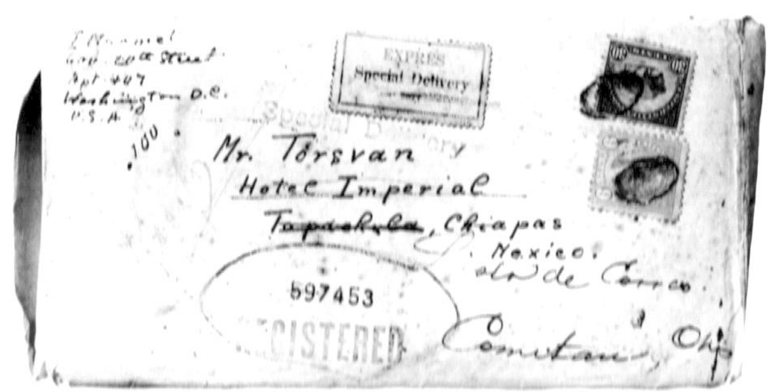

Letter from Irene Mermet to Traven, 1928.

Traven in Chiapas.

Photographs taken by Traven in Chiapas.

uf einer kleinen Bahnſtation, wo der Nachtzug für zwei Minuten hielt, um die Poſt zu erledigen, zwei oder drei Fahrgäſte aufzunehmen oder abzuſetzen, kamen etwa zwanzig bis fünfundzwanzig Männer in den Zug geſtiegen. Es war zwiſchen ſieben und acht Uhr und bereits ſtockdunkle Nacht.

Es kam nie vor, daß auf dieſer kleinen Station ſo viele Leute einſtiegen, aber weder der Stationsmeiſter noch das Zugperſonal dachten darüber nach. Es konnten ja Männer ſein, die irgendwo zu Markte fahren wollten, oder die in den Minen gearbeitet hatten und ſtreikten, oder die in andern Minendiſtrikten Arbeit ſuchen wollten.

Sie waren alle Meſtizen, hatten alle ihre großen Strohhüte auf, Hoſen und Hemd an. Sandalen oder Stiefel an den Füßen. Alle waren in ihre Decken gehüllt, da die Nacht kühl war. Da nach Einbruch der Dunkelheit auf kleinen Stationen keine Fahrkarten verkauft werden, kamen ſie ohne Fahrkarten, die ſie im Zuge löſen konnten. Die Station war ſtockfinſter, nur der Stationsmeiſter hatte ſeine Laterne und die Zugbeamten, die eil-

Dust jacket and first page of the first German edition of *The Treasure of the Sierra Madre*, 1927.

Cover of the April 1936 issue of *Büchergilde*, celebrating "10 years of B. Traven."

Ernst Preczang, late 1930 s.

Ansicht eines Teiles der Geschenke, die B. Traven aus seinen Sammlungen den werbetätigen Mitgliedern der Büchergilde Gutenberg Zürich überwiesen hat. Den Reichtum an Farben kann man nur ermessen, wenn man die Gegenstände vor sich sieht.

B. Traven stiftet neue Werbepreise für die Mitglieder der „Büchergilde Gutenberg"

Wie in den Heften Nr. 9, 10, 11 und 12 der «Büchergilde» 1935 bereits mitgeteilt wurde, hat uns B. Traven eine große Anzahl von indianischen Halsketten, gefertigt aus Muscheln des Pazifischen Ozeans, sowie zierliche kleine irdene Töpfchen, Schüsselchen, Kännchen, Kasserolen indianischer Herkunft als Werbe-Preise für unsere werbetätigen Mitglieder gestiftet. Diese seltenen und schönen Gegenstände fanden so viel Anklang unter unsern Mitgliedern, daß, als wir ihm davon Mitteilung machten, B. Traven den dritten Teil seiner Sammlung der Büchergilde Gutenberg zum Geschenk machte. Mit den Halsketten und den irdenen Schüsselchen, die wir bereits in Zürich haben, handelt es sich um mehr als dreitausend verschiedene Gegenstände, die B. Traven uns übergeben will, mit der ausdrücklicher Bestimmung, sie unter den Mitgliedern, die wenigstens zwei neue Mitglieder werben, als Preise zu verteilen auf dem Wege der Auslosung. Unter den Gegenständen, die uns in den nächsten Wochen zugeschickt werden, befinden sich: Reichbemalte Fruchtschalen der Tarascan-Indianer, indianische Schokoladenbecher, indianische Schokoladenquirle, Handtaschen aus feinem Bastgeflecht, ungemein zierliche kleine Körbchen, geflochten aus den

47

A page from *Büchergilde*, March 1936. Announcement of prizes donated by Traven for members.

22.

1.

The burros were loaded. ~~They were standing~~ with their packs on their backs ~~and~~ [They] waited patiently for Dobbs to kick them as a signal that it was time to shuffle off. Now and then they turned their heads ~~back~~ [ward] to Dobbs, [looking for] ~~Partly because they wanted to indicate that Dobbs had forgotten something that is to give them~~ the few handfuls of corn ~~they~~ [They usually gave them got] ~~thought they had a legitimate right to expect for Breakfast. Partly they were looking back because they could not understand~~ [and wondering] why Dobbs ~~was~~ [did not] ~~hesitating to~~ holler them on their way, for they were ~~used~~ [accustomed] to march the moment the[ir] ~~had the~~ packs ~~well tied upon the saddles.~~ [were loaded.]

~~The forenoon was well advanced.~~

Dobbs had ~~had~~ more trouble ~~to do the~~ loading than he had expected. It was not easy to pack the burros properly without the help of another man. One cannot ~~well~~ pack ~~at~~ two sides at the same time. ~~By the help of~~ [With] many oaths and kicks Dobbs ~~had~~ finally succeeded in his task, [b]ut much time had been lost and it was ~~now really late, close to noon.~~ [almost noon.]

~~Dobbs~~ [He] was ready to march, [but] ~~He~~ just ~~wanted~~ [as he was going] to shout at the animals ~~to go now when~~ he thought of Curtin ~~once more. The whole morning through he had thought of Curtin but not so much as of a dead but more as of a person temporarily absent as it happened frequently while they worked at their mine.~~ That Curtin was dead [he did not yet fully comprehend] ~~and therefore absent~~ for ever from ~~now on this had not been fully entered the mind of Dobbs yet.~~ He could not think ~~yet~~ of ~~a~~ Curtin, with whom he had been so long, as gone for ever and so suddenly. If Dobbs ~~would have~~ [had not] been alone with his thoughts ~~for the only company~~ he might have ~~got rid of any thought about~~ [forgotten about] Curtin in a few hours. But being alone in the wilderness he ~~seemed to~~ [thought he] hear[d] the voice and the laughter of Curtin unceasingly.

~~Though at the very moment when he was to march off~~ he ought to

The Treasure of the Sierra Madre.

Editorial

masas

S. C. L.

DONCELES 30
APARTADO 8092
TEL. ERIC. 2-04-03
MEXICO, D. F.

México, D. F. Mex.,
August 8, 1939.

Mr. Alfred A. Knots Inc.
501 Madison Ave.
New York City, N. Y
U. S. A.

Gentlemen:-

I beg you to inform me if there is any possibility to obtain the film rights on B. Traven's novels "Bridge in the Forest" and "Hanged's Revolt", and under Which price and conditions.

The company which desires to realize them is form my - point of view, the best in this country.

Thanking you in advance for your courtesy, I remain

Yours truly.

E L Mateos

Esperanza López Mateos.
MANAGER.

Esperanza Lopez Mateos's letter to Alfred A. Knopf, Inc.
Esperanza Lopez Mateos.

El C. MANUEL TELLO
Secretario de Relaciones Exteriores de los Estados Unidos Mexicanos

A todos los que la presente vieren, sabed:

Que EL SEÑOR TRAVEN TORSVAN,
se ha presentado en la Secretaría de mi cargo solicitando naturalizarse mexicano, con fundamento en LOS ARTICULOS 21, FRACCION I, 22 Y 29 de la Ley de Nacionalidad y Naturalización vigente; ha acreditado llenar todos los requisitos legales, hecho formal renuncia de su propia nacionalidad como NORTEAMERICANO y protestado adhesión, obediencia y sumisión a las Leyes y Autoridades de la República; en virtud de lo cual y por acuerdo del C. PRESIDENTE DE LOS ESTADOS UNIDOS MEXICANOS se le concede la naturalización, otorgándose la presente para que pueda acreditar que ha adquirido los derechos y obligaciones que competen a los mexicanos conforme a la Constitución y demás Leyes de la República.

Dado en la ciudad de México, el día TRECE del mes de SEPTIEMBRE de mil novecientos ~~cuarenta~~ CINCUENTA Y UNO.

MEXICO

Nombre del interesado: TRAVEN TORSVAN.
Nombre del padre: BURTON TORSVAN.
Nombre de la madre: DOROTHY TORSVAN.
Nacionalidad anterior del interesado: NORTEAMERICANA.
Lugar de su nacimiento: CHICAGO, ILL, USA., MAYO 3 DE 1890.
Estado civil: SOLTERO Profesión u ocupación: AGRICULTOR.
Color: BLANCO Ojos: AZULES Barba: - - - Pelo: GRIS.
Estatura exacta: 1,60 MTS.
Sabe leer y escribir: SI SABE.
Señas particulares: NINGUNA.
Nombre de la esposa: ----
Lugar de su residencia: ----
Nombre y edad de los hijos menores: ----
Lugar de su residencia: ----

Declaro, bajo protesta de decir verdad, que los anteriores datos son ciertos, así como que las huellas digitales y fotografía que obran en esta carta son de mi persona.

(FIRMA DEL INTERESADO)

MANO DERECHA: PULGARES, INDICES, M..., ANULARES, MEÑIQUES
MANO IZQUIERDA

Traven's naturalization certificate, September 13, 1951.

Gabriel Figueroa.

File   Treasure of the Sierra Madre

Dear Hal Croves:

Just arrived at the Hotel Reforma - can you call around 6:00 or come by - most anxious to see you.

John Huston.

314

Note from John Huston to Hal Croves.

Gabriel Figueroa.

Mañana
DESCUBRE
LA
IDENTIDAD
DE
B. TRAVEN!

Luis Spota's report in *Mañana*, August 7, 1948.

Rosa Elena Lujan at Calle Durango 353.

The library at Calle Rio Mississippi 61.

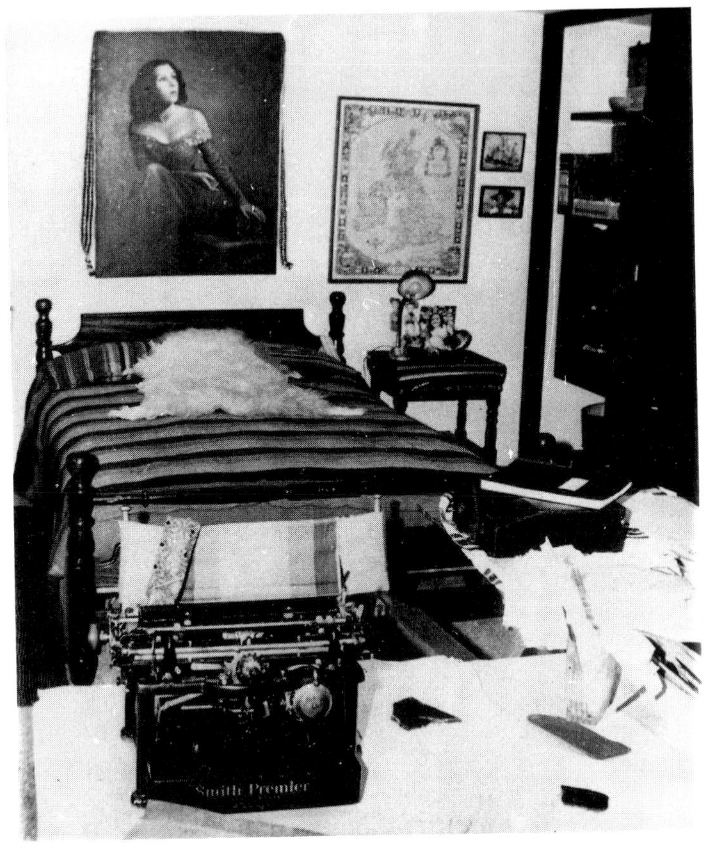

"The Bridge."

Traven and Rosa Elena Lujan's visit to Hamburg for the film premiere of *Das Totenschiff*, 1959.

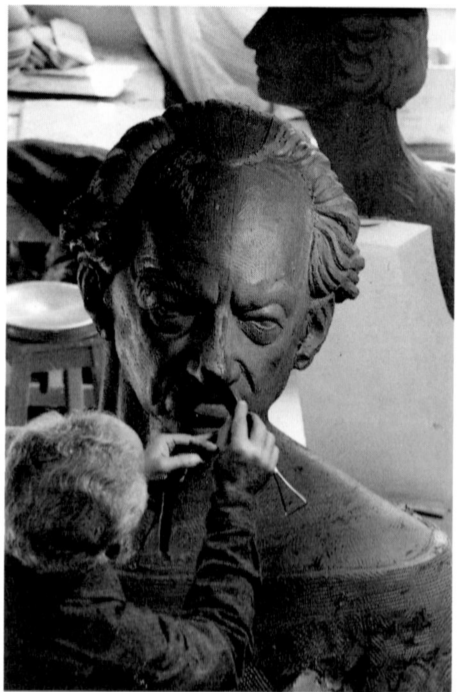

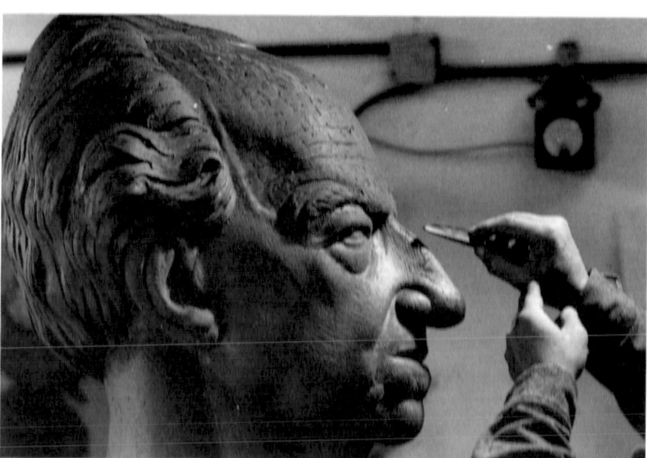

Federico Canessi working on the Traven bust.

AUD. 243/68. RPsreg-21

Nº 207943

DEPARTAMENTO
DEL
DISTRITO FEDERAL

En nombre de la República Mexicana y como Oficial del Registro Civil de este lugar, certifico ser cierto que en el libro 1-7a del Registro Civil que es a mi cargo, a la foja 378 se encuentra asentada una Acta del tenor siguiente:

OFICIALIA 7a
DEL REGISTRO CIVIL
MEXICO, D. F.

PARA CERTIFICADOS DE LAS ACTAS DEL REGISTRO CIVIL DEL DISTRITO FEDERAL

CONFRONTADA

Valor de la hoja $ 5.50 URGENTE

ACTA DE DEFUNCION

En México, Distrito Federal, a las once horas del día veintisiete de marzo de mil novecientos sesenta y nueve, ante mi Licenciado, José Ignacio Fernández Oficial del Registro Civil, comparece el señor, Juan Vega y exhibe un certificado médico en el que se hace constar el fallecimiento de 1 adulto, TRAVEN TORSVAN CROVES con los siguientes datos:

GENERALES DEL FINADO

Lugar de Nacimiento: Chicago Illinois, Estados Unidos de Norteamérica Edad: 78 años
Nacionalidad: Mexicana por naturalización Ocupación: Escritor
Domicilio: Rio Mississipi 61 Colonia Cuauhtémoc
Estado Civil: Casado con Rosa Elena Luján
Padres: Burton Torsvan y Dorothy Croves, finados

Enfermedad: Nefroesclerosis-Adenocarcinoma, Prostatica
Día y hora del fallecimiento: ayer a las 11 horas 20 minutos
Lugar del fallecimiento: su domicilio
Lugar de inhumación: Se concedió permiso para la incineración del cadaver en el panteón Civil. (Dolores)
Médico que certifica: Federico Marín Preciado
Domicilio del Médico: San Luis Potosí 48

GENERALES DEL DECLARANTE

Edad: veintiseis años Ocupación: empleado
Estado Civil: soltero Domicilio: Rosas Moreno 151

TESTIGOS

Nombres:	José Nieves	Victor Vega
Edad:	veintisiete años	veintiocho años
Ocupación:	empleado	empleado
Domicilio:	Rosas Moreno 151	
Parentesco:	ninguno	ninguno

Leída la presente acta, la ratifican y firman los que saben: Doy Fe. Lic. J. I. F. Juan Vega.-José Nieves.-Victor Vega.-"Rúbricas".
MARGINALES: Partida Núm.- 377.- Trescientos setenta y siete.-TORSVAN CROVES TRAVEN.- - - - - - - - - -ES COPIA FIEL DE SU ORIGINAL QUE EXPIDO EN LA CIUDAD DE MEXICO A LOS TREINTA Y UN DIAS DEL MES DE JULIO DE MIL NOVECIENTOS SESENTA Y NUEVE.

EL OFICIAL DEL REGISTRO CIVIL.

LIC. JOSE IGNACIO FERNANDEZ G.

OFICIALIA 7a
DEL REGISTRO CIVIL
MEXICO, D. F.

Official copy of Traven's death certificate.

Applicant is the son of William Marut and Helene Marut (nee Ottorrent) and was born he says at San Francisco, Cal on —. He ran away from home when he was ten years of age, having signed on as a ~~[illegible]~~ kitchen boy on a ship bound for Australia (1892 - summer) after 5 or 6 weeks he left there, ~~[illegible]~~ and proceeded to India. Then to Singapore and from there to Rotterdam finally (1895) From there on another ship to India and after 18 mos cruise returned to Rotterdam (1897) Then to Germany and on another boat from Hamburg proceeded to ~~[illegible]~~ to Rio & and from there to Frisco. and return to Rio. (1899) From Rio to N. Y.

and having changed there proceeded to Rotterdam (1900) Stayed in Rotterdam waiting for [illegible] (1901) Then to Germany ~~[illegible]~~ remaining there & from there to Vienna where he took up the study of language. Later he obtained position in Vienna & later became a full fledged actor under the name Langer. (1907) Then to Germany Berlin where he opened a theatrical agency till then to Frankfort, where he obtained work as actor and traveled through ~~[illegible]~~ Germany. Then to [illegible] as actor to 1912. From 1912 to 19[illegible] [illegible] 1916 to 1919 at Munich P. P. [illegible]

Made appln [illegible] 1914 but [illegible] [illegible]

The London c.v., 1924.

11

We had brought over to Antwerp a cargo of cotton from New Orleans in the Tuscaloosa. She was a fine ship, yes, a first rate steamer, American built, home at New Orleans. She had fine quarters for the crew and the food was all right, sure. Second mate? No, sir, I was not ~~the~~ second mate on that ~~boat~~ bucket, no not. I had signed on just as a plain deckhand, painting, doing odd jobs, being kept busy all the day long, you know. Just forty five dollars a month. If you never spend a cent you may call yourself a well ~~do~~ to do chap after twenty years.

I did not bother about going ashore because I hated that town, ~~its people had placed a foul trick on me a year previous~~ there are so many mean sailors ashore. However, the last evening before we sailed homeward bound in ballast, I became tired of the look of the quarters and I wanted to see a street, just a street that not swayed. It was only for the benefit of my eyes to make them a nice present.

When asking the first mate for ten dollars advance he said: 'No, old man, I don't give you ten, just five, not a dime more.'

'I can do nothing with five, I want ten,' I insisted. So ~~I~~ he gave me ten and said: 'Don't go drunk, boy, it's a dangerous place.'

Now wasn't that an insult? It was, because the skipper himself, all the mates and all the engineers had been drunk twice each day while [illegible] day by the wharf.

'No, sir,' I said 'I never took a drop of that poison, I am a teetotaler, bone dry, sure, sir that [illegible] I am.'

'Ah. That's all right!' he said and out of [illegible]

First version of *The Death Ship*, 1923–24.

government in the world" to do away with passport requirements—"and when will Germany follow?")

Thoughts of "propaganda" for his own works were not far off when Traven repeatedly offered Preczang and Schönherr authentically Mexican objects to be used for lectures, promotional evenings, and exhibitions. He sent not only photographs he had taken of Mexico and its people (some of which, bearing his own commentary, later appeared as background illustrations to his novels in *Die Büchergilde*). Above all, he repeatedly sent handmade Indian art objects and articles from the daily life of the Indians—objects that would gradually be replaced by mass-produced varieties and that thus would soon have "enormous value," as he informed Schönherr on January 5, 1928. After all, the individually crafted items, made with "patience and a sense of beauty," contained the "personality," the very "soul" of the artisan. A curious hodgepodge of exotic pieces amassed itself in the course of time at the Büchergilde office at Dreibundstrasse in Berlin: Indian rugs and serapes, hats and sandals, ceramics, purses made of hemp, tobacco pouches, obsidian tools, arrowheads, little baskets woven from hair, feather arrangements, wood carvings, clay figurines, toys of all descriptions, drinking bowls and other containers, flutes, a saddle, a grating stone, silver votive offerings, archeological objects from Mayan civilization, some of which Traven himself had found or excavated, and even souvenirs of tropical fauna: the wings of a moth ("thousands" of an even larger species were his "constant nightly companions") and a scorpion (but just a small one, for "I did not dare send a large black scorpion, because I know for sure that not only every person, but even every object in your office would turn pale, especially when I add that I share my sleeping quarters with hundreds of them"). But he did not spare his publisher the gift of the "rattle of a rattlesnake," which he himself "saw in the nick of time and caught." (He made great strides in this art form as well: "I have killed rattlers with thirty-four rings"—very big specimens, in other words, and therefore old and crafty ones.) On occasion his packages of folk art and natural specimens also include printed matter: "the magazine of the Federation of Mexican Unions," for example, but also a bourgeois Mexican newspaper, the pictures in which he explained pedantically with reference to his own travel book or to the ever turbulent political environment. (Traven took pains to keep the Büchergilde up to date on Mexican political happenings, reporting on the government's confrontations with rebels, shootings of reactionary officers, the church's schemings, the important role played by workers' organizations, exploitation of the Indians even in postrevolutionary times, and also immigration restrictions for Communists, of which he approved.) In his letter of January 5, 1928, he included a photo of striking Wobblies in Colorado that appeared in a U.S. newspaper: "Show this picture to those who want to move to the promised land of freedom, North America."

Some of Traven's offerings were specifically labeled as gifts or as loans. Still others were to be sold in Europe, with Traven suggesting the retail price. The proceeds were to be used for advertising his books. In the mid-1930s, he also offered special prizes for those most successful at recruiting new Büchergilde members: Indian shell necklaces, pottery, and even a "lion skin" on one occasion, as well as Mexican magazines and American comics; *Die Büchergilde* made frequent mention of such incentives. Traven volunteered to offer ten or even fifteen percent of his royalties for "propaganda, advertising, and newspaper ads" to promote not only his own works but also those of other Büchergilde authors. He further liked to speculate whether a certain book would draw new readers or scare off existing members and whether the risk was worthwhile. In this regard, he advocated a more daring path: Members who cared for "sweet novels" and who had no taste for Traven "should be allowed to drop by the wayside. The same is done when transporting large herds of cattle across the country, and the practice has proved effective. You would scarcely believe the similarities between a half-wild herd of cattle and a herd of human beings." The "bourgeois world of ideas," he wrote to Schönherr on January 5, 1928, should not find expression through the Büchergilde. "You must not make any concessions to the lassitude and intellectual laziness of the readers." His model in this case was—of all people—Henry Ford. When he returned from his next trip, he added, he would try "to work out a complete propaganda plan for recruiting new members."

From his remote headquarters, Traven thus made all sorts of attempts to help manage the Büchergilde and refashion its image. At the same time, and characteristically, he was firmly opposed to a rigidly defined program and a sharply focused image. "I do not like anything set in stone," he wrote to Preczang on August 8, 1926, in response to a request from June 8 for a few lines about the "value of proletarian book clubs." Traven continued with a passage that sounds like a motto for Traven the anarchist:

> The book club which today seems useful and necessary may tomorrow be an obstacle to the free and unimpeded development of human expressive potential and expressive power. The thing is not to determine anything rigidly; always apply fire to the seat of the pants so that we don't fall asleep over our pretty programs and constitutions. . . . All I can say in this regard is the following: Dear members of the Büchergilde, everything that you are doing and have done is beautiful and outstanding. But please, tomorrow—or, even better, this evening—do everything completely differently. Perhaps it will become even more outstanding, perhaps everything will be destroyed. It doesn't matter. Just do it differently and don't be conservative, otherwise you'll become barren and dried out. . . .
>
> There are so few people, particularly among Socialist and Communist workers, who can put up with it when someone topples their idols. It is so sad to witness that even workers, those on whom the hope of the world rests, have their own idols and bibles and catechisms which one cannot touch.

One gains a better understanding of Traven's situation in these early years in Mexico when one pursues the fate of each of his books as discussed in the correspondence.

In regard to *The Cotton-Pickers*, Preczang, having consulted with his colleagues, responded as early as September 15, 1925, that the Büchergilde would accept the novel "on the condition that you expand the work to normal book length." In his reply of October 11, Traven reported that the novel had been "completed" in the meantime and that he would send it off to Berlin the following week. "Now you will, I suppose, finally be satisfied, as far as the question of length is concerned." The title, however, had become less appropriate because the new second part depicted the vagabond lifestyle of the expatriate American Wobbly against a new backdrop: Gales, formerly the cotton picker, appears as a baker, oil driller, ranch hand, cattle drover and, above all, it seems, a strike agitator wherever he goes. Traven deviated from the original subject matter (thus necessitating a change of title) since his first "novel" essentially recorded what he himself had experienced or observed during his first months in Mexico. The extent to which the narrative parallels the author's own living and working experiences (and not those of an undocumented legendary "other man") is revealed by Traven's offhand autobiographical comment on October 11, 1925, which is to justify the new direction in the second part of the novel: "Here one cannot pick cotton the whole year through. There are times when one has to do something else." The unassuming picaresque novel apparently was meant to be, and cannot be anything but, a record of day-to-day events transposed into fiction—which does not mean, of course, that Traven "experienced" or witnessed every episode in precisely the manner depicted in the novel. One can scarcely transform an autobiography into a novel without creative fantasy, the desire to spin a good yarn, and literary talent. With this qualification, Traven's frequent claim that his writings were authentic is doubtless justified. "Life, life as it is really lived, is so difficult to label," he says in his letter of October 11. "It is simply life and nothing else." This authentic life included, not least, the realm of the erotic and sexual, which represented something else entirely "out here in the world" than in the bourgeois Germany of the 1920s:

> I am going on the assumption that members of the Büchergilde are not at the same time members of a morality league. Should that be the case, you would have to cut pages 53–81 of the second part, for these pages include a description of the "Señoritas' Quarter." The life of geishas and *bajaderes* deviates somewhat from the traditional prettifying conception. But when I depict life, I want to depict it as it is and not the way people want to have it depicted. I write for men and for women who want to know how things really look out here in the world. For that reason my writings are not meant as schoolbooks or as Christmas presents for demure and chaste young girls.
>
> If you cut that passage, you would remove an irreplaceable part of the work; for the "Señoritas" play as important a role for men here, particularly for workers, as your club dances where boy meets girl. Here one just heads for the goal or one takes a vow of celibacy and goes out of his skin. Here every pleasure has its price, even those that men over where you are can have for nothing, due to the overabundance of women and girls.

His depiction of the social and political environment in *The Cotton-Pickers* was just as true-to-life, bordering on journalistic reportage, he noted; it reflected the situation under Calles's presidency:

> No other work is to be had just now. The big American oil companies fire 800 to 1,000 people every week and that puts

> great pressure on the employment market. The companies intend to lead the government back to supporting capitalist interests, while the government is dedicated to continuing its determined support of workers' interests.
>
> I would like to note that the events of the strike, as depicted in the second book, correspond to real events; from this you can see that the government here is not as lukewarm as many of the so-called workers' governments in Europe. The government here takes up the cause of the workers against the capitalists. In Vera Cruz the Chamber of Commerce closed down to protest the government's labor policy.

As mentioned earlier, Traven's comments in no way imply that he saw himself solely as a writer of the working class. In this same letter of October 11, 1925, he even said that it had never been his intention to write "only" for a workers' audience; on the contrary, he doubted whether his present and future writings would "always appeal to workers." Preczang informed Traven that his works had the greatest appeal among workers and claimed that the bourgeois press ignored his novels "with very few exceptions." Traven, for his part, did not in principle value the worker who read his works any more than the capitalist reader. Referring to the business practices of the workers' newspapers, he said, "The worker is not infrequently a wretched egoist exploiting others as he does not wish to be exploited."

The Cotton-Pickers is thus not intended as a novel for a particular class, but rather as an adventure story accentuated by social criticism and spiced with humor. Traven sent off the first and second "book" to the Büchergilde in mid-October 1925, as noted in his letter to Preczang of October 15, 1925, in which he also demanded, as he would continue to do in later years, that the typescript be returned to him. "The Second Book is much, much better than the First, with much richer contents, much livelier, much richer in color; it far outshines the First Book," he announced. He now proposed *Der Wobbly* as a title: "If the readers don't know what it means, they'll learn soon enough." A propos of the readers, Traven adopted no false modesty: He hoped that in spite of stylistic inconsistencies between the two parts—though these were unavoidable due to the subject matter, he contended—his book would double the membership of the Büchergilde. (He had even higher expectations for *The Death Ship*.)

Whether the Büchergilde shared this optimism or not, *Der Wobbly* was accepted on December 11, 1925, by telegram, though not for the Büchergilde but for its commercial affiliate, Buchmeister Press, since one publisher could not bring out two Traven novels at more or less the same time, as Traven himself had feared in regard to *The Death Ship*. But even representation by two publishers could not guarantee the high level of sales that Traven was counting on: The editor reminded him of the "extraordinarily bad" economic conditions in Germany. Nonetheless no time was lost in typesetting and printing—the process occurred so quickly that Traven did not even receive proofs. One reason for the hurry was that *Vorwärts*, namely "Comrade Schikowski," wanted to begin serialization of the second part by late May or early June, with the book to come out two or three weeks later, as Preczang explained on May 14, 1926. On June 8, Preczang wrote: "*The Wobbly* is already typeset and printed for the most part. The book should appear this very month. *Vorwärts* wants to begin its serialization of the work any day now." (The second book did appear in the newspaper as *Der Wobbly* from June 9 to July 22.) There is no reason to doubt the supposition that the novel was in fact published in book form in June 1926; the claims in Recknagel's biography—on the one hand that *The Wobbly* was first published in August and on the other that it appeared in Buchmeister Press in May 1926—not only contradict each other but also are both undocumented. On August 8, 1926, having just returned from the Palacios expedition (May–August), Traven asked Preczang for six copies of *The Wobbly*. (Registered packages sent to him had been returned in his absence.)

The story of Traven's discovery is the story of the discovery of *The Cotton-Pickers*. (From 1928 on, book editions bore this title.) Recknagel cites a letter from Traven to Preczang dated November 18, 1929, that reveals this event as a major turning point in his life. Had he not received word from the Büchergilde of their interest in his work, Traven noted in retrospect, "I would probably have ended up again in some remote oil camp in a corner of Central America or in the boiler room of some vagabond tramp steamer, or God knows where." "Hardly at all or only very rarely" can one find in the history of literature an act of faith such as Preczang's initial letter, he contended. No other publisher had noted that in the chapters published by *Vorwärts* "a new voice [had begun] to call out, albeit from far away." "Thus not only do books have their fate, but also the authors of books and the discoverers of authors and books." This "new" element in Traven's books, which the Büchergilde was quick to appreciate and which made them unique not only in German literature but in Mexican and American literature as well, Traven himself attempted to characterize in a letter to Johannes Schönherr of November 24, 1927: His works afforded an authentic "insight into the conditions of workers in Central America and Mexico" that would certainly be of particular interest to "German workers." (*The Death Ship*, he added, was in its own way no less authentic and timely; newspaper reports confirmed again and again "how many death ships sail the seas.")

Traven also asked for six copies of *The Death Ship* in the letter of August 8, 1926, in which he requested his copies of *The Wobbly*. Though it makes its appearance in the correspondence with the Büchergilde only after *The Cotton-Pickers*, *The Death Ship* preceded *The Wobbly* in subject matter and in Traven's work on it. And it was, in fact, published before *The Wobbly*, in April 1926—Traven's first novel to appear in book form. While waiting to see whether the manuscript of *The Death Ship* would be accepted by the Büchergilde, he wrote to Preczang on October 11, 1925, that publication of the work was "very important" to him since he was trying to "make the public get up and take a closer look at the consequences of what are called passport and visa requirements." He seemed to put more importance on the novel's pointed social criticism than on the broader question of a person's identity and the rights of the individual. And the social criticism may also have been the deciding factor for the socialist Büchergilde. In any event, the Büchergilde came to a quick decision. A cable of October 19 announced acceptance of the novel; a letter (apparently lost) provided confirmation but recommended many cuts. Traven discussed the suggestions in detail in his letter of November 9, 1925, saying that he did not wish to be "unreasonable, as long as nothing is changed in the work's character and intention." The book's intention, he noted, was to show "where the enemy stands" and who he is, namely "international bureaucracy and state absolutism which is surfacing so rapidly and with such disastrous results" in Russia, the United States, and Europe. Preczang seems not to have wanted to tamper with this aspect of the work. He apparently took exception above all to certain remarks that the "old" German unions had played into the hands of the state and the capitalists to the detriment of the workers. (Traven claimed, incidentally, that the American unions had done the same, resulting in the formation of the IWW.) Traven played the pragmatist: To avoid frittering away valuable time with such "little corrections" and resuscitating outdated discussions, he simply recommended deleting controversial passages. "It is not my intention to stir up workers against each other."

He took more interest in the matter of the "conclusion, which you would like to see changed." While claiming that he was not sufficiently well informed about political issues "to make quick judgments of what is right and wrong," he felt "on more solid ground" in questions of his works' "artistic form." To Preczang's concern that the reader would be "tormented" with the question of what becomes of the first-person narrator, who is left shipwrecked at the end of the novel, floating alone on the high seas and overcome with hallucinations, Traven defended the novel's conclusion in basically the same way he would in the short essay "My Novel *The Death Ship*," which appeared in *Die Büchergilde* in March 1926. But his discussion in the letter to Preczang was more extensive as well as more direct and more personal. Only one who himself has spent "several days and nights" shipwrecked can see the conclusion as the "only one possible," Traven claimed. His letter reveals the wealth of insights hidden between the lines at the novel's end:

> Consciousness for the past twenty-four hours has been nothing but the consciousness of a man stricken with fever, with delusions and mental confusion, whose sense of distance and judgment has disintegrated (judgment whether water is as solid a surface to stand on as hard earth). Now it is about to be extinguished completely. The last spark of the dying consciousness is kindled once more, not by the mind but by the animal instincts. The instincts, not the mind, undergo the shock of beginning to be alone, of having to help one's comrade out of one's egoistic sense of self-preservation, to avoid being left alone. This final flaring up of the last remnant of consciousness by experiencing the tragic event through the instincts so shake up the man that he sees a blurred collage of forms (which for months had filled his existence): God, captain, death ship, signing on, the door of the crew's quarters, and the death of his comrade—though the whole seems to be logically connected, as is so often the case with those suffering from mental illness. But this last incredible expenditure of the remaining bit of consciousness hurls the man into a state which is tantamount to

death. The great silence begins. He is no longer able to narrate anything. He is extinguished. What happens with him from now on is not his action, but the action of others. Whether he is thrown ashore (the action of the waves) or is saved by a ship (the action of men) or dies (the action of fate), he is unable to relate. He can do that no more than an unborn child beneath its mother's heart can tell what is happening to it. Any additional sentence at that point would be no conclusion, but rather the start of a new novel. I am considering writing this new novel. But it is in fact a new novel. The authors of earlier periods of civilization made it easier for themselves. They killed off all their characters, and the novel or play was over. Even in *Hamlet*: Polonius, Ophelia, King, Queen, Laertes, Hamlet—all dead. That's one sort of conclusion. I can't do that. We are no Werthers, no Romeos or Juliets. We have to live. We have to endure it. And only when we are extinguished is there a conclusion of sorts. But the narrator was not extinguished. The fact that "He" narrates must be sufficient [proof] for the reader that he survived. In what form he survived, in what form he was saved—these questions have nothing to do with this novel.

There would be a conclusion to satisfy the average reader. The conclusion at the end of the Second Book, directly after the death ship's dancing song. "They get each other," the lover and the beloved. The rosy blush of sunset. You have everything there. But no novel about real life ends like that. The novel begins after they have got each other, the novel which we can recognize as the only possible novel in our epoch of civilization. August Strindberg saw that early on. After they get each other, the tragedy begins. After "He" has begun to long for his Yorikke, his fate begins. Fate treats him so tormentingly that he learns to love the Yorikke as a paradise, the same Yorikke which once seemed to him the most devilish torment in hell.

Now I could change the conclusion by relating to the reader everything that I have said in this letter. In which form? As a monologue? I know that any monologue or reflection is ruled out for purely practical reasons, since the thought process ceases. Should I deceive the reader and tell him that such thoughts, such monologues are possible in this situation? I can't do that. Should I let the waves whisper and end with a fairy tale atmosphere? I would like to offer the reader a greater gift, since I hope that he is a reader of our period of civilization. I want to give him the gift of moving him to draw his own conclusion. I wish that after reading the novel the reader will continue to

> think for himself, continue to experience things for himself, continue to write for himself. I don't want to empty out the reader, I want to inspire him to consider how things go from here. Only what he himself thinks is his possession, not what I write.

The reaction from Berlin was conciliatory. Preczang agreed on December 11, 1925, to Traven's comments about cuts and about the novel's conclusion; only eight shorter "polemical comments" would be left out, "which we cannot put before our readers without inciting protest and debate." Details about royalty payments were also resolved satisfactorily. So the manuscript went directly to the typesetter, and *The Death Ship* was to appear in early March.

The only thing to actually appear by the end of March was Traven's Büchergilde essay on *The Death Ship*, and even that suffered from haste, in Traven's opinion, though he did believe that "it is often a disadvantage when one has too much time for reflection." He reflected further on the novel's conclusion on March 29, 1926: In principle he did not like "the somewhat religious-sentimental turn at the end," but unfortunately it was realistic, for workers had been brought up believing in reward or punishment in the hereafter. He himself would have preferred the dying man cursing the gods mightily, he said.

Production of the novel itself was delayed, as *Die Büchergilde* informed its readers in March 1926, citing—surely not without an eye to effective advertising—"severe storms on the Atlantic" that slowed down "the passage of the proofs." Traven himself had brought up this reason for delay on February 9, 1926. He did what he could, under the circumstances, to forgo stylistic improvements and he made only the most necessary corrections. "As a rule I do not like to read proofs. Who enjoys it?" In the same letter he said he was more interested in seeing the book furnished with illustrations, particularly of New Orleans and Louisiana. (Nothing came of this, since the photos were not sharp enough and illustrations were perceived by the Büchergilde as "contrary to the book's character," as Preczang informed the author and photographer on March 5.) The novel was finally launched in late April. "It has already been three weeks since *The Death Ship* left the harbor," the editor began his letter of May 14, 1926. He also communicated the first enthusiastic responses from readers but at the same time downplayed the author's great expectations, reminding him of poor economic conditions in Germany. Traven addressed these issues on August 8, having just returned from Chiapas: "A book that is received that well right away—something must be amiss here. I would prefer it if people would curse more." He was deeply impressed by the way the book had been produced: "The whole make-up is appealing with its simplicity and inobtrusive elegance."

The Death Ship subsequently trailed off as a subject in the correspondence. Reprints in newspapers were touched on here and there; Traven was so interested in the reprint issue that he even recommended marketing strategies to Preczang. Preczang, for his part, suggested that Traven write a screenplay, to which Traven, who later became so preoccupied with film versions of his works, answered that he would agree only if a film company first expressed definite interest. But right away he was gripped by the idea and in this connection launched into his own interpretation of the work, which is extremely informative, not least in regard to the question of Traven's engagement with proletarian causes:

> In adapting the work I would put the main emphasis—in *The Death Ship*—on the character of Stanislav; for Stanislav, not the novel's "I," is the greater personality. Stanislav is the really great, strong, and conscious proletarian. He stands above the law, above the petty morality; he is a deserter, prankster, pickpocket, burglar, passport counterfeiter, signature counterfeiter—not because of a defect in his soul but because he has been compelled by his proletarian condition. Basically he is a true, full-blooded proletarian, healthy to the bottom of his soul, who is fanatically devoted to truly honorable work, constructive work. His destructive behavior arises from the defects of the capitalist system. The "I" in *The Death Ship* is only a secondary figure. And in the film scenario I would attempt to group all the action more around Stanislav than around the "I." Stanislav is the truly conscious man without a country, an international figure; the human core of the proletariat of the future lies in people of Stanislav's caliber. To be sure, I do not yet know whether that can be depicted in a film.

In the 1960s Traven made similar remarks regarding *The Death Ship* and about Stanislav in particular.

Twenty years after Traven's earliest discussion of film as a means of communicating his work, his first novel to be made into a film appeared on the screen: *The Treasure of the Sierra Madre* (Warner

Brothers, 1948). This novel, too, formed a central topic of conversation with the Büchergilde in their early correspondence. Traven's letter to Preczang of August 8, 1926, contains a shot out of the blue: "I currently have another MS at hand." The Union Deutsche Verlagsanstalt had declined *The Treasure of the Sierra Madre*, because—Traven cited a letter from that publisher's editor—it was "more an adventure and gold prospectors' story than a novel"; the work lacked a "resolution of the plot" as well as female characters; the depiction was thus not suitable for publication in "a German family magazine." Traven viewed this final criticism as "reassuring," he said in his letter, and thus offered the manuscript to Preczang. While agreeing with the criticism, he reinterpreted it positively: The women appearing in family magazines "have been made somewhere out of cake dough . . . , for I know women too, and when they appear in my works [a woman actually does appear in *Treasure*, he noted], there's usually a hailstorm." He admitted that the novel lacked clear rising and falling action, but with good reason: The plot was not structured like this "for the simple reason that life does not play itself out that way. . . . I depict life the way I have seen it and the way I have experienced it, intellectually and physically." Again, he claimed authenticity:

> The book *The Treasure of the Sierra Madre* describes in its first part the life of workers in the oil fields of Mexico that I know—know only too well. In the further passages the life of workers is depicted who go prospecting for gold. Gold-prospector novels are no better than sea novels. And I intended for a change to look more closely at the "family-magazine romanticism" of the gold miners. It could be eminently useful for many a German worker who has seen the American strike-it-rich films to find out what a poor proletarian the "independent" gold miner is, even when he finds a few nuggets.

On October 1 Preczang cabled to Mexico City: "Treasure accepted." The manuscript, he wrote on October 10, was "gobbled up" by the editors; the book would make it, even if its social criticism was not as "pointed and apparent" as in *The Death Ship*. Traven was in complete agreement with his critic on this point but stressed that in the novel he could have said much about the "murderous exploitation of workers in the oil fields . . . that would not be dissimilar in many regards to *The Death Ship*. For the workers in some industries here are already dead men":

> The many cripples and men beaten to death, burned and maimed in the course of exploitation of human labor in the oil fields are a grisly indictment of the system. Here, too, it is the free worker, the free contract worker who bleeds, loses arms or legs, or dies thinking he is free because he earns two or three hundred dollars per month. If he has work at all. If he has none, he whimpers but still goes on believing that he is a free man. And because they are free American workers, they slave away 12 hours per day, in only two shifts. Mexican workers don't do that, they work only eight; they also won't put up with half of what the free Americans do. But Americans all have the idea they could someday become billionaires. That is the trick they use to muzzle them here. . . .
>
> But I never leave out the flowers growing near a dung heap, for that would be bias. For the world has dung heaps and flowers, sorrows and joys, death ships and ships where they serve good butter and where the stokers and coal drags are treated like princes. But because some writers paint only ships where opera arias are sung all day long, equilibrium can be restored to the world only if ships are occasionally depicted as they really sail about.

Traven struck the same chord when he returned to *Treasure* in a letter of March 20, 1927: He was unable to "make things beautiful" as the bourgeois press (and not only the bourgeois press) demanded. "And so I have to do without the blessing of the artistic and literary popes, and roll about in the dust full of contrition."

A month to the day later, on April 20, 1927, writing to Preczang, he already held a copy of the new novel in his hands in Tampico and could scarcely contain his joy at the quality and beauty of the printing, particularly the ornamental capitals at the chapter heads.

> And the binding! Yellow like the glittering treasure sought after in the novel, red like the rage and greed and blood that the glittering treasure engenders, and a bit of green, recalling the forest, field, and quiet bliss of those who get nothing out of gold and to whom it means nothing. The cover presents such a beautiful and yet unobtrusive symbol of the red-skinned fellow man, represented from within, from his own feelings.

Curiously, in the midst of this aesthetic evaluation by a social critic—which Traven purported to be in *The Treasure of the Sierra Madre* as well—Traven insisted that the conditions and events he depicted were not artful fiction but a precise recounting of actual experiences. The very next day he sent Preczang an illustrated page from the newspaper *El Universal* showing Mexican bandits to give him an idea of how "the readers should imagine the bandits who ambushed that train [in *Treasure*] and later besieged the prospectors." He sought to prove the documentary character of his writing even with facts that happened subsequently:

> Judging from the pictures alone, you can imagine that with such people you can expect neither mercy nor pity. The bandits illustrated here spread terror for weeks on end in the countryside around the capital city. They attacked men and women, Mexicans and Americans, and not only robbed them, but also left them behind without a stitch of clothing, after they had mistreated their victims in the most barbarous manner. How many of their victims they murdered cannot be determined, since dead men tell no tales. In not all but in many cases the women were brutally raped, indeed in the most bestial and unnatural manner.

This railway ambush episode from *Treasure* gained much publicity. Preczang sent the text to "several hundred newspapers" to be reprinted. And Traven confirmed the realism of particularly this part of his novel in a further retrospective letter to Preczang of May 7, 1927, speaking of yet another ambush that had occurred in the meantime:

> This new ambush eclipses by far all earlier train ambushes. The train was accompanied by fifty-one soldiers of the First Mexican Field Artillery Regiment. These soldiers were terrific, they defended the train for three and a half hours. Then forty-eight soldiers and officers lay dead, with the remaining three so seriously wounded that there was no chance of their survival. More than a hundred passengers were killed, including twenty children less than ten years old. One family alone lost eight children. It occurred just as in my depiction. The bandits fired without pity into the crowd of passengers, stabbing with bayonettes, knives, and machetes. The cars were doused with gasoline and petroleum and set ablaze, burning the wounded and those who could not get out quickly enough. Words cannot describe the scenes which ensued as the emergency train came into the main train station in Mexico City carrying the survivors. Three men went crazy, one woman committed suicide at the station. The bandits' war cry during the attack was "Long live

> Christ our King"—"Viva Christ [*sic*] El Rey." The Catholic clergy disputes that three Catholic priests led the bandits. But all the passengers said they had seen the three priests, and some said that during the killings one of the priests screamed into the cars: "The scourge of God is upon you!" I assume that the German newspapers reported on this train ambush as well.
>
> The government is now rooting out the bandits from that area. The peace-loving population has been called upon to leave the region within two days. Then the military will move in and raze twenty-five towns and villages there with the help of military planes. A horrid solution, but the only effective one. Soldiers cannot enter that region, due to the mountains. They are shot down in the narrow passes. The villages and towns are the bandits' hideouts, and when these hideouts are destroyed, the bandits have to move on, for they are helpless without their families and the families need homes, villages, and towns.

In his very first letter to the Büchergilde, Traven had mentioned a further project: the collection of stories that was originally to include "The Bridge in the Jungle" and was to bear the same title. At first nothing came of the suggestion, nor could anything come of it, since the author, ambitious and busy by necessity, bombarded his newfound publisher with publication plans that were still very much in the making. Preczang understandably showed diplomatic restraint, all the more since "The Bridge in the Jungle" was to be the centerpiece of the collection, and Preczang considered the minutely detailed concluding passage as "going into too much detail," while Traven obstinately saw this detail work as a particular virtue. So discussion of the project was silenced for the moment; *The Cotton-Pickers* and *The Death Ship* dominated the correspondence.

Then, curiously, the novella suddenly resurfaced. While the "Bridge" manuscript still lay unevaluated in the editorial offices of *Vorwärts*, Traven wrote on January 18, 1926, to Preczang, who had sent it there, that "The Bridge in the Jungle" would be "substantially expanded":

> In the last few months something has happened with one of the novella's main characters (Mr. Sleigh) which compels me to write it up. S. had to be taken to a hospital in Texas, where a few days after arriving he died under circumstances which the doctors cannot understand and explain. As soon as I heard of his death, I spoke with natives who knew him longer than I had and they "lifted the veil" a bit. If Dr. Sch[ikowski] publishes

> the novella as it is, that would do no harm, for the planned expansion is as independent as the Second Book of *The Cotton-Pickers.*

This much is clear in the matter: The text that *Vorwärts* acquired after long indecision was the version Traven had sent originally. The book version of 1929, however, while longer than the *Vorwärts* text, is not a reworking of the sort that Traven intimated here: It included no addition that was "as independent as the second part of *The Cotton-Pickers.*" So it remains unclear whether a second part was ever written or if one of the stories eventually published in *The Bush* was originally intended as a second part of *The Bridge in the Jungle.*

The project of a collection of stories came to the fore again when Preczang wrote unexpectedly on March 31, 1927, to suggest such a collection, ideally "with a humorous bent," though he did not refer to the earlier plan for such a collection. Given the communications barriers, it is ironic that Traven wrote almost simultaneously, on April 3, 1927, suggesting the same idea to Preczang. To be sure, he had in mind combining only two stories, "The Night Visitor" and "The Bridge in the Jungle." He wished to "rewrite the final part [of the latter] a bit, since I don't like some elements any longer." As an alternative he again mentioned expanding "The Bridge" by a second, quasi-independent section, "for the figure of Mr. Sleigh is tormenting me and wants to come into print. Mr. Sleigh died a very unusual death in the fall of 1925. I had visited him just ten days earlier, when we had planned a journey up the Tamesi in December of that year." (Is "Sleigh" Alex Smith or the "B." of the Tampico/Columbus diary?) Preczang, it turned out, was more interested in a new, independent story than a second part to the existing novella.

Before Traven could learn that, however, he had already taken action. On May 7 he announced that "in a few days" he would send material for two volumes in the Büchergilde's planned Kleine Gildenbücher (Little Guild Books) series, first "The Bridge in the Jungle," as it was to appear from May 14 to June 24, 1927, in *Vorwärts*, and second "short novellas with a humorous or tragicomic shading" for the collection Preczang had suggested. Some of them were as yet unpublished, he noted, "and are thus completely original." "The Night Visitor" was also to be included, with the last ten sentences "changed a bit" from the version that had appeared in *Westermanns Monatshefte* in 1926, in accordance with Preczang's request for humorous coloring. The novella was to be taken as "more tragicomic . . . than gloomy and mysterious"; and the recasting of the conclusion "revealed" this "tragicomic underlying character" more clearly than the original conclusion. "In addition, the novella's basic character has much in common with *The Treasure*. In the story "The Night Visitor" the glittering treasure also goes back to where it came from, back to the dirt."

After some wrangling about the texts to be included, one can assume, the collection *The Bush* emerged in 1928 (it was expanded in the second edition of 1930), while *The Bridge in the Jungle* first appeared in 1929—though not as a volume in the new Little Guild Books series but as a regular Büchergilde book offering. The delay was probably due to two reasons: The length of the original version published in *Vorwärts*, did not seem sufficient for a regular Büchergilde volume; and the starkly realistic depiction of the drowned child's corpse decomposing in the tropical heat was thought to be excessive (Preczang at least had that partly in mind in his criticism of the conclusion as "going into too much detail"). However, the (expanded) version that finally appeared in book form in 1929 contained all the physiological details, which were no doubt offensive to many readers. In fact, in a letter to Schönherr of October 16, 1927, Traven had expressly defended the realistic depiction of repulsive detail against the average reader's "bourgeois false piety." The decomposing body of a child was only a "deep shadow," he wrote,

> which becomes necessary in order to allow the lights to shine all the more brightly. The main thing is not the child's stinking corpse but rather the sad struggle between disgust and love in the soul of a mother who must look on helplessly as the dearest thing she possesses is transformed before her eyes into the ugliest thing one can imagine, a stinking cadaver. The pain of a mother who sees her child lying before her cold and stiff like a marble statue is certainly great; but how much more moving must be the pain of a mother who sees her child lying before her as a stinking carcass oozing pus which she cannot even protect any longer from dung-flies and worms, and from which she sees herself driven away instinctively due to her robust health. Just yesterday she had hugged and kissed him and today it disgusts her if she even comes near him. But I can only relate this horrifying incident—far more horrifying than Mary's experience

standing before her son's cross—when I depict the child's corpse as it is. And it was exactly the way I describe it—that is the way I saw it and that is the way every child's corpse appears after a certain amount of time. Here in the tropics it just happens more quickly, and it is more shocking here than elsewhere, since so little time lies between life and decomposition. A human being, who a mere ten hours earlier was dancing, is now a decomposing mass. In the mind's eye he is still a happy person without a care in the world. One who has not seen that and experienced it certainly cannot feel it.

But there should actually be no need for a long, wordy explanation. The child's corpse looked just as I depict it; and if I may not describe something as it appeared in reality, then I do not see why I should write at all.

When the novel finally appeared, *Die Büchergilde* published a long explanation from the author elevating the simple story of the death of an Indian boy and his mother's sorrow to mythic proportions and at the same time sounding the motif (of which Traven spoke so often) of the dignity of the "primitives":

The entire course of the action, with the exception of the exposition at the start of the story, transpires within twenty-one hours. In these twenty-one hours, one witnesses the life of an entire people and at the same time that of an individual. The "bridge over the river in the jungle" ceases to be a wooden bridge; in the minds of the people gathered here, it is transformed in those twenty-one hours into the center of the universe, into the starting point, the focal point of all worldly and otherworldly life. And when the people finally cross the bridge together in order to reveal their unanimous sympathy and great pity for a mother in the depths of despair; and when an Indian cuts a notch in the bridge with his machete as a memorial, the "bridge in the jungle" reaches its third transformation: During this time it becomes for those present the final point of all that exists, is coming into being, and is happening.

I do not believe that in all of world literature, to the extent it is known to us and belongs to our cultural sphere, there exists a book which depicts for a European reader the deepest agony of a nonwhite, of an Indian mother in the same or similar form as this book. . . . Until the revolution in Mexico which began in 1910—and particularly under the dictatorship of Porfirio Díaz—the Indian was viewed as an animal which could talk, laugh, and cry. It was expressly denied—by the state, the church, and in literature—that the Indian had a soul.

I am confident in my hopes that I have succeeded in revealing to the Europeans in this book that the Indian displays no differences of any sort from our race in regard to his feelings and emotions. And when I say in this book—though with other words: "It is *my* mother suffering here, it is *my* child, *my* brother, *my* heart and flesh and blood which stands here defenseless and helpless before a pitiless fate!" I think that I have sufficiently clarified what I mean, even if I avoid any other explanation which would only obscure my simple idea unnecessarily.

Land of Springtime and *Art of the Indians*

A year before *The Bridge in the Jungle* appeared in book form, another project had been finalized after similarly protracted negotiations with the Büchergilde: the Chiapas travel book finally titled *Land des Frühlings* (*Land of Springtime*) (1928). Ernst Preczang had made overtures about this book in his initial letter of July 13, 1925. In his immediate reply to Preczang, Traven essentially embraced the idea, and the thought of embarking on an expedition cropped up shortly thereafter. On October 11, 1925, Traven asked specifically whether the Büchergilde was interested in "'Travels and Adventures in Mexico,' accompanied by numerous photographs taken by the author." He had been planning such a journey, he informed Preczang, for two [!] years already and would journey perhaps as far as Peru, but "only to gather material for my books." He would have to ask for an advance to finance the expedition, to buy mules and equipment. Preczang reacted with enthusiasm and generosity "in the matter of dollars." But the advance seems not to have been necessary once Traven was given the chance to take part in the Palacios expedition. On August 8, 1926, he informed Preczang that he had returned from Chiapas to Mexico City two days earlier "with nothing in my pockets." "My expedition came about somewhat sooner than I would have liked." It cost him $1,500, "though the Mexican government was kind enough to help me out with three mules from their stock and generously helped finance the 2,400 km railway journey." In regard to the book, he noted that he had to give some thought to the "form," not the "content." The illustrations constituted one of the form problems. Much of the ensuing correspondence deals with the selection of photographs, their quality (they were developed in an unfavorable climate and under very primitive conditions), their placement in the book, the reproduction method and their color tone, the type of paper to be used, and so on. Are illustrations even necessary? Traven asked. Could he reproduce Indian stone drawings? At one point he even brought up the possibility of a separate volume of illustrations.

As early as March 5, 1927, Traven wrote that he could "finally" send the manuscript of the "travel book," which he originally called "Reise im Sonneland" ("Travel in the Land of the Sun"). "To tell the truth, I didn't really know whether I would ever be able to write it. I had to spend so much time searching for the appropriate and congenial form for such a book, so that I could interweave my thoughts with the subject matter, creating a unified result, and so that the reader feels and experiences what is going on. Had I been asked to treat the subject in a purely scholarly manner, I would have had a real fright." With the eye of a connoisseur he made light of scholarly books about Mexico and their genesis that he had observed at close range. Readers turning to Traven's book, however, "from that moment on glimpse into the heart and soul of Mexico and feel the breath of the Mexican people. I think that's more important than reading about mummified facts." But he had written not only a book about Mexico as a land of exotic charm for Europeans, he went on to say, but also a timely critique of social, economic, and political problems arising at this time in the history of the world from the clash of less developed countries and the great industrial powers. *Land of Springtime* was thus meant to be Traven's contribution to an understanding of current politics and the future of the entire planet:

> My approach is to focus on the state about which the least is known. In every respect the state [of Chiapas] is a faithful reproduction, in miniature, of all of Mexico. And because the state in all aspects of its character belongs just as much to Central as to North America, I saw it as the state which could be viewed as the ideal "original cell" through which one can best study the whole body and its functions. For everything which appears in such complicated and tangled forms in the centers of highly developed civilization is revealed here, in this state, in the simplest, most natural and elementary form imaginable.

Though the book is in essence a book about Mexico and remains throughout a book about Mexico, it nonetheless goes further to address all the questions that occupy people today, particularly the economic and political problems that the whole working class around the world is facing today. That was unavoidable. On the contrary, if I had attempted to avoid such questions and problems, it would not have become a truthful book about Mexico. Mexico is already, and will become increasingly so in the coming two decades, the economic and hence political focal point of capitalist and imperialist world politics, but at the same time it is, curiously, also the focal point of anticapitalist and anti-imperialist world politics.

I have had to deal with issues of race in the book in order to show that what is going on in Mexico is first and foremost the awakening of the Indian race. The opinion is widespread in Europe, particularly among the workers, that the Indians have all but died out, since people seem to talk and write only about the Indians dying out in the United States. I hope that I succeed in showing readers of my book that the Indian lives on and that he has begun to raise his voice in world politics, that here on this continent the indigenous race, entitled to its patrimony, has awakened, a race that no one would have thought could shake up the fate of the world. The proletariat in Mexico, Central America, and Peru consists solely of Indians and those of mixed blood. The awakening of the Indian race here has thus become synonymous with the proletarian movement. But since we are also dealing with the awakening of a race which has been repressed until now, the proletarian movements in these countries differ in several important points from those in Europe and the United States.

All in all, it seems fair to say that my book is the first book of exploration conceived and written from the perspective of the modern proletariat. In this way it distinguishes itself from all other travel books, and in this way it also distinguishes itself greatly from the "books of traveling philosophers."

This comprehensive, sociopolitical perspective seems to relegate the book's depiction of the land and its people to a secondary role. But Traven put equal emphasis on those aspects—geography, flora and fauna, customs and mores, folklore, history, archeology, and ethnology. He thus remarked that his depiction of the country and its inhabitants was authentic, in contrast with the usual travel books. The romantic conceptions commonplace in Europe were to be rectified by firsthand documentation. His claim to authenticity and realism for his nonfictional work was the same as that for his novels:

> I have done my part, I have ridden through jungle and rain forest, waded through swamps and morass, swum across rivers and climbed steep cliffs, crept into unexplored caves, I have offered myself to bloodthirsty vampires, and sought out wild and half-wild Indians—all this to get photographs for the Büchergilde that no one else has. . . .
>
> A slew of photographers in Mexico flood the world with books and pictures of "Beautiful Mexico." These pictures have created a certain image of Mexico, particularly in Europe. For that reason hundreds of those reading my book will find something, at least in the illustrations, to turn their conception of Mexico on its head. If I succeed in that, I will again be content for a while, having perpetrated another heresy. For those pictures which the whole world has tired of looking at after more than a hundred years and which are believed to be "the real Mexico" all come from a small geographical area, the Federal District and the state of Mexico, an area scarcely a quarter the size of Chiapas. It is, of course, the longest- and best-known part of Mexico and is the tourists' sole destination. It is the only region that 95 percent of the foreigners living in Mexico know, since it surrounds the capital city and can be reached on Sunday excursions. It is thus more or less like the Mark Brandenburg which surrounds Berlin. There the Spree forest, with a few Wends in colorful outfits, must ever and again serve to give the countryside color and character.

The true Indian is a proletarian, according to Traven's theme of the "awakening of the Indian race" that underlies the novels of the Mahogany series as well. There is nothing romantic about the Indians. Traven wrote to Preczang on March 22, 1927:

> People still believe only too easily that the Indians run around all day long wearing war paint, that they all resemble the illustrations on the covers of Indian storybooks. I hope to do my part to let people see the Indian as he really is: a simple, hardworking peasant who must exert himself mightily to support himself and his family and has not the slightest inclination to go on the war path or perform mysterious snake dances every evening.

It is clear how the focus on world politics and the focus on the land and the people of Mexico are interrelated, inextricably in fact, for Traven. He felt that the Latin American Indians (who, he liked to think, had not come from Asia but were the earth's original inhabitants who had migrated in the opposite direction) held in their hands the future of the world, together apparently with the proletariat of the industrial nations, but he maintained that the Indians' value system would form the basis of the culture of the future. *Land of Springtime* outlines this scenario, offering a plethora of details in a not particularly systematic fashion.

The author may have feared he had overstepped his bounds with his publisher. A concerned Traven wrote to Johannes Schönherr on June 20, 1927, asking whether his manuscript had been accepted. He could easily cut one hundred, even two hundred, pages; he had also sent a map of Chiapas, which he had drawn himself using "a rusting pen dripping ink everywhere" and working "under the most primitive of conditions": on the floor of his wooden shack at a temperature of 40 degrees Celsius with a tropical thunderstorm raging. For a title, he proposed "Metate and Zarape" to Schönherr on August 1, 1927, with the possible addition of the subtitle "Journey to the Land of Eternal Springtime." In mid-October he sent back the proofs, somewhat late, for "I was returning from a short trip to an Indian celebration, when I was held up by the military rebellion which broke out recently in an attempt to install reactionary elements in power. The rebels had encamped between Mexico City and the place where I was, and the proofs lay in Mexico City, waiting for me." In this letter Traven also spoke of the many changes and additions he had made in the proofs, simply because every day he experienced something new that rectified some of his "purely personal views." He added that there was "probably no country today where everything is in such a state of flux and daily change as is the case here." Accordingly, the book is infused with the spirit of the immediate present—it was only later that Traven, in the guise of his agent Hal Croves, maintained that the book had been written before the revolution of 1910 (Croves made the assertion to journalist Judy Stone in the 1960s, intending to cover the trail leading back to Germany and Marut).

On November 24, 1927, in a letter to Schönherr, Traven once again spoke of his travel book as "unique in its genre," as it was neither a dry scholarly treatise nor "an adventure story meant for entertainment." Further, he claimed once more that the work "for the first time" depicted an "expedition of this kind" from a "proletarian and antibourgeois point of view." As such, it would not be suitable as a travel guide. "That is one of its great advantages, I think. But the reader will see a new world taking shape before his eyes, which he had no idea existed until then," he wrote.

> I am certain that the European worker in particular, upon reading this book, will in many substantial and decisive points experience a change in his feelings and his understanding of his position in society, his opportunities for development, and the tools available for his struggle. He will find a kindred spirit in his Indian proletarian brother. And here is yet another difference. The bourgeois travel books, without exception, highlight the differences between peoples, while this travel book demonstrates the unbreakable bond between men and thus between peoples. The intelligent European worker will learn from this book that here—as with all foreign peoples—things are simply "done differently" from the way they are done back home, but that one's goals in life, the motivations, the drive towards the light, towards beauty and freedom, are the same everywhere.

Only three weeks later Traven had two advance copies of *Land of Springtime* in his hands in Mexico City. The physical makeup of the "exquisite work" surpassed all his expectations. He overflowed with praise for the "quiet, simple, tasteful, and truly harmonious unity and perfection of this masterpiece of the German printer's craft."

A book so tied to the world political situation at that moment naturally has less to say one or two generations later—or may have a different message. For the new edition of 1950, Traven cut much that was outdated and changed many factual details. And in 1966 he told Judy Stone that the work would not be published in English because the text was "out of date."

He had a point. Traven's free-and-easy and not unbiased use of the term *race* in his speculations on the future of world politics is problematic today. One also raises one's eyebrows at his often simplistic, romanticizing contrast of the Indian's "culture" against the white man's "civilization." His animosity toward the "colonialistic" Catholic church in Mexico and the "imperialism" of American capitalists must be understood in terms of Mexico's internal political situation in the 1920s—marked by tensions between the pro-labor government and such forces. Traven's prediction that Mexico would become the focal point of world politics and economics because of its natural resources and the potential of its untapped "race" remains to be fulfilled.

Nonetheless, some of the themes have a certain resonance today. *Land of Springtime* is no handbook on current problems of less developed nations, but it contains thoughts that are relevant now as before. Traven's frequent warning against the whites' superiority complex over those of darker skin may be considered noteworthy for its early date. Another point deserving attention is his view that the white people and thus the entire European-American world make the individual, with his ambition and efforts to "be somebody," the centerpiece of their value system, while the Central American natives see the individual as part of a large social or communal fabric in which individual self-assertion and the rise of "authority" are held in check. The opposition of these basic forms of human existence is a seminal thought in Traven's works, prefigured in Marut's views and still powerfully present in the Mahogany Novels of the 1930s. It explains how the European anarchist managed to feel at home in far-off Mexico (in particular in the heart of Chiapas, which furnished him with the raw material for *Land of Springtime*); it finally sheds some light on why the author, his star in ascendance, guarded his anonymity or pseudonymity while at the same time, in spite of his anarchistic past and Mexican Indian present, he was strongly influenced by the Western conception of the individual. How else can one explain a man who strives to remain invisible yet, as evidenced by his letters to the Büchergilde, virtually boasts of his own worth and significance in world literature? Traven's contrast between individual and communal ways of looking at the world gained a new timeliness in the 1960s, the era of the counterculture, and has not lost its appeal today. All the more since Traven did not offer unreserved praise for a primitive lifestyle while dismissing out of hand the dubious blessings of civilization. In *Land of Springtime*, one also reads the following:

> To live happily and well in an Indian commune one has to have been born and bred in such a commune. Even an Indian industrial worker in Mexico could not enjoy the material things in an Indian commune that he today possesses or could possess working as a hired hand in the city. The primitive living conditions in an Indian commune appear downright idyllic when one hears tell of them. But when one must live in these primitive conditions, life for a civilized human being becomes so poor,

> so drab, so dry, and so colorless, that one scarcely considers it worth living.
>
> In the midst of this industriousness, which cannot be found in such concentration even in the United States, the Indian lives as a representative of a half-civilized and in part totally uncivilized race, which still goes hunting with spear, bow, and arrow. Though life in a commune may appear ideal for one who views it from afar, it can only be called a downright sorry life in comparison with the rich life led by his Indian brother who works for good wages in the city. The Indian in the commune has no share in civilization. However much poison it injects into the lives of people, this same civilization can at the same time make people's lives so rich that one is willing to take the poison in the bargain as a bitter aftertaste.

Traven did not, in fact, reduce the situation to an either/or dichotomy of Western civilization versus Indian culture, though he is so characterized in some literary histories. Rather, he presented a subtly nuanced and thus still interesting contrast. Just as "civilization" has its advantages, as the preceding passages demonstrate, so too does the world of the Indians have its dark side: The enslavement by the large landowners was still accepted by the Indians in the 1920s; the ox carts on the jungle paths, depicted with such a loving brush in the novels, must rightly yield to the railroads—"the merry singing, guitar playing, and dancing around the campfires of the carreteros" will disappear along with them, but so too will the backbreaking labor that "brutalizes" the peon. "Romanticism is always what has been. But the true beauty of life, the only sense one can find in life, comes from change, from alteration, from motion." *Land of Springtime* thus closes not with nostalgia but with an appeal to Mexicans "not to fall asleep again" after the revolution of 1910; the hour has come for Mexico, this "land so overabundantly blessed by nature," to play its role in the world, by using its riches "for itself and to the benefit of the rest of mankind."

In this book Traven came to the realization that his homeland of choice was a place "where one can get to the bottom of all matters and all wisdom of the world."

Those interested principally in the author himself will see in this book how the former Marut comes alive in his new environment, even if the many photographs do not show him in the flesh. In the more narrative sections of the work we see Traven among Tzotzil Indians and hacienda owners. He visits village schools, accompanies a doctor on his rounds among the Indians; he rides, accompanied only by his guide Felipe, through thick brush, studies the strange fauna in areas rarely seen by a white man, and explores old Spanish cities such as San Cristóbal las Casas, for weeks the starting point of his daily expeditions. He reminisces that he had served "for a while as a private tutor for an American farmer's family in Central America," which in principle there is no reason to doubt. Concrete recollections of his early days in the bungalow in Tamaulipas are also interesting: "On the evening of the first day I sat on a crate and read by candlelight . . . when I suddenly saw a full-grown giant scorpion on the floor before me, scampering off at full speed. I managed to catch him before he could disappear into a crack in the floorboards."

Land of Springtime appeared with the date 1928. Subsequently, the author probably turned to *The White Rose*, where the contrast between "civilization" and "culture" is more crassly drawn. A second nonfiction work begun in this period sounds a more conciliatory note, as did *Land of Springtime*: the book eventually entitled *Kunst der Indianer* (*Art of the Indians*). It may have been finished as early as the summer of 1929. For on August 5 of that year Preczang wrote: "It has naturally been with great pleasure that I have agreed to your proposal to publish the work about Indian art. It is extraordinarily informative and will help root out certain prejudices that many give voice to here. The asinine pride of the 'white man' who thinks himself above the 'colored man' meets a convincing opponent in you and your works." (Marut's *Torch of the Prince* had struck a similar note.) *Art of the Indians* is a rich manuscript with photographs, drawings, and contributions from various authors concerning the natives' many types of artwork and handicrafts. It remained unpublished. Traven explained in the first issue of the *BT News* (1951) that "various chapters had been superseded in the meantime," while in 1933 he scared off the National Socialist usurpers of Büchergilde Gutenberg with the warning that their publication of the book would constitute copyright violation of the artists and authors whose works he "mentioned and used." Only excerpts have appeared in print: the essay "Spielzeug" ("Toys") in the *Typographische Mitteilungen* (*Typographical Report*) of December 1929, where publication of the book is announced for the end of 1930; other published sections are "Der Künstler" ("The Artist") and "Die Mexikanische Nationaltracht" ("The Mexican National Costume") in the *BT News*. The chapters "Las Pulquerías" ("The Pulquerías") and "El niño mexicano como artista y creador" ("The Mexican Child as Artist and Creator") appeared in Spanish translation on July 3, 1974, in the Mexican magazine *Siempre*.

The theoretical speculations on art in *Art of the Indians* are unmistakably Traven's own. Traven generally took pleasure in talking about the principles underlying art, as when he wrote to Preczang on March 29, 1926, that the task of all art is "to make people happy," but that happiness is "also that which is able to stimulate people to contemplation or the development of new ideas." It thus comes as no surprise that in *Art of the Indians* Traven made ample use of the opportunity to talk about the general value of art. But even these theoretical considerations were formulated to pave the way for an art that is uniquely contemporary or future-oriented, an art he saw emerging from a union of the impulses of the most modern North American art and of Mexican folk art. In the version of the chapter on art theory, "The Artist," published in the *BT News* in 1953, he sketched only the most basic principle: A people cannot exist without art, and for good reason, for art can achieve what religion only attempts or claims to achieve, namely "the enrichment and beautification of life, since it is the only means of escaping the drabness of daily life." Art thus provides an answer to the question "Live to what end?" At the same time, Traven avoided endowing art with the nimbus of the otherworldly. "The artist should not serve as my God, or as an authority," but should reveal his humanity in his work and thus appeal to his audience: "The artist should reveal to me in his work that he is my earthly brother, full of concerns like me, full of longing like me, full of the urge to be free of intellectual or emotional chains like me, and full of earthly drives and shortcomings like me." He expresses what "my soul feels." "Only the artist can make us into human beings and make us conscious that we are human beings." "There is but one who can save us from all of our spiritual anguish, and that is the artist."

In an unpublished version of the chapter, ten times the length of the text published in the *BT News*, Traven embellished on this credo, which is neither original nor profound. In this version he stressed above all the timeliness that art must possess to produce the desired effect. It may come as a surprise for some that in this regard Traven did not have "proletarian art" in mind. If anything, dadaism, not proletarian art, pointed toward the future in Traven's eyes; he characterized the latter as "the saddest" of art forms, which was created to serve a single class, not "mankind," and which has consequently degenerated to the level of propaganda. "Proletarian art [*Proletkunst*] creates hatred in people, in the proletarian as well as the nonproletarian." Nor should contemporary art, if it is to take the place of religion, merely imitate the art of other periods. One can achieve "the liberation of man from daily life" and the enrichment of man "in his soul" with an art that is truly contemporary. Such an art is not remote from everyday reality (unlike all art created in preceding epochs, according to Traven, from Greek temples to Reims Cathedral, from altar paintings to Rembrandt—such works have nothing to say to us anymore). The art that Traven has in mind is usable art (*Gebrauchskunst*), created to fill present-day needs. Skyscrapers and giant bridges, automobiles and high-speed locomotives are artworks in Traven's view, against which the great names of art history pale in comparison. Such formulations, though reminiscent of futurism, seem uncultured and scarcely defensible even with the maxim that the end justifies the provocative means. In any event, the end is to spread the word of the "new means of expressing the feelings, the emotions, the longings of modern man." These come from America, the continent to which the future belongs once the European (and particularly English) world domination is overcome. And however modernistic this conception of art may seem, for Traven it remains a mere transitional stage. For modern art can become the art of the future only if it joins with the native Indian folk art, particularly the art of Mexico. Mexico "is the only country on the American continent which has its own art and its own culture, which as a result of the strong Indian influence is indigenous American art and culture. Mexico is also the only country on the American continent which has a purely American folk art, an art which grows from the people and which is rooted in the people itself." Traven sees an affinity between the ultra-modern North American and native Indian "means of expression" and "will to expression." This enables "objectivity and intellect" from the north to be "united" with "romanticism, variety, and heart" from the south, creating an art that is appropriate for contemporaries—but perhaps inappropriate for even the next generation. Traven notes with heroic resignation that a great artist and "truly great human being" is one who, like "the greatest painter on our continent, paints on whitewashed walls masterpieces that will have pealed off long before he will have completed his last painting."

The reference is to Diego Rivera, in whose circles Traven moved then. At the end of this otherwise very impersonal essay, he reported that in the Academy of Fine Arts in Mexico City, Diego Rivera had discovered a young Indian painter with great natural gifts and made him his assistant. The student had meanwhile risen to the ranks of the "great painters of Mexico." "His art and technique are Indian—an influence of which the Academy struggled to rid him."

While it remains unclear precisely how Traven envisioned the synthesis of North American and Indian-Mexican artistic directions, it is interesting from a biographical point of view to note how Traven's experiences in his new land molded his theoretical outlook. The displaced European saw the promise of art in everything that was not "European" but "American"—though this included everything from the New York skyscraper to the clay pot from Chiapas.

Battling Censorship

Traven's correspondence with Büchergilde Gutenberg on the genesis of *The White Rose* (1929), the last book to appear in the Tampico period, apparently no longer survives. The retrospective letter of Bruno Dressler, head of the publishing house, about this book from June 16, 1937, is therefore of particular interest. It shows that the work was the subject of debate because of its alleged anti-Americanism (more accurately its anticapitalism). Judging from Dressler's letter, Traven had apparently complained that the Büchergilde had made and printed "changes" in his manuscripts without authorization. Dressler stressed that such changes had been made early on with the author's approval. "In one particular case"—a reference to *The Carreta*—time constraints precluded getting his approval, though an attorney and "a specialist on religion" had been consulted. More drastic, we gather from Dressler's letter, were the cuts made in the text of *The White Rose* as submitted by the author: The editors had rejected the two first chapters, some seventy typed pages, since they "were not closely related to the subject matter which followed in *The White Rose*." Dressler, for his part, at the time advocated Traven's fashioning "a new novel" from this material. It never came to that; a fifty-six-page typescript that may represent the original beginning of the novel—it bears no title—is preserved in the estate.

Dressler's letter of 1937 is an attempt to appease Traven in response to his numerous complaints about his treatment by the Büchergilde. Traven's tone must have been shrill. Nor was this the first occurrence of tensions. As mentioned earlier, the two had almost come to a parting of the ways toward the end of the Tampico period, in the fall of 1929. On October 5, 1929, Preczang had sent Traven Manfred Georg's article about him from *Die Weltbühne*, encouraging Traven to write a letter to the editor, "planting new riddles for the gentlemen who are racking their brains over you." (As a starting point, he suggested that Traven clarify that Erich Knauf, who had begun working at the Büchergilde only in 1928, was not responsible for discovering Traven but rather that Preczang himself was.) Traven actually set to work on such a letter to Manfred Georg: The carbon copy of the first page is in the estate (though it is unclear whether the letter was ever completed or sent). More important is his answer to Preczang of October 26, 1929, not least because it throws further light on the stormy beginnings of the publication of *The White Rose*.

Since Preczang approached him in all confidence, Traven replied expecting the same confidentiality. This "completely private expression of my feelings" unexpectedly revealed a bitterness that must have been building up over the years and now had the potential of leading to a "break," as Traven put it. Georg had sparked the controversy by printing in his essay excerpts of a letter Traven had sent to the Büchergilde, which Knauf had made available to Georg. However, all of Traven's letters to the Büchergilde were by mutual consent to be kept strictly confidential. This constituted a breach of faith in his opinion; he would "never again" reveal his "intimate thoughts" to the Büchergilde. Now as before Traven still essentially supported Büchergilde Gutenberg and its basic principle: "I care for the Büchergilde, and those wonderful people who toil away there to raise up this wonderful proletarian institution and hold it aloft. I have said before that I consider such an institution more important for the liberation of the proletariat than political parties and unions. And that conviction is growing stronger." But for precisely that reason they must now get to the root of the problem threatening their relationship: the "autocratic stance of the management" at the Büchergilde. He thought that "leaders" were beginning to infiltrate the publishing house who were out to "run this institution into the ground . . . just as they have run the proletarian unions and parties and newspapers into the ground for their personal advantage." The "whole relationship" is "by no means so blossomy and rosy as it may appear from the outside":

> I have the definite feeling that a union autocrat is sitting somewhere in there on the crimson chair of the New Holy Socialist Unionist Inquisition, a New Holy Inquisition, which must protect the "proud" building of the Party and the Union from disturbances. Until today I did not know the identity of the Grand Inquisitor of the Holy and All-True and All-Righteous Catholic Socialist Unionist Church. But in your letter I find a name and now I know that the head pope appears to be Mr. Dressler. I have never exchanged a letter with the Lord of the Bookprinters' Hosts. I do not know him. But I will bet you ten good dollars that he is the man who is making my life so hard. The real grand inquisitors always remain in the background.

He had had confidence only in Preczang (who now had a part-time position in the editorial department) and Schönherr (who had left the organization), Traven said. He had none in Knauf and his superiors on the board.

This autocracy, manifested as "censorship," would reappear again in the 1937 discussion with Dressler. In his October 26, 1929, letter to Preczang, Traven took particular exception to the cuts in the manuscript of *The White Rose* made by the "union autocrats and party popes." Censorship of this sort "will probably compel me one day to say good-bye to the Büchergilde." Traven reacted so violently because the passages that were struck included his opinions on unions and political parties—apart from the omission of the original beginning and a "humorous legal proceeding in heaven" for which the Büchergilde feared charges of blasphemy. He put particular importance on the expression of those political opinions because he had developed them not based on articles read in magazines, but rather

> in long experience as a working proletarian, not as a salon proletarian or literary proletarian, but as a proletarian who stood in the ranks, because his economic situation compelled him to do so. Based on a feeling of comradeship and the desire to help

> in the revolutionary fight to liberate my former comrades, I wish to tell the worker what I think about his pampered unions and parties, what I think about his leaders who, just like the Christian religion, promise him a paradise far off in the future, while they themselves, the leaders—not only in the United States but also in England and especially in Germany—treat the proletarian unions and parties as pawns for their personal advantage in order to install themselves permanently as cabinet members or presidents, police chiefs, chief administrators, lord mayors, inspectors of schools, and chancery councillors. The leaders have gained personal economic freedom, while the proletariat is just as bad off today as when the socialists could not gain any high office. In the United States, certain bosses will sell the unions for a tidy sum which goes right into their own pockets. Mr. Knauf, upon censoring my latest book, stated that I cannot generalize from that incident, since that sort of thing does not happen in Germany. But it does happen in Germany much more frequently than in the United States.

Such censorship, Traven said, confirmed that he was "in the right" in his assessment of the German unions and parties: "Union leaders" and socialist delegates and cabinet members "barter the ideals of the workers . . . for their personal economic and social independence," namely for their own positions of power. They betray the proletariat and play into the hands of the "reactionary" parties by "agreeing to" antilabor legislation, such as the abolition of the eight-hour workday. German workers (but English and French workers as well) had only been promised paradise for seventy years. But in Mexico and Russia, where workers had little or no union or political organization before the revolution, workers assumed a position of power "as in no other country." Traven thought it important to voice this view, as he did not want to be considered an "ass" by the "intelligent workers" in Europe. Just as, he said, he did not hold his tongue in the presence of captains, engineers, and factory supervisors, he now refused to allow the Social Democratic management of the Büchergilde to dictate his behavior.

All this, then, underlay the anarchist's strident reaction to the unionist publisher's "autocratic" censorship, above all of *The White Rose*. "I hope for a publisher who doesn't try to control my speech. And if capitalist publishers have more respect for my freedom of expression, this is yet another proof of how rotten the workers' movement must be." He said he might move to another publisher, however much he was "on the whole . . . truly dedicated" to Büchergilde Gutenberg.

The differences did not appear to be irreconcilable; Traven even intimated that he might be wrong. The storm passed. Preczang responded with a friendly, conciliatory letter (November 19, 1929) and let it be known in the November issue of *Die Büchergilde* that Traven, out of loyalty to his publisher, had instructed that his books be sold only to Büchergilde members until July 1, 1930, and promised that he would offer every new book first to the Büchergilde. A typed page found in the estate offers further evidence of such loyalty, bearing the title "A Short Factual Correction of Your Essay." In it, apparently an addendum to the letter to Georg, Traven again expressed the sociopolitical views cut by the publisher who was "otherwise so congenial and whom he treasured" and concluded with a conciliatory shrug of the shoulders: "But every institution exercises censorship." When the series of novels following *The White Rose* began to appear in 1931, it, too, bore the imprint of Büchergilde Gutenberg.

6

ACAPULCO AND MAHOGANY

The Pariah's Ascent, 1930–1957

Jungle Novels: Exoticism and Social Critique

Five novels, a volume of stories, and a travel book had all been published within four years. Their rapid succession and large press runs, their Mexican setting (with the exception of *The Death Ship*) and unfamiliar author, surrounded by mystery even then—this ensemble of unusual factors took the German book market by storm. By 1930, the end of his first period of exile, "B. Traven" was a known quantity. The fame of the man who still sought anonymity as he had on the day of his arrival in Mexico was conspicuous and unretractable. Of the German edition of *The Death Ship* alone, 100,000 copies were in print, *Die Büchergilde* reported in June 1931; by 1936, the total circulation of Traven's works in German approached a half million. This was an extraordinary literary success, even by today's standards—all the more so because Traven's books were not what Germans dismiss as *Unterhaltungsliteratur* ("light reading"). In 1930, the noted critic Kurt Tucholsky celebrated Traven as a sensational new phenomenon (in the high-brow *Weltbühne*, no less)—in spite of Tucholsky's very low regard for the author's stylistic or even linguistic abilities. But not only was Traven successful in Germany at the start of the new decade—he was a success throughout the world, as *Die Büchergilde* noted in 1931:

"Five years ago, Traven was still unknown, and today he is a commanding figure in world literature. In addition to the German editions of his works published by the Büchergilde Gutenberg, editions are currently available or in preparation in Swedish, Norwegian, Danish, Dutch, French, Spanish, Yugoslavian, Polish, Hungarian, Czech, and Russian. Negotiations are under way for a British and an American edition. This is a global literary success—accomplished within a few years—the likes of which precious few authors can enjoy."

If Traven had been so inclined, he might have now taken a moment to draw a breath and look back on his accomplishments. He did not, of course; but even without such a pause it is clear that 1930 marked a new period in his literary and personal life.

In the 1930s Traven's literary pursuits gained a new contour as he consciously set out on the path from which he would not deviate for the rest of the decade. From 1931 to 1940 the six Mahogany novels appeared, depicting the forced labor of the Indians in the mahogany camps in southern Mexico. The six novels form a thematic, interrelated whole, unlike the early novels, which are linked mainly by their Mexican setting (except *The Death Ship*, of course). This Caoba cycle (*caoba* is "mahogany" in Spanish) begins with *Die Carreta* (*The Carreta*) and *Regierung* (*Government*), which appeared in Berlin in 1931; it continues during Büchergilde Gutenberg's World War II exile in Zurich with *Der Marsch ins Reich der Caoba* (*March to the Montería*) in 1933 and *Die Troza* (*The Troza* [meaning "tree trunk"]) and *Die Rebellion der Gehenkten* (*The Rebellion of the Hanged*) in 1936 and culminates in *Ein General kommt aus dem Dschungel* (*General from the Jungle*), published in 1940 by Allert de Lange in Amsterdam (a year after the Swedish translation brought out by Axel Holmström in neutral Sweden). (The "Indian legend" *Sonnen-Schöpfung* [*The Creation of the Sun and the Moon*] of 1936 was largely taken from *The Carreta*.)

The Mahogany cycle itself, no less than its publication history, mirrors contemporary political developments. It treats, in epic and often somewhat didactic fashion, the conditions and events in southern Mexico that led directly to the revolution of 1910 against the dictatorship of Porfirio Díaz; in particular it depicts the Spanish landowners' exploitation of the Indians in the logging camps, the notorious *monterías* in Chiapas. (Traven's guide in the jungle in the

1920s, Amador Paniagua, had himself worked in such a camp.) But in spite of all the local color and authentic detail, Traven surmounts the limits of a purely historical narrative. His picture of social injustice, capitalist greed, and the personal caprice of those in power and their henchmen attains a degree of generality that makes its social and political *j'accuse* applicable to analogous situations at other times and places, in particular to Europe at the time of the National Socialist takeover. Allusions to Hitler are not hard to uncover in the later novels of the series, and even *Government* was thought to be a roman à clef aimed at the National Socialist dictatorship. Nor was its message lost on the Nazi censors, who put the novel on their first list of forbidden books. Their opponents took full advantage of this interpretation. The Mahogany novels were hailed in 1937 as antifascist "literature of struggle" by *Das Wort*, a magazine published in Moscow for German émigrés: "They not only depict repression and exploitation, they also show a way out."

The Mahogany series gains such extended significance not least because the Indians of Latin America, in Traven's view, stood for victims of repression in general. He saw an analogy between the Indians and the European proletariat and viewed his series as an epic about the liberation of this underclass, exploited and deprived of its rights, in *every* society: The ruling class digs its own grave; by exploiting, it sparks the will to revolt, which suddenly breaks loose, unrestrainable. This is how the Zurich *Büchergilde* presented the ideological potential of the series in June 1936. That Traven had a hand in this interpretation is evident from the remark in the text that even in present-day Mexico, capitalism ruled with repressive measures like those depicted in the novels; the Mexican sources offered as evidence could only have been provided by Traven.

This shows that in addition to the historical accuracy and universality of the message of the Mahogany novels, Traven put paramount importance on their actuality, their depiction of current-day Mexico. Immediately upon publication of the first two novels of the series, he pointed out the particular importance of this aspect. These were indeed *historical* novels about the final years of Díaz's dictatorship, he noted; and the depiction did gain more general validity, as if to say: "government is the same everywhere, it is always the repression of part of a people to the advantage of another part of the same people." At the same time, however, the novels are "documents," he claimed, that bring to life the *current* situation in Mexico. One of the key contributions, in Traven's analysis, is that the Mahogany series reveals "the true causes of the revolutions and rebellions which have stirred up the Mexican people for twenty years." Nor was his claim to authenticity empty rhetoric. As proof that the events described in the novels did not happen much before the date of publication, he recalled, for example, that the Indian revolt against a decree of the governor described in Chapter 10 of *Government* "occurred on New Year's Day, 1929." Incorporating recent events into a historical novel seems perfectly reasonable from Traven's perspective, since "in that far-off region depicted in the book, a region wholly unknown in Europe and known only very superficially to but few Mexicans themselves, all the circumstances reported in *Government* and in part already in *Carreta* are still the same today, in 1931 (nineteen hundred thirty-one), without a single exception, just as they were woven into the plot of the novel." This emphasis on authenticity, familiar from Traven's writings in the 1920s, thus gained a particular immediacy and urgency, even if it took the form of the author's claim that he was stuck up to his saddle in swamp waters, that he had to drink from muddy pools—like the Indians in *March to the Montería*—and that he had "rolled down" into ravines and had cut up his face and hands in a thorny patch in the jungle.

Traven's ambitious project, combining authenticity of portrayal and a poignant critique of the policies of the contemporary Mexican government, afforded him a real entrée to his chosen homeland. He must have had the idea for the series at the latest in 1927, when the publication of *The Treasure of the Sierra Madre* threatened to relegate him to the ranks of adventure-story writers. Even then he had grasped the sociopolitical significance of the Mexican revolution of 1910—"this powerful event on the world stage and this mammoth cultural phenomenon"—when he formulated the theme of his future series of novels:

> I know the courage, the dedication, the sacrifice—unknown and inconceivable in Europe—with which the proletarian Indian in Mexico fights for his liberation to reach the light of day. It is a struggle for liberation the likes of which has never before been seen in the history of mankind, not even in the history of

> the struggling proletariat. To date I have not succeeded in making a single chapter of this struggle for liberation accessible to the European working class in objective, historical form or in a work of art. For all the writer's or poet's tools as I have possessed them to date fail me when faced with the enormity and variety of the cultural, societal, and economic side effects and logical consequences of this Indian-proletarian struggle for liberation.

He had not presented a recent act of rebellion in *Land of Springtime*, he explained in a letter to Johannes Schönherr on November 24, 1927, because that would have required "depicting the whole Mexican revolution. I will perhaps do that one day, and if I succeed, it will be a very good book, for it is the most interesting revolution that has ever taken place."

When the first volumes of the six-part cycle were completed, Traven thought of the revolutionary impetus his depiction could spark, particularly in the Europe of the 1930s. With a veiled but unmistakable reference to political developments in Germany—which affected him decisively—he stressed in *Büchergilde* of September 1934 that it was not the task of his publisher to educate the reader in a certain political direction. There were other institutions for that. A novel was far more capable of heightening and sharpening political consciousness—leading to appropriate action at the critical moment:

> Certain powerful novels can lead to socialism just as well, and more surely I contend, than *Das Kapital* or books by Lenin or Engels. But it is not the task of Büchergilde Gutenberg to lead workers to socialism, but to educate them into individuals of solid character who know their place in relationship to their environment, who know how to find their own way in this world, who can tell the difference between comedians and apostles, and whose own character tells them right away what stand to take when any sort of political or economic collapse takes place.

Traven was speaking not only about literature in general, but clearly also about his Mahogany series—mere adventure stories set in an exotic milieu did not interest Traven. Political upheaval in Mexico as well as in Europe now required the refugee's full attention, though he had not exactly been a stranger to political issues in his works of the 1920s. The final two volumes of the series, the *BT News* reported in 1951, were no longer intended merely as a general moral support for the European opponents of fascism, but as a usable tool for them; Traven wanted "to encourage the repressed people of Europe and show them how things have to be done, and that no dictatorship is invincible."

Uncertain Idyll: The Orchard on the Pacific

The work on the Mahogany series marked a turning point not only in Traven's literary production but also in his personal life.

During his years of commuting between Tamaulipas and the capital, Traven had met María de la Luz Martínez, a Mexican of Indian descent. Practically nothing is known about her. Recknagel's contention that she had been a teacher at the Escuela Francisco Madero in Mexico City seems to rest on a single reference in *Land of Springtime* ("I know a young Indian woman who is a teacher . . ."), but is this reference explicitly to María de la Luz Martínez? According to Luis Spota's sensational report in *Mañana* in 1948, Martínez had been married to Traven, whom she called "Mister," since 1930, but actually started living with him only in 1948. María de la Luz Martínez, Spota said, "studied" in Eagle Pass, Texas; she traveled every year to visit her parents in Los Angeles and New York; Traven, he added, also traveled each year to North America, though unaccompanied. María de la Luz Martínez told Heidemann too that she had been married to Traven. Traven's will states that he had been married only once, to Rosa Elena Luján, and there is no reason to doubt this.

María de la Luz Martínez owned El Parque Cachú, Traven's principal residence during this stage in his life (he lived in separate quarters, according to a letter Traven wrote to Bodil Christensen on August 11, 1948). El Parque Cachú was a modest orchard of three hectares with a garden restaurant just outside of Acapulco—not yet a garish resort, but rather a sleepy town like many others in the state of Guerrero on the west coast of Mexico. Traven lived there, on the Avenida Costa Grande 901 (also called Camino del Pie de la Cuesta), for some twenty-five years beginning in 1930, according to Spota: behind a high wire fence and thick brush, under the nut and mango trees. In his report, Spota reproduced a flyer for the garden restaurant that captures the ambiance: Rural calm and fresh air, along with books and magazines in English and Spanish, beckon the visitor; there one could enjoy sandwiches, fish, juice, cold beer, and "above all the aristocratic cashew fruit, which contains all the vitamins required for your good health." An English text, reproduced in Spota's report, made El Parque Cachú appealing to visitors from abroad:

Visitors Welcome

> Surely, you have enjoyed cashew nuts and you have liked them; but you have never seen a cashew tree, never seen or tasted a cashew fruit, never seen a cashew nut in the raw. Come and rest in the shade of the most aristocratic tree of the tropics:

The Divine Cashew Tree

> One mile and one eighth from the center of Acapulco on the highway to Pie de la Cuesta.
>
> Welcome:
> We close at 9:00 P.M.
> CASHEW PARK
> Parque Cachú

Traven by no means remained tied to the spot, however. He continued his romance with multiple addresses, having his mail and his royalty payments sent not to Acapulco but to his collaborator Esperanza López Mateos or her brother-in-law Gabriel Figueroa or various post-office boxes, and occasionally even to Tamaulipas (such as letters from Bruno Dressler, the head of Büchergilde Gutenberg, in 1937 and 1938). The address of the publisher Alfred Knopf in New York or Curtis Brown, Traven's London agent, was also occasionally given as a return address. Traven disappeared for weeks and not infrequently for months or even years, according to Señora Luján—to Chiapas, Mexico City (where Figueroa occasionally provided him with a room, when he wasn't staying at the Pánuco hotel), Texas, California, and even England and continental Europe in 1954 and 1956. He had led a similar peregrine existence in the earlier years, of course. In 1931 he recalled having lived more than two years among the Indians, and in a letter to Otto Jamrowski in 1933 he spoke of his "frequent and long expeditions" during which he had been cut off "from all contact with civilization, and from mail deliveries as well, in one case [in the 1920s or 1930s?] for a period of 18 months." He apparently visited Texas frequently during the

Acapulco years; he earned a pilot's license there in the 1930s, according to his widow, and owned a small plane with Major James Cashburn (or perhaps Casburn) in San Antonio. Traven maintained his pied-à-terre in Acapulco until he married Rosa Elena Luján in San Antonio, Texas, on May 16, 1957, and moved with her to Mexico City.

It was not until July 1931 that Traven gave notice at his bungalow in Columbus near Tampico. Not that the accommodations in Acapulco were much more comfortable than the hut in the jungle. Traven himself did not live in the main building (which housed María de la Luz Martínez, her sister Elvia, and her brother Gilberto), but in a clay cottage in the rear of the orchard, guarded by several dogs and out of sight of passersby. Spota described the structure as "a very modest hut with clay walls painted red and with a shingled roof" that the "novelista" had put on himself. The walls sported framed photos of Franklin Delano Roosevelt and General Marshall as well as a few small landscapes; the furnishings consisted of an old typewriter on the desk at the window, an iron bedstead in an adjoining room, books everywhere, a battery-powered radio, petroleum lamps, and similar minimal comforts. Electricity was added only in 1954, when Traven had an additional small house built on the property, an *oficina* for Rosa Elena Luján (at that time Señora Montes de Oca). Nor was there running water at first. María de la Luz Martínez ran the restaurant with the hired help and kept house, while Torsvan, as he was known there, occupied himself with the fruit trees and, according to Spota, started studying ants—a diversion from his main pursuits at the primitive writing desk. He continued his game of hide-and-seek: Some of his professional and financial correspondence was signed Martínez or Casa M. L. Martínez.

In spite of his perpetual flight from a fixed identity, Traven allowed the details of his biography—the fictionalized version, of course—to be entered into the official record at the dawn of this new stage in his life. On July 12, 1930, he obtained what was apparently his first foreigner's registration card in Mexico under the name Traven Torsvan, occupation "engineer." He does not seem to have pulled this occupation entirely of the air—there are other references to this profession, and his library still contains N. Hawkins's *Aid to Engineers' Examinations* (New York, 1914). Only later did Torsvan adopt the name Hal Croves as well, reportedly derived from the

Christian name of his Scottish grandfather (Halward) and his mother's maiden name (Dorothy Croves). When and why he did this is unclear. The collaboration with John Huston on the filming of *The Treasure of the Sierra Madre* in 1946–1947 cannot have been the occasion, though this is usually assumed; the earliest occurrence of the pseudonym that I found is on an envelope addressed to Hal Croves by Esperanza López Mateos—postmarked June 29, 1944. This Croves regularly presented himself as B. Traven's agent, claiming in his correspondence with publishers, editors, and film professionals that he spoke for Traven but that he himself was not Traven. In 1953 Croves even obtained from the Mexican State Department a document acknowledging him as Traven's fully authorized representative.

Traven—"el gringo" to his neighbors—held fast to his claim of American citizenship during his stay in Acapulco, now for the first time "officially": Not only does the registration card of 1930 identify Traven Torsvan as a North American from Chicago, but Traven also went so far as to write a letter—signed "T. Torsvan c/o Martínez, Acapulco, P.O. Box 49"—to the American embassy in Mexico (June 5, 1941) volunteering for nonmilitary duty in the United States. A curious move for the pacifist and anarchist Marut/Traven! The best explanation is that he made the proposal to divert attention from his dangerous German past. One can view Torsvan's explanation in the Spota interview in a similar light: He could not adopt Mexican citizenship during the war because he did not want to create the impression that he was failing in his allegiance to his (American) homeland. He was not naturalized in Mexico as Torsvan until 1951. The following year the *BT News* published the official biography of B. Traven to dispel all speculations about his identity: Traven's roots, like Torsvan's, were to be found in the American Midwest.

The move to Acapulco in 1930 did not signify that Traven, the former day laborer, had finally reached financial security through his writings. In fact, his complaints of financial problems came with increasing frequency after 1930, when he began composing his epic novel cycle, and lasted well into the 1940s. In the letter to Bodil Christensen of August 11, 1948, when the first film based on a book of his had already been released, he noted (in English): "If you should happen to come down here don't fail to look me up. I am sure Mrs. M. can put you up somehow, but understand everything is primitive . . . more often than not there is just enough money around to have a meal of rice and beans." There is little reason to doubt such statements, particularly when one considers that the Mahogany cycle did not enjoy the impressive sales of some of the earlier novels and that the Nazi takeover effectively cut Traven off from the German (though not the entire German-speaking) market. Nor did the translations of his books provide much additional income. "I am now most concerned with the translations," he wrote to his editor Ernst Preczang in 1933. "We have to make a decision here. Some of my books have been translated into fifteen languages, and all I have seen to date from these numerous translations is a few small advances paid by the publishers."

The correspondence with his Swedish publisher, Axel Holmström in Stockholm, affords a glimpse into the author's economic condition in an exile that took on a new dimension in 1933. Holmström, himself an anarchist with a militant past, had published Traven's novels since 1929, without always making prompt royalty payments. On October 21, 1933, for example, Traven wrote to Holmström (in English, as always) that his income had so declined as a result of political developments in Germany that he now saw himself in the "worst conditions I have encountered for many many years." He was thus forced to postpone the expeditions on which he was to collect material for future books. Whether he was able to undertake them again later in the 1930s is not clear from the surviving documents, but he could scarcely have completed his novel series without further explorations in Chiapas. Still, even as the final part of the cycle was completed, his fiscal complaints sounded just as loudly as in 1933. On April 26, 1939, Traven reminded Holmström that now the author was in worse shape than his financially troubled publisher: "But it's now me who has a very hard time. In fact not even as a sailor or a factory worker, yes, not even when I was out of a job, have I had such hard times to overcome as at present." Even more dramatic—not self-pitying, but also not without a sense of pride—was Traven's description of his sorry state in a letter to Preczang of May 15, 1939. His "material conditions" had been "such for several years," he said,

> that—as I know people—they would be viewed as hopeless by every other human being, and presumably the majority would have put a violent end to their physical existence.

> You know that for a number of years I enjoyed a lavish income, by German standards, on the average 250 to 350 dollars each month, sometimes more, sometimes less. But I spent all this money on the trips necessary for continuing my work; for as the money came mostly from proletarians, I didn't feel I possessed it; rather the money, as I saw it, was given to help me do further service to those who had entrusted it to me. I could afford to do that since I was certain the B.G. would continue to grow, allowing me to get back all the money I invested in my work, so that if I should find myself required to dip into the reserves, I would not have to come on hard times. You, as a well-known and great poet—far greater than I as far as true poetry and art are concerned—know that when authors are unable to build up any material reserves, they unexpectedly find themselves faced with financial chaos if they fail to find a publisher for a work on which they have labored a year or more—or, having found one, find no readers, or so few that the publisher doesn't consider it wise to take any more risks with the author.
>
> That is more or less the general state of affairs. However miserable my own circumstances at present—more miserable than you could ever imagine—I am convinced that you are no better off. I live in a country where I need no heat, except perhaps when I wish to take a hot bath. I can make it through the entire year here with a single suit of clothes—I have only one—since there is no snow or ice here. Besides that—believe it or not—I can get by on less than the minimum wage of an Indian day laborer who has no skills and can neither read nor write. That is a real accomplishment if one is not an Indian. I am also much younger than you, I am unflappable by nature, and I always have the chance that my ship may come in again loaded with treasure. In the meantime it is floating somewhere out there, engulfed in fog, with no wind in the sails. But it will still make it into the harbor. I have no doubt of that.

The outbreak of war saw a further decline in his fortunes: Royalties were not forwarded from a number of countries, payments did not reach him, and foreign-currency regulations made financial transactions difficult, even among neutral countries. Correspondence was interrupted for years in some cases, while sales of the books were sluggish, due partly to shortages and rationing of paper. The correspondence with Holmström offers a lively insight into the situation. The American editions, which Traven authorized once the

German market ceased to exist, enjoyed meager sales, owing not least, ironically, to the author's desire to limit advertising. The authorized Mexican editions that began to appear in the 1940s fared little better. No wonder that Traven, his options dwindling, swamped his Swedish publisher—one of the few in the neutral countries—with suggestions for translating his works and reprinting stories in Swedish newspapers and magazines though there were only a small number of readers to count on. He even sent Holmström a promotional piece on the American filming of *The Treasure of the Sierra Madre* to help boost sales—along with the usual request for overdue payments. "Times are awfully tough for me, worse than I ever expected. . . . In the long run one gets tired of having a tough time even down here where no bombs are dropping down on us," he wrote to Holmström in 1941. In 1945 the situation was just as critical: For practically two years contact even with Holmström, in neutral Sweden, had been interrupted by problems with mail deliveries; Traven had not even been able to have his letters—with their requests for payment—forwarded through the Mexican or American embassies. His urgent tone in a letter of February 28, 1945, comes as no surprise: "Fact is I need the money badly enough." For two years, according to this letter, he had not even had word from his agent in Zurich, Josef Wieder, who generally handled royalty payments from continental Europe. In the war years, Traven's isolation, self-sought at first, thus brought perils far different from those of the past. In the 1920s and even 1930s, a free flow of royalty payments allowed him to remain in isolation—a dead man's living, so to speak. This life line was virtually cut off during the war. All the more noteworthy is Traven's letter of December 9, 1947, to Ernst Preczang, whom he addressed as "forever most deeply esteemed, unforgettable to my dying day." "B.T.," as he typed at the end of the letter, had just heard from Preczang for the first time since 1939 and, flushed with the joy of their reunion, now related that he had forwarded money to Preczang in exile in Switzerland on several occasions during the war; "it was about 1,250 Swiss francs." Similarly, in the letter to Holmström of February 28, 1945, Traven, though in financial straits himself, instructed that 250 Kroner be taken out of his honoraria and forwarded to the widow of his Swedish translator, Eugen Alban, "in case that she finds herself economically in need." Holmström's first royalty payment arriving after the war's end worked like a charm: "The money was badly, very badly needed, believe you me." And when Traven, in a letter to Josef Wieder, resumed his relationship with the Büchergilde after a hiatus of several years, he concluded without mincing words: "Can't any more money be coaxed from the B.G.?" Prices in Mexico were "outrageous. . . . The cheapest New Year's Eve dinner costs 50 pesos."

Traven's fortunes began turning only after the late 1940s, when sales of his novels picked up and the film versions started appearing. But these new sources of income notwithstanding, wealth and a "comfortable" lifestyle came to him only later in life. Never, however, did Traven's financial plight inspire him to consider moving from Mexico—a position he eloquently explained in his letter to Preczang of January 11, 1934:

> In spite of the seemingly enormous income I had in the past years, I own nothing—no villa, no house, no hut, no corner of land, no furniture, no fixed residence, and only the most necessary clothing. This by way of warning you that I won't suggest Mexico for you. I know better climes for you, where you could live like a prince, and where I would like to live, if I weren't bound by every fiber of my being to this continent, where I first saw the sun and expanses that first taught me the meaning of the infinite.

Traven's financial difficulties starting in the 1930s did strain his relationship with his main publisher, Büchergilde Gutenberg. His dissatisfaction with the Büchergilde, after their near parting of ways in 1929, came to a head twice in the 1930s: in 1933, when the political situation in Germany began to encroach on him in far-off Mexico, and again at the end of the decade. Royalties certainly played a role, though they were not the most prominent factor. Traven spoke of royalties in an aside in his letter of May 23, 1933, to the Büchergilde, which by that time had been transplanted to Zurich: "I offered my books to the B.G. for royalties which were ridiculously small in comparison to what bourgeois publishers offered me, on the sole presupposition that the B.G. was in fact the organization that had been presented to me," that is, that the Büchergilde was an institution serving the working class. Since the "character" of the Nazified Berlin Büchergilde was unacceptable, Traven added that "all contractual rights" were to be transferred forthwith to the Zurich Büchergilde. But his rejection of the National-Socialist Büchergilde and his support of its free counterpart did not altogether eliminate the tension between author and publisher that had been simmering for years. Traven's retreat from the Berlin Büchergilde was dictated by the forces of political change. But as Traven saw it, another, likewise unsavory transformation in the Büchergilde itself had taken place even before the Nazi takeover. And the move to Zurich had not reversed this trend but had paradoxically intensified it.

In the year before the Nazi takeover, the Büchergilde—Bruno Dressler in particular—had in Traven's view considered adapting to the new political situation, "exactly as the morally degenerated" Social Democrats had done in the early 1930s, he stated in a letter of October 14, 1933, to Ernst Preczang, who in mid-September had left the Zurich branch of Büchergilde Gutenberg in disagreement with the management. Indeed, the Büchergilde seemed for several years to have "departed from its original spirit and begun to turn Social Democratic," Traven wrote, recalling his critical letters of 1929. In other words, the Büchergilde management blew with the wind like the Social Democrats who had elected "Herr Feldmarschall" Hindenburg and one day "will have to elect the crown prince in order to prevent anything worse from happening. Decomposition always begins with the act of basking in one's own triumphs and one's own imposing grandeur." The retreat from the workers' true political interests was inseparable in Traven's view from corruption and greed, self-enrichment, and the search for personal success. The Büchergilde had grown too flexible politically for his taste—in 1929 and now in October 1933, after he had stood firmly by his publisher over the summer of that year. "The managers' struggle for the bacon costs the workers a delay in their liberation which is difficult to make up." Censorship of his works by the editors opened his eyes again to what he saw as political acquiescence and greed in the increasingly bourgeois publishing house. So Traven again entertained the idea of changing publishers:

> I can say that in all likelihood I would have broken with the B.G. if the takeover had not occurred. One can work far better with bourgeois publishers—believe me, Ernest [*sic*] Preczang—than with groups where the infighting never ceases about who is to stand at the helm. With a bourgeois publisher I can really say what I want in my books; that is something that I unfortunately could never do with the B.G. I always had to fear that

I might lose the favor of the Central Committee or of Mr. Severing and Company.

Such sentiments, heartfelt before, were all the more so in 1933: Preczang, whose politics Traven never questioned, no longer held a position of authority, and Traven saw himself, he continued, "left high and dry" more than he had ever been. He had followed the Büchergilde into exile in Switzerland in early 1933 only because Preczang was thought to assume leadership. "[It had been] my intention to look for a publisher in Germany or somewhere else in German-speaking territory and to take my leave of the B.G.," he told his editor. Now that the Büchergilde had become a "business" instead of a "democratic institution of the workers," why should he not think of business himself? "If I can look at it solely from a business perspective I will always prefer a bourgeois publisher; because with a bourgeois publisher my works will end up where I want them every bit as well," and he would enjoy higher royalties to boot.

In the crisis of 1933 Traven did not put such musings or threats into action. Just a few months later, on January 11, 1934—the Berlin Büchergilde had meanwhile acknowledged Traven's withdrawal—he sent a many-paged letter to the Zurich Büchergilde attesting to his unbroken loyalty. With all-knowing pedantry, he now offered all manner of suggestions—even directives—aimed at seeing his publisher prosper. While still insisting that his address be kept strictly under wraps (to avoid his being disturbed while working), he hoped to take a more active role in managing the Büchergilde and mapping out its business strategy, not least with an eye to giving himself and his works more visibility. First he attempted to have Preczang brought back into the fold since, Traven contended, Preczang had the clearest understanding of proletarian interests, to which the publishing house and book club would have to continue to be committed, however commercial they became. Whatever happened in Preczang's case, Traven said that he attached great importance to keeping the functions of editor and business manager separate. In regard to the publishing program, Traven advised that only those works be accepted that "the modern worker requires in his struggle for existence and in his striving for freedom." Goethe and Dostoyevsky were to be excluded, and even Jack London, with whom Traven had felt so much in common, was passé. The number of titles offered was too large; and books should be sold only to members, as this would increase membership (the service done to the cause would more than offset the loss of revenue). The man in Mexico even had definite proposals regarding book format—and not only of his own works (the worker wanted a book he could stick in his pocket, Traven claimed).

The *Büchergilde* magagzine could be improved by essays on various topics—suggestions flowed effortlessly from Traven's pen—to ignite a "fresh spirit" and "enthusiasm for our cause." The publisher could take a further step in this direction by intensifying "propaganda" efforts (the Büchergilde was a "business enterprise" as well, Traven reminded the management). He even envisioned a contest for the best advertising ideas, spelling out the prizes, and proposed rewarding those who enlisted new members. Lectures and radio programs with Mexican music would be worthwhile endeavors. He even made suggestions about how to run board meetings. "The goal is to boost the B.G. and develop it into a powerful institution," he asserted. Traven saw himself as a fitting authority in such matters, claiming to have the objective gaze of one "so far removed from the tumult in Europe." And as the world political climate worsened, with his own fate hanging on the Swiss Büchergilde, he translated his enthusiasm into very concrete terms, contributing a number of objects for the Büchergilde's promotional campaign in 1936, including rare Indian shell necklaces that he had collected over the years. On the occasion of this gift he published an essay in *Büchergilde*, in which he again expressly stated his loyalty to his publisher. Büchergilde interests now came above all else in his eyes, even if his relationship with his publisher was not the most financially auspicious. He was primarily concerned with the workers' cause, and hoped the Büchergilde could become their "most important cultural community":

> I put great importance on the flourishing and growth of the Büchergilde Gutenberg Zurich-Prague; I want to see the Büchergilde Zurich grow larger and more influential than the Büchergilde in Berlin ever was; in addition to the third of my collection en route to Zurich, I hope to present the second and perhaps even the final third, with the exception of a few items, to the members of the Büchergilde Zurich-Prague—and I do this not with sadness, but with a heart brimming with joy at the thought of serving an institution which I hope will become the largest and most significant cultural community of European

> workers. This has nothing to do with promoting sales of my own books, for every member knows or can imagine that I can sell my books elsewhere and perhaps for more substantial personal profit. All authors, not merely myself, benefit from an increase in the membership, and over the last three years more than one author of the Büchergilde Zurich has sold more books than I have. Of this the management is well aware. And if it should happen that in the next three years the same relatively small number of my books is sold, or even less, this would not weaken my interest in the Büchergilde Gutenberg Zurich-Prague in the least, but, strange as it may sound, might actually heighten it. I am determined to do everything I can, through greater or lesser personal sacrifice, to aid the growth of the Büchergilde Zurich-Prague in the course of 1936. I have selected 1936 as the year in which to apply all my energies and all my material possessions to insure that on 31 December 1936 the Büchergilde Gutenberg will have 15,000 more members than it had in January. If that should occur, I would of course not be fully satisfied, but unspeakably happy nonetheless, all the more so if I could be convinced that my own contribution during this year had made such an increase possible.

This statement appeared in an issue of the magazine dedicated to "Ten Years of Traven," which also featured an essay on Traven by Preczang (writing as Ben Spoer) entitled "Ein fabelhafter Kerl!" ("A Wonderful Guy!"). The loyalty was clearly reciprocal.

Nonetheless, in the long run the emigration of the Büchergilde to democratic Switzerland paradoxically threw a shadow on Traven's relations with the organization through which he maintained contact with his readers. The Swiss bourgeoisie—to admittedly simplify the matter—had replaced the German working class as the Büchergilde's—and Traven's—public. Traven himself apparently realized this shift relatively late. In his letter of January 11, 1934, in which he insinuated himself into managerial issues, he had still insisted that the exiled Büchergilde be conducted as a *Swiss* institution, since the fall of Austria and Czechoslovakia appeared likely. But on October 29, 1938, he wrote to Bruno Dressler:

> The German workers understood my books and my intentions far differently than the Swiss ever could. The German workers and readers of my books had a five-year war behind them, they had fought it out in revolutions and street battles, they had experienced the degeneration and political corruption

> of their party big-wigs and union bosses, they saw the fascists and new evangelists march in, without having the opportunity to fight them. They were an army of people to whose heart I spoke, who understood me, who grasped not only the sentences that I wrote, but who also understood and felt the truth of those sentences that I didn't write, the ones I forced them to think for themselves.
>
> The Swiss members of the B.G. live on different soil, they have had fundamentally different experiences in the course of the last twenty-five years. For Swiss readers, my books are good novels, interesting and worth reading, but they are not works which instill in them a sense of solidarity. This was the case with German readers, just as my Spanish public is beginning not merely to read my books, but to experience them. The Swiss interpret the struggles of the Indian proletariat as the struggles of people as far removed from them as the Chinese in their current struggles. The German and now the Spanish readers of my books identify completely with the proletarian struggles in Mexico; they experience their own struggles, hopes, disappointments, defeats, betrayals, and victories. This makes it difficult for me to produce a new book which would appeal to the management. I can only write what I have experienced, or only write what is right and can be nothing but right according to my best knowledge and experience, since to do otherwise would of necessity be lying. I cannot depict proletarian struggles that I have lived through with a view to bringing a smile to the faces of trade union administrators. The slave who breaks his chains does not give a damn about a Socialist program or a Communist Manifesto.

Traven spoke with equal candor about tensions with the Büchergilde in a letter to Holmström of April 26, 1939: "I am under the impression that this institution [the Büchergilde Gutenberg] has gone soft during the last three years, and I can't agree with many of the books which that organisation has brought out lately."

This statement reflected not only Traven's disappointment at the change in the Büchergilde's public but also his dissatisfaction with a restructuring in the Büchergilde's hierarchy: Josef Wieder, a Swiss native living in Zurich who had served as Traven's "legal representative" since 1933, had, after considerable quarreling, left the management of the Zurich Büchergilde as of January 1, 1939, while Traven retained him as his sole authorized representative for continental Europe. Also lurking behind his comment to Holmström about the Büchergilde's "softening" in the late 1930s was, however, his disappointment at the Büchergilde's rejection of his novel *General from the Jungle*. On April 15, 1937, Bruno Dressler had informed his star author that the final component of the novel series, then titled *Der Dschungel-Marschall* (*The Jungle Marshal*), had divided the editors: "one group did not feel comfortable with the book's subject matter, while the other group desired cuts in the second part of the manuscript," as a result of which Dressler suggested that Traven review the text. The author, whose readers already numbered in the millions, would scarcely have been obliging, particularly as the news came from Dressler, whose business practices Traven had criticized extensively in 1929. Allert de Lange in Amsterdam, not the Büchergilde, would publish the novel, and then only some three years after the completion of the manuscript—which could not have reduced the friction between the Büchergilde and the author.

Büchergilde Gutenberg had "published my new books," Traven explained to Dressler on January 14, 1939,

> not for their revolutionary content, but for financial reasons; and my new books were greeted there not with enthusiasm, but with the asthmatic sighs of nervous petit-bourgeois, of people who call themselves labor leaders, but who blow with the wind. And in Switzerland, if it should come to pass, they would prostrate themselves before the fascists just as quickly and fawningly as they had in Germany.

Traven separated formally from Büchergilde Gutenberg (Zurich), announcing to Dressler in the same letter:

> According to my estimation the Büchergilde Gutenberg currently has at least five thousand members who will thank me for leaving the corporation of Büchergilde authors, so that I will not have to face the day, near at hand, when I am thrown out of the Büchergilde. These five thousand members, upon learning of my decision will, along with you, the board, and the perfumed literature committee call out from the bottom of their soul: "Praise be to God in heaven and Jehova to boot that we are finally rid of this unwashed, lice-ridden vagabond, and can purify our book list of this wretched spot of dirt, so that we can at last occupy ourselves with real literature." I share this opinion with you, the board, and the apple-polishing literature committee.

Traven's dissatisfaction is still evident in his letter of March 27, 1939, to Dressler, which brings up the matter of *General from the Jungle* again:

> In all your letters of the last two years, you write that the members want to know what has become of the rebels. I can only tell the members how it is, not how the management would like to hear it. Do you imagine that arms fall from the sky to rebels with no arms, or that they are sent by the non-intervention committee in Christmas packages so that the rebellion can go on? . . .
>
> Don't think, Mr. Bruno Dressler, that I cannot sell the book. It will go like hot cakes with maple syrup. You can bank on that. To this day I have offered it nowhere else, after Mr. J. Wieder assured me so often that the book was good and advised me not to destroy it under any circumstances. I did this solely for the sake of B.G. members, not for the management, or for you, but exclusively out of consideration for the members and the proletarian members in particular; the pastors and intellectuals and complacent bourgeois in the B.G. won't buy my books anyway. And that can only help me and my books.

In addition to the Büchergilde's increasingly bourgeois clientele, Wieder's departure from the publishing house, and the Büchergilde's rejection of *General in the Jungle*, the author's material condition in early 1939 may have contributed to the friction with the Büchergilde as it had ten years earlier. Traven intimated as much in his letter to Preczang of May 15, 1939, claiming once again that it was only for the sake of the proletarian cause that he had published his works for years through the Büchergilde Gutenberg.

After Traven's break with the Büchergilde, Josef Wieder was the only one authorized to represent Traven's interests in continental Europe. The German-speaking public was lost for the most part, in any event. Financial ruin was an all too real possibility for Traven. Wieder touched on the author's precarious position in a letter to Axel Holmström of June 20, 1939: "Mr. Traven must think of getting his royalties these days if he is not to perish. Things are going so badly for him now that he even has to make increased demands to the Büchergilde in order to survive."

Further difficulties arose. While Traven officially no longer had a role to play in German literary life and at best continued to be read in secret and sold clandestinely, he was anybody's fair game: The man who was so particular about copyright was suddenly helpless, and plagiarists were free to plunder his works without fear of retribution from their far-off, disempowered author. The crassest instance—besides the novel *Kesselbum* by Tex Harding (discussed in Chapter 2)—was *Der Kampf um die Weltmacht Öl* (*The Struggle for the World Power, Oil*) by Anton Zischka, published by Wilhelm Goldmann in Leipzig in 1934. In the May 1935 issue of the Zurich *Büchergilde* Traven demonstrated that Zischka lifted an entire chapter more or less verbatim from *The White Rose*. Aside from making such a statement in his publisher's magazine—which could not be distributed in Germany in any event—Traven was powerless.

The Nazi takeover isolated Traven as much from his reading public as he had isolated himself from Nazi Germany. The historical events, which directly affected Traven's relations with his publisher, warrant a closer examination.

Blacklists and Bonfires

After the National Socialists "assumed" power in Germany on January 30, 1933, little apparently changed for the Büchergilde for a quarter of a year. In March Büchergilde director Bruno Dressler wrote assuringly to Traven that the euphoria surrounding Hitler would soon yield to grim economic reality. But on May 2, the Büchergilde's Berlin headquarters on Dreibundstrasse were occupied by SA troops; the German Workers Front annexed the press, employees were ordered to leave, and Dressler and others were taken into "protective custody." Some leading figures, including Preczang and later Dressler, fled to Switzerland; others were threatened into staying on in Berlin. An SA company commander, Otto Jamrowski, headed the publishing house and book club under its old name, while the previous management reconstructed its organization in Zurich as the Genossenschaft Büchergilde Gutenberg and continued "the Guild's work as it had been earlier defined." At first the book club had only 6,000 members, but at the outbreak of the war it had 26,000 members, and more than 100,000 by war's end; by the end of 1948, the club had published 383 titles, with a total printing of almost four and a half million volumes.

The Nazi takeover did not mean that all Büchergilde titles were withdrawn from circulation; not even all of Traven's books were banned. But Traven had the honor of appearing on the first blacklist of undesirable authors, with *The Carreta* and *Government.* This list, compiled by a commission of Berlin librarians but apparently binding for the entire Reich, was published on May 16, 1933, in the German book dealers' journal *Börsenblatt für den deutschen Buchhandel.* The practical purpose of the list was to name books "which *may* be withdrawn in the process of sanitizing public libraries. Whether they *all must* be suppressed," the explanatory notes instructed with astounding pragmatism, "depends on the extent to which the gaps can be filled by good *new acquisitions.*" The ban on *The Carreta*—which *Völkischer Beobachter* had condemned on February 21 as a product of an "unfeeling, destructive intellect" incapable of "constructive thought"—was soon lifted; and *The White Rose,* in spite of a call from the Berlin *Börsenblatt* for its inclusion on the list, remained available for the time being, as did the other Traven books. But within a few weeks of the initial action against Traven, in accordance with an "order of the Reichspräsident for the protection of the people and the state," *The White Rose,* along with *The Carreta* and *Government,* was "confiscated" in Germany, and in February 1934 *The Death Ship* was "confiscated and withdrawn from circulation in the state of Prussia." One can assume that Traven's books were not only banned but burned as well, since the books that went up in flames on May 10, 1933, at the Berlin Opernplatz and elsewhere in Germany were gathered on the basis of the original blacklist.

Books were forbidden and burned based on "literary-political" considerations. "We are fighting," the notes to the blacklist stated, "against phenomena destructive to our native manner of thinking and living, i.e., against *asphalt literature,* which is written predominantly for metropolitan man, to strengthen him in his lack of relation to his environment, to the people, to every sense of community, and to uproot him completely. It is the literature of intellectual nihilism." Ironically, the Büchergilde Gutenberg claimed that Traven's strength came from the abundance of those very qualities that the Nazis said he lacked; the antagonists thus judged the works according to the same criteria: "On the basis of its understanding of pure folkdom alone . . . this book [*Government*] would rightly have stood at the top of the Third Reich's recommended reading list," the Zurich *Büchergilde* boasted in May 1934. Still, the censor had not forbidden Traven's books haphazardly. In the instructions on how to use the blacklist, Traven was listed as the sole example of "Group 3": cases in which it was debatable whether the books were to be "destroyed" or "sequestered."

How did Traven react?

His general attitude toward the new regime was predictable. As early as November 1932 *Die Büchergilde* had published a letter from him on the decisive role of books in the intellectual and practical liberation of the worker:

> Far more important for the proletarian than the fascist fighting for the bone is that he keep a clear head, that he not give up hope, that he not fall prey to emotional collapse, that his intellectual abilities do not fall asleep, that he stay awake and remain fully alert, so he may be ready when he believes that his hour has sounded. The Nazi is the one who has something to worry about, for he is the reaction, the brake on the wheel of the economic and intellectual development of mankind.

The occupation and takeover of the Berlin Büchergilde elicited a powerful response from Traven. In his first letter to the Zurich Büchergilde, of May 23, 1933, answering its report of the expropriation, he noted that he had composed his last two letters to Dressler in such a way that the "progenitors of the new race," into whose hands they had surely fallen, would learn what people in the United States and Mexico thought of the "fools shouting about resurrection" and that the Nazis would "not be very happy" about it. He unmistakably viewed the National Socialists as synonymous with the capitalists, attempting to ingratiate themselves with the workers in order to rob them of their ideals. The "labor leaders"—ever ready to turn in the proletariat after 1914—would only too happily offer their assistance, he contended. If the Büchergilde should reorient itself to the new course, "I will not go along." At this point he did not know whether his books had been banned, but he expressly hoped that they had been, though at the same time he rightly foresaw that the new masters would attempt to continue selling at least some of his books to "create the impression that I support this change." He thus beat the "shirts" (as he liked to call the Nazis) to the punch: He prescribed in this letter that all contractual rights, domestic and foreign, be transferred immediately to the new Zurich Büchergilde. "Better to go to the devil and hell than to make concessions which are degrading in cases like this." Since he had never been a German citizen, he noted, the Nazified

Büchergilde in Berlin could not confiscate his rights anyway. Should they continue to publish Traven's works, decisive action would have to be taken through diplomatic or other channels. Traven thus took an unequivocal stand, even before he knew with certainty whether and how he would be affected by the new course. He felt revulsion not only at the new ideology but also at the Führer personally:

> The Nazis don't have a single friend abroad, not even among the capitalists, and not even in Italy. Adolphus is such an unsympathetic character—in appearance, to say nothing of his overblown gestures—that because of him personally one mistrusts and despises even things which might possibly be good in the movement. In his worst moments the German kaiser was not so hated and unpopular as this impossible Adolphus.

Soon after this letter (on May 27 and again on June 29) Traven wrote again to the Berlin management. These letters, mentioned in Traven's communication with the new head of the Berlin Büchergilde, Otto Jamrowski, on September 30, 1933, apparently have not survived. Most disturbing to Traven was the possibility that those now in control would simply appropriate his books and his name and thus create a false impression. Regarding his new novel, *March to the Montería*, which the Zurich Büchergilde was to publish amid great fanfare as its first new Traven book, he wrote on June 8 to Preczang: "We must at all costs combat every attempt to publish the book within the German Reich." Similar were his remarks to Preczang two days later:

> My goal is not to leave any doubt about my position toward the political buffoons in Germany. I cannot rid myself of the suspicion that these people will take any literature which has achieved any standing in the civilized world and exploit it to their own ends, though not necessarily for financial gain—though I believe they would try that too. One way or another they would appropriate the literature which has arisen in the era of the Holy Resurrection, particularly if the author is not a Jew, but more Nordic than Adolf himself. Reviews of my work in the Nazi press, with few exceptions and those only recently, were always favorable. That arouses my suspicion—and even more the fact that they have not banned all of my books, but only four.
>
> I therefore now wish to ban from Germany also those books that those jerks have not banned and that they are apparently hoping to use for some purpose or other.

> Losing the profits I might have by leaving the books in circulation means nothing to me. In matters like this I prefer clarity to profit.

At the same time, Traven stressed that his break with the Nazis not be used for promotional purposes, however much he understood that this would be the best recommendation for his books. He may have feared the wrath of reactionary circles, a bane to him since his Munich days. He continued in this letter of June 10, 1933:

> I have expressly forbidden my English publisher, who will be bringing out *The Death Ship* this autumn, to use in any sort of advertising the fact that my books are banned in Germany. That sort of promotion has proved very helpful in selling all other forbidden German books in England.

Nonetheless, the Zurich *Büchergilde* announced the new novel in July 1933 as a sign that Traven "remains true to the old conception of the Guild and his cooperation attests to where the true Büchergilde is located." Traven himself chose to underscore the novel's exotic elements; in the letter of June 8, 1933, accompanying the manuscript bearing the subtitle "A War March," he described the new work:

> A war march without glockenspiels, oboes, or clarinets. A war march, rather, with blaring horns; heavy timpani; drums by the score; deafening cries; shrill whistling; the crack of whips; wild cursing; the tumult of pack animals sinking into the swamp or straying from the narrow mountain paths and plunging into the abyss; death moans of torturers and cannibals, punished by Indians; the construction and collapse of bridges; the crackle of evening campfires; the hiss of hungry tigers; the dull cries of great apes; the rebellion of mutinous Indians; the murmuring waters of powerful forest streams; the babbling of garrulous brooks in the jungle. That is the instrumentation of this war march which, like every war march, ends with the arrival at the scene of the battle.

While Traven's contacts in Zurich responded, the Berlin Büchergilde cloaked itself in silence. Fearing the worst as a powerless émigré with no legal recourse, Traven acted through the Zurich headquarters to demand the return of his manuscripts, photos, Indian craft collections, letters, and contracts, as well as royalty payments amounting to $70,800, for which he had written to Berlin in May and June, presumably in the two previously mentioned letters.

The situation became more acute when, as the result of a suit brought by the Buchmeister Verlag, the Berlin District Court issued a temporary order on July 22, 1933, forbidding the Swiss Büchergilde from marketing Traven's books until further notice. In practical terms this meant that the Berlin Büchergilde could continue selling Traven's books on its own, "with the exception of *Government* naturally," as Wieder wrote to Traven on August 21, urging him to fight the decision (as if this were necessary). On August 23 Wieder insisted for a second time: Traven, he wrote, must distance himself publicly and in writing to avoid seeming in the eyes of the world to go along with the Nazis. The September issue of the Berlin *Büchergilde*—as of June 1933 there were two separate publications, in Zurich and Berlin—in fact used Traven's name to promote its own program: "An author of world stature to first appear in the Büchergilde: B. Traven."

Not least, this last affront must have acted on Traven like a red flag and incited him to act. He composed an "open letter" of more than seven pages to the head of the Berlin Büchergilde, Otto Jamrowski, dated September 30, bringing up the Berlin Büchergilde's unauthorized use of his name in the second paragraph. He also wrote Jamrowski a seven-page cover letter, bearing the same date, in which he threatened to publish the open letter if the Berlin management did not immediately and unconditionally agree to his demands. The tone of the cover letter is rabid. Jamrowski had not won his place at the Büchergilde through his talent, Traven contended, but rather through his political orientation. "Only yesterday, German people, you paid homage to Goethe." Traven stressed that only he held the copyright; he had withdrawn it from the Berlin Büchergilde, and its marketing of his works was thus illegal; the power of his name would be sufficient to convince the world of his rights: "You may be sure that as soon as I publish the open letter that will be the end of your Guild." He wished to show Jamrowski "the power an author has, and with what effect he can exercise his power once he gets his dander up"—a new variation of the superiority complex that Traven often exhibited in his lonely exile. In particular, the Berlin Büchergilde, he asserted, had no right to publish the manuscript of *Art of the Indians*, since that would require authorization from a number of contributors, most of them Mexican, who directly or indirectly helped create the book.

The demands—the fulfillment of which Traven specified as the sole means of keeping him from publishing the open letter—amounted to a radical break between author and publisher. Traven forbade the Berlin Büchergilde to publish and market his books, and he declared that his manuscripts were to be "handed over," as were contracts and correspondence and the "ethnological collections, newspapers, magazines, maps, plans, photographs, drawings, records, and originals and copies of lectures" that Traven had made available to the Büchergilde; remaining copies of his books and their printing plates were to be offered at cost to his representative Wieder; the Berlin *Büchergilde* was to carry a notice to the effect that the Büchergilde Gutenberg Berlin would no longer represent Traven's books; finally, he was to receive an accounting for all outstanding domestic and foreign royalties by October 31, 1933.

The open letter itself, entitled "The 5,000 Mark Scandal"* and addressed to Otto Jamrowski as the "accountable director" of the "National-Socialized Büchergilde Gutenberg," was ostensibly composed on September 30 in "London, W.C. 2" (no doubt a reference to the address of Traven's English agent, Curtis Brown), though a cover note to Wieder bears the date "September 18, 1933." The latter contains the instruction "In case Berlin fulfills my demands, this open letter must not be published, either now or in the future." The Berlin Büchergilde, the open letter stated, continued to market Traven's intellectual property and listed his books in its catalogues—with the exception of *Government*—as if nothing had happened, hoping that this deception would keep the publishing house in business. Traven ripped into this hypocrisy and boundless display of greed with the most acerbic terms. "I here declare before the world that I do not have the least connection with you or with the Third Reich," he claimed, heaping further denunciatory verbiage on the new Büchergilde director. Traven turned the tables on the Nazi propagandists when he labeled the new Büchergilde's practices as "un-German" and "Jewish," turning their own anti-Semitic language against them. The manner in which the usurpers dealt with *Gov-*

*The title was a reference to the fact that the Berlin court, according to Traven, had set a fine of 5,000 marks per day and per offense if Traven stated publicly that he had withdrawn all rights to his books from the Büchergilde Berlin or allowed his books to be published by another press or awarded translation rights on his authority.

ernment was typical, he noted. That book, from the first line to the last, was aimed against dictatorship and offered the clearest demonstration of his political sentiments; until they realized that, the people in Berlin "hawked it" for two months, but now it was not mentioned at all so as not to jeopardize sales of the other Traven titles. The last straw, however, was that *Government* was banned only in the German market, while the Berlin Büchergilde "had the nerve" to sell the novel abroad "in order to scare up the money with which they could erect the cultural facade of the New Germany and establish the dictatorship." The open letter concludes with a political flourish the author must have savored: "Good-bye [in English], Büchergilde Gutenberg Berlin, farewell. Heil! Undefeated in the field. A stab in the back. Long live the Fourth Reich! Built up with a single line. Animated by 40 million hearts!" He typed his signature: "B. Traven."

The reaction from Berlin was negative at first. A certain Herr Justi informed Traven on October 9, 1933, that Jamrowski, "with whose business practices we were not in agreement," was no longer director of the Büchergilde. Yet the new man acted as dismissively as one would have expected from his predecessor: "We reject your proposals"; the ethnological collection "etc." would be returned, however. In regard to publication of the open letter, Justi simply said, "we leave it to you." Justi seems to have had as little final authority as Jamrowski, though. For only a week later, on October 16, 1933, the Berlin Büchergilde and Josef Wieder as Traven's representative signed an agreement transferring all rights to Wieder and recognizing all of Traven's demands, save that the remaining copies of *Government* could not be exported to Switzerland without a special permit for the time being. (The Berlin office also sent Wieder the manuscript of *Art of the Indians* and informed the publishers of translations of Traven's works about the new state of affairs.) Traven retrieved the original of his open letter, which today is found among his papers: He apparently considered it important that this prominent episode in his political biography not escape the notice of historians.

Thus concluded Traven's break with Nazi Germany. As of January 1, 1934, his books could no longer be sold in Germany. If Austria were to fall to the fascists, Preczang wrote on November 21, 1933, Traven's income "would fall to a pitiful level." In a telling detail of Traven's complete break with and antagonism toward Nazi Germany, in 1933, writing as "L. M. Martínez," he typed on a piece of mail, "Please don't send with German ship.

Fiasco with Forethought: The American Editions

After he cut himself off from the German market, Traven naturally depended more than ever on revenues from translations. He now attempted, via the Büchergilde's Zurich headquarters, to make the publishers of translations of his works keep up with their royalty payments, and his subsequent efforts to open additional non-German-speaking markets thus come as no surprise. In particular, he seems to have pinned his hopes on conquering the American market.

The thought of publishing American or British editions was by no means new in that critical year 1933, when Traven was compelled to rethink his role in the literary world as a result of political reality. In 1929—when he was considering a break with the Büchergilde—he had already signed an agreement with Doubleday in New York for all rights to the American and British markets, including those for film and theater. Traven insisted, however, that advertising for his works be kept at a minimum—his novels were not to be hawked "like cigarettes, car tires, toilet soap, toothpaste, and the latest mattresses." No mention was even to be made of the author's name. As a result, Doubleday, who in Traven's eyes was interested only in "making big money," soon lost interest and Traven bought back the rights "for a considerable sum," as *Die Büchergilde* reported in December 1931. This was not merely a publicity ploy, as one might have expected from the man who has been accused of exploiting his own mystery to help sales of his works. Signing himself "B. Traven," he wrote from Mexico City on July 10, 1931, to a certain Mr. Adler: "Yes, it is correct what you have been told. I have bought back from Doubleday, Doran & Co. all the American and British book rights, stage rights, and picture rights. But that does not mean that I am looking for another American publisher. For the time being I am fed up with American publishers." A year and a half later, Traven sang the same tune: on December 21, 1932, just weeks before the events that would compel him to reconsider his position, he informed Kurt Wagenseil in Munich, "I am interested in neither an English nor an American publisher for my books, and I have not authorized or asked anyone to find an English or American publisher for me." That was no caprice, as it might have appeared in his 1931 letter to Mr. Adler. Half a year earlier, on July 9, 1932, Traven had in no uncertain terms informed Raymond W. Postgate of London that he would use all legal means available to block American editions of his books: "I am quite willing to spend my last nickel to prevent my books being on the American market as long as I do not wish to have them there."

Postgate headed the London branch of Alfred A. Knopf. Knopf himself had discovered Traven a short time previously. An anonymous essay entitled "On the Trail of B. Traven," appearing on July 9, 1938, in *Publishers Weekly*, recounts this discovery, which would eventually lead to the *Sierra Madre* film and, ultimately, financial security. Knopf heard the name Traven, the "best writer of his kind" since Jack London, for the first time in February 1932, on a business trip to the Universitas Press in Berlin, which was licensed to publish editions of Traven's novels. "Not unnaturally," Knopf immediately instructed Traven's London agent, Curtis Brown, as well as Postgate to establish contact with Traven regarding U.S. rights. Traven's initial reaction was negative. He had claimed, the essay related, that American publicity methods reduced authors to trapeze performers, sword swallowers, and circus animals. But sometime after the summer of 1933, according to this essay, Traven apparently had a change of heart and granted Knopf permission to publish his books in America. (That agreement predates the publication of the London editions, translated by Eric Sutton and Basil Creighton and published by Chatto & Windus since 1934.) Traven and Knopf quickly came to an understanding: In 1934 *The Death Ship* appeared, followed in 1935 by *The Treasure of the Sierra Madre*, *The Bridge in the Jungle* in 1938, and *The Rebellion of the Hanged* in 1952. Nothing came of Traven's plan to transpose *The Death Ship* into the period of the Second World War, which he suggested to Knopf in a letter of August 12, 1947.

The manuscript of *The Death Ship* that arrived in New York in 1933 was couched in an English that would have raised the eyebrows of most readers. As Knopf editor Bernard Smith reported, the text was so Germanic in vocabulary and syntax that it could never have made it into print. And for good reason: Traven himself had translated the novel (as he was to translate the other novels Knopf would bring out), at the same time giving free rein to his lifelong passion for rewriting, cutting, and inserting new material. Knopf asked Traven to agree to a revision by Smith. Traven asked for sample pages and was favorably impressed. After instructing Knopf that only grammatical, syntactic, and orthographic changes were to be made, he authorized Smith to rework the entire manuscript. "This entailed treating about 25 percent of the text," Smith recalled. "In any given paragraph there was sure to be at least one impossibly Germanic sentence, and sometimes an entire paragraph had to be reconstructed." Smith stressed that his contribution in no way involved what could be considered literary or creative work on the three novels he revised. He had merely turned Traven's translations into acceptable English. It was clear to Smith from the beginning that English was not the translator's mother tongue; the syntactic thread was German, and even in Smith's reworked version the German original rears its head from time to time.

Smith described his literary midwifery in *The New York Times Book Review* of November 22, 1970. "B(ashful). Traven," he stated in no uncertain terms, had his own view of the genesis of the novels—Traven claimed that the text sent to Knopf was the "original English version." Knopf accordingly billed *all* the English versions of Traven's novels—not only *The Death Ship*—as the English originals. The most cursory comparison of the English and German texts of course leads one to the same conclusion Smith drew, namely that Traven's claim of an "amerikanische Urschrift" ["original American text"] simply does not hold water. Nonetheless, even the Büchergilde Gutenberg publicly accepted Traven's story. Shortly after the appearance of the American editions, it ironically had two of the novels—*The Death Ship* and *The Treasure of the Sierra Madre*—translated into German "from the American original," that is, from "the English version originally written by Traven." *Die Brücke im Dschungel* followed in 1955, translated from the "original American edition" of *The Bridge in the Jungle*.

In his agreement with Knopf, Traven insisted that any publicity contain no reference to his place of residence, his background, or his personal life—although his demand to curb publicity had derailed his previous attempt to find an American publisher. Traven instructed Smith that any inquiries sent to Knopf regarding Traven's biography and personality were to receive the curt reply that nothing at all was known about the author. Traven himself offered the following explanation in a letter to the American journalist Herbert Arthur Klein:

> I write to propagate ideas, not to make a profit. My books came to readers precisely by the same means they came to you, that is, individual recommendation. . . . Mr. Knopf does not advertise my books outside of the trade press. This is according to my specific instructions. My work carries all the publicity I need and all I want. If my books are not considered good no publicity can make them any better.

Smith told BBC producer Will Wyatt the enticing detail that Traven assured himself that Smith opened all his mail personally—lest an outsider discover that the novels came from Mexico. The publicity-shy hermit of Acapulco went to particularly bizarre lengths to cover his trail when Smith wrote Traven that he and his wife were planning a Mexican vacation in the fall of 1936 and hoped to meet the author face to face. Traven answered, Smith recalled in the *Times* article, that he himself would at that time be traveling to California, "Dakota," and Wisconsin, "where I have to see some people how they are doing." Yet he insisted, in his curiously German English, that the Smiths undertake the journey. They never met Traven in the flesh on their trip, but he made his presence felt in a curious manner. He arranged for a certain "Miss Mary" to serve as the Smiths' guide. They were instructed not to ask her any questions about Traven—though she would have had difficulty communicating with them in any event (she "does not speak very well English," Traven explained in a note to Smith). Miss Mary provided the Smiths with a total of thirty-five single-spaced typed pages of day-to-day sightseeing suggestions that clearly came from Traven himself. Not surprisingly, Mr. and Mrs. Smith had the strange sensation that Traven was somehow with them, hiding somewhere in the background, amused at his own subterfuge.

This maneuver was characteristic of Traven's knack of drawing attention to himself by becoming invisible. Another intriguing example comes from one of his "outrageously long letters" to Alfred Knopf, dated November 21, 1933. He first made the usual points: Publicity was to be kept to a minimum; his books were important, not his private life. But then he served up a tantalizing list of the "mystery stories" surrounding his identity then making the rounds in Europe: The author of the Traven best-sellers was said to be

President Calles, Jack London, a general from the Mexican revolution, a nephew of the German kaiser, an American soldier of fortune in Nicaragua, the wealthiest Pacific ship owner, the richest Mexican landowner who held one of the largest sugar plantations and refineries; some said he was married to the daughter of President Calles, that he was wanted by the police in New York, Chicago, Detroit, and Los Angeles for murder, bank robbery, or a holdup, while others pegged him as an escaped convict from Fort Leavenworth or San Quentin (a Japanese mail boat had fished him out of San Francisco Bay!); still others said he did not exist at all but was merely the invention of publishers or was long dead or an Arctic explorer.

Why the aversion to publicity in America? In his letters to the Büchergilde in this period and in the correspondence with his Swedish publisher, Traven did everything he could to encourage what he called "propaganda." And wasn't revenue from the translations one of his chief concerns, now that the Nazis had driven him from the German market? Why then did he advise against advertising the American editions? Bernard Smith suspected that this was merely clever marketing on Traven's part, that by shrouding himself and his whereabouts in mystery he heightened the appeal of his books. This is certainly a simplistic explanation. Could the aversion to publicity in the United States point to a skeleton in Traven's past there, or to his belief that there was one, as the playful letter to Knopf might suggest? Was he perhaps thinking of his extremely anti-American article "America, the Promised Land of Freedom," published in *Die Büchergilde* of January 1930, in which he claimed that U.S. workers—particularly socialists, communists, pacifists, and anarchists—had neither freedom of speech nor any other "real freedom"? Did he dread sharing the fate of Upton Sinclair, cited in the article, who was ignored because he had openly spoken his mind about American legal conditions? Or was he thinking of Halldor Laxness, also mentioned in the article, who followed Sinclair in criticizing injustice and was threatened with deportation? "Eager reporters," *Die Büchergilde* stated in September 1931—before the appearance of the first American translation—had attempted to get information about the mysterious Traven through the German embassies in both Mexico and Washington. In December of that year, *Die Büchergilde* predicted that Traven's withdrawal of his books from the American market would unleash a host of speculations that he was wanted by the American authorities. Was all this mere sensationalism? Or did Traven's flight from the (American) public eye point to some wrongdoing, real or imagined? What is he referring to, for example, in his confession to Knopf of August 12, 1947: "I was traveling, hiding out is more correct, in the Sierra de Oaxaca for reasons somehow related to an article which appeared several months ago in a widely read magazine"?

Traven's behavior in regard to the American editions is even more curious when one considers his behind-the-scenes attempts to *promote* publicity. On the one hand, he wrote to Knopf: "This fact that nobody even mentions my book is a very good sign." On the other hand, in 1935 and 1936 he corresponded extensively with Herbert Arthur Klein, relentlessly urging the journalist to initiate a discussion of him in the American press. Klein had reviewed *The Death Ship* and requested that Traven send information for use in articles. Traven responded with unbounded enthusiasm, as if nothing about him had ever before made it into print. But even with Klein he stressed that he put little stock in American publicity ("It flares up and dies at sunset. Nothing behind"). Yet the main thrust of their correspondence was to provide the energetic young journalist with material for essays on Traven. Klein was not to forget, Traven said, that fifty magazines and newspapers in the British Empire were eagerly waiting to publish "intelligent" articles about Traven. Indeed, Traven saw nothing wrong with sketching out the articles himself for his admirer. Klein thus might well consider starting a piece with his own activities as a correspondent in Germany and express his surprise that workers there did not talk about cars or radios but about Gorky, Sinclair Lewis, Upton Sinclair—and B. Traven, whose name he had often heard in Germany. He—Klein was to write—had not met anyone in these circles who had not read all the books of "that strange man, B.T." Such was the introduction Traven envisioned for an American audience. Traven went even further: He recommended appropriate American magazines as well as prospective essay titles to Klein: "Adventure Yarns or Philosophy?" "Unknown B.T. and Why?" "Fiction or Propaganda?" (Traven even furnished an answer to this last question: He did not wish to change anything, he only wished to open the eyes of his fellow men so that they might change the world if they considered it necessary). Such interest in publicity in America is certainly curious for a writer purporting to eschew any promotion there.

Traven's maneuver had little or no effect. *Publishers Weekly* stated on July 9, 1938, based on information provided by Knopf, that only 3,288 copies of *The Death Ship* and only 2,692 of *The Treasure of the Sierra Madre* had been sold. And in a letter to Knopf of September 23, 1937, Traven noted that of his total advance of $1,000 for *The Death Ship*, $309.01 had not yet been covered by royalties from sales of the book. So he now wished to have that amount deducted from the advance for *The Bridge in the Jungle*. Knopf would be relieved to know, Traven pointed out, that *The Death Ship* would now be sailing ahead without any debt weighing it down.

His gesture scarcely helped to put wind in the sails. In fact, Traven attempted on his own to launch the English translation of another of his books through another publisher—an understandable move, and then again surprising in light of his aversion to American publicity. He turned to Raymond Everitt, an editor at Little, Brown in Boston, on April 27, 1939, suggesting the publication of a collection of his Mexican stories, to be called "Swallowed by the Bush, Bone and Soul"—a title far too sensational for that publisher. Traven recalled in the letter that Everitt had learned of the stories through Traven's London agent, Curtis Brown, but had at first declined to publish them because the collection lacked unity; yet he had said he would look at the manuscript again when he returned to Boston. (The stories in question amounted to the English equivalent of *Der Busch*.) In a 3½-page, single-spaced letter, Traven now attempted to change the editor's mind, claiming that the collection was unified by its constellation of themes; the unity of his books always "consists more of the unity of one or more problems than of characters." Traven then offered his own interpretation of the *Bush* novellas, seeing the influence of the tropical jungle on humans as their unifying theme:

> As to the technic used I know quite well that the whole book will make the impression as if very losely [*sic*] knit together to make it appear like a novel. . . .
>
> If in a collection of short stories in book-form a love story is followed by a detective story and this by a story about a lost gold mine, then a story about an American jane stranded in China and found by her sailor brother in a Russian night club in Shanghai, one story having for its background a ranch in Arizona, the other a bolshevic training camp for North-Pole aviators, well, then you cannot blame the reader, less so can you

> blame the would-be buyer if he says to the book-seller: "I git that better in True Romances and there it'll set me back only two bits, why the hell am I going to pay for [*sic*] two bucks if I kin git it for two bits and with pitchas too."

Traven's book was decidedly "not of the same ilk. Here the reader is not constantly thrown from Alaska to Italy, from a penthouse to a film studio, from a love affair to a murder committed by a cross-eyed man with a wooden leg. In the case we have before us the reader will, practically permanently, remain under the impression that he is reading a novel and not a collection of short stories." The letter could hardly have come from Traven's pen without a reference to the educational value of this "good book." He counseled the editor not to think twice about taking the risk. Still, his partisanship in his own case did little good. The book did not make it into print.

Traven's efforts at self-promotion did not end here. A few years later he paradoxically took it upon himself to help increase sales of one of his books published by Knopf. *The New Republic* of January 25, 1943, contained an advertisement for "The Story of an American Sailor Aboard a Death Ship. The most exciting and sensational sea story of this time," available in the only "authentic" edition for two dollars through Casa M. L. Martínez, Post Office Box 2520, Mexico City. Mina Klein, Herbert Klein's wife, ordered a copy and received a letter from Traven himself as Martínez, in which he maintained that the book had no equal in the whole world. Mrs. Klein was instructed to read it and then send it to a friend, preferably one in the navy or merchant marine, in the army or the marine corps—Traven, as always, was loath to let slip an opportunity of educating strangers about the right way to think or act.

This eccentric tactic did not, however, contribute much to total sales of the American edition of *The Death Ship*. If Traven had expected that the American market would change his fortunes, he had, on the whole, miscalculated. It was only in the 1960s, when Lawrence Hill of Hill & Wang became Traven's publisher and Traven had apparently overcome his fear of publicity, that the American market took part in the worldwide upswing in Traven's popularity. Knopf's edition of *The Treasure of the Sierra Madre* was the sole exception—but as a result of the film version of 1948. In any event, in 1955 Traven saw himself compelled to take the unusual step of negotiating with Knopf over the return of all rights and the repurchase of the plates and of the remaining copies of his books published by Knopf.

Thus ended a chapter in Traven's life that had started more than twenty years earlier, when the self-styled American was forced to find a new public among his "compatriots." (He had attempted unsuccessfully to do the same in the mid-1920s, before his novels appeared in German.) The occasion in the 1930s had been the Nazis' rise to power. As late as December 1932, he had displayed a lack of interest in the American market; his attempts to gain a foothold there in 1933 can thus be viewed in the context of his opposition to fascism.

The Spanish Civil War and German Exiles in Mexico

A few years after the start of his relationship with Knopf, the Spanish Civil War gave Traven the opportunity to make a more concrete statement of his opposition to fascism.

During the Spanish Civil War the republican Solidaridad Internacional Antifascista turned to the author of *The Death Ship*, hoping to win him over as a contributor to *Timon* , a magazine published in Barcelona. Traven's answer to "Comrade Herrera" appeared on May 22, 1938, in the Barcelona daily *Solidaridad Obrera* as "Una carta de Bruno Traven," signed "B. Traven." Traven wrote:

> Salud!
>
> I greet you and all workers, peasants, and Republican soldiers who are fighting so heroically in Spain against the fascist monster. I salute the great men and women whom Spain has brought forth in these times of struggle, who with their lives are silently writing a new history of humanity.
>
> Your letter, comrade Herrera, is the first to reach me from your country.
>
> Your invitation—for which I thank all members of the S.I.A.—represents the greatest honor bestowed on me to the present day. Unfortunately I am not in a position to accept this honor for reasons of which you certainly had no idea when you made me this offer.
>
> My command of German is very limited, far more limited than my knowledge of Spanish—which is seriously limited, as you can tell from the mistakes in this letter. On various occasions

I have stated in German magazines that I am not a German, by extraction, race, or blood. I spent time in Germany on only one occasion, before the 1914 war, and my knowledge of the country and its language and people is too limited for me to be able to judge the literary works of German writers.

I was born in North America and English is my mother tongue. As for judging English literary works, there are men in England at your disposal with more talent and fame than I have, and with them you will not be inconvenienced by the distance separating us which would impair my collaboration. Nonetheless, comrades, you have my sincerest thanks for your invitation.

If someone were to offer me a trip to Germany, all expenses paid, with every luxury, a guarantee of my own security, and thousands of dollars besides, rest assured that I would refuse the offer. So small is my desire to see that country in its state of enslavement today; I say the same to you in regard to the Italian "empire." An "empire" which is being broken into ever smaller pieces.

But on the other hand if the Spanish government (for Spain has but one government) would honor me with a passport and pay for the expenses, I would gladly accept the offer, so great is my desire to see and get to know Spain in the midst of its glorious struggle. But no, comrades, I would not go. I would take the money and buy cotton, evaporated milk, coffee, and cigarettes here and send them off to you directly. For however much I would like to visit Spain, I know that you need such things to win the war more quickly, while my presence in Spain is necessary neither to win the war nor to furnish you with good advice. You know very well what you need and what you want. You don't need a writer, not even one from the ranks of the revolutionary workers, to tell you how to improve your situation. You have had too many advisers, far more than you needed. If instead of the millions of words which they sent to you, you had a triple-engine plane for every million and a machine gun with plenty of ammunition for every hundred, you would have won the war over a year ago. Comrades, every unnecessary word is like a lost cartridge for you.

I would like to help you in some manner. Although my works have been translated into seventeen languages, I have no house and no money, only the most necessary clothing. I offer these details about my personal condition since it saddens me that I cannot help you as the Pope helped Pancho of Salamanca, whose jaw is still dropped in awe [a reference to Franco].

Nonetheless I do have something that I take great joy in putting at your disposal. I have my library. It is not large or luxurious. Why do I need it, when it can be of use to Spanish comrades in the war? This library includes magazines in English and Spanish. If you are interested in all my books and magazines, write to me, and I will send them to you. I will take care of the transportation costs. Send me the address.

Magazines and books are useful for hospitals, in the trenches, and for camps and schools where the new officers [or civil servants] are trained.

Everything I own is yours. I don't have to tell you that I wish you victory from the bottom of my heart, for I know that the workers, peasants, and Republican soldiers will emerge with total victory, even if the Italian and German invaders send in another 50,000 poor slaves and let them be slaughtered like sick cattle, hoping to get back the millions of marks and lire they have already lost on the peninsula.

You will enjoy victory before December, I believe. Perhaps your struggle will last longer. One year, two years. Who knows. But it's not a question of that: however long it takes, victory will be yours.

More than through your weapons, you will be victorious as a result of your sensible and progressive ideas. The republic of 1931 was only paper, and for that reason it couldn't survive. The republic born during this war, however, will be a republic arising from the blood of the people, from unimagineable suffering, superhuman sacrifices, it will be erected by heroic deeds, the likes of which have never before been seen in human history.

For these reasons, the republic which will remain after this struggle will last because its foundation will be so strong that it can never again be attacked by the enemies of progress, of civilization, and of humanity.

That is what I wished to tell you, Spanish comrades, and I thank you for your attention.

Salud!

B. Traven

In spite of the rhetorical flourishes, one has the overwhelming impression that Traven (whose loneliness and eagerness for communication is revealed throughout this letter) put his convictions above all else. The same voice can be heard in the novels.

The fact that Traven's offer of assistance came from Mexico had an unmistakable political symbolism. The government of President

Lázaro Cárdenas (1934–1940) stood firmly against the fascists. At that time Mexico was the only country besides the Soviet Union that did not recognize the Austrian Anschluss; and when the Spanish Civil War ended, Mexico proved more willing than any other country to take in the Spanish antifascists and members of the international brigades. Spain's republican government in exile established its headquarters in Mexico City, and Mexico did not recognize the Franco government. Thus Traven's land of choice developed into the Latin American bastion of antifascism.

Not only the German supporters of a republican Spain enjoyed a warm welcome in Mexico, but also the antifascist émigrés from Hitler's Germany. Numerous intellectuals and well-known writers took refuge there beginning in the mid-1930s: Otto Rühle, Theodor Balk, Anna Seghers, Bodo Uhse, Egon Erwin Kisch, Gustav Regler, Ludwig Renn, Alexander Abusch, Franz Pfemfert (Marut's kindred spirit from the *Brickburner* period), to name but a few. When Ernst Toller, Marut's comrade-in-arms in Munich, visited Mexico in 1937, the refugees from Nazi Germany founded the Liga pro Cultura Alemana, which was joined by the Heinrich-Heine-Klub in 1941 and the publishing house El Libro Libre the following year. These anti-Nazi intellectual organizations nonetheless were positioned precariously in a country that was officially antifascist: The German émigrés from earlier periods were generally nationalistic and provided a network for Nazi intelligence. The Nazis were an active political presence, not only in the underground, being involved in the coup attempt of General Saturnino Cedillo (1938) and threatening antifascist émigrés. The political climate in Mexico, particularly in Mexico City where Traven spent a good deal of time in these years, was thus highly explosive.

One could imagine that Traven, himself a victim of the Nazi blacklists, would have had contact with the exiled German intellectuals—who, for example, in May 1942, 1943, and 1944 commemorated the anniversary of the book burnings in large-scale ceremonies. The opposite was the case. True, he was not completely inaccessible to the exiled opponents of the Nazis: His estate includes a letter from Thomas Mann dated December 15, 1936, asking Traven (one assumes; the letter bears the generic appellation "Dear Sir") to support the "German literary emigration" by signing a proclamation; how Traven reacted is unknown. But he did take great pains to avoid any contact with the circles of German émigrés in

Mexico. This must have been difficult for him—all the more so as the emigrés saw in Traven not only an intellectual kindred spirit but also a model for how to behave in exile in Mexico, as Traven must have known. On August 21, 1941, he informed his Swedish publisher, not without a sense of pride, that on the occasion of the four-hundredth anniversary of Morelia, capital of the state of Michoacán, a dramatic adaptation of *The Rebellion of the Hanged* was performed; this piece had opened the season of the Teatro de las Artes on August 1, and seven further performances were planned. Ludwig Renn confirms this in his afterword to *The Cotton-Pickers* in the edition of the East Berlin publishing house Verlag der Nation (1954):

> Now the energetic young people [an amateur theater group] got help from a professional actor from the school of Stanislavsky and Max Reinhardt and performed an adaptation of Traven's novel "The Rebellion of the Hanged." The performance by what was originally an amateur company was so splendid that it was commissioned by the Secretary for Public Education to tour through the entire large country of Mexico. The troupe offered free performances in all the larger towns for an audience composed of all strata of society. Never before had Mexico seen good theater, only inferior North American troupes. The Mexicans were captivated by the force of the revolutionary play. Traven has that effect, and it is the effect that he intends.

Ludwig Renn was at that time professor at the University of Morelia. If his comments suggest that German émigré circles had a hand in bringing about Traven's initial success on the stage in Morelia, Traven never gave any sign of appreciation. The German and Austrian refugees in Mexico never saw him face to face. Even when he mentioned the "more than fifty performances" of *The Rebellion of the Hanged* that first introduced him to broad segments of the population, he made no mention at all of the antifascist German exiles in Mexico.

It nonetheless remains curious that on the rare occasions when Traven did mention the German émigrés as his devotees and admirers, he distanced himself from them. In the *BT News*, for instance, he faulted the way the exiles promoted his books in Mexico:

> European émigrés, who had fled to Mexico from the Nazis, published some of his books in Mexico, without asking him

> for permission or paying him royalties, since they saw themselves obligated, as they put it, to make Traven's books known to the Mexican people. It required great efforts on the part of Traven and a special decree from the Mexican president to put a stop to sales of these pirated editions. The responsible parties had the effrontery to maintain that Traven had long since died in Puebla and that his books could thus be printed without permission and without paying royalties.

The unauthorized translations Traven referred to are probably those he named in the foreword to *Puente en la selva* (Mexico City, 1941): *La rosa blanca* (translated by Pedro Geoffroy Rivas and Lia Kostakowsky, Mexico City, 1940) and *La rebelión de los colgados* (translated by Pedro Geoffroy Rivas, Mexico City, 1938). But if the German antifascist exiles in fact played a role in publishing these translations, there is no indication that it was meant to be a quasi-official homage to Traven.

What matters in any event is that Traven felt sure that it was the antifascist refugees who made life difficult for him by publishing the unauthorized Spanish editions. The new editions stirred up unwanted publicity, threatening to disrupt his already uncertain idyll on the Pacific, and they helped fan the rumor that the author was dead and that his literary legacy was free for the asking.

Though curious at first glance, Traven's effort to keep his distance from the German exiles gains plausibility when seen from this vantage point. But under the circumstances did it not make more sense for Traven to come to terms with the German exiles in Mexico? Why instead his radical withdrawal from them—creating an exile within an exile? Why did he keep his antifascist compatriots at arm's length when he could have joined their cause, which was also his own?

In fact, the exiled Germans represented a threat to him; they had come dangerously close to uncovering his secret or at least one of his secrets: that Traven and Ret Marut were one and the same. Traven's reaction was vehement, as can be seen from later documents, such as a letter of July 20, 1948, to Ernst Preczang, in which Oskar Maria Graf and Egon Erwin Kisch are identified as responsible for starting the Marut stories. A *BT News* article ("Die Mühlen Gottes mahlen langsam, aber . . ." ["The Mills of God Grind Slowly But . . ."]) mentions besides Kisch the journalist Heinrich Gutmann as the guilty party. Gutmann, one of the founders of the Liga pro

Cultura Alemana, it says, was found dead one day in a Mexico City street "with his head beaten in," which the article's author sees as a fitting end. He was "the first to circulate the mischievous Traum-(Traven)-Marut story and directly upon his arrival in Mexico he published extensive articles about it (surely to introduce himself in the most positive light at the same time), and also told this story to every newly arrived émigré."

Clearly, Traven's situation in Mexico in the 1930s and 1940s gained tragically ironic overtones as the trauma of the past compelled him to conceal himself from the very people who could have relieved his painful lack of communication. The man who forever led a life on the run now had to flee from the fugitives.

Esperanza López Mateos

The *authorized* Spanish versions of Traven's works that started appearing in 1941 were translated by Esperanza López Mateos, who played a pivotal role in Traven's life. She was the sister of Adolfo López Mateos, who served in the early and mid-1950s as Mexico's secretary of labor and from 1958 to 1964 as the country's president. From the early 1930s Esperanza was married to her cousin Roberto Figueroa, brother of Traven's friend Gabriel Figueroa, the well-known cameraman who filmed some of Traven's novels. It was thus no coincidence that film brought Esperanza and Traven together. Gabriel Figueroa, as he told Wyatt and confirmed to me as well, had read *The Bridge in the Jungle* and wanted to produce a film based on the book. According to the *BT News*, however, Esperanza herself came upon the novel in a Mexico City bookstore (in English, one assumes) and was taken by it at once—not surprising, as her political orientation ran close to Traven's. Esperanza wrote to Alfred Knopf on August 8, 1939, on letterhead of the Masas Press, where she worked at the time (in addition to her political acitivities and administrative duties at the Instituto de Cardiología): "I beg you to inform me if there is any possibility to obtain the film rights on B. Traven's novels 'Bridge in the Forest' and 'Hanged's Revolt,' and under which price and conditions. The company which desires to realize them is from any point of view, the best in this country." (The titles are curious: *The Rebellion of the Hanged* was not yet available in English—though it was in Spanish—nor was *The Bridge* available under the title Esperanza used.)

Traven had refused her the film rights, Figueroa told Wyatt. When E. López Mateos subsequently requested permission to translate Traven's works into Spanish, Traven at first declined (according to Figueroa)—no doubt because of "serious personal reasons," which must refer to his fear of publicity. But when she then took it upon herself to translate *The Bridge in the Jungle*—from the English—on her own and at her own expense, Traven welcomed the venture. Only then, apparently, did the two meet face to face, having corresponded to that point via Knopf. Traven insisted, Rosa Elena Luján has related, that the two meet on neutral ground, in a small town in the state of Michoacán in western Mexico. They took the same train, recognizing each other only upon disembarking. Whether this story is true or another of Traven's clever inventions, *Puente en la selva* was the first authorized Spanish version of a Traven novel, published in Mexico City in 1941 by A. P. Márquez. That same year, Esperanza became not only Traven's authorized Spanish translator but also his private secretary, letter writer, and agent. She later held copyrights to his books.

Esperanza sparked Traven's interest in reaching the Spanish-speaking market. As late as March 1939 the Zurich *Büchergilde* remarked that Traven had banned Mexican editions so that he could "write in peace." He did an about-face two and a half years later: "I still have no new book to offer you," he wrote on August 21, 1941, to Holmström, "because I am now very busy looking for getting my books out for the Latin American public and this takes up all my time at present." From this time, Traven's mail and royalties often came to Esperanza's Mexico City address, Avenida Coyoacán 1106 in the Del Valle quarter. She had his "unrestricted confidence," Traven informed Holmström on February 21, 1946. Esperanza also traveled to Switzerland in 1947 as Traven's representative, negotiating with Josef Wieder in Zurich and visiting Davos as well. Through 1951 she translated seven other Traven works for various Mexican publishers (though none for Masas): *Tesoro en la Sierra Madre* (1946), *Una canasta de cuentos mexicanos* (1946), *La carreta* (1949), *La rebelión de los colgados* (1950), *El barco de la muerte* (1950), *Gobierno* (1951), and *La rosa blanca* (1951). She translated for the most part from English, not from the German originals (according to the *BT News*, she learned German in the late 1940s and from then on translated from German). She committed suicide in 1951, but until late 1953 she was listed along with Wieder as editor of the *BT News*, and copyright notices bearing her name did not disappear until 1954.

Once she became associated with Traven in the Spanish-speaking world, Esperanza emerged as yet another candidate for author of the Traven novels. In a letter of July 30, 1946, Traven exhorted his Swedish publisher Holmström to deny this claim publicly—in a Mexican magazine, no less. The reporters, Traven claimed, hounded Señorita Mateos endlessly. "At various times, private detectives kept watch on her house for weeks on end; her letters were intercepted, her servants were bribed, and she was followed by secret agents wherever she went."

Esperanza López Mateos was "for ten years" Traven's "most faithful, his truest and his most honest representative," as Traven wrote, in English, some time after her death to a Señor Margáin. Nor was their relationship strictly professional. Esperanza was Traven's closest friend for almost a decade. During his visits to Acapulco and elsewhere he remained in contact with her, sending her books, magazines, and on one occasion a bottle of scorpions in alcohol along with sketches by Otto Dix entitled *War*. "Don't look at them at night," Traven warned her, "you might get bad dreams." The playful wit of this inventor of private myths surfaced in a letter of January 29, 1943, to Esperanza, in which he commented on a portrait photo of a well-known personality that had appeared in a magazine: She would also find the inverted V between the eyebrows on "a certain man whom you think you know. The mark on the right cheek you will find with a certain man exactly on the same spot, you may measure it and you'll find that there is hardly a difference of three or four hair-breadths." But, he went on to say, the family mark clearly visible in the photograph on the right earlobe appeared on the left ear of

> a certain man, whom you ought to know better, and this has been the mystery of the clan for the last thousand years, this mark is always changing from the left ear to the right and back again to the left, but it is always there and results from a definite custom which was in use for many thousand years before the mark stabilized. It is all written up in an old Bible, and I think, he, the one pictured, owns that bible, and it has always been that Bible which for centuries has caused all members of the clan to hate one another and never see each other, never speak to one another and not only ignore, but deny their existence.

> And so I cannot return the picture because I don't want you to know more than you actually know; and that's already more than you should ever have known.

This letter begins "Dear Woman." A week earlier he had sent a letter to "Dear Señorita Mateos" about their joint project of founding a publishing house. Esperanza advocated calling the venture Rayo, while Traven chose Tempestad. His explanation was illuminating: "I still insist Tempestad is better and so far the best I could discover. . . . Tempestad has so many meanings just if you come to think of [*sic*]. A tempest stirs up your soul and mind, all your physical body, it shakes you all over and through and through but not to destroy you, no, after the tempest is over the atmosphere is clear, the sky is clear and blue again, the sun comes out, you feel easy in mind and heart, you as the whole nature are refreshed and energetic, full of dynamics, ready to tackle the hardest job. Everybody having read a book published by Editorial Tempestad should feel exactly as he felt after a heavy tempest, clear of mind, younger, ready and willing to conquer the world, daring to write a book ten times better than the one he just read." Nothing came of the project.

Esperanza's death shook Traven deeply. He wrote to the American author Sanora Babb and her husband, cameraman James Wong Howe, on October 31, 1951:

> After long and horrible sufferings which she, heroine that she always was, tried so very hard not to let anybody know about Esperanza died.
>
> Mexico, no, the Americas have lost one of the most wonderful and extraordinarily highly gifted women with dear Esperanza.
>
> At this moment there is nothing else I can say except this: May she rest in peace.

He was still haunted by her memory a year and a half later. On February 6, 1953, he wrote again to Babb and Howe:

> As to E. I am not over it yet and have been unable to adjust myself to her leaving. I see her still everywhere, wherever we have been together, be it in a café, or restaurant, or in a certain street, or in a certain park, or in a certain movie.

On November 25, 1953, he wrote to Sanora Babb: "As to E. and how I feel I cannot write about it."

Political Journalism at War's End

Esperanza saw her dream of a film version of a Traven novel realized with John Huston's *Treasure of the Sierra Madre* (1948), featuring Humphrey Bogart and Walter Huston. Before this breakthrough into the film medium, which introduced Traven to a far greater audience than he had ever enjoyed in print, Esperanza helped increase Traven's visibility in a different direction—the political sphere. Just as Marut had turned to political journalism in the final year of the First World War with *The Brickburner*, Traven, in the final year of the Second World War, published articles on contemporary political developments.

As the Second World War drew to an end, Traven understandably wished to express himself publicly on global political trends. He must have felt under considerable pressure during the war. As he kept his distance from the German antifascist émigrés, with whom he might have made common cause, he must have observed with clenched teeth the nationalist or even pro-Hitler Germans in Mexico. In his letter to Josef Wieder in late 1946 resuming his ties to Europe, he suddenly vented his long pent-up bitterness on political developments, pulling no punches in speaking of the Germans. He said he was "convinced that [the Germans] will start swinging again in twenty or thirty years." He did not condemn any of the former Büchergilde workers for their political orientation during the Nazi years, he claimed. All the more harsh was his verdict of the Germans in Mexico (the original German text reveals how much his command of his native tongue had deteriorated): "And just as in 1919 they are starting here to spread their tear-jerking stories about the lot of the poor, tormented Germans under foreign occupation, how they suffer and are suppressed by the powers which call themselves democratic nations." These Mexico Germans, like their compatriots in Germany, had saluted Hitler's victory "with thunderous roars and truckloads of champagne." Many Germans, he conceded, had no doubt remained "upright," but "maybe because they had more luck at not being caught by the Gestapo spies." "Ten months before the War was over," he told Wieder, he wrote an essay that "did not paint the Germans in a very favorable light"—the distinction between Germans and Nazis was blurred, as in his earlier remarks. He had sent the piece "to some twenty newspapers and magazines in the U.S., but none of them printed it. One newspaper replied: 'We are not about to print dynamite.' The article was published in Mexico several weeks ago." He invited Wieder to translate and publish it. The essay in question, undiscovered to date, appeared on November 9, 1946, in *Mañana*, "a certain important magazine in Mexico," as Traven informed Holmström (whom he encouraged to translate the text, while mentioning the "dynamite"). Another political essay had appeared even before the *Mañana* article.

Traven's political analyses were far from sophisticated. Rather, they merit our attention as public statements of his political activism. Traven's pacifism had not changed since his *Brickburner* days, though it was now wedded with a more profound skepticism.

This is particularly evident in the first of the two articles, "La tercera guerra mundial," which appeared in 1945 in the magazine *Estudios sociales*. "One does not need to be a prophet to predict that a new World War is inevitable," the essay began—half a year after the end of the Second World War. The Allies, the article contended, now had the opportunity to divide the world up among themselves, naturally through armed conflict. Such a conclusion was evident in 1945 not only because the Second World War was not propagandized as the "war to end all wars" as had been the First, but, more important, because democracy had not emerged as the clear victor. To the contrary, Traven wrote, the result of the Second World War had been ideological confusion: the democracies continued to acknowledge the Franco regime, which had come to power through the Nazis and the fascists; they gave no sign of abandoning their conviction that fascism was the sole bastion against bolshevism. (Churchill, to whom this passage referred above all, had the "*idea del mundo*" of a police sergeant.) The war had not been waged to root out fascism, Traven claimed, but to temper it: to replace its brutal leaders with more normal, human figures in the name of a so-called democratic spirit that signified little practical change, however. The fascist leaders had been dangerous because the future of capitalism was as insecure under them as under communist totalitarianism. The Western Allies had thus waged the war solely to bolster capitalism, in spite of all the talk of democracy and human rights. But their efforts had been in vain: The artificial democracies of the postwar period would sooner or later be transformed into the "wildest bolshevism" that the world had ever seen. Stalin, Traven continued, was the only one to see that; so he could afford to sit idly by while the British liberated Greece. "Since 1917 bolshevism has grown fat as a result of the stupidity perpetrated by democratic governments."

Traven stressed two factors that would lead to a new world war: the expansion of the American navy and a peacetime draft. "Giant fleets were never built solely for undertaking pleasure cruises or for viewing the landscape." He saw the danger coming from the military "caste," consolidated into a major power base ("*una institución permanente*") that viewed war as inevitable. Its existence thus justified, the military would directly or indirectly aid in planting the seeds of conflict. Traven considered three scenarios plausible for the start of the next war, which would break out before 1950: Russia and England against the United States, England and the United States against Russia, and the United States against England (with Russia remaining neutral). "Lasting peace would be possible if the superpowers wanted true peace," he wrote. "The fact is, however, that no government is or ever was interested in lasting peace." War would thus result, and the United States would provide the financing as it had for the last two wars. A ray of hope remained, however: General Marshall was not enthusiastic about a draft. Traven hailed him as "one of the greatest and most sincere sons of a democratic America"—only to conclude with the satiric cry to found and defend empires. "And why not? Yes, why the hell not?"

The second foray into political writing, published in *Mañana*, was entitled "Dónde y cuándo perdió Alemania la guerra" ("Where and When Germany Lost the War"). An editor's note mentioned the role of Esperanza López Mateos and her rumored identity with Traven, which the editor did not endorse. It was through her, he stated, that the hitherto unpublished text came to the magazine, having been composed in October 1944 and translated into Spanish in November 1944. *Life*, *The New York Times*, *The New Republic* and other publications had considered printing the essay too risky: "We can't print dynamite."

Where and when did the Germans lose the war? Traven offered ten popular answers and then provided his own—a startling solution, even if one dismisses it as the speculation of a political amateur with no firsthand information. According to Traven's analysis, in September 1939, within only two weeks of the outbreak of the war, as Soviet troops marched into Poland and Hitler and Stalin established a partition plan, the Germans had already lost the war. Stalin emerged as the real mastermind, even more strongly than in Traven's 1945 essay. Stalin, who more than any other understood Hitler and took him seriously, carefully prepared long beforehand the chain of events that led to the war and the end of the war. His nonagression pact with Germany (August 24, 1939) was calculated to win time. His occupation of eastern Poland, the Baltic, and Bessarabia was a cunning act of aggression against Hitler, with whom he appeared to be on good terms at the time. For Stalin had realized that before Hitler could begin his campaign of world domination, he would need the granaries of the Ukraine and the Russian oil fields. Based on information from his own secret service and his correct interpretation of Hitler's ultimate intentions, Stalin thus knew "immediately that the Nazis' invasion of Poland [in early September 1939] was actually the first step of the march toward Russia"—the "Drang nach Osten," as Traven identified it (in German). Stalin foresaw not only that Hitler ultimately aimed at conquering the Soviet Union but also that Germany was in no position to do so at that time. Stalin's diplomatic prowess in pursuing his *own* goals of gaining access to the Baltic and control over the Dardanelles therefore lay in his ability to entice Hitler into war against Russia. "The Nazis were to attack not when they wanted it, but when Stalin did," Traven wrote. The embarrassing "comedy" of the Russians invading Finland in the winter of 1939–1940 was intended solely to incite the Germans to attack Russia, to make them believe that it was a lame giant, a Goliath who could not deal with the David of Finland. When Russia finally did bring the Finns to their knees, the Nazi propagandists attributed the victory to the strategic assistance rendered by a German general—exactly as the Russians would have desired. "The Nazis were so impressed by their effective lies that it never occurred to them that Stalin had staged the little comedy for the sole purpose of forcing the Nazis into war with Russia soon thereafter, at a time when England and quite possibly the United States would already find themselves at war with Germany." Stalin's calculation was of course correct, Traven said. Hitler attacked in the summer of 1941. But by occupying eastern Poland and expanding the Russian sphere of influence westward, Stalin had already mapped out the course of the war: His gambit signaled the beginning of the end of the Nazi dream of world domination. If Stalin had not marched into Poland in mid-September 1939, Traven contended, "Russia might still exist today, but England would not, at least not in Europe." He concluded with the grotesque twist: "The day will come when the picture of Saint George will have to look like Stalin. Why not?"

It makes little sense to discuss the accuracy of Traven's facts or the merits of his political analysis. It is nonetheless significant to realize that Traven's political philosophy not only had its roots in his Munich period in a general way, but also fit particularly well in the Mexican political landscape: opposition to bourgeois capitalism, fascism, imperialism, and militarism are motifs both from *The Brickburner* and the postrevolution Mexican politics that Traven welcomed. In this sense these essays reveal just how fitting was Marut's reemergence in Mexico. There he found more than merely shelter and protection from persecution. His voice, a lone cry amid the turbulent final years of the German empire and the early years of the Weimar Republic, could count on resonance in Mexico. And the desire for resonance—resonance around the world, social and political resonance—had increasingly become Traven's driving force in the final quarter century of his life.

The Treasure of the Sierra Madre and Other Films: The Trials of Publicity

After the completion of the Mahogany cycle and especially with the arrival of Esperanza López Mateos's political activism and entrepreneurial spirit, Traven underwent a marked change in the way he viewed his work. He now strove for a new and broader appeal than he had previously desired or thought possible—in the 1940s, Traven discovered film as a medium. He turned to film about a year after Esperanza's letter expressing interest in acquiring the film rights to his works. In a letter of August 29, 1940, Traven asked the Hollywood agent Paul Kohner to consider the possibility of a screenplay based on *The Bridge in the Jungle*. Traven did not see film primarily as a profit generator—his concept of film was the antithesis of what is normally associated with Hollywood. "The picture should, in a way, be no picture at all as we have come to accept pictures. It should be an entirely new kind of symphony . . . so strong that the audience even imagines to smell the exotic perfumes of the jungle and the cheap soap which the women used when bathing." Traven sought to redefine film not only in aesthetic but also in ideological terms. The plot of *The Bridge in the Jungle*, he noted in the letter to Kohner, would be insignificant in a film version. Films of the future "will be pictures in which the plot is superseded by the idea, by the basic argument which led up to the plot, and the plot will be used merely to make visible the tendency the writer had in mind and wanted to drive home." Similar impulses had been evident in music since the days of Haydn; directors could now realize in their films what Beethoven and Mozart as well as Verdi and Rossini had achieved. Without discussing Traven's conception of music and opera, we may say that his conception of film recalls his *Brickburner* activism as well as the reformist tendencies of his Mexican novels.

Traven's turn to film—several of his novels were to be filmed with his cooperation into the 1960s—comes as a surprise only when one recalls that before 1940 Traven had expressed nothing but disinterest in screen versions of his works. When Preczang in the 1920s brought up the idea of a *Death Ship* film, Traven opposed the project. And when the German film production company Ufa announced in 1931 that it hoped to produce a *Death Ship* film, *Die Büchergilde* stated that Traven had "repeatedly" declined offers from the film industry; he was not, however, opposed in principle to the idea of film adaptations that preserved the sociopolitical impetus of the originals:

> Traven reserves for himself an undistorted presentation of his works as film, and no offer of dollars, regardless how great, can sway him from his principles. In late March a Berlin daily published a notice that the actor Albers intends to produce a "Death Ship" film for Ufa and that for this reason they wished to find "the supposedly unlocatable author B. Traven," so that a contract could be signed. This notice bears all the earmarks of a publicity stunt. Traven will not consider doing business with the Ufa of Mr. Hugenberg. A "Death Ship" film with a happy ending—that would please them just fine. Traven does not write to make money, he writes to give expression to his worldview and to stiffen the spines of workers of all countries against profiteers like the Ufa people.

Traven apparently did not think at the time that the film industry would want to back a production that could amount to a battle in the struggle of the oppressed, as his books did. This may also have been one of the reasons that he withdrew the film rights from

Doubleday, Doran in New York, though he had no intention of awarding them elsewhere. And even in 1938, in serious financial straits, Traven passed up the opportunity to have several of his novels filmed by the French company Synops. (It is unknown whether Traven answered a request from Bernhard Diebold in Zurich of July 20, 1937, asking if Traven would permit the agency Filmstoff Vertrieb Thema to offer Traven's books to film producers.) It was only around 1940, no doubt under the influence of Esperanza, that Traven seems to have accepted the proposition that he could achieve his sociopolitical, didactic goals as effectively on film as with the printed word—more effectively, in fact, through the mass appeal of the medium. In the meantime, he had of course lost a great segment of his readership through political events.

It was still several years before his first film—*The Treasure of the Sierra Madre*—appeared, in January 1948. Warner Brothers had acquired the film rights in 1941 and had signed John Huston as director. Traven, via his agent Paul Kohner, was then invited to come to Hollywood to discuss Huston's prospective screenplay. Traven answered on November 17, 1941 that Huston should rather come to Mexico before starting on the screenplay to get a flavor for the ambiance of this book about gold prospectors—and of his other novels as well, which would also be suitable film subjects. Pearl Harbor was attacked twenty days later; Huston was drafted and producer Henry Blanke convinced Warner Brothers to hold off production until the end of the war. Contact was resumed only in 1946. Huston initiated an intensive correspondence with "Croves," who wrote interminably about the fine points of the screenplay. Though Huston authored the screenplay, Traven had meanwhile penned a script and sent it to Huston.

Huston naturally wanted to meet Traven; he told Traven he would come to Mexico City, since Traven apparently disliked traveling north. Huston arrived and waited for almost a week in his hotel without hearing a word from the mysterious author. Finally one day, Huston relates in the Traven chapter in his autobiography *An Open Book*, a slight man appeared in Huston's hotel room at dawn and handed Huston—still in bed—a business card identifying him as Hal Croves, translator from Acapulco and San Antonio. Croves brought a letter from Traven explaining that he was ill but that his friend Hal Croves knew just as much about Traven's works as the author himself and was authorized to answer all questions in his place. The two met again in Acapulco, where Croves proved himself very knowledgeable about Traven's works but less than adroit at deep-sea fishing—Evelyn Keyes, Huston's wife at the time, recalls in her autobiography that Croves, the erstwhile seaman, wore a suit and tie on their Pacific excursion.

Shooting started in Tampico in the spring of 1947. After only a week the Mexican government halted production; the Americans were accused of showing Mexico in a bad light. Production resumed only after two of Huston's friends—one was Diego Rivera—appealed to the Mexican president. In April the film crew, following the trail of the novel's gold prospectors, headed into the Sierra Madre to a village near San José Purúa in the state of Michoacán, some 130 miles west of the capital, where local Indians watched and worked on the production. Traven kept up his incognito—Hal Croves had been hired by Huston for $100 per week ($150 in some versions) as a technical adviser. In this capacity he explained in lavish detail to his American colleagues what Traven would want regarding various aspects of the filming; he considered Huston's father, Walter Huston, much too young for the part of the prospector Howard, for example. Croves never let on to being Traven, though he clearly shared at least one trait with the author—acute camera shyness.

The release of *The Treasure of the Sierra Madre* in January 1948 sparked considerable publicity in the American press—with much of the attention directed to the behind-the-scenes stories of filming in Mexico and Croves's mysterious presence. The film was called by *Life* magazine "one of the half a dozen or so in recent years which genuinely deserve to be called 'great.' " *Time* labeled Walter Huston's performance the greatest of his long career; Humphrey Bogart had also found his best role to date, while John Huston had established himself among the first rank of directors. Both magazines also spoke of the curious incidents involving Croves during filming. Croves wrote complaints to the editors of both *Time* and *Life*, correcting their depictions of his role. He was most intent on setting the record straight that he was not Traven, as the magazines had at least conjectured. He played the old theme with a new variation: If he were Traven, Huston would have paid him closer to $1,000 per week; if the $100 per week paid to Croves had really been meant for Traven, that would represent an unbelievably low opinion of Traven, "the man, or the woman, as the case might be, whose story gave Mr. John Huston the chance of his lifetime." The tone of self-importance recalls the correspondence of the isolated émigré. Huston, who had intimated that Croves and Traven were one, would never again get a chance to film a Traven novel, Croves added in his letter to *Life*. "A writer of books like the ones Traven created and which have been published in 20 different countries will be read, loved and admired, or, yes, perhaps severely criticized still when nobody any longer can remember a movie director who, once upon a time, long, long ago, did a picture based on a story by said writer."

In spite of this prophecy of short-lived fame for the movie (unfulfilled, of course), Traven took inordinate pride in the film's success. As mentioned earlier, he tried promoting the film in Sweden even before production began: He had sent promotional copy to his publisher Holmström on February 5, 1947, which was to be forwarded to some one hundred newspapers and magazines. When the movie was released, Traven delighted—understandably—in the praise accorded both the director and actors. As late as 1951 he had a notice published in the *BT News* that he also intended for wider circulation in the press:

> The film, after the novel of the same name by B. Traven, ran for many weeks in Mexico City's largest cinema, with each of the three daily shows sold out. A monumental success, when one considers that in Mexico a film rarely stays on the program for more than a week. At 4 Mexican dollars per ticket, the theater took in 22,700 Mexican dollars the first Sunday the film ran. In New York the film also sold out weeks in advance. The critics called the film the most significant work since the creation of the sound picture. Most of the film was to be shot outside the studio. Individual scenes were shot in Tampico, the rest in the Sierra Madre, only a small part in a forest in California, and only 5% in the studio. The studio work was necessary, since strong winds on a certain mountain both night and day made filming impossible. So the mountain was shot from all sides, reconstructed with wood and plaster in the studio, and fitted with trees and bushes brought in from Mexico. That required six weeks of work at a cost of 60,000 dollars. With the exception of the death of Cody Lacaud in a fight with the bandits (in the novel he is left behind in the Sierra Madre), nothing in the novel's plot was changed. The screenplay had to be submitted to the author for approval. In addition, Traven sent one of his colleagues to oversee the filming so that nothing would be pret-

> tified. It is well known that the film garnered three Oscars. In addition, the Screen Writers' Guild awarded the author of the novel a special citation for best adventure story. Traven is the only author to date so honored who was not present to receive the award.

A success of such magnitude could only stir up the old question of the author's identity. Both *Time* and *Life* made the case of "Mexico's Mysterious Stranger" more interesting than the mystery of the film's success. "The mysterious B. Traven," *Time* wrote, "has an enormous following in Europe, but nothing is known of him except that he has lived invisibly, somewhere in Mexico, for many years." *Life* introduced him as "the mystery man of modern letters," and included a report by Dwight Whitney, who had allegedly "smoked out" Traven, but in fact merely passed on some of the stories of Croves's antics in San José Purúa. *The New York Times* was equally fascinated by the "invisible and mysterious" Traven—and equally unable to come up with tangible evidence. The only thing known for certain was that no one knew anything or would divulge anything about him. Huston hardly exaggerated in *An Open Book*: "The question of his identity became a matter of public controversy. Everyone was talking about the B. Traven mystery." The prize supposedly offered at this time by *Life* for unmasking the real Traven further powered the rumor mill.

Traven himself could have foreseen that such publicity was inevitable. Long before the filming, he had written to journalist Herbert Arthur Klein:

> Please cut out that goddamn mysterious if you mention my name or my work. There is no mystery about me, truly, not even a dot of a mystery. I am such a plain mug that any time a captain of a tramp will sign me on as a stoker and never even think that I might have some intelligence enough to be a fair A.B. All my mystery is that I hate columnists, feature writers, sobsisters, reviewers who don't know anything about the book they talk about. There is no greater joy and satisfaction for me as to be unknown as a writer if meeting somebody or going places. Only this way I can be myself and have no obligation to act up. Only in this way I can say what I really wish to say without being reminded by some high-stuffed or high-brow that a writer of such a great reputation shouldn't talk so silly. If this attitude of mine is called mystery . . . I wonder what one expects

> of somebody who is really a mystery . . . Over there in Hollywood every man who can write four lines with only one mistake in spelling calls the [*sic*] Greta Garbo the Mystery woman. What is so mysterious about her? Everybody knows everything about her, even the name and birth dates of her great-grandparents and the interior decoration of the rooms she slept in while on a trip in Italy with Leopold the Great.

(The comparison with Greta Garbo is amusing. Traven seems to have admired her greatly; in 1946 he instructed his Swedish publisher Axel Holmström to send Garbo an article about her from a Mexican newspaper along with copies of three Traven books.)

The public guessing game about Traven's identity reached its most fevered pitch with the interview, covering several days, into which the young Mexican journalist Luis Spota ensnared the innkeeper Torsvan in Acapulco in late July 1948. Spota, having cornered his prey, published a sensational report that resonated far beyond Mexico's borders. Spota's coverage was unique in that it brought the author himself on the stage—with the result that Torsvan admitted to being Traven. After August 7, 1948, when Spota's extensive article, complete with photos, appeared in the Mexican weekly *Mañana*, Torsvan could no longer take refuge in the role of the harmless gringo living inconspicuously in a tropical orchard on the edge of a sleepy Acapulco.

The interview, which also has the singular advantage of affording a vivid impression of Traven's concrete, physical presence, was more accurately an ambush. Spota claimed to have long been interested in Traven. But *The Treasure of the Sierra Madre* provided the immediate impetus for his project. After the film the shadowy figure of Hal Croves was asking to be "unmasked." According to Spota's own report, the scene played out as follows.

Spota got his first clue through a Mexican friend who was involved in the filming; it suggested that Traven (Croves) resided in the state of Guerrero. When Spota subsequently discovered (he was very vague about his method of discovery) that a post office box had been rented under the name Berick Traven Torsvan at the Banco de México in Mexico City since 1934, he knew he was on to something. The renter of the box, he learned, had left instructions that he could be reached via certain post office boxes in Mexico City. Who paid for these boxes? A certain María de la Luz Martínez, Spota learned. The house in Mexico City, in which she had lived, according to available information, had already been torn down by the time Spota started following this trail. It was then back to Torsvan. Incredibly, Spota did manage to uncover the card at the alien registration office that Traven Torsvan had filled out on July 12, 1930. The card identified a man with American citizenship, born on March 5, 1890, in Chicago, 1.68 meters tall, blond, straight nose, white skin, blue eyes, no beard or mustache, no special marks, unmarried, engineer by profession, native language English, speaks Spanish, Protestant faith, entry in 1914 via Ciudad Juárez. "By chance" Spota then got his hands on Torsvan's 1942 identity card listing his address as Acapulco.

On July 17, 1948, Spota and a colleague arrived at the garden restaurant El Parque Cachú in Acapulco, posing as government officials on vacation. A shy, short man approached them; he was wearing an ancient straw hat, old flannel trousers, an old shirt, and worn-out canvas sandals, and he was carrying a high-quality camera. His face was wrinkled, thin, and tanned, his eyes blue, his thin lips almost invisible, his hair sandy with touches of gray, his hands calloused; fragile but muscular and in the best of health—such was Spota's first impression of the innkeeper and novelist. (At their next meeting two days later, Traven was carefully groomed and better dressed.) He was a highly unusual man, according to María de la Luz Martínez: "He is not sociable, he has no friends, he speaks with no one, and works a lot in the garden and in his 'oficina.' " He nonetheless sat talking with Spota over beer for four and a half hours at their first encounter. Torsvan did remain rather taciturn, offering two or three sentences in his "good Spanish" and then falling silent. In any case, he did not shrink from the uninvited guests. He claimed to be an American of Swedish extraction (on one of the following days he was of Norwegian and "20 percent"[!] Scottish extraction); he had been in Mexico since 1913, he said, but was not naturalized. (If someone presented a birth certificate, he added two days later, who could prove that this person is in fact the one listed on the document?) The finca seemed to keep him well occupied, as he put into it "the sweat of his work, drops of blood, and even tears."

When the *Mañana* detectives returned two days later, Traven was combatting insects, especially ants. They talked for hours again. The gringo claimed to have done away with 32,000 ants on a single day. The conversation turned to the struggle between the Israelis and the Arabs and then to the Bible. The host advised his guests where to buy the "most complete" Bible in Mexico City and supposedly attempted to convert Spota's colleague to Protestantism.

At this point, Spota was not yet certain that his partner in conversation was the novelist B. Traven. Again, chance came to his aid. He had convinced someone at El Parque Cachú to let him look at all incoming letters for 10 pesos each. On 20 July he set his eyes on a document that solved the mystery ("*termina el misterio*"). The letter in question, from Gabriel Figueroa, was addressed to "Estimado Sr. Martínez." Figueroa, writing at the request of Esperanza López Mateos, enclosed a letter from Josef Wieder "para el Sr. Traven." This letter concerned a royalty payment that Traven had complained about not receiving. Esperanza—then in the hospital—had scribbled a short note about this financial transaction to Traven ("V." for "Viking," her pet name for Traven) at the bottom of Wieder's letter. Thus mail for Traven was being forwarded through Esperanza López Mateos, Traven's translator (so identified on the title page of Traven books), it was addressed to Martínez, and it arrived at El Parque Cachú, residence of Berick Traven Torsvan!

On the day he saw the Figueroa letter, Spota and his colleague talked with the innkeeper for five hours in the house and garden. They discussed North American and Mexican politics, the therapeutic qualities of cashew juice, the plight of the Indians, and even Traven, "the author of the books," as if he were someone else. But in the "last minute" of the conversation Torsvan let down his guard. "When I was working in the oil fields, they called me the Swede. That irked me so much that I decided not to use my typically Scandinavian name Torsvan any longer. Since then I've called myself B. Traven." *Myself*! The suspect played right into the hands of the sleuths, confirming that the fruit farmer Torsvan and the Nobel hopeful Traven were the same. Not that Torsvan had shied away from discussing Traven earlier in their talks, but he had spoken of him only in the third person. Since 1934–1935 Traven had not written a single line, Torsvan claimed; after the thirtieth page of *La rebelión de los colgados*, one could note a definite break: "It seems that the author experienced a crisis, an illness, some anomaly." His legal representative, Esperanza López Mateos, had been in Davos a year earlier—and Davos, Torsvan noted, was not only a sanitorium for those with respiratory ailments, as Thomas Mann depicted it in

The Magic Mountain, but also a center of therapy for mental patients. "You may think of that what you will!" Did Torsvan wish to imply that the author of the novels was in an asylum, having given up writing after some sort of breakdown? The suggestion was clear enough, though it was not a statement of fact. In any case, Torsvan denied being B. Traven. "I am not the man you think I am. B. Traven is my cousin. But he is no longer alive; he is dead. I am Torsvan."

A few days later, on July 26, Spota grabbed the bull by the horns. He and a photographer shadowed the gringo on his daily walk to the post office and the newspaper stand. The camera started clicking and Torsvan ran off in a panic. His pursuers cornered him; they all agreed to sit down in a bar over a beer. "But everyone pays for himself," said Torsvan. He wanted to be left in peace. No, he was not Traven. The author of the books had left the country years earlier to avoid "difficulties." Where he went Torsvan did not know, nor could he reveal Traven's real name. The writer, his cousin, called himself Barbick Traven, while he, Torsvan, used the name Berick. Why the similarity? "One of our ancestors, a Norwegian sailor, was shipwrecked off the coast of Maine in the United States. In a village called Barbick they treated him so well that he vowed he would name his children after the town. That is why my cousin and I have such similar names." "Mr. Traven is a simple man, he has never hurt anyone, and he does not want any honors. He only wants to live in peace"—just like Torsvan. He had been offered honorary Mexican citizenship—Torsvan now suddenly spoke of Traven in the first person—but he did not want any honors or banquets. His Swiss publishers said he could have Swiss citizenship and even the Nobel Prize, but he didn't want the publicity. The author had been offered $250,000 a short while before for delivering a few lectures, but he declined. The attempt to distinguish between Torsvan and Traven yielded to a curious confusion of identities.

Compounding the confusion, Torsvan went on to admit to some involvement in the Traven novels. The innkeeper with the calloused hands who spent his days wiping out colonies of ants discussed Traven's novels with a tone of authority and even claimed to have furnished the author with the "theme" of *The Bridge in the Jungle* (based on a real incident, he said). A remarkable admission, for here Traven himself offered a version of the "other man" hypothesis—in a dire emergency and with the clear intention of throwing off his interrogator, who had come too close to his secret. Torsvan was not Traven, but he—and not only he—had given the author some help with his work. "I am sure that B. Traven did not write his books alone," Spota quoted Traven as saying. "If you carefully examine his works, you will find sections which only a woman, a very intelligent woman, could have written. . . . I do not know if that was Señorita Mateos. . . . But it is evident that he had help ["*colaboración ajena*"]. . . . Traven has seen very little of what he wrote about; indeed, I can almost say that the majority of his subjects were told to him by others. He worked in Tampico in the office of an oil company; he never went into the bush and never came in contact with the people. For that reason there are so many mistakes in all his novels. . . . Only someone who does not know this country could have written what B. Traven wrote." Torsvan, on the other hand, claimed to know Mexico well; he had even discovered an unknown Indian tribe in Chiapas (no, he replied, not the Lacandones), he confided the next day to his difficult guests.

As a farewell gesture, Torsvan invited Spota and his colleague—but not the photographer—one more time into his house, which was guarded by a pack of dogs. In the mud hut he served them a roasted wild goose and told them the parable of the man who goes on a wild goose chase and returns with nothing, having seen but a "phantom." In other words: Anyone who saw B. Traven in Torsvan was on the wrong trail. Certainly he, Torsvan, was a writer: He penned articles for American magazines, many of which had been returned as unusable; he even suggested that Spota write an essay about ants based on materials that Torsvan could provide—the essay would be published under Spota's name, of course. Did Torsvan hope to stage a working relationship with Spota, as he supposedly had enjoyed with Traven?

The world-famous B. Traven was none other than the innkeeper Berick Traven Torsvan in Acapulco. That was Spota's sensational revelation in *Mañana* on August 7, 1948.

Before the story could make the rounds in Europe, Torsvan was already denying it. The Mexican daily *El Universal* published his rebuttal only four days later, on page one of its August 11 issue, and the same text appeared on August 14 in the Mexican weekly *Hoy* (which on July 31 had curiously published its own solution to the "*misterio*"). T. Torsvan summarily and indignantly dismissed all major points of Spota's story. Certainly, the royalty payment from

Wieder to Traven via the López Mateos/Martínez address was meant for him—as a royalty not for the Traven books but rather for Torsvan's representing the author's interests in Mexico and the United States, as well as for some four hundred photographs taken by Torsvan that had appeared in various Traven books and articles. The renowned author Traven would, in any case, command considerably higher royalties; his income from the *Sierra Madre* film alone would amount to thousands of dollars per month. Besides, Traven had left Mexico in 1930 because of difficulties with unspecified authorities. Most of Traven's mail was still addressed to Mexico and was also sent from Mexico, but only so publishers and readers could more easily accept the authenticity of Traven's books. (It is curious how the theme of deception played an important role in this deceptive maneuver itself.) Indeed, some circumstances led Torsvan to believe that the author of the books had died some time ago; all the honors paid to him, including "*posiblemente*" the Nobel Prize, thus came too late. (In statements like this Torsvan skillfully promoted both his own interests—being left alone—and the fame of B. Traven, as he did with the reference to the *Sierra Madre* success.) Although he did not know whether Traven was still alive, he, Traven Torsvan, was one of only three people who were in a position to identify the person or persons who was (or were) the world-famous author; yet no one could bribe any of these three into breaking faith, not even with $100,000.

But for a moment, the old man left himself exposed in his desperate game of cat-and-mouse with the reporter. He explained the coincidence of his first name and that of the author's pseudonym as follows in his letter to the newspapers: If Spota had more experience in life, he would know that there is no more secure way of fleeing into anonymity than by assuming the name of a living person who—by certain twists of fate, "*por ciertas coincidencias*"—*could* be the one borrowing the name. Literature abounds with such cases, he noted (a reference to Ret Marut, who presented himself to the London police as Otto Feige?). Torsvan clearly alluded to Marut, as he remarked in his rebuttal that Traven's first book had been written in 1916—the year in which *To the Honorable Miss S . . .* by Richard Maurhut appeared in Munich. Even with his back against the wall, Traven was participating in that biographical striptease he found so irresistible when he penned his novels.

At the conclusion of this long rebuttal, Torsvan once again turned to self-promotion while protecting his own privacy: "Until 1920, Mexico and the Mexicans were internationally more or less undiscovered, unknown, and scarcely acknowledged. Solely through the books of B. Traven, currently published throughout the world with some twenty million copies sold to date, Mexico has won the place among the nations of the earth which is owed to its size and stature." But only Traven and not he, Torsvan, deserved recognition. Torsvan was being dragged without reason into this affair, "which in the last six years has grown from a microbe to a monster which seems to darken the entire sky of Mexico." Grandiloquence in the guise of modesty: yet another variation of the lone man self-condemned to anonymity, yet preoccupied with his fame.

Torsvan's story—had he left it at that—might have settled the matter. But a few weeks later, the publisher of *Mañana* received a typed letter from B. Traven in London, writing that Spota was in error: He, Traven, the author of the novels, was in fact living in London; he was not the innkeeper on the Camino del Pie de la Cuesta. Spota immediately had the letter examined for authenticity at the laboratory of the Instituto Politécnico Nacional. The stationery, it turned out, came from Mexico, and both typewriter and ribbon corresponded to those that Torsvan used at his house in Acapulco. Another Traven canard: In desperation, he had sent the letter from Acapulco or Mexico City (where he stayed briefly with Gabriel Figueroa following the interview) to his English agent, requesting that it be forwarded to *Mañana*, postmarked London. Spota's fame was secured, Torsvan's cover blown for good.

Torsvan's reaction was almost hysterical—if anything was published about him, he would emigrate, he told Spota. Or he would kill himself, as Spota later reported to Wyatt. Naturally Traven had a lot at stake: His peaceful days of anonymity in the orchard were apparently over, requiring him to find a new place to stay and to create a new incognito—a reasonable assumption for the man on the run, though he ended up staying in Acapulco to the mid-1950s.

A further circumstance made Traven's situation even more precarious at this time and helps to explain his extreme reaction to Spota's intrusions: Traven's German past, his life as Marut, threatened to come to light in spite of all efforts to the contrary. Axel Holmström had written to the author on February 22, 1947, that

Traven was rumored to be the Brickburner from Munich. (As late as 1960, in the *BT News*, Traven struck back with a vengeance against the identification with Marut in an article signed "Josef Wieder," though this formal distinction makes little difference.) In the very week of the Spota interview, on July 20, 1948, Traven wrote to his former editor Ernst Preczang, lashing out against the Marut theory. (That same day Traven talked for hours with Spota, who might have brought up the Ret Marut story, which is in fact mentioned in the *Mañana* article.) Traven's panic-ridden letter was sparked by an incident that involved him in a personal way. Preczang had forwarded a letter from Irene Zielke addressed to "Traven" and dated June 1948. Irene Zielke introduced herself as the daughter of Ret Marut, with whom she had not had any contact for thirty years. Two ghosts from the past had thus come back to haunt him: Marut and his alleged daughter. In his response to Preczang of July 20, Traven treated both as complete strangers. He first addressed the issue of the daughter, casting an interesting light on his precarious personal situation: His incognito, the source of his personal freedom, in fact allowed all sorts of people to meddle in his affairs.

> It is remarkable how many techniques some people will use to get close to people who have a name. This young lady is number nine of the illegitimate children in search of a father who have directly or in a roundabout way addressed themselves to me over the last ten years from five different countries. Four years ago a woman in Saskatchewan, Canada, wrote through her lawyer, insisting she was my real mother and that we were separated while I was still a child. She came to this conclusion through the detailed descriptions of Saskatchewan snowstorms in one of my books. She demanded regular support payments as were due a mother from her son. Other family members have surfaced, even from Czechoslovakia and Poland; but also from Chicago, from relatives of a certain Victor Bruno, who disappeared there thirty years or so ago and went to Mexico. One of the widely read magazines in New York published an article claiming I must be that long-lost Victor Bruno who wrote stories in the same style as I. As a result of that story I came to be called Bruno, though that is not my name.

Traven returned Irene Zielke's letter to her—as an enclosure to his letter to Preczang of July 20—and informed her in another enclosed note, written in English and dated August 10, 1948, that he could not be her father. He had "never" been in Germany and in 1912, the year she told Preczang she was born, he was serving in the "U.S. Pacific Merchant Marine."

Regarding the identification with Marut, Traven had the following desperate words for Preczang on July 20:

> The Fred Maruth story is very old, as you will also read in the letter to the philosophy student [Irene Zielke]. It started in 1929 when you were still living in Berlin, invented by a certain Oskar Maria Graf who wanted to get his name in the papers. The story made it into twenty or more newspapers, in Austria and Sweden as well. This reporter said that the author's real name was "Der Thraum," an anagram for Red Maruth. The story was also printed in Mexican newspapers. I did not respond in the German press, though I wrote the editor of a Mexican newspaper telling him to watch out for German reporters, mostly Jewish émigrés, since they would write anything imaginable as long as it brought in money. Graf came to Mexico and found Erwin Kisch, said to be the wildest of the German reporters, and from whose loud-mouthed articles no one can be safe. The F. Maruth story was as good as dead at the time. But Oskar M. Graf whispered it to Kisch in the café where they sat every day, and that became a sort of gold mine for Kisch. He wrote the story in a hundred variations, and there was no newspaper or magazine in German anywhere where he did not send one or the other variation hoping to make money. In this manner the story also came to England. A few months ago it also appeared in a newspaper in Stuttgart. I finally got tired of these lies and J. Wieder followed up with a letter to the newpaper's publisher, who then asked O. M. Graf for an explanation. Graf responded that he had in fact fabricated the story but that he had always viewed it merely as an unsubstantiated, interesting hypothesis that gave him something to write about. He admitted that he could not submit a shred of evidence that his story was true. The newspaper published Graf's explanation at J. Wieder's insistence and regretted falling victim to a frivolous reporter.

Though dangerously close to being unmasked, Traven indulged in his typical antics, praising himself in the third person. "If only half of what I have read about that formidable F. M. [Fred Maruth] were true, he must have been one of the most important people on earth." Again, self-praise as a gesture of self-preservation from the man who has annihilated himself but does not want to be ignored. One article called Marut the greatest contemporary philosopher, Traven noted!

This letter to the old German friend bore only the typed signature "B.T." The correspondent thus left no doubt that while not identical with Marut, he was—as before—the author of the novels. Torsvan/ Traven had never seen Preczang face to face, to be sure. With those he met in person he distinguished between Torsvan and Traven—as Torsvan with Spota ("*Yo no soy Traven*") or Croves working as "Traven's representative" on the *Sierra Madre* filming. Croves's relationship with the American writer Sanora Babb illustrates well the lengths to which he would go even in the early 1950s to distinguish himself from B. Traven. In a letter to Croves, Sanora Babb had referred to a Traven story as his own, prompting this correction: "It isn't mine, it is T.'s story and remains his although I had to make a few changes." When Croves visited her for tea one day and she unintentionally referred to him as the author of the novels, she received a note from Croves that very evening demanding that she never again address him as if he were Traven—and the next morning Croves came to retrieve the note. And yet Traven viewed Sanora Babb as a close friend and was acutely concerned about her well-being ("Life is worth more than any book one can write," he wrote to her on one occasion). The result was a poignant struggle to maintain his "secret" and keep a close friend.

It was the *Sierra Madre* film that unleashed the torrent of unwanted publicity culminating in the Spota interview. One might have thought the hermit in Acapulco would have learned his lesson. The opposite was the case. In spite of being tormented by the publicity hounds, Traven apparently remained convinced that film was the medium best suited to disseminating his ideas. With readers in the millions, he would have seen the film audience as an ideal target; at the same time he must have realized that his literary medium, the German language, was increasingly slipping away from him, while English and Spanish remained beyond the pale as means of literary expression. Thus in his last decades, while bringing few new works to market, Traven grew intensely interested in film versions of his novels and stories. (He also tried his hand at writing a radio play, with a version of *The Death Ship*.) As Croves he wrote screenplays and assisted with production even when someone else wrote the script, as had been the case with *The Treasure of the Sierra*

Madre. Traven's eagerness in this regard is nicely illustrated in the biography of his Hollywood agent Paul Kohner. Kohner, who had been instrumental in putting together the *Sierra Madre* deal, encouraged Croves one day to write a screenplay with a suitable role for Kohner's wife, the Mexican actress Lupita Tovar. Only a few weeks later a manuscript of more than five hundred pages reached Kohner, "a good story"—presumably *Mercedes Ortega Lozano*—but completely unsuitable for a film. Traven had as little luck with his five-page film scenario for the Mexican fairy tale *Macario*, which he sent on October 16, 1950, to the cameraman and director James Wong Howe.

Croves wrote with equal gusto to Humphrey Bogart, whom he had met in San José Purúa. Addressing him as "Bogey" in a long letter of March 23, 1953, Croves tried to win over the actor for the lead in a film based on a Traven novel—the work was unnamed and is unidentifiable—embarrassingly playing up the merits of this "great story" and of the renowned Bogart as well, whom he invited to Acapulco for discussions. Bogart did not agree to the proposal, and the project fell by the wayside. Typed, one imagines, in the clay hut under the fruit trees, Traven's plot outline clearly indicates his views on the clash between American consumerism and Indian self-sufficiency—similar to the short story "Assembly Line." Traven's sketch for the film, which was never produced, runs as follows:

> Let's call him Edwards. He is an adventurer, a soldier of fortune, who, when the story begins, is working for an American company as an explorer which job leads him to an out-of-the-way section in unknown parts of Mexico. He finds the natives simple and peaceful people with no authorities to pester them. Because of their entire lack of what he thinks is true civilization he, being an American and white, despises them and makes no effort to conceal his contempt for them. Many events happen while he is in that region and he comments constantly on the stupidity and silly superstition of those people. A member of that Indian community meets with an accident and he, Edwards, is suddenly under the impression that these people blame him for said accident in that he has brought them bad luck. At a certain episode when everybody is in the grip of an extremely heavy tension, Edwards, an unwelcome stranger and who, as everyone knows, hates these simple folks and their way of living and thinking, is falling into a sort of hypnosis and sees, in his imagination, these people hacking him into pieces while he in

> his desperation yells "The Marines are coming, we have the situation in hand. Hurray, Hurray." (This his imagination with his struggle against the impact of these Indians who slaughter him will be photographed.) He comes out of his nightmare and reaching the climax of the story he sees a native woman in deep sorrow on account of her having lost a very beloved one. When he, near the end of the story, realizes that in fact, though not by intention, he really was responsible for the accident which occurred, he learns that what these people lack in civilization they have tenfold in their kindness for other human beings, they have great hearts and souls where he feels merely a limited tolerance. In the meantime he discovers what he had set out to find in that section, that is, a certain rough material which if properly exploited will change the simple and peaceful way of life of these people and make them as hungry for money and as heartless as he used to be. Foreseeing such consequences he reports back to his company that in this section of the country there is no trace of any basic material useful to industry.
>
> Reactions: He, Edwards, in his conscience will feel a hero, because he conquered what is most difficult to conquer, his own self and his ruthless selfishness. Five per cent of the audience will call Edwards a sap, because he abandoned a twenty million dollar business for what they believe purely sentimental reasons. The real bulk of the audience, any audience anywhere on earth will love him for what he did and be happy that he saved that idyllic part of the country from being converted in only another industrial center with all the misery and soullessness that goes with it. He walks away a man greater than he was before he came in contact with these simple people.

A year prior to Croves's letter, the *BT News* reported that *The Bridge in the Jungle* would be filmed in Mexico. The announcement reflected Traven's newfound interest in the film medium:

> The Mexican press is now reporting that the renowned Mexican film producer Julio Bracho, having recently outdone himself with the success of "La Ausente" [The Absent Woman], has acquired the rights to "Puente en la Selva" and will be producing a film version. Bracho and the Mexican cameraman Gabriel Figueroa, who made a name for himself with such films as "Maria Candelaria," "The Pearl," "Enamorada," and "La Malquerida," are less interested in creating a box-office hit than an excellent work of art. The celebrated film actress Maria Elena Marques has been chosen for the role of Señora Garza, the

mother of the Indian boy. She has long been acquainted with Traven's book and stated publicly years ago that she, the mother of two children herself, wished nothing more fervently than to play the role of the mother in this film. Bracho's greatest concern at this point is to find an Indian boy who corresponds in all respects to Traven's marvelous depiction.

Nothing came of this film project, as was also the case with *Mercedes Ortega Lozano* (1945), a reworking in English of the story "Dennoch eine Mutter" ("Frustration"), about which Traven wrote on several occasions to Holmström in 1945–1946. In a letter to his English agent Curtis Brown, Traven discussed this "film-novel" about a Mexican woman working in a Texas hotel who pretends to herself and the world that she has a son:

> Since the day I wrote the short story "Frustration" which Miss Daly knows, I have pondered over the basic idea what to do about it as to make it a more substantial work, for I think the character was crying for being developed into something greater than the limitations of a short story would permit. I thought of doing the novel in the usual form. But soon I realized that the usual form would make necessary lengthy explanations of details which most of them would be boresom to the reader. So I decided to tell the story by sheer actions and dialogues, and boil down necessary descriptions of scenery to sort of pictorial impressions. In its actual form it is left to the reader to puzzle about explanations and let him reach his own conclusions which, whether they are right or wrong from the author's point of view, are his very own. Some readers will conclude that the heroine is insane yet harmless, other readers will say that she is just a liar, still others will insist that her wounded pride forces her to act the way she does or she would lose her self-respect if she acted different. Women readers will have by far more different opinions than male readers are likely to have. My Mexican translator for the Spanish version got so enthusiastic about the book that she translated inside three weeks to get it out and have it read by prospective Mexican publishers. And she is a highly educated and very sensitive lady where literature is concerned. If the reader, you yourself not excluded, on having finished the book, will and can remain under the impression that he, or she, by his mental eyes has just seen a moving picture or listened to a drama over the radio, I shall feel satisfied that the work is taken as I wanted readers to take it. And I am convinced

> that in England as in all war-ridden countries there will be at present and in times to come thousands of characters like Mercedes with the difference only that all, or most of them, will act and do in secret what Mercedes is acting and doing openly, unbelievable as this character may appear at first sight. At second sight you will quickly realize that Mercedes is not an accident or just a by-product. She is real and fully alive and she has her counterparts everywhere if you take the trouble to look behind the curtains where humans try hiding their innermost thoughts and minds.

Traven, as "H. Croves" and "representante legal de B. Traven" once again awarded an option on the film rights for *The Bridge in the Jungle* in 1956, this time to his friend Gabriel Figueroa; the director Fred Zinnemann showed some interest, but the project came to naught as it had in 1952. Likewise fruitless was Traven's attempt with Josef Wieder in 1956 to organize a joint German-Mexican production of his *White Rose* screenplay, which he had written in English. "Even Jacinto and some of the subordinate Indian characters can be played by German actors," he wrote on November 1, 1956, in his greatly deteriorated German. Figueroa would be in charge of the outdoor shots, while the actors would be "processed in" as had been done with *The Treasure of the Sierra Madre.* The tireless impresario spoke in the same breath of an American version, which could easily be made from the German, though nothing came of this plan either.

In spite of these failed attempts—and there may have been others—a number of Traven works did make it onto the screen in the 1950s and 1960s: *The Rebellion of the Hanged* in 1954, in a Spanish and English version with screenplay by Hal Croves; *Canasta de cuentos mexicanos* in 1955 (a series of the three stories "Eine unerwartete Lösung" ["An Unexpected Solution"], "Der Grossindustrielle" ["Assembly Line"], and "Bändigung" ["Obedience"]), and *Macario* in 1959 (screenplay by Hal Croves). All three were Mexican productions with Gabriel Figueroa as cameraman. *The Death Ship* followed in 1959 as a coproduction of the German Ufa with Producciones José Kohn of Mexico City (screenplay by Hans Jacoby). *The White Rose* was completed in 1961, with Figueroa again as cameraman, though the Mexican government prevented its release until 1975. (Reinhold Olschewsky, who appeared in the lead, also directed this Mexican production.) *Días de otoño* (1962) was the last Traven film to appear during his lifetime.

Hal Croves was involved to a varying degree with each of these films, though surely most intensively with the production and advertising of *The Rebellion of the Hanged* and *La rebelión de los colgados*, about which the *BT News* repeatedly reported. Croves's collaboration on this film thus merits special consideration, the more so as it gives a general impression of Traven's concern with the film medium.

Shooting of *Rebellion* lasted nine weeks, concluding on April 23, 1954. In the *BT News* Traven described the production in terms strongly reminiscent of his remarks on the drudgery of writing in the tropics almost thirty years earlier. The jungle scenes were shot in Chiapas, the company was "tormented by the tropical heat, drenched by tropical downpours, and plagued by insects and reptiles of every kind. One of the actors failed to survive these hardships." Traven made no secret of the clashes among director, producer, and the author's representative Croves. The latter was described as "an uncommonly energetic man with dark eyeglasses who is completely uncompromising and would never allow even the faintest modification to be made to Traven's work." He even saw to it that the original director was replaced by Alfredo Crevenna, who was more accommodating to Croves's desires. But this time it was not Croves but assistant director John Bright who was suspected to be B. Traven, as the *BT News* dutifully informed its readers, commenting for its part only that B. Traven—once again—was not in Mexico.

Croves, in a letter to Sanora Babb of June 22, 1954, gave a lively account of his part in the production:

> I had to do the script, had to do the casting, had to hurry hundreds of miles over the whole country to find the right locations. The most difficult thing was to locate a genuine jungle, an authentic jungle, where you could bring the heavy equipment close enough to do the picture with all the essentials audiences ask of a picture of today. The equipment had to be brought several hundreds of miles by train, ferried across one of the biggest rivers we have in Mexico, then again shipped by train and finally rolled on bad roads close to where we needed it. Right now we are getting in the music, sound effects, corrections of speeches, the fading ins and fading outs, the screen credits and the backgrounds of those titles, well, all the thousand of little details necessary to round up the picture. It will be a great picture. It would have been ten times better still if I had had my way all through. At one episode I separated from the pro-

> ducer, telling him that I am no longer responsible for the picture and that I in the name of the author protest against what he is doing, I am a peaceful individual, I guess you know that. But we had now and then the most terrific fights he and I, fights that lasted for hours while the production was suspended. He is a Checoslovakian and so of course he doesn't know a thing about the Indians, the mahogany camps, the way those people described by the story live, work and think.

Producer José Kohn, in an interview published in the *BT News*, recalled the snakes, scorpions, and tarantulas that bit and stung the cast and crew during shooting in the mahogany forests—further testimony, in Traven's analysis, that he was not writing mere adventure stories, but recording "what really happened." The film, the Mexican government's choice for best film, premiered at the Venice Biennale on 28 August 1954—"under sensational circumstances," as the mysterious B. Traven was rumored to be present incognito at the festival. The journalists had a field day, though for once the tables were turned. The *BT News* reported, "Pedestrians on the Lido tugged at the beard of a Spanish journalist, thinking it false and that B. Traven lurked beneath." He was naturally not in Venice, the article added. (He was in fact there, Señora Luján insists.)

Traven attributed the film's failure to garner an award at the Biennale (though it was one of three that should have) to politics. The "sensational success" of *La rebelión de los colgados* in Mexico City was all the more welcome. Traven gleefully described the mammoth crowds at Mexico City's largest cinema: "Thousands failed to get tickets," expressing again the sense of self-importance of the recluse who sought to be acknowledged but not discovered. He must have derived immense satisfaction from seeing his view vindicated that film could alert the masses to their plight. *La rebelión* confronts social injustice in Mexico in the most drastic terms imaginable. While the film limits itself specifically to the exploitation of the Indians in the mahogany camps, its general message speaks to the suppressed masses of the uneducated, the working people:

> The film ran in other Mexican cities at the same time. Remarkably, it enjoyed the greatest success in cities and towns where most of the viewers were illiterate and thus had not read either the rave reviews or the book itself. In the lines formed in front of the movie theaters, one could see elegant women clad in fur coats beside poorly dressed Indian women, and all

> of them left the theater taken by the film. That is a curiosity that journalists and film directors find puzzling.

The *BT News* later reprinted lengthy excerpts from German reviews of the film. Traven was clearly interested not only in the Mexican cause but also in the response from Germany. Isolated from Germany and everything German, he felt the connection all the more strongly and thus the need to be acknowledged—though never recognized—in his homeland.

Traven's turn to film and a public that numbered in the millions may be seen as a symptom of the general upsurge in his popularity some time after 1945. During the Second World War and the immediate postwar era, Traven titles had not sold particularly well. With *The Treasure of the Sierra Madre*, at the latest, Traven's fortunes had turned, not only in the German-speaking countries (where, besides the Büchergilde, Traven now published through S. Fischer, Wolfgang Krüger, Kiepenheuer, Rowohlt, Sigbert Mohn, Universitas, Volk und Welt, the Europäische Verlagsanstalt, and others and also gained entrée to the lucrative paperback market). From the mid-1950s, his international fame loomed ever larger, with a new generation of readers discovering Traven as "their" author, their contemporary and kindred spirit, and elevating him to the level of a kind of cult figure. In some ways this resonance had been foreshadowed in the 1920s and 1930s, though to a more limited degree. The contrast was most striking in the United States: The American edition of *The Treasure of the Sierra Madre* sold 2,692 copies by 1938, while by 1948 sales of the paperback edition alone were said to have reached 410,000; and on September 15, 1955, Croves wrote to Sanora Babb that American sales had passed the million mark. True, this book ranks as an exceptional case in the reception of Traven in the United States. Nonetheless, the sales figures that the author himself collected for his novels reveal a clearly impressive international presence in the postwar years:

> Until June 30, 1950, the books by B. Traven had been published in sixteen different languages. In English (New York City and London), in Swedish (Stockholm), in Finnish (Helsinki), in Norwegian (Oslo), in Danish (Copenhagen), in Dutch (Amsterdam), in Spanish (Mexico City and Madrid), in French (Paris and Lausanne), in Czekish (Prague), in Italian (Milano), in Slovakian (Bratislava), in Serbian (Belgrade), in Hungarian (Buda-

> Pest), in Polish (Warsaw), in German (Berlin, Leipzic, Hamburg, Zurich, Vienna), in Russian (Moscow).
>
> Not counting the great number of reprints, his books had, until June 30, 1950, reached one hundred and forty-five different editions. "The Death Ship" is considered one of the most successful of Traven's books. Of this book alone the German edition sold more than two hundred thousand copies, the Russian edition, according to reports, sold more than two and a half million copies.
>
> In such small countries as is Slovakia, now a state of Czecoslovakia, and with only 2,500,000 inhabitants, "Rebellion of the Hanged" sold forty thousand copies and while this is written the book is still selling strong and at the original price. "Rosa Blanca," a book which goes peddling for ten years from one American publisher to the other, sold in the same little Slovakia until December 31, 1950, twenty thousand copies. In Sweden, also a small country, with less than 7,000,000 population, "Treasure of the Sierra Madre" sold within three months twenty-two thousand copies.
>
> In Holland, 7,500,000 population, "Treasure of the Sierra Madre" sold within twelve months fifty-two thousand copies.
>
> At present the French writer Philippe Jaccottet is translating "The Death Ship" into French again to prepare an entirely new edition to be published in Paris by Edition Albin Michel and in Lausanne, Switzerland, by Guilde du Livre.
>
> All books by Traven are vehemently directed against dictatorship in any form. This most likely was one of the main reasons why, wherever Nazis controlled a country, including their own Germany, the books by Traven were taken out of bookstores and libraries, persons found in possession of a Traven book went to prison or concentration camp. When Yugoslavia was occupied by the Nazis, any person having a Traven book was executed. Because of this fact when the war was over not one copy of a Traven book could be found in Yugoslavia and new translations had to be made.

Soon after the war, media interest in Traven also reached its height and did not let up through the late 1960s (and beyond): An increasing number of articles appeared on Traven, mainly in dailies and lighter magazines, but also in more serious journals. The sensationalists kept the fires burning about the Traven "mystery": Most striking are the *Stern* stories from the 1960s as well as the curious reference book *Wie sie schreiben, wie sie aussehen* ("How They Write, What

They Look Like"), in which the article on Traven is accompanied not by a portrait photo, as is the case with all the other renowned authors, but by a gray rectangle. Serious discussions about the timeliness of Traven's philosophy also surfaced here and there, as in 1955 in the East Berlin *Sonntag*, which carried a debate on the extent to which Traven's anarchistic view of society could be acceptable in a Marxist state. Were Traven's novels not infused with a pessimistic, antihumanistic sense of resignation, a flight from civilization into the realm of the primitive, leaving little room for commitment to the masses' struggle for liberation? Did his books not lack a sense of faith in the people, in revolution, in self-sacrifice? Through his air of disinterest, wasn't Traven playing into the hands of the capitalists? Or did his sympathy with those robbed of their rights serve as a sufficient sign of constructive hope, qualifying him as a friend of the working class? Didn't this sympathy reveal a power to shake up the reader, in spite of the anarchist's ideological shortcomings? Traven had had an easier time of it in East Germany shortly after the war, as a supposed Marxist critic of capitalist society. Such is the view championed in Herbert Roch's *Deutsche Schriftsteller als Richter ihrer Zeit* (*German Authors Sit in Judgment over Their Time*), in which Traven appears alongside Lessing, Lichtenberg, Schiller, Büchner, Heine, Thomas Mann, and others in condemning the common front of capitalism and bourgeois-democratic sentiment.

The *BT News* offered a wealth of information on Traven's rise in popularity after the end of the Second World War. From 1951 to 1960, this newsletter was sent gratis to publishers and other interested parties as a news and promotional device. Josef Wieder was listed as editor for the thirty-six mimeographed issues, first along with Esperanza López Mateos and from 1956 on with Rosa Elena Luján. Traven's role in producing the news stories and editorial pieces is not always entirely clear. Some are Wieder's handiwork, evident from the style alone; in many cases, at least the raw material can only have come from Traven or someone close to him, though he may not be fully responsible for specific formulations and though pseudonyms used are not always fully transparent. Wieder no doubt edited everything in any case—as is documented with Traven's previously mentioned background story on the filming of *The Death Ship*, the typed original of which is contained in the Traven estate along with other *BT News* materials. Regardless of the precise extent of Traven's role, the *BT News*, which could not have come into existence without at least Traven's general approval, chronicles the author's chain of successes and does everything imaginable to heighten his success, trying to make B. Traven the focal point of literary discussion.

News *and* promotion. The "news" included announcements regarding new Traven publications and new foreign-language editions, with figures on the size of the print runs. According to these figures, by 1950 Traven had 145 editions of fifteen books in print, while in 1956 more than 250 editions of his books were available in twenty-three languages. To cite a typical case: In 1956 a new edition of the Czech translation of *The Treasure of the Sierra Madre* was necessary, after 100,000 copies had been sold. "News" also entailed updates on film productions as well as on radio and television offerings; reports abounded on radio plays, operas, lectures, the inclusion of Traven in textbooks, and the like. Reviews of Traven's books and the films based on them were a frequent feature; quotations and long excerpts from his works were often used to illustrate a point, as were occasional essays by Traven and reports based on information he provided. He would thus contribute material on his friction with the Nazis as well as for a column on "Little-known Mexico," discussing such topics as women's career opportunities, divorce practices, the relation between church and state (there were scarcely any monks or nuns in Mexico, one column disclosed), not to mention the report "Mexico City Is Sinking." Bordering on the promotional were Traven's not infrequent reminders that he did not fabricate his material but wrote the truth, whether it be about the insurance swindles with death ships or forced labor in the mahogany camps. This truthfulness, this authenticity gave Traven's books "such incredible power and strength," the newsletter reported, that everyone, even Traven's ideological enemies, read them—the German printer, the Russian worker, the Swedish student, the American mathematics professor, and, last but not least, the Dutch tulip grower.

The focal point of the *BT News* surely lay in the area of publicity—though this was of course the ultimate function of its informational aspect as well. After all, the texts could be reproduced without cost, and frequently articles—such as excerpts from *Art of the Indians*—as well as unpublished stories were offered for publication in newspapers or periodicals. The praise of Traven, coming either from him directly or at least with his authorization, often borders on the embarrassing. The issue is not merely one of ill-chosen adjectives. Traven, for example, liked to repeat the tale of the attempt to award the innkeeper in Acapulco the Aztec order. Traven's "discoverer," none other than Spota, sought him out with reporters and photographers "so that the world could celebrate him [Spota] as the great man who could introduce the renowned author to the President of Mexico, who could then award the Aztec order, the highest Mexican honor, to the long-lost poet of the Mexican Indians. Few European newspapers carried the story of how the Mexican President had to be sent back to Mexico City without success, because the man who had been 'discovered' was not Traven." (Spota himself had not even mentioned the Aztec order in *Mañana*.) "Humble as he is," Traven more than once referred in the *BT News* to the premium supposedly offered by *Life* from 1946 to 1957 for whoever would unmask Traven. While the *BT News* had the goal, stated in the preface to its first issue, of combatting the "rumors" and "lies" about the author that proliferated particularly after the success of the *Treasure of the Sierra Madre* film, it in fact did its best to keep the rumor mill turning with reports on the many theories of Traven's identity. As new legends came up—including that of an authors' collective in Honduras ("Did Traven Never Exist?") and that of the Slovenian shepherd with the short fingers—they were seized upon and corrected, as were the sensational reports by Wolfgang Cordan and others, who in their turn attempted no new identifications, to say nothing of the tales—told with relish—of the usurpers trying to publish under the Traven name. Reference was made to the grisly death that had greeted those spreading false rumors about Traven. Apart from denying such stories, the *BT News* revealed nothing; it merely served up anew the old stories of Traven's youth in the American Midwest, with general references to the novels as a portrait of the author's life. Traven (or Wieder, with Traven's authorization) most keenly combated the Marut identification, which was the result of Recknagel's research as well as an assertion spread by the circle of German émigrés in Mexico (namely Heinrich Gutmann and Egon Erwin Kisch). The Marut story was dismissed as categorically as that of the Slovenian shepherd.

Some of the corrections border on the macabre, as in the denial of the announcements that Traven was long dead or in an insane asylum. The *BT News* by its very existence was meant to be evidence of the opposite, yet it refused to enlighten its readership by telling them once and for all who Traven was.

Between the Languages: Traven's Literary Production After the War

Rumors of Traven's death were not to be taken lightly. Anyone who tried to usurp Traven's copyright and name put the author in a precarious position: He was being forced either to declare himself or to let the literary pirates have their way. But he had another, though less effective, way to prove his existence: literary activity. The apparent literary hiatus following *General from the Jungle* (1940) understandably elicited the sundry reports of Traven's death; Traven himself had even suggested as much in the Spota interview. Not without irony, therefore, the *BT News* reported in 1951 that Traven had agreed to a Mexican edition of his short stories, "in order to prove that he was still alive." Traven devotees wondered why no new Traven work had appeared for years, the magazine noted in 1954. Traven's production of screenplays based on his novels, which occupied him increasingly in the final two decades of his life—the estate includes stacks of such screenplays in various versions, unproduced for the most part—was naturally not as visible as his novels had been in the 1920s and 1930s. Similarly, the dramatization of *The Death Ship* of 1955 (by B. Traven and R. E. Luján, according to the title page) was published only in manuscript form, while the radio play version still lies unpublished in the estate. Nonetheless, the quarter century after the Second World War saw Traven actively involved in specifically literary production—and thus gave proof of his existence, sorely needed in the face of widespread skepticism.

During this period Traven thoroughly revised his novels for new editions (just as he had radically reworked the originals when he produced the English versions for Knopf)—perhaps the least conspicuous of his literary activities in this period. New chapters were added, and extensive passages cut, replaced, or inserted. Traven cut *Land of Springtime* quite drastically for the 1950 edition, thinking much of the material outdated. Numerous stylistic modifications were also made in that book and in others. "Traven revises all his books before a new printing," reported the first issue of the *BT*

News in 1951. Traven firmly embraced his right to revise. On August 24, 1964, he wrote, in English, to Fritz J. Raddatz, then editor at the German publishing house Rowohlt (the letter bears the typed signature "R. E. Luján"):

> All this brings us to a point: you know there's a controversy all over the world whether an author should revise, change or edit himself a book after its publication, that is, for future publications in the same language. Some are of the opinion that once a book has been written an author should not "touch" it anymore and leave it exactly as it was first written. Well, Traven does not believe in this, he thinks an author may revise, re-write, or whatever he pleases to do with his books to better them for future readers. Usually he makes very small changes, though.
>
> Of course, you know very well he is not the only author who does this. Many others make considerable changes in new editions. Thomas Mann, I believe, made changes in his novels "Felix Krull" and "Lotte in Weimar."
>
> As a rapid composer, Traven often has to make changes in successive editions. Perhaps the best contemporary example of similar behavior is Vladimir Nobakov [sic] (Lolita), who wrote several books first in Russian; others in German; on arriving in USA, he began to write and publish in English. We have been told that after he was famous for "Lolita," he supervised the translations of his Russian books into English, with considerable changes.

In the 1950s Traven began cutting references in the novels to matters German, hoping to give greater credence to his posture as an American with scant familiarity with Germany; critics had in fact cited such references in an effort to refute the American background that Traven claimed.

Translations represented another important area of Traven's literary activity in this period, consisting primarily (though not exclusively) of English versions of stories published in the collection *Der Busch*. *The California Quarterly* published "Der Grossindustrielle" as "A Legend of Huehuetonoc" in 1952. Traven corresponded extensively with Sanora Babb, the editor of the journal, trying (in vain) to get other stories published. (According to a note to "A Legend," the story was translated by Esperanza López Mateos, who had presented a Spanish version in the *Canasta* of 1946; Esperanza can scarcely have translated from German into English, however; at the very least Traven must have been involved in some way in the production of the English version: Probably he had actually prepared such a version for Esperanza for the 1946 collection.) "Visitor from Nowhere," which appeared in 1953 in the journal *Cosmos Science Fiction and Fantasy* was "Nachtbesuch im Busch," better known in English as "The Night Visitor." The *Busch* story "Medizin" appeared as "Effective Medicine" in August 1954 in the unlikely magazine *Manhunt*, while "Ein Hundegeschäft" from the same volume was published in 1957 as "Indian Trading" in the periodical *Short Stories.*

Translations, even when they involved revision, must have represented a sort of literary stagnation, as did, in a sense, the screenplays, radio plays, and dramatizations, to say nothing of the revisions, of his own novels. However intensive this "estate management," Traven must have felt the need to overcome the halt in production dating back to the late 1930s. With the exception of *Aslan Norval*, his new literary works in this period were primarily short stories—an art form he approached with some hesitation. "Someone may be a great novelist[;] that does not mean that he also is great in writing short stories. As you yourself know these are two different arts," he wrote to Sanora Babb on September 10, 1951. Raskin found a notebook from 1948 containing new story ideas in English, and I uncovered some pieces of paper in the estate containing thumbnail plots. Here are a few examples:

> Six doctors meet in a little village to die there because they don't wish to die where they were known to be great. One cures the other.
>
> U.S. G.I. killed in action. Cannot be buried in Texas because of his Mexican origin. The corpse goes hitch-hiking. [A throwback to Marut's "Story of the Unburied Corpse"!]
>
> Story of the man who when down on his heels was helped by a well-to-do citizen and brought back to good standing. The man thus helped slowly cultivated a terrific hatred against his benefactor until he no longer could bear it and so killed him. After this he felt happy and happily went to the chair.
>
> Let the man who loves the jungle be a Don Quixote. He sees all things in an unnatural blurred way. Lives forever under the illusion of what he thinks that jungle life has to be but is not. Cannot get away from that illusion. Leads him to all kinds of

trouble in life. Writes the most fantastic jungle adventures liked by the public, all untrue.

Contrary to the widespread impression of a work stoppage after *General from the Jungle* (1940), some of the literary projects of the next three decades actually came to fruition, though the level of productivity was clearly not what it once was. Also, aside from the fairy tale *Macario*, such works did not approach the quality of some of the early novels and stories; not surprisingly, the modest corpus of works created late in Traven's life never really did reach the public's awareness.

As a rule, Traven seems to have composed these late works in English (which is also true of the unpublished "film-novel" *Mercedes Ortega Lozano* [1945]). The main postwar work, the novel *Aslan Norval* (1960), was written in German but had to undergo major linguistic and stylistic corrections by at least one third party, Johannes Schönherr, before publication; Traven's German in these late years was in a sorry state, as reflected for instance in the letter to Preczang about Irene Zielke mentioned earlier. The decision to write in English in this late period was thus understandable—if there was such a decision. For one cannot always be certain whether a given story may only have *appeared* first in English or whether an English version printed later than the German version represents a translation or an original. (Since Traven was not fully at home in either language, definitive answers are hard to decipher; a case-by-case, word-by-word investigation would be required.)

Macario, the best-known and most accomplished work of Traven's last thirty years, leaves open no such questions. The Zurich Büchergilde published *Macario* in 1950 in a German version identified as a translation from the English ("The Healer"); Hans Kauders was named as the translator, and the total lack of Anglicisms clearly rules out Traven's work. The English "original version," or *Urform*, as the *BT News* called it, doubtless correctly, in November 1959, is to be found in a typescript text (carbon copy) in Harvard University's Houghton Library, entitled "The Uninvited Guest." It appeared in 1953 in revised form under the title "The Third Guest" in the American magazine *Fantastic*, from which it was then reprinted in *The Best American Short Stories* of 1954. *The New York Times* discovered it there, declaring it the best short story of the year. Nothing came of the plan in the early 1950s to make the story the centerpiece of a collection to be called *Ungeladene Gäste* (*Un-*

invited Guests). Traven did allow Kauders's translation of *Macario* to be published as "Der dritte Gast" ("The Third Guest") by Volk und Welt (East Berlin) and by Europäische Verlagsanstalt in their collection *Der dritte Gast und andere Erzählungen* (1958). But he so radically refashioned Kauders's text (the ending in particular) for a separate edition of the story published by Bertelsmann that only then did a work in authentic "Traven German" result—Anglicisms and all. (The text was "reworked from the bottom up by the author and thus deviates in numerous instances from the previous version.")

Macario is the story of a pact with Death that to a German reader is reminiscent of the Grimms' "Godfather Death." Yet *Macario*'s setting is thoroughly Indian-Mexican, and though Traven surely knew the Grimms' fairy tales, there is no reason to doubt Señora Luján's claim, published in Traven's lifetime, that the story was based on "*una leyenda indígena.*" Macario is a desperately poor Indian woodsman living a hard life on the edge of the tropical rain forest and harboring a single wish: to enjoy a roast turkey once in his life without having to share it with anyone. The wish is fulfilled and—so one must interpret the fairy tale's plot—he has a dream. The Devil appears to him, followed by Christ in the guise of a pilgrim. Both ask him for a mouthful of meat; Macario refuses both, but not Death, who joins him as the "third guest." Addressing him as "Godfather," Macario gives him half the turkey; for he knows that the remaining minutes of his life are numbered. In return, Death gives the Indian an elixir that he says can cure all diseases—except when Death appears at the head of the sick person, indicating that the case is incurable. Macario becomes a renowned doctor, and his fame reaches Europe. But he meets his fate when he comes to treat the viceroy's son: Death stands at the head of the bed, just as fate would have it, "apparently predetermined from the very moment of birth." The miracle worker is in danger of being burned alive, but death grants him release: That very evening after going into the jungle with his roast turkey, Macario is found under the tropical trees, half the turkey lying uneaten before him. "He was dead. A broad, beautiful smile lay on his face." He had died "exceedingly happy"—happy because his life's wish was fulfilled. Yet he shares this happiness with Death; in his happiness he finds Death and in Death happiness. Veiled social criticism? Cynicism about human nature? Or, more likely, a serene resignation?

Three stories first published in Spanish in *Una canasta de cuentos mexicanos* (1946) were also no doubt translated by Esperanza López Mateos from English originals. The English versions of these stories, which one may take as the originals (they were written around 1945), were published as "An Unexpected Solution," "A Customer Broke a Tooth," and "Ceremony Slightly Delayed." The *BT News* announced publication of "An Unexpected Solution" and "Ceremony," noting that "B. Traven writes detective stories as well, which may come as something of a surprise to many of his readers." These two stories were first published in German ("Eine unerwartete Lösung" and "Leicht verschobene Zeremonie," respectively) in the East Berlin Volk und Welt collected stories in 1968, while the German version of the third story, "Seele eines Hundes" ("A Customer Broke a Tooth"), first appeared in the collection of Mexican stories entitled *Der Banditendoktor* in 1955. Here, too, the late story "Eine wahrhaft blutige Geschichte" ("A Truly Bloody Tale") appeared for the first time; a Spanish version was included in the *Canasta* of 1956 and an English one in the *Texas Quarterly* of 1963 as "Foreign Correspondent." The story "Dennoch eine Mutter" ("A Mother Nonetheless"), which appeared in Germany in 1951, first appeared in English as "Frustration" in the 1961 collection *Stories by the Man Nobody Knows*, though Traven had composed the English text in 1946 at the latest. The German public enjoyed a new version of the story in 1967, in a translation by Gabriele Pallat entitled "Hochzeit um elf" ("Wedding at Eleven"). "To Frame or Not to Frame" and "His Wife's Legs," first introduced to German readers in the collected stories (*Erzählungen*) of 1968, originally appeared in English, the language in which they were apparently also first written.

The late stories and indeed Traven's entire literary production of his last decades, including the final years discussed in the following chapter, by their very paucity reveal that his primary interest was elsewhere: in the film medium—commencing at the latest with filming of *The Treasure of the Sierra Madre* and gaining particular intensity following *The Rebellion of the Hanged.*

Rosa Elena Luján

Work on the film *The Rebellion of the Hanged* brought a major change in Traven's personal life. In 1953, American film director

William (Bill) Miller introduced screenwriter Croves to Señora Rosa Elena Montes de Oca in Mexico City. Miller thought she could assist Croves with the translation (Spanish and English versions of the screenplay were written at the same time). The two recognized each other immediately: They had met in 1936 or 1937 through mutual acquaintances, the Danish sisters Bodil and Helga Christensen, whom Traven knew from his university days in Mexico City. Croves was Traven Torsvan then, and Señora Montes de Oca was Señorita Luján. A striking dark-eyed, black-haired beauty, Señora Luján came from a landowning family from the northern state of Chihuahua that was long prominent in Mexican history; her father had been a high-ranking military officer. She was born in 1915 in Progreso in the Yucatán, where her family had temporarily taken refuge during the revolution. Señora Montes de Oca translated Croves's screenplay of *The Rebellion of the Hanged* into Spanish and then gradually took on the tasks formerly attended to by Esperanza López Mateos. By the summer of 1954, Traven had instructed that royalties be transferred to "Account R. E. Luján" at Mexico City's Banco de Londres y México. Later that summer, the two traveled to Europe—by which time the gringo was of course no longer the "agent" of the author of the novels to Rosa Elena Luján, but that author himself. They visited Antwerp, where the "American sailor" Gales had begun his odyssey; they were also in Venice and Verona, Paris and Amsterdam; the train took them through Germany, though they did not make any stopovers—after three decades incognito, the journey may have been more traumatic than sentimental (in contrast to Traven's short visit to London two years later).

As a reflection of Traven's trust, beginning in 1956 Rosa Elena Luján is cited in print as the copyright holder for his books and copublisher of the *BT News*. Her translations of several stories were published in 1956 as *Canasta de cuentos mexicanos* (not the same selection as Esperanza López Mateos's collection *Una canasta de cuentos mexcianos* of 1946). In the meantime, she had been divorced in 1955 from Carlos Montes de Oca, a Mexican businessman from one of the country's most prominent families; she had custody of their two daughters from this marriage, Chele (Rosa Elena) and Malú (Maria Eugenia). "He feels so very, very lonely," Traven wrote her on March 2, 1955. "It seems to be his destiny, or part of his destiny, to feel always lonely and be always lonely. This has been the cause of his many mis-elations in his life, his many mistakes he did and which could have been avoided had he in good time met somebody in whose presence he would not feel so terribly alone."

Two years later, on May 16, 1957, Traven Torsvan and Rosa Elena Luján were married in San Antonio, Texas.

7

FINAL YEARS IN MEXICO CITY

Renowned in Seclusion, 1957–1969

The House on Calle Río Mississippi

It was only in the last twelve years of his life, after decades of leading an unsettled existence, that Traven found a sense of security beyond that granted by a pseudonym. His honeymoon had brought him to New Orleans, home port of the freighter that strands Traven's double Gales in Antwerp and is remembered as a world of happiness on the sailor's odyssey aboard "death ships." The symbolism would not have escaped Traven: He had come full circle; the "American sailor" of the autobiographical novel had returned home. Traven had grown up without regular family ties, without a father, siblings, cousins, aunts, and uncles, and from an early age also without a mother, it seems. Now he had a family for the first time, a feeling of domesticity, and soon enough his own home of solid luxury—where he could fittingly have received homage as the grand old man of letters, had that been his desire.

From the summer of 1957 until his death in late March 1969, Traven was not separated from Rosa Elena Luján a single day, as she noted in her essay "Remembering Traven." She dedicated herself to B. Traven and his work. Regarding the touchy matter of the "mystery" or "secret" surrounding his early life (beyond the identity of Traven and Marut), Rosa Elena Luján demonstrated tact. "I rarely asked questions," she said in the essay, "because I knew he hated them, and he would stop talking immediately. 'Stop poking,' he would say." "I wanted only what he wanted," she told journalist Kevin M. Kelleghan. In "Remembering Traven" she wrote:

> Some people think that I changed Traven. If I did it was certainly not intentional, because what I admired most about him was his ability to live the way he pleased. He always said that he would never let fame, glory, or money change him, and these things never did alter his personality or life style. Sometimes, Traven would say, "It's not good to be too happy. It's like having too much money. And if you have too much money it's because you have taken it from someone else."
>
> Perhaps his habits changed most in that he lived a settled life with me. He had never married before and although he gave different birth dates I knew that he was about thirty years older than I. So he was more than 60 when he married for the first time. We loved and respected each other exactly the way we were. When we got married we made a pact that each one would be completely free and independent. However, it was never necessary to impose this pact. Traven and I enjoyed working and traveling together. During our married life we were never separated for more than three or four hours.
>
> He was the one who changed me; he gave Elena, Malú and me a new and different view of the world. He made us conscious that people were homeless and starving. Previously, I had had a sense of Christian charity, but not an understanding of social injustice and the need for basic social change. Traven gave us this important education.

Upon returning from their honeymoon in May, Traven and Rosa Elena Luján settled down in Mexico City, remaining there, with the exception of short trips, until the end of Traven's life. Along with Señora Luján's teenage daughters, Chele and Malú, they first moved into a high-rise apartment building on the Paseo de la Reforma, the capital city's main street, near the Plaza de los Ferrocarriles and not far from the Hotel Reforma. Quarters were tight. Traven would often withdraw to a corner of the apartment with his typewriter and work late into the night (in his first months of marriage he wrote *Aslan Norval*, a novel of the love and marriage between an aging man and an elegant younger woman). The earthquake of the summer of 1957, which toppled the Column of Mexican Independence, the Angel of Freedom, seriously damaged their apartment house. Rosa Elena and one of her daughters gained temporary shelter in the city, while Traven and the other daughter stayed in the apartment, until they all moved in December to the seventh floor of a high-rise in the center of town at Calle Durango 353.

It was here that Señora Torsvan based her "Literary Agency R. E. Luján" to manage her husband's literary, financial, and legal affairs, communicating through P.O. Box 2701 at Mexico City's central post office. As Traven's authorized representative, Rosa Elena Luján now kept a watchful eye on such issues as royalties, contracts, licenses, copyrights, translation rights, options, and the use of Traven's texts for radio, theater, records, television, film, and so on. She took care of most of the business and literary correspondence, even typing letters in German from Traven's drafts—she did not know the language—either in Traven's or her own name. And naturally her "literary agency" was adroit in protecting—and cultivating—the "mystery." One bizarre example of the lengths to which Traven would go to shake anyone from his trail is a letter, in German, from R. E. Luján dated May 31, 1962, to Ernst Vollenweider, who had sent Traven a copy of his travelogue *Roland fliegt nach Mexiko: Ein junger Zürcher erlebt Mexiko* (*Roland Flies to Mexico: A Young Man from Zurich Experiences Mexico*):

> Your book went to Argentina, Uruguay, Bolivia, and Chile, following the trail of our author B.T.; but whenever the book would arrive, he had already left. The book was sent on after him, finally catching up with him in Guatemala, where he at last had a chance to read it. He dictated a letter via night telephone, the text of which I translate for your convenience.
>
> "Write to Mr. Vollenweider that I thoroughly enjoyed receiving a copy of his book. The way he saw and described the country is just how Mexico appears to one visiting it for the first time and who can only stay for five weeks.["]

A detailed critique of the book followed, instructing the Swiss recipient about Mexico and further explaining to the landlubber the nautical term *Knoten* ("knot").

Rosa Elena Luján also typed her husband's German manuscripts, including *Aslan Norval*. She translated from English the works not yet available in Spanish: *Macario* (1960), *General from the Jungle* (1966), *The Cotton-Pickers* (1968), *March to the Montería* (1973), and *The Creation of the Sun and the Moon* (1977). She also compiled two collections of stories in Spanish, translating parts of them herself: *Canasta de cuentos mexicanos* (1956) and *El visitante noc-*

turno (1967). Finally, Rosa Elena Luján helped with Traven's screenplay work. The dramatization of *Das Totenschiff* (*The Death Ship*) bears her name beside Traven's on the title page, though Señora Luján attributes this more to Traven's generosity than to a substantive contribution.

Durango 353 was a respectable home in a middle-class neighborhood—decorative plazas and gardens interrupted the monotony of the quiet street. By 1963 their situation had so improved—owing not least to Rosa Elena's mastery of Traven's finances—that in September the family could purchase a modern three-story house on a palm-lined side street to one of the most prestigious stretches of the Paseo de la Reforma in one of the more elegant parts of central Mexico City. Traven spent the remaining years of his life here, at Calle Río Mississippi 61. (The house in Cuernavaca, which the two had purchased early in their marriage, was so in need of repair that the family stayed there only rarely.)

Today Calle Río Mississippi is a noisy street with nondescript 1970s-style high-rises and tourist restaurants; yet some of the Mediterranean villas from Traven's day still stand, with their wrought-iron grating and colonial gates, patios, and colorfully tiled fountains. The date palms that towered over the middle of the boulevard into the 1970s were removed when the street was widened to accommodate increased traffic. A kiosk at a busy corner hawks an assortment of pulp fiction and news, with the stand of a street vendor and a cheap liquor store nearby, across the street from an upscale hotel with disco. This quarter of the "Paris of Central America" is a marriage of contrasts, as it was in Traven's day: European and Indian, elegant and primitive, modern and traditional. Street musicians abound in the area, Indian women beg or sell tamales, their piercing black eyes in wrinkled faces, their bodies clad in dark cloaks, their children at their side falling asleep late at night on the sidewalk on a colorful serape, clasping the wilted roses they were to have sold—children who open their eyes wide for a moment when a passer-by presses a coin into their grimy hands. Not far from there, American and European cars skirt past the imposing bank facades, the fashionable boutiques and art galleries, the garish apartment houses and ministry offices on the Reforma, the multi-starred American hotels with their banal luxury. Farther on, young fire-eaters risk throat cancer for a handful of tourist pesos, cripples hang out in front of baroque churches filled with gold, and the *beau monde*, wearing capes and gowns, stream from the opera house, the marble Palacio de Bellas Artes, passing the outstretched hands of the Indios on their way to the bars, whose names on shiny brass ring strange to the Aztec descendant: Ambassadeur, Cosmopolitan, Carlton.

Traven spent the last years of his life here, the years in which he had "made it," the years also of his personal happiness. World fame, however, did not give him a sense of self-importance. He moved in Mexico's best circles and went to the opera and concerts; but he led a simple life as he had always desired. He took long walks through the city almost every day, going as far as the main post office several miles away in the old town center at the Zócalo, with its impressive official buildings from the colonial period. In 1968 he walked down to the Reforma to see the student demonstrations. The gray-haired man who spoke Spanish with a mid-European accent knew his way around the city, where he had lived on and off since the 1920s. He was always exploring it anew, finding the most authentic out-of-the-way eating places and Indian stores and appreciating the old city's architectural charms. He often took his wife and her daughters—who soon became "his" daughters—to restaurants in the elegant Zona Rosa on the other side of the Reforma or to small ethnic eateries discovered on his walks. One can easily conjure up the image of this inconspicuous man, meticulously groomed and wearing a tailor-made suit, standing among the tourists and natives watching the mimes perform as they still do almost every evening in the Zona Rosa: the renowned author anonymous, unobserved, free, in "his" city. "I want to be able to go to the newspaper stand at the corner, to go into a restaurant, to ride the bus, without having people stare at me," his widow recalls him saying. In the midst of the hustle and bustle of the metropolis, his wish was fulfilled, albeit with a few unpleasant interruptions. Alan Cheuse quotes Señora Luján: "My husband was one of the freest men who ever lived. His desire for privacy was part of that freedom."

The gray-green home on Calle Mississippi was Traven's oasis. Unprepossessing from the outside, within it exudes elegance and a sure sense of style. The author who spent his life concerning himself with the proletariat, both European and Indian, who was bitterly familiar with life's brutalities, might seem strangely out of place amid such wealth: the paneled library and reception room on the ground floor with leather club furniture, the shelves of Traven books reaching the ceiling; the spacious living room with fireplace, Oriental rugs, and concert grand piano, appointed with silk, crystal, and silver. The oils, watercolors, and graphics throughout the house represent the country's top artists: Diego Rivera contributed a sketch of a frog bearing a resemblance to himself, which calls out "Chelena" (Señora Luján) with a doleful look; also represented are Leopoldo Méndez (graphics illustrating *The Rebellion of the Hanged*), Orozco Romero (an oil portrait of Rosa Elena in a ball gown), Federico Cantú, Guillermo Meza, and Julio Castellanos. From the dining room with its marble table one enters the small garden, the patio with lemon and rubber trees, blossoming bushes, and flowers behind high ivy-covered walls. The enclosed sitting area is adorned with Indian masks and ceramics, including a reproduction of the famed head of a Maya chief from Palenque, the original of which is in the Museo Nacional. On the patio, where one can sit in the sun every month of the year, Traven would feed his poodle Gigi, his terrier Tabasco, and his monkey Lalo. The household also included a parrot. Traven would raise plants here in tin cans—avocados, lemons, and anything else he could grow from seed; he would then give the plants to Indians.

The third floor was Traven's domain; aside from his wife, no one had access to the "bridge," as he called it. He would work here, surrounded by books, manuscripts, and memorabilia from many decades, as well as expedition equipment, cameras, binoculars, boots, pith helmet, riding gear, a Colt.45, and gifts from Indians (including bow and arrows from the Lacandones). Even in his last year, he would sit over his papers or Remington typewriter late into the night, until his wife would "interrupt" him. "Si, mi vida, I'm coming, I'll stop now."

"I want to be free, not a slave to money, not a slave to fame," Traven is reported to have said, and above all he did not want to be a slave of bureaucracy. Freedom was synonymous with work, however, even in his final decade as the grand old man of Mexican literature. Tirelessly he would write down ideas or turns of phrase, probably intended for future projects. He tried his hand at deciphering Mayan writing and strove even in his final years to master Indian languages such as Zapotec (his vocabulary lists still exist); his archeological pursuits would sometimes give him a bad conscience, family members relate, for skirting more pressing problems he felt compelled to confront as a political writer in the widest sense. Writing was his life. "The motto of Traven's life was work," wrote Austrian journalist Hans Erich Lampl after Traven's death, reporting on a visit with Traven in 1967. "If you are bed-ridden, unable to work or be creative," Traven said at that time, "it is much better to shoot yourself, as Hemingway did."

The bridge was thus more a sanctuary for creative work than a room for studying. (Traven does not seem to have kept up to date with the literary scene or even to have reread the classics, though on occasion—as far back as *The Death Ship*—he made literary allusions in the most unexpected places: In a letter to Ernst Preczang in 1934, he alluded to a passage in Schiller's drama *Fiesco*, and in a discussion of a screenplay Paul Kohner had sent him for review he remarked late in life: "Be Mexican and don't recite the speech of Mortimer in Shiller's [*sic*] play, Mary, Queen of Scotland.") On occasion, his work on the bridge may in fact have seemed almost compulsive, and his widow recalls that sometimes Traven even rented a hotel room to complete a particularly pressing project or escaped to a neighbor's home to avoid being disturbed.

Still, the bridge was not always the scene of creative ferment. The workroom had a small balcony overlooking the Calle Mississippi, where Traven liked to feed the birds, which were not yet scared off by the traffic, as they are today. His dogs kept watch over him in this oasis within an oasis. Señora Luján could not confirm Recknagel's story that a backpack containing Traven's expedition equipment always stood next to the bed on the bridge, ready for use at a moment's notice—which Recknagel cited as tangible evidence that the gringo from Munich always felt hunted, ready to cast off his life of luxury and to retreat again into namelessness.

The books on the bridge offer a hint of Traven's complex past. When I surveyed the library's contents in 1983, little seemed to have changed since Traven's death. Here were Traven's own works in various editions and translations, from paperbacks to a deluxe illustrated edition on handmade paper. Issues of *The Brickburner* were on hand, and even a copy of *An das Fräulein von S . . .* (To the Honorable Miss S . . .). A glance around the room revealed an issue of *Das Forum* (November 1918), a pacifist left-of-center literary and cultural magazine, and a barely used German high school anthology, *Deutsches Lesebuch für höhere Lehranstalten* by Heinrich Bone, in two parts. There were also books by anarchist Rudolf Rocker, with whom Traven is said to have been in contact for years, though no correspondence between the two is preserved in the estate of either; pamphlets dedicated to Traven by Charlot Strasser, one of Traven's first new contacts after landing in the New World; art portfolios from the Seiwert circle in Cologne, such as his *Welt zum Staunen* and other prints from the Kalltal Community. Max Stirner's *Der Einzige and sein Eigentum*, which Recknagel reported seeing on the bridge, also hearkens back to the Marut period, as do the two hundred or so "Little Blue Books" Recknagel uncovered there and viewed as the educational treasury of the self-schooled émigré. Numerous tracks lead back to Germany: In 1983 the shelves still featured many Tauchnitz editions of the series *British and American Authors* in addition to numerous Grieben and Meyer travel guides on regions of Germany through which Marut apparently made his way after the failed revolution in Bavaria (Bavaria, Thuringia, the Rhineland, Taunus, Eifel, Hunsrück, the Rhön region, Spessart, and also Rothenburg and Cologne), a guide to Luxembourg, and Justus Perthes's German *See-Atlas* (eleventh edition by Hermann Habenicht, Gotha, 1922). Dietrich Stürmer's book about Maximilian Harden, *Der geheimnisvolle Gewaltige* (*The Mysterious Man of Power* [Leipzig, 1920]) could be found there as well. A thick German-English, English-German dictionary of 1859 (by Thieme and Preusser) no doubt assisted during Traven's early writing attempts in Mexico as well as in his everyday dealings with Americans and Englishmen in the oil fields and cotton plantations of Tamaulipas. Also pointing to the earliest period in Mexico were the brochures and magazines promising an entrée to the English-language magazine market. I also found archeological and historical books about Mesoamerica as well as books about the Indians of Mexico, their art, their mythology, and their languages. On a scrap of paper that fell from one of the books, Traven had written, "The Creation of the Sun, a fable written by B. Traven, based on prehistoric Mexican Mythology. The names of the characters or locations mentioned in the work are taken from the language of the Tzeltal Indians who live in the state of Chiapas (Southern Mexico)." Interestingly, the library also included *Revolt in the Desert* (in German) by T. E. Lawrence, whose fascination with anonymity has elicited comparisons with Traven; Traven is also said to have had works of Rimbaud, another man of mystery, in his possession. The *Dada-Almanach* of 1920 was there, as was Tristan Tzara's *Vingt-cinq poèmes* with a handwritten dedication from the author—to whom? Another curiosity: William C. Russell's *The Death Ship* (1901), which has nothing to do with Traven's novel aside from the title. I have already mentioned Bang's *Denied a Country* in a German edition of 1918. Music books of German folk songs and opera arias abounded. Under stacks of magazines, kept apparently because of their reports on Traven, I stumbled unexpectedly on the small brochure "This Week in New Orleans," dated May 18, 1957, a memento of Traven's honeymoon. Though he tried so hard to avoid fame, the aging Traven religiously preserved magazine clippings about himself (which his publishers sent and which he occasionally used to pique the interest of new publishers): Torsvan/Croves was thus surrounded by proof of his identity with Traven.

Family and Friends

A hermit, then, confined to his cell on the third floor of Calle Mississippi 61? Traven did occasionally retreat fully into his work. But friends and family also give a very different impression of the aging "Skipper," as he was called by those close to him. When he came "below deck" from the "bridge" (Traven adopted nautical terminology throughout the household), he was again the paterfamilias, ready for games and fun, for stories about his adventures at sea or in China, India, Australia, and other far-off lands, for banter or serious discussions, for play with the dogs, the monkey, or the parrot. He never spoke with guests about the problems of writing—according to the surprised testimony of such disparate witnesses as the American journalist William Weber Johnson and the Mexican playwright and diplomat Rodolfo Usigli. The "Skipper" played the piano and violin, recited poems by Heine, and spoke French and on rare occasions German (primarily with his godson Gabrielito Figueroa); English was Traven's preferred tongue even among his family.

He was fond of a certain formality at home in his dress, in table manners, in the daily routine—an attitude hard to reconcile with the proletarian whom Will Wyatt's thesis made Traven out to be. Dinners, his wife and family recall, were "formal occasions even when there were no guests present." A proletarian like Otto Feige from Schwiebus would hardly change for dinner, as Traven did, according to his family.

"Usually the 'skipper' came below . . . at seven p.m.," Rosa Elena Luján writes in "Remembering Traven." He then would have a drink, she recalls, Tequila, beer, or scotch; he would talk of politics, the news, the children's interests and problems. No topic was taboo for the daughters; they could speak with the Skipper about sex or religion with equal freedom. During the evenings he would sometimes teach them German or French or act out scenes from a play. He would have them recite Portia's monologue, for example, while they wore costumes they had made themselves. "Traven enjoyed it all. He had the marvellous ability to look at the world through the eyes of a child," Rosa Elena Luján recalls. "We took Elena [Chele] and Malú with us wherever we went, to showings of paintings and culture, to the ballet and the theatre, to conferences, and on short trips in Mexico to Mazatlán or Acapulco. On long trips abroad we preferred to go alone. When our daughters were away from home for long periods at school in the States or in Paris he wrote to them at least once a week."

Another of Rosa Elena's snapshots records Traven's love of animals (even in the 1920s, as a new arrival in Mexico, he is said to have carried around a small monkey):

> After breakfast he watered the plants and took care of our small garden. One of his obsessions was to plant trees. He never owned land himself, but over the course of his life he planted hundreds of trees with his own hands throughout the Republic, no matter whose land it was or where it was.
>
> He also fed the animals himself, including Lalo our monkey, who, before drinking the warm milk the Skipper offered him, searched his pockets for something interesting. Common things like eyeglasses and handkerchiefs were a bore and he threw them on the grass. Then my husband would patiently pick them up. But when Lalo discovered a box of chiclets he would shout and jump with delight into Traven's arms. Then he would fall on his back, holding himself only by the long, black tail circled around the Skipper's neck. Poor Lalo! When he fell in love with our next-door neighbor, a beautiful brunette, he became impossible and we had to find him a new home.
>
> Traven also loved and respected dead animals. When our dear friend, the playwright Rodolfo Usigli was Mexico's Ambassador to Norway, he sent us three reindeer skins as a Christmas present. I thought that they looked beautiful on top of the rug in front of the fireplace. But when my husband saw where I had placed

them he said, "No, no, I will not have anybody step on such noble, proud animals."

In spite of the aging Traven's avoidance of strangers (a back entry allowed him an easy escape to the bridge when he wished to avoid guests), he enjoyed socializing with those he trusted. The consummate host, attentive though somewhat hampered by hearing problems, lively in conversation—such are the memories of the visitors whom business or professional interests brought to the Calle Mississippi. One of these was Lawrence Hill, formerly of Knopf, who published Traven's works in the 1960s under the Hill & Wang imprint and later continued publishing them through his own firm, Lawrence Hill & Company. During Hill's visit to Mexico City in the summer of 1967, Traven surprised his guest by appearing "as if from nowhere" and greeting him "cordially." According to Hill's description in a letter to the editor of *The New York Times Book Review*, Traven was a man of medium height and stern bearing (apparently only to strangers). He looked younger than his claimed seventy-seven years (he was in fact eighty-five, assuming that 1882 was the year of his birth) and spoke English with a German accent. A few days later Hill and his wife lunched at Traven's home along with William W. Johnson and his wife and the Israeli painter Igal Maoz. "The luncheon was an elegant affair. Traven was very much the gracious continental host. His wife, a charming and beautiful woman in her mid-forties, stayed close beside him to repeat remarks he missed." Johnson had similar memories of his meeting with Traven at the home on the Calle Mississippi.

Hans Erich Lampl, an Austrian correspondent for a Norwegian paper, also wrote of a meal at Traven's home. He had gained entrée in late November 1967 through the recommendation of Usigli, then Mexican ambassador to Oslo. Lampl too noted the German accent. He also thought his host was ten or more years younger than he really was (again assuming his birth was in 1882). His hair was white, he was fragile, "a leptosome type (delicate, bony), with sharply defined, aristocratic features"; he didn't see well and was hard of hearing, his voice wavered and from time to time he was lost in thought, but "when he speaks of the rights and dignity of man, his voice could be that of a twenty-year-old"; at such moments his excitement expressed itself in his face and gestures. He spoke with Lampl about Ibsen, Strindberg, and Hamsun. The Austrian concluded that his host—he presented himself as Croves, although

Lampl was aware of his true identity—knew Vienna well; Lampl was convinced that Traven was there in 1910 during the "scandal" surrounding *Glaube und Heimat* (a sensationally successful play by the Tyrolean writer Karl Schönherr dealing with Catholic persecution of Protestants in the seventeenth century). Traven himself recalled spending a night under the stars in the Vienna Woods, as he spent nights elsewhere on numerous occasions—a reference to his years of flight from Munich perhaps. He also recalled a voyage to Budapest. "It is long ago. Soy viejo."

Regarding his works, Traven commented that "the real hero" of *The Death Ship* was not the American sailor Gales, but his Polish comrade Stanislav—as he also told Judy Stone. His conversation with Lampl then touched on politics, focusing on the superpowers' manipulation of smaller nations (an oblique reference to Poland perhaps; he did mention Finland); the Germans, Russians, and Americans were brought down a peg in this context. Mexico, on the other hand, was the land of peace, the land of the future after the decline of the current world powers. National socialism was criminal from the very beginning; communism, which in principle had healthy roots, degenerated to that level. "El neonazismo? Bah!" Traven spoke of his love for the elements, for the earth, the sky, and the sea. He loved people, "although they make it so difficult to keep loving them. It is much simpler with animals and flowers." Lampl continued: "He goes out onto the patio and talks with the bird." (The following anecdote was considered significant enough to be included in the introduction to the monumental leather-bound *Obras escogidas*, a selection of Traven's works: "What sort of name do you want?" Traven asked his dog, listing off the states of Mexico: Chiapas, Tamaulipas, Campeche, and so on. The dog's responses were construed to be in the negative until Traven came upon Tabasco; the dog seemed to nod and was called Tabasco thereafter.)

Traven's close friends found his home a warm meeting place. His friends were not many, his widow stresses, but they were that much closer. They knew his "secret"—that Hal Croves was not Traven's representative but the author himself—and they kept his secret, protecting him from inquisitive journalists. Traven, even in his final years, could walk through the streets of his beloved city without having passersby turn to stare. He could visit restaurants, movies and concerts, theater and opera performances, and the Chapultepec Park (where he went just a few days before his death)—even after Spota's richly illustrated report appeared in Mexico City and after the German and American magazines claimed to have solved the mystery in the 1960s. Traven's friends were by and large associated with film and the creative arts rather than the literary world. He avoided shop talk, however much he at times enjoyed speaking of his novels with someone like Judy Stone or Hans Erich Lampl. Apart from Luis Suárez, the noted journalist and editor of *Obras escogidas*, the literary members of Traven's circle included above all the playwright and critic Rodolfo Usigli who also held high diplomatic posts from time to time. Writing about his conversations at Calle Mississippi 61, Usigli recalled Traven's love of children and animals more vividly than any comments Traven had made about his work as a writer. With a glass in hand, the Skipper discussed "everything"—mundane happenings, his friends and their views—but not literature. He sometimes seemed lost in thought, but he never lost the thread of the conversation.

Traven's acquaintances from the American colony in the 1960s included Esther Turner, the wife of John Kenneth Turner, whose sensational exposé on the forced-labor camps in the Yucatán, *Barbarous Mexico* (1911), forms a sort of companion piece to the Mahogany cycle. A somewhat incongruous member of the Traven circle was Joaquín Zapata Vela, a specialist in military law. Traven knew few politicians, since he never directly involved himself in the country's political affairs, though he followed political developments closely to the end of his life (as Rosa Elena Luján wrote in an unpublished biographical sketch). Nonetheless among his friends was Mexican President Adolfo López whose personal protection he sought in 1963, when *Stern* reporters were dogging his trail. His friend Gabriel Figueroa saw to it that the former Ret Marut was given a telephone number through which he could reach López Mateos (the brother of Traven's translator and collaborator Esperanza) day or night.

Traven's closest friends came from the world of the arts and film (in which Rosa Elena Luján had been at home while she was still Señora Montes de Oca). Esperanza's cousin Gabriel Figueroa was a prominent member of this group. Traven had often stayed with him on visits to the capital during his years in Acapulco and had found temporary asylum with him after the brouhaha surrounding the Spota interview. Figueroa, today the revered nestor of Mexican film, collaborated on several films based on Traven novels and thus was partially responsible for Traven's fame in the author's later years. A charcoal sketch of Traven by Figueroa's wife, Antonieta, has hung in the library of the Traven archive in Cuernavaca since 1983. It depicts a contemplative old man with delicate features and a trace of humor and *joie de vivre*—the Traven of the Calle Mississippi. The story of Figueroa's first meeting with Traven is quite telling. Traven was scheduled to meet Esperanza in a café in Mexico City; she fell ill and asked her cousin to go in her place. From Esperanza's description, Figueroa immediately identified Traven. Asked whether he was Señor Croves, he carefully eyed the stranger and said no. When Figueroa returned, after leaving to phone Esperanza, Traven was gone. Hollywood agent Paul Kohner, husband of the Mexican actress Lupita Tovar, was also close to Traven. He represented Traven for years, but in 1950 Traven broke with him suddenly, and it was only in the late 1960s, during one of Kohner's frequent visits to Mexico City, that the two were reconciled. "Paul and Traven embraced. When Traven kissed Lupita, there were tears in his eyes. 'What a pity,' he said, 'that it took so long!' "

Among his close friends were also a number of creative artists, especially Diego Rivera (who died in late 1957) and David Alfaro Siqueiros. The two great Mexican muralists shared Traven's leftist leanings though they had sufficient differences with him to ensure lively debate. Unlike the two artists, whom Traven had come to know in the imperialist-anarchist turbulence of the mid- and late 1920s, Traven was not a Communist. Rivera had paved the way for Trotsky's Mexican exile in the 1930s and helped the revolutionary settle close to him in the Coyoacán section of the city, though Rivera later embraced Stalinism. Siqueiros spent time in jail following an attempt on Trotsky's life. In 1966, Siqueiros introduced Traven to his collaborator Igal Maoz, whom Traven subsequently tried to promote. Maoz first encountered Traven's works in a kibbutz, where he heard the cotton pickers' song as set by Hanns Eisler. Alberto Beltrán, founder of the newspaper *El Día*, also counted among Traven's artist friends in the final years. He is most noted as a graphic artist (Traven's *Creation of the Sun and the Moon* of 1968 features his illustrations). Others included such famous Mexican artists as Rufino Tamayo, Leopoldo Méndez, and Manuel Rodríguez Lozano. The sculptor Federico Canessi was often at Traven's house in these final years. He fashioned the larger-than-life bust (1965) that shows Traven as an energetic, eternally young man with a visionary gaze.

Canessi was also responsible for the sculptural work on the Milpaso dam in Chiapas, about which Traven intended to make a documentary film in the 1960s. Not to be overlooked among Traven's intellectual circle is Traven's physician, Rivera's brother-in-law Federico Marín, who knew "el sueco" from the 1920s, when Edward Weston and Tina Modotti had their circle of intellectuals, artists, and politicians in Mexico City.

Marín and Canessi were interviewed in 1974 by Theo Pinkus, the Swiss book dealer, publisher, and literary agent. Pinkus related the comments of these friends—vivid snapshots of "Hal Croves" in his final period, when he enjoyed his greatest fame:

Marín:

> Hal, as his friends called him, was a worldly saint, of unbelievable kindness. He never thought ill of anyone, he forgave mistakes and human shortcomings. Whenever anyone expressed reservations, he would explain that he had the advantage of being stone deaf.
>
> He had great sympathy for young people; he was occupied with problems of the new generation and of the Indians who lived in wretched conditions.
>
> He never coveted money. He supported several Indian families. He sympathized with all the physical and mental sufferings of his fellow men, particularly of those whom he truly loved as brothers.

Canessi:

> The Skipper—as his friends would call him—was a true sage, although one didn't always know from where he took his wisdom. When I was working on a mural at the Milpaso dam in Chiapas, he once accompanied me. He told the engineers so much about Chiapas and its villages that they stood there with their mouths open. He knew the forest like the back of his hand, he had penetrated its most forbidding corners and had learned much about the Indians—he wept and laughed with them.
>
> Should I commit an indiscretion which he would surely not forgive? For many years he contributed money for the preservation of a ruin in Chiapas. He often paid the doctors who had to see the sick in the jungle. How often did he appear like a Saint Nicholas, loaded with gifts for the Indian children who experienced so little joy. . . .

> He detested playing with parables, detested artificial phrases, dirty tricks and disorder. He was all the more orderly, all the more simple, and he hid his true personality to avoid standing out. I do not believe that his life was a mystery. I believe that his modesty caused him to live in anonymity.

Managing the Literary Legacy

Aside from *Aslan Norval* (discussed later in this chapter), Traven's literary production during the final years in Mexico City was scant. He was certainly brimming as always with plans and ideas for new works, particularly stories, which he would draft in outline form. An idea for a story is noted on a calendar page as late as September 1967. Nothing came of such ideas, however, and even the revised version of *Land of Springtime*, which Traven planned in 1962 for the Fackelträger Press in Hannover, never made it into print. The main works to appear, as was the case in the later Acapulco years to a certain extent, were English translations or reworkings of stories that had long ago appeared in German. It is not always clear who deserves the credit for the translations. The English versions appeared in American magazines, and some of them were collected in *Stories by the Man Nobody Knows*. Some English texts were reprinted as well during these years, including *Macario* in *The Texas Quarterly* and a chapter from *The Cotton-Pickers* in the magazine *Fling*. Similar cases may come to light but are unlikely to change our view of Traven; if anything, they will reinforce the impression that the author now more than ever played the role of manager of his own literary estate, often in collaboration with his authorized representatives in New York (Scott Meredith) and in London (Curtis Brown).

And that was indeed a considerable task—for Traven himself no less than for his agents—given the tremendous upsurge in Traven's popularity after the Second World War. Traven described the situation in Germany to Max Schmid in 1961, speaking of his comeback after the Second World War (the German letter concludes with a typed "R. E. Luján" but was certainly written by Traven): "In the meantime an entirely new generation had come of age that knew nothing of T., a generation for whom even T's older works are new. Such books currently enjoy sales in West Germany which could not even have been dreamed of in the best times of the Weimar Republic."

Even in the United States Traven's writings (beyond *The Treasure of the Sierra Madre*, of course) began to gain popularity. *Short Story International* introduced him to the American public as "Mexico's most famous writer" in its edition of March 1963. And from 1966, the Hill & Wang editions began to appear in the United States, bringing the "man nobody knows" to a new circle of readers. The Knopf editions had enjoyed very modest success in the 1930s, but now a new generation of Americans would discover Traven afresh. In this regard Traven (or Rosa Elena Luján with his agreement) corresponded extensively with Lawrence Hill. One leitmotif in the correspondence is Traven's desire to become widely known in America and to take an active role in the production of the English texts; in some cases he either translated the works himself or revised existing English versions for the new editions. No longer did he talk of limiting the "propaganda," a word he used in both German and English in reference to advertising and promotion. To the contrary, as an old man Traven seems to have enjoyed seeing his works finally succeed in the United States—the land from which he claimed to hail. He must have taken equal pleasure at the prospect of the deluxe two-volume Mexican edition of his selected works, *Obras escogidas*, published after his death in 1969, in the country where he had also originally wished to keep his works from appearing.

The main activity remained in the German market, however, and Traven's interest in developments there was naturally keen. After he had parted with Büchergilde Gutenberg in 1939 and once the war was over, numerous German-language publishers began selling Traven's works on the open market (rather than primarily to book club members as the Büchergilde had done).

Of course the Büchergilde, in Frankfurt after the war, did continue to sell Traven titles even after its relations with the author had soured. It had apparently entered into agreements with Traven's agent Josef Wieder that were valid into the postwar period, to judge from a German letter to Max Schmid in 1961 signed by Rosa Elena Luján but no doubt authored by Traven. According to this letter, Traven had tried for five years (indeed, since 1948) to free himself from the Büchergilde, enjoying only partial success. Josef Wieder had died in the meantime. The *BT News*, which he had published, was discontinued (the last issue is dated April 1960); the Zurich-based Theo Pinkus became Traven's agent "for German-language editions and the Socialist countries." Pinkus had already dedicated himself to promoting Traven in the Eastern bloc countries while Wieder was alive. Tensions with the Büchergilde dissipated in the 1960s, and Büchergilde Gutenberg gradually became Traven's primary publishing house once again, a role it clearly retains today.

Still, other publishers were also instrumental in broadening Traven's audience. Rowohlt was particularly prominent in the author's final decade, and Traven did his part to promote its new editions of his works. The self-propaganda was apparently unavoidable, as it had been in the decade of the *BT News*. Traven sent Rowohlt reviews of earlier editions of his books. According to a cover letter dated January 26, 1962, one of these reviews mentioned "Albert Einstein's view of the works of B. Traven," no doubt a reference to Lionel Hale's article from the London *News Chronicle* of January 18, 1934, which in fact states that Einstein considered Traven the one author whose works he would take along to the proverbial desert isle. Traven even wrote promotional copy for the press and for the Rowohlt editions, though none made it into print. His texts call attention to the numerous translations and detail the size of the print runs for certain editions as well as play up film versions. His comments on *The Cotton-Pickers* are revealing:

> By April 1960 Traven's *The Cotton-Pickers* had appeared in twenty-six editions and in the following languages: English, German, Dutch, Danish, Norwegian, Swedish, Czech, Croatian, Polish, Hungarian, Bulgarian, Slovenian, Russian, and Hebrew.
>
> The first edition of the book in German appeared in 1926 with a run of 25,000. By 1932 some 70,000 copies had been printed; the novel had also been serialized in thirty-eight German-language newspapers.
>
> . . .
>
> Like many, perhaps most, other authors Traven first had to write a half million words before producing a work that made him one of the most widely read authors in twenty-six countries. He personally does not consider *The Death Ship* his best work. Someone once said: "No master has yet fallen from the sky." As one can see, this is also true of B. Traven.

Traven composed a similar text on *The White Rose*. In spite of all the self-promotion, however, he did not see only financial gain in the Rowohlt editions. He put a great deal of effort into linguistically refashioning his work dating back to the 1920s, wishing such texts to be the valid versions, which were then also published in the Büchergilde's *Werkausgabe* (*Collected Works*). Still, he was hardly unaware that his German had deteriorated considerably since the first edition of the novels. He wrote in English to Rowohlt on November 30, 1962, he said, because "I'm out of a German secretary" (which he never had)—a veiled admission of his weakening hold on the German language, one may assume.

Another aspect of Traven's estate management was his involvement in film versions of his novels and stories—or at least his lively interest in such projects, which made his works accessible to millions, above all in Mexico and North America, where he originally had not even wished to see his works appear in print. Traven's interest had begun with the filming of *The Treasure of the Sierra Madre* in the late 1940s and continued with the filming *The Rebellion of the Hanged* in 1953–1954. In his final years Traven maintained an interest in film, though he took a less active role in the production of *Macario* (1959), *The Death Ship* (1959), and *The White Rose* (1961). Recknagel provides an idea of Traven's involvement (in the guise of Hal Croves) in such films, basing his story on information from Gerti Villarejos: "Hal Croves could be seen only rarely at the film studio in Mexico City. When he was present—according to Reinhold Olschewsky [the main lead in *The White Rose*]—he offered advice and directions to the actors in a friendly and modest way. During a rehearsal Olschewsky suggested to Hal Croves that a scene be changed. Hal Croves responded that he first had to speak with B. Traven. But after only a half hour we had 'B. Traven's authorization.'" This contrasts markedly with Croves's more active participation in the filming of *The Rebellion of the Hanged*.

Traven (as Croves) expressed his interest in film in the final years most directly through his work on screenplays. His efforts, however, did not always make it to the screen. For *The Death Ship*, for example, Traven wrote several screenplay versions, none of which formed the basis for the 1959 film. The same is true of his 1957 screenplay for *The Bridge in the Jungle* (a film was produced after his death); and the film version of *The White Rose* (*La rosa blanca*) was based on Philip Stevenson's script, not Traven's 1960 treatment. The film *Días de otoño* (based on "Dennoch eine Mutter" ["Frustration"]) was based on the screenplay of Julio Alejandro and Emilio

Carballido (1962), not Traven's. Some works that Traven turned into screenplays were never filmed at all. The Traven estate contains, for example, a script labeled "Playing with Bombs. Screen Play by Hal Croves. Based on B. Traven's Story The History of a Bomb" (undated, possibly from the early 1950s). In other cases Traven merely made an outline, as in "Las hijas del general" ("The General's Daughters"); he also is said to have composed an outline (for William Miller) for a film on Pancho Villa. A documentary on David Alfaro Siqueiros was planned in the early 1960s but never completed. Nor did anything materialize from his 1966 idea for a film on the Milpaso dam in Chiapas.

The Traven novels and stories that finally became films thus give a scant impression of the extent of his screenplay work. The success of the Traven films that did materialize was rather unusual for those times, however. The triumphs of *The Treasure of the Sierra Madre* (screenplay by John Huston) and *The Rebellion of the Hanged* (screenplay by Hal Croves) have already been mentioned. Traven discussed *Macario* (screenplay by Hal Croves), also a box office hit, in a letter of February 17, 1961, to Sanora Babb:

> The picture has turned out the greatest artistic and financial success the Mexican Film Industry has ever enjoyed since the first film was done in Mexico.
>
> It ran at the Alameda Theatre which seats 3,260 for fourteen consecutive weeks, weekdays three, Saturday and Sunday four functions. The Alameda advertised in the papers congratulating the producer saying that the theatre in its twenty-four years of existence has never once had a box-office success similar to this film which means a lot if you consider that the Alameda had the run of the most famous pictures among them "Gone with the wind."
>
> After the picture had been on at the Alameda for fourteen weeks it was shown in two other movies for five weeks more. During the first week of November it ran at eight movie houses simultaneously.

La rosa blanca was not released until 1975, a delay that was politically motivated more than it was an affront to the novelist who was gaining fame as a film author. The Mexican government apparently did not wish to offend its neighbor to the north, which might see itself depicted in the film as brutally capitalistic and imperialistic. Traven mentioned another bit of behind-the-scenes intrigue in 1961, the year the film was shot: The leading actress, Christine Martell, had married the son of then Mexican president Miguel Alemán after "the pic was finished." Her husband's offense at his wife's nude scenes resulted in their being cut—and yet the film was still banned. In his conversations with Judy Stone, Traven (as Croves) claimed not to know the reason; even President Alemán could not do anything about the ban. "This story about the picture," he added, "in my opinion is almost as good as the book." The case certainly raised a stir, in a scenario that typified Traven's involvement with publicity in his later years: He became a Midas in the age of global communication. Everything the camera-shy recluse touched, everything that touched him, turned into publicity; he gained publicity even from his setbacks, his defeats, and, as with the *Rosa blanca* case, his very removal from the public.

While desiring the utmost publicity for his books, Traven must have felt ever more acutely the need for personal privacy. His house in the metropolis, protected by walls and an iron gate, was ideal for the isolation he craved. Unlike the orchard on the Pacific or the bungalow in the bush, his house on Calle Mississippi afforded him the opportunity to weave himself more deeply into his cocoon.

His escapes from this cocoon—his travels—were generally related to his long-standing passion for Chiapas and to film. Traven's last great journey, with Rosa Elena Luján of course, was in connection with the *Death Ship* film of 1959 (the *BT News* reported that rumors of the filming had been in circulation for years). Its Mexican producer, José Kohn, an exile from Bohemia, had met Traven through Gabriel Figueroa and had bought the film rights for $35,000. He collaborated with the German film company Ufa, and shooting began in May at Málaga harbor and in studios in Berlin (directed by Georg Tressler and starring Horst Buchholz). The screenplay by Hans Jacoby was presented to Hal Croves for approval before shooting began. Traven's estate contains "A few notes and observations about the Jacoby script" and "Memorandum on the Screen Script 'Das Totenschiff,'" dated April 24, 1959. Traven suggested numerous changes in details—for example, the former seaman regretted that the ships' flags were "set the wrong way"; perhaps he recalled the small notebook in which Marut had drawn flag signals as a young man. Traven, in spite of his many complaints, which he also expressed to Jacoby in person (as R. E. Luján recalls), thus appeared to have no objections in these notes to the more substantive plot changes: the insertion of a scene featuring a belly dancer in a North African bordello and the invention of Mylène, whom the sailor meets on his journey through French provinces. Nor does Traven seem to have had any objections to updating the depiction of Gales as the "prototype of the eternal DP [displaced person]." After a well-publicized dispute over finances between Kohn and Ufa head Arno Hauke that eventually involved the Berlin court (Traven as Croves had cabled Ufa from Mexico City that he annulled "film rights Traven Death Ship"), the film premiered on October 1, 1959, at the Hamburg City Theater. Traven and his wife traveled to Germany for the occasion, first to Berlin (where Rosa Elena Luján de Torsvan registered them at the Berlin Hilton on September 13 under the name Torsvan-Croves and "Torsvan called also Croves"). Traven had an operation on September 14 to combat his worsening hearing problems. Before the couple traveled on to Hamburg, Traven insisted on showing Rosa Elena the monument to Kaiser Wilhelm I in Grunewald.

Shortly after the movie's premiere in Hamburg, photos of Croves appeared in the papers (though cameras had been forbidden at the event), causing Croves to remark that "naturally" he was not Traven. Journalists revived the "mystery"; and the *BT News* fanned the fires by publishing three articles, one of them detailing the "prehistory" of the film based on the "world-famous book." "That Traven writes his stories on brown wrapping-paper with pencil is an invention of the reporters," according to the article "Vorgeschichte" ("Prehistory"), written by Traven himself, as indicated by a typescript preserved in the estate. "He wrote all his works with a typewriter," the article asserted, including *The Death Ship*, which he claimed at the time of its publication would "set the world on fire." The "message" of the novel, and that of the film to a lesser degree, could be summed up in a few words: "Two world wars that had been waged and won for freedom and democracy had robbed the individual of all his freedom, reducing him to a mere number. And if he can't present his number properly stamped, he finds himself deprived of man's fundamental freedom, the freedom of movement," according to the article "B. Travens weltberühmtes Buch 'Das Totenschiff' verfilmt!" ("A Film of B. Traven's World-Famous Book *The Death Ship!*"). Traven here contrasted the book and the film, singling out two motifs in the film that were not faithful to the novel and its "message." By putting undue weight on the "love story," Tressler "almost strangled the real story of the book." And "The brutal murder of the First Officer of the 'Yorikke,' carried out in the lowest gangster style, is not even hinted at in the book, and apparently serves no other purpose in the film than to give the viewer yet another rehashing of the Hollywood-style shoot-'em-up. . . . The true and deeply moving drama of the individual whom a heartless bureaucracy robs of his freedom of movement was presumably not engrossing enough."

Anonymity and Its Discontents: *Aslan Norval*

Traven did not leave Mexico in his final decade. But even at home he became painfully aware of the fragility of his protection against the outside world—particularly against the journalists who tried to corner him in the 1960s. The hope that he could gain publicity for his books while himself remaining hidden in the wings proved illusory because of the popularity of his books after the war and of the films inspired by them. Journalists were not the only threat from the outside, however. The public had found other ways of insinuating itself into the idyllic retreat on the Calle Mississippi.

Traven's name came up again in the 1960s as a candidate for the Nobel Prize (mention of the prize had surfaced in Traven's correspondence with his Swedish publisher Axel Holmström shortly after the war and again in connection with the Spota affair in 1948). In 1963, the year of Heidemann's first search for Traven, the critic Fritz J. Raddatz had inquired whether he could nominate Traven for the international Prix Formentor. Traven responded (in English) that there were more deserving candidates; besides, he added, he continued to do all he could to avoid personal publicity. In this case Traven was successful in heading off the publicity. But in 1967 a Stockholm newspaper openly advocated Traven's candidacy for the Nobel Prize.

Recknagel's detective work since the late 1950s identifying Traven as Ret Marut further stirred publicity in this period. The reaction from Mexico was a frantic rebuttal (signed by Traven's agent Josef Wieder) published in 1960 in the *BT News*, which rehashed the "official biography" (birth in Chicago as the son of Norwegian immigrants, and so on). Once again, Traven withdrew into an invented past.

This "past" offered little security against intrusions such as the fraudulent Traven manuscripts discussed in Chapter 2. Attempts to sell publishers unknown, "authentic" Traven novels not only added to the sensational atmosphere surrounding the author but also tarnished his reputation and thus affected his financial interests. But above all, they forced Traven to deny his authorship and thus brought about even more undesirable publicity. And the annoyance caused by such fraud no doubt impinged on Traven's creative energies. He could in principle set the record straight only by appearing in public before a court of law—impossible for the man preoccupied with his own anonymity. Josef Wieder, beyond articles in the *BT News*, had no choice but to publish in 1958 in a German book trade journal an announcement that must be unique in literary history:

Warning
Manuscripts of any sort, purportedly written
by the world-famous author
B. Traven
which are offered to book publishers or newspaper editors or
by anyone other than
B. Traven's
authorized representative,
named below,
or which are not authenticated by him
are crude counterfeits
which criminally abuse the name B. Traven.
J. Wieder, Zurich 9/47, Switzerland
B. Traven's legally authorized representative since 1933

Ironically, the defense against such wily false Travens would soon backfire on the real Traven. For the same year the announcement appeared, Traven had completed *Aslan Norval*, his first novel since *General from the Jungle* (1940). Publishers who had been offered the work viewed it as yet another counterfeit—not least because of its highly atypical subject matter and perceived substandard quality of writing. This was yet another infringement on the privacy and cocoonlike isolation of the famed author, who faced a choice of evils: of confronting the danger or ignoring it. In spite of widespread doubts of the novel's authenticity, first among prospective publishers and then among the public after it appeared under the Desch imprint (1960), a look through the Traven estate refutes any such suspicions.

There we find three typescript versions of the work, containing handwritten corrections by Traven and Schönherr (whose corrections Traven sometimes emended yet again). The affair over the authenticity of the novel, which the aging author had hoped would signal his comeback, instead stirred up old rumors. Was the author of *The Death Ship* even alive? some asked. Part of Traven's rationale for publishing *Aslan Norval* may well have been to prove that "B. Traven" was still alive, but in the end, the negative criticism of the novel, of its style and its emphasis on sex, must have told Traven that his creative powers were waning.

The attacks of the literary critics were indeed hurtful. East and West German critics vied for the honor of discrediting the celebrated figure—if he was indeed Traven and not a clever impostor. The novel tells the story of a super-rich, exquisitely beautiful American named Aslan Norval who is married to an aging tycoon. She has an affair with a young man, but her husband wins her back in the end. It is also the story of Aslan's project to build a cross-country canal from New York to San Francisco, which is depicted as more socially meaningful than stockpiling atomic weapons or exploring space. This plot was not perceived to live up to the claims made in the 1958 announcement of the novel in the *BT News*: The work, according to Traven's mouthpiece, aims at "giving us new direction by uprooting the foundations of the gnarled and hopelessly confused world of ideas in which we are all helplessly cooped up and which is preoccupied almost exclusively with war and the possibilities of war."

Friedrich Sieburg, a prominent conservative critic, wrote in 1960 in the *Frankfurter Allgemeine Zeitung* of the "empty secret" of B. Traven, peppering his critique with adjectives such as "colorless," "un-American," "old-fashioned," "boring," and "wooden." In the East German *Neue deutsche Literatur*, Pierre Unau published an article in the same year entitled "Traven or Not Traven?" in which he claimed that Traven seemed to write like a sixteen-year-old who had heard educational radio broadcasts of the Voice of America and the *Communist Manifesto*. "This isn't Traven!" Unau wrote—not the proletarian author, not the Traven "whom we love." *Aslan Norval* was tasteless and banal, he continued, hardly what one would expect from a Traven work. Recknagel was the first to take *Aslan Norval*'s sociopolitical message seriously ("peaceful efforts at improving society" and so on). Few echoed his sentiments—even

Traven (as Croves), in his interview with Judy Stone in 1966, seemed to consider publication of the novel a miscalculation and the work itself an artistic misstep.

Only once during the time of the controversy about *Aslan Norval* did Traven allow himself to be drawn out of his reserve. In the *BT News* of March 1959, when the novel was not yet available in print, he countered the objections raised by publishers to whom the manuscript had been offered. One senses the wounded pride of the man used to success: Those making the "extremely hurtful" claim that the book was of an "erotic nature" from the first page to the last underestimated it; *Aslan Norval* was in any event far from pornographic. Regarding the view that printing the novel would harm Traven's reputation, the author responded that he had neither a good nor a bad reputation as a writer—none at all in fact and hence none that could be damaged. A lame excuse, but full of the bitter animosity of one wounded by the experience that anonymity has its grave risks.

Traven's authorship of *Aslan Norval* is not discussed in the *BT News* rebuttal but is taken as self-evident. After publication of the book in the spring of 1960 Traven made special mention of this point of contention in a letter to the Swiss journalist Max Schmid, who would soon become known in Travenology as a representative of the "other man" hypothesis. The letter, dated June 9, 1961, is signed "R. E. Luján" but is in German; hence it is by Traven himself:

> As long as books have been written, countless times a debate has raged on whether a certain work was really written by the one named as its author, since it varied or seemed to vary from the style, form, or basic philosophy of other works of the same author whose authenticity did not stand in doubt.
>
> For years, T. has been accused of having but one string on his violin, playing it to excess, and peopling his supposedly narrow world with poor, enslaved, tortured Indians on the one hand and brutal exploiters and blood-suckers on the other.
>
> Like everybody else T. has the undisputable right to move with the times to keep from being left behind. People should praise him for being able to write about something other than only Indian proletarians, who are beginning to disappear here as well, though much more slowly than in the U.S. and Europe.
>
> T. is no politician, no world reformer, no propagandist, no partisan. He is a storyteller and, as he stated in a magazine thirty years ago, he tells the story as he sees it, as he saw it, or as he

> thinks he sees it. Under his name he has written numerous detective and similar stories, published only in English so far. Anyone who knows only his novels would not recognize them as his.
>
> And now he comes out with a book in which no enslaved Indios are martyred; instead, a beautiful and intelligent woman is the focus of attention who tries in her own way to solve the most pressing problem of our time, the atom bomb. And on the spot the tale is fabricated that T. could not possibly have written this book.
>
> We are surprised that you, Herr Schmid, an intelligent dramatist and no doubt familiar with T.'s books, do not search in his books for what is true T. and could not have been written by anyone else in the world but T. Instead, you single out an essentially isolated sentence, only a marginal comment taken from a newspaper, strictly speaking, and on that basis align yourself with the judgment of superficial critics.
>
> "The attempt was made to rein in the expansion of Bolshevism with dollars, *not with Western ideology and culture which at the core are entirely sound.*"
>
> If, Herr Schmid, instead of highlighting the entire final phrase ["fourteen" words, the German original says] you had done so only with *at the core*, you would have revealed that you know how to read T.

The healthy core of Western ideology, Traven explained in the following section of the letter, striking back at his critics, was the democratic countries' legal system, which does not limit the individual's freedom of movement or thought, as dictatorships do. That the author of *Aslan Norval* embraced this system proved his identity with the author of the other Traven novels, for this ideology was "T.'s authentic and most sincere view of the world. . . . T. sees no difference in the dictatorship of the church or the dictatorship of the Nazis or the dictatorship of Mussolini or the dictatorship of the Bolshevists—misleadingly called dictatorship of the proletariat—or the dictatorship masquerading as 'land reform' which today is running rampant in Cuba."

Hiding in the Limelight: Encounters with Journalists

Given the sensitive tone of the letter to Schmid and likewise of the reply to critics of *Aslan Norval* in the *BT News*, it comes as no surprise that Traven did all he could to sidestep reporters, who posed the gravest threat to his seclusion. "Croves" would brush aside journalists with the story that "Traven" was traveling, as usual, in the south of Mexico. Traven's dread of published photos and reports was so acute—he even let Gabriel Figueroa appeal for protection to the Mexican president—because he feared being "kidnapped" to Germany, according to Figueroa's conversations with Will Wyatt. More than forty years had passed since Ret Marut's name stood on the wanted list of the *Bavarian Police Record*. While his fears can scarcely have been well founded, his trauma must have been real enough. When Heidemann was hot on his heels in 1963, Traven fell victim to a nervous blindness, his family reports. One night he burned papers in the fireplace—perhaps papers from his Marut past. In ironic contrast, Traven also had to live with the rumors that he had died or was a patient in a mental hospital. One West German fan wrote to him in 1967, after reading Heidemann's report in *Stern*, that he was delighted to hear that the author was actually still alive. The same year *Revista de la Universidad de México* published a feature article on Traven (with a full-page photo of "Traven [not Croves] y su esposa") focusing on the dialectic of the author's obsession with secrecy and his world fame; the article further saluted the journalists interloping in Traven's hermetic world as detectives of the highest caliber.

Journalists did in fact gain entry to Calle Mississippi 61 on a number of occasions during these years. Lampl visited in November 1967, while Heidemann did so in December 1966. Two additional interviews were given in 1966: to Mexican journalist Luis Suárez, to whom Traven trustingly spoke as the author of the books, and to reporter Judy Stone from San Francisco (Marut's official "place of birth"), with whom Croves continued his game of cat and mouse concerning his identity, unsuccessfully, as it turned out.

With all his publicity dodging, why did Traven grant these revealing interviews? Was it to counter the Marut rumors with his "official" biography? He did not particularly need an interview for this purpose, having made the case in writing on numerous occasions. Three years earlier Gerd Heidemann's determined attempt to gain access to Traven, then on Calle Durango, had been fruitless; and it had resulted nevertheless in his publication in *Stern* of "Das Rätsel Traven gelöst" ("The Riddle of Traven Solved"). In spite of its title, the article offered no new information (it claimed Traven's identity with Bibeljé, the customs officer from Mecklenburg) but deeply shook Traven nonetheless. Traven had also routinely declined interviews with other journalists, as Suárez noted in his report, including one with *Quick* reporter Johannes Leeb, who had made a name for himself as the coauthor of a book on the Nuremberg trials. Why then Traven's sudden willingness to appear before the public?

The interviews, like the letters to the Büchergilde in the 1920s, most likely offered Traven a chance to break out of his self-imposed isolation and enter into some sort of communication with his readers. They seem to represent his attempt to experience personally the recognition due him, a form of self-assertion that allowed him to draw close to his public, no matter how briefly. Stone's report in particular reveals how "Croves" is able to enjoy the attention given to "Traven" in the interview. Speaking of the author in the third person, Traven vicariously enjoys his self-worth to the full, as he had years earlier in the Spota interview.

Suárez's interview was the first to appear. "*Siempre* finally unmasks the most exciting literary mystery of the century and presents B. TRAVEN to the world!" read the headline to *Siempre*'s five-page illustrated report on October 19, 1966. For the first time, Suárez boasted, a journalist could say "This is B. Traven," without the author denying the claim. Neither Suárez nor Traven revealed anything, however. The journalist had agreed not to mention even the street address in Mexico City (only interior photographs were permitted). And regarding Traven's country house, the article stated that Traven had never been there nor did he know its location. The name Croves did not come up in the interview (only the first name Hal). It was "Traven" or "Traven Torsvan" who was interviewed, as the author of the works. Suárez elicited hardly any new information—only well-known stories, rumors, facts, and the official biography of the American who did not know German, this time the son of a fisherman. When the conversation turned to the Bavarian revolution, Traven restated his creed that the work was important, not the author, and a harmless letter was printed that made that point. Traven had no "secret," Suárez reported; the press had pursued its own interests in stirring up controversy. All the while, in contrast to the interview with Spota almost two decades earlier, the distinction between Torsvan and Traven was fully abandoned. Traven also stressed the identity of life and work and his drive to live for his work to the very end. Asked whether he was satisfied with his extensive *oeuvre,* Traven answered with a clear no: "Because I'd like to do more. Write more and live more." And in everything he wrote he admitted to a "Mexican viewpoint"—the unofficial national laureate at the peak of his career.

Suárez provided some details about Traven's physical appearance: a man of (supposedly) seventy-six years, medium height, blond hair with streaks of gray, receding at the temples, his eyes tired behind glasses, a hearing aid in his right ear. He moved with a certain caution. One had to speak slowly with him. He himself spoke slowly, haltingly and with harsh pronunciation, his *r* giving away the nonnative speaker of Spanish. The Suárez interview caused a sensation in Europe and the United States as in Mexico. Suárez himself reported on the reaction abroad in *Siempre.*

Judy Stone made less of an international splash with her own report on her discussions which had begun before the Suárez interview (May 1966) and continued in November and December of that year. She published her results first in the San Francisco magazine *Ramparts* in September and October 1967 and in final form in *The Mystery of B. Traven* in 1977.

Traven (as Croves) refused to open up during their long discussions on Calle Mississippi, in restauraunts in the Zona Rosa, and on their excursion by car to San José Purúa. He firmly maintained that he was not Traven—scarcely believable even as far back as the trip to Germany in 1959. Croves did claim to be an authority on Traven's works and views, however. Though Traven was busy traveling in the tropical regions of Mexico, Croves had written to Stone, Croves himself was "really eager" to speak with her. "You may be assured that your trip will turn out to be an unforgettable one" as there was so much to see and learn. To perfect the cover, Croves in the interview repeated the story that Traven had written his works before the Mexican revolution, during the regime of Porfirio Díaz (until 1910)—thus long before 1924. Traven had been captured by Pancho Villa around 1914, Croves recalled. Ret Marut—who therefore could not have been Traven—was dismissed as a "political charlatan" who had probably not been involved in the Bavarian revolution at all. And Croves repeated the old chestnut that the work, not the author, was important; Traven's works did reveal the author's views, but not actual biographical details. This interview serves as a prime example of how Traven fervently sought contact with the public, establishing contact, however, only in the third person. (In the case of Suárez, he made contact on the condition that no mention be made of either his address or his current pseudonym, Croves.)

The Stone interview also reveals, more clearly than Traven's usual toying with the press, that the nervous old man saw his entire existence at stake. He knew he was playing with fire and, though ever on guard, Croves occasionally came dangerously close to revealing that he was Traven. He sensed that his visitor, who was becoming a friend in the course of the interviews, had long seen through this ruse. His very first words, spoken with a German accent, showed him on the defensive: "Forget the man! What does it matter if he is the son of a Hohenzollern prince or anyone else? Write about his works. Write how he is against anything which is forced upon human beings." His farewell to the woman whose news story could spell danger for him had the same nervous ring: "We have enjoyed having you. Don't spoil it." And earlier in their meetings, Stone wrote, "He kissed me goodbye and admonished pleadingly, 'Don't write anything that might hurt us.' He smiled shyly and they [Traven and his wife] left." On another occasion Rosa Elena Luján asked Stone if she could forgo reporting on the meetings entirely; her husband had said he would reward the journalist with lifelong friendship if she did not write about him.

Croves called on his full repertoire of themes in the conversations with Stone. He discussed Traven's—and his own—opposition to communism and fascism alike. He attacked the Nazis for their anti-Semitism. Croves illustrated their treatment of Traven with his typical flair for embellishment, if not outright invention. When the Nazis conquered a country such as Hungary, Yugoslavia, or Czechoslovakia, "one of their first orders" was to burn Traven's books. Anyone buying one of his books was ordered shot. But there was another side to the Nazis' reception of Traven, Croves noted: *General from the Jungle*, published in 1940 in Amsterdam, sold poorly in Holland until the Germans marched in. The Nazi soldiers were so intrigued by Traven that the entire print run of five thousand copies was sold out within a week. Traven's works have something to say, Croves went on; they are not merely light reading. And he drew the contrast with Joseph Conrad, as had previously been done in *The Death Ship* "Birth Notice." Croves spoke of Traven's love for the Indians, another favorite topic. Their religion was "far better" than the Judeo-Christian religion, particularly the Indians' notion of life after death, which expressed Traven's philosophy in mythical terms. The Aztec paradise was a place of hard labor, harder than on earth. Georg Büchner played with a similar idea of the afterlife in *Woyzeck* (the basis of Alban Berg's opera) to drive home satirically the plight of the proletariat. In Mexico the scenario was taken more positively: In paradise the Indians must "shape the clouds, guide the lightning," and so on.

The conversations naturally touched on individual novels. Traven considered *The White Rose* a seminal work, holding up "the value of the soil" against the accomplishments of the industrialized world. This was not only the theme of this novel, Croves said, but also the thread running through all of Traven's works: "This nearness to the soil is the most frequent and most important element in Traven's books." Croves maintained, "I would never classify Traven as an intellectual. He is so very close to earth as an intellectual never can be and never will be." The man who for years had led an unsettled life among the Indians but who owed his present comfortable existence to the book and film industries turned against civilization: The American consumer-oriented society dominated by radio and television "and all that" was not his milieu. "Traven likes to see birds sing in the morning, trees misting in the morning." A critic had rightly noted that Traven's basic convictions ran parallel to those of Thoreau. Even *The Death Ship* sounded the theme of longing for one's own piece of land.

Turning to *The Death Ship*, Croves restated that the American sailor Gales was not the truly important character; but Stanislav, who represented "a real person," was the key to the novel. Croves naturally could not say *why* Stanislav was such a key figure, who he was, and how Traven came to know him. He was, after all, not Traven: "How could *I* know Stanislav?" He was more forthcoming in explicating the novel itself:

> It's not just the story of an American sailor. It has a deeper meaning. It's not only about passports. It's that human beings under modern conditions are forced. . . . If you have no passport, you can't return to the idea of the human soul and the human being has been lost entirely. In such lines as I now tell you, we come to the fundamental idea on which the book is based. The American consul says, "How do I know who you are? You haven't got a birth certificate." "You see me, I must be alive," Gales answered. "Yes, I see you, but if I report you to Wash-

ington, there is no proof." Gales says, "Perhaps you even deny that I am alive." "Officially, I deny your existence. Officially, you are not alive."

This was the novel's "fundamental idea," Croves said. It was also Traven's fundamental experience in life: the question of human identity and a person's rights in a bureaucracy that assigns unique numbers to each member of civilized society but does not make him a self, an individual with unique personal qualities. Without papers one is dead, a nobody; but with bureaucratic papers as the sole means of "identification," Traven implied in his books, one is little more than that. Human beings can be human only when they are identified using means other than I.D. documents, as in the primitive Indian communities, for example, where living conditions were far worthier of human beings. A utopian and nostalgic picture, but at the same time an invigorating challenge for Traven.

Croves's commentary on *Aslan Norval* was strange: By limiting his role to that of Traven's agent, Croves could distance himself from this atypical work of the aged author. Croves's claim that the book did not live up to the standard of the earlier Traven novels sounds like an echo of the widespread criticism of the work. The work was stylistically poor, he said, focused too much on sex, in fact not written at all in the Traven style. In his "personal opinion," it should not circulate under Traven's name. Sincerity or subterfuge? Was the clever author merely expressing his regret at not choosing a different pseudonym for his last book, two decades after the Mahogany series was completed? Or had he come to see in the meantime that *Aslan Norval* represented a decline?

When Judy Stone's report appeared in *Ramparts* in 1967, Traven was very much a topic of conversation throughout the world, in Europe above all. In May, Heidemann had published his second and long-awaited report in *Stern*. The same month, *Westdeutscher Rundfunk* broadcast a five-evening documentary on Heidemann's detective work that had led to the discovery of Traven in Mexico City. The international press, led by the Germans, was quick to join in this new and, it appeared, final phase of the manhunt, whether in criticism or acceptance of the findings. After his years of investigations around the world, Heidemann was offering no run-of-the-mill solution to the mystery: The father of the famous writer was no less than Kaiser Wilhelm II. The immediate rebuttal from Traven's wife on May 17, 1967, in *Siempre*—she denied telling Heidemann that her husband was a bastard son of the kaiser, his mother a singer of Norwegian descent—added more spice to the controversy rather than putting it to rest.

In the summer of 1963 Heidemann had not gained access to Traven. He had cornered Rosa Elena Luján in the main post office as she was picking up mail from P.O. Box 2701. She spoke with him "for a total of thirteen hours" but ruled out an interview with Traven. She finally granted the reporter a meeting with her husband in early December 1966. In the resulting *Stern* report Heidemann did not mention Croves; Traven apparently had abandoned at least this subterfuge. Heidemann said he spoke with *Traven*, and his use of "Mr. Traven" met with no objections—something Hal Croves and T. Torsvan would normally not have tolerated. But had the host—wearing a hearing aid and described in *Stern* as "effectively deaf"—actually understood his guest? Ferdinand Anton, the archeologist friend of the Travens' who accompanied Heidemann on this memorable visit, reported that "Rosa Elena Luján de Torsvan" had admonished the two visitors beforehand not to speak German with their host nor to ask him if he was Traven (which they did not). Anton added: "We did not present ourselves as reporters or detectives, but as an archeologist and his assistant, and we had come to talk about Mexico." The guests, too, were thus practicing a sort of deception—highly significant (if Anton remembers correctly). For it shows that Traven had not chosen this December afternoon to end his decades-long charade with the public, to reveal his "secret," just as he had had no such intention when he talked to Suárez. Traven was thus not intentionally "giving himself up," as Heidemann claimed. To the contrary, he had unwittingly stumbled into a trap, as it must have appeared to him when he read in *Stern* that one of his guests had been an investigative journalist—and one who presented the sensational Kaiser Wilhelm theory as gospel, citing none other than Rosa Elena Luján as his source!

Heidemann's story, which purported to solve the "tantalizing riddle of modern literature," the secret of the "most mysterious writer of the twentieth century," deeply upset and enraged Traven. His instinct to flee must have been revived, to judge from R. E. Luján's letter to Judy Stone of June 21, 1967. Traven's world, Hal Croves's cocoon, built up and protected so carefully over the decades, had seemed to offer security in his old age but was now threatening to collapse. For the *Stern* story, published in Hamburg, revived not only the legend of Traven's noble ancestry but also the ghost of Marut, the bit actor and Munich revolutionary on the wanted list. And all this was presented as the factual, not hypothetical, background of the man who a few years earlier had been fêted at the Hotel Atlantic in Hamburg as a leading figure of world literature. The "other man" also made his appearance in *Stern*—likewise as "fact": The experiences of a certain August Bibeljé (identified with Traven in the *Stern* article of 1963) had provided Traven with the raw materials for *The Death Ship* and *The Treasure of the Sierra Madre*, it was claimed.

Traven clearly could not have predicted that it would come to this when he descended the stairs from the bridge at five o'clock that winter afternoon to greet the guests seated by the fireplace:

> The white-haired man of medium height seems frail and almost transparent.
>
> With small, careful steps he approaches the reporter and extends a strong hand which shakes a bit, his head held at a slight angle.
>
> Traven smiles warmly. Thick glasses make his bright blue eyes unnaturally large, though he can scarcely see ten meters away. He is effectively deaf, in spite of his hearing aid.
>
> He tries to read his guests' lips—they speak in English, for he does not wish to speak German, his wife points out.
>
> Traven offers them a drink. They have mescal, a strong liquor made from the thornless agave. The old man has four shots, and his wife says: "He is still a man, a real man."
>
> Dinner is at Traven's favorite spot, Bellinghausen, a formerly German gourmet restaurant. His wife drives the white Chevrolet 66, license-plate 662 NS. Traven has another drink and increasingly opens up.
>
> Heidemann shows him pictures from Chiapas. Traven, in a deep voice full of energy, tells colorful tales of his travels and experiences there, speaking English with an unmistakable German accent. He asks whether certain people are still alive and is touched that they all remember him so well.
>
> His wife has to repeat most of the conversation into her husband's hearing aid at a specific pitch.
>
> He is not put off by the reporters calling him "Mr. Traven." His only response: "You have to understand me, my life belongs to me alone, only my books belong to the public."
>
> A quick farewell comes two hours later. Traven seems absent and tired, and wishes the reporter "Good luck!"

Ferdinand Anton provided a few further details. Their host wore one blue and one yellow slipper (so that he could distinguish between them easily with his myopia). They drank tequila, mescal, and comiteco, and "Torsvan" spoke about the Indians in a number of Mexican states. He spoke about Traven "sometimes in the third person, sometimes in the first person," and also talked about "the theater, some politics, and the Congo." Munich seemed off limits. "After dinner the delicate, aristocratic-looking Traven takes the bones from his wife's plate and wraps them in a paper napkin. 'For Tabasco, one of my dogs, he likes them so much.' When we were back out on the street, out of nowhere comes the question: 'Do the Bierkellers in Munich still have the political importance?' The question hangs unanswered on the Calle Londres in Mexico City."

Last Words and a Lasting Secret

So we find Traven in late 1966: The world seemed to be growing ever more removed from the old man, his hearing and sight failing. (He was in all likelihood eight years older than he claimed, born in 1882 rather than 1890.) He still had flashes of youthful élan; and all accounts attest to his warmth among those who were simpatico as well as to the special intimacy between Traven and his wife. But there could be no doubt that the end was near, particularly after a serious illness in 1963–1964. "I was working so hard," he wrote to Sanora Babb on October 28, 1964, "without sufficient rest and no vacation that I suffered a terrific breakdown and which brought me very close to the end of my theather [*sic*], earnestly speaking, my medicos had little hope to get me through and out of it. I am still far from being myself again as you perhaps can see from this letter. All confused, because my eyesight also suffered, so did other faculties. I only can repeat to you and Jimmy to come up here for a week or two." Judy Stone provides a further detail: "He looked at her [Rosa Elena] fondly and said she had almost literally pulled him back from death a few years ago when he was very ill." It must have seemed a new lease on life for him. In the letter to Sanora Babb he noted cryptically (the context provides no further clues): "Right now I am practically on my way to Chiapas, preparing sort of something for future generations so to say." Traven survived this difficult period as he would the trauma of the *Stern* report in the summer of 1967.

What went through Traven's head in the final years after his serious illness, one can only speculate. If he did know his identity—the identity of his father and mother—he must have wondered whether it would be right to hand over this information to posterity. The day he died, Traven authorized his wife to acknowledge that he had been Ret Marut. Was that all he had to reveal?

Anonymity had its risks. That must have become increasingly clear to him in the final years. On the back of a calendar page from May 1967 is scribbled (in English): "Anonymity its threats. Possibilities of danger." But nowhere, as far as I can tell, did Traven even hint at the truth behind his anonymity, or, more properly, pseudonymity. He may well have had *no* secret to reveal regarding his true roots or his true name. He may not have known himself or may not have known with absolute certainty.

Mystification was not Traven's principal occupation in his final years. Rather, he dedicated himself primarily to the daily "work" which to him was far more important than the "person" hunted by the paparazzi and the literary sleuths. His October 1964 letter to Sanora Babb concluded with a mention of the many projects on which he was currently working. Traven said he must write to Sanora's husband, the director and cameraman Jimmy Howe—about what he did not yet know, "because I have several projects which have not matured sufficiently that I could say something definite about." Projects, plans, drafts, new editions (particularly for the U.S. market)—these molded Traven's daily routine to the very end. Among his more ambitious plans in the final years were a book on the life of Benito Juárez, the Indian who took on the Mexican presidency after the execution of Maximilian (an outline exists in the Traven estate) and a history of the Luján family.

About three weeks before his death, Traven visited Bodil Christensen, the Danish friend from his days at the university in Mexico City who had introduced him to his future wife in the 1930s. Christensen now lived on Avenida Cinco de Mayo in the capital. She recalls the visit:

> He stood in the hall and handed me a copy of *The Creation of the Sun and the Moon* and said "This is Traven's last book." There was a special way that he looked at me, a special way he said the words "last book." At first I thought that he meant Traven's most recent book, but then I realized that he meant that this was the end, that there would be no more books. I

> wanted to say "You mean *your* last book," but I never did. I knew he was Traven and he knew that I knew he was Traven, but neither of us ever said so.

The day Traven said farewell to his old friend may well have been the same on which he said his official, legal farewell. On March 4, 1969, he insisted on going to his attorney to sign and notarize his will (which his widow says had been ready for two years). Rosa Elena tried to dissuade him, but that afternoon he went to the office of Juan Manuel G. de Quevedo on Avenida Juárez, where he signed the will in the presence of Federico Canessi, Alberto Beltrán, and Federico Marín. Not that he had been ill. That evening a friend came to the house and "they drank until 4 a.m. He awakened me with champagne," his wife recalls, "he would often do that."

In his will, his "*primero y único testamento*," Traven states that he was the American Traven Torsvan Croves, born on May 3, 1890, in Chicago, son of Burton Torsvan and his wife Dorothy, née Croves; husband of Rosa Elena Luján; writer by profession; naturalized as a Mexican citizen on September 13, 1951. In his long literary career, the document continues, he used "names such as" B. Traven and Hal Croves; before marrying Rosa Elena Luján he had not been previously married, either under his true name ("*nombre propio*") or under a pseudonym. His wife is named as both executrix and sole heir to his property, the majority of which consists of the various rights to his works of all types. She is the only one authorized to execute Traven's wishes regarding his writings and to control the literary estate. In this regard Traven emphasizes that he has authorized no one as his biographer; his biography should not be written without the approval of his wife and heir. If she should die before him or at the same time, the rights of inheritance would be transferred to his stepdaughters Rosa Elena and María Eugenia.

On the morning of March 4, on which he had made his will legally binding by his signature, Traven wrote the following lines, most likely his last, capturing for the last time his life's dominant theme (the passage, written in English in a frail hand, begins at the top of a large sheet of paper, as if more was to follow):

> This world with all its troubles, shortcomings, disappointments, pains, problems, unwelcome events, occasional hailstorms is after all, still too beautiful to abandon even if you are sick, tired of life or close to a hopeless end. Stick it out. Keep

on fighting, don't give up. Spit Death in its face and turn the other way. The sun is still in the sky surrounded by stars.

Traven was to live three more weeks. Though not actually sick, he was becoming weaker; he was in good spirits and working to the end and was confined to his bed only in his final hours. Rosa Elena Luján has recalled:

> I remember the day he died. He had been revising his novel *The Carreta*. He put aside the manuscript. Malu and I were in the room. He started to say something to us and then stopped suddenly in the middle of a sentence. A tear dropped from his eye and fell on my palm. . . . Just before he died he told me that I could reveal to the world that he was Ret Marut the Bavarian anarchist.

Traven died on Wednesday, March 26, 1969, on the bridge. At his side were his stepdaughters and wife; it was 5:50 P.M.; the rays of evening light were streaming through the broad windows. Rosa Elena recalled, "He died kissing my hands and saying he loved me." Federico Marín confirmed the death of his friend. Shortly thereafter—Luis Suárez had been notified—photographers, reporters, and radio and television crews swarmed through the house on Calle Mississippi.

The death certificate, issued the following day, bore the same pseudonym as the will, one that Traven rarely used in this form: "Traven Torsvan Croves," born in Chicago, seventy-eight years old, naturalized Mexican citizen, writer by profession, son of Burton Torsvan and Dorothy Croves, married to Rosa Elena Luján; cause of death: sclerosis of the kidneys and prostate cancer; cremation at Panteón Civil in Mexico City. The hour of death given in the official certificate, 11:20, is incorrect. Traven would have enjoyed that. Even in death, as so often in life, he managed to escape society's enslaving demand for the facts.

NOTES

Preface

ix with more than thirty million readers worldwide by now: See pp. 4–5 about this estimate.

x *Vorbilder für Deutsche*: Ed. Peter Glotz and Wolfgang R. Langenbucher (Munich, 1974). Other school texts include *Vagabunden: Three Modern German Stories*, ed. Wolfgang Paulsen and Fred L. Fehling (New York, 1950); Bruno Traven, *Macario* (Spanish), ed. Sheilah R. Wilson (Boston, 1971); Beck, Bergmann, and Boehncke, *Das Traven-Buch* (see especially p. 18); Werner Glenewinkel and Werner Hennings, *B. Traven im Unterricht: Zur Didaktik des Nord-Süd-Dialogs* (Bielefeld, 1982); Glenewinkel and Hennings, *Anpassung oder Widerstand? Ein Arbeitsbuch zu technischem Fortschritt und gesellschaftlichem Wandel am Beispiel von B. Traven "Die Weisse Rose"* (Bielefeld, 1982).

x a sort of forerunner by Brecht . . . " 'alternative lifestyle' ": Werner Helwig, *Die Tat* (Zurich), April 19, 1969, p. 40. Brecht, Helwig reported, had a "silent admiration" for Traven and remarked that "*The Death Ship* was one of those nameless works of world literature in which he found something of himself anticipated." Brecht's face "lit up" when Helwig told him his work revealed "a great fondness for Traven's style and manner." On the beat generation, see Drewey W. Gunn, *American and British Writers in Mexico 1556–1973* (Austin, Texas, 1974), p. 218; on the "hero of the 'alternative lifestyle,' " see Harry Pross, "Ein Mann namens Feige," *Stuttgarter Zeitung*, March 24, 1979.

xi "The only date known for certain": *Stern*, April 15, 1982, p. 100.

xi "My life story . . . would not disappoint": *Die Büchergilde*, March 1926, p. 34.

xii the author's presentation of Traven' life "predominantly through his literary works": Recknagel, *B. Traven*, p. 34.

Chapter 1

3 Bruno Kreisky's thank-you note: Traven estate.

3 H. C. Hansen: See *BT-Mitteilungen* (*BT News*), no. 32, December 1958.

3 Einstein's favorite author: Lionel Hale, "Einstein's Desert-Island Author," *News Chronicle* (London), January 18, 1934. Clipping in the Traven estate.

4 "probably the most mysterious figure in contemporary letters": *Die Welt*, March 31, 1969, p. 8.

4 A few days before the *Welt* notice: All statements about Traven's death and funeral are based on newspaper reports in the clipping file in the Traven estate as well as on Stone, *The Mystery of B. Traven*, pp. 83–87; William Weber Johnson, "Pilgrimage to the Sierra Madre," *Life*, May 30, 1969, section between pp. 20 and 21; Luis Suárez, "Al borde del fin, Traven pensó en un escopetazo al estilo Hemingway," *Siempre*, April 9, 1969, pp. 12–15; and Jesús Sánchez Hermosillo, "Sólo la muerte reveló el misterio," *Impacto*, April 16, 1969, pp. 40–44. Señora Luján also provided information.

4 "Few writers": Traven estate.

4 Extensive pictorial essays: On April 5, 9, and 16, respectively.

4 32 million in 1982: *Stern*, April 15, 1982, p. 106.

5 "The Governor's Palace in Tuxtla Gutiérrez": *Land des Frühlings*, pp. 349–51.

8 a fact that had been established for some time: See also Suárez, "Al borde del fin" and William Johnson, "A Noted Novelist Who Lived and Died in Obscurity," *Los Angeles Times Calendar*, April 13, 1969, p. 12.

8 "As soon as I feel the hour of death": *Der Ziegelbrenner* (*The Brickburner*), no. 4, July 27, 1918, p. 94.

9 "*I am nothing*": *Der Ziegelbrenner*, no. 4, July 27, 1918, p. 84.

9 Tampico diary: Traven estate.

9 He was also chairman: *Der Ziegelbrenner*, no. 18–19, December 3, 1919, p. 15.

10 Marut expected a death sentence: See *Der Ziegelbrenner*, no. 18–19, December 3, 1919, p. 15, and *BT-Mitteilungen*, no. 25, April 1957. Many of Marut's "coconspirators" were indeed condemned to death; see Chapter 4, p. 140.

10 "Two soldiers felt a spark": *Der Ziegelbrenner*, no. 18–19, December 3, 1919, p. 20.

10 an American sailor named Gales: In the English editions overseen by Traven, the name is Gales; in the German editions it is Gale. *Gales* is used throughout this book.
12 "the greatest literary mystery of this century": Paul Theroux, (London) *Times*, June 22, 1980, p. 44.
13 "Lucky he who can be someone else!": Georg Büchner, *Leonce und Lena*, act I, scene 1.
13 "Only he who has lived life": *BT-Mitteilungen*, no. 9, October 1952. On the *BT-Mitteilungen*, see Chapter 6, pp. 353–56. [533–36]

Chapter 2

17 *Das Totenschiff*: The novel was "sold out in four weeks," Traven wrote in a note on the filming of the book. Traven estate; see also *BT-Mitteilungen* (*BT News*), no. 35, November 1959.
17 selling 120,000 copies: *Die Büchergilde*, April 1936, p. 65.
17 "Anyone who applies for a job": *Die Büchergilde*, March 1926, p. 34; repeated in *BT-Mitteilungen*, no. 6, March 1952.
18 "trader among the wild Indian tribes": Quoted from *Die Büchergilde*, April 1936, p. 52.
18 "It is clear that works": *Die Büchergilde*, March 1927, p. 35.
18 "We are asked": *Die Büchergilde*, February 1928, p. 18.
19 "Next to nothing is known": *Die Büchergilde*, November 1931, p. 351.
19 " 'Who is this man?' ": Letter from B. Traven to Johannes Schönherr, January 5, 1928.
19 "Der Bungalow": *Die Büchergilde*, February 1928, pp. 19–22.
20 the many hardships he encountered: See Chapter 5, p. 220.
20 But that irked him: Letter from B. Traven to Johannes Schönherr, January 5, 1928.
20 in the 1950s and 1960s, the nondescript gringo: See, for instance, *BT-Mitteilungen*, no. 4, n.d. (1951); no. 28, August 1957; no. 17, December 1954.
20 "There are dead men": *Der Ziegelbrenner* (*The Brickburner*), no. 3, March 16, 1918, p. 49.
21 "who are dead from their first day in school": *Der Ziegelbrenner*, no. 3, March 16, 1918, p. 49.
21 "revealed more about himself": *Die Büchergilde*, September 1931, p. 287.
21 repeated in his own *BT News*: *BT-Mitteilungen*, no. 3, n.d. (1951).
21 "I know the courage": *Die Büchergilde*, February 1928, p. 26.
22 between his citizenship and his nationality: In his 1938 letter to the Spanish Republicans (see Chapter 6, p. 316), he denied that he was German by "race" or "blood"; he could claim neither German

"citizenship" ("*Staatsangehöngkeit*") nor German "nationality" ("*Volkszugehörigkeit*"), he wrote on October 16, 1927, in a letter to Johannes Schönherr.

22 His "true countrymen": *Die Büchergilde*, February 1928, p. 25.

23 Traven was very upset: See Chapter 5, pp. 242 and 273.

23 "Workers . . . should not respect": Manfred Georg, "Kennen Sie B. Traven?" ("Do You Know B. Traven?"), *Die Weltbühne*, vol. 25, part 2, pp. 484–85.

24 *Vier neue amerikanische Dichter*: Zurich, 1929.

24 letter to Strasser: Charlot Strasser, *Arbeiterdichtung* (*Workers' Literature*) (Zurich, 1930), p. 193.

24 "The typesetter who sets my book": Strasser, *Arbeiterdichtung*, p. 196.

24 as Traven sometimes chose to maintain: He claimed this version, for example, in the third issue (n. d., 1951) and in the eighth issue (July 1952) of *BT-Mitteilungen*.

24 "doesn't know proper German" . . . "awful Americanisms": Peter Panter [Kurt Tucholsky], "B. Traven," *Die Weltbühne*, vol. 26, part 2 (1930), p. 800.

25 "His mother tongue is English": Strasser, *Arbeiterdichtung*, p. 193.

25 he did not need to look further than his own statements: See Chapter 2, pp. 18, 19.

25 "Traven und sein amerikanischer Verleger": *Die Büchergilde*, December 1931, p. 381.

25 "Numerous newspapers now think they have discovered": *Die Büchergilde*, September 1932, p. 160.

26 B. Traven surely read that: The press reports cited in *Die Büchergilde* may not have been simply plucked from thin air. Only Traven himself could have known for sure, having been involved in political controversies even before his Marut period. See, for example, *Der Ziegelbrenner*, no. 18–19, December 3, 1919, p. 10.

26 he did so in a tone of amusement: See Chapter 6, pp. 310–11.

26 a seemingly unconnected digression: Fragment of *The Death Ship*, ca. 1923–1924. Traven estate.

26 every skipper automatically thought "cutthroat": *Das Totenschiff*, p. 181.

26 his "own judge": See Chapter 3, p. 79.

27 English nationality . . . was changed: Recknagel claims that the change was made at the beginning of the war (*B. Traven*, p. 38). However, this is not indicated on either side of the registration card.

27 Marut was officially registered: Bayerisches Hauptstaatsarchiv, Abt. IV, Akte "I. Armee-Korps, 2033."

27 After 1930 Traven thus returned: In the 1930s, Traven gave the American version even to Americans, such as the bibliophile Harry W. Schwartz, who published Traven's letter stating "I am an American born in the U.S.A." in 1937. Harry W. Schwartz, *This Book Collecting Racket* (Chicago: Normandie House, 1937), pp. 80–81.

27 "*The Death Ship* is": *Die Büchergilde*, June 1936, p. 100.

27 Traven says nearly the same: *The Death Ship* (New York: Knopf, 1934), pp. 109–10; compare *Das Totenschiff*, p. 122.

28 "Traven, the author of *The Death Ship*": *Leipziger Volkszeitung*, September 24, 1947.

28 Shortly after the Second World War: William W. Johnson, "Trying to Solve the Enigma of the *Sierra Madre*," *Smithsonian*, March 1983, pp. 164–65; see also Johnson, *New York Times Book Review*, April 17, 1966, p. 42.

29 Traven liked to regale his friends: *The Night Visitor and Other Stories*, p. viii.

29 Traven himself published extensive biographical information: "Wer ist B. Traven?" ("Who Is B. Traven?"), *BT-Mitteilungen*, no. 8, July 1952.

30 "B. Traven, of Norwegian descent": *BT-Mitteilungen*, no. 25, April 1957.

30 the yearning for exotic, primeval, far-off lands: See *Der Ziegelbrenner*, no. 4, July 27, 1918, p. 81.

30 "The only thing one knows for sure": *BT-Mitteilungen*, no. 11, August 1953.

31 his occupations: See Chapter 5, p. 178.

31 Smith attested to the presence of Germanisms: *New York Times Book Review*, November 22, 1970, p. 2. Also see Chapter 6, p. 309.

31 the strong German accent in his English: See Karl S. Guthke, "*Das Geheimnis um B. Traven entdeckt*"*—und rätselvoller denn je* ("*The Mystery of B. Traven Solved*"*—And Stranger Than Ever*) (Frankfurt: Büchergilde Gutenberg, 1984), pp. 37–38, 61–62.

31 comical Teutonic flavor: Guthke, "*Das Geheimnis um B. Traven entdeckt,*" pp. 61–62.

32 "Many of Traven's books are set": *Sonntag*, February 1, 1948.

32 He did not meet face to face: See Chapter 6, pp. 318–19.

33 The story was exposed: See Wolfgang Cordan, "Ben Traven-Torsvan: Ein Schriftsteller und seine Trommler" ("Ben Traven-Torsvan: A Writer and His Drummers"), *Die Kultur*, October 15, 1958, p. 9.

33 a thousand dollars a week: See Chapter 6, p. 332.

33 he bristled when addressed as Bruno: Dwight Whitney, *Life*, February 2, 1948, p. 66.

33 disguised again as Croves: Reported in *Stern*, October 17, 1959, p. 44.

33 He reportedly employed: Recknagel, *B. Traven*, p. 295.
33 he scheduled a rendezvous: See Chapter 7, p. 380 and note.
33 Traven arranged for a young woman: See Chapter 6, p. 310.
33 William Johnson reported: "Trying to Solve the Enigma," p. 160.
34 Luis Spota interview: See Chapter 6, pp. 335–41.
34 Wolfgang Cordan sparked: *Frankfurter Allgemeine Zeitung*, June 29, 1957.
34 Cordan answered them: *Die Kultur*, October 15, 1958, pp. 9–10.
34 agitated attacks on Cordan's piece: *BT-Mitteilungen*, no. 27, August 1957; no. 28, August 1957; no. 32, December 1958.
34 "to combat the never-ending stream": *BT-Mitteilungen*, no. 6, March 1952.
34 Traven was a son of the last German kaiser: See Chapter 7, pp. 399–400.
34 An interview with Mexican journalist Luis Suárez: See Chapter 7, pp. 395–96.
34 Otto Feige from Schwiebus: See Chapter 3, pp. 87–97.
34 such as that in *Stern*: April 15, 1982, pp. 100–12.
35 None of the investigations: *BT-Mitteilungen*, no. 26, July 1957.
35 a letter to Alfred Knopf: See Chapter 6, pp. 310–11. Compare *BT-Mitteilungen*, no. 3, 1951; no. 5, August 1951.
35 In the letter to William Johnson: Johnson, "Trying to Solve the Enigma," pp. 162–64.
35 Gertrud Düby reported: *Sonntag*, February 1, 1948.
35 Edvard Welle-Strand thought he had met Traven: Reprinted in Beck, Bergmann, and Boehncke, *Das B. Traven-Buch*, pp. 35–37.
36 The *BT News* revived the story: *BT-Mitteilungen*, no. 34, May 1959.
36 When Gerd Heidemann was rummaging: Heidemann, *Postlagernd Tampico*, pp. 251–57.
36 Adolfo López Mateos . . . turned out to be: *BT-Mitteilungen*, no. 18, August 1955.
36 Charles Miller . . . recounts this story: *The Night Visitor and Other Stories*, p. xi.
37 Rodríguez himself related this rejoinder: *Siempre*, April 1, 1964, pp. 26, 86.
37 the *BT News* returned to both López Mateos legends: *BT-Mitteilungen*, no. 34, May 1959.
37 referring also to *Life* magazine: *Life*, March 10, 1947, pp. 13–16.
37 The *BT News* did not fail to play up this canard: *BT-Mitteilungen*, no. 15, July 1954.
37 An anonymous article: *Sie*, October 2, 1949, p. 8.
39 But a follow-up report: As late as 1958, the *BT News* was still waiting. *BT-Mitteilungen*, no. 31, November 1958.

39 The *Frankfurter Allgemeine Zeitung* . . . reported: Karl Kerber, "Ein gewisser Traven" ("Someone Calling Himself Traven"), January 20, 1960, p. 24. The story first appeared in the Slovenian weekly *Tedenska tribuna*, whose editor sent an English translation to the *BT News* (*BT-Mitteilungen*, no. 36, April 1960).

40 The last issue of the *BT News*: No. 36, April 1960.

40 "Who'll Laugh Along?": *BT-Mitteilungen*, no. 25, April 1957.

41 "London merely pretended": Johnson, "Trying to Solve the Enigma," p. 164.

41 his life "bore far greater similarity": Strasser, *Arbeiterdichtung*, p. 195. In his book *Vier neue amerikanische Dichter* (Zurich, 1929), Strasser had mentioned the identification of Traven with Jack London (p. 137).

41 Another was . . . Ambrose Bierce: See, for example, Wyatt, *The Secret of the Sierra Madre*, p. 17.

41 A scholar approached Heidemann: Heidemann, *Postlagernd Tampico*, p. 287.

42 the candidacy of Herbert Baldus: *Die Büchergilde* (Berlin), September 1933, p. 44.

42 "could be none other than": Rolf Vápenik, "B. Traven from a Czech Point of View," in Schürer and Jenkins, *B. Traven: Life and Work*, p. 273.

43 his friend Traven must have had: Stone, *The Mystery of B. Traven*, p. 87.

43 Ohly's own testimony: "Ein höchst problematischer Autor" ("A Highly Problematic Author"), *Die Welt*, October 16, 1948.

44 an interview with . . . Luis Spota: See Chapter 6, p. 338.

44 "Bavarian of Munich": See Chapter 1, p. 9.

44 Traven was in an insane asylum: *BT-Mitteilungen*, no. 9, October 1952; no. 10, May 1953.

44 "the veil masking the author's true personality": *Novedades* (Mexican daily newspaper), March 2, 1952, as quoted in *BT-Mitteilungen*, no. 7, May 1952.

44 "some of [Traven's] books": Reported in *BT-Mitteilungen*, no. 4, n.d. (1951).

44 denied the story; dismissed the rumor: *BT-Mitteilungen*, no. 5, August 1951; no. 6, March 1952.

44 denying his rumored suicide: *BT-Mitteilungen*, no. 28, August 1957.

44 the newsletter recalled: *BT-Mitteilungen*, no. 34, May 1959; no. 36, April 1960.

45 "a hundred reasons": *BT-Mitteilungen*, no. 15, July 1954.

45 "literary pirates": This is the title of an article by Johannes Schönherr in *Greifenalmanach*, 1963, pp. 182–202.

45 Heinz W. Schilling from Bochum: *BT-Mitteilungen*, no. 15, July 1954; no. 16, September 1954.

45 the astounding story of two alleged Traven typescripts: *BT-Mitteilungen*, no. 20, February 1956; no. 30, August 1958.

45 the *BT News* corrected itself: *BT-Mitteilungen*, no. 20, February 1956; no. 21, June 1956; no. 22, August 1956.

46 While held in an English internment camp: Ronald Stent, *A Bespattered Page?* (London, 1980), p. 180.

46 The letter was printed: "B. Traven: The Man and His Work," *Tomorrow*, vol. 7, no. 12, pp. 43–44.

46 in a letter to Wolfgang Paulsen: Wolfgang Paulsen, "Ist Traven nun verheiratet oder nicht?" ("Is Traven Married or Isn't He?"), *St. Galler Tagblatt*, April 25, 1958.

46 Other such usurpers of fame: *BT-Mitteilungen*, no. 7, May 1952; no. 8, July 1952.

46 he had copied pages on end: There is a reminder of this case in *BT-Mitteilungen*, no. 25, April 1957.

46 this was not simply a matter of individual sentences: *Die Büchergilde*, September 1936, pp. 149–52.

46 "The beginning of the 'Kesselbum' ": Reported in *Die Büchergilde*, September 1936, p. 152.

47 back side of a calendar page: Traven estate.

47 "If I do not personally sign this letter": *BT-Mitteilungen*, no. 30, August 1958.

48 "awful Americanisms": *Die Weltbühne*, vol. 26, part 2 (1930), p. 800.

48 "Since not much work can get done": *Land des Frühlings*, p. 267.

49 Amador Paniagua also doubtless furnished: See Chapter 5, p. 192.

49 Mexican journalist Luis Spota: See Chapter 6, pp. 338–39.

49 a series of articles: *Tages-Anzeiger* (Zurich), November 2, 1963–January 4, 1964. Schmid published these articles under the pseudonym Gerard Gale. Essentially unaltered, his thesis is presented under his real name in *Das B. Traven-Buch*, pp. 119–45. The version in the *Tages-Anzeiger* presents the articles as a "collaborative effort." The afterword to the edition of Ret Marut's *Khundar* (Egnach: Clou, 1963), which likewise supports the "other man" hypothesis, was written by "Gerard Gale (B. Traven-Archiv), Zürich/Leipzig." Schmid's theory is discussed in detail later in this chapter.

49 One version that made the rounds: *Tagesspiegel* (West Berlin), July 5, 1959, p. 32.

50 the claim put forward: *News from Neasden*, no. 13, Spring 1981, pp. 9–10.

50 His name was not given: This case, strictly speaking, falls between the two "other man" versions: The claimant's name and identity were not given, but he could be contacted through his representatives.

50 At least this is what Bilbo wrote: Recknagel, *B. Traven*, pp. 27–28.

50 He again maintained that he was Traven: Robert Neumann, *Ein leichtes Leben* (*An Easy Life*) (Vienna, 1963), pp. 61–63. Bilbo's claims were also reported in *BT-Mitteilungen*, no. 31, November 1958.

51 "always referred to himself": Wolfgang Cordan, "Ben Traven: Ende der Legenden."

51 "Much could be said about the Hess-Traven collaboration": Wolfgang Cordan, "Ben Traven–Torsvan: Ein Schriftselles," p. 9.

51 The denials to which Cordan was referring: *BT-Mitteilungen*, no. 27, August 1957; no. 28, August 1957.

51 One of the "living witnesses": Heidemann, *Postlagernd Tampico*, pp. 264–67.

52 Gerd Heidemann . . . believed: Heidemann, *Postlagernd Tampico*, p. 58.

52 Heidemann discovered that August Bibeljé: Heidemann, *Postlagernd Tampico*, p. 219.

52 "not a person, B. Traven is a joint enterprise": "Travens Tod" ("Traven's Death"), *Der Monat* (Munich), September 1967, pp. 75–79.

52 The report of Harmut Wilmes: "Eine Kölnerin behauptet: Ich bin die Witwe des Phantoms B. Traven" ("A Cologne Woman Maintains: I Am the Widow of the Phantom B. Traven"), *Kölnische Rundschau*, August 24, 1980.

53 incontrovertible evidence of Will Wyatt: Will Wyatt, "A Mystery Solved," BBC-TV, December 19, 1978; and *The Secret of the Sierra Madre*.

53 the novels that began appearing in Germany in mid-1925: The earliest short story appeared on February 28.

53 Thus several reviewers of Wyatt's book: Guthke, "*Das Geheimnis um B. Traven entdeckt*," p. 45.

53 "Traven nuts": *Times* (London), June 19, 1980, p. 18.

53 "The question remains open": Wolfgang Bittner, *Neue Zürcher Zeitung*, May 14, 1982, p. 39.

53 "anyone who traded his own identity": *Stern*, April 15, 1982, p. 106.

53 "that several narrators, writers, and translators had taken part": Beck, Bergmann, and Boehncke, *Das B. Traven-Buch*, p. 18.

53 "role played by other participants": Beck, Bergmann, and Boehncke, *Das B. Traven-Buch*, p. 81.

54 "Only one thing is certain": Max Schmid in *Das B. Traven-Buch*, p. 120. What follows in this paragraph is based on Schmid, pp. 120–22.

55 *Dictionary of Literary Biography*: vol. 9, part 3, 1981, especially p. 103.

55 "conclusive evidence of the existence of such an 'other man' ": Max Schmid, *Tages-Anzeiger* (Zurich), November 9, 1963.

55 which neither Schmid nor Baumann attempted to pin on an "other man": That was Baumann's position in his 1976 book. Baumann now claims that the later novels, too, were reworkings of someone else's English originals; see his article "The Question of Idioms in B. Traven's Writings," *German Quarterly*, vol. 60 (1987), pp. 171–92.

56 the "other man" hypothesis is untenable: For a more detailed argument, see Guthke, "*Das Geheimnis um B. Traven entdeckt,*" and Guthke, "Who Wrote Traven's Works?," *German Quarterly*, vol. 60 (1987), pp. 623–31 (followed by Baumann's rejoinder).

57 The occasional traces of delusions of grandeur: See Chapters 1 and 5.

57 the "Marut equals Traven" equation has been halfheartedly questioned: See Wolfgang Paulsen, *Germanistik*, vol. 6 (1965), p. 493; Augustin Souchy, *Geist und Tat*, vol. 22, no. 4 (1967), p. 250; Richard Gott, *Punch*, June 18, 1980, p. 982; Nicolas Walter, *Spectator*, June 21, 1980, pp. 17–18, and *The Times Literary Supplement*, January 1, 1982, p. 13; and Lothar Creutz, *Die Weltbühne*, vol. 22 (1967), p. 1309.

58 "the thesis gaining in credibility": Beck, Bergmann, and Boehncke, *Das B. Traven-Buch*, p. 18.

58 the letters Irene Mermet . . . wrote to Traven: The letters are preserved in the Traven estate.

58 "a question of faith": *Die Weltbühne*, vol. 22, 1967, p. 1309.

58 "has very weighty reasons": See the unsigned article "Das Rätsel um den Dichter B. Traven" ("The Mystery About the Writer B. Traven"), *Münchener Stadtanzeiger*, February 25, 1949, p. 4.

59 Gales . . . remarks that he needs no papers: *The Death Ship* (New York: Knopf, 1934), p. 48.

Chapter 3

63 "probably the most mysterious figure": *Die Welt*, March 31, 1969, p. 8.

63 "the greatest literary mystery of this century": Paul Theroux, *The Times* (London), June 20, 1980, p. 44.

63 Captain Bilbo: Discussed in Chapter 2.

63 *Traven* means "the traveler": Recknagel, *B. Traven*, p. 28.

63 *Traven . . . trauen . . . betrauen*: Charles Miller, "B. Traven in the Americas," *The Texas Quarterly*, vol. 6, no. 4 (1963), p. 209; George

Woodcock, "On the Track of B. Traven," *The Times Literary Supplement*, August 27, 1976, p. 1053.

64 the city of Lübeck: Marc Kuhn, "Ist das Rätsel B. Traven gelöst?" ("Has the Riddle About B. Traven Been Solved?"), *Volksrecht* (Zurich), July 20, 1967.

64 Traven's widow herself made the Traven/Trave connection: Heidemann, *Postlagernd Tampico*, p. 237.

64 the picture . . . that Judy Stone reported: Stone, *The Mystery of B. Traven*, p. 85.

64 One rumor has it: Recknagel, *B. Traven*, p. 32.

64 Ada Traven, the story continues: *Die Welt*, October 16, 1948.

64 no Ada Traven is documented in the personnel records: I was so informed in a letter from the Dumont-Lindemann Archives at the Theater Museum of Düsseldorf.

64 a type of storm god: Recknagel, *B. Traven*, p. 39.

64 Traven's plans . . . under the name Tempestad: Letter from B. Traven to E. López Mateos, January 23, 1943. Also see Chapter 6, p. 324.

64 "The storm draws near!": *Der Ziegelbrenner* (*The Brickburner*), no. 5–8, November 9, 1918, p. 105.

65 Leopold Spitzegger: *Plan*, vol. 1, no. 8 (1946), p. 670.

65 Manfred George: *The New Republic*, March 24, 1947, p. 35. Georg changed his name to George when he immigrated to America.

65 The Maurhut hypothesis circulated: See Richter, *Der Ziegelbrenner*, pp. 170, 390.

65 In response to a reader's letter: *Der Ziegelbrenner*, no. 5–8, November 9, 1918, p. 148.

65 the suspicion that Traven was an illegitimate child: See, for example, Wyatt, *The Secret of the Sierra Madre*, p. 95.

66 "In Mexico there are no illegitimate children": *BT-Mitteilungen* (*BT News*), no. 26, July 1957. Compare *Land des Frühlings*, pp. 154–55.

66 "I can choose my own country": Wyatt, *The Secret of the Sierra Madre*, p. 183.

66 His prodigious talent for spinning yarns: See Rosa Elena Luján's Introduction to *The Kidnapped Saint and Other Stories*.

66 The life stories told by the *Death Ship* sailors: *Das Totenschiff*, p. 182.

66 "I don't think he could have told the truth": Raskin, *My Search for B. Traven*, p. 106.

66 like the narrator of *The Death Ship*: *Das Totenschiff*, p. 125.

66 the interview with Luis Spota: See Chapter 6, pp. 337–38.

67 he would easily change his stories: See Wyatt, *The Secret of the Sierra Madre*, pp. 183–86.

67 Anyone can present a birth certificate: See the discussion of the Spota interview in Chapter 6, p. 336.

67 The registration form filled out in Munich; the Munich register of occupations: Munich Stadtarchiv.

68 Heinrich Maret: Mentioned in *Das Buch der Deutschen in Amerika* (*The Book of Germans in America*) (Philadelphia, 1909), p. 366.

68 It is revealing to recall a story: Recknagel, *B. Traven*, pp. 59–60.

68 "The man without a country is free": *Der Ziegelbrenner*, no. 9–14, January 15, 1919, p. 93.

68 which does more to confirm the German background: See Karl Guthke, *"Das Geheimnis um B. Traven entdeckt"—und rätselvoller denn je* (*"The Mystery of B. Traven Solved"—And Stranger Than Ever*) (Frankfurt: Büchergilde Gutenberg, 1984), pp. 35–38.

68 Rosa Elena Luján reportedly said: K. H. Bodensiek, "B. Traven: Aufhellungen eines geheimnisvollen Dichterlebens" ("B. Traven: Elucidation of the Life of a Mysterious Writer"), *Der Literat*, vol. 10, no. 3 (1978), p. 53. On Traven's own claim of having American origins, see Chapter 2, pp. 24–32; see also Wyatt, *The Secret of the Sierra Madre*, pp. 267–73, 280.

68 She made similar remarks: Wyatt, *The Secret of the Sierra Madre*, pp. 183–84.

69 as his widow has in fact stated: See Chapter 3, p. 102.

69 "the Germany of my most sublime childhood dreams": *Der Ziegelbrenner*, no. 4, July 27, 1918, p. 79.

69 this British coloration cannot be isolated from Traven's German accent: For more details, see Guthke, *"Das Geheimnis um B. Traven entdeckt,"* pp. 35–38, 52–62.

69 "once again, that one can fully express": B. Traven to Manfred Georg, October 21, 1929. Carbon copy in the Traven estate.

70 Traven was not speaking the truth: See also Chapter 5, p. 171.

70 When Marut filled out: See Chapter 4, p. 163.

70 If that is true: See Chapter 2, pp. 31–32, and Chapter 3, p. 102.

70 "with a slight accent": Recknagel, *B. Traven*, p. 59.

70 The daughter could not speak from personal experience: See Chapter 4, pp. 114–15, and Chapter 6, p. 342.

70 "He was a quiet, withdrawn man": Letter from Maria Ludwig-Morian to Rosa Elena Luján, April 20, 1969. Traven estate.

71 Kurt Tucholsky declared so: *Die Weltbühne*, vol. 26, part 2 (1930), p. 800.

71 *Proletarian Writers of the Thirties*: (Carbondale, Ill.: Southern Illinois University Press), 1968.

71 "official biography": See Chapter 2, pp. 28–30.

71 Traven must have been pleased: Strasser, *Arbeiterdichtung* (Zurich, 1930), p. 194.

72 "than I have felt under any government": "The World Revolution Is Under Way," *Der Ziegelbrenner*, no. 15, January 30, 1919, pp. 5–6, 12.

72 "greatest opponents": *Der Ziegelbrenner*, no. 15, January 30, 1919, p. 3.

72 to which Marut admitted on occasion: See, for example, *Der Ziegelbrenner*, no. 4, July 27, 1918, p. 79.

72 his remark in his theater days: See Chapter 4, p. 111.

72 the son of Emil Rathenau: Ange-Dominique Bouzet, "La nouvelle piste Traven," *Libération* (Paris), December 13, 1990, pp. 23–25.

72 "Quarta classmates": *Der Ziegelbrenner*, no. 5–8, November 9, 1918, p. 136. In the German Gymnasium, grade levels began with the Sexta and progressed to the Prima.

73 Lawrence Hill referred to: *New York Times Book Review*, December 27, 1970, p. 10.

73 "Our family history can be traced back": *Der Ziegelbrenner*, no. 4, July 27, 1918, pp. 88–89; See also *Der Ziegelbrenner*, no. 16–17, March 10, 1919, p. 21.

73 His collaborator Esperanza López Mateos: Letters in the Traven estate.

73 María de la Luz Martínez: See Chapter 6, p. 284.

74 he dismissed Ben, Benno, Bernard, and . . . Bruno: See *BT-Mitteilungen*, no. 1, January 1951; no. 5, August 1951; no. 30, August 1958.

74 several Marut stories: See Chapter 4, p. 120.

74 Marut allegedly told Elfriede Zielke: Recknagel, *B. Traven*, p. 60.

74 When Marut applied for an American passport in 1917: Wyatt, *The Secret of the Sierra Madre*, p. 271.

74 working as a bootblack, newspaper boy: See Chapter 2, pp. 28–30.

75 Less certain is the assertion: Recknagel, *B. Traven*, p. 60.

75 Elfriede Zielke . . . believed this version: Recknagel, *B. Traven*, p. 60.

75 In connection with his "Application for Registration": See Chapter 3, pp. 76–77.

75 Traven emphasized that he himself had traveled: "Herr Anton Zischka schreibt ein Buch" (Mr. Anton Zischka Writes a Book"), *Die Büchergilde*, May 1935, p. 79.

75 "B. Traven's depiction of the boiler room": *BT-Mitteilungen*, no. 3, n.d. (1951).

77 "vocabulary of the docks of Rio": *Der Ziegelbrenner*, no. 4, July 27, 1918, p. 80.

77 he likewise claimed to have visited Asia: *Der Ziegelbrenner*, no. 5–8, November 9, 1918, p. 131.

77 general statement that he "lived abroad": *Der Ziegelbrenner*, no. 1, September 1, 1917, p. 1. See also *Der Ziegelbrenner*, no. 5–8, November 9, 1918, pp. 136–37.

77 "was familiar with practically all countries": *Der Ziegelbrenner*, no. 15, January 30, 1919, p. 6.

77 He insisted on speaking at *Brickburner* events: See Chapter 4, p. 141.

77 Traven sleuths have speculated: See Chapter 2, pp. 25–26.

78 in his handwritten English draft: See Chapter 2, p. 26.

78 "It's not what we do that burdens us": *Der Schatz der Sierra Madre*, p. 69.

78 "Another reason for the heavily guarded incognito": Ulrich Schnapauff, "B. Traven: Die Jagd auf den bekannten Unbekannten" ("B. Traven: The Search for the Unknown Celebrity") *Die Welt*, March 31, 1969, p. 8. Also see Chapter 6, pp. 310–12.

78 "When you have a name that keeps coming up": *Die Troza*, p. 89.

79 "and there will be no more codes of law": *Der Ziegelbrenner*, no. 9–14, January 15, 1919, p. 94.

79 "Where my homeland is, you ask?": *Das Totenschiff*, p. 203.

79 "Once they are all burned": *Die Rebellion der Gehenkten* (*The Rebellion of the Hanged*), p. 210.

79 "Only then, when no registers or a single document": *Die Rebellion der Gehenkten*, p. 200.

79 "without a passport, without a visa": *Die Büchergilde*, March 1926, p. 35.

79 "What I do is law because *I* do it": *Der Ziegelbrenner*, no. 5–8, November 9, 1918, p. 147.

80 "Not because I am an egoist": *Die Büchergilde*, March 1926, p. 34; this statement is referred to again in *BT-Mitteilungen*, no. 6, March 1952.

80 "become a murderer under certain circumstances": *Der Ziegelbrenner*, no. 23–25, March 20, 1920, pp. 38–39.

80 "Our system of justice continues to adhere": *März*, vol. 10, no. 2, May 27, 1916, p. 156.

80 One who cannot prove his innocence: *Das Totenschiff*, p. 199.

81 or did he?: One might consider the hidden allusions to his Marut identity, which Traven, who did not want to be Ret Marut, occasionally made in his novels, such as the reference to the obscure town of Crimmitschau, where Marut had had an acting engagement, in *Die Brücke im Dschungel* (p. 122). Beginning in the early 1950s, Traven excised such telltale clues to his past from new editions of his books (Recknagel, *B. Traven*, pp. 151, 203, 214). See also Chapter 4, p. 110.

81 in those years he told: *Der Ziegelbrenner*, no. 18–19, December 3, 1919, p. 10.

81 "He was given two days": *Das Totenschiff*, p. 199.

81 "A story of strike breakers": *Das Totenschiff*, p. 202.

82 "The creative man should have no other biography": This followed Traven's remark that he wanted to be his own judge in his own case. *Die Büchergilde*, March 1926, p. 34.

82 "that he does not want his books to appear": *Die Büchergilde*, December 1931, p. 381. See the previously mentioned quotation from Schnapauff. Also see Chapter 6, pp. 310–12 and Chapter 2, pp. 25–26, where speculations about the interest of European authorities are cited. In an undated statement of principle entitled "Die Frage der Uebersetzungen" ("The Question of Translations") and addressed to his editor Ernst Preczang, Traven declared, perhaps without further implications: "In publishing English translations, it must be explicitly agreed that translation rights apply only to England, Ireland, the English Dominians [*sic*], and the English colonies, not however to the U.S.A., which must be expressly excluded." Copy in the Institut für Arbeiterliteratur, Stadtbibliothek Dortmund.

82 a letter to . . . Alfred Knopf: See Chapter 6, pp. 310–11.

83 a new hypothesis: See Chapter 3, pp. 98–102.

83 "I gave up my study of theology prematurely": *Der Ziegelbrenner*, no. 9–14, January 15, 1919, p. 89.

83 his dissertation: Rostock, 1965.

83 Lübbe considered it "certain": "Das Revolutionserlebnis," p. 10.

83 Recknagel followed suit: See Chapter 3, p. 86.

83 he still considered the matter conjectural: Recknagel, *B. Traven*, p. 341, note 92.

83 included Trefny's expulsion: Recknagel, *B. Traven*, pp. 44–47.

83 as had Recknagel: Recknagel, *B. Traven*, p. 47.

84 reproduced in Recknagel's book: Recknagel: *B. Traven*, p. 45.

84 Gerd Heidemann's sensational report: summed up in Heidemann, *Postlagernd Tampico*, pp. 242–44; also see Chapter 7, p. 400.

84 "legend of the 'Hohenzollern Prince' ": Recknagel, *B. Traven*, p. 31.

84 Ferdinand Anton . . . maintained: *M* (Offenburg), May 5, 1970, p. 103.

84 in an article that Traven touted: "B. Traven: The Man and His Work," *Tomorrow*, vol. 7, no. 12 (1948), p. 43. See Chapter 2, p. 46.

84 German worker named Wil'm . . . "only stranded princes and dukes": *The Death Ship* (New York: Knopf, 1934), pp. 68–69, 123.

85 "as a 'stranded prince' he found his way": Recknagel, *B. Traven*, p. 139.

85 Traven, writing to Esperanza López Mateos: January 29, 1943. Carbon copy in the Traven estate.

85 this reference is clearly tongue in cheek: See Chapter 6, pp. 323–24.
85 "Forget the man!": Stone, *The Mystery of B. Traven*, p. 3.
85 Señora Luján had denied the reports: Stone, *The Mystery of B. Traven*, pp. 83–84; Raskin, *My Search for B. Traven*, p. 49–50.
85 she published a rebuttal to Heidemann: *Siempre*, May 17, 1967, p. 5.
85 Traven remarked: Heidemann, *Postlagernd Tampico*, p. 242.
85 while Traven was alive: Heidemann, *Postlagernd Tampico*, p. 244.
85 Señora Luján noted in her introduction: *The Kidnapped Saint and Other Stories*, p. vi.
85 the catalogue to the exhibition: *Literaten an der Wand*, edited by Hansjörg Viesel, Berlin, 1976.
86 The column reported: *Nouvelle Revue*, vol. 24, no. 4, October 15, 1883, p. 667.
86 "This mistress was probably": Exhibition catalogue, *Literaten an der Wand*, p. 69.
87 Wyatt, painstakingly retracing this path: Wyatt, *The Secret of the Sierra Madre*, Chapter 20.
87 the well-researched history of the German theater of Cincinnati: Ralph Wood, "Geschichte des deutschen Theaters von Cincinnati," *Deutsch-Amerikanische Geschichtsblätter*, vol. 32 (1032), pp. 411–522.
87 "The B. Traven archivists": Kuhn, *Stuttgarter Zeitung*, May 27, 1967, p. 70; *Volksrecht* (Zurich), July 20, 1967; see also the obituary in *Die Welt*, March 28, 1969, p. 21.
87 Will Wyatt's sensational solution: "A Mystery Solved," BBC-TV, December 19, 1978.
88 The breakthrough for Wyatt's discovery: See also Guthke, "*Das Geheimnis um B. Traven entdeckt,*" pp. 18–32.
88 The file revealed: Wyatt, *The Secret of the Sierra Madre*, pp. 273–74.
88 "well acquainted with that town": Wyatt, *The Secret of the Sierra Madre*, p. 275.
88 discussed by both Raskin and Wyatt: Raskin, *My Search for B. Traven*, p. 243; Wyatt, *The Secret of the Sierra Madre*, pp. 210, 276, 278.
89 a date Marut stated on other occasions: See Chapter 3, p. 67 and Chapter 4, p. 111.
89 The father . . . was Adolf Rudolf Feige: Wyatt, *The Secret of the Sierra Madre*, pp. 300, 306, 310.
89 The only word from him: Wyatt, *The Secret of the Sierra Madre*, pp. 318, 335.
89 Both brother and sister recognized photographs: Wyatt, *The Secret of the Sierra Madre*, pp. 322–23, no. 37.

89 photograph from about 1902: Wyatt, *The Secret of the Sierra Madre*, illus. no. 37.

89 "The full life of this extraordinary man": Wyatt, *The Secret of the Sierra Madre*, p. 5.

89 they *expected* that the photos Wyatt presented to them: Wyatt, *The Secret of the Sierra Madre*, p. 323.

90 as Wyatt assumes: Wyatt, *The Secret of the Sierra Madre*, p. 335.

90 The letter, quickly revealed to have come from Mexico: See Chapter 6, p. 341.

90 Details from this background profile: Wyatt, *The Secret of the Sierra Madre*, pp. 281–82. National Archives, Washington, D.C. The complete text is printed in the German original of this book: Karl S. Guthke, *B. Traven: Biographie eines Rätsels* (Frankfurt: Büchergilde Gutenberg, 1987), pp. 652–53.

91 The petition was denied: Wyatt, *The Secret of the Sierra Madre*, p. 284.

91 "his identity has never been absolutely established": Wyatt, *The Secret of the Sierra Madre*, p. 285.

91 Wyatt himself admitted: Wyatt, *The Secret of the Sierra Madre*, p. 314.

91 economic considerations commonly dictated: Wyatt, *The Secret of the Sierra Madre*, p. 215.

91 "very weighty reasons": See Chapter 2, p. 58.

91 How else could he have come by such detailed information: Wyatt, *The Secret of the Sierra Madre*, pp. 301, 307, 312.

92 the birth date that Marut "always" gave: Wyatt, *The Secret of the Sierra Madre*, p. 300.

92 Marut is not documented there as an actor: See Chapter 4, p. 111.

92 Schwiebus lies on the periphery: Wyatt, *The Search for the Sierra Madre*, p. 304.

93 He read Cooper's *Leatherstocking Tales: The Death Ship* (New York: Knopf, 1934), p. 187; *Der Ziegelbrenner*, no. 5–8, November 9, 1918. Compare *Das Totenschiff*, p. 183, where Stanislav reads "Indian and sea stories" instead of Cooper.

93 German-Polish nationality: *Der Ziegelbrenner*, no. 4, July 27, 1918, p. 83; no. 5–8, November 9, 1918, p. 150; no. 9–14, January 15, 1919, p. 80; no. 16–17, March 10, 1919, p. 1. It is conceivable that in Stanislav Traven created a memorial to the real Otto Feige. In the original English text of *The Death Ship* (printed in the appendix to the original German edition), Stanislav is named Berthold.

93 Marut was a German or grew up in Germany: See Chapter 3, p. 70.

93 German was Traven's mother tongue: See Chapter 3, p. 73.

93 Jan Berg et al., *Sozialgeschichte der deutschen Literatur* (Frankfurt: Fischer, 1981), p. 211.

93 except Raskin: Raskin, *My Search for B. Traven*, p. 243.

93 Nicolas Walter: *Times Literary Supplement*, January 1, 1982, p. 13; *Spectator*, June 21, 1980, pp. 17–18.

93 Michael Baumann: *Dictionary of Literary Biography*, vol. 9, part 3, 1981, p. 103.

93 Wolfgang Bittner: "Wie hiess B. Traven wirklich?" ("What was B. Traven's Real Name?"), *Neue Zürcher Zeitung*, December 25, 1982.

93 The latest Traven book: *Der Mann, der sich verbarg* (Stuttgart, 1983).

93 The basis for Hetmann's reservation: Hetmann, *Der Mann, der sich verbarg*, p. 146. Wyatt's thesis is also rejected by Hugo Pepper in his comments in *Bücherschau* (Vienna), October–December 1979, pp. 1–7; by Heiner Boehncke in his review in *Germanistik*, vol. 30 (1989), pp. 511–12; and by H. D. Tschörtner in *Die Weltbühne*, October 17, 1989, pp. 1342–43. Bernd Fischer does not consider it proved in his contribution to the Helmut Kreuzer Festschrift *Erkundungen* (Göttingen, 1987), p. 182.

94 Travenologist Theo Pinkus: Hetmann, *Der Mann, der sich verbarg*, p. 240.

94 H. D. Tschörtner pointed out: *Sonntag*, no. 47 (1982), p. 12.

94 Feige "spent some time in the US": Recknagel, *B. Traven*, p. 126.

94 "But how can Otto Wienecke alias Feige": Recknagel, "Neues über Traven" ("New Traven Studies"), *Neue Deutsche Literatur*, vol. 30, no. 12, December 1982, p. 169.

94 Wyatt, incidentally, had learned: Wyatt, *The Secret of the Sierra Madre*, p. 278.

99 *Allgemeines Theater-Lexikon*: Vol. 7, Altenburg and Leipzig, 1842, p. 190.

100 in a conversation with Señora Luján about the playbill: See Wyatt, *The Secret of the Sierra Madre*, p. 184. Señora Luján confirmed this to me. A photocopy of the playbill of uncertain date is in the Traven estate.

100 "I believe" Traven's mother was named: Raskin, *My Search for B. Traven*, p. 47.

100 *Biographisches Bühnen-Lexikon der deutschen Theater*: Munich, 1892.

100 The Gotha peerage: See the indexes to all the Gotha handbooks in Thomas von Fritsch, *Die gothaischen Taschenbücher* (Lüneburg, 1968).

100 *Almanach für Freunde der Schauspielkunst*: Later titled *Deutscher Bühnenalmanach* (*German Theater Almanac*), the almanac was published for the years 1836–1871. Both it and its continuation, Ernst Gettke's *Almanach der Genossenschaft deutscher Bühnen-Angehöriger* for 1872–1888, list the activities of German theaters and their companies year by year.

100 "Ludwig von Sternwaldt, *recte* v[on] Warnstädt": Gettke, *Almanach*, vol. 9, 1881, pp. 126–27.

100 noted in the birth register of Braunschweig: Braunschweig Stadtarchiv.

101 Her obituary: Gettke, *Almanach*, vol. 13, 1885, p. 70.

102 Traven told Señora Luján: *The Match!* (Tucson), May 1974, p. 6.

102 the year Marut claimed to have left America: See Chapter 3, p. 70.

102 the claim that his father had been an impresario: See Chapter 3, p. 67.

102 Traven's oft-claimed Scandinavian heritage: In addition to the *Uradel* Gotha (1900–1939), see Christopher von Warnstedt, "Kurze Geschichte und ältere Genealogie des Geschlechts von Warnstedt," *Der Herold*, vol. 3 (1943), pp. 141–84.

102 his family could be traced back: *Der Ziegelbrenner*, no. 4, July 27, 1918, pp. 88–89.

102 "emigrated to America": *Jahrbuch des deutschen Adels*, vol. 3 (1899), p. 732.

103 where the name Traven is documented (in Lübeck, for example): "Personenkartei," Lübeck Stadtarchiv.

103 Jürgen von Warnstedt and Charlotte von Warnstedt: *Jahrbuch des deutschen Adels*, vol. 3 (1899), p. 732. They died in 1836 and 1868, respectively.

103 an old noble family: Henning Oldekop, *Topographie des Herzogtums Holstein*, vol. 1 (Kiel, 1908), p. 63. Regarding the Marut family, see *Lexicon over Adelige Familier i Danmark, Norge og Hartugdömmene*, vol. 2 (Copenhagen, 1787). The Landesarchiv Schleswig-Holstein informed me that various persons named Marut(h)e appear as fourteenth-century knights and pages in the *Schleswig-Holsteinische Regesten und Urkunden*. The name is not found in the von Fritsch index.

103 he doesn't need any papers: *The Death Ship* (New York: Knopf, 1934), p. 48.

103 he does not know whether his family name: *The Death Ship* (New York: Knopf, 1934), p. 113.

103 after six months of research at Traven's house: *Liberation*, July–August 1977, p. 19.

104 letter from Traven . . . to Lewis Gannet: The letter has no handwritten signature but merely a typewritten "B. Traven" at the bottom. Houghton Library, Harvard University.

104 Gotha peerage in French: *Almanach de Gotha: Annuaire diplomatique et statistique 1910* (Gotha: Justus Perthes).

Chapter 4

109 *Neuer Theater-Almanach*: The association's German name was Genossenschaft Deutscher Bühnen-Angehöriger. From 1915, the publication was called *Deutsches Bühnen-Jahrbuch*.

110 In the résumé that Marut put on record: Printed in the Appendix to the German original of this book: Karl S. Guthke, *B. Traven: Biographie eines Rätsels* (Frankfurt: Büchergilde Gutenberg, 1987).

110 One can follow his stage career: See Johannes Schönherr, "Wer ist B. Traven?," *Greifenalmanach*, 1964, pp. 247–56, and Recknagel, *B. Traven*, pp. 48–66.

110 Crimmitschau out of the blue: *Die Brücke im Dschungel*, p. 122.

110 he casually referred to Suhl: *Das Totenschiff*, p. 176.

111 Photocopies of the correspondence: Published in part by Recknagel, *B. Traven*, pp. 61–65.

111 "personal conditions": Undated letter from Marut to the Lindemanns. Recknagel (*B. Traven*, p. 61) dates the letter as December 2, 1911.

111 "as a solo dancer": Recknagel, *B. Traven*, p. 62; see also Recknagel, *B. Traven*, p. 58.

111 In the official Düsseldorf registration form: Reproduced in the German original of this book: Guthke, *B. Traven: Biographie*, p. 146.

112 The Munich Alien Registration Office noted: Bayerisches Hauptstaatsarchiv, Abt. IV, Akte "I.Armee-Korps, 2027, Ausländerüberwachung."

112 His Munich registration form: Munich Stadtarchiv.

112 the financial records of the Schauspielhaus: Heidemann collection.

112 playbills, theater reviews, letters from and to the Düsseldorf theater: Heidemann collection; Recknagel's chapter "Ret Marut" in *B. Traven*.

113 Letters from Marut to Hans Franck: H. D. Tschörtner, "Unbekannte Briefe Ret Maruts aus dem Jahre 1914," *Neue deutsche Literatur*, vol. 32, no. 12 (1984), pp. 156–63.

113 Marut, on behalf of Franck: Carbon copies of letters in the Heidemann collection.

113 The Danzig director: Photocopy of letter in the Traven estate.

113 *The Vikings . . . Honor* and *Heimat*: See Recknagel, *B. Traven*, pp. 51–58.

113 *Alcestis* and *The Merchant of Venice*: See Recknagel, *B. Traven*, pp. 64–65.

113 *Minna . . . Don Carlos*: Heidemann collection.

114 "Ret Marut had a small build": Quoted in Götz Ohly, "Ein höchst problematischer Autor" ("A Highly Problematical Author"), *Die*

Welt, October 16, 1948. The photograph is reproduced in the German edition of this book: Guthke, *B. Traven: Biographie*, p. 159.

114 The facts and dates of it: See Recknagel, *B. Traven*, pp. 51–74.

114 "In August 1913": Recknagel, *B. Traven*, p. 61.

115 A register of the students: See Recknagel, *B. Traven*, p. 71.

115 Mermet was the name of her adoptive father: See Recknagel, *B. Traven*, p. 72. She took to the stage as Irene Alda in Düsseldorf in Niebergall's *Datterich* in June 1915. Playbill in the Heidemann collection.

115 on November 24, 1915: Registration form, Munich Stadtarchiv.

115 Munich Occupational Register: "Gewerbeliste" in Munich Stadtarchiv.

115 The Munich University Archives: Letter from Prof. Laetitia Boehm, October 31, 1983.

116 the personal wealth he hinted at: See, for example, *Der Ziegelbrenner* (*The Brickburner*), no. 4, July 27, 1918, p. 79.

116 *Lieder eines Menschen*: Individual poems are dated from early 1906. The title page bears the name Ret Marut (without any indication of when the name was written).

117 *Die Geschichte vom unbegrabenen Leichnam*: This novella appears in the Büchergilde volume of the same title, vol. 13 of *Werkausgabe*.

117 "A certain Ret Marut": *Simplicissimus*, December 10, 1918, p. 462.

117 "if necessary, I can send more": Recknagel, *B. Traven*, p. 64.

117 in the German press: The newly located pieces were reprinted in the Appendix to the German original of this book: Guthke, *B. Traven: Biographie*.

118 The widely scattered publication of his pieces: See Armin Richter, "B. Traven als Feuilletonist," *Zeitschrift für deutsche Philologie*, vol. 91 (1972), pp. 585–606; introduction to B. Traven/Ret Marut, *Das Frühwerk*, ed. R. Recknagel (Berlin, 1977); Recknagel, *B. Traven*, pp. 393–94 (Bibliography). For interpretation, see Peter Küpfer, *Aufklären und Erzählen: Das literarische Frühwerk B. Travens*, dissertation, Zurich, 1981.

118 "Marut must have undergone major emotional shocks": Quoted from Schönherr, "Wer ist B. Traven?," p. 252.

119 the author "can be recognized in his works": See, for example, *Die Büchergilde*, March 1926, p. 34.

119 "performed behind the front": Recknagel, *B. Traven*, p. 64.

120 "Deceivers": Listed with a reference to *Vorwärts* in the table of contents to *Die Himmelfahrt* (1913).

120 "eternal gratitude for giving life to her child": Traven, *Werkausgabe*, vol. 13, *Die Geschichte vom unbegrabenen Leichnam* (*The Story of the Unburied Corpse*), pp. 112–13. This volume contains all the Marut stories. Dates given in the text are publication dates.

120 "He stood for a moment in the hallway": Traven, *Werkausgabe*, vol. 13, p. 14.

121 "Papa was a pilot": Traven, *Werkausgabe*, vol. 13, p. 117.

121 "Bubi must always love Mama": Traven, *Werkausgabe*, vol. 13, p. 117.

121 Bubi, looking out the upstairs window: *Werkausgabe*, vol. 13, p. 124.

121 "Don't be in no hurry": *Werkausgabe*, vol. 13, p. 177. English translation: Peter Silcock, trans., *To the Honorable Miss S . . . and Other Stories*, pp. 92–93.

123 "a pile of crumbled, filthy gray bones": *Werkausgabe*, vol. 13, p. 288.

123 "The Actor and the King": The story first appeared in 1919 in *The Blue-Speckled Sparrow*, but was written several years earlier. See p. 119.

123 "You smiled": Traven, *Werkausgabe*, vol. 13, p. 115; English translation: Silcock, *To the Honorable*, p. 29 (adapted).

123 "Höflichkeit der Könige": *Der Ziegelbrenner*, no. 5–8, November 9, 1918, p. 132.

124 "Now let me tell you one thing": Traven, *Werkausgabe*, vol. 13, p. 289.

125 the tender, fleeting moments of human companionship: See, for example, "Geschichten vom Bahnhof" ("Stories of the Railway Station"), mentioned earlier.

125 "And no one knows who he is": Traven, *Werkausgabe*, vol. 13, p. 171. English translation: Silcock, *To the Honorable*, p. 102.

125 "But in the fathomless depths of their eyes": Traven, *Werkausgabe*, vol. 13, pp. 257–58. English translation: Silcock, *To the Honorable*, pp. 96–97.

126 "split his heart": Traven, *Werkausgabe*, vol. 13, pp. 201–02.

126 "I would never have thought that the cannon thunder": Traven, *Werkausgabe*, vol. 13, pp. 149–50.

127 "What care I for life and fatherland?": Traven, *Werkausgabe*, vol. 13, pp. 205–06. English translation: Silcock, *To the Honorable*, pp. 105–06.

127 the crowned heads conduct war like a family squabble: Marut, in the story "The Politeness of Kings," stresses that the First World War was literally a family dispute among royalty.

128 the officer's existential crisis: See Chapter 4, p. 114.

128 *The Brickburner* . . . gives expression to the drive to flee: *Der Ziegelbrenner*, no. 4, July 27, 1918, p. 81.

129 "Indizien": *März*, vol. 10, no. 2, May 27, 1916, pp. 155–57. Also see Chapter 3, p. 80.

129 Götz Ohly was one such occasional collaborator: See Ohly's unsigned article "Das Rätsel um den Dichter B. Traven" ("The Riddle of the Writer B. Traven"), *Münchener Stadtanzeiger*, February 25, 1949, p. 3. The Marut estate contains indications that Ohly's assertion was correct. Literary collaboration by the painter Franz Wilhelm Seiwert has been suggested. See p. 158.

129 Irene Mermet's involvement in *The Brickburner*: See Richter, *Der Ziegelbrenner*, pp. 21–23.

129 "to furnish with his publication": Richter, *Der Ziegelbrenner*, p. 18.

129 "I never wanted to work for the fall of Germany": *Der Ziegelbrenner*, no. 9–14, January 15, 1919, p. 27.

130 "of the opinion that a pencil I have bought": *Der Ziegelbrenner*, no. 16–17, March 10, 1919, p. 11.

130 *Die Fackel* as a model for *The Brickburner*: See *Der Ziegelbrenner*, no. 9–14, January 15, 1919, pp. 90–91 and Richter, *Der Ziegelbrenner*, pp. 41–45. Issues of *Die Fackel* are preserved in the Marut estate.

130 "I scream": *Der Ziegelbrenner*, no. 4, July 27, 1918, p. 84.

130 the Brickburner's pinings to emigrate to exotic climes: See *Der Ziegelbrenner*, no. 16–17, March 10, 1919, p. 4.

131 "Die Zerstörung unseres Weltsystems durch die Markurve": *Der Ziegelbrenner*, no. 20–22, January 6, 1920.

131 "By understanding the Markurve": "Die Zerstörung," p. 43.

131 "I stand in the center-point of the universe": "Die Zerstörung," p. 44.

131 "no magazine or newspaper in the conventional sense" . . . "We do not have a single subscriber": Richter, *Der Ziegelbrenner*, pp. 379–80.

132 Reaction to *The Brickburner*: See Richter, *Der Ziegelbrenner*, pp. 152–62.

132 *The Brickburner* . . . did have a worldwide circulation: *Der Ziegelbrenner*, no. 23–25, March 20, 1920, p. 40.

132 the average number of copies printed: Richter, *Der Ziegelbrenner*, pp. 39–40, and see also p. 27.

132 Difficulties with censorship: See *Der Ziegelbrenner*, no. 9–14, January 15, 1919.

132 private funds, which Marut . . . claimed to have at his disposal: See Richter, *Der Ziegelbrenner*, pp. 28–30. The Marut papers indicate that in February 1918 Marut and Irene Mermet each pledged to put up 10,000 marks when they founded the Ziegelbrenner-Verlag.

132 the true "human being" whom Marut saw emerging: See Richter, *Der Ziegelbrenner*, pp. 48–52.

133 "no more precious commodity": *Der Ziegelbrenner*, no. 23–25, March 20, 1920, p. 8.

133 collective of individuals, of "selves": *Der Ziegelbrenner*, no. 35–40, December 21, 1921, p. 13.

133 *Der Selbe*: Reprinted in the appendix to the German original of this book: Guthke, *B. Traven: Biographie.* Typescript with corrections by hand, Heidemann collection.

133 "The World Revolution": The article was also printed separately and according to Marut sold more than 12,000 copies. *Der Ziegelbrenner*, no. 15, January 30, 1919, pp. 13–14.

133 "*I can belong to no party*": *Der Ziegelbrenner*, no. 15, January 30, 1919, pp. 1–2, 13; see also *Der Ziegelbrenner*, no. 18–19, December 3, 1919, p. 4.

134 Wolfgang Essbach has, however: Essbach, "Das Prinzip der namenlosen Differenz: Gesellschafts-und Kulturkritik bei B. Traven," in Beck, Bergmann, and Boehncke, *Das B. Traven-Buch*, pp. 362–403, especially pp. 376–83. Also see Küpfer, *Aufklären und Erzählen*, pp. 103–11, 142–44; Richter, *Der Ziegelbrenner*, pp. 48–52; Walter Fähnders and Martin Rector, *Linksradikalismus und Literatur* (Reinbek, 1974), vol. 1, pp. 309–19; Angelika Machinek, *B. Traven und Max Stirner* (Göttingen, 1986). An advertisement for Stirner's *Kleinere Schriften* appears on the inside cover of *Der Ziegelbrenner*, nos. 5–8 and 9–14. For the nineteenth- and twentieth-century ideological and historical contexts, see also George Woodcock, *Anarchism* (Cleveland, 1962); Wolfgang Abendroth, *Sozialgeschichte der europäischen Arbeiterbewegung* (Frankfurt am Main, 1965), especially pp. 87–95; and David Miller, *Anarchism* (London, 1984).

134 "The most important thing is not the state": *Der Ziegelbrenner*, no. 9–14, January 15, 1919, pp. 11, 94.

135 "And if I do not recognize the government?!": *Der Ziegelbrenner*, no. 35–40, December 21, 1921, pp. 9–20.

137 he himself stood "so far to the left": *Der Ziegelbrenner*, no. 18–19, December 3, 1919, p. 11.

137 "In a Munich paper of 27 July 1917": *Der Ziegelbrenner*, no. 1, September 1, 1917, pp. 20–21.

137 It anticipates Traven's attribution of the Second World War: See Chapter 6, p. 326.

137 The First World War, with its "murders" and "tears" . . . Capitalism alone: *Der Ziegelbrenner*, no. 3, March 16, 1918, pp. 54–55; no. 15, January 30, 1919, p. 12.

138 To combat it: *Der Ziegelbrenner*, no. 16–17, March 10, 1919, p. 1.

138 Marut even cited Goethe: *Der Ziegelbrenner*, no. 5–8, November 9, 1918, p. 108.

138 he protested against a new state: *Der Ziegelbrenner*, no. 16–17, March 10, 1919, p. 23; no. 18–19, December 3, 1919, p. 11.

138 in the name of peace and order: *Der Ziegelbrenner*, no. 15, January 30, 1919, pp. 1–13.

138 a "more lively, a richer, a stronger life": *Der Ziegelbrenner*, no. 1, September 1, 1917, pp. 5–6.

138 Marut relentlessly condemned them: *Der Ziegelbrenner*, no. 18–19, December 3, 1919, p. 7; no. 35–40, December 21, 1921, p. 17. See also Richter's chapters on war, the state, the press, and the church: *Der Ziegelbrenner*, pp. 53–106.

138 "The state convulses in its death throes": *Der Ziegelbrenner*, no. 18–19, December 3, 1919, pp. 9, 25.

139 Berlin and, in the final stages, Cologne: Richter, *Der Ziegelbrenner*, pp. 24–25.

139 "itinerant press": *Der Ziegelbrenner*, no. 18–19, December 3, 1919, p. 14.

139 "The highest authority": Allan Mitchell, *Revolution in Bavaria, 1918–1919* (Princeton, 1965), p. 101. My discussion of political events in Bavaria is also indebted to the following studies: Tankred Dorst, ed., *Die Münchner Räterepublik* (Frankfurt am Main, 1966); Armin Richter, "Ret Marut und die Sozialisierung der Presse," *Publizistik*, vol. 16 (1971), pp. 279–93; Hansjörg Viesel, ed., *Literaten an der Wand: Die Münchner Räterepublik und die Schriftsteller* (Frankfurt am Main, 1980).

140 death sentences were pronounced: Dorst, *Die Münchner Räterepublik*, p. 187.

140 Marut's role in these political devlopments: See Richter, "Ret Marut," and Viesel, *Literaten an der Wand*. The relevant Marut texts appear in these studies.

140 "Since the day the revolution broke out": *Der Ziegelbrenner*, no. 9–14, January 15, 1919, p. 8.

141 since "I had more important things to do": *Der Ziegelbrenner*, no. 15, January 30, 1919, p. 15.

141 "They pounded their chairs on the floor": *Der Ziegelbrenner*, no. 15, January 30, 1919, p. 16.

141 a concrete variant of his anarchistic anonymity complex: *Der Ziegelbrenner*, no. 16–17, March 10, 1919, p. 5.

141 That is how he wanted it: *Der Ziegelbrenner*, no. 16–17, March 10, 1919, p. 6.

141 Marut had again unleashed his scorn of the press: *Der Ziegelbrenner*, no. 15, January 30, 1919, p. 20.

142 which also circulated as a flyer: Richter, *Der Ziegelbrenner*, p. 97.

143 his membership in the "Preparatory Commission": *Der Ziegelbrenner*, no. 18–19, December 3, 1919, p. 15.

143 the minutes of the Central Council meeting of April 8, 1919: Staatsarchiv München, trial documents of Erich Mühsam, p. 293.

143 the arrest warrant: Staatsarchiv München, Akte Staatsanwaltschaft München I, 3122: "Rädelsführer."

143 in the Central Committee meeting on April 17, 1919: Staatsarchiv München, trial documents of Ernst Toller, p. 151.

143 "I will anticipate my later work": *Der Ziegelbrenner*, no. 18–19, December 3, 1919, p. 15.

144 Armin Richter's research: For the following discussion I am indebted to Richter, "Ret Marut."

144 the man who previously could not do enough: *Der Ziegelbrenner*, no. 9–14, January 15, 1919.

144 "To work toward the realization of the Council system": *Der Ziegelbrenner*, no. 18–19, December 3, 1919, p. 21.

145 "Presse-Freiheit oder Befreiung der Presse": Marut's plan also appeared in 1919 in the magazine *Der Mitmensch: Hefte für sozialistische Literatur*, vol. 1, no. 1, pp. 27–29.

145 Also not published was a piece: Richter, "Ret Marut," pp. 396–97.

145 Marut condemned this brutality more than once: See especially *Der Ziegelbrenner*, no. 18–19, December 3, 1919, pp. 14, 12.

145 He dedicated the issue: *Der Ziegelbrenner*, no. 23–25, March 20, 1920, p. 1.

145 "a friend of the Brickburner got two years": *Der Ziegelbrenner*, no. 18–19, December 3, 1919, pp. 14, 13.

146 fifteen years in jail or execution: *Der Ziegelbrenner*, no. 18–19, December 3, 1919, p. 15.

146 "As M sat in the Maria Theresia café": *Der Ziegelbrenner*, no. 18–19, December 3, 1919, pp. 15–20.

150 "Since that hour in which Marut succeeded in escaping": *Der Ziegelbrenner*, no. 18–19, December 3, 1919, p. 20.

150 Marut's letter to Marta Haecker: Heidemann collection.

151 "M, as long as he still possessed even the least bit of freedom": *Der Ziegelbrenner*, no. 18–19, December 3, 1919, pp. 21–22.

151 "In some sixty cities, village, and towns": A curious detail: Traven's estate includes a train ticket for the Gotteszell-Viechtach line in Lower Bavaria.

151 "as good as wiped out": *Der Ziegelbrenner*, no. 18–19, December 3, 1919, p. 14.

151 "put into five rooms far away from each other": *Der Ziegelbrenner*, no. 18–19, December 3, 1919, p. 14.

152 the former superintendent of the apartment house: See Recknagel, *B. Traven*, p. 104.

152 "I . . . continued to operate the *Brickburner* press: Letter from Marta Schubert-Haecker to B. Traven, Traven estate.

152 Items seized in a search of the woman's apartment: *Der Ziegelbrenner*, no. 18–19, December 3, 1919, p. 1.

153 since the Viennese printing firm cited could not be verified: Richter, *Der Ziegelbrenner*, pp. 24–25.

153 Traven, late in his life, told the Austrian journalist Lampl: See Chapter 7, p. 378.

153 "[Marut] fled to Cologne": Götz Ohly, "A Highly Problematic Author," *Die Welt*, October 15, 1948.

153 The passport was "stolen in Belgium": *Münchener Stadtanzeiger*, February 25, 1949, p. 4.

153 Wollenberg . . . told Heidemann: Heidemann, *Postlagernd Tampico*, pp. 98–99; also *Stern*, May 7, 1967, p. 68.

153 Marut may have met the anarchist Rudolf Rocker: It has been maintained that Marut/Traven was in touch with him. Recknagel, *B. Traven*, pp. 389, 465, without documentation.

153 Rocker . . . had particularly good connections: Rocker, *Aus den Memoiren eines deutschen Anarchisten* (Frankfurt am Main, 1974), pp. 312–13, 387–89.

154 Enticing potential clues are the travel and hiking guides: See Chapter 7, p. 374.

154 "Is Traven a German?": *BT-Mitteilungen* (*BT News*), no. 3, n.d. (1951).

154 But if one believes: See Chapter 4, p. 110.

155 "during the Kapp putsch of 1920": *Biographisches Staatshandbuch*, vol. 1, 1963.

155 the painter Franz Wilhelm Seiwert: My earliest piece of evidence for the Seiwert-Marut association is a carbon copy of a letter from Marut to Seiwert, dated April 3, 1919, in the Marut estate. Seiwert's portrait of Hoelz appears in *Franz W. Seiwert, 1894–1933: Leben und Werk*, ed. Uli Bohnen (Braunschweig, 1978), p. 67. See also Hoelz, *Vom Weissen Kreuz zur Roten Fahne* (Berlin, 1929).

155 It was foreign territory: Bohnen, *Franz W. Seiwert*, p. 25.

155 a circle of friends and like-minded people: The following discussion of Marut, Seiwert, Mermet, and their circle follows Bohnen, *Franz W. Seiwert*, pp. 8–30. See also Seiwert, *Schriften*, ed. Uli Bohnen et al. (Berlin, 1978).

156 Ret Marut and Irene Mermet . . . found refuge around 1920: Bohnen, *Franz W. Seiwert*, pp. 11, 25.

156 As late as May 1932: *a bis z*, vol. 3, no. 24, p. 96.

157 at the latest in the spring of 1919: See the earlier note for page 155 about the letter from Marut to Seiwert dated April 3, 1919.

157 Their association may also have been brought about: *Der Ziegelbrenner*, no. 9–14, January 15, 1919, p. 91.

157 Seiwert's portfolio of woodcuts: An illustration is in Bohnen, *Franz W. Seiwert*, p. 235.

157 at least one scholar maintains that Marut wrote it: Recknagel, *B. Traven*, p. 124.

157 more than fifty: K. H. Bodensiek, "B. Traven—Aufhellungen eines geheimnisvollen Dichterlebens," *Der Literat*, vol. 20, no. 3 (1978), p. 53.

157 she remained in contact with Seiwert: See Chapter 5, p. 182.

158 "And there is Ret Marut": Seiwert estate. See Bohnen, *Franz W. Seiwert*, p. 215.

158 "Gegensatz": *Der Ziegelbrenner*, no. 35–40, December 21, 1921, pp. 9–20.

158 "Totengänge des Hyotamore von Kyrena": *Der Ziegelbrenner*, no. 3, March 16, 1918, pp. 49–53.

158 "Khundar": *Der Ziegelbrenner*, no. 26–34, April 30, 1920 (entire issue).

158 only "possibly" the author . . . "so fundamentally related": Bohnen, *Franz W. Seiwert*, pp. 22–25.

159 "Marut was taken by the Anarchistic Association": Heidemann, *Postlagernd Tampico*, p. 225.

159 the segment of it that Recknagel claims: Recknagel, *B. Traven*, p. 329.

159 with Götz Ohly's passport: See Chapter 4, p. 153.

159 the "passport" of his Cologne friend Anton Räderscheidt: See Bohnen, *Franz W. Seiwert*, p. 28.

159 The little we know about the period between Marut's departure: The information in this section is based on Wyatt, *The Secret of the Sierra Madre*, pp. 209–20, 264–86, and on copies of documents from the Marut file of the U.S. Department of State (National Archives) owned by Rosa Elena Luján and/or me. See also Raskin, *My Search for B. Traven*, pp. 242–44, and the documents reproduced in the German original of this book: Guthke, *B. Traven: Biographie*, pp. 240–42, 246–47, 250. Rolf Recknagel's polemics against Wyatt in "Neues über Traven," *Neue deutsche Literatur*, vol. 30, no. 12 (1982), pp. 165–70, are not adequately documented.

160 The résumé (not in Marut's own hand): Printed in the Appendix to the German original of this book: Guthke, *B. Traven: Biographie*.

161 the magazine *Freedom*: See Wyatt, *The Secret of the Sierra Madre*, p. 216.

161 "The Tyranny of Passports" and "Mexican Workers' Fight for Freedom": *Freedom*, August 1923, pp. 39, 41.

161 "Revolutionary Mexico": *Freedom*, December 1923, p. 67.

162 " 'With unassisted effort' ": *Freedom*, August 1923, p. 41.

162 "In some form or other": *Freedom*, December 1923, p. 67.

163 The final document: Copy in the possession of Rosa Elena Luján.

163 a fire in 1910 in Pillkallen: See Chapter 4, p. 111, about Marut's presence in Pillkallen.

163 His application for an American passport was declined: Raskin cites a further attempt by Marut in Holland in April 1917. Raskin, *My Search for B. Traven*, p. 242.

163 "Applicant's memory seems to fail him": Copy in the possession of Rosa Elena Luján, who also has a copy of the rejection of Marut's application from the State Department dated April 23, 1917.

164 "Height 1.65–1.68 meters": Letter from H. Dorsey Newson to Boylston Beal. Copy in possession of Rosa Elena Luján. "Dark hair" contradicts other documents, especially Traven's Mexican I.D. cards, reproduced in the German original of this book: Guthke, *B. Traven: Biographie*, p. 37.

164 "This man is reported to have sailed": Archives of the U.S. Department of State.

165 "a letter Traven wrote to Ernst Preczang: Quoted by Recknagel, *B. Traven*, p. 16. I am unaware of the whereabouts of this letter; Recknagel does not print it in toto.

Chapter 5

169 " 'Up then, let us go into the wilderness' ": *Der Ziegelbrenner* (*The Brickburner*), no. 26–34, April 30, 1920, p. 72.

170 "The Bavarian of Munich is dead": Notebook in the Traven estate.

170 as an old man he was still overcome: See Chapter 7, p. 394.

170 El Aguila addressed a letter: Traven estate.

171 alien registration card issued in 1930: The 1930 and 1942 I.D. cards are reproduced in the German original of this book: Karl S. Guthke, *B. Traven: Biographie eines Rätsels* (Frankfurt: Büchergilde Gutenberg, 1987), p. 37.

173 "thirty-five miles" from Tampico: Letter from Traven to Ernst Preczang, August 5, 1925.

173 "But if one wishes to get to know the bush and the jungle": "Der Bungalow," *Die Büchergilde*, February 1928, pp. 21–22.

173 Traven left it to "literary sleuths": "Der Bungalow," *Die Büchergilde*, February 1928, p. 19.

174 "The mosquito plague during certain hours": "Der Bungalow," *Die Büchergilde*, February 1928, pp. 20–21. The shifting tenses in this essay are Traven's.

175 "There is no rent left to be paid": Letter from Traven to Smith & Co., July 6, 1931. Carbon copy in Traven estate. Traven's statement that he lived there six, not seven, years may be due to either Traven's mistake or his allowance for having been absent from the bungalow for long stretches of time.

176 Traven's letters to his German publisher: The correspondence is discussed extensively in relation to the genesis of the early Mexican novels later in this chapter.
176 *The Brickburner*'s sole Mexican subscriber: *Der Ziegelbrenner*, no. 23–25, March 20, 1920, p.40.
178 "His books, which are always based on what he himself has seen": *BT-Mitteilungen* (*BT News*), no. 8, July 1952.
178 "He has worked as an oil man": Quoted from *Die Büchergilde*, April 1934, p. 52.
179 which appeared in similar form: *Die Büchergilde*, March 1927, p. 35; *Die Weltbühne*, vol. 25, part 2, p. 484 (discussed in Chapter 2).
179 he noted that he wished to see: Letter from Traven to Ernst Preczang, January 24, 1926. Schönherr estate.
179 made a few pesos taking portraits: See also p. 200.
179 "planting cotton again": Letter from Traven to Ernst Preczang, March 29, 1926. Schönherr estate.
180 a telegram informing him of her arrival: Telegram in Traven estate.
180 George McCrossen recalled that his wife: Wyatt, *The Secret of the Sierra Madre*, pp. 238–39.
180 she wrote to Malet and McCrossen: Letter of July 30, 1924. A photocopy of the letter is in the possession of Rosa Elena Luján.
181 Irene Mermet wrote on March 28, 1925: Wyatt, *The Secret of the Sierra Madre*, p. 239.
181 she wrote to Dora Malet . . . and George McCrossen: Wyatt, *The Secret of the Sierra Madre*, p. 239.
181 According to Recknagel: *B. Traven*, p. 74.
181 Among Traven's papers Wyatt found: Wyatt, *The Secret of the Sierra Madre*, pp. 194–95; see also Chapter 5, pp. 170–71, in this book.
181 Her letter to Traven of May 5, 1927: Letter in the Traven estate.
181 she later sent him a typewriter: The Traven estate contains an undated note asking if Traven wanted a typewriter. Also see Chapter 5, p. 228.
182 letter dated January 23, 1928: Letter in Traven estate.
182 an obsession with writing: Recknagel, *B. Traven*, p. 36.
182 "Doesn't any reader of *Fanal*: "Where Is the Brickburner?," *Fanal*, vol. 1, no. 7 (1927), p. 112.
184 Traven at that time moved among leftist groups: See Marín's comments in Raskin, *My Search for B. Traven*, p. 37. Traven is not mentioned in the biography *Sandino* by Gregorio Selser (New York and London, 1981).
184 "a very radical labor organization": *Der Wobbly*, p. 37.
185 Traven's descriptions of Wobbly activities: See Philip Jenkins, "Traven and the Wobblies," in Schürer and Jenkins, *B. Traven*, pp. 199–215.

185 On May 7, 1927, he sent Preczang: See also Chapter 5, p. 244.
186 the role played by the Indian: See also Chapter 6, p. 281.
186 "brother of the European proletarian": *BT-Mitteilungen*, no. 4., n.d. (1951).
186 March 29, 1926, letter to Preczang: Schönherr estate.
186 Traven . . . circulated among the artists and politicians who gathered around Rivera and Siqueiros: I am not aware of any written evidence of his association with Rivera and Siqueiros in those years. See Marín's statements in Raskin, *My Search for B. Traven*, pp. 36–39. Preczang thanked Traven on August 5, 1929, for a book about the Mexican muralists.
187 which Traven alluded to in his letter of January 20, 1927: See Chapter 5, p. 184.
187 he left some of his "things" back in Mexico City: Letter from Traven to Ernst Preczang, March 22, 1927.
188 "There was furious activity in the city": Mildred Constantine, *Tina Modotti* (New York: Paddington Press, 1975), pp. 67–68.
189 "Torsvan had so much trouble pronouncing the *o* in Spanish": Raskin, *My Search for B. Traven*, pp. 185–86.
190 *BT News*'s assertion that Weston helped him join the expedition: *BT-Mitteilungen*, no. 28, August 1957.
190 He is listed as a Norwegian photographer: *En los confines de la selva lacandona*, p. 209; also see p. 6. Baumann's view (*German Quarterly*, Fall 1987, pp. 636–37) that Traven did not "participate" in the expedition makes too much of the "Norwegian photographer's" independent role in the enterprise, which was, in any case, rather disorganized in its early weeks before it got fully under way. Baumann himself cites evidence showing that Traven was sponsored by the government as an associate of the group (Palacios's own statement in his report that Torsvan participated in the first part of the expedition). In addition, of course, there are the card and the authorization identifying Torsvan as a member of the expedition (discussed later).
190 Torsvan's identification card: Traven estate.
190 the *BT News* decades later derided: *BT-Mitteilungen*, no. 6, March 1952.
190 "An Important Mexican Scientific Expedition": Carbon copy of typescript in the Traven estate. Reprinted in the German original of this book: Guthke, *B. Traven: Biographie*, pp. 699–701.
191 he began the expedition along with the team of scientists: Compare *En los confines de la selva lacandona*, p. 11 with these dates. A photo of the first page of the diary appears in the German original of this book: Guthke, *B. Traven: Biographie*, p. 293.

191 "At night they camp and they start again": See Wyatt, *The Secret of the Sierra Madre*, p. 190.

191 arriving on August 6: Letter to Preczang, August 8, 1926. My reconstruction of Traven's journey is based on Recknagel's account (*B. Traven*, pp. 211–12) as well as on passages in *Land of Springtime* and *En los confines* (particularly p. 209). In *Land of Springtime* Traven states that he took the photos appearing in the book from May to October 1926 (preface to the section of illustrations). Did he thus return later in the year to Chiapas from Mexico City? Vitorino Trinidad assured Heidemann in 1963 that Traven did not return to Mexico City until the end of October 1926. The authorization might then point to just an interruption of the expedition. Trinidad described Traven's independent trips as short "excursions" undertaken from San Cristóbal Las Casas. Interview with Heidemann, typescript in Heidemann collection.

191 their conversations with Heidemann in 1963: Interview with Heidemann, typescript in Heidemann collection.

192 Erich Knauf wrote to the Swedish publisher: Arbetarrörelsens Arkiv, Stockholm.

192 Amador Paniagua remembered this expedition: Typescript, Heidemann collection.

192 "This week I am again going on a long trip": Letter from Traven to Serena Koenig, July 1, 1931. Carbon copy in the Traven estate.

192 Amador Paniagua told Heidemann: Typescript in the Heidemann collection.

192 he would probably have returned: See *Siempre*, May 7, 1969, p. 36.

192 "These trips are necessary": *Die Weltbühne*, vol. 25, part 2 (1929), p. 486.

193 *Siempre* published the list of items Traven planned to take: *Siempre*, May 7, 1969, p. 36. The typescript list is preserved in the Traven estate.

193 on the otherwise Spartan expedition of 1926: Letter from Traven to Johannes Schönherr, November 24, 1927.

193 a certain E. Yarela in San Cristóbal: Letter in the Traven estate.

194 "This writer has, with a few short interruptions": *BT-Mitteilungen*, no. 4, n.d. (1951). Also see *Die Büchergilde*, September 1931, p. 260.

194 In 1963 she told Gerd Heidemann: Typescript in the Heidemann collection.

194 the stranger arrived with seven horses . . . brought along a record player: Confirmed by other sources interviewed by Heidemann.

195 Ricardo Albórez . . . told Heidemann in 1963: Typescript in the Heidemann collection.

195 not 1930 as Recknagel claims . . . first met in 1927: Recknagel, *B. Traven*, p. 216. Heidemann's typescript.

195 conditions remained more or less unchanged in the 1920s: See Chapter 5, pp. 268, 281–82.
195 many of the large landowners from the area felt attacked: *BT-Mitteilungen*, no. 27, August 1957.
195 The claim of an otherwise unknown Fred Gaudat: *BT-Mitteilungen*, no. 27–28, August 1957.
196 The notes Traven made on his journey of 1928: Traven estate.
197 I examined the typed version: Traven estate. Raskin prints a few lines of text (*My Search for B. Traven*, p. 75), largely identical to but also somewhat at variance with the entry dated December 29, and gives as his source a small notebook.
203 "Before I sold a book to Germany": Wyatt, *The Secret of the Sierra Madre*, p. 104; also see p. 204 later in this chapter.
203 noted in the *BT News* as well: *BT-Mitteilungen*, no. 26, July 1957.
203 On November 1, 1926, the editor of *National Geographic*: Traven estate.
204 In a letter dated November 23, 1926: Traven estate.
205 which *The Brickburner* had excoriated: *Der Ziegelbrenner*, no. 9–14, January 15, 1919, pp. 7–8.
205 On March 27, *Vorwärts* editor John Schikowski wrote: Letter in the Traven estate.
205 his debut in *Vorwärts* . . . rejection letters: See Chapter 4, p. 117.
205 *Simplicissimus* informed him on October 3, 1925: Letter in the Traven estate.
205 In the meantime Traven's "The Story of a Bomb" had already: See also Karl S. Guthke, "Die Metamorphose eines Expressionisten: B. Travens Anfänge," *Zeitschrift für deutsche Philologie*, vol. 103 (1984), pp. 538–51.
205 "editors of German newspapers and magazines": *BT-Mitteilungen*, no. 35, November 1959.
206 Büchergilde editor Johannes Schönherr recalled: Schönherr, "Wie B. Traven entdeckt wurde," *Greifenalmanach*, 1962, p. 150.
208 both of which appeared in *Vorwärts*: "Die Gründung des Aztekenreiches," August 7, 1925; "Götter der alten Mexikaner," March 14, 1926.
208 He attempted journalistic essays: See Chapter 5, pp. 204–5.
208 that publication's regular columns: "Mannigfaltiges" ("This and That"), "Bunte Geschichten" ("Mixed Bag of Stories"), and "Humor-Witz-Scherz" ("Humor, Wit, and Jokes").
208 "Lebensgeschichte eines erfolgreichen Mannes": Typescript in the Traven estate. See Chapter 2, p. 32.
208 Other unprinted articles may have been similar reworkings: See Chapter 5, p. 204.

209 the Traven titles . . . were embraced by readers: See the bibliographies in Recknagel, *B. Traven*, pp. 430–31, and Peter Küpfer, *Aufklären und Erzählen: Das literarische Frühwerk B. Travens*, dissertation, Zurich, 1981, pp. 348–51.

209 as *The Brickburner* had attempted at the close of the Empire: See "The Gathering Storm," *Der Ziegelbrenner*, no. 5–8, November 9, 1918, p. 105.

209 his projected publishing program . . . , which he hoped to name Tempestad: See Chapter 6, p. 324.

209 Kurt Tucholsky realized this: See Chapter 6, p. 279.

210 the wagon wheel rotting away in the courtyard: *Die weisse Rose*, p. 23.

210 Those hoping to find psychological sophistication: See, for example, Anthony West, "The Great Traven Mystery," *The New Yorker*, July 22, 1967, pp. 82–87; Gert Ueding, "Ein Panorama des Elends und der Versklavung," *Frankfurter Allgemeine Zeitung*, June 5, 1982 (Supplement "Literatur"); and Wolfgang Kiessling, *Brücken nach Mexiko*, Berlin, 1989, p. 164.

210 he stated his own critique of society: See Chapter 6, p. 305.

211 heated discussions took place in East Germany in the 1950s: See Chapter 6, p. 353.

212 the state "reveals" its "omnipotence": *Das Totenschiff*, p. 167.

212 "It used to be that the princes were the tyrants": *Das Totenschiff*, p. 47.

212 Bureaucracy is "fate": *Das Totenschiff*, p. 51.

212 people without papers have "no right to live": "Mein Roman *Das Totenschiff*" ("My Novel *The Death Ship*"), *Die Büchergilde*, March 1926, p. 35.

212 Traven continued to stress the timeliness of the subject matter: *BT-Mitteilungen*, no. 18, August 1955; no. 25, April 1957.

212 in the 1920s fraud of this sort: See Peter Koch, "Das Totenschiff," *Versicherungswirtschaft*, vol. 24, no. 20 (1969), pp. 1210–11.

212 "They were dead men": *Das Totenschiff*, p. 148.

212 Traven deromanticizes the traditional view of the sailor: *Das Totenschiff*, p. 11. On Conrad, see the "Birth Notice," p. 236.

213 The American consul in Paris tells Gales: *Das Totenschiff*, p. 55.

213 "without a country and never born": *Das Totenschiff*, p. 58.

213 "And so I gave up my good name": *Das Totenschiff*, p. 125; see also p. 182.

213 "I *have* a homeland": See Chapter 3, p. 68.

213 "He who enters here": *Das Totenschiff*, p. 109.

213 "Where is my homeland?": *Das Totenschiff*, p. 203.

214 It is a land of nameless faces: *Der Wobbly*, p. 9.

215 this American is well versed in things German: *Der Wobbly*, pp. 85–87; see also *Der Wobbly*, p. 131.

215 the confrontation of the "colored peoples": *Die Brücke im Dschungel*, p. 171.

216 "The curse of civilization and the reason nonwhite peoples": *Die Brücke im Dschungel*, p. 170.

216 "If the people who live in this great land do not wear shoes": *Land des Frühlings*, p. 423.

216 "the jungle sings its eternal song": *Die Brücke im Dschungel*, p. 124.

217 "all equal when gold is involved": *Der Schatz der Sierra Madre*, p. 69.

217 "dregs of the cities": *Der Schatz der Sierra Madre*, p. 183.

217 never "fight over gold": *Der Schatz der Sierra Madre*, p. 135.

218 "People worked here": *Die weisse Rose*, p. 202.

218 Traven does make a forced attempt: *Die weisee Rose*, pp. 189–92.

218 The essay bears the signature "R.E.L.": Carbon copy of typescript (in German) and of the letter to Rowohlt in the Traven estate.

219 "Impenetrable jungle covers the broad plains": *Der Busch*, p. 195.

220 "It would make for another interesting story": Carbon copy in the Traven estate.

221 "I finally have a chance to send you the novel": Letter from John Schikowski to Traven, August 6, 1925. Traven estate.

222 What was the Büchergilde?: In the following paragraphs I am indebted to Bernadette Scholl, "Die Büchergilde Gutenberg, 1924–1933," *Börsenblatt für den deutschen Buchhandel*, Frankfurt edition, no. 76, September 23, 1983, pp. B89–109. See also Helmut Dressler, *Werden und Wirken der Büchergilde Gutenberg*, Zurich, 1947.

222 their prospectuses were designed: Scholl, "Die Büchergilde Gutenberg," p. B90.

223 life can be "worth living": *Die Büchergilde*, August 1925, p. 115.

223 "dedicated to the ideals of a working class": *Die Büchergilde*, April 1936, p. 53.

223 "The new novel displays the strong points": *Die Büchergilde*, March 1927, p. 35.

224 his comments on *Land of Springtime*: Letter from Traven to Ernst Preczang, March 5, 1927.

225 "to get on its legs and secure a place": Letter from Traven to Ernst Preczang, September 10, 1925.

225 Instead, he offered philosophical explanations: See Chapter 2; see also Chapter 5, pp. 241–42.

226 "Dear Mister Traven!": Letter from Ernst Preczang to Traven, July 13, 1925. Photocopy in Fritz-Hüser-Institut für deutsche und ausländische Arbeiterliteratur, Stadtbibliothek, Dortmund.

234 the same Ullstein that *The Brickburner* . . . had years earlier blasted: See *Der Ziegelbrenner*, back covers of nos. 3 and 4, March 16, 1918, and July 27, 1918.

235 "will set the world's horizons ablaze": *BT-Mitteilungen*, no. 25, November 1959.

235 "Birth Notice!": Original in the possession of the Büchergilde Gutenberg.

237 "originally written in American": *BT-Mitteilungen*, no. 35, November 1959.

237 when the English original of part of the novel . . . came to light in the estate: See Chapter 2, p. 25.

237 The work progressed so quickly: Recknagel, *B. Traven*, p. 14.

237 as the "other man" hypothesis posits: See Beck, Bergmann, and Boehncke, *Das B. Traven-Buch*, p. 120.

238 "to compose a book on speculation": Letter from Traven to Ernst Preczang, Recknagel, *B. Traven*, p. 14.

240 An American bank in Tampico went bankrupt: Letter from Traven to Ernst Preczang, October 21, 1926. Schönherr estate.

240 "Here the state is not so concerned about the citizens": Letter from Traven to Ernst Preczang, December 2, 1926.

241 welcomed his royalties "with ardent enthusiasm": Letter from Traven to Ernst Preczang, October 21, 1926. Schönherr estate.

241 "That's right, Mr. Preczang, take care": Letter from Traven to Ernst Preczang, August 8, 1926.

241 "One is in an enviable position if one cannot be reached": Letter from Traven to Ernst Preczant, April 3, 1927.

241 "I have no intention of coming to Germany any time soon": Letter from Traven to Büchergilde Gutenberg, August 21, 1927. Schönherr estate. Only the second page of the letter is in the Schönherr estate; hence it is not known whether the letter was addressed to Schönherr or Preczang.

242 "After this experience, I will write": Letter from Traven to Ernst Preczang, October 26, 1929.

243 "I did not dare send a large black scorpion": Letter from Traven to Johannes Schönherr, January 5, 1928. The rest of the paragraph is based on this letter.

244 The proceeds were to be used for advertising his books: Letter from Traven to Ernst Preczang, April 5, 1927.

244 Traven volunteered to offer ten or fifteen percent: Letter from Traven to Ernst Preczang, March 20, 1927.

244 Members who cared for "sweet novels": Letter from Traven to Ernst Preczang, November 19, 1925.

245 his books as discussed in the correspondence: Statements similar to those quoted from Traven's letters to the Büchergilde may be found in his letters to Schikowski. See the catalogue of Auction 56 (November 14–16, 1990) of Galerie Gerda Bassenge, Berlin, pp. 655–59.

247 In this same letter of October 11, 1925: Also see the quotation from this letter in Chapter 3, pp. 71–72.

247 Preczang informed Traven that his works had the greatest appeal: Letters from Ernst Preczang to Traven, August 5, 1929, and February 23, 1927.

247 "The worker is not infrequently a wretched egoist": Letter from Traven to Ernst Preczang, December 2, 1926.

247 He had even higher expectations for *The Death Ship*: See Chapter 5, p. 242.

248 since one publisher could not bring out two Traven novels: Letter from Traven to Ernst Preczang, November 19, 1925; letter from Preczang to Traven, December 11, 1925.

248 The editor reminded him of the "extraordinarily bad" economic conditions: Letter from Ernst Preczang to Traven, March 5, 1926.

248 *The Wobbly* was first published in August: Recknagel, *B. Traven*, p. 386.

248 it appeared in Buchmeister Press: Recknagel, *B. Traven*, p. 16.

248 Recknagel cites a letter from Traven to Preczang: Recknagel, *B. Traven*, pp.16–17.

249 And the social criticism may also have been the deciding factor: See the retrospective collection of the publisher's "Announcements" in the May 1940 issue of the Zurich *Büchergilde* (p. 75): "The stirring novel of a ship laborer, *Das Totenschiff*" (February 20, 1926). "*Das Totenschiff*. This novel is a human document and a document of the disgrace of our capitalistic age" (February 24, 1926). "*Das Totenschiff*. No one who reads this latest offering of the Büchergilde Gutenberg will remain unmoved or be able to put it aside" (March 6, 1926). "*Das Totenschiff*. There is no comparable work in German, nor perhaps in world literature. The narrative style of the author, a German-American sailor, has a quality that is totally unique. With unparalleled force, this novel combines sensitive emotional portrayal, angry and unrelenting realism, bitter outrage for the injustices committed against the working class, and an extravagant sense of humor" (March 17, 1926). "*Das Totenschiff*. This adventure story by the American sailor B. Traven, currently living in Mexico, is the tale of a proletarian sailor whose ship departs without him, leaving him without legal identification papers in a strange country. His experiences with various consuls to whom he must give proof 'that he was born' are the most biting satire yet written about international bureaucracy. The outcast's grandiose gallows wit celebrates victories that arouse in us a grim laughter" (March 31, 1926). "*Das Totenschiff*. Novel by B. Traven. A sailor portrays not only the bureaucracy of consuls but also the insidious evils of capitalism, how it steals on land and at sea and rides roughshod over the lives of men. The author writes from personal experience of the brutal power of money, which shrinks from no crime and holds the poorest in a bondage incomprehensible to the 'free worker.' A stirring book!" (April 7, 1926) "*Das Totenschiff*. The novel of the Nameless Ones, the 'ghosts,' the dead who still breathe and labor but who are obliterated from the list of the living because they have no papers. A novel of people 'who cannot prove that they were born.' Based on the real-life experiences of a proletarian, who wields language with the force of a powerful tool" (April 10, 1926). Note translated by Doris Sperber.

249 A cable of October 19 announced acceptance of the novel: *Die Büchergilde*, April 1936, p. 54.

250 his discussion in the letter to Preczang was more extensive as well as more direct and personal: Ten days after this letter, on November 19, Traven sent off a business letter, dictated by dire financial straits. Two days later, on November 21, he spoke of difficulties in the transfer of funds.

252 "it is often a disadvantage when one has too much time": Letter from Traven to Ernst Preczang, January 18, 1926.

252 "the somewhat religious-sentimental turn at the end": Letter from Traven to Ernst Preczang, March 29, 1926. Schönherr estate.

252 "severe storms on the Atlantic": *Die Büchergilde*, March 1926, p. 48.

253 he even recommended marketing strategies to Preczang: Letter from Traven to Ernst Preczang, March 20, 1927.

253 Preczang . . . suggested that Traven write a screenplay: Letter from Ernst Preczang to Traven, February 24, 1927.

253 he would agree only if a film company first expressed definite interest: Letter from Traven to Ernst Preczang, May 7, 1927.

253 In the 1960s Traven made similar remarks: Stone, *The Mystery of B. Traven*, p. 62.

254 Traven was in complete agreement with his critic: Letter from Traven to Ernst Preczang, December 2, 1926.

256 "Judging from the pictures alone, you can imagine": Letter from Traven to Ernst Preczang, April 21, 1927.

256 Preczang sent the text to "several hundred newspapers": Letter from Ernst Preczang to Traven, May 3, 1927.

257 Traven obstinately saw this detail work as a particular virtue: Letter from Traven to Ernst Preczang, October 11, 1925; see also Preczang's letter of September 15, 1925, quoted on p. 239.

258 The text that *Vorwärts* acquired after long indecision: Traven's letters to Ernst Preczang of August 8, 1926, and March 5, 1927.

258 Preczang . . . was more interested in a new, independent story: Letter from Preczang to Traven, May 3, 1927.

259 The length of the original version . . . did not seem sufficient: This according to a letter from Bruno Dressler dated June 16, 1937, in answer to Traven's reminder that the Büchergilde had "declined this work repeatedly." Traven estate.

260 "The entire course of the action": *Die Büchergilde*, March 1929, pp. 36–37.

261 the thought of embarking on an expedition cropped up shortly thereafter: See Chapter 5, p. 233.

261 Preczang reacted with enthusiasm and generosity: Letter from Preczang to Traven, December 11, 1925.

264 "I have done my part": Letter from Traven to Ernst Preczang, March 27, 1927.

264 "People still believe only too easily": See *BT-Mitteilungen*, no. 4, n.d. (1951), where Traven takes exception to the images of "fantastically painted" Indians brandishing tomahawks and wearing scalps on their belts, as popularized by the "fairy tale books" of Cooper and Karl May. See also *Die Büchergilde*, September 1931, p. 261.

265 who, he liked to think, had not come from Asia: *Land des Frühlings*, p. 132.

265 "I was returning from a short trip to an Indian celebration": Letter from Traven to Johannes Schönherr, October 16, 1927.

265 Croves made the assertion to journalist Judy Stone: Stone, *The Mystery of B. Traven*, p. 68.

266 "quiet, simple, tasteful": Letter from Traven to Johannes Schönherr, December 14, 1927.

266 For the new edition of 1950, Traven cut much that was outdated: One can follow this in the *Werkausgabe* of the Büchergilde Gutenberg, Appendix to vols. 16 and 17.

266 in 1966 he told Judy Stone: Stone, *The Mystery of B. Traven*, p. 68.

266 his often simplistic, romanticizing contrast of the Indian's "culture": *Land des Frühlings*, pp. 95, 223.

267 the white people and thus the entire European-American world: *Land des Frühlings*, pp. 201–11.

267 "To live happily and well in an Indian commune": *Land des Frühlings*, p. 254.

268 In the midst of this industriousness": *Land des Frühlings*, p. 60.

268 The enslavement by the large landowners was still accepted by the Indians: *Land des Frühlings*, p. 368.

268 "the merry singing, guitar playing, and dancing": *Land des Frühlings*, pp. 363–64.

268 *Land of Springtime* thus closes not with nostalgia: *Land des Frühlings*, p. 428.

268 "where one can get to the bottom of all matters": *Land des Frühlings*, p. 429. The only previous critical discussion of *Land des Frühlings* has been Michael L. Baumann's "B. Traven: Realist and Prophet," *The Virginia Quarterly Review*, vol. 50 (1977), pp. 73–85.

269 He reminisces that he had served "for a while as a private tutor": *Land des Frühlings*, p. 204.

269 "On the evening of the first day I sat on a crate": *Land des Frühlings*, p. 171.

269 It remained unpublished: *Die Büchergilde* announced the work for the last time in October 1931, p. 302.

269 in 1933 he scared off the National Socialist usurpers: See Chapter 6, p. 305.

269 *Typographische Mitteilungen*: In the section "Das Schiff" ("The Ship"), pp. 71–73.

270 other published sections: *BT-Mitteilungen*, no. 12, December 1953; no. 20, February 1956.

270 "Las Pulquerías" . . . and "El niño mexicano como artista y creador": *Siempre*, July 3, 1974, pp. 40, 42–45, 118.

270 the task of all art is "to make people happy": Letter from Traven to Ernst Preczang, March 29, 1926. Schönherr estate.

270 In the version of the chapter on art theory: *BT-Mitteilungen*, no. 12, December 1953.

270 In an unpublished version of the chapter: Traven estate. Printed in the Appendix to the German original of this book: Guthke, *B. Traven: Biographie*.

272 The retrospective letter of Bruno Dressler: Traven estate.

272 Traven had apparently complained: See also Chapter 5, p. 249, regarding *The Death Ship*.

273 a fifty-six-page typescript that may represent the beginning: The typescript is printed in the German original of this book: Guthke, *B. Traven: Biographie*, pp. 701ff.

273 Manfred Georg's article: *Die Weltbühne*, vol. 25, part 2 (1929), pp. 484–86.

273 Traven actually set to work on such a letter to Manfred Georg: See Chapter 3, p. 69.

276 Traven . . . had instructed that his books be sold only to Büchergilde members: *Die Büchergilde*, November 1929, p. 168.

276 "A Short Factual Correction": Carbon copy in the Traven estate.

Chapter 6

279 Of the German edition of *The Death Ship*: *Die Büchergilde*, June 1931, p. 191.
279 by 1936, the total circulation: *Büchergilde*, April 1936, p. 65.
279 Kurt Tucholsky celebrated Traven: *Die Weltbühne*, vol. 26, part 2 (1930), pp. 793–800.
280 "Five years ago, Traven was still unknown": *Die Büchergilde*, October 1931, p. 300.
280 The Mahogany cycle itself: There is a plot summary of the Mahogany series in *BT-Mitteilungen* (*BT News*), nos. 5–9, August 1951–October 1952. Reprinted in the Appendix to the German original of this book: Karl S. Guthke, *B. Traven: Biographie eines Rätsels* (Frankfurt: Büchergilde Gutenberg, 1987). For a discussion of the Mahogany series, see Winfried Pogorzelski, *Aufklärung im Spätwerk B. Travens* (Frankfurt, 1985).
280 Traven's guide in the jungle in the 1920s: Heidemann, *Postlagernd Tampico*, p. 276. Also see Chapter 2, p. 49 and Chapter 5, p. 192, in this book.
281 "They not only depict repression and exploitation": *Das Wort*, vol. 2, no. 4–5 (1937), p. 127.
281 He saw an analogy between the Indians and the European proletariat: "The Indian is . . . the Indian brother of the European proletarian" (*Die Büchergilde*, September 1931, p. 261).
281 This is how the Zurich *Büchergilde* presented the ideological potential: June 1936, pp. 98–99.
281 Immediately upon publication of the first two novels: The succeeding quotations in this paragraph are from *Die Büchergilde*, September 1931, pp. 260–61, except where noted otherwise.
282 the author's claim that he was stuck up to his saddle: *BT-Mitteilungen*, no. 3, n.d. (1951).
282 "I know the courage, the dedication, the sacrifice": *Die Büchergilde*, February 1928, p. 26; repeated in *BT-Mitteilungen*, no. 4, n.d. (1951), supposedly from a letter of October 18, 1927.
283 "Certain powerful novels can lead to socialism": *Büchergilde*, September 1934, p. 147; from Traven's letter to Büchergilde Gutenberg of January 11, 1934.
283 The final two volumes of the series: *BT-Mitteilungen*, nos. 3 and 4, n.d. (1951).
284 "to encourage the repressed people of Europe": *BT-Mitteilungen*, no. 4, n.d. (1951).
284 Recknagel's contention that she had been a teacher: Recknagel, *B. Traven*, p. 220.

284 According to Luis Spota's sensational report: "¿Por que no me dejan en paz?" ("Why Don't You Leave Me in Peace?"), *Mañana*, August 7, 1948. See Chapter 6, pp. 335–39.

284 María de la Luz Martínez told Heidemann: Heidemann, *Postlagernd Tampico*, p. 149.

284 he lived in separate quarters: Raskin, *My Search for B. Traven*, p. 184 (also p. 104).

285 In 1931 he recalled having lived more than two years among the Indians: In *Die Büchergilde*, September 1931, p. 260, and in *BT-Mitteilungen*, no. 4, n.d. (1951).

285 "frequent and long expeditions": Letter from Traven to Otto Jamrowski, September 9, 1933. Carbon copy in the Traven estate.

286 he earned a pilot's license: The estate contains a copy of *The Navigation of Air Craft* by Logan C. Ramsey (New York, 1929). See also Raskin, *My Search for B. Traven*, p. 79.

286 Nor was there running water: Raskin, *My Search for B. Traven*, p. 104.

286 his first foreigner's registration card. Reproduced in the German original of this book: Guthke, *B. Traven: Biographie*, p. 37.

286 his library still contains N. Hawkins's *Aid*: See also Chapter 5, p. 178.

286 reportedly derived from the Christian name of his Scottish grandfather: Stone, *The Mystery of B. Traven*, p. 83.

287 though this is usually assumed: See, for example, Recknagel, *B. Traven*, p. 373.

287 an envelope addressed to Hal Croves . . . postmarked June 29, 1944: Traven estate.

287 In 1953 Croves even obtained from the Mexican State Department: Letter from Traven to Sanora Babb, December 15, 1953.

287 a letter—signed "T. Torsvan c/o Martínez": Carbon copy in the Traven estate.

287 He could not adopt Mexican citizenship during the war: See p. 336.

287 He was not naturalized in Mexico until 1951: The document is in the Traven estate. Reproduced in the German original of this book: Guthke, *B. Traven: Biographie*, pp. 494–94.

287 Traven's roots, like Torsvan's, were to be found in the American Midwest: See Chapter 2, p. 29.

288 "I am now most concerned with the translations": Letter from Traven to Ernst Preczang, June 17, 1933.

288 Traven's description of his sorry state in a letter to Preczang of May 15, 1939: *Volksrecht* (Zurich), July 20, 1967.

290 He even sent Holmström a promotional piece: Letter from Traven to Axel Holmström, February 5, 1947.

290 "Times are awfully tough for me": Letter from Traven to Axel Holmström, August 21, 1941.

290 Traven's letter of December 9, 1947, to Ernst Preczang: Heidemann collection.

290 "The money was badly, very badly needed": Letter from Traven to Axel Holmström, October 12, 1945.

291 Prices in Mexico were "outrageous": Undated letter from Traven to Josef Wieder (late 1946). Carbon copy of pages 2 and 3 in the Traven estate.

291 "In spite of the seemingly enormous income": Letter from Traven to Ernst Preczang, January 11, 1934. Copy, Stadtbibliothek Dortmund; not identical with the letter of the same date to the board of the Büchergilde.

292 "exactly as the morally degenerated" Social Democrats had done: Letter from Traven to Ernst Preczang, October 14, 1933. *Volksrecht* (Zurich), July 20, 1967.

292 "departed from its original spirit": Letter from Traven to Ernst Preczang, July 7, 1932. Carbon copy in the Traven estate.

292 "I can say that in all likelihood": Letter from Traven to Ernst Preczang, October 14, 1933.

293 Jack London, with whom Traven had felt so much in common: See Chapter 2, p. 41.

294 "I put great importance on the flourishing and growth": *Büchergilde*, April 1936, p. 69.

295 "Ein fabelhafter Kerl!": *Büchergilde*, April 1936, pp. 51–65.

295 "The German workers understood my books": Letter from Traven to Bruno Dressler, October 29, 1938. *Volksrecht* (Zurich), July 20, 1967.

296 Josef Wieder . . . had . . . left: Letter from Traven to Axel Holmström, April 26, 1939; letter from Josef Wieder to Holmström, January 9, 1939; letter from Ernst Preczang to Traven, undated (Traven estate); introduction, *BT-Mitteilungen* (Berlin: Klaus Guhl Verlag, 1978), pp. 8, 12. See also the announcement of 1958 on p. 390. Traven's letter to Preczang of December 9, 1947, sheds some light on the tensions: "My dealings with the B.G. were conducted through an attorney, because the B.G. refused to speak with W[ieder] or hand over the accountings to him." Heidemann collection.

297 "one group did not feel comfortable": Letter from Bruno Dressler to Traven, April 15, 1937. Traven estate.

297 Büchergilde Gutenberg had "published my new books": Letter from Traven to Bruno Dressler, January 14, 1939. *Volksrecht* (Zurich), July 20, 1967.

297 "According to my estimation": In the Introduction to *BT-Mitteilungen*, p. 14, this text is attributed to a letter dated May 8, 1939.

298 "In all your letters of the last two years": Letter from Traven to Bruno Dressler, March 27, 1939. *Volksrecht* (Zurich), July 20, 1967.

298 "Mr. Traven must think of getting his royalties these days": Letter from Josef Wieder to Axel Holmström, June 20, 1939. Arbetarroerelsens Arkiv, Stockholm.

299 Traven demonstrated that Zischka lifted an entire chapter: *Büchergilde*, May 1935, pp. 76–80.

299 Bruno Dressler wrote assuringly to Traven that the euphoria: According to Traven's letter to the Büchergilde of January 11, 1934.

299 on May 2, the Büchergilde's Berlin headquarters . . . "the Guild's work as it had been earlier defined": *Die Büchergilde* (Zurich), July 1933, p. 114.

299 At first the book club . . . by the end of 1948: *Büchergilde* (Vienna), October 1949, pp. 164–65; letter from Ernst Preczang to Traven, June 15, 1933; *BT-Mitteilungen*, no. 35, November 1959. See also Helmut Dressler, *Werden und Wirken der Büchergilde Gutenberg* (Zurich, 1947), pp. 59, 108.

300 This list . . . was published on May 16, 1933: *Börsenblatt für den deutschen Buchhandel*, no. 112, pp. 357–58.

300 The ban on *The Carreta* . . . and *The White Rose*: *Büchergilde* (Zurich), May 1934, Supplement.

300 *The White Rose* . . . was "confiscated": *Die Büchergilde* (Zurich), July 1933, p. 128.

300 in February 1934 *The Death Ship*: *Börsenblatt*, no. 29, February 3, 1934, p. 112.

300 the books that went up in flames on May 10, 1933: Josef Wulf, *Literatur und Dichtung im Dritten Reich* (Gütersloh, 1963), p. 42.

300 "On the basis of its understanding of pure folkdom": *Büchergilde*, May 1934, Supplement.

300 In the notes to the blacklist: *Volksbücherei und Nationalsozialismus*, ed. Friedrich Andrae (Wiesbaden, 1970), pp. 167–68.

301 "Far more important for the proletarian than the fascist": *Die Büchergilde*, November 1932, p. 191.

303 "remains true to the old conception of the Guild": *Die Büchergilde*, July 1933, p. 114.

303 for which he had written to Berlin: Letter from Traven to Josef Wieder, July 20, 1933. Carbon copy in the Traven estate.

304 "with the exception of *Government* naturally": Letter from Josef Wieder to Traven, August 21, 1933. Traven estate, with additional documents pertaining to this lawsuit.

304 Traven, he wrote, must distance himself: Letter from Josef Wieder to Traven, August 23, 1933. Traven estate.

304 "An author of world stature": *Die Büchergilde* (Berlin), September 1933, p. 54.

304 "open letter": Letter from Traven to Otto Jamrowski, 30, September 30, 1933. Traven estate.
304 seven-page cover letter: Carbon copy in the Traven estate.
306 "We reject your proposals": Letter from Justi to Traven, October 9, 1933. Traven estate.
306 the Berlin Büchergilde and Josef Wieder . . . signed an agreement: Typescript copy in the Traven estate.
306 The Berlin office also sent Wieder the manuscript: Letters from Josef Wieder to Traven, October 27 and 28, 1933. Traven estate.
306 As of January 1, 1934: Contract between Josef Wieder and the Büchergilde Berlin. Typescript copy in the Traven estate.
306 Traven's income "would fall to a pitiful level": Letter from Ernst Preczang to Traven, November 21, 1933. Traven estate.
307 "Please don't send with German ship": Envelope in Heidemann collection.
307 He now attempted: Letter from Traven to Ernst Preczang, June 17, 1933.
307 *Die Büchergilde* reported in December 1931: p. 381.
307 "Yes, it is correct what you have been told": Letter from Traven to Mr. Adler, July 10, 1931. Carbon copy in the Traven estate. A similar statement occurs in the *Büchergilde* article of December 1931, p. 381.
307 "I am interested in neither an English nor an American publisher": Letter from Traven to Kurt Wagenseil, December 21, 1932. Carbon copy in the Traven estate.
308 "I am quite willing to spend my last nickel": Letter from Traven to Raymond W. Postgate, July 9, 1932. Carbon copy in the Traven estate.
308 "On the Trail of B. Traven": *Publishers Weekly*, July 9, 1938, pp. 105–6.
308 That agreement predates the publication of the London editions: Bruno Dressler's letters to Chatto & Windus of June 20 and July 11, 1932, reveal, however, that the English publisher was interested in bringing out Traven's works in English at that time. The sales of the British translations were just as unsatisfactory as those of the American translations, as one may gather from Traven's letter to Chatto & Windus of April 28, 1936, and Chatto & Windus's letter to Traven of November 2, 1937 (carbon copy). All letters mentioned are in the library of the University of Reading, England (Chatto & Windus Archives).
309 After instructing Knopf that only grammatical: Letter from Traven to Alfred Knopf, September 23, 1937.
309 Smith described his literary midwifery: *The New York Times Book Review*, November 22, 1970, pp. 2 and 56.

309 "amerikanische Urschrift": *BT-Mitteilungen*, no. 3, n.d. (1951); see also no. 23, November 1956.

309 it ironically had two of the novels . . . translated into German: *Das Totenschiff*, 1937 and 1940; *Der Schatz der Sierra Madre*, 1942. Also see *Büchergilde* (Zurich), May 1940, p. 74; January 1942, p. 27.

309 *Die Brücke im Dschungel*: See *BT-Mitteilungen*, no. 23, November 1956.

309 Traven instructed Smith that any inquiries sent to Knopf: Smith, *New York Times Book Review*, November 22, 1970, p. 2.

310 "I write to propagate ideas": Raskin, *My Search for B. Traven*, pp. 131–32.

310 Smith told BBC producer Will Wyatt: Wyatt, *The Secret of the Sierra Madre*, p. 111.

310 one of his "outrageously long letters": Letter from Traven to Alfred Knopf, November 21, 1933: Carbon copy in the Traven estate.

311 Bernard Smith suspected: *The New York Times Book Review*, November 22, 1970, p. 2.

311 "America, the Promised Land of Freedom": *Die Büchergilde*, January 1930, pp. 12–14.

311 "Eager reporters": *Die Büchergilde*, September 1931, p. 287.

311 *Die Büchergilde* predicted that Traven's withdrawal of his books: December 1931, p. 381. Also see Chapter 3, p. 82.

312 "This fact that nobody even mentions": Letter from Traven to Alfred Knopf, December 11, 1934. Carbon copy in the Traven estate. Some critics did in fact give *The Death Ship* a warm welcome; see Anthony West, "Traven's 'Death Ship'—Authentic, Hypnotic, and Maybe Alchemical," *The New York Times Book Review*, November 10, 1985, p. 62. See also the excerpts reprinted from reviews of the London edition in *Büchergilde* (Zurich), May 1934, section between pp. 72 and 73.

312 in 1935 and 1936 he corresponded extensively with Herbert Arthur Klein: See Wyatt, *The Secret of the Sierra Madre*, pp. 103–8.

313 only 3,288 copies of *The Death Ship* and only 2,692 copies of *The Treasure*: *Publishers Weekly*, July 9, 1938, p. 106.

313 He turned to Raymond Everitt: Letter from Traven to Everitt, April 27, 1939. The Pennsylvania State University Library.

314 an advertisement for "The Story of an American Sailor": E. R. Hagemann, "¡Huye! A Conjectural Biography of B. Traven," *Inter-American Review of Bibliography*, vol. 10 (1960), pp. 380–81.

314 Mrs. Klein was instructed to read it: Wyatt, *The Secret of the Sierra Madre*, p. 108.

314 but as a result of the film version of 1948: See p. 351.

314 the return of all rights and the repurchase of the plates: See *BT-Mitteilungen*, no. 34, May 1959. Traven's letters to Sanora Babb dated September 15 and October 25, 1955, give the impression that only *The Rebellion of the Hanged* was bought back. Señora Luján explained to me that the typesetter's plates of all the books published by Knopf were returned to Traven, as well as the remaining copies of *Rebellion*.

315 He had attempted unsuccessfully to do the same: *BT-Mitteilungen*, no. 26, July 1957, contains a reminder of this.

315 "Una carta de Bruno Traven": *Solidaridad Obrera* (Barcelona), no. 1893, May 22, 1938, p. 4. In the faulty and excessively free German translation published by Augustin Souchy in 1952 as "A Letter from Bruno Traven" in the magazine *Die freie Gesellschaft* (vol. 4, no. 36–37, pp. 20–22), the letter is signed "Bruno Traven," which throws the entire text into question.

318 The political climate in Mexico: See Wolfgang Kiessling, *Exil in Lateinamerika* (Frankfurt am Main, 1981), pp. 144–59.

318 in May 1942, 1943, and 1944 commemorated the anniversary: See *Dort wo man Bücher verbrennt*, ed. Klaus Schöffling (Frankfurt am Main, 1983), pp. 123–24, 131–32, 138–39, 140–41. See also Marianne O. de Bopp, "Die Exilsituation in Mexiko," *Die deutsche Exilliteratur 1933–1945*, ed. Manfred Durzak (Stuttgart, 1973), pp. 175–82, and Hans Albert Walter, *Deutsche Exilliteratur 1933–1950*, vol. 2 (Stuttgart, 1984), pp. 337–61.

319 Even when he mentioned the "more than 50 performances": *BT-Mitteilungen*, no. 3, n.d. (1951).

319 "European émigrés, who had fled to Mexico from the Nazis": *BT-Mitteilungen*, no. 4, n.d. (1951).

320 threatening to disrupt his . . . idyll: See also p. 322.

320 Oskar Maria Graf and Egon Erwin Kisch are identified: See p. 343.

320 "Die Mühlen Gottes mahlen langsam, aber . . .": *BT-Mitteilungen*, no. 6, March 1952.

321 Gabriel Figueroa . . . had read *The Bridge*: Wyatt, *The Secret of the Sierra Madre*, p. 161.

321 Esperanza herself came upon the novel: *BT-Mitteilungen*, no. 6, March 1952.

321 "I beg you to inform me if there is any possibility": Letter from Esperanza López Mateos to Alfred Knopf, August 8, 1939. Traven estate.

322 "serious personal reasons": *BT-Mitteilungen*, no. 4, n.d. (1951).

322 But when she then took it upon herself: Wyatt, *The Secret of the Sierra Madre*, p. 161.

322 Traven insisted . . . that the two meet on neutral ground: See Traven, *Obras escogidas (Selected Works)* (Mexico City, 1969), vol. 1, p. 44.

322 Esperanza became not only Traven's authorized Spanish translator: See also *BT-Mitteilungen*, no. 34, May 1959.

322 Traven had banned Mexican editions so that he could "write in peace": *Büchergilde* (Zurich), March 1939, p. 44.

322 Esperanza also traveled to Switzerland in 1947: See introduction to *BT-Mitteilungen*, p. 8. Regarding Davos, see p. 337. E. L. Mateos's stay in Europe (Switzerland and Czechoslovakia) for the year 1947 is also established by letters from her to Gabriel Figueroa in his possession.

322 she learned German in the late 1940s: *BT-Mitteilungen*, no. 34, May 1959.

323 copyright notices bearing her name did not disappear: Introduction, *BT-Mitteilungen*, pp. 7, 8, 10.

323 "At various times, private detectives kept watch": *BT-Mitteilungen*, no. 34, May 1959.

323 "most faithful, his truest and his most honest representative": Letter from Traven to Señor Margáin, undated. Carbon copy in the Traven estate.

323 "Don't look at them at night": Letter from Traven to Esperanza López Mateos, December 24, 1942. Carbon copy in the Traven estate. Traven's letters to Esperanza cited here are all in English.

323 "a certain man whom you think you know": Letter of Traven to Esperanza López Mateos, January 29, 1943. Carbon copy in the Traven estate.

324 while Traven chose Tempestad: Letter from Traven to Esperanza López Mateos, January 23, 1943. Carbon copy in the Traven estate.

325 the political sphere: That it was Esperanza who cleared Traven's path as a political commentator into the Mexican press is revealed in the editor's note accompanying Traven's political essay in *Mañana* (discussed later).

325 In his letter to Josef Wieder in late 1946: See p. 291.

326 The essay in question, undiscovered: *Mañana*, November 9, 1946, pp. 19–23.

326 "a certain important magazine": Letter from Traven to Axel Holmström, February 5, 1947. An English version of the article is preserved in the Traven estate.

326 "La tercera guerra mundial": *Estudios sociales* (Mexico City), November/December 1945, pp. 9–16.

329 letter of August 29, 1940: John Huston, *An Open Book* (New York, 1980), p. 139.

330 before 1940 Traven had expressed nothing but disinterest: Not before 1946–1947, as Recknagel contends. *B. Traven*, p. 283.

330 Traven opposed the project: See Chapter 5, p. 253.

330 "Traven reserves for himself an undistorted presentation": *Die Büchergilde*, June 1931, p. 191.

330 he withdrew the film rights: Letter from Traven to Mr. Adler, July 10, 1931. See Chapter 6, p. 307.

331 Traven passed up the opportunity: Traven's notes on Josef Wieder's letter of August 6, 1938. Traven estate.

331 a request from Bernhard Diebold . . . of July 20, 1937: Carbon copy in the Akademie der Künste, Berlin.

331 Warner Brothers had acquired the film rights: For this paragraph, see Huston, *An Open Book*, pp. 140–41.

332 Evelyn Keyes . . . recalls: Keyes, *Scarlett O'Hara's Younger Sister* (Secaucus, N.J.: Lyle Stuart, 1977), p. 113.

332 the Americans were accused of showing Mexico in a bad light: Huston, *An Open Book*, p. 143.

332 Production resumed: In addition to the Traven chapter in Huston's *Open Book*, see Stuart H. Kaminsky, "Gold Hat, Gold Fever, Silver Screen," *The Modern American Novel and the Movies*, ed. Gerald Peary and Roger Shatzkin (New York: Frederick Ungar, 1978), pp. 53–62.

332 "one of the half a dozen or so films": *Life*, February 2, 1948, p. 63.

332 *Time* labeled Walter Huston's performance: February 2, 1948, p. 80.

332 Both magazines also spoke of the curious incidents: *Life*, February 2, 1948, p. 66; *Time*, February 2, 1948, p. 82.

332 Croves wrote complaints to the editors: His letters appeared in both *Life* and *Time* on March 15, 1948.

332 Huston would have paid him closer to $1,000: *Time*, March 15, 1948, p. 14.

332 "the man, or the woman": *Life*, March 15, 1948, p. 23.

333 "The film, after the novel of the same name": *BT-Mitteilungen*, no. 2, February 1951.

334 "Mexico's Mysterious Stranger": *Time*, February 2, 1948, p. 80.

334 "The mysterious B. Traven": *Time*, February 2, 1948, p. 82.

334 "the mystery man of modern letters": *Life*, February 2, 1948, p. 66.

334 "invisible and mysterious" Traven: *New York Times*, January 18, 1948, section 2, p. 5. See also *New York Times*, January 24, 1948, p. 11.

334 "The question of his identity": Huston, *An Open Book*, p. 145.

334 "Please cut out that goddamn mysterious": Letter from Traven to Herbert Arthur Klein, October 11, 1941, cited in Huston, *An Open Book*, pp. 139–40.

335 he instructed his Swedish publisher: Letter from Traven to Axel Holmström, July 30, 1946.

335 After August 7, 1948: Spota, "¿Por que no me dejan en paz?," *mañana*, pp. 10–26.

336 Torsvan's 1942 identity card: Reproduced, along with the 1930 card, in the German original of this book: Guthke, *B. Traven: Biographie*, p. 37. The Acapulco address is on the reverse side of the card, reproduced in Spota, "¿Por que no me dejan en paz?," p. 18.

339 on July 31 had curiously published: An article by José Giacomán Palacio claimed that the famed author was living as Torsvan in Acapulco. *Hoy*, July 31, 1948, p. 10.

340 Traven's first book had been written in 1916: *El Universal*, August 11, 1948, p. 12. The sentence is absent in *Hoy*.

340 Traven was participating in that biographical striptease: See Chapter 4, p. 110.

341 the publisher of *Mañana* received a typed letter: *Mañana*, April 19, 1969, p. 53.

341 where he stayed briefly with Gabriel Figueroa: Wyatt, *The Secret of the Sierra Madre*, p. 160.

341 Or he would kill himself: Wyatt, *The Secret of the Sierra Madre*, p. 155.

342 As late as 1960: *BT-Mitteilungen*, no. 36, April 1960.

342 Traven wrote to his former editor: Letter from Traven to Ernst Preczang, July 20, 1948. Heidemann collection; carbon copy in the Traven estate.

342 the Ret Marut story: "Red Marut," *Mañana*, August 7, 1948, p. 16.

342 Preczang had forwarded a letter from Irene Zielke: Typescript copy of her letter in the Heidemann collection.

342 with whom she had not had any contact: As stated in Irene Zielke's letter. See also Ferdinand Anton, "Aber Traven sind sie alle," *M*, May 5, 1970, p. 100; Heidemann, *Postlagernd Tampico*, pp. 204–6.

342 informed her in another enclosed note: Letter from Traven to Irene Zielke, dated August 10, 1948. Copy in the Heidemann collection. Reproduced in the German original of this book: Guthke: *B. Traven, Biographie*, p. 168.

344 "It isn't mine": Letter from Traven to Sanora Babb, October 28, 1953.

344 When Croves visited her for tea one day: Wyatt, *The Secret of the Sierra Madre*, pp. 122–23.

344 "Life is worth more than any book": Letter from Traven to Sanora Babb, February 6, 1953.

344 He also tried his hand at writing a radio play: *BT-Mitteilungen*, no. 3, n.d. (1951).

345 "a good story": Frederick Kohner, *The Magician of Sunset Boulevard* (Palos Verdes, Calif.: Morgan Press, 1977), p. 134.

345 his five-page film scenario for . . . *Macario*: Letter from Traven to James Howe, October 16, 1950. Houghton Library, Harvard University.

345 Addressing him as "Bogey": Letter from Traven to Humphrey Bogart, March 23, 1953. The letter runs five pages. Carbon copy in the Traven estate.

345 the short story "Assembly Line": The story, incidentally, enjoyed both an opera and television adaptation in Germany. See *BT-Mitteilungen*, no. 12, December 1953; no. 14, April 1954; and no. 26, July 1957.

346 "The Mexican press is now reporting": *BT-Mitteilungen*, no. 6, March 1952.

347 *Mercedes Ortega Lozano*: See *BT-Mitteilungen*, no. 15, July 1954 ("Film-Roman"). In the Traven estate is a "Screenplay by B. Traven." Among the correspondence with Holmström is a title page "Mercedes Ortega Lozano. The History of a Biological Instinct Miscarried. A Novel" (in English). See Chapter 7, pp. 385–86 on the film version of 1962.

347 Traven discussed this "film-novel": Letter from Traven to Curtis Brown, May 25, 1946. Carbon copy among Holmström's Traven correspondence in Stockholm.

348 Traven . . . awarded an option: Materials in the manuscript department of The Pennsylvania State University Library; screenplay in Traven estate.

348 "Even Jacinto and some of the subordinate Indian characters": Letter from Traven to Josef Wieder, November 1, 1956. Carbon copy in the Traven estate.

348 *Días de otoño*: See Chapter 7, pp. 385–86.

349 Traven described the production: *BT-Mitteilungen*, no. 15, July 1954.

350 Producer José Kohn . . . recalled the snakes: *BT-Mitteilungen*, no. 17, December 1954.

350 the Mexican government's choice: *BT-Mitteilungen*, no. 15, July 1954.

350 B. Traven was rumored to be present incognito: *BT-Mitteilungen*, no. 16, September 1954.

350 Traven attributed the film's failure: *BT-Mitteilungen*, no. 17, December 1954.

350 "Thousands failed to get tickets": *BT-Mitteilungen*, no. 17, December 1954.

350 "The film ran in other Mexican cities": *BT-Mitteilungen*, no. 17, December 1954.

351 lengthy excerpts from German reviews: *BT-Mitteilungen*, no. 19, December 1955.

351 The American edition . . . sold 2,692 copies: See p. 313. Hagemann, "¡Huye!," p. 379.

351 "Until June 30, 1950": Undated typescript in English. Carbon copy in the Traven estate.

352 An increasing number of articles appeared on Traven: See the bibliography in the Appendix to Recknagel, *B. Traven.*

352 *Wie sie schreiben: Wie sie aussehen*: Hamburg: Rowohlt, 1956.

353 a debate on the extent to which Traven's anarchistic view: *Sonntag*, March 6, March 13, March 20, April 10, June 10, 1955, p. 8 in each.

353 *Deutsche Schriftsteller*: (Berlin, 1947), pp. 131–36.

353 condemning the common front of capitalism and bourgeois-democratic sentiment: See p. 326, for a discussion of Traven's political essay attacking this common front.

353 Traven's previously mentioned background story: *BT-Mitteilungen*, no. 35, November 1959.

354 by 1950 Traven had 145 editions: *BT-Mitteilungen*, no. 1, January 1951; no. 24, January 1957.

354 In 1956 a new edition of the Czech translation: *BT-Mitteilungen*, no. 20, February 1956.

354 This truthfulness, this authenticity: *BT-Mitteilungen*, no. 3, n.d. (1951).

355 "so that the world could celebrate him": *BT-Mitteilungen*, no. 8, July 1952.

355 "Humble as he is": *BT-Mitteilungen*, no. 11, August 1953.

355 it merely served up anew: *BT-Mitteilungen*, no. 6, March 1952.

355 Traven . . . most keenly combated: *BT-Mitteilungen*, no. 6, March 1952.

356 "in order to prove that he was still alive": *BT-Mitteilungen*, no. 4, n.d. (1951).

356 Traven devotees wondered why no new Traven work: *BT-Mitteilungen*, no. 15, July 1954. See also no. 29, March 1958.

356 was published only in manuscript form: *Das Totenschiff* (Zurich: Europa).

356 the radio play version still lies unpublished: See also *BT-Mitteilungen*, no. 3, n.d. (1951); no. 18, August 1955.

357 "All this brings us to a point": Letter from Traven to Fritz J. Raddatz, August 24, 1964. Carbon copy in the estate.

357 critics had in fact cited such references: *BT-Mitteilungen*, no. 26, July 1957; Recknagel, *B. Traven*, pp. 151, 203, 214.

357 "A Legend of Huehuetonoc": *The California Quarterly*, vol. 1, no. 2 (Winter 1952), pp. 56–63. The better-known English title is "Assembly Line."

357 Esperanza can scarcely have translated from German to English: See p. 322 on her competence in German.

358 "Visitor from Nowhere": *Cosmos Science Fiction and Fantasy*, vol. 1, no. 2 (1953), pp. 1–43.

358 "Effective Medicine": *Manhunt*, vol. 2, no. 6 (August 1954), pp. 31–42.

358 "Indian Trading": *Short Stories*, March 1957, pp. 115–27.
358 "Six doctors meet in a little village": Raskin, *My Search for B. Traven*, pp. 246–47.
359 "The Third Guest": *Fantastic*, vol. 2, no. 2 (1953), pp. 5–36, 89.
359 *The Best American Short Stories*: Ed. Martha Foley (Boston: Houghton Mifflin), pp. 328–62.
359 declaring it the best short story of the year: *BT-Mitteilungen*, no. 35, November 1959.
359 Nothing came of the plan: See *BT-Mitteilungen*, no. 3, n.d. (1951).
360 a separate edition of the story: Published by Bertelsmann, Gütersloh, 1961. Printer's copy with Traven's revisions in the Traven estate. The following quotation is from the editorial commentary of the Bertelsmann edition.
360 Traven surely knew the Grimms' fairy tales: See *Land des Frühlings*, p. 205.
360 "*una leyenda indígena*": *Política*, vol. 1, no. 11 (October 1960), p. 3.
360 quotations from *Macario*: *Werkausgabe*, vol. 14, pp. 303, 306–7.
361 they were written around 1945: According to a letter from Traven to Axel Holmström, July 30, 1946.
361 "An Unexpected Solution": *Short Stories*, June 1957, pp. 62–67.
361 "A Customer Broke a Tooth": *Modern Reading*, vol. 20 (Winter 1951–52), pp. 44–55.
361 "Ceremony Slightly Delayed": *The Saint Detective Magazine*, vol. 8, no. 4 (October 1957), pp. 88–104.
361 "B. Traven writes detective stories": *BT-Mitteilungen*, no. 27, August 1957.
361 Volk und Welt collected stories: I am using the "Lizenzansgabe", *Erzählungen*, ed. Werner Sellhorn, 2 vols. (Zurich: Limmat, 1968).
361 "Seele eines Hundes": *Der Banditendoktor* (Fischer-Bücherei, 1955).
361 "Foreign Correspondent": *Texas Quarterly*, vol. 6, no. 4, pp. 173–75. The text itself reveals that it was written in June 1951 (*Werkausgabe*, vol. 15, p. 111). Traven sent an English version to Sanora Babb on June 12, 1951. Carbon copy of her letter in the Traven estate.
361 "Dennoch eine Mutter": Cologne *Neue Illustrierte*, May 9, 1951, pp. 25–30, 35.
361 "Frustration": *Stories by the Man Nobody Knows* (Evanston, Ill.: Regency Books, 1961).
361 Traven had composed the English text in 1946 at the latest: See letter from Traven to Curtis Brown, Ltd., May 25, 1946; see p. 347.
361 "Hochzeit um elf": *Kontraste*, vol. 7, no. 6, pp. 35–37.
361 "To Frame or Not to Frame": *Selected Writings*, no. 5 (1946), pp.

101–4; published in German as "Der Silberdollar" ("The Silver Dollar").

361 "His Wife's Legs": *Accused*, vol. 1, no. 4 (1956), pp. 116–20; published in German as "Die schönen Beine seiner Frau."

361 *Erzählungen*: Volume 2, pp. 349–73, contains valuable bibliographical information.

362 Señora Rosa Elena Luján's background: Raskin, *My Search for B. Traven*, Chapter 19.

362 Traven had instructed that royalties: Letter from Traven to Sanora Babb, June 22, 1954.

362 beginning in 1956 Rosa Elena Luján is cited in print: Introduction, *BT-Mitteilungen*, pp. 7, 10.

362 "He feels so very, very lonely": Raskin, *My Search for B. Traven*, pp. 245–46.

Chapter 7

367 "Remembering Traven": The essay appears as the introduction to *The Kidnapped Saint and Other Stories*.

368 "I wanted only what he wanted": Typescript of interview of Rosa Elena Luján by Kevin M. Kelleghan, 1969 (?). Traven estate.

368 "Some people think that I changed Traven": "Remembering Traven," in *The Kidnapped Saint and Other Stories*, p. ix.

369 *Roland fliegt nach Mexiko*: Zurich, 1961.

369 "Your book went to Argentina, Uruguay, Bolivia, and Chile": Letter from R. E. Luján to Ernst Vollenweider, May 31, 1962. Max Schmid collection.

370 By 1963 their situation had so improved: On Traven's economic situation, see, for example, R. E. Luján's letter of July 7, 1962, to the Swiss Writers' Guild (Schweizerischer Schriftsteller-Verein): "We are happy to hear that the Christmas contribution was so well received and welcome. Traven does not overlook other writers' organizations in Europe either. He could not render this assistance earlier because he by no means has the hundreds of thousands or even millions that he is always said to have; in fact his economic situation has improved only recently, when some of his works were filmed, which he had previously not allowed." Max Schmid collection. During this period Traven sent money not only to the Swiss Writers' Guild but also to Austrian and German writers' associations. The funds were intended for "professional authors sick or otherwise in need of help" and were given on the condition that they would be acknowledged "without expression of thanks" and without any publicity (letters from R. E. Luján to the Swiss Writers' Guild of December 16, 1961, and July 7, 1962, and carbon copy of a letter from R. E. Luján to the Kurt Desch publishing company of April 30, 1962). Max Schmid collection.

371 In 1968 he walked down to the Reforma: Raskin, *My Search for B. Traven*, p. 138.

371 "I want to be able to go to the newspaper stand": Rosa Elena Luján had similar recollections in her interview with Kevin Kelleghan. Typescript in the Traven estate.

371 "My husband was one of the freest men who ever lived": Rosa Elena Luján, quoted by Alan Cheuse, "The Treasure of the Calle Mississippi," *Los Angeles Times*, February 15, 1976, p. 3.

372 "Si, mi vida": "Remembering Traven," in *The Kidnapped Saint and Other Stories*, p. ix.

372 "I want to be free, not a slave to money": Rosa Elena Luján's remarks to Kevin Kelleghan.

373 "The motto of Traven's life was work": From the Spanish translation of Lampl's interview, "Cita con Traven," *Hojas de crítica*, supplement to *Revista de la Universidad de México*, vol. 23, no. 8 (1969), p. 6. The interview was first published in *Aftenposten* (Oslo), April 14, 15, 22, 1969. Regarding the idea of suicide à la Hemingway, see also Luis Suárez, "Al borde del fin, Traven pensó en un escopetazo al estilo Hemingway," *Siempre*, April 9, 1969, pp. 12–15.

373 In a letter to Ernst Preczang: January 11, 1934. Copy in Stadtbibliothek Dortmund.

373 "Be Mexican and don't recite the speech of Mortimer": Note from Traven to Paul Kohner. Traven estate.

373 Recknagel's story that a backpack containing Traven's expedition equipment: *B. Traven*, p. 320.

373 *Deutsches Lesebuch für höhere Lehranstalten*: Cologne, 1868, 1871.

374 *Welt zum Staunen*: Kalltalpresse, 1919.

374 Recknagel reported seeing on the bridge: *B. Traven*, p. 329. I did not see this book.

374 "Little Blue Books": *B. Traven*, p. 328. I did not see these volumes.

374 Also pointing to the earliest period in Mexico: See Chapter 5, p. 203.

374 I also found archeological and historical books: See Chapter 5, p. 202.

375 He never spoke with guests about the problems of writing: William Weber Johnson, "A Noted Novelist Who Lived and Died in Obscurity," *Los Angeles Times Calendar*, April 13, 1969, p. 12; Rodolfo Usigli, *Conversaciones y encuentros* (Mexico City, 1973), p. 161.

375 "formal occasions even when there were no guests present": John Huston, *An Open Book* (New York, 1980), p. 146, quoting one of Traven's stepdaughters.

376 "Traven enjoyed it all": Rosa Elena Luján, "Remembering Traven," in *The Kidnapped Saint and Other Stories*, pp. vii-viii.

376 "After breakfast he watered the plants and took care of our small garden": "Remembering Traven," in *The Kidnapped Saint and Other Stories*, p. x.

377 According to Hill's description: *The New York Times Book Review*, December 27, 1970, p. 10.

377 Johnson had similar memories of his meeting with Traven: Johnson, "A Noted Novelist Who Lived and Died in Obscurity."

377 Hans Erich Lampl . . . also wrote of a meal at Traven's home: Lampl, "Cita con Traven."

378 Traven commented that "the real hero": See Chapter 7, p. 398.

378 The following anecdote was considered significant enough: Introduction to *Obras escogidas*, 2nd edition (Mexico City, 1980), vol. 1, p. 21. First published in 1969.

379 Writing about his conversations at Calle Mississippi 61: Usigli, *Conversaciones y encuentros*, pp. 161–62.

379 A somewhat incongruous member of the Traven circle: *Obras escogidas*, vol. 1, p. 19.

379 whose personal protection he sought: See Figueroa's account as reported by Wyatt, *The Secret of the Sierra Madre*, p. 163.

379 Traven had often stayed with him on visits to the capital: Wyatt, *The Secret of the Sierra Madre*, p. 160. Confirmed by Figueroa's remarks to me.

380 The story of Figueroa's first meeting with Traven: Wyatt, *The Secret of the Sierra Madre*, p. 162.

380 it was only in the late 1960s: Frederick Kohner, *The Magician of Sunset Boulevard* (Palos Verdes, Calif.: Morgan Press, 1977), p. 137.

380 Siqueiros: Traven offered Siqueiros a public tribute in *Siempre*, February 8, 1967, p. 5.

380 Igal Maoz, whom Traven subsequently tried to promote: Letter from Traven to Sanora Babb, October 31, 1966.

380 Maoz first encountered Traven's works in a kibbutz: Stone, *The Mystery of B. Traven*, p. 71.

381 Pinkus related the comments of these friends: *Wochenpost*, March 22, 1974, p. 15.

382 The English versions appeared in American magazines: *Stories by the Man Nobody Knows* (Evanston, Ill., 1961). Among the stories (not all are in the collection) were "Burrow Trading" ("Eselskauf"), *Short Story International*, March 1963, pp. 7–19, purportedly after the version that had appeared in the Mexican magazine *Diana*, July 1962; "Sun Creation" ("Sonnen-Schöpfung"), *Fantasy and Science Fiction*, April 1964, pp. 16–27, and *Mexican Life*, July 1965, pp.

22–25, 42–45; "Tin Can" ("Geschichte einer Bombe"), *The Texas Quarterly*, vol. 6, no. 3 (1963), pp. 30–38, and *Short Story International*, June 1964, pp. 95–107; "Midnight Call" ("Der Banditendoktor"), *Short Story International*, November 1964, pp. 83–107, and *Mexican Life*, May 1965, pp. 7–8, 43–65; "Submission" ("Bändigung"), *Argosy*, November 1965, pp. 63–81; "A Saint in Pain" ("Der ausgewanderte Antonio"), *Michigan Quarterly Review*, Fall 1965, pp. 266–73; "Love, Justice and a Bomb" ("Geschichte einer Bombe"), *Argosy*, February 1966, pp. 82–93. The book edition of *The Creation of the Sun and the Moon* (1968) was mentioned earlier. Regarding "Frustration," see Chapter 6, p. 361.

382 *Macario* in *The Texas Quarterly*: vol. 6, no. 1 (1963), pp. 47–72.

382 a chapter from *The Cotton-Pickers*: *Fling*, vol. 9, no. 1 (1966), pp. 35N-37, 44, 66.

382 "In the meantime an entirely new generation": Letter from Traven to Max Schmid, June 9, 1961. Carbon copy in the Traven estate.

383 "Mexico's most famous writer": *Short Story International*, March 1963, p. 19.

383 It had apparently entered into agreements with Traven's agent: Letter to Max Schmid, June 7, 1961. Carbon copy in the Traven estate.

384 Theo Pinkus. See Frederik Hetmann, *Der Mann, der sich verbarg: Nachforschungen über B. Traven* (*The Man in Hiding: Searching for B. Traven*) (Stuttgart, 1983), pp. 234–36.

384 Tensions with the Büchergilde dissipated: See Pinkus's comment in Hetmann, pp. 246–47.

384 Traven sent Rowohlt reviews of earlier editions of his books: This according to correspondence preserved in the estate (carbon copies of letters sent to Rowohlt).

384 Lionel Hale's article from the London *News Chronicle*: Clipping in the Traven estate.

384 "By April 1960 Traven's *The Cotton-Pickers*": Carbon copy in the Traven estate (in German).

385 "Hal Croves could be seen only rarely at the film studio": Recknagel, *B. Traven*, p. 295.

386 "Las hijas del general": Outline in the Traven estate.

386 A documentary on David Alfaro Siqueiros was planned: Raskin, *My Search for B. Traven*, p. 134.

386 Traven mentioned another bit of behind-the-scenes intrigue: Letter from Traven to Sanora Babb, June 28, 1961.

387 "This story about the picture": Stone, *The Mystery of B. Traven*, p. 57.

387 the *BT News* reported that rumors of the filming: *BT-Mitteilungen* (*BT News*), no. 29, March 1958. See also "Hauke & Kohn," *Der*

Spiegel, July 22, 1959, pp. 51–52. The discussion that follows is based on this article, on Recknagel, *B. Traven*, pp. 286–91, and on documents in the Traven estate cited later in this paragraph.

387 "A few notes and observations" . . . "Memorandum on the Screen Script": Carbon copies, in English, in the Traven estate.

387 "set the wrong way": "Memorandum."

387 the small notebook in which Marut had drawn flag signals: Marut estate.

388 causing Croves to remark that "naturally" he was not Traven: *Hamburger Abendblatt*, October 5, 1959, p. 10.

388 the *BT News* fanned the fires by publishing three articles: All three articles are in *BT-Mitteilungen*, no. 35, November 1959.

389 mention of the prize had surfaced: Letter from Traven to Axel Holmström, May 25, 1946.

389 Traven responded . . . that there were more deserving candidates: Traven's response was printed in *The Texas Quarterly*, vol. 6, no. 4, p. 207. His letter is dated May 24, 1963.

389 in 1967 a Stockholm newspaper openly advocated Traven's candidacy: Gunnar Müllern, "Mysteriet Traven," *Aftonbladet*, June 3, 1967, p. 5. Clipping preserved in the Traven estate.

389 a frantic rebuttal: *BT-Mitteilungen*, no. 36, April 60.

390 "Warning / Manuscripts of any sort": Announcement placed by Josef Wieder in *Börsenblatt für den deutschen Buchhandel*, Frankfurt edition, September 30, 1958.

391 "giving us new direction": *BT-Mitteilungen*, no. 29, March 1958.

391 Friedrich Sieburg . . . wrote in 1960: Reprinted in his *Zur Literatur 1957–1963*, ed. Fritz J. Raddatz (Stuttgart, 1981), pp. 178–80.

391 "Traven or Not Traven?": Pierre Unau, "Traven oder nicht Traven?", *Neue deutsche Literatur*, vol. 8, no. 11, pp. 165–68.

391 "peaceful efforts at improving society": Recknagel, *B. Traven*, p. 307.

392 in his interview with Judy Stone in 1967: See Chapter 7, p. 399.

392 "As long as books have been written": Letter to Max Schmid, June 9, 1961. Carbon copy in the Traven estate.

394 he feared being "kidnapped" to Germany: Wyatt, *The Secret of the Sierra Madre*, p. 163.

394 One West German fan: Letter in Traven estate.

394 The same year *Revista de la Universidad de México* published a feature article: vol. 22, no. 1 (1967), pp. 1–3.

394 Lampl visited in November 1967: Discussed earlier in this chapter.

394 "Das Rätsel Traven gelöst": *Stern*, August 25, 1963, pp. 8–11.

395 "Croves" is able to enjoy the attention given to "Traven": Stone, *The Mystery of B. Traven*, pp. 69, 74, 79.

395 *Siempre*'s five-page illustrated report: No. 695, pp. 5–9, 70; partly repeated in the introduction to *Obras escogidas*.

395 For the first time, Suárez boasted: *Obras escogidas*, p. 9.
396 Suárez himself reported on the reaction in *Siempre*: No. 699, November 16, 1966.
396 "You may be assured that your trip will turn out": Stone, *The Mystery of B. Traven*, p. 51.
396 Traven had written his works . . . who had probably not been involved in the Bavarian revolution at all": Stone, *The Mystery of B. Traven*, pp. 59, 68, 69, 79.
396 Traven's works did reveal the author's views: Stone, *The Mystery of B. Traven*, p. 55.
397 "Forget the man!": Stone, *The Mystery of B. Traven*, p. 47.
397 "We have enjoyed having you": Stone, *The Mystery of B. Traven*, p. 80.
397 "He kissed me goodbye": Stone, *The Mystery of B. Traven*, p. 64.
397 On another occasion Rosa Elena Luján asked Stone: Stone, *The Mystery of B. Traven*, p. 78.
397 But there was another side to the Nazis' reception of Traven: Stone, *The Mystery of B. Traven*, p. 54.
397 And he drew the contrast with Joseph Conrad: Stone, *The Mystery of B. Traven*, p. 63.
398 In paradise the Indians must "shape the clouds": Stone, *The Mystery of B. Traven*, p. 68. See also *Land des Frühlings*, p. 80.
398 "This nearness to the soil": Stone, *The Mystery of B. Traven*, p. 59.
398 "Traven likes to see birds sing" . . . Thoreau: Stone, *The Mystery of B. Traven*, p. 58.
398 Even *The Death Ship* sounded the theme of longing for one's own piece of land: Stone, *The Mystery of B. Traven*, p. 62.
398 the American sailor Gales was not the truly important character: Stone, *The Mystery of B. Traven*, pp. 62, 72. See Chapter 5, p. 253, and Chapter 7, p. 378.
398 Croves naturally could not say *why* Stanislav was such a key figure: Stone, *The Mystery of B. Traven*, pp. 62, 72.
398 "It's not just the story of an American sailor": Stone, *The Mystery of B. Traven*, p. 61.
399 In his "personal opinion," it should not circulate under Traven's name: Stone, *The Mystery of B. Traven*, p. 69.
399 Heidemann had published his second and long-awaited report: "Wer ist der Mann, der Traven heisst"," *Stern*, May 7, 1967, pp. 58–71, 170–73. See also Heidemann, "Ich fand B. Traven," *Konkret*, nos. 6–9 (1967). Regarding the television series mentioned subsequently in the text, see "Wer ist der Mann," p. 66.
399 The international press, led by the Germans: See Recknagel, *B. Traven*, pp. 442–44.

399 she denied telling Heidemann that her husband: *Siempre*, May 17, 1967, p. 5. In conversations with me as well, Rosa Elena Luján has repeatedly denied having made this assertion.

400 She spoke with him "for a total of thirteen hours": Recknagel, *B. Traven*, p. 295.

400 "We did not present ourselves as reporters or detectives": Ferdinand Anton, "Aber Traven sind sie alle," *M*, May 5, 1970, p. 105.

400 Traven was thus not intentionally "giving himself up," as Heidemann claimed: Heidemann, *Postlagernd Tampico*, p. 283.

400 to judge from R. E. Luján's letter to Judy Stone: Stone, *The Mystery of B. Traven*, p. 84.

401 "The white-haired man of medium height seems frail": Heidemann, "Wer ist der Mann," pp. 172–73.

402 Ferdinand Anton provided a few further details: Anton, "Aber Traven," pp. 105–6.

402 "He looked at her [Rosa Elena] fondly": Stone, *The Mystery of B. Traven*, p. 61.

403 On the back of a calendar page from May 1967: Traven estate.

403 "He stood in the hall": Raskin, *My Search for B. Traven*, p. 185.

404 That evening a friend came to the house: Mary Blume, "Clearing up the Mysteries of Author B. Traven," *Los Angeles Times*, July 19, 1970, p. 21.

404 Details of Traven's will: From *Siempre*, April 9, 1969, p. 15.

404 "This world with all its troubles, shortcomings, disappointments": Traven estate.

405 "I remember the day he died": Jonah Raskin, "In Search of Traven," *The Radical Reader*, ed. Stephen Knight and Michael Wilding (Sydney, 1977), p. 82. See also Raskin, *My Search for B. Traven*, p. 103.

405 "He died kissing my hands and saying he loved me": Rosa Elena Luján, quoted by Blume, "Clearing up the Mysteries of Author B. Traven."

405 The death certificate: Certified copy in Traven estate.

405 Even in death, as so often in life: Even in his will he managed to give conflicting information. The date of birth May 3 ("*tres de mayo*") contradicts the more frequently claimed March 5 ("*5 marzo*"), as on the identity card of 1930.

BIBLIOGRAPHY

Works by B. Traven

Unless otherwise indicated in the Notes, references to Traven's works are to the first German editions published in book form, as given here. Any work published in English is listed here following its German original, with the date of its first English edition and its U.S. publisher (if it is in print).

Novels and Nonfiction

Das Totenschiff. Berlin: Büchergilde Gutenberg, 1926. *The Death Ship*. New York: Alfred Knopf, 1934; New York: Lawrence Hill Books, 1972.

Der Wobbly. Berlin: Buchmeister-Verlag, 1926. *The Cotton-Pickers*. London: Robert Hale, 1956; London: Allison & Busby, 1983.

Der Schatz der Sierra Madre. Berlin: Büchergilde Gutenberg, 1927. *The Treasure of the Sierra Madre*. London: Chatto & Windus, 1934; New York: Hill and Wang, 1984.

Der Busch. Berlin: Büchergilde Gutenberg, 1928. References in this book are to the 1930 edition.

Land des Frühlings. Berlin: Büchergilde Gutenberg, 1928.

Die Brücke im Dschungel. Berlin: Büchergilde Gutenberg, 1929. *The Bridge in the Jungle*. New York: Alfred Knopf, 1938.

Die weisse Rose. Berlin: Büchergilde Gutenberg, 1929. *The White Rose*. London: Robert Hale, 1965; New York: Lawrence Hill Books, 1979.

Der Karren. Berlin: Büchergilde Gutenberg, 1931. *The Carreta*. London: Chatto & Windus, 1936; London: Allison & Busby, 1984.

Regierung. Berlin: Büchergilde Gutenberg, 1931. *Government*. London: Chatto & Windus, 1935; London: Allison & Busby, 1983.

Der Marsch ins Reich der Caoba: Ein Kriegsmarsch. Zurich, Vienna, Prague: Büchergilde Gutenberg, 1933. *March to Caobaland*. London: Robert Hale, 1960. *March to the Montería*. London: Allison & Busby, 1983.

Die Troza. Zurich, Prague: Büchergilde Gutenberg, 1936.

Die Rebellion der Gehenkten. Zürich, Prague: Büchergilde Gutenberg, 1936. *The Rebellion of the Hanged*. London: Robert Hale, 1952; New York: Alfred Knopf, 1952; London: Allison & Busby, 1983.

Ein General kommt aus dem Dschungel. Amsterdam: Allert de Lange, 1940. *General from the Jungle*. London: Robert Hale, 1954; London: Allison & Busby, 1985.

Macario. Trans. from the English by Hans Kauders. Zurich: Büchergilde Gutenberg, 1950. *Macario*. Revised edition. Gütersloh: Bertelsmann, 1961. (English translation in *The Night Visitor and Other Stories*.)

Aslan Norval. Vienna, Munich, Basel: Kurt Desch, 1960.

Sonnen-Schöpfung. Zurich, Vienna, Prague: Büchergilde Gutenberg, 1936. *The Creation of the Sun and the Moon*. New York: Hill & Wang, 1968; reissued New York: Lawrence Hill Books, 1977.

Collected Works

In German

Werkausgabe. Frankfurt: Büchergilde Gutenberg, 1977–1982; reprinted Zurich: Diogenes, 1982.

In English

Stories by the Man Nobody Knows. Evanston, Ill.: Regency Books, 1961.

The Night Visitor and Other Stories. Introduction by Charles Miller. New York: Hill and Wang, 1966; London: Allison & Busby, 1983.

The Kidnapped Saint and Other Stories. Introduction, "Remembering Traven," by Rosa Elena Luján. New York: Lawrence Hill Books, 1975.

To the Honorable Miss S. . . and Other Stories. Trans. Peter Silcock. New York: Lawrence Hill Books, 1981.

Books About B. Traven

The following studies are cited frequently in the Notes. Translations in brackets are for readers' reference and do not indicate that the books exist in English translation.

Beck, Johannes, Klaus Bergmann, and Heiner Boehncke, editors. *Das B. Traven-Buch* [*The B. Traven Book*]. Reinbek: Rowohlt Taschenbuch Verlag, 1976.

Heidemann, Gerd. *Postlagernd Tampico: Die abenteuerliche Suche nach B. Traven* [*General Delivery, Tampico: The Adventurous Search for B. Traven*]. Munich: Blanvalet Verlag, 1977.

Raskin, Jonah. *My Search for B. Traven*. New York: Methuen, 1980.

Recknagel, Rolf. *B. Traven: Beiträge zur Biografie* [*B. Traven: Contributions to a Biography*]. 3rd edition. Leipzig: Philipp Reclam, 1982.

Richter, Armin. *Der Ziegelbrenner: Das individualistische Kampforgan des frühen B. Traven* [*The Brickburner: Individualistic Polemical Journal of the Early B. Traven*]. Bonn: Bouvier, 1977.

Schürer, Ernst, and Philip Jenkins. *B. Traven: Life and Work*. University Park: The Pennsylvania State University Press, 1987.

Stone, Judy. *The Mystery of B. Traven*. Los Altos: William Kaufmann, 1977.

Wyatt, Will. *The Secret of the Sierra Madre: The Man Who Was B. Traven*. New York: Doubleday, 1980. (Pagination differs from that in the British edition, *The Man Who Was B. Traven*. London: Jonathan Cape, 1980.) All references are to the American edition.

Method of Citation

Published Sources

Quotations from Traven's works, unless otherwise noted, were translated from the first-edition German texts given in the Bibliography. They were not taken from English translations, where such exist, because English translations are not always based on the first German edition.

Quotations from *Der Ziegelbrenner* (*The Brickburner*) are cited from the edition of Klaus Guhl Verlag (Berlin, 1976). Quotations from *BT-Mitteilungen* (*BT News*) are from the Klaus Guhl Verlag edition, introduction by "Kilian Schott" (Berlin, 1978).

Quotations from the Büchergilde Gutenberg's magazine for 1933–1945 are from the Zurich *Büchergilde* unless the Berlin *Büchergilde* is indicated. The Zurich Büchergilde published its journal under the title *Büchergilde* beginning in January 1934 to differentiate it from the Berlin Büchergilde's publication, *Die Büchergilde*.

Handwritten and Typescript Sources

Orthography and punctuation in cited passages written in English by B. Traven have not been normalized.

Quotations from the most important correspondence are cited by date only. The original correspondence is held by the following:

From B. Traven to Sanora Babb (and James Wong Howe): Houghton Library, Harvard University.

From Rosa Elena Luján to Lawrence Hill: Hill & Wang, Inc., New York.

From B. Traven to Axel Holmström: Arbetarrörelsens Arkiv, Stockholm. (Also includes letters from Josef Wieder to Axel Holmström and carbon copies of Holmström's responses to Traven and Wieder.)

From B. Traven to Alfred A. Knopf: Alfred A. Knopf, Inc., New York.

From B. Traven to Johannes Schönherr: Originals in the Schönherr estate, in the possession of Dr. Wolfgang Schönherr, Jena; copies at Verlag Volk und Welt, Berlin.

From B. Traven to Ernst Preczang: A few letters are cited from the text printed in the "Kultur-Spiegel" supplement in the Zurich newspaper *Volksrecht*, July 20, 1967, and in Recknagel, *B. Traven*, pp. 14–17. Most of the Traven–Preczang correspondence is cited from the (typed) originals of Traven's letters and the carbon copies of Preczang's letters, both held by Büchergilde Gutenberg, Frankfurt. The following letters are cited from typescript copies held by Büchergilde Gutenberg: Traven to the Zurich Büchergilde, May 23, 1933; Traven to the Board [Vorstand] of the Zurich Büchergilde, January 11, 1934; Preczang to Traven, February 24, March 31, and May 3, 1927. In the case of the Traven-Preczang letters not held by Büchergilde Gutenberg, the source of the letter is given in the Notes.

INDEX

R

S

Born and raised in Germany, Karl S. Guthke immigrated to the United States in 1956. After teaching at the University of California at Berkeley and the University of Toronto, he joined the faculty at Harvard University, where he has held the position of Kuno Francke Professor of German Art and Culture since 1978. He is the author of several books on literary and cultural history, including *The Last Frontier: Imagining Other Worlds, from the Copernican Revolution to Modern Science Fiction.*

Robert C. Sprung holds a B.A. in classics and German from Harvard University and an M.A. in modern languages from the University of Cambridge. He is founder and president of Harvard Translations in Boston.